1981

# THE EMERGENCE OF SOCIAL WELFARE
## AND SOCIAL WORK
### Second Edition

# The Emergence of Social Welfare and Social Work,

## SECOND EDITION

NEIL GILBERT and HARRY SPECHT

University of California, Berkeley

F.E. PEACOCK PUBLISHERS, INC. ITASCA, ILLINOIS 60143

To Barbara and Riva

# CONTENTS

PART III    SOCIAL WORK

# INTRODUCTION

# INTRODUCTION

Social welfare is an emerging institution and social work an emerging profession. Both originated as human responses to the problems of social change and the difficulties of life in modern industrial society. All industrialized societies devote a significant part of their resources to social welfare, and all have developed some sort of professional practice that is similar to American social work.[1] Therefore, although both institution and profession are relatively young, they represent significant social inventions that influence the conditions of life in modern society.

As social designs, the profession and the institution represent relatively new ideas that are changing rapidly in response to the needs and values of the community. During this century alone, social welfare in the United States has undergone dramatic changes. At the turn of the century it was organized almost exclusively as a voluntary activity supported by charitable impulse. Until the 1930s, support for social welfare programs came primarily from state and local governments along with voluntary charitable organizations. Since then the federal government has assumed an increasingly larger role in social welfare, and today it is the major funding source. Expenditures for social welfare constitute the largest item in the federal budget.[2]

The growth and development of the profession of social work in this century has been just as dramatic. Until the late 1800s, the profession did not exist in either an organizational or scientific sense. Until this century, social work involved various forms of charitable activity voluntarily offered as a matter of individual conscience.[3] By 1915 there was sufficient development of the organizational, ethical, scientific, and theoretical aspects of this profession for the National Conference of Charities and Corrections to consider the question "Is Social Work a Profession?" Responding to this question, Dr. Abraham Flexner analyzed the criteria of a profession and concluded that social work was not eligible to claim professional status.[4] Despite this assessment, by the 1920s several schools of education for social work had been established, and a number of professional organizations had been founded. By midcentury a unified national organization of professional social workers had been formed (the National Association of

Social Workers) as well as an accrediting body for educational programs conferring degrees in social work (the Council on Social Work
Education). Currently in the United States there are over 250 accredited schools offering degrees in social work at the bachelor's, master's, and doctoral levels. In addition, there are many professional
journals.[5]

Along with the phenomenal growth of the institution and the
profession, another change is currently taking place. That is, social
welfare and social work are coming to be seen as programs and
services that are necessary and important to everyone, not only the
poor, the sick, and the handicapped. For example, Title XX, one of
the 1975 amendments to the Social Security Act, established a statutory framework which would allow states to provide comprehensive
social services on a universal basis.[6] The framework, however, represents a potential that has yet to be implemented. These kinds of
societal developments in social welfare are not achieved rapidly or
easily, as the readings in this book will attest.

Our intention in this book is to introduce students to important sets
of ideas associated with the emergence of social welfare and social
work. The readings in Part I are concerned with the changing nature
of the responsibility society assumes for the welfare of its members,
the role of public and private efforts in these collective endeavors,
the functions of social welfare and how they fit into the institutional
structure of modern society, and the directions in which social welfare appears to be headed. The readings in Part II illustrate how
analysis and interpretation of needs and problems of existing social
arrangements affect the development of social welfare and social
work. These readings provide examples of how ideas derived from
a sociological perspective operate as an intellectual stimulus to institutional and professional developments. Part III deals with conceptions of the nature and development of professionalism in social
work, the organizational context in which practice takes place, and
the new directions professional practice seems to be taking.

To set the framework for this book, we will briefly review the
relationships among the topics around which the readings are organized: social welfare, sociological critique, and social work.

## THE INSTITUTION AND PROFESSIONAL PRACTICE

The institution of social welfare is older than the profession of
social work. The institution serves as a mechanism for mutual support, expressing the collective responsibility of the community for
helping its members. It consists of a series of programmatic arrangements for meeting needs through the allocation of income and ser-

vices outside of other institutional channels such as the family and the market.[7] These programmatic arrangements are administered by people from many professions, including public health, nursing, city planning, public administration, teaching, and social work. Among these professional groups social work is most strongly identified with social welfare because it provides the largest proportion of personnel for the diverse areas of the institution. In addition, social work training is geared primarily to the broad range of social welfare programs. This is unlike city planning and public administration, in which the training is concerned primarily with planning and management of the physical side of urban development, or nursing, public health, and teaching, in which the training tends to be focused around a more circumscribed set of professional interventions and programmatic arrangements.

Social welfare programs can be distinguished broadly in terms of arrangements concerned with income maintenance and those concerned with social services. Historically, programs for income maintenance developed first because social welfare emerged as an institution dealing with problems of economic dependency and insecurity. The history of social welfare as an institution can be read in large part as the history of the development of labor legislation. That this system of mutual support evolved in relation to the need to earn a living is not surprising because this is one of humankind's foremost needs. Social work also began with a concern for problems of economic dependency but the profession's purview expanded rapidly to include many other social problems. This occurred, we think, because of the rapid change in this century in ideas about what people are entitled to expect from their government. Increasingly, income maintenance is perceived to be a guaranteed *right* rather than a benefit that is awarded on the basis of a judgment of the applicant's worthiness. Increasingly, personal social services, such as child care and care of the aged, are being defined as services that should be available to everyone in the community.

In most societies, security of family income is the first area around which social welfare provisions are established. Once these monetary provisions are established as almost automatic fiscal transactions, eligibility determination does not require very highly trained personnel. Thus, while income maintenance is among the most compelling of human needs, it is also the one which can be handled most easily as a financial transaction that does not require the intervention of a professionally trained helper. However, many of the other kinds of problems that are dealt with in the personal social services, such as family disorganization, juvenile delinquency, and care of the aged and mentally ill, are rich fields for the development of professional methods of intervention. For that reason, even though financial need may be the original cause of many problems, social work as a profession has tended to develop its professional methodologies in working directly with individuals and groups and in the management of therapeutic, rehabilitative, and preventive programs.

Professional social work services provided to those in need include counseling, education, advocacy, information giving, and referral. But the relationship between the profession and the institution is more complex than that of an agent carrying forward the institutional agenda. The profession also has responsibilities for creating, maintaining, and reforming the institutional context within which it operates.

This dual responsibility is to directly aid clients in need, and to attend to the institutional structure within which these services are offered. This duality is a source of confusion and strain in the profession. The strain is reflected in the inescapable realities of practice that confront professionals with difficult moral dilemmas. Should society's resources be devoted to helping people who have been damaged by the inequities and inadequacies of the social system, or to finding ways to change the system so that its inequities and inadequacies are eliminated? Are the remedial functions of social work a disservice to the poor and needy because they help the system to survive by carting away and repairing the wounded—particularly those who are the greatest political nuisances—thereby retarding social change?

These dilemmas are, essentially, insoluble. Some of the confusion that surrounds this dual responsibility is reflected in the names given to schools engaged in the education of professional social workers: *School of Social Wefare* (University of California, Berkeley), *School of Applied Social Sciences* (Western Reserve University), *School of Social Service Administration* (University of Chicago), *School of Social Work* (University of Alabama), *Graduate School of Social Service* (Indiana University), and *School of Social Policy and Community Service* (State University of New York at Buffalo). If we add to this partial list of names for master's degree programs in social work the many names of departments that offer undergraduate majors and degrees in social work (e.g., *Sociology, Social Work, Social Services, Social Welfare and Corrections, Behavioral Sciences, Health and Social Services,* and *Urban Life and Social Science*), the reader can see the difficulty of sorting out the basic terminology of the field.

By and large, regardless of the names, the educational programs we have mentioned are concerned with training practitioners to provide direct services to those in need. With few exceptions the training of social welfare specialists—practitioners prepared to deal with activities related to the development and reform of the institution—has not been emphasized in the United States as an important area separate from the training of social workers for direct services. (An outstanding exception is the Florence Heller School for Advanced Studies in Social Welfare at Brandeis University. However, this school offers training only at the doctoral level.) The situation is considerably different in United Kingdom where training for "social administration" (the equivalent of what we refer to as "social welfare") is differentiated from social work practice and is recognized as an important field of study in its own right.

This situation appears to be changing in the United States. Since the latter part of the 1960s, many schools of social work have organized their programs along lines designated as "clinical track" and "social change track," "direct service" and "indirect service," and the "micro-level" and "macro-level" of practice. (Some schools add "mezzo-level.") Other schools have sought to resolve the dilemmas posed by the conflicting objectives of social work by utilizing a "generalist" framework for practice whereby a professional works with all kinds of problems—of individuals, groups, organizations, and communities.[8] Thus the dual responsibility of the profession in relation to the institution, which has long been recognized in theory, seems to be gaining a formal role in the structure of professional training.

Society's response to social work and social welfare is a dual one too. Americans support and take pride in their efforts to care for their sick, needy, dependent, and handicapped citizens. Such people as Jane Addams, Dr. Martin Luther King, Jr., Dorothea Dix, Cesar Chavez, Dr. Robert Coles, and Dr. Albert Schweitzer—people who have dedicated their lives to serving the poor—are much admired. There must be a strong base of support among the polity for the Welfare State to survive. But at the same time, many Americans feel that the State (and especially the Welfare State) is too costly. Many believe that it saps resources, and they wonder whether these resources are being used fairly and wisely. Are *all* those recipients *really* needy? Evidence of wrongdoing is not hard to come by: There are thousands of programs and some of them are, indeed, mismanaged; there are millions of recipients and some of them are, indeed, cheating. Sentiments against social work and social welfare may become strong as is the case at the beginning of the 1980s.

There is an ebb and flow in the American attitude toward social work and social welfare. We are a reluctant Welfare State.

## PROFESSIONAL PRACTICE AND SOCIOLOGICAL CRITIQUE

In its efforts to provide for mutual support, the institution of social welfare is concerned both with rehabilitation of individuals who have personal problems and with the management and reform of society's need-meeting structures. In practice, social workers are engaged in both rehabilitation activities, and management and reform activities.

*Rehabilitation activities* include counseling, education, advocacy, information giving, and referral. These activities are the major subject matter of social casework, social group work, and those aspects of community organization in which direct services are provided to community groups. Currently there has been great interest within the profession in the development of a "generalist" approach which integrates these different methodologies of direct services. The largest numbers of professional social workers will always be needed to provide these direct services. These are personally engaging activities and constitute an attractive career to those who enjoy being involved with others and sharing intimate and sometimes troubling personal experiences.

*Managerial and reform activities* are concerned with bringing about a better adjustment between human needs and social resources by creating organizational arrangements through which society can deal with recognized social problems, deviancies, and maladjustments. These activities are the major subject matter of the indirect services—community organization, planning, administration, and evaluation—for which the social welfare specialist is trained. A smaller, but currently growing, number of professional social workers undertake these functions. Generally the work here is drier and less personally engaging that in the direct services, involving as it does an orientation toward research, policy analysis, and program development.

There is another type of activity that is closely related to social reform and which has substantial influence upon its direction. This activity involves the description and analysis of social problems. We call it "sociological critique" because it seeks to assess patterns of human interaction in order to explain where and why social institutions fail. While many academic disciplines contribute to these activities, the major intellectual force flows from sociology. August Comte, Karl Marx, Ferdinand Tönnies, Max Weber, and Hênry de Saint-Simon are some of the early sociologists who provided analyses of society, critiques that encouraged the consideration of alternative means for organizing communities. As noted in the first textbook of American sociology: "Sociology was born of the modern ardor to improve society."[9]

During the period following World War I through the 1920s, social work was considered by many to be "applied social science." Since that period the relationship between social work and sociology in the United States has declined as sociological orientation has moved away from application toward the theoretical aspects of problem analysis and social work moved from sociological toward psychological and psychoanalytic theory. However, the relationship is still quite evident in social work education on the undergraduate level. Many programs offering an undergraduate major or a degree in social work are located in departments of sociology and social science. The situation is somewhat different in United Kingdom and Germany, where the influence of sociology on social work at all educational levels is very strong, with sociologists exercising intellectual hegemony over the social work profession.

Because sociological critique has an influential bearing on social work practice, it is important to recognize the distinctions between these two types of activities. Sociological critique points up what is wrong with society. Its function is not to refine the operation of the welfare system, but rather, to be dissatisfied with what is. The intellectual analyses of many social critics may be backed up by strong personal commitments. Some who are engaged in social-critiquing activities are not satisfied with being merely academic; they participate actively in experimenting with and attempting to implement their ideas for social reform. Richard Cloward, Frances Fox Piven, Frank Riessman, Michael Harrington, Nathan Glazer, and Daniel Patrick Moynihan are among those who combine the academic and theoretical orientation of sociological critique with efforts at practical application. But for the most part this combination is more the exception than the rule. The university offers the major possibility of permanent careers for those engaged in research and analysis of social problems. To some degree the insulation of the academic environment is necessary to allow sociological critique to be objective and fearless of reprisals from institutional spheres that might be offended by the critique.

There are elements of tension and reciprocity in the relationships among sociological critique, social welfare, and social work. The institution of social welfare and the profession of social work constitute important sources of data for the study of social problems. Many social work practitioners are intellectually and emotionally drawn to sociological critique because it often expresses the problems and frustrations experienced in practice. The ideas of sociological critique provide a source of innovation and change in social welfare programs and social work technology. Many students come to the field of social work stimulated by the ideas of sociological critique they encounter in their undergraduate work in the social sciences. For these students, the reciprocal elements between sociological critique and social work practice often stand out more sharply than the conflicts.

But there is also a built-in strain between social work practice and sociological critique because social work practitioners invariably have to come to grips with the implications of sociological critique.

The descriptions and cause-effect analyses of social problems such as poverty, juvenile delinquency, and mental illness suggest new programs and technologies for improving social welfare. But it is the social work practitioner's job to apply these ideas. This results in three potential sources of tension. First, there are usually competing theories generated by sociological critique that have different implications for rehabilitation and reform activities in social work practice. Second, sociological critique often yields assessments of practice that are less than flattering. Social workers who have devoted their lives to developing professional skill will not be enthusiastic about analyses that suggest that their functions are socially irrelevant, or worse, oppressive and reactionary. Finally, when ideas of sociological critique are transformed into new programs and methodologies, they often fall short of expectations, and the new arrangements quickly become the target of new sociological critique, leaving the practitioners wondering whether they can ever do anything right.

Thus, the interaction among reform, rehabilitation, and sociological critique is a source of both vigor and conflict in the emergence of social work and social welfare. While each of these activities stimulates and inspires the others, not infrequently each also undermines and frustrates the aspirations of the others.

## SELECTION OF READINGS

In preparing the chapters of this book and selecting readings we have addressed an audience with a social science background. Our readers, we expect, have mastered introductory materials in history, economics, sociology, and psychology, and they may already be acquainted with some of the authors from whom we have selected readings.

We tended to select articles that deal with subject matter at a high level of generalization. For example, Reading 5, "The Role of Redistribution in Social Policy," by Richard Titmuss, and "Issues in Welfare Reform," Reading 8 by Martha Ozawa, deal with issues that crosscut social welfare programs in all industrial societies. Our basic criterion in the selection of readings was whether they analyzed or described major ideas that illuminate the interesting and universal aspects of the emergence of social welfare and social work. In the introduction to each chapter, we mention additional readings that students might find useful in further exploration of the subject matters.

The book is organized in three Parts. Each Part consists of one or more chapters. There are three chapters in Part I, one chapter in

Part II, and three chapters in Part III. There is an introduction to each of the seven chapters.

## Part I

The readings in the three chapters of Part I, "Social Welfare," focus upon the evolution of social welfare from three perspectives: (1) as it emerged in the transition from preindustrial to industrial society, (2) the place of social welfare in the institutional context of modern society, and (3) the directions in which social welfare seems to be headed.

The articles presented in the first chapter analyze the development of social welfare in the context of the great social, political, and economic changes following in the wake of industrialization. As these changes occurred, new institutional arrangements were required to perform necessary societal functions such as mutual aid, production, distribution, and social control which had previously been centered in the traditional network of social relationships.

The articles in the second chapter offer a series of divergent views concerning the primary functions served by the institution of social welfare. The questions of how and where the evolving institution of social welfare fits into the overall framework of these new institutional patterns have been answered in different ways.

The third chapter describes some of the important features of contemporary social welfare activities and attempts to predict the directions in which they are headed. Whatever conceptual problems and disagreements exist in defining precisely the functional boundaries of the institution are not due to a lack of concrete, ongoing, social welfare activity in society. While the functional boundaries are vague, we can distinguish the broad shape, content, and direction of contemporary social welfare. The relationships between public and private efforts in the provision of services, the shape of social insurance programs, and trends in service delivery are reviewed.

## Part II

The readings in Part II, "Sociological Critique," consist of examples of social problem analyses that have influenced the direction of social work and social welfare. The readings examine causes and potential solutions of the problems of alienation, mental illness, poverty, and the fragmentation of the family.

## Part III

The readings in Part III, "Social Work," are organized in three chapters. Chapter five is concerned with the emergence of social work as a profession. The readings in this chapter reflect the ongoing concern of social work with the attributes of a profession and the dilemmas and problems of professionalism in social work.

Most social workers practice in agencies (which are usually bureaucracies), and most social work services are financed by large governmental and voluntary agencies. Chapter six is devoted to discussion of the organizational context of social work practice.

The final chapter attempts to give some idea of the present status of the profession. In addition, the readings in this chapter deal with current issues in social work in this decade.

## NOTES

1. For example, the following is a list of the proportions of Gross National Product above 5 percent allocated for social security expenditures in selected countries in 1966 and 1970:

|               | *1966* | *1970* |
|---------------|--------|--------|
| Germany       | 19.6   | 22.6   |
| Belgium       | 18.5   | 19.5   |
| Netherlands   | 18.3   | 23.0   |
| France        | 18.3   | 20.9   |
| Italy         | 17.5   | 21.1   |
| Australia     | 9.0    | —      |
| Israel        | 8.3    | —      |
| United States | 7.9    | —      |
| Japan         | 6.2    | —      |

Source: Harold L. Wilensky, *The Welfare State and Equality* (Berkeley: University of California Press, 1975).

2. For example, the following is a list of social welfare expenditures on public programs for selected fiscal years 1928–29 to 1975–76 in the United States. The first row shows total expenditures on social welfare of all levels of government, and the second row shows the percentage of the federal budget on social welfare (see page 13).

In 1977, federal expenditures on social welfare programs constituted approximately 60 percent of expenditures by all levels of government (Alma McMillan, "Social Welfare Expenditures Under Public Programs, Fiscal Year 1977," *Social Security Bulletin,* 42:6 (June 1979), pp. 4–5).

|                           | 1928–29 | 1949–50  | 1959–60  | 1969–70   | 1975–76   |
|---------------------------|---------|----------|----------|-----------|-----------|
| Total expenditures of all levels of government (in millions) | $3,921  | $23,508  | $52,293  | $145,856  | $331,366  |
| Percentage of federal budget allocated for social welfare | 30.9    | 26.2     | 28.1     | 40.1      | 56.0      |

Source: Social Security Administration, U.S. Department of Health, Education, and Welfare, *Social Security Bulletin: Annual Statistical Supplement*, 1976 (Washington, D.C.: U.S. Government Printing Office, 1980).

3. See Howard Goldstein, *Social Work Practice: A Unitary Approach* (Columbia: University of South Carolina Press, 1973), pp. 20–55, and Reading 14, "Origins of the Profession" by Harry Specht.

4. Abraham Flexner, "Is Social Work a Profession?" *Proceedings of the National Conference of Charities and Corrections* (Chicago, 1915), pp. 576–90.

5. Allen Rubin, *Statistics on Social Work Education in the United States,* 1979 (New York: Council on Social Work Education, 1980); *Colleges and Universities with Accredited Undergraduate Social Programs,* 1979, and *Schools of Social Work with Accredited Masters Programs,* 1979 (New York: Council on Social Work Education, 1979).

Examples of a variety of professional journals are: *Social Work; Journal of Social Service Research; Social Service Review; Administration in Social Work; Social Work Research and Abstracts; Health and Social Work; Practice Digest;* and *Social Security Bulletin.*

6. Neil Gilbert, "The Burgeoning Social Service Payload," *Society,* 14 (May–June 1977), 63–65.

7. "Income" and "Services" is a shorthand expression for the types of social provision allocated through social welfare arrangements. For a more detailed analysis of social provisions see Neil Gilbert and Harry Specht, *Dimensions of Social Welfare Policy* (Englewood Cliffs, N.J.: Prentice-Hall, Inc., 1974), pp. 81–102.

8. Generalist approaches to practice are discussed in: Harry Specht and Anne Vickery, *Integrating Social Work Methods* (London: George Allen and Unwin Ltd., 1977); Goldstein, *Social Work Practice;* Harriet Bartlett, *The Common Base of Social Work Practice* (New York: National Association of Social Workers, 1970); and Allen Pincus and Anne Minahan, *Social Work Practice: Model and Method* (Itasca, Ill.: F. E. Peacock Publ., 1973).

9. Lewis Coser, *The Functions of Social Conflict* (New York: Free Press, 1956), p. 17.

*Part I*

# SOCIAL WELFARE

# Chapter One

# EMERGENCE OF THE INSTITUTION

The origin of social welfare in Western society has many roots, some of which extend far back to the religious teachings of the ancient Christians and Jews, which stressed compassion and charity for the poor. In the first selection in the chapter, "The Background," Walter Trattner describes how various elements of religious law and tradition maintained that the poor were victims of misfortune with a right to assistance, which those well-off were duty-bound to provide. These early religious customs furnished the basic moral authority for the emergence of social welfare. However, it is in the transition from preindustrial to industrial society that the main root from which contemporary social welfare arrangements have grown can be found. The institution of social welfare, as we know it today, emerged out of society's varied efforts to cope with changes in economic and social relationships fostered by the breakdown of feudalism, the Reformation, and the emergence of a capitalist orientation by the end of the Middle Ages. This was a tumultuous period during which traditional forms of social relationships and values were overwhelmed by the forces of change. In the process they were transformed to accommodate to the reality of social existence in an industrial society.

What was this reality? Social theorists of the nineteenth century distinguished many elements in the transformation of community life that marked the shift from preindustrial to industrial society. The

French sociologist Émile Durkheim analyzed the change in the basis of social cohesion, which he described as moving from mechanical solidarity to organic solidarity. In a peasant community, the integration of the individual—his sense of being a part of the whole—derived from the likeness that was all about him in work, values, and beliefs. This likeness was reinforced by tradition and produced a form of mechanical solidarity described by Durkheim as follows:

> The social molecules which can be coherent in this way can act together only in the measure that they have no actions of their own, as the molecules of inorganic bodies. That is why we propose to call this type of solidarity mechanical. The term does not signify it is produced by mechanical and artificial means. We call it that only by analogy to the cohesion which unites the elements of an inanimate body, as opposed to that which makes a unity out of the elements of a living body.[1]

As the division of labor necessary to perform industrial tasks increased, a new form of social cohesion emerged which was based upon the interdependence of people. The sense of social solidarity that came from likeness was replaced by what Durkheim referred to as organic solidarity. Community life became highly diversified, like an organism with numerous units performing different functions, all of which are required to keep the system in working order.

The German sociologist Ferdinand Tönnies sought to capture the essence of the transformation of community life by analyzing this phenomenon in terms of what has become a classic typology: Gemeinschaft and Gesellschaft. These polar ideal types are logical constructs which attempt to extract the core elements of the phenomena under investigation. Gemeinschaft reflects elements of the social system of peasant or tribal communities, and Gesellschaft the corresponding elements in urban communities. Some of the characteristics of these community types are summarized in Table 1.

According to Tönnies, Gemeinschaft social relationships are based upon the idea of a natural distribution which determines and is in turn supported by a sacred sense of tradition. Thus:

> The relationship between community and feudal lords, and more especially that between the community and its members, is based not upon contracts, but upon understanding, like that within the family. The village community, even where it encompasses also the feudal lord, is like one individual household in its necessary relationship to the land.[2]

As the feudal society began to crumble, so did the "individual household," and with it went the stability and security it had provided for its members. While imposing a strong order of constraint on individual freedom, feudalism offered a form of social insurance against unemployment, disaster, old age, and other exigencies of life. With its collapse, individual freedom increased, along with uncertainty and hardship. New social arrangements were required to mitigate these hardships, to reduce uncertainty, and to stabilize community life. It is in this context that the institution of social welfare emerged.

The readings in this chapter describe the early types of social arrangements devised to deal with the problems of economic insecurity and social control that resulted from a declining feudal economy and a rising capitalist state. The beginning of social welfare as we know it today can be traced to the development of the English Poor Law of 1601. English poor law embodied the conflicting strains between the desire to reinforce the feudal structure and the increasing assumption by government of responsibility for the poor. The various statutes that were codified in the Poor Law of 1601 are analyzed by Walter Trattner in Reading 1, "The Background." This act amounted to more than government relief to substitute for the system of mutual support that had been provided under feudal custom. It also served as a mechanism for social control by requiring registration of need, distinguishing between the impotent and the nonimpotent poor, and securing work for those strong enough to be in the labor force. To a lesser degree, the poor laws also served a socialization function by authorizing local officials to assume responsibility for apprenticing the children of the poor so they might become industrious, self-supporting citizens. However, as a cornerstone of the modern institution of social welfare, the most prominent feature of Elizabethan poor law was its endorsement of the principle of public obligation for the economic well-being of the people.

A number of statutes followed the Poor Law of 1601. Some were repressive measures, such as those embodied in the Law of Settlement of 1662, which buttressed the Act of 1531 in restricting the movement of the poor from their parishes. Another such measure provided for establishment of the workhouse in 1772, the wretched conditions of which were considered both a necessary discipline for the poor and a deterrent to the choice of public relief by the able-bodied. Other statutes were positive efforts to deal with relief for the poor, such as the Gilbert Act of 1782, which sought to provide assistance to the able-bodied poor in their own homes and to mitigate the demoralizing effects of the workhouse system. One of the pivotal experiments in relief tried during this period (and certainly the most absorbing one) was the well-intentioned effort to provide a guaranteed minimum wage under the Speenhamland Law of 1795. Analyzing this effort and its unintended consequences, Karl Polanyi shows how the Speenhamland allowance system depressed wages, reduced productivity, and demoralized workers.[3] These devasting effects of Speenhamland prepared the way for the Poor Law Reform of 1834, under which public responsibility for the able-bodied poor was considerably diminished and extremely harsh conditions were imposed upon those who sought public relief. With the Industrial Revolution in England almost completed, public protection against economic risk was at its nadir, and the able-bodied were left to fend for themselves in the open marketplace.

In the United States, arrangements for social welfare followed the general patterns of the English experience. The specific character of early social welfare activities in the United States is examined by James Leiby in Reading 2, "The Poor Law, 1815–1845." Leiby points out how social welfare developments in the United States were influenced by the English poor law principles of public responsibility, local responsibility, relatives' responsibility, and individual responsibility for self-help. He also reveals certain distinctive features of the American experience under which 19th century social welfare legislation was more of a state than a federal concern. One of the important differences in the evolution of English and American social welfare activities concerns the utilization of "indoor relief." The workhouse was a harsh environment for placement of the poor, emphasized in the English poor law reform of 1834 as a method to deter pauperism. During this period such institutions for the poor also developed in the United States. However, as Leiby indicates, the American movement in this direction was relatively short-lived and without the political support given in England.

The final selection in this chapter, "The Changing Balance of Status and Contract in Assistance Policy" (Reading 3), by Samuel Mencher, provides an overview of the development of assistance policy from the preindustrial poor laws through contemporary arrangements for social security. Mencher's framework for examining assistance policies in the light of the changing social relationships that marked the transition from the feudal period to modern times draws attention to three elements: (1) the growth of contractual relationships which culminated in the Poor Law Reform of 1834, (2) the rise of new status relationships reflected in relief policy toward the end of the 19th century, and (3) the mixture of status and contract relationships characteristic of government responsibility for relief in the capitalist welfare state.

While the institution of social welfare is composed primarily of programs under public auspices, voluntary or private efforts account for a substantial proportion of social welfare activities. Public programs in the United States evolved more slowly than those in England, leaving the voluntary sector in this country with an important role in carrying out welfare functions. The voluntary sector developed out of two streams of activity that often intermixed: philanthropic endeavors of the upper classes, and self-help efforts at the grass roots. Leiby (Reading 2) describes the communitarian movements which were a special and extreme form of rural self-help efforts. In regard to urban self-help arrangements Oscar Handlin offers a penetrating account of the experience of immigrants who came to the United States in the nineteenth century and adjusted to life in a foreign land.[4] One of these adjustments involved the creation of new social arrangements among the immigrants as they banded together for mutual protection and assistance in coping with the uncertainties of a strange and unstable environment. The formation of these rural and urban voluntary associations was one of the stirring features of the emergence of social welfare in the United States.

TABLE 1

Characteristics of Tribal and Urban Communities

|                | Gemeinschaft | Gesellschaft |
|----------------|--------------|--------------|
| Social structure | Simple | Complex |
| Relationships | Private—Family | Public—Strangers |
| Self-expression | Conformity | Individualism |
| Social control | Religion—Custom | Law |
| Ownership | Communal | Private property |
| Will to associate (basis of human relationships) | Natural (relationships are ends in themselves) | Rational (relationships are means to ends) |
| Payment for service | Usage of land and commodities | Money |

## NOTES

1. Émile Durkheim, *The Division of Labor in Society,* trans. George Simpson (New York: Free Press, paperback ed., 1965), p. 130.

2. Ferdinand Tönnies, *Community and Society* (Gemeinschaft and Gesellschaft), trans. and ed. Charles Loomis (New York: Harper Torchbooks, 1963), p. 59.

3. Karl Polanyi, *The Great Transformation* (New York: Holt, Rinehart and Winston, 1944), pp. 77–102.

4. Oscar Handlin, *The Uprooted* (New York: Little, Brown and Co., 1951), pp. 170–200.

# 1  The Background

## WALTER TRATTNER

The basic tenets and programs of any social welfare system reflect the values of the society in which they function and, like all other social institutions, they do not arise in a vacuum; they stem from the customs, statutes, and practices of the past. Therefore, one cannot understand efforts to help the needy without first comprehending the foundations on which they were built. And since the practice of assisting people in need as we know it in America did not originate in this country but was transplanted from the Old World to the New during the colonial period, we must go back in time, perhaps even to antiquity, to begin our study of American social welfare.

Hospitality to strangers, for example, was recognized as a virtue even among primitive peoples. Hammurabi, the famed ruler of Babylonia some two thousand years before Christ, made the protection of widows and orphans, and the weak against the strong, an essential part of his code. Buddhism, founded about 400 B.C., taught that all other forms of righteousness "are not worth the sixteenth part of the emancipation of the heart through love and charity."

The ancient Greeks frequently discussed the matter. Aristotle (384–322 B.C.) spoke of man as a social animal and, as such, one who had to cooperate with and assist his fellow men. He also said it was more blessed to give than to receive. And, in fact, the words "charity" and "philanthropy," and the concepts for which they stand —humanity, brotherhood, love for mankind—are of Greek origin.[1] Hence, the ancient Greeks, and the Romans after them, had a variety of ways of relieving distress and helping those in need, some of which we might not recommend today, such as slavery, concubinage, and euthanasia. However, they also had such other practices as daily allowances or pensions for the crippled, public distribution of grain for the needy, and institutions for the custodial care of various unfortunates, especially youngsters orphaned as a result of fathers lost in battle.

Even more important for the history of American philanthropy and social welfare, however, are the ancient Jewish doctrines which teach the *duty* of giving and, equally important, the *right* of those in need to receive. Throughout the Old Testament, the ancient Hebrew collection of historical books, laws, proverbs, psalms, and prophetic writings that go as far back in time as the late eleventh century B.C., one finds commandments to be charitable to the unfortunate—the sick, the old, the handicapped, and the poor.[2] Thus, for example, the Scriptures state not only that "one might break off his iniquities" by showing mercy to the poor, but that "thou shalt not harden thy heart nor shut thy hand" to the poor, and that "it is forbidden to turn away a poor man . . . empty-handed." Moreover, such "charity should be given with a friendly countenance, with joy, and with a good heart."

Not only is everyone who can afford to do so obliged to contribute to charity, but according to the Old Testament, all those in need are obliged to take it. Thus, for example, according to Jeremiah: "Whosoever is so much in need of charity that he cannot live unless he receives it—as, for instance, a man who is old or sick or in constant pain,—but takes none out of pride, is guilty of bloodshed and is responsible for his own life; so that he has nothing for his suffering, save punishment and sin."

The Talmud, a collection of Jewish law and tradition (based upon Biblical texts and rabbinical commentaries on those texts) codified around 500–400 B.C. and adopted as the rule of Jewish life, and still considered as the source of authority among orthodox Jews today, prescribes exactly how charitable funds are to be collected and distributed, including the appointment of *gabbaim*, or tax collectors, to administer the system.

How much should be given a poor man? The Talmud provides the answer: "Sufficient for his needs in that which he wanteth." Thus, if someone is hungry, "he should be fed; if he needs clothing, he should be clothed; if he lacks household utensils, they should be purchased for him. . . . each and everyone should be supplied with what he needs" (Deut. 15:8).

Christianity carried on this tradition. Its emphasis upon good deeds, love of one's enemies, and entry into heaven through mercy and charity, stemmed, of course, from Old Testament doctrine and Hebraic law and custom. Since Jesus, Peter, Paul, and all the founding fathers of the Christian church—including the first fifteen bishops in Jerusalem—were Jews, it is not surprising that the New Testament no less than the Old contains many verses that stress charity. The text that perhaps more than any other weaves together the threads of early Christian-New Testament teaching on charity is the description of the Day of Judgment in St. Matthew, especially: "And the King shall answer and say unto them, Verily, I say unto you, Inasmuch as ye have done it unto one of the least of these my brethren, ye have done *it* unto me."

The Decretum, a compilation of papal decrees, canons of church councils, and commentaries of church lawyers codified in the twelfth century which, along with subsequent decrees and writings, is considered Canon (church) Law and (like the Talmud for Jews) the authoritative source of law for Christians, contains an elaborate discussion of the theory and practice of charity. Study of the Decretum clearly reveals that the leading principle underlying early Christian social welfare policy was similar to the Hebrew idea that preceded it—poverty was not considered a crime. And while discretion was to be observed in bestowing assistance, and careful rules were elaborated for discriminating among the various classes of needy people,[3] generally speaking, evidence of need overrode all else. It was assumed that need arose as a result of misfortune for which society, in an act of justice, not charity or mercy, had to assume responsibility. In short, the needy had a right to assistance, and those better off had a duty to provide it.

In practice, these ideas operated in a variety of ways. At the outset, when the church was small and its early followers owned no private property, there was little need to establish any formal social services. While there was some poverty, it was not a social problem. Those suffering misfortune were among close friends and associates who, as a matter of course, came to their assistance; mutual aid, in other words, sufficed to meet the needs of the faithful.

However, with the passage of time, the end of persecution (as marked by Emperor Constantine's conversion to Christianity in the fourth century), an increase in members and wealth, and greater ease of travel, church fathers found it more and more necessary to establish a formal system of charities. Beginning in the sixth century, the monasteries that emerged served as important agencies of relief, especially in rural areas. Some monastic orders, in fact, were organized to help the needy. Receiving income from their lands and from donations, legacies, and collections, they not only gave generously to those who came to their doors, but carried food and other provisions to the poor in the community.

With the evolution of feudalism by the eleventh century, there was little uncared-for distress, at least in theory. Most people were serfs who, by virtue of their lack of freedom, were protected by their liege lords or masters against such hazards as sickness and unemployment. Those who received no such protection, especially in the rapidly emerging cities, often were helped by social, craft, and merchant guilds. While, for the most part, the guilds provided benefits for their own members (who, because of their craft or trade, were somewhat removed from the immediate threat of poverty), they also provided assistance to others. Thus, many maintained "works of charity" for the town poor—they distributed corn and barley yearly, fed the needy on feast days, provided free lodgings for destitute travelers, and engaged in other kinds of intermittent and incidental help.

A more important source of aid to the needy during the Middle Ages was the hospital. Medieval hospitals did not merely provide medical assistance to the ill; rather, they housed and cared for weary travelers, for orphans, the aged, and the destitute, and, in general, provided a variety of services for all those in need. Most early hospitals were attached to monasteries or were found along main routes of travel. Soon, however, they appeared in cities and later were taken over by municipal authorities, thus forming a link between ecclesiastical and secular charity. By the middle of the fourteenth century, there were hundreds of such institutions in England alone. They varied in size from those caring for a dozen or so people, to others accommodating up to several hundred.

Most important, however, in terms of administering medieval poor relief was the aid dispensed by ecclesiastical or church authorities at the diocese or parish level. The bishop of each diocese was charged with the duty of feeding and protecting the poor within his district. He was, in fact, directed to divide the total revenue of the diocese, which came from the church tithe, and distribute a fixed portion—from a third to a fourth—to those in need. In most cases, though, the diocese was divided into several parishes and, in practice, it was the parish priest who became directly responsible for relieving distress.

Most priests were diligent in carrying out their duties, and the money available to care for the poor was sufficient for the need. Therefore, by the "high" Middle Ages, a highly developed and effective system of poor relief had been established. Because the church was a *public* institution and the tithe a compulsory tax, it could be argued that the system as regulated by the church was the prototype of the one that arose under the famous English Poor Law of 1601. With the rise of the modern state, which in the middle of the sixteenth century absorbed the church, civil authorities naturally became responsible for administering the system of poor relief conducted earlier by church officials.

In the meantime, however, certain social and economic upheavals occurred. The general dissolution of feudalism and the manorial system resulted in social disorder and serious hardship for many, especially agricultural laborers forced from the land. The growth of commerce and international trade and the rise of a money economy with its elements of capital investment, credit, interest, rent, and wages also affected the incidence and nature of poverty. So too did the industrial revolution and development of the factory system, which, in urban centers, gave rise to masses of persons with specialized skills who experienced not only seasonal but also cyclical unemployment.

In England, conditions were made worse by the so-called enclosure movement, which resulted from the growth of the woolens industry. As the demand for wool increased, and with it the price, it became extremely profitable for landowners to turn their fields into pastures and to raise sheep. Since sheepraising could not be done on small fields, this upset the earlier feudal system of tillage, which rested on landlords dividing their estates into small tracts and parcelling them out to tenants (or serfs) in return for certain specified services. Enclosure thus led to the further destruction of rural homesteads, the scattering of many more cottagers, and a sizeable increase in the number of unattached persons without the means of support.

Then a series of natural calamities—crop failures, famine, pestilence, and especially the dread Black Death (or bubonic plague), which occurred in 1348–49 and killed almost a third of England's population—produced further suffering and hardship for many. Finally, the growth of corruption and the general decay of the church in England and elsewhere ultimately led to the Protestant Reformation and, in 1536, the dissolution of the monasteries and other church property by Henry VIII; many of those who had lived or had been employed in ecclesiastical institutions were turned out and forced to join the ranks of poor wanderers.

Taken together, these developments—the breakdown of the medieval economy, the social structure with its relatively fixed order of things, and the church with its entire framework of charity—meant for many people the loss of the economic security given to a serf by his master, and the social, economic, and spiritual security given by the church to its members during the Middle Ages. This, in turn, resulted in a tremendous increase in unemployment, poverty, vagabondage, begging, and thievery, especially in the growing commercial centers to which many of the needy naturally gravitated.

In an effort to do something about these conditions, especially to suppress the restless wandering of the landless and to keep laborers in the state of servitude from which they were just emerging, Edward III, as early as the mid-fourteenth century, initiated a series of restrictive measures. Although sometimes considered the beginning of Parliamentary involvement in welfare policy, they basically were repressive statutes aimed more at regulating labor than assisting the needy. Among these, the most important was the Statute of Laborers. Proclaimed in 1349 (a year after the Black Death, which had caused labor shortages and demands for higher wages among the poorer classes), the measure fixed maximum wages, placed travel restrictions on impotent and unemployed persons, and in effect compelled the jobless to work for any employer willing to hire them. The law also forbade the giving of charity to "sturdy" and "valiant" almseekers, a practice which allegedly induced mobility or laziness and unemployment; all able-bodied persons would be forced to work in their place of residence at a rate of wages fixed by law.

The social and economic changes that occasioned the statute, however, were far more powerful than the law designed to stop them. The progress from feudalism toward a capitalistic-democratic society continued, not always peaceably. As a result, in the sixteenth century, other measures were enacted which further attempted to repress vagrancy and mobility. In 1531, for example, Parliament passed a statute that provided severe punishment for able-bodied beggars. They were to be brought to the market place and "there to be tyed to the end of a carte naked and be beten with whyppes throughe out ... tyll [their bodies] ... be blody by reason of suche whypping."

The act, however, also contained constructive features concerning relief of the poor; it decreed that mayors, justices of the peace, and other local officials "shall make diligent search and inquiry of all aged poor and impotent persons which live or of necessity be compelled to live by alms of the charity of the people," and assign such people areas where they may beg. While still primarily a punitive and repressive measure designed to limit begging, by making a distinction between the able-bodied who refused to seek work and the poor who could not work and thus needed relief, and authorizing the latter to beg, and even setting aside areas where they might do so, the state actually took the first step toward administering an organized network of relief.

In 1536, with the passage of the Act for the Punishment of Sturdy Vagabonds and Beggars—the Henrician Poor Law—the government exercised further responsibility for the relief of persons in economic distress. While the measure made the penalties for begging even more severe (including an elaborate schedule of branding, enslavement, and execution for repeated offenses), it also ordered local public officials to obtain resources, through voluntary contributions collected in churches, to care for the poor, the lame, the sick, and the aged. Thus, instead of merely setting up machinery for legalizing begging and confining it to the impotent poor, as the previous statute had done, this measure attempted to eliminate the need for alms-seeking, making the parish the unit of local government for poor relief.

Furthermore, the act permitted local officials to use the funds they collected to provide work for "such as be lusty or having their limbs strong enough to labor." A perceptive and novel feature of the measure, then, was its recognition of the fact that the able-bodied were not always able to find jobs. In such cases, parish officials could furnish work for those in need. They also were given the authority "to take ... children under the age of fourteen years and above the age of five years, in begging or in idleness, and to appoint them to masters of husbandry or other crafts or labors to be taught, by which they may get their living when they shall come of age." Another important feature of the statute was the provision for compensating alms collectors, thus anticipating by many years the development of paid public welfare workers. By the provisions of this act, then, the state, through civil and church authorities, assumed legal responsibility for the relief of *all* its poor, old and young, impotent and able-bodied alike. It was a serious attempt to cope with the economic and social problems of the age.

Although local officials—mayors, governors and head officers of every city and the church wardens or two others of every parish—were required to provide assistance to the destitute, funds for the purpose were to be raised through voluntary contributions in churches. Therefore, the next logical step was introduction of a compulsory assessment when donations proved insufficient. This came in 1572 with the enactment of a measure stating that the justices of the peace and other local officials "shall by their good discretions tax and assess all and every the inhabitants dwelling in all and every city, borough, town, village, hamlet and place" for the care of those in economic distress. The statute also created a new public official, the overseer of the poor, who was charged with the duty of providing work relief for the able-bodied unemployed, a job more clearly defined and made mandatory by the provisions of yet another measure, enacted four years later.

By the late sixteenth century, then, the government had perceived that punitive measures directed at vagrants were insufficient to preserve order, let alone the general good of the realm. Based on acceptance of the obligation to help those people who could not provide for themselves, a series of measures relating to poverty, vagrancy, and relief of the poor had been enacted that attempted to deal with the problem of economic security in light of the changing religious, social, and economic conditions of the period. The principle of relief locally financed and administered for local residents had been established. Public officials administered a system of assistance that included both direct grants-in-aid to the unemployable and a policy of apprenticeship and work relief for the able-bodied. Taken together, these measures embodied most of the principles written into the famous Poor Law of 1601.

The immediate background of the famous statute was the worsening times of the 1590s—a decade of food scarcity and widespread famine, of inflation and high prices, of insecurity and great suffering. Rioting, thievery, and social disorder again became widespread. Lawmakers, not only fearful of insurrection, but also compelled to recognize the existence of large-scale involuntary idleness and suffering due to difficult conditions, felt the need to act.

This, too, was the age of mercantilism, an era of paternalism, and of faith in the government's capacity (and, indeed, need) to arrange the affairs of man. The interests of the state, especially the desire to build up a strong, self-sufficient economy, were dominant. And since the means of accomplishing this were by "setting the poor to work" and turning the country into "a hive of industry," direct and active government intervention was required to overcome the threat of insecurity and the prevailing social disorder; hence, the Poor Law of 1601.[4]

Like its predecessors, the Elizabethan Poor Law, which was to stand with but minor revisions for almost 250 years, contained harsh, repressive features. Parents, insofar as they had the means, were legally liable for the support of their children and grandchildren. Likewise, children were responsible for the care of their needy parents and grandparents. More important, vagrants refusing work could be committed to a house of correction, could be whipped, branded, or put in pillories and stoned, or even be put to death.

On the other hand, the measure had many constructive features —especially its assumption that the state had a responsibility to supplement ordinary efforts to relieve want and suffering and to insure the maintenance of life. It further conceded that there were helpless or needy people who not only deserved such assistance but who had a legal right to it. In addition, the statute defined three major categories of dependents—children, the able-bodied, and the impotent— and directed the authorities to adapt their activities to the needs of each: for needy children, apprenticeship; for the able-bodied, work; and for the incapacitated, helpless, or "worthy" poor, either home ("outdoor") or institutional ("indoor") relief.

The law firmly established the principle of local responsibility, at the lowest level, for the care of those in need. In executing the measure, the parish was to act through its church wardens and a small number of "substantial householders" who would be appointed annually by the justices of the peace to serve both as overseers of the poor and as collectors of the revenue—a wholly secular or civil position. Funds necessary for carrying the act into effect were to be raised by taxing every householder in the parish.[5]

So while the basic principles of public assistance did not originate in 1601—for poor relief had been a matter of public concern long before that time—the Elizabethan Poor Law brought together, in a single coherent statute, the "inconsistent and erratic relief legislation of the previous" years, firmly placing its operation in the hands of civil authorities and establishing a definite system of obligatory financing outside of the church. According to Karl de Schweinitz, author of *England's Road to Social Security,* it culminated a development that started in 1531, or perhaps as early as 1349.

Written to bring order out of chaos and with an eye toward preserving stability in case of future social and economic crises, the statute recognized the existence of involuntary unemployment and of need, and firmly established the individual's right to public assistance. For the most part, it was a broad, permissive act. From what evidence we have, we can say that it was put into effect throughout England with a fair degree of efficiency and success. Although it did not eliminate all human suffering, many of the needy were helped, the able-bodied put to work, and the children apprenticed.[6] The statute also provided the pattern for the poor laws in the American colonies, in the original thirteen states, and in the subsequent ones as they entered the Union.

## NOTES

1. Charity comes from *caritas,* or love (brotherly love); philanthropy comes from the words *philo,* or love, and *anthropos,* or mankind.

2. This is especially true, however, of the Pentateuch, or the first five books of the Old Testament, sometimes called the Torah. Within the Pentateuch, the book of Deuteronomy, the law book, is most important for these purposes. The Hebrew faith, derived largely from Moses, rested upon a belief in one God, Maker and Ruler of all, who demanded good behavior, economic and social justice, and true humility from all His worshippers.

3. A man's first responsiblity was to his family, especially his parents, then to his neighbors, and after that, to strangers. Even among strangers, however, a rather highly elaborate hierarchy existed.

4. Actually, although the 1601 Act (the 43 Elizabeth, Chapter 2) is the most famous and is thought of as the most important poor law, it was in fact anticlimactic. In 1597 and 1598, a comprehensive poor law was enacted which brought together all the previous legislation on the matter; about the only thing the latter measure added to its predecessor was the extension of liability for support to grandparents. As Karl de Schweinitz has pointed out, the 1601 statute has been considered a landmark in the relief of economic distress largely because it was the last rewriting of the total law.

5. The justices of the peace, who fixed the rate of assessment, also had the authority to raise revenue from other parishes should local funds prove to be insufficient.

6. Perhaps it should be mentioned that while the state gave notice (through passage of this act) that the poor were to be cared for from public funds, the state was quite willing, if not anxious, to allow parishes to look after their poor through voluntary (or private) relief, if they elected to do so. Hence, the same Parliament that passed the Poor Law of 1601 encouraged private philanthropy through enactment, the same year, of the Law of Charitable Uses which, in the words of W. K. Jordan (*Philanthropy in England, 1480–1660*), "was far more important to the history of Tudor-Stuart philanthropy than the great Elizabethan Poor Law of the same year." According to Jordan, until 1660, the mainspring of the English charity system remained private, both in organization and in financing. The Trust Law directed the spirit of generosity into the founding of numerous free private schools, hospitals, almshouses, dispensaries, and the like. In short, private philanthropy at least complemented public relief at this time, providing a second cluster of institutions and services for the needy.

# BIBLIOGRAPHY

Beer, Max. *Social Struggles in Antiquity.* New York: International Publishers, 1925.

————. *Social Struggles in the Middle Ages.* New York: International Publishers, 1929.

Campbell, Anna M. *The Black Death and Men of Learning.* New York: Columbia University Press, 1931.

Coll, Blanche D. "Perspectives in Public Welfare: The English Heritage," *Welfare in Review* 4 (March 1966): 1–12.

Coulton, G. G. *The Medieval Village.* Cambridge, Mass.: Cambridge University Press, 1931.

de Schweinitz, Karl. *England's Road to Social Security.* Philadelphia: University of Pennsylvania Press, 1943.

Feinberg, Louis, ed. *Section on Charity from the Shulhan Arukh.* New York: Charity Organization Society, 1915.

Hands, A. R. *Charities and Social Aid in Greece and Rome.* Ithaca, N.Y.: Cornell University Press, 1968.

Jordan, W. K. "The English Background of Modern Philanthropy," *American Historical Review* 66 (January 1961): 401–08.

————. *Philanthropy in England, 1480–1660.* New York: Russell Sage Foundation, 1959.

Leonard, E. M. *The Early History of English Poor Relief.* Cambridge, Mass.: Cambridge University Press, 1900.

Marshall, Dorothy. *The English Poor Law in the Eighteenth Century.* London: George Routledge, 1926.

Marts, Arnaud. *The Generosity of Americans.* Englewood Cliffs, N.J.: Prentice-Hall, 1966.

————. *Man's Concern for his Fellow-man.* Geneva, N.Y.: Marts and Lundy, 1961.

Mencher, Samuel. *Poor Law to Poverty Program.* Pittsburgh: University of Pittsburgh Press, 1967.

Nichols, Sir George. *A History of the English Poor Law, 3 Vols.* London: P.S. King, 1900.

Niebuhr, Reinhold. *The Contribution of Religion to Social Work.* New York: Columbia University Press, 1932.

Owen, David. *English Philanthropy, 1660–1960.* Cambridge, Mass.: Harvard University Press, 1964.

Polanyi, Karl. *The Great Transformation.* Boston: Beacon Press, 1957.

"Poor Law," *Encyclopaedia Britannica,* Vol. 18 (Chicago: William Benton, 1971): 226–32.

Queen, Stuart. *Social Work in the Light of History.* Philadelphia: J. B. Lippincott, 1922.

Thorndike, Lynn. "The Historical Background," in Ellsworth Faris *et al.,* eds., *Intelligent Philanthropy.* Chicago: University of Chicago Press, 1930.

Tierney, Brian. *Medieval Poor Law.* Berkeley: University of California Press, 1959.

Ullman, Walter. "Public Welfare and Social Legislation in the Early Medieval Councils," in *Councils and Assemblies.* Cambridge, Mass.: Cambridge University Press, 1971.

Webb, Sidney and Beatrice. *English Local Government: English Poor Law History, Part I, The Old Poor Law.* New York: Longmans, Green, 1927.

————. *English Poor Law Policy.* New York: Longmans, Green, 1910.

# 2  The Poor Law, 1815–1845

## JAMES LEIBY

The story of practical provision for the dependent, defective, and delinquent in the years 1815–1845 is largely a blank. Our main sources are legislation, reports by administrators, and studies by reformers. Legislation tells us what was supposed to be; administrative accounts are typically perfunctory or defensive; and reformers concentrated on exposing faults and advocating causes. Ordinary administrative circumstances and events are left to the imagination. Moreover, both theory and practice rested on contemporary assumptions about the nature of the community and the social duties and rights within the community, and these must be made clear.

As a concrete image and a practical matter, people thought of society and government in terms of the locality in which they lived. State government was remote; it was a body of legislators meeting for a few weeks every second year, passing laws that told local officials to bestir themselves. It is difficult to imagine now how isolated and self-sufficient local communities were. Most families raised their own vegetables, butchered their own meat, and milked their own cow; crossroads stores carried items like salt, sugar, tea, and tobacco. Even a town house often had a sizable garden and a cow in the barn. News consisted of neighborhood gossip, and church affairs were the most frequent occasion for organized social life.

The concept of community that ordered these experiences was still, after two centuries in the new world, the European (specifically English) village, for what alternative was there? Accordingly, it was assumed that neighbors would have the same cultural background; Irish, German, and other immigrants drew off by themselves. Church and government, public and private, would be naturally linked in common life. There would be some of patrician leadership; a few unfortunate dependents, crippled, perhaps, or widows; and probably some ne'er-do-wells or rogues.

This traditional picture of the community, which implied a stable population, a well-established culture, and a hierarchical class structure, was often incongruent with the new world, where settlements were relatively fast-changing and formless. After 1815 it seemed more and more archaic. The growing market economy pressed in on local self-sufficiency and directed men's attention to centers of trade.

From *A History of Social Welfare and Social Work in the United States* by James Leiby, pp. 35–47. Copyright © 1978 by Columbia University Press. Reprinted by permission of the publisher and author.

It brought potent influences on state government with regard to transportation, banking, and economic regulation. The organization and reorganization of political parties gave new zest and scope to the competition for votes, in which statewide and even national linkages were advantageous. In building their congregations, evangelists competed with established preachers. Generally and very unevenly, local communities lost their central place in contemporary thought about common problems and resources. On the one hand, individuals became more enterprising; on the other, some larger societal organization began to seem more significant. It is helpful to look at practical arrangements for social welfare in the perspective of these changing features of social life.

The most comprehensive and positive responses to the disorganizing factors just mentioned were the dozens of utopian communities that took form during these years. In general, they illustrated the freedom and opportunity that prevailed in the nation and its reliance on voluntary association. No power forced these people to join together, nor did any stop them, so long as their communal life did not outrage conventional decency (which it sometimes did). In outer form their little societies looked much like rural villages; in this framework they established fellowships that guaranteed cradle-to-grave security as a matter of right and personal solicitude, without relying on the elaborate schemes and bureaucratic administration that have characterized the twentieth century. In some respects their goals were similar to ours, but their means were different, just because of the sentiments that underlay their community rights and duties.

Some of the communitarians, like those who settled in Amana, Iowa, or the Rappites in Indiana, were German sectarians who obviously tried to reconstruct the European village. Others, like the Shakers (the largest and longest lived of these groups), the Perfectionists at Oneida, New York, and Transcendentalists at Brook Farm, were Anglo-Americans but drew their membership from different regions or classes. Most were united by peculiar, even fanatic, religious doctrines, but some, like Robert Owen's colony at New Harmony or the two score "phalanxes," formed in the model prescribed by the French reformer, Charles Fourier, were aggressively secular. Most failed, but many earned not only security but substantial wealth. Somewhat similar to these groups were the Mormons, who gathered strength in the years before 1845 and brought to the territory of Utah enduring forms of the New England town and its cooperative enterprises.

Unlike twentieth-century welfare programs, which typically meet a specific category of need or problematic behavior, the communitarians went directly to the heart of the matter. They held their property in common, at least in part, so that everyone had a share, as in a family. They also arranged strong indoctrination and social control to ensure that everyone felt a personal and mutual responsibility for the common life. Their discipline demanded the ascetic virtues of the Protestant ethic, excepting its worldly emphasis on competition and "success." These places were much like monasteries, with frequent occasions for confession, criticism, and correction of misbehavior, often by techniques resembling present-day encounter groups.

Obviously these communities realized ideals and offered satisfactions that had deep roots in our culture and have a continuing appeal, and it is not clear why they did not multiply and adapt themselves to changing circumstances. Doubtless the concept of the village commune became increasingly archaic in economic, social, and intellectual terms. Economically, the communitarians did not meet the market demand for large-scale and opportunistic investment and production. They wanted not economic progress but relatively simple and stable modes of work that would enhance their common life. Still, they might have adapted if it were not for the prerequisite of a religious or quasi-religious conviction that separated them from the world of nonbelievers, and the strong self-discipline and social control required by the common life. A sympathetic observer and historian, writing in 1874, thought that many communes did succeed in providing security and comfort. His main criticism was that they were parochial, boring, lacking the stimulation and culture of the urban metropolis.[1] By that time it was apparent that the country's future lay in great diverse cities, not rural villages, and utopians of the next generation would think of a national revolution, perhaps violent but preferably peaceful, rather than groups of people withdrawing to make themselves an example to others.

In any case the communitarians in the years 1815–1845 gave concrete expression to many notions underlying welfare institutions in the period. They elaborated the tradition that social relations were best ordered in the form of a face-to-face community much like a rural village; that the group was properly united by a common moral authority—usually the Bible and supplementary divine revelations, rightly interpreted—which laid down how people ought to act and respond to others; that within this framework people were more or less equal children of God, stewards of His bounty, sharing in it among the vicissitudes of life.

The communitarians were an extreme. In the rest of the rural democracy, social solidarity and sharing were ideals left mostly to the individual conscience. Here the poor law was a testimonial, more or less respected, to the ancient order of society. It was part of our English and, beyond that, our Christian heritage. If people had been good Christians, no public poor law would have been necessary. Private almsgiving and congregational charity would have done the job. In fact in England poor relief had been left to individuals, churches, and monasteries until the sixteenth century. There was then no public relief, tax supported and administered by government officials. Between 1534 and 1601 there were major changes in this situation. England turned Protestant, and its hierarchy of bishops and priests became responsible to the king rather than the Pope. Furthermore, English monasteries, which inclined toward Rome, were secularized, ending their important work of poor relief. Hence, the king and Parliament began passing legislation to help the local congregations—the parishes of the Church of England—do the job better. Laws gave parish officials who looked after church property the power to tax the congregation if voluntary contributions were not sufficient; other regulations governed the administration of parish relief and eligibility for such relief. These statutes, enacted between 1534 and 1601, were summarized and codified in the second chapter (i.e., act) of the 43rd Parliament of Queen Elizabeth, held in 1601. When Englishmen settled America and felt the need for some similar provision, colonial legislators reenacted versions of the act just as they followed English patterns in their other legislation. In these forms it remained our fundamental provision for the needy until the Great Depression of the 1930s.

What principles laid down in 1601 seemed relevant more than three centuries later, despite the great changes of society and thought in the intervening years? One was *public responsibility*. This meant simply that the law designated officials (called "overseers of the poor") and charged them with a duty. The parish, or whatever local government, had to appoint such officials, and they had to relieve the poor. The central government (acting through the courts) might punish localities that did not carry out its intentions. This was not like the situation in France, nor like that in Quebec and Louisiana, where Frenchmen had settled. There matters were left to private individuals and the church, in the older pattern.

A second principle was *local responsibility*. In England the parish was a geographic area as well as a congregation; every part of the realm was served by a parish church (which might be quite distant in sparsely settled areas), just as, later on, every part of the land would be in a postal district served by a local post office. The parish congregation was held to be responsible for its own poor. It should not push them out on other parishes; if they became needy elsewhere, it should receive them back. This idea was formalized in the settlement law of 1662 (also brought to America), which laid down the conditions by which a newcomer could gain a settlement: renting a substantial property for some stated length of time or paying taxes or serving as a public official of the place. The law supposed that others, looked upon as transients, should return (or be returned) to their own parish for relief. In its assumption that everyone was rooted in his place of settlement and its denial of the fact and desirability of increasing mobility of labor, especially among the poor, it was a backward-looking and cruel feature of relief.

A third principle was *relatives' responsibility.* The parish did not have to provide if there were parents, grandparents, or (adult) children or grandchildren who could do so. Officials of course looked into this possibility.

Finally, the overseers were authorized to put the poor to work. Children were bound out as apprentices or unfree workers; there was a market for this kind of child labor. Adults might be employed at various tasks, in a workhouse or outside. This provision went back to a fundamental notion underlying the poor law, the "work ethic," which held that people ought to support themselves insofar as they were able, that they not to live in idleness by begging from those who did work, and that there were degrees of responsibility between complete self-sufficiency and complete dependency: dependents ought to help themselves as much as they could, even if it were only a little.

In short, people were expected to look out for themselves and their families. If they got into trouble, they would turn first to their relatives and neighbors, just as we do today. If these resources were inadequate, the community was morally obliged to share with them through the poor law, but on the other hand officials were justified in seeing that individuals or members of the family did not evade their responsibilities. The poor law is sometimes said to have established a right to relief, but in its historical context it long antedated the Lockean notion of individual rights and was originally founded on religious obligations and mutual responsibilities.

In England the poor law was enacted by Parliament, the national legislature; in America, by the several colonies (and later territories and states as they were formed). Consequently poor relief in the United States was seen as a state rather than a federal problem. The state poor laws, like their prototype, made the local communities responsible and delegated administration to them. There was no state agency to supervise localities until 1863 (in Massachusetts), and in fact very little state supervision until the 1920s. The principal check was an occasional investigation of a scandal.

As for practical arrangements, there were in general two types. In New England, and wherever Yankees went as they moved across the country, communities were organized in "towns" or townships—a settlement and the surrounding land. Settlers had a parish church (often Congregational) in the English pattern. Town business was handled by part-time unpaid citizen committees, including the overseers of the poor. Elsewhere the pattern of settlement was more scattered—isolated farms and a crossroads store and church, rather than the compact New England town. In some states the Anglican or Dutch Reformed Church had been established and had tried to maintain a territorial parish organization, but by 1815 the church had long since lost practical importance. Except among Yankees, the county was the center of government for poor relief as for other local services, such as roads or criminal justice. Here the elected county supervisors or commissioners had the authority to help those in need. Often these gentry were elected from separate districts and each handled problems in his district as they arose, referring momentous or expensive decisions to the collective body.

The poor law revision in Pennsylvania was particularly important because it was copied in the law governing the Northwest Territory and in the acts of the great states carved out of it or settled farther to the west. Northern Pennsylvania had been settled largely by Yankees who held to the town system; in the rest of the state the county system was usually favored. The law accommodated both arrangements.

In the cities—seaports or river ports—the town fathers usually delegated authority to a poormaster, and often there were specialized institutions and hospitals for the homeless sick. The big picture is a varied response depending on local problems and traditions, whatever the law.

In the typical case under the poor law as it appeared in the great rural expanses, the breadwinner was incapacitated or the family broken and the ordinary informal sources of support were not available. Of course the general plane of living was very low by today's standards. To be needy was not to lack the means of decent life but to face a threat to survival.

If a needy family had a home and was able to help itself but unable to support itself completely, the overseers might give it an allowance or arrange to pay its bills at the store or its rent. This was called "home relief" or, if the family got food, rent, or medical care rather than money, "relief in kind." If families or individuals were unable to care for themselves or needed supervision (in the case of the mentally disordered, for example), the overseers fitted them into some functioning family unit and paid their host for the service. If there were many such cases, the overseers would seize upon a time when the community was likely to assemble (election day, perhaps) and conduct an auction or "vendue" to dispose of their charges. They would present the cases to the citizens and ask for bids for their care. The low bidder would get the contract and the responsibility. Often bidders would undertake to care for several or all of the cases and in effect operate a private poorhouse on a public subsidy. Sometimes the caretakers were themselves on the margin of dependency, and in effect they were relieved along with their charges by a single grant. Sometimes they hoped to put the paupers to appropriate and useful chores. When the overseers delegated the care of the poor to one or two households, this was called "farming out the poor." This approach was advantageous because it simplified the overseers' work, the budgeting of costs, and also such supervision of the arrangements as the overseers chose to exercise. The overseers also "bound out" (i.e., apprenticed) orphans or the children of those on relief.

As both population and problems increased in some of the little communities, the expedient of farming out the poor became less satisfactory. Here the notion of a public almshouse or poorhouse took hold. Its proponents had several aims. One was humanitarian, to end the humiliating and embarrassing auction of the poor, the mercenary bidding on human misery: much better to have an established place of refuge for these unfortunates, with an official responsible for their care. So in eighteenth-century America religious or ethnic groups sponsored a few private almshouses to look out for their own, and a few public bodies took this step. It was easy to see the possible economy in such a institution: almshouse keepers might devise ways to put inmates to helping one another or perhaps to some elementary work for self-support or profit (oakum picking, for example: pull discarded ropes into fibers used for calking seams in wooden ships). In rural places authorities might buy a "poor farm" where residents helped with chores as they were able (this was a different meaning of "farm" from the delegation or "farming out" of the care of the poor). So much for the impotent or handicapped. With regard to children and the able-bodied poor, it was easy to imagine a program that would realize their potential and train them for the future. This training might be work managed so strictly that it would deter loafers from taking advantage of charity. In the sense of an agency for training and deterrence, the institution was called a "house of industry" or a "workhouse."

These ideas, all familiar in 1815, soon began to take on a new urgency. One growing problem was that of dealing with the people who were lost in the increasing stream of immigration and migration; another, the need for assistance to manufacturers and shippers who had to face new competition from England after the War of 1812 and, later, the Panic of 1819, which affected commerce, especially in the West. A third factor was the experience of England, then in the throes of the industrial revolution, where various schemes for the management of the poor and needy had been tried, studied, and found wanting, and where in the ascendancy of economic liberalism, the problems of poverty and pauperism were receiving systematic and critical scrutiny.

In the postwar crisis of 1817 in New York, businessmen, physicians, and clergymen—men who could see the problems, felt some patrician and Christian responsibility to face them, and knew what the English were thinking—set up a Society for the Prevention of Pauperism. Similar organizations of concerned citizens appeared in Philadelphia in 1817 and in Baltimore (the third-largest city in the country) in 1820. These voluntary efforts were followed by public commissions to investigate the poor laws in Massachusetts (1821), New York (1824), and the City of Philadelphia (1827). Taken together, these bodies and their reports represented a new approach to new conditions. Whereas eighteenth-century discussion about the needy had been mostly religious—charity sermons to encourage giving, for example—in the nineteenth-century people took a harder look. They asked what were the causes of need, what might be done to prevent it, and what might be done to get dependents back to self-sufficiency. They tried to take a systematic, critical view and to develop their plans in a rational way. They took steps toward a science of social welfare and a profession of social work.

Although these people often spoke of "the poor" and "poverty," the center of their concern was the extreme of indigence: "paupers" and "pauperism," or dependence on public or private charity. Mere poverty was familiar among the "laboring poor," who lived from hand to mouth. Dependency was different and more important because, according to the teaching of liberal economic theory, the money spent on charitable relief had to come from somewhere, and it either reduced the amount that was available for self-sufficient workers to share with their families or—equally serious—reduced the amount that wealthy capitalists would otherwise invest in labor-saving and wealth-producing investments. Although charity was certainly a moral responsibility, it was also, in terms of economic theory, a burden on the self-supporting and productive classes and a drag on economic progress.

Just as liberal economists thought that universal poverty was not an inevitable condition of society, that many people might escape it, that by studying political economy in a rational spirit leaders could learn how a nation could produce more and therefore have more to share, so they believed that, through analysis and wise policy, pauperism or dependency might be much reduced. Given the moral assumptions of the Protestant ethic that guided their own lives, it is not surprising that these early students of pauperism found that many of its causes indicated that the needy one himself was to blame, partly or wholly, for his plight.

In its first report (1818) the New York Society for the Prevention of Pauperism listed nine causes of dependency: ignorance (the pauper did not see the opportunities in his situation or did not know how to take advantage of them); idleness (he preferred to loaf); intemperance in drinking (he could not control himself); "want of economy" (he spent his money foolishly); imprudent and hasty marriage (before the couple was prepared to undertake the responsibilities of family life and parenthood); lotteries (which tempted the poor with the hope of easy gains); pawnbrokers (who encouraged the poor into personal debt at high interest rates); houses of prostitution ( a distraction from proper family life and a threat to health); and finally the numerous charitable organizations of the city (which allowed themselves to be exploited by crafty beggars).[2]

The practical proposals of this first report were the following:

1. Divide the city into small districts and appoint district visitors who would acquaint themselves with indigent families "to advise them with respect to their business, the education of their children, the economy of their houses" and "to administer encouragement or admonition, as they may find occasion." This proposal looked backward to the informal, personal social controls of the village.
2. Help the "laboring classes" make the most of their earnings by promoting savings banks, mutual-benefit societies, and life insurance.
3. Enforce settlement laws more strictly.
4. Prohibit street begging (by which paupers could appeal to the undiscriminating generosity of bypassers).
5. Provide employment in houses of industry or materials for the poor to work on at home, as they ordinarily did in the system of "domestic industry."

These observations about the causes of pauperism and the practical proposals that resulted were plausible enough so that intelligent and well-meaning people would often reiterate them during the century, and much of our story will show how and why they proved to be superficial. For now it is enough to note that these early appeals did not attract much support or have much consequence. In 1823 the New York Society changed from its broad goal to a program of encouraging free education for children and a "house of refuge" for juvenile delinquents, and soon thereafter it expired.

The state commissions in Massachusetts (1821) and New York (1824) had a more specific charge—to study the administration of public charity under the poor law—and came to more specific recommendations. The Massachusetts report discussed the possibility of simply eliminating public relief, as some English theorists had proposed, but it recognized that "the present system of . . . public or compulsory provision for the poor is too deeply riveted in the . . . moral sentiment of our people to be loosened by theories, however plausible . . . "[3] Instead, it endorsed another English argument that opposed *home relief* and favored *indoor relief* in "Alms Houses having the character of Work Houses or Houses of Industry." Such institutions with their strict regimen would discourage mere loafers from applying for help, it was thought, and would at least employ the poor in partial self-support. Later reports repeated this logic, which supported the ongoing change from "farming out" the poor to building regular public institutions. So, in the 1820s and 1830s, the county poorhouse or township poor farm became part of the American landscape.

These early proponents of indoor relief had plans that were more radical than they were actually able to effect. They had in mind a general system in which every community would have its poorhouse, and accordingly outdoor relief and farming out the poor would be largely eliminated. The new institutions would be run in a strict, economical, and deterrent fashion under some central supervision. This was the way the English were heading, toward their momentous poor law reform act of 1835, which made the workhouse the instrument to deter pauperism.[4]

Ironically, however, as the English poor law reform, centering on the workhouse, was debated and put into operation in the 1830s, the American movement died out. In America the poorhouse appeared in places where local authorities thought it would be cheaper or decidedly less trouble than home relief or farming out the poor. No central authority supervised its administration. Sometimes it was businesslike, sometimes not. In any case it was more custodial than deliberately deterrent. One reason that poor law reform died out in America was the notable prosperity of the 1830s. Another, of more enduring significance, was the hostility English working men expressed toward the workhouse (which they called "the bastille"). Because the English laboring class did not have the vote the middle class there was able to sustain the reform. In America most white men had the vote and the middle class was much less distinct and militant. Furthermore, English immigrants were often prominent in such labor organizations as took form. In these circumstances neither Whigs nor Democrats would have found much advantage in pursuing the notion of workhouses for deterrence. In any case it was not pursued.

The American situation as of 1837 was summarized by the English traveler Harriet Martineau in her account, *Society in America*. A conscientious observer, she was already a famous advocate and popularizer of English liberalism, in particular its poor law reform. "The pauperism of the United States is, to the observation of a stranger, nothing at all," she said.

> It is confined to the ports, emigrants making their way back into country, the families of intemperate or disabled men, and unconnected women, who depend on their own exertions. The amount altogether is far from commensurate with the charity of the community; and it is to be hoped

that the curse of a legal [i.e., public] charity, at least to the able-bodied, will be avoided in a country where it certainly cannot become necessary within any assignable time.[5]

This was the situation in the country at large, but already conditions in "the ports"—Boston, New York, Philadelphia, Baltimore, and New Orleans—foreshadowed much trouble. Meanwhile, however, there were also hopeful signs as men began to distinguish among different kinds of problem people and devise special institutions to deal with them in a more rational and practical way.

## NOTES

1. Charles Nordoff, *Communistic Societies of the United States; From Personal Visit and Observation* (New York: Hilary House, 1961, first published 1875), pp. 416–18.
2. Society for the Prevention of Pauperism in the City of New York, *First Annual Report* (New York, 1818), reprinted in Ralph E. Pumphrey, and Murial W. Pumphrey, *The Heritage of American Social Work* (New York: Columbia University Press, 1961), pp. 59–62.
3. Massachusetts, General Court, Committee on Pauper Laws, *Report* (1821), reprinted in Pumphrey, *Heritage of American Social Work,* pp. 62–66; the quote is from p. 65. Other reports of this period are reprinted in *The Almshouse Experience: Collected Reports* (New York: Arno Press, 1971).
4. In English usage, soon adopted in America, "indoor relief" meant relief for people who lived in an institution, subject to its discipline; "outdoor relief" meant relief for people who lived outside the institution in their own homes.
5. Harriet Martineau, *Society in America,* 2 vols. (New York, 1837), II, 289.

# 3   The Changing Balance of Status and Contract in Assistance Policy

## SAMUEL MENCHER

The effect of assistance on dependency has probably been the most persistent problem of social policy since the period of the Reformation. Although the nature of assistance[1] and the concept of depen-

Reprinted from *The Social Service Review,* 35 (March 1961): 17–32, by permission of the University of Chicago Press. © 1961 by The University of Chicago.

dency have changed markedly during the last four centuries, the expectation, or, more accurately, the fear, has persisted that any effort resulting in benefits beyond those obtainable through the normal economic institutions of society will discourage maximum assumption of responsibility and inevitably decrease the total welfare of society. With increasing knowledge of the social and psychological components of behavior, the concept of dependency has been increasingly broadened, but the ultimate criterion for assistance policy has remained within the economic sphere.

The extent to which individuals may be expected to be independent or to rely on their own resources has varied, but within its own norms each society has struggled with the effects of further redistribution of its economic wealth. For example, contemporary society accepts the cost of schooling as a common responsibility, but the foster placement of children continues to be chargeable to the parents' account. The major problems of society, however, have concerned direct financial aid rather than the provision of objects or services, for, as Pigou notes, the latter tend to be "neutral" in their effect on incentive for income.[2] Since the goal of assistance policy has been to increase the individual's desire or ability for self-support, or at least certainly not to discourage it, assistance policy has struggled primarily with issues related to the productive or potentially productive individual.

Thus dependency, for practical purposes, involves the inability or unwillingness of the able-bodied members of the population to provide for themselves and for those considered to be their legal or natural dependents. From the first, the poor law programs of England and western Europe after the Reformation, and even before, distinguished between the "impotent" and the "employable" poor. Though the definition of the classes has changed, there has been continuous acceptance of social responsibility for the "impotent" poor. Basic issues of assistance policy in regard to this group have arisen only as the employable group has been affected. For example, to what extent should the employable groups be held responsible for impotent individuals attached to them? To what extent should individuals who are at any time incapable of employment, whatever the reason, be expected to provide from their previous earnings for their present incapacity or lack of employment?

The purpose of this paper is to analyze the concepts and theories which form the background of contemporary thinking about the relationship of assistance and dependency. This analysis will be presented primarily in terms of the continuing conflict between "status" and "contract" relationships since the period of the Reformation. The concepts of status and contract are broadly derived from Sir Henry Maine.[3] Status, as used here, refers to relationships which are determined essentially by membership in the group, whether it is the family, the community, society as a whole, or any particular institution of society, such as a religious or commercial organization. In a status society, rights and responsibilities are inherent in the relationship of the individual to the social unit. The term "contract" will refer to relationships which are specifically and purposefully entered into, and rights and responsibilities are determined by their acceptance in free exchange.

The distinction between the impotent and the employable illustrates well the difference between status and contract. The continued assistance of the impotent has been on a status basis. No matter what the pressures toward a contract society, extenuating circumstances have resulted in the protection of members of the group, such as children or the handicapped, who are considered incapable of managing their own affairs and cannot therefore be held responsible according to the contract code of society. It is the employable group, however, whose assistance has been directly affected by the attitudes of society toward dependency according to the emphasis on status or contract relationships in particular periods.

From the point of view of status and contract, assistance policy since the Reformation may be roughly divided into three periods: (1) the growth of a contract society between the Reformation and the early nineteenth century; (2) the revival of status relationships in the nineteenth century; and (3) the mixture of status and contract in the twentieth century. Naturally, as in all social phenomena, sharp distinctions tend to be more academic than actual. In the three periods, overlappings occur particularly in the continuance of traditional modes and in the development of new practices. While much of the evidence presented will be related to the English scene, the analysis pertains generally to both British and American assistance policy.


I


The factor most sharply distinguishing the modern from the medieval period has been the changed emphasis on work and effort. Certainly in the four centuries since the Reformation the dominant goal of Western society has been the increasing of man's productivity. However, this emphasis on work and productivity, so integral to contemporary life as to make almost banal any reference to it, represented a fundamental break with earlier eras. The relatively sudden and great attention given to work as reflected in all the institutions of society following the Reformation indicates the significant and revolutionary nature of the change.[4] On the religious side, work became the duty of man before God, and, on the temporal side, labor became more than the means of man's satisfying his own needs; it enriched the wealth of the community and nation. Work had never previously achieved a similar position as a universal value.

In the static feudal economy of the medieval period, the gains that could be obtained from increased productivity, whether in agriculture or in industry, were relatively of little consequence. The feudal society was essentially self-sufficient and non-enterprising. The new economy, ushered in first by the Commercial Revolution and then by the Industrial Revolution, had virtually no limits to its expansion.

The increased wealth, approved by social and religious sanctions, flowing from commerce and industry was directly related to increased effort. The medieval concept of labor as the basis of value was inherited by the new society, and its leading theorist and exponent, Adam Smith, assumed labor to be the "real measure of the exchangeable value of all commodities."[5] However, while labor may have been considered the basis of economic value in the Middle Ages, economic value itself was of much less significance than in the period commencing with the Reformation.

Support from the newly arising religious institutions was especially important if the emphasis on labor and property was to take firm hold. The medieval Church had hardly given sufficient encouragement to devotion to labor or the accumulation of property to satisfy the needs of a commercial society. The new economy of the Reformation had to overcome not only a static feudal economy but also a system of religious values which, in effect, subordinated temporal to spiritual interests. The medieval Church's emphasis on poverty and other-worldliness conflicted sharply with the demands of the developing economy. It cast doubt on the value of worldly labor and questioned the intrinsic right of property. The fundamental weakness of the Church's charitable policy, according to a nineteenth-century Protestant historian of Catholic charity, was its failure to appreciate the importance of work and property, for "a healthy charity is only possible where healthy moral views of work and property prevail."[6]

Since the Reformation, much has been made of the "demoralizing" effect of the Church's indiscriminate almsgiving, which, in reality, was not so great as to justify the amount of attention given it.[7] This demoralizing influence was the threat to a society founded on work and property of a system of charity which permitted other ways of obtaining a livelihood than through productive labor. This criticism, applied to a system of charity flourishing in an era before the ultimate value of work and property was recognized, has, however, remained a classic gauge of the effectiveness of welfare programs since that time.

The medieval Church's approach to work and property and its related philosophy of charity was particularly important for assistance policies after the Reformation, because the Church, either directly through its own institutions or through its influence on lay society, had established the tradition of charitable help. If the emerging society was to continue the practice of philanthropy it must be organized in such a fashion as to distinguish clearly the new relationship between work and property, on the one hand, and charity, on the other.

The emerging commercial society must not only change existing notions of the importance of work but must also take into account the existing attitudes toward labor itself. For several centuries before the Reformation, efforts had been made to enforce the laborer's attachment to his place of employment. While some of these efforts were no doubt motivated by a desire to maintain a ready supply of local labor, they were also indicative of the generally slack attitude of the working population and of the need for strong measures of control.[8] The increasing severity of legislation for this purpose reflects the ineffectiveness of such a policy.

The laboring classes, breaking away from feudalism, sought to escape from the obligation of work as from other feudal requirements. For the most part, they did not have a lengthy experience as small landholders or craftsmen to develop habits of effort and workmanship. The craft guilds, the main institution for medieval and Renaissance workmanship, had only a limited membership, and their exclusiveness prevented any wide diffusion of their influence.[9] The agricultural classes were soon dispossessed of their rights as small property holders as the movement toward enclosure and large-scale farming developed. If the lower classes found no stimulus within their own lives to obtain satisfaction from work, they saw little in the lives of their betters to provide an impression of work as a pleasurable activity. As Veblen has so cogently observed, freedom from work has been a traditional mark of upperclass status. During no period was this more true than during the period preceding the Reformation.

The new entrepreneur classes who proclaimed with such gusto the importance of work as the only acceptable way of living and attaining God's grace did not, however, foster an appreciation of work as an agreeable activity in itself. Work for them was a task and a duty, and its very unpleasantness symbolized its sacredness. Work was a discipline, not a satisfaction. For the classical economist, work could be equated with the renunciation of leisure and freedom of choice. While the entrepreneur classes found sufficient incentive directly from their material gains and ultimately from being among God's chosen, there was little to motivate the laboring classes. Their status was low; they had little to gain from the new religious philosophies; and the work tasks assigned to them were both unpleasant and poorly rewarded.

Finally, the laboring classes saw no advantage in the emphasis on freedom or laissez faire which marked the new economy. The transition from a status society of established and fixed relationships to a contract society of fluid agreements based on material gain presented few advantages to the lower classes. In this arrangement, the worker was stripped of the security formerly provided by the status system and was forced to rely solely on the market value of his labor. However, the development of an open economy was vitally important to the entrepreneur classes, and the possibility that the lower classes might "depend" on the previous guaranties of support through status in a manorial or religious community would hinder the free operation of the new society.

The poor laws of England and western Europe of the sixteenth century must be viewed against the background of an emerging contract society seeking to establish an assistance policy consistent with an emphasis on work both as a value in itself and as a source of economic value. The sixteenth-century poor laws attempted to meet the new needs and to remedy the previous assistance policies by the following reforms:

1. An organized community system of relief was substituted for informal or status-oriented approaches. Through providing a clear, tax-supported method of assistance, the new acts helped make obsolete the earlier habits of philanthropy which provided little social control over labor. Some of the sixteenth-century legislation in England and on the Continent even made specific reference to the prohibition of private philanthropy outside the community-administered program. The Sorbonne authorities disapproved of these measures because they conflicted with the Catholic ethic of charity, and it is likely that the English provisions were also too radical a departure from traditional status practices to be effective, as they were not included in the eventual codification of the poor laws under Elizabeth.

2. The sixteenth-century acts made a clear distinction between the "employable" and the "impotent" poor. The distinction was vital for any effective administration of assistance in a contract society. Thus, those exempted from the contract system and those responsible to it were defined. Individuals unable to market their labor value were still to be protected by the community or, in other words, to be maintained in a status relationship.

The Elizabethan poor law, like the systems of assistance on the Continent around the time of the Reformation, provided for the finding of work for the employable who were not engaged in labor. This provision was to be the source of much controversy by the beginning of the nineteenth century. While recognizing work as the only basis of livelihood for the able-bodied, it continued the traditional status responsibility of the community for all the poor. The possibility of confusing work and assistance was also present, and this threatened the core of the new contract society.

3. The mutual liability for support of parents and children was extended by the Elizabethan poor law to grandparents. This measure had dual significance. By expanding the responsibility of the employable or those with previous income from employment, it narrowed the sphere of community responsibility and increased the numbers dependent on the contract system of wages. By enforcing family responsibility it helped stabilize the labor market.

Societies faced with the problem of social control of labor frequently have resorted to incentives outside the immediate work situation. The feudal economy provided serfs with their own small plots of land, and even slave economies encouraged the growth of family life. In the sixteenth century, when one of the main problems was irregularity of attachment to the labor market, the enforcement and extension of family responsibility might well act as a leavening force on the lower classes who had neither the possession of property nor the personal investment in a skill to stabilize their work interest.[10]

Thus the English poor law established by the beginning of the seventeenth century the basic policies of (1) work as the only approved source of livelihood for those defined as employable and (2) the separation of the employable from any reliance on the community's provision of assistance. The law, however, was not entirely consistent. If aid were extended to the employable because of their membership in the community, then work ceased to be the only measure of their value, and contract was not the only basis of livelihood. Not, however, until some two centuries later, were the contradictions in both the letter and the spirit of the law fully faced.

During the period before 1834, the poor law system showed many deviations from the emphasis on work and contract. The Elizabethan poor law, as already noted, while not accepting responsibility for the relief of the able-bodied poor, had empowered the parishes to provide work for the employable. This early policy, reflecting the mercantilist philosophy of the time, eventually culminated in the Speenhamland practice of the late eighteenth and early nineteenth centuries of subsidizing wages with relief. The clear distinction between work and assistance, so important to a contract society, was thus dimmed.[11]

The doctrine of laissez faire or the complete acceptance of contract relationships in assistance policy reached its ultimate expression in the poor law reform in 1834. Although their strategy might differ, the goal of such leading advocates of reform as Sir George Nicholls and Nassau Senior was the total abolition of any benefits for the employable group.[12] The most ardent proponents of reform would have done away with the poor law entirely, for, from their point of view, there was no risk befalling the able-bodied or his dependents for which he should not have provided during his period of employment.[13] In effect, the Commission of 1834 concluded that a system of assistance founded on status privileges was far inferior to the normal rigors of the economic market. The investigations of this Commission, along with conditions considered prevalent under pre-Reformation philanthropy, have provided strong foundations for the classic argument of the relationship of assistance and dependency.

However, the succeeding history of poor law administration indicates a failure of the effort to force the employable poor to remain totally dependent on the contract value of their own labor or conversely totally independent of any status right to social support. Able-bodied poor continued to resort to public relief, and succeeding poor law commissions were constantly faced with the growth of relief rolls. What is pertinent is not that the Commission of 1834 and the later commissions and boards did not understand the causes of poverty, or failed to apply appropriate remedies to it, but rather that, despite their strenuous efforts, the poor law remained a resource for the able-bodied.

As suggested above, traditional paternalism continued to frustrate any system which refused to recognize the dependency of the poor on the wealthier elements of the community. Of more significance was the fact that, by the time the doctrine of laissez faire had become completely accepted, it was no longer fully applicable. The concepts of natural rights and of individualism, like the labor theory of value, had their roots in the "handicraft and petty trade" era before the growth of large-scale manufacture and commerce.[14] An assistance policy, therefore, founded on an out-moded scheme of social and economic relationships had little likelihood of success. The poor law guardians continued to provide, albeit poorly, outdoor relief to the able-bodied and their families. The doctrine of status, recognizing the dependence of the individual on the resources of the group, was maintained in practice, if not in theory.

The Reform Act of 1834 may be considered the high-water mark of the doctrine of contract as applied to assistance programs in England. The doctrine of contract was reinforced by closely associated economic and social theories. Thus assistance was criticized, not only because it upset the natural harmony of the economic market, but because it reduced the wealth of the nation both by withdrawing labor from productive work and by providing goods to nonproductive members of society. Since, in the minds of some nineteenth-century classical economists, the only justification for consumption was the creation of further wealth, the assistance recipient was viewed as a drain on the resources of the nation.[15]

This approach to consumption, however, meant that employed labor itself was considered to require only sufficient subsistence to make possible its continued engagement in production. Any further compensation would have led to unproductive consumption. Thus the principle of "less eligibility" established by the Commission of 1834 meant that, in reality, those dependent on the assistance system would receive less than was necessary for subsistence. Here again, as with denying assistance to the able-bodied, the contract aspects of the program were thwarted by the traditional status elements in poor law administration. While the entrepreneur of the early Industrial Revolution might look upon labor as an abstract and easily replaceable unit in production, the poor law guardians continued to see assistance recipients as persons or families and frequently indulged them beyond the budgetary limits established by the poor law boards.

The adoption of the principle of less eligibility also reflected the utilitarian pleasure-pain psychology of the period. According to the utilitarian view, behavior is motivated by the seeking after pleasure and the avoidance of pain, and if through the practice of less eligibility idleness could be made sufficiently unpleasant or painful in comparison with work, then work, no matter how undesirable, would be preferred over idleness. Since the conditions of the working class in the beginning of the nineteenth century were especially poor, and the estimate of their character by the influential elements of society was particularly low, a strong policy was required to motivate the lower classes toward work.[16] This the Act of 1834 attempted to do not only through the principle of less eligibility but also through the application of the workhouse test.

Finally, the contract view of the dependency of the poor received much support from what may be termed the pessimistic social and economic theories of the period. Both Malthus and Ricardo stressed the inevitability of poverty and subsistence wages. The laws of population and economics and the miserliness of nature condemned the lower classes to constant poverty. In fact, there was little room for help since any relief would eventually only make heavier the burden of the working population.

## II

The second major phase in assistance policy had its inception during the period of poor law reform in the early part of the nineteenth century and continued in England until the beginning of the twentieth century. In the United States its duration was somewhat longer. This second phase was marked by a renewal of status relationships, with the foundation of an established contract society. The nineteenth-century resurgence of status in assistance policy differed in several important respects from earlier practices. These differences were largely influenced by changes in the role and philosophy of both the upper and lower classes and in the concept of the nature and purpose of society itself.

Although the dominant development of the previous period was directed toward the establishment of a contract scheme of relationships, elements of the previous status system continued to be active. However, during the period of emphasis on contract relationships, the concept of status was gradually transformed. In the earlier period, the giving of assistance to the poor was the recognition of a natural relationship between the wealthy and the deprived classes. Whether because of traditional feudal or local rights or because of a religious duty of sharing with the poor, charity was a mutual relationship the acceptance of which required no special behavior on the part of the recipient, unless it was to pray for the salvation of his benefactor. In fact, the advantage of the relationship, according to later critics, fell to the wealthy to whom the poor were merely a convenient object of pity. As for the poor, the complaint was made in the beginning of the sixteenth century that many "wolde not take almes as a free benefyte with thankes: but lordly claymed it as it had been a trybute due unto them by lawe."[17] All that was desired in this period of transition from the feudal to the commercial society was described in the following:

The poor man agayne loueth the ryche man as hys benefactoure of whom he hath his lyuynge and by whose ayde he is holpen him he thanketh for all he hathe to him he gyveth manye blessynges and good prayers as a token of gratytude and he rendereth theym hertely and as lyberally as he can. For no other cause dyd nature mengle poore and ryche togyther but that poore men shulde receyve benefytes of ryche men.[18]

This was far less than the status relationships of nineteenth-century charity sought to accomplish. True, gratitude has been one of the main elements of charitable giving since the disruption of the medieval system when status endowed definite rights. Any system of status relationships which involved voluntary giving and which did not result in automatic benefits to the giver required at least some such justification as gratitude or recognition on the part of the recipient. In the nineteenth century, however, gratitude alone was not sufficient; gratitude was merely the sign of "worthiness" or readiness to be helped.

While for some patrons of nineteenth-century charity the satisfaction of gratitude was sufficient, these brought upon their philanthropy the same disrepute as had come to characterize pre-Reformation assistance. However, the new approach to status relationships in assistance sought to accomplish what, in the eyes of its supporters, had not been achieved either by the traditional status pattern as exemplified by public relief or by the emphasis on contract. The voluntary nature of giving in accord with the contract motif involved a discretion and selectivity which would counteract any expectation of assistance as an obligation of the rich to the poor.[19] However, in return for the voluntary self-sacrifice of the rich there were to be obligations on the part of the poor: " 'We are willing to give up the life we care for,' Arnold Toynbee said, but we ask 'one thing in return' "— a change in the way of life of the poor.[20]

The new system of status relationships in assistance, introduced by such men as Chalmers, thus differed from the old in recognizing the possibility of change in the poor. This represented a significant shift from the philosophy of all previous assistance policies. Whether denying assistance under the principles of contract relationships or extending it in the traditional pre-Reformation pattern, there had been no expectation of effecting any change in the poor themselves. The poverty of their condition was sufficient evidence of the unworthiness of the poor under early Protestant doctrine.

Whatever conflict there may have been between the contract position of the earlier Protestant ethic and the status approach of the nineteenth century, the ultimate goal for the lower classes was the same—the self-maintenance of the able-bodied poor. The new philanthropists abhorred any assistance policies that might encourage the able-bodied poor to prefer social support to independent effort. If anything, the supporters of the new status philanthropy, as exemplified by the leaders of the Charity Organization Society, were the most ardent opponents of any system of assistance providng the able-bodied poor with any status claim on the wealth of the community. They sought when possible to protect the poor from the "demoralizing" experience of public assistance, but they were equally critical of private efforts that encouraged status dependency. The COS preserved its own resources for those poor who demonstrated the potential of meeting the commitments of a contract society and relegated to the public authorities those who could not manage without status support.

At the same time the new philanthropy was employing status relationships founded upon the unequal social position of master and servant to effect the independence of the working class, the position of the working class, and to some extent the nature of work itself, had begun to change. Partly as a result of the evangelical faith and interest in the improvement of their condition and partly as a result of forces within the working class itself, the working class achieved a position of respectability in the latter half of the nineteenth century that it had not had previously. A statement such as that made by the economist Alfred Marshall before the Royal Commission on the Aged Poor in 1893 would have seemed inconceivable before the Commission of 1834:

> I am convinced that the leaders of the working men would be as firm as anyone in insisting that scamps and lazy people should be put to a severe discipline; . . . in fact I believe that probably the professional tramp is even more odious to large classes of working men than he is to the rest of society.[21]

In fact, one of Marshall's main criticisms of the work of the Commission was that it had not taken pains to sound out labor's views on the problems of the poor.

Meanwhile a changed attitude toward labor had been growing among employers themselves. George Friedmann compares the attitude toward labor prevalent in the early period of the Industrial Revolution with America's "debauch" of its natural resources. As with other resources, an interest in conserving labor resources accurred. He wrote:

> Toward the close of the century, it became evident that the supply of labor was not inexhaustible, and that it was expensive, all the more so as the workers were organizing both to defend their value on the labor market and the elementary guarantees of their well-being. Social legislation was devised and refined.[22]

Other important and closely related changes which were to effect reforms in assistance policy were an "optimistic" view of the economic potential of society as contrasted with the pessimism of Malthus and Ricardo and a belief that the purpose of society was to provide satisfactions for its members. While work maintained its place as the most important human function, it ceased to be the only end of life and became more closely related to other social goals.

During the second half of the nineteenth century, the industrial economy of England, America, and western Europe flourished with boundless vigor. The preoccupation was no longer with the sufficiency of production, but rather with the development of markets to absorb current production and to make possible its continued growth. The superfluity of goods lent to a concentration on "consumption and selling" and the satisfactions to be obtained from the products of industry.

The concern of the economist with maximizing satisfactions paralleled the growing interest in conserving human resources. While the emphasis on satisfaction resulted in a welfare economics to a large

extent founded on utilitarian ethics, the emphasis on human resources resulted in a social policy to be effected by political action.
Thus Alfred Marshall, as a formulator of the new economics, stated
that additional income for the poor increases the "total happiness"
more than an "equal amount" for the rich "because the happiness
which an additional shilling brings to a poor man is much greater
than that which it brings to a rich one."[23] As a contributor toward
government policy, he commented:

> That a man ought not to be allowed to live in a bad home, that extreme
> poverty ought to be regarded, not indeed as a crime, but a thing so
> detrimental to the State that it should not be endured, and that every-
> body who, whether through his own fault or not, was in effect incapable
> of keeping together a home that contributed to the well-being of the
> State, that person should, under the authority of the State, pass into a new
> form of life.[24]

The new economics and the new view of the role of the state in
the latter part of the nineteenth century were laying a foundation for
a status system of assistance vastly different from that espoused by
the growing movement of private philanthropy of the same period.
The individual-centered private philanthropy sought through the
instrument of the master-servant status relationship to remove the
individual from reliance on society. The new economics concerned
itself with the satisfactions of individuals as they affected the total
welfare of the community.[25] While these approaches differed in this
respect, both agreed in aiming toward the financial responsibility of
each individual for himself and his dependents. The new philosophy
of state intervention, however, recognized the individual's reliance
on society as a resource if his contract relationships were to be adequately fulfilled.

Although there were important differences between the two approaches to assistance policy as evidenced in the Poor Law Commission of 1905—one emphasizing voluntary, personal, and unequal
status relationships and the other, common social responsibility—
they both assumed that assistance, unless carefully controlled, would
be preferred by those eligible to independent effort. There was
greater understanding of the causes of dependency than in earlier
eras, and it was recognized that all the evils previously attributed to
assistance policies alone were the result of many influences. However, the belief remained that, whatever may have caused individuals to need assistance, the provision of assistance itself was sufficient
to keep them in a state of dependency. After all, work was still
considered an unpleasant responsibility which all would avoid if it
were possible.

It is noteworthy that both the Webbs, who supported a highly organized program of state services, and the leaders of the COS, who looked askance at state intervention, opposed pension systems.[26] Both feared the temptation to rely on status benefits, particularly on the part of the working class. When the Webbs spoke of "universal provision" it was largely in regard to services, for the Webbs had almost as little faith in the moral responsibility of the lower classes for work and independence as did the members of the COS.[27]

Thus, by the beginning of the twentieth century there was a shift away from the strict contract position of assistance policy, although the new practices rested, in many respects, on the same tenets as the old. The view of work as a commodity and of the worker merely as a purveyor of a commodity had been undermined, and the distinction between the working class and the society which it served had also been dissolved to a large extent. In effect, some return to a status system had taken place, but not sufficiently for the worker to rely for his economic security on the wealth of society.

However, behind this general position were several factors, already noted, which presaged the development of the third phase of assistance policy: (1) the growth of a strong labor movement concerned with the security of its members, (2) the shifting emphasis in industry from exclusively technological concerns to the human problem of personnel, and (3) the increasing recognition that sound economic and social policy depended on more than productivity and that other factors must be taken into account to assure the economic welfare of society.

## III

The third or most recent phase of assistance policy, like those preceding it, has been marked by the inclusion of earlier principles and practices and by the development of new modes reflecting the contemporary scene. The search for an acceptable system of relationships between the employable worker and society, the major concern of assistance policy since the Reformation, has resulted in a new compromise between the principles of contract and status.

The growing importance of the labor movement drew the attention of society to ways of satisfying the needs and demands of the working class for economic security. The solution, however, could not be found, as it was to some extent in the nineteenth century, through status relationships reflecting inequality of social position. Any scheme giving the worker status rights to security must necessarily reflect the equality being achieved by the working class in society as a whole. No system of assistance, however, could guarantee this equality if it conflicted sharply with the contract mores. Exemption from contract relationships involved *ipso facto* some degree of inferiority. Justice according to the contract mores meant the protection of the individual's or the group's bargaining position in a contract relationship, not the guaranty of any assumed rights to a share of the social resources.

Any satisfactory scheme of assistance in twentieth-century England and the United States must, therefore, bridge the gap between contract and status relationships. It must provide the security of status rights without conflicting fundamentally with the contract mores. Thus the major innovation in England and America was social insurance, which represented a suitable compromise between the principles of status and contract. Employability and attachment to work were the core of eligibility for social insurance. The contract relationship of employment was extended to include protection against the risks of injury, sickness, age, survivorship, and even lack of employment. Though the public assistance programs affecting the able-bodied, which had somehow managed to weather the opposition of four centuries, continued, the goal was to replace them with the new insurances. The presence of the insurances would make reliance on assistance based on status relationships even more invidious.

The new programs themselves had, of course, strong status elements. Their establishment or promotion by public institutions rather than by private corporations and their implicit guaranty of security by society indicated a considerable shift from the philosophy that any interference with the responsibility of the able-bodied for their own financial security would lessen their desire for work and independence and consequently have dire effects on the welfare of society as a whole. Although the pessimistic predictions of Malthus and Ricardo had long been discarded, and new social and economic theories had replaced the emphasis on labor value and laissez faire, the fear of the consequences of any status share in the wealth of society remained. The acceptance of the social insurances indicated that the pressures toward a status relationship had taken precedence over, though they had not replaced, the insistence on contract.

The insurances, however, as already noted, were careful to include safeguards for the contract system. The insurances were available only to the employed and their dependents; they required a real attachment to the labor market; they did not provide enough benefits either to compete with wages from employment or to make possible even a minimal standard of living without additional "independent" provision; and, at least in the United States, they aimed to reflect differences in habits of industry and skill. The requirements for benefits, principally the contribution of the worker and/or his employer, gave a sense of contract right. It was this contract right that needed to be controlled so as not to become a status right.

Although in principle the new programs emphasized the responsibility of society as a whole for the welfare of the individual, in practice the core of status relationships developed around the employment situation itself. The employer's contribution to the insurances was symbolic of the employer's or, more generally, the economic institution's responsibility for the welfare of the contributors to production. While employers may have been concerned basically with obtaining maximum work effort, the twentieth-century business organization proceeded from the premise that the best way of obtaining the worker's contribution was through viewing him as a member of a social unit rather than as an abstract commodity.

Labor, too, particularly in the United States, viewed the business organization as the major source of economic security. Some labor leaders even opposed the development of public social security programs and preferred a system of welfare benefits based on agreements between labor and management. Paralleling the growth of public programs was a vast extension of welfare benefits under employer and union aegis to which employers made a large contribution. While these programs formally arose out of the contract relationship between employers and employees, in fact they reflected the recognition on the part of both groups of the status responsibilities of business organizations toward their employees.

It may seem paradoxical that the very institutions which were originally responsible for introducing and enforcing the contract concept should offer the most clear-cut example of status recognition. However, it may be noted that historically those institutions which have had the major role in society have generally provided the focus for status relationships. In a work-centered culture, therefore, it is not surprising that economic institutions should assume this function.

Concomitant with the new relationships on the economic scene, important but less obvious changes were taking place in the meaning of work itself. The position of respectability achieved by labor, the changing view of labor by management, the concept of the plant as a social institution, were all indicative of the changing nature of work. Whatever the specific factors, such as the shorter work week or improved working conditions, work was no longer the same unpleasant sacrifice defined by the classical economists nor were workers the same "sturdy beggars" of the early poor laws. After some four centuries, work became part of the normal pattern of western culture and at least for the working class was freed to some extent from the compulsive sense of duty with which it was originally introduced.[28]

The significance of work to the economy of society also changed perceptibly. Regardless of its moral justification, work in a scarcity economy was essential to provide for the immediate needs of society. As western nations, and particularly America, moved to an economy of abundance, the relative importance of work diminished. The advantages to be obtained from additional work decreased, and increased productivity often created embarrassing problems of distribution. As machine technology improved to the point of automation, the relationship of the wealth of a nation to the quantity of its human labor power became more and more obscured.

The shift in emphasis from production to consumption by the economists of the latter part of the nineteenth century was given further impetus by the new economics of the Keynesian school. The theory of full employment stressed the value of keeping the economy at its full productive capacity. However, the means of achieving full production were largely dependent on consumer demand. Consumer capacity thus became of focal importance to the economic welfare of society. Since Keynesian economics questioned the automatic adjustment of the factors of the economy, the development of consumer capacity became an important function of governmental policy.

This approach to economic welfare was significant for assistance policy. While assistance policy has been largely concerned with the avoidance of any practice that might deter the worker from attachment to the normal labor market, the new emphasis on stimulating consumption indicated that the primary concern was with maintaining the worker's capacity to consume rather than with maintaining his sense of responsibility to the contract relationships of the labor makret. In essence, the theory of full employment reinforced the status relationship of the able-bodied worker in society by combining his roles of worker and consumer. Beveridge, in applying Keynesian economics to assistance policy, stated:

> The redistribution of income that is involved in abolishing want by Social Insurance and children's allowances will of itself be a potent force in helping to maintain demand for the products of industry, and so in preventing mass unemployment.[29]

For Beveridge, full employment was a social as well as an economic doctrine. Full employment freed the worker from the threat of poverty and at the same time made more possible the selection of personally satisfying work.

Thus, full employment emphasized the combined status responsibility of society for both insuring sufficient consumer income and providing adequate employment opportunities. In effect, this was a radical reversal of the contract view of society with its foundation in laissez faire and individual responsibility and with its reliance on economic pressures to maintain attachment to work—a tedious duty to be avoided at the slightest pretext.

A new concept of status relationships of the worker to his place of employment and to society has, thus, taken its place alongside, and to some extent has superseded, the effort to maintain contract principles in assistance policy. The social insurances have come to be determined more by their "social" than by their "insurance" aspects, as benefits have tended to reflect need more than contributions. The "social assistance" programs, such as family allowances and universal non-contributory old age pensions, in some western nations have recognized status relationships without reference to contract rights based on employment.

## CONCLUSIONS

The development of assistance policy has been examined from the point of view of status-contract relationships for the purpose of understanding the basis of contemporary programs. It has been suggested that the most realistic indicator of assistance policy is the treatment of the able-bodied or employable worker. Assistance policy has been divided into three phases and attitudes toward work; the position of the laboring class and the relationship of work and the worker to society have been related to the concepts of status and contract in assistance policy. The three periods described are: (1) the development of contract relationships between the poor laws of the Reformation and the poor law reform of 1834 in England, (2) the revival of status relationships during the nineteenth century, and (3) the mixture of contract and status in the twentieth century.

It is clear that none of the above periods represents a "pure culture" of the status or contract type. In each, the declining or ascending elements of one or the other are present. However, the resolution of the status-contract balance reached in assistance policy at any one time often reflects attitudes and developments that have already passed their zenith in society generally. For example, contemporary assistance policies place an emphasis on work and the position of the laboring class which more accurately reflects nineteenth- than twentieth-century conditions. There is present in both private and public welfare a contract philosophy that questions any right beyond what has been contracted for in the economic market and a fear of status relationships which must be controlled to avoid the ubiquitous potentiality of dependency. The resulting practices vary from the negative pressures of utilitarian pleasure-pain psychology to the patronizing loss of dignity through personal controls.[30]

At this point it seems that few factors remained to support the original sixteenth-century equation of assistance and dependence; yet the fear of dependency has continued to be one of the besetting concerns of contemporary society and sources of opposition to assistance policies. The concept of dependency has outstripped the original emphasis on independent contract for labor value. Freudian psychology, so influential in professional social work, has emphasized the basically dependent nature of man.[31] Independence has almost replaced work as a value, and any program which tends to "relieve" man from the vicissitudes of life is viewed both as a symptom of and a stimulus to dependency. To the extent that the current concept of dependency is merely a "putting of old wine into new bottles," it needs to be re-examined in light of its historical roots.

## NOTES

1. The term "assistance" is used broadly throughout this paper for all programs, whether public or private, which provide financial support.

2. A C. Pigou, *The Economics of Welfare* (4th ed.; London: Macmillan & Co., 1950), pp. 720 ff.

3. Sir Henry Sumner Maine, *Ancient Law* (London: John Murray, 1906).

4. Erich Fromm, *Escape from Freedom* (New York: Rinehart & Co., 1941), p. 93.

5. Adam Smith, *The Wealth of Nations* (New York: Modern Library, 1937), p. 30.

6. Gerhard Uhlhorn, *Christian Charity in the Ancient Church* (New York: Charles Scribner's Sons, 1883), p. 126.

7. W. J. Ashley, *An Introduction to English Economic History and Theory* (4th ed.; London: Longmans, Green & Co., Ltd., 1914), Part II, p. 312.

8. *Ibid.,* p. 338.

9. Emil Lederer, "Labour," *Encyclopedia of Social Sciences* (New York: Macmillan Co., 1932), VIII, 616.

10. It is interesting to note that the status responsibilities of the worker were increased at the same time that those of society were lessened. This has remained as one of the conflict points of contemporary assistance policy, for there is an inherent contradiction in the expectation of status responsibility in a contract-oriented society.

11. Reinhard Bendix, *Work and Authority in Industry* (New York: John Wiley & Sons, 1956), p. 60.

12. Thomas Mackay, *A History of the English Poor Law* (New York: G. P. Putnam's Sons, 1899), III, 33 ff.

13. *Ibid.,* pp. 153–54.

14. Thorstein Veblen, *The Instinct of Workmanship* (New York: B. W. Huebsch, 1922), pp. 340–41.

15. See Nassau William Senior, *An Outline of the Science of Political Economy* (London: Allen & Unwin, 1938), pp. 55–56.

16. Lewis Mumford, *Technics and Civilization* (New York: Harcourt, Brace & Co., 1934), pp. 172–73.

17. "The Ypres Scheme of Poor Relief," trans. William Marshall (1535), in *Some Early Tracts on Poor Relief,* ed. F. R. Salter (London: Methuen & Co., 1926), p. 42.

18. *Ibid.*, p. 70.

19. See Beatrice Webb, *My Apprenticeship* (New York: Longmans, Green & Co., Ltd., 1926), pp. 191–92.

20. As quoted in *My Apprenticeship*, p. 177.

21. Alfred Marshall, *Official Papers* (London: Macmillan & Co., 1926), p. 210.

22. George Friedmann, *Industrial Society* (Glencoe, Ill.: Free Press, 1955), p. 29.

23. Alfred Marshall, *Principles of Economics* (8th ed.; London: Macmillan & Co., 1927), p. 474.

24. Marshall, *Official Papers*, pp. 244–45.

25. I. M. D. Little, *A Critique of Welfare Economics* (2d ed.; Oxford: Clarendon Press, 1957), pp. 72–73.

26. Mary Richmond, prominent in the COS in the United States, was also critical of pension systems. See "Motherhood and Pensions" in *The Long View* (New York: Russell Sage Foundation, 1930), pp. 350–64.

27. It should be noted that reformers of welfare policy have frequently been members of the middle class with a highly refined sense of guilt. See Beatrice Webb's *Diaries*, 1912–1924, ed. Margaret I. Cole (London: Longmans, Green & Co., Ltd., 1952), p. 70.

28. See David Riesman, "Some Observations on Changes in Leisure Attitudes," in *Individualism Reconsidered* (Glencoe, Ill.: Free Press, 1954), particularly pp. 208–09; also Eugene A. Friedmann and Robert J. Havighurst, *The Meaning of Work and Retirement* (Chicago: University of Chicago Press, 1954).

29. William H. Beveridge, *Full Employment in a Free Society* (New York: W. W. Norton & Co., 1945), pp. 255–56.

30. See Grace F. Marcus, *Some Aspects of Relief in Family Casework* (New York: Charity Organization Society, 1929). Although this interesting study was conducted some thirty years ago, it is still applicable to current relief practices. See also J. P. Kahn, "Attitudes toward Recipients of Public Assistance," *Social Casework*, XXXVI (October, 1955), 364–65.

31. Lucille Austin has deprecated the tendency in casework to overstress the "pull toward dependency," as follows: "It is easy to see how this concept of dependency gave reinforcement to earlier sociological ideas that dependency was enticing and careful efforts had to be made to guard against it. As those concepts were tested in practice, questions were raised about their validity. Experience showed that many people achieved independence in spite of obstacles and maintained it with pleasure" ("The Place of Relief in the Treatment of Dependency," in *Relief Practice in a Family Agency* [New York: Family Welfare Association of America, 1942], p. 26).

# Chapter Two

# THE SOCIETAL CONTEXT OF SOCIAL WELFARE

The institution of social welfare is unlike other major societal institutions on at least two counts: It is broader in scope, and it is less well established. Upon reflection, this statement should stimulate some curiosity. If it is not as well established as other institutions, how did social welfare get to be so broad in scope? To understand why this state of affairs characterizes the institution we must consider how the idea of social welfare fits the concept of a social institution.

Social institutions are networks of relationships that are widely accepted as the normal way to carry out essential societal functions such as child rearing, production and distribution of commodities, and social control. These networks of relationships are concretely manifest in organizational forms with which we are all familiar: the church, the university, and the political party, to name a few. Thus, the concept "institution" is often used on two levels of abstraction; for example, we may speak both of a religious institution, such as St. John's church, and of *the* institution of religion, or the "Church." In the former sense, institution refers to a single organizational unit, while in the latter it implies the sum of organizational units that carry the primary responsibility for performing an essential function.

Social institutions are not limited to performing single functions. On the contrary, a given institution usually serves many functions. The church, for instance, engages in socialization and in recreational and sometimes even political activities, though its main function is that of an agency which fulfills spiritual needs. While the major social institutions may perform many important functions, they are distinguished and achieve normative acceptance primarily on the basis of their core function. The crux of the issue regarding the institution of social welfare, therefore, is the question: What is or should be the core function of social welfare?

The readings in the preceding chapter indicated some of the functions performed by social welfare arrangements, such as redistribution of income, social control of the poor, assistance for the aged and disabled, socialization of the children of the poor, and general provisions for social security. But which of these functions distinguishes social welfare activities from those of familial, religious, political, and economic institutions? Is the core function security, control, redistribution, socialization, assistance, or something else?

One answer to these questions is to view the institution of social welfare as consisting of a series of arrangements necessary to compensate for the imperfections and limitations of other major social institutions in meeting human needs. According to this view, social welfare serves all of the functions noted above under the general rubric of "mutual support." As observed in the first selection in this chapter, "Policy and Social Institutions" (Reading 4), by Gilbert and Specht:

> Mutual support functions come into play when individuals are not able to meet their needs through major institutions which operate to carry out the other social functions we have described. This may occur for a wide variety of reasons such as sickness, loss of a wage earner, or inadequate functioning of the economic institutions. In technologically under-developed societies, mutual support activities are carried out primarily by the family. As societies have become more complex, other groups, organizations, and agencies develop to carry out mutual support activities, such as the church, voluntary agencies, and government. *The institution of social welfare is that pattern of relationships which develops in society to carry out mutual support functions.*

This definition of the function of social welfare helps to explain why the institution is broader in scope than others, because mutual support activities cut across a wide range of institutional sectors. These activities are relative to and dependent upon the extent to which human needs are met through the primary activities of religious, familial, political, and economic institutions at any given point in time. The relative and diffuse quality of mutual support activities complicates efforts to delineate the institution of social welfare as a separate and distinct entity.

There are a number of reasons why the institution of social welfare is less well established than the other major social institutions. First, as noted above, it is difficult to discern a core function for the pattern of relationships designated as social welfare that is distinct from functions served by older established institutions. Second, there is a fair amount of disagreement concerning the question of whether mutual support activities are a true representation of the main purpose of social welfare. Many critics have observed that beneath the humanitarian facade of mutual support, social welfare arrangements are essentially devices for the social control of the poor and underprivileged.[1] And finally, the institution of social welfare is not established on as firm ground as other institutions because there are divergent views within society concerning the desirability of mutual support activities. Many people deem these activities as nothing more than temporary corrective arrangements for meeting needs that are not at the time being served through regular or "normal" institutional channels. This perspective reflects the "residual" view of social welfare identified by Wilensky and Lebeaux.[2] As a residual mechanism social welfare activities are perceived as second-rate substitutes for meeting needs that somehow fail to be met through traditionally preferred institutional channels such as the family and the market economy. In contrast to the "residual" view, the "institutional" conception defines social welfare as an established pattern of activities serving important, on-going and legitimate functions in modern society.

Another reflection on the institutional versus residual status of social welfare is found in Wolins' analyses of "type B welfare programs," which substitute for and are perceived as less desirable than "type A welfare programs," which consist of need-meeting arrangements that have achieved institutional status. He examines a number of areas, such as adoption and old age security (which later became Supplemental Security Income) that have experienced a transition from B to A type welfare programs. Based on these experiences, Wolins suggests several requirements must be met for social welfare programs to move from residual to institutional status: evidence of program effectiveness; conformity or appearance of conformity with community values; impact on large numbers of people; and a recipient group capable of political organization.[3]

The institutional and residual perspectives suggest some of the conceptual problems and disagreements that surround the idea of social welfare. The readings in this chapter present alternative views on the primary functions of social welfare and how social welfare activities fit into the institutional framework of democratic-capitalist societies. In Reading 5, "The Role of Redistribution in Social Policy,"

Richard Titmuss explores the "iceberg phenomena" of social welfare, uncovering what he considers to be the submerged elements of the welfare state. Emphasizing the redistributive functions of social welfare arrangements, Titmuss argues that conceptual frameworks for analyzing social welfare arrangements have been too narrow and tend to exclude arrangements that benefit the middle and upper classes more than the poor. For Titmuss, the analysis of the redistribution effects of social welfare would include what he refers to as "fiscal welfare" (e.g., income tax deductions) and "occupational welfare" (i.e., private pensions and other benefits connected with employment), as well as the forms of direct public provisions of services and cash that constitute the prevalent conception of social welfare.

Most social welfare activities are conducted under government auspices. Thus, any case for expanding the institution of social welfare is, in part, a case for increasing the range of governmental interventions into other institutional sectors such as the family and the market economy. What are the proper functions of government? Under what conditions are government interventions in the market economy justified? In contrast to the socialist views presented by Richard Titmuss, these questions are addressed from the viewpoint of classical liberal economics in Reading 6, "The Role of Government in a Free Society," by Milton Friedman. According to Friedman, much of what we would consider social welfare activity is justified on paternalistic grounds, where government intervention is warranted to protect people who cannot be held responsible for their own well-being. This viewpoint, of course, envisions social welfare as being concerned with the limited function of handling arrangements for the incompetent. Friedman notes that social security programs, among a host of other government activities, are not justified in terms of the criteria for government intervention outlined in his article. From Friedman's perspective, social welfare has a circumscribed and residual function in our society.

## NOTES

1. For example, see Frances Fox Piven and Richard Cloward, *Regulating the Poor* (New York: Pantheon Books, 1971), and Betty Mandell, "Welfare and Totalitarianism: Part 1. Theoretical Issues," *Social Work*, 16 (January 1971): 17–25.

2. Harold Wilensky and Charles Lebeaux, *Industrial Society and Social Welfare* (New York: Free Press, 1965), pp. 138–47.

3. Martin Wolins, "The Societal Function of Social Welfare," *New Perspectives: The Berkeley Journal of Social Welfare*, 1 (Spring 1967), pp. 1–18.

# 4   Policy and Social Institutions

## NEIL GILBERT AND HARRY SPECHT

Social welfare policy is an elusive concept used frequently as a synonym for social policy and public policy, both of which are broader in scope and more inclusive than the concerns of this book. Social welfare policy is identified with public policy because enactment of most social welfare policies involves expenditure of the public dollar. Government spending in this area (see Figure 4–1) has been increasing, and amounted to 71 percent of the $268 billion spent for social welfare activities in 1972. Total social welfare expenditures in 1972 accounted for 25 percent of the gross national product. Even when private dollars pay for program support they are often augmented by public funds.

However, public policy includes more than just social welfare activities. It encompasses the broad range of goods and services supported by public funds, such as defense, aerospace research, and transportation.

FIGURE 4–1

Percent Public and Private Social Welfare Expenditures in Constant Dollars, Selected Fiscal Years 1959–60 through 1971–72

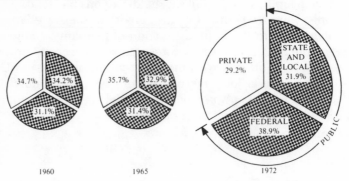

From Alfred M. Skolnik and Sophie R. Dales, Social Welfare Expenditures, 1971–72, *Social Security Bulletin*, Vol. 35, No. 12 (December 1972).

Similarly, the term social policy is often used to designate a more extensive range of activities than we would subsume under the heading of social welfare. For example, Gil defines social policies as

From Neil Gilbert and Harry Specht, *Dimensions of Social Welfare Policy* (Englewood Cliffs: Prentice-Hall Inc. 1974). Reprinted with permission of the authors and Prentice Hall, Inc. Copyright © 1974 by Prentice Hall Inc.

Elements of a society's system of social policy, a system of interrelated, yet not necessarily logically consistent, principles and courses of action, which shape the quality of life or level of well-being of members of society and determine the nature of all intrasocietal relationships among individuals, social subsystems, and society as a whole.[1]

According to this definition, social policy includes all the courses of action that impact on human relationships and the quality of life in a society. T. H. Marshall's definition, though somewhat more circumscribed, comes closer to what we would designate as social welfare policy.[2] For him it is "the policy of governments with regard to action having a direct impact on the welfare of citizens by providing them with services or income." Specifically, the "central core" of programs included under this definition are social insurance, public assistance, health and welfare services, and housing. At the periphery, but still within bounds, are programs dealing with education and delinquency prevention.[3]

Even the term "policy" has several nuances.[4] For Kahn it is the "standing plan";[5] Rein explains policy as the substance of planning choices;[6] and Mangum describes it as "a definite course of action selected from among alternatives, and in light of given conditions to guide and determine present and future decisions."[7] On this matter we defer to Webster and simplicity. The meaning of policy that we will use is that it is "a course or plan of action." This book is about the decisions and choices which inform the course or plan of action in public and private voluntary agencies. What binds and delimits these decisions and choices is that they inform action addressed to the functioning of a particular institution—the institution of social welfare.

By limiting our discussion of policy in this way we skirt the conceptual swamp of social policy, public policy, and social welfare policy distinctions, but enter the thicket of institutional delineation as we attempt to describe the "institution of social welfare."

All human societies organize life into enduring patterns that carry on essential social functions.[8] "Institutions" are networks of relationships that are generally accepted as the way of carrying out these essential social functions.[9] "Essential social functions" are human activities such as childrearing and the production, consumption, and distribution of goods. For example, all societies develop institutions for socialization that are networks of relationships within which responsibilities and expectations for raising and training the young are distributed. Socialization, of course, is not limited to children. The function has meaning for all stages of the life cycle.

One primary institution seldom exhausts the patterns a society uses to deal with any particular essential function. While the primary institution for socialization in our society is the family, it is by no means the only one. Religious and educational organizations and social service agencies also assume some responsibilities for socialization, but this is not the primary or core function of these institutions.[10]

For our purposes, there are five social functions around which the major institutional activities of community life develop: (1) production-distribution-consumption, (2) socialization, (3) social control, (4) social integration, and (5) mutual support. These functions represent the organization of basic human activities necessary in day-to-day living. We shall comment on each of them briefly, paraphrasing from both Johnson's and Warren's descriptions.[11]

1. *Production-consumption-distribution* has to do with the processes of producing, distributing, and consuming those goods and services required for living. This includes the modern business corporation which is the principal provider of such goods and services as well as other institutions, whether industrial, professional, religious, educational, and governmental, which provide goods and services. For the individual these institutions affect his way of earning a living and providing for family needs for goods and services. For the community, the ways in which these functions are carried out will determine the extent to which its members are self-supporting and in receipt of what is required for healthful functioning.

2. *Socialization,* which we mentioned above, involves those processes by which society transmits prevailing knowledge, social values, and behavior patterns to its members.

3. *Social control* refers to the arrangements by which a society influences the behavior of its members to achieve conformity with its norms. Formal government, which has coercive power to enforce universally applicable laws through the police and the courts, is a primary institution of social control. However, many other social units, including the family, the school, the church, and social agencies assume responsibilities for carrying out this function.

4. *Social integration* has to do with the relationships among units in a social system. Members of a particular institution or of the system-as-a-whole must be loyal to one another and the system must achieve some level of solidarity and morale in order to function. Socialization refers to mechanisms for teaching people how to behave; social control functions have reference to the means for governing or coercing that behavior; and social integration refers to the means of getting people to *want* to behave, e.g., to value and to abide by the rules of the system of social control, socialization, and so forth. The social agencies which carry out these social integration functions are those concerned with the development of social values and norms and include the church, the family, and the school.

5. Finally, *mutual support* functions come into play when individuals are not able to meet their needs through the major institutions which

operate to carry out the other social functions we have described. This may occur for a wide variety of reasons such as sickness, loss of a wage earner, or inadequate functioning of the economic institutions. In technologically underdeveloped societies, mutual support activities are carried out primarily by the family. As societies have become more complex, other groups, organizations, and agencies develop which carry out mutual support activities, such as the church, voluntary agencies, and government. *The institution of social welfare is that patterning of relationships which develops in society to carry out mutual support functions.*

## THE INSTITUTION OF SOCIAL WELFARE

In the very simplest of societies, all of the functions noted above are carried out by one social institution, the family. As societies become more complex, individuals and groups specialize in these social functions, and with this specialization other institutions evolve, such as religious, political, and economic institutions. These four types of institutions—familial, religious, political, and economic—are generally recognized as the major social institutions of society.[12] Each institution serves more than one function; at the same time each is closely associated with a primary or core function (see Table 4–1). The institution of social welfare is, by comparison, more functionally diffuse than the others. That is, family, religious, political, and economic institutions intersect at the periphery but contain primary functions which can be defined in fairly discrete and independent terms, while the primary function of social welfare—mutual support —is defined in terms that are relative to and dependent upon the other institutional functions. Mutual support activities come into play only when human needs are not being met via family, political, religious, or economic activities. This is clearly expressed in the literature where various efforts to describe and conceptualize the distinctive features of social welfare policy tend to emphasize objectives concerning integration,[13] distribution[14] and social control.[15]

Functional diffusion is the quality that complicates efforts to delineate the institution of social welfare as a separate and distinct entity. Indeed, it lends weight to the conception that social welfare serves mainly a residual function wherein its activities are perceived as necessary only when those who are served by the "normal" institutional channels are unable to benefit, either through personal failings and exceptional needs or when these "normal" channels fail to perform appropriately. Viewed as a residual, temporary substitute for the failures of individuals and major institutions, social welfare is seen as a rather negative and undesirable set of activities. Supporters of this view argue that it is inappropriate to place social welfare alongside of and on equal standing with the major societal institutions of Table 4–1.

TABLE 4–1
Institutional Functions

| Institution | Primary Function |
| --- | --- |
| Family | Socialization |
| Religion | Integration |
| Economics | Production–distribution–consumption |
| Politics | Social control |
| Social welfare | Mutual support |

Speaking at the Conference of Charities and Corrections in 1915, Dr. Abraham Flexner expressed this residual conception of social welfare in comparing social work with the recognized professions:[16]

A good deal of what is called social work might perhaps be accounted for on the ground that the recognized professions have developed too slowly on the social side. Suppose medicine were fully socialized; would not medical men, medical institutions, and medical organizations look after certain interests that the social worker must care for just because medical practice now falls short? The shortcomings of law create a similar need in another direction. Thus viewed, social work is, in part at least, not so much a separate profession as an endeavor to supplement certain existing professions *pending their completed development.* [Emphasis added]

Competing with this conception is the "institutional" view of social welfare as a distinct pattern of activities serving not as a safety net to catch the pieces after all else has failed, but as an integral and "normal 'first line' function of modern industrial society."[17] Perceived thus, as a basic social institution, social welfare carries none of the stigma of the "dole" or "charity." Rather, it is seen as the normal and accepted means by which individuals, families, and communities fulfill their social needs and attain healthful living.

Whether the institutional or residual conception of social welfare prevails depends in large measure upon how we comprehend both the causes and the incidence of unmet needs in society. In both conceptions, the major institutional structures are viewed as ineffective to some degree in meeting people's needs. The fundamental issues are: To what extent is this an anomaly reflecting mainly the deficiencies of some individuals and a small margin of institutional malfunctioning? To what extent is it a regularly anticipated consequence reflecting the inherent limitations of both institutional adaptations to change and individual efforts to deal with the exigencies of life in modern industrial society? In other words, is it the workman and a few of his tools that occasionally may be faulty? Or, are both inherently imperfect given the complex and uncertain demands of the job? An answer of "very much" to the first question and "very little" to the second relegates social welfare to the status of a residual activity which, as Figure 4–2 suggests, serves as a safety net for the basic institutional structure. Reverse these answers and social welfare emerges as a basic social institution.

FIGURE 4–2
Conceptions of Social Welfare

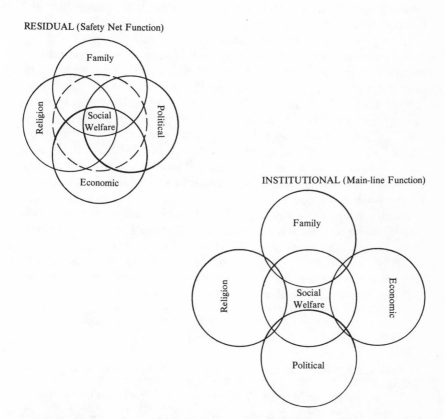

The answers to these questions, however, remain equivocal. In this regard, Wilensky and Lebeaux's assessment of the status of the competing conceptions of social welfare in the United States is still accurate.

While these two views seem antithetical, in practice American social work has tried to combine them, and current trends in social welfare present a middle course. Those who lament the passing of the old order insist that the second ideology is undermining individual character and the national social structure. Those who bewail our failure to achieve utopia today, argue that the residual conception is an obstacle which must be removed before we can produce the good life for all. In our view, neither ideology exists in a vacuum; each is a reflection of . . . broader cultural and societal conditions. . . . With further industrialization the second is likely to prevail.[18]

In sum, social welfare may be characterized most accurately as an emerging institution whose core function is mutual support. Historically, mutual support activities are secondary functions of other institutions, mainly family and religion. Modern times have brought increasing demands on such activities as our conceptions of need and standards of well-being have changed. The limitations of existing major institutions to meet these demands as well as individual vulnerabilities to the forces of change in urban industrial society are becoming more apparent. However, the extent to which these limitations and vulnerabilities are perceived to exist varies greatly among segments of society. An elaborate system of public and private agencies has developed for the express purpose of providing mutual support. Thus, the relative importance of this activity as a distinct pattern begins to emerge, a pattern of activity comprising the major set of relationships and programs to which our discussion in this book is addressed.

Finally, while social welfare is described here as an emerging institution, there are certain eligibility requirements for social welfare benefits that lend credence to the residual conception. Because it is unlikely that these eligibility conditions will be eliminated entirely from social welfare concerns, it seems that the residual conception will linger even as social welfare approaches institutional status.

## NOTES

1. David A. Gil, "A Systematic Approach to Social Policy Analysis," *Social Service Review*, Vol. 44, No. 4 (December 1970), 411–26.
2. This distinction between "social policy" and "social welfare policy" is discussed by George Rohrlich, "Social Policy and Income Distribution," *Encyclopedia of Social Work*, Vol. 11, ed. Robert Morris (New York: National Assn. of Social Workers, 1971), pp. 1385–86.
3. T. H. Marshall, *Social Policy* (London: Hutchinson University Library, 1955), p. 7.
4. See Chapter 2 [not reprinted here] for discussion of distinctions that are made between policy and program.
5. Alfred Kahn, *Theory and Practice of Social Planning* (New York: Russell Sage, 1969), p. 13.
6. Martin Rein, *Social Policy* (New York: Random House, 1970).

7. Garth Mangum, *Emergence of Manpower Policy* (New York: Holt, Rinehart and Winston, 1969), p. 130.

8. For a probing, in-depth examination of functional analysis, see Robert Merton, *Social Theory and Social Structure*, 2nd ed. (London: The Free Press of Glencoe, 1964), pp. 19–84.

9. Harry M. Johnson, *Sociology: A Systematic Introduction* (New York: Harcourt Brace, 1960), p. 22.

10. The term institution is commonly used on two levels of abstraction. For example, there is the religious institution (such as St. John's Church) and the institution of religion. In the former sense this concept implies an organization or agency that performs a social function; in the latter it reflects the sum of organizations and agencies with the primary responsibility for performing this function.

11. Roland Warren, *The Community in America* (Chicago: Rand McNally, 1963), pp. 9–20; and Johnson, *Sociology,* pp. 51–66.

12. For a detailed discussion of these institutions, see William Ogburn and Meyer Nimkoff, *Sociology* (Cambridge: Houghton Mifflin, 1940), pp. 552–740; Robin Williams, Jr., *American Society* (New York: Alfred A. Knopf, 1951); and Francis Merrill and H. Wentworth Eldredge, *Culture and Society* (Englewood Cliffs, N.J.: Prentice Hall, 1952), pp. 462–82. In some cases education is also included on this list, though we consider it within the larger institution of social welfare.

13. For the emphasis of integration see, Kenneth Boulding, "The Boundaries of Social Policy."

14. For the emphasis of distribution see, Richard Titmuss, "The Role of Redistribution in Social Policy," *Commitment to Welfare* (London: George Allen and Unwin, 1968).

15. For the emphasis on social control see, Martin Wolins, "The Societal Functions of Social Welfare," *New Perspectives: The Berkeley Journal of Social Welfare*, Vol. 1, No. 1 (Spring 1967), 1–17.

16. Abraham Flexner, "Is Social Work a Profession?" Presented at the Conference of Charities and Corrections, May 17, 1915.

17. Harold Wilensky and Charles Lebeaux, *Industrial Society and Social Welfare* (New York: Russell Sage, 1958), p. 138.

18. Wilensky and Lebeaux, *Industrial Society and Social Welfare,* p. 140.

# 5   The Role of Redistribution in Social Policy

## RICHARD M. TITMUSS

In the literature of the West, concepts and models of social policy are as diverse as contemporary concepts of poverty. Historically, the two have indeed had much in common. They certainly share diversity. There are today those at one end of the political spectrum who

From *Social Security Bulletin,* 28 (June 1965): pp. 14–20.

see social policy as a transitory minimum activity of minimum government for a minimum number of poor people; as a form of social control for minority groups in a "natural" society; as a way of resolving the conflict between the religious ethic of compassion and undiluted individualism. In this view social policy is not good business. Statistical estimates of the national income per capita look healthier if the infant mortality rate rises. At the other end of the political spectrum there are writers like Macbeath who has comprehensively stated that "Social policies are concerned with the right ordering of the network of relationships between men and women who live together in societies, or with the principles which should govern the activities of individuals and groups so far as they affect the lives and interests of other people."[1]

Somewhere between these extreme visionary notions lives a conventional, textbook, definition of social policy.[2] The social services or social welfare, the labels we have for long attached to describe certain areas of public intervention such as income maintenance and public health, are seen as the main ingredients of social policy. They are obvious, direct and measurable acts of government, undertaken for a variety of political reasons, to provide for a range of needs, material and social, and predominantly dependent needs, which the market does not or cannot satisfy for certain designated sections of the population. Typically, these direct services are functionally organised in separate and specialised ministries, departments or divisions of government, central and local. They are seen as the "social policy department." What they do is thought to be explicitly redistributive; they politically interfere with the pattern of claims set by the market. They assign claims from one set of people who are said to produce or earn the national product to another set of people who may merit compassion and charity but not economic rewards for productive service. In short, they are seen as uncovenanted benefits for the poorer sections of the community. And because these separate functional units of social service are accountable to the public their activities are, in large measure, quantifiable. We can thus measure the size of the presumed burden (as it is conventionally called) on the economy.

This, I propose to argue, is a very limited and inadequate model of the working of social policy in the second half of the twentieth century. In its distance from the realities of today it is about as helpful (or unhelpful) as some recent models of economic man maximising his acquisitive drives. Later, I attempt to support and illustrate this statement by examining some of the lessons of experience of nearly 20 years of so-called "Welfare Statism" in Britain. First, however, I want to briefly consider one or two of the factors which have contributed to this limited concept of social policy—particularly in relation to its role as a redistributive agent.

Perhaps the most important causative factor in Britain has to do with the heritage of the poor law (or public assistance). Less than 60 years ago social policy was, in the eyes of the middle and upper classes, poor law policy. This model of "welfare use" was part of a political philosophy which saw society as an adjunct of the market.[3] As Karl Polanyi puts it, "Instead of economy being embedded in social relations, social relations are embedded in the economic system."[4] The essential, though financially reluctant, role of the poor law was to support industrialism and the attempt in the nineteenth century to establish a completely competitive, self-regulating market economy founded on the motive of individual gain. It thus had to create a great many rules of expected behaviour; about work and non-work, property, savings, family relationships, cohabitation, men-in-the-house, and so forth.[5] Poverty, as Disraeli once said, was declared a crime by industrialism. Laws about poverty became associated with laws about crime.

This system, which legally survived in Britain until 1948, inevitably involved personal discrimination. The stigmata of the poor law test, moral judgments by people about other people and their behaviour, were a condition of redistribution. The requirements of poor law and public assistance administration were, we can now see, remarkably attuned to the characteristics of bureaucracy drawn by Weber and others.[6] It was theoretically a neat and orderly world of eligible and ineligible citizens; of approved and disapproved patterns of dependency; of those who could manage change and those who could not. From its operation for over a century Britain inherited in 1948 a whole set of administrative attitudes, values and rites, essentially middle-class in structure, and moralistic in application. The new social service bottles of 1948 had poured into them much of the old wine of discrimination and prejudice. It has taken nearly two decades of sustained programmes of new recruitment, training, retraining and intraining, and the appointment of social workers to the public services, to eradicate part of this legacy of administrative behaviour.[7]

The history of the poor law and public assistance is thus still important to an understanding of social policy concepts today. If one disregards the social costs of industrialism, of allowing a large part of the disservices of technological progress to lie where they fall, then the system (of public assistance) was clearly redistributive. It directly benefited the explicit poor. Those in the greatest need did receive some benefit. But with the limited instruments of policy and administrative techniques to hand in the past, the system could only function by operating punitive tests of discrimination; by strengthening conceptions of approved and disapproved dependencies; and by a damaging assault on the recipients of welfare in terms of their sense of self-respect and self-determination. Within the established pattern of commonly held values, the system could only be redistributive by being discriminatory and socially divisive.

All this is now well documented in the archives of social inquiry and is somewhat ancient history. Equally well-known is the story of society's response to the challenge of poverty during the past 30 years or so: the discovery that this system of public aid was administratively grossly inefficient; the discovery that it could not by its very nature absorb the new dimensions of social and psychological knowledge and that, therefore, it could not function effectively both as a redistributive agent and as an agent to prevent social breakdown; and the discovery that the system was fundamentally inconsistent with the need to grant to all citizens, irrespective of race, religion or color, full and equal social rights.[8]

Gradually in Britain, as we tried to learn these lessons, we began to discard the use of discriminatory and overtly redistributive services for second-class citizens. The social services on minimum standards for all citizens crept apologetically into existence. In common with other countries we invented contributory national insurance or social security and provided benefits as of right. The actuary was called in to replace the functions of the public assistance relieving officer. Free secondary education for all children, irrespective of the means of their parents, was enacted in 1944 as part of a comprehensive educational system. Public housing authorities were called upon in 1945 to build houses for people and not just for working-class people. A limited and second-class health insurance scheme for workingmen was transformed, in 1948, into a comprehensive and free-on-demand health service for the whole population.[9]

All these and many other changes in the direct and publicly accountable instruments of social policy led to the notion that, in the year 1948, the "Welfare State" had been established in Britain. While there was general political consensus on this matter there was, on the other hand, much confusion and debate about cause and effect.[10] There were many, for instance, who thought that these policy changes were brought about for deliberately redistributive reasons and that the effects would be significantly egalitarian. This, perhaps, was understandable. Direct welfare in the past had in fact been redistributive (considered apart from the effects of the fiscal system). Therefore it was natural to assume that more welfare in the future would mean more redistribution in favour of the poor. There were others however (among whom I count myself), who believed that the fundamental and dominating historical processes which led to these major changes in social policy were connected with the demand for one society; for non-discriminatory services for all without distinction of class, income or race; for services and relations which would deepen and enlarge self-respect; for services which would manifestly encourage social integration. From some perspectives these major changes in policy could be regarded as ideological pleas to the middle- and upper-income classes to share in the benefits (as well as the costs) of public welfare.

Built into the public model of social policy in Britain since 1948 there are two major roles or objectives: the redistributive objective and the non-discriminatory objective. To move towards the latter it was believed that a prerequisite was the legal enactment of universal (or comprehensive) systems of national insurance, education, medical care, housing and other direct services.

What have we learnt in the past 15 years about the actual functioning of these services? What has universalism in social welfare achieved? Clearly, I cannot give you a full account of all aspects of this development during a period when, for 13 of these years, the Government in power was not, in the early stages at least, entirely committed to the concept of the "Welfare State." I shall therefore concentrate my conclusions, brief and inadequate though they are, on the theme of redistribution.

Up to this point I have dealt only with what I sometimes call the "Iceberg Phenomena of Social Welfare." That is, the direct public provision of services in kind (e.g. education and medical care) and the direct payment of benefits in cash (e.g. retirement pensions and family allowances).

I now turn to consider two other major categories of social policy which have been developing and extending their roles in Britain and other countries over much the same period of time as the category we call "the social services." Elsewhere, I have described the former as "Fiscal Welfare" and "Occupational Welfare."[11] These are the indirect or submerged parts of the "Iceberg of Social Policy." In both categories a remarkable expansion has taken place in Britain during the past 20 years.

All three categories of social policy have a great deal in common in terms of redistribution. They are all concerned with changing the individual and family pattern of current and future claims on resources set by the market, set by the possession of accumulated past rights, and set by the allocations made by government to provide for national defence and other non-market sectors. Social welfare changes the pattern of claims by, for instance, directly providing in-kind education or mental hospital care either free or at less than the market cost. Fiscal welfare changes the pattern of claims by taking less in tax (and thus increasing net disposable income) when a taxpayer's child is born, when its education is prolonged, when men have ex-wives to maintain, when taxpayers reach a specified age, and so on. An individual's pattern of claims on resources is today greatly varied through fiscal welfare policy by his or her change in circumstances, family responsibilities, and opportunities available (and taken) for prolonged education, home ownership and so on. In Britain, the United States and other countries the tax system has recently been regarded as an alternative in certain areas to the social security system; as a policy instrument to be used to provide higher incomes for the aged, for large families, for the blind and other handicapped groups, and for meeting part of the costs of education which today may last for up to 20 years or more.[12]

Occupational welfare, provided by virtue of employment status, achievement and record, may take the form of social security provisions in cash or in kind. Such provisions are legally approved by government and, as in the case of fiscal welfare, they may be seen as alternatives to extensions in social welfare. Their cost falls in large measure on the whole population. It is thus, like social welfare and fiscal welfare, a major redistributive mechanism.

In Britain, occupational welfare may include: pensions for employees; survivors' benefits; child allowances; death benefits; health and welfare services; severance pay and compensation for loss of office (analogous these days to compensation for loss of property rights); personal expenses for travel, entertainment and dress; meal vouchers; cars and season tickets; residential accommodation; holiday expenses; children's school fees at private schools; sickness benefits; medical expenses; education and training grants and benefits ranging from "obvious forms of realizable goods to the most intangible forms of amenity"[13] expressed in a form that is neither money nor convertible into money.

A substantial part of these occupational welfare benefits can be interpreted—again like fiscal welfare—as social policy recognition of dependencies; the long dependencies of old age, childhood and widowhood, and such short-term dependencies as sickness and the loss of job rights.

The populations to which these three categories of welfare relate differ, but a substantial section of people may be eligible for benefits in respect of all three. In Britain, most of the social welfare services (except national assistance and university education) are universalist and citizen-based; they are open to all without a test of means. Thus, access to them does not depend upon achieved or inherited status. Fiscal welfare relates to a smaller population; only to those who pay direct taxes and not those who pay property taxes and social security contributions. Occupational welfare relates to the employed population and, at present, predominantly favours white-collar and middle-class occupations. Benefits are thus related to achievement.

All three categories of welfare are, as we have seen, redistributive; they change the pattern of claims on current and future resources. They function redistributively as separate, self-contained systems and they do so also in relation to the whole economy. Here is one example. Many private pension schemes, which include manual and non-manual workers, tend to redistribute claims on resources from lower-paid to higher-paid employees. This happens because the lower-paid workers change jobs more frequently; in doing so they do not have credited to them the full amount of pension contributions or premiums. It is estimated in Britain that the cost of full preservation of pension rights for all employees in the private sector (an objective in the present Government's proposals for the reform of social security) could add 15 to 25 percent to the actuarial costs of private schemes.[14] Moreover, as at present organised, the cost to the Treasury (the whole community) of private pension schemes substantially exceeds the Treasury contribution to social security pensions for the whole population. The pensions of the rich are more heavily subsidised by the community than the pensions of the poor.[15]

This in part happens because occupational welfare and fiscal welfare benefits are fundamentally based on the principles of achievement, status and need. If there is need, then the higher the income the higher is the welfare benefit. By contrast, social welfare benefits generally take account only of needs—the need for medical care, for education and so on irrespective of income or status.

I have now described in very general terms three categories of social policy redistribution—with particular reference to their operation in Britain. At present, they are publicly viewed as virtually distinct systems. What goes on within and as a result of one system is ignored by the others. They are appraised, criticised or applauded as abstracted, independent, entities. Historically, they have developed different concepts of poverty or subsistence; different criteria for determining approved dependencies; different standards of moral values in determining eligibility for welfare. Some examples will illustrate this point.

The social policy definition of subsistence as developed in the fiscal system for determining exemption from taxation, income needs in old age, and so on, differs markedly from the definition used in public assistance.[16] In some areas of policy the fiscal definition of poverty is employed, as, for instance, in determining grants to university students.[17] In other and similar areas of policy the public assistance definition is employed—as, for instance, in determining aid for poor parents of 16-year-old children at school.[18] It is odd, when you come to think of it, that dependency at age 16 is assessed at a lower standard of assistance than dependency at 18 or even 23 (in the case of medical students and graduates).

We have in fact two standards of poverty for determining aid from the community; highly subjective and unscientific; both employed to assist dependent states; a working-class standard and a middle-class standard. The former has been investigated, studied, measured and argued about for long by sociologists, social workers and economists, and made the subject of many books and doctoral theses. By contrast, the latter has been virtually ignored.

One further example of double standards operating in different categories of welfare may be selected from a large field—this one to illustrate the role of moral values in social policy.

In the category of social welfare, cash aid from public funds for unsupported mothers, and their children may be stopped if it is believed that cohabitation is taking place. This is an event—or a relationship—that can rarely be legally proved. It is hardly a scientific fact. We have in Britain a cohabitation regulation,[19] you have a man-in-the-house regulation.[20] They amount to the same thing; they cannot be spelt out in precise operational terms. Their application in practice depends in large measure, therefore, on hearsay and moral judgement.

The same problem of to give or not to give aid arises in the category of fiscal welfare. As an example I quote from a memorandum by Lord Justice Hodson to a Royal Commission on Marriage and Divorce: "A super-tax payer may, and quite frequently nowadays does, have a number of wives living at the same time since after divorce his ex-wives are not treated as one with him for tax purposes he can manage quite nicely since he is permitted" (a social policy decision) "to deduct all his wives' maintenance allowances from his gross income for tax purposes leaving his net income comparatively slightly affected."[21]

In both instances redistribution takes place; the community renders aid in these situations of need and dependency. But while the decision to help the public assistance mother may involve judgements about moral behaviour, in the case of the taxpayer the decision is automatic and impersonal. The logic of the double standard is not apparent. If one is socially acceptable and approved behaviour then why not the other?

Now I must begin to draw these reflections together. What have been the lessons of experience in Britain about the actual functioning of these three categories of welfare during the past 15 years? Obviously, I cannot give you more than a fragment of an answer, and even this involves over-simplifying to a dangerous degree. To analyse and measure the redistributive effects of this process of the social division of welfare would be an immensely complex task—even if the essential statistical data were available which, in many areas, they are not. All I can offer are a few generalised conclusions.

The major positive achievement which has resulted from the creation of direct, universalist, social services in kind has been the erosion of formal discriminatory barriers. One publicly approved standard of service, irrespective of income, class or race, replaced the double standard which invariably meant second-class services for second-class citizens. This has been most clearly seen in the National Health Service. Despite strict controls over expenditure on the Service by Conservative Governments for many years it has maintained the principle of equality of access by all citizens to all branches of medical care. Viewed solely in terms of the welfare objective of non-discriminatory non-judgemental service this is the signal achievement of the National Health Service. In part this is due to the fact that the middle-classes, invited to enter the Service in 1948, did so and have since largely stayed with the Service. They have not contracted out of socialised medical care as they have done in other fields like secondary education and retirement pensions. Their continuing participation, and their more articulate demands for improvements, have been an important factor in a general rise in standards of service—particularly in hospital care.[22]

But, as some students of social policy in Britain and the United States are beginning to learn, equality of access is not the same thing as equality of outcome. We have to ask statistical and sociological questions about the utilisation of the high-cost quality sectors of social welfare and the low-cost sectors of social welfare. We have to ask similar questions about the ways in which professional people (doctors, teachers, social workers and many others) discharge their roles in diagnosing need and in selecting or rejecting patients, clients and students for this or that service. In the modern world the professions are increasingly becoming the arbiters of our welfare fate; they are the key-holders to equality of outcome; they help to determine the pattern of redistribution in social policy.

These generalisations apply particularly when services in kind are organised on a universalist, free-on-demand basis. When this is so we substitute, in effect, the professional decision-maker for the crude decisions of the economic marketplace. And we also make much more explicit—an important gain in itself—the fact that the poor have great difficulties in manipulating the wider society, in managing change, in choosing between alternatives, in finding their way around a complex world of welfare.

We have learnt from 15 years' experience of the Health Service that the higher income groups know how to make better use of the Service; they tend to receive more specialist attention; occupy more of the beds in better equipped and staffed hospitals; receive more elective surgery; have better maternity care; and are more likely to get psychiatric help and psychotherapy than low income groups—particularly the unskilled.[23]

These are all factors which are essential to an understanding of the redistributive role played by one of the major direct welfare services in kind. They are not arguments against a comprehensive free-on-demand service. But they do serve to underline one conclusion. Universalism in social welfare, though a needed prerequisite towards reducing and removing formal barriers of social and economic discrimination, does not by itself solve the problem of how to reach the more-difficult-to-reach with better medical care, especially preventive medical care.

Much the same kind of general conclusion can be drawn from Britain's experience in the field of education. Despite reforms and expansion during the past 15 years it is a fact that the proportion of male undergraduates who are the sons of manual workers is today about 1 percent lower than it was between 1928 and 1947. Although we have doubled the number of University students the proportion coming from working-class homes has remained fairly constant at just over a quarter.[24]

The major beneficiaries of the high-cost sectors of the educational system in "The Welfare State" have been the higher income groups. They have been helped to so benefit by the continued existence of a prosperous private sector in secondary education (partly subsidised by the State in a variety of ways including tax deductibles), and by developments since 1948 in provisions for child dependency in the category of fiscal welfare.[25] Take, for example, the case of two fathers each with two children, one earning $60,000 a year, the other $1,500 a year. In combining the effect of direct social welfare expenditures for children and indirect fiscal welfare expenditures for children the result is that the rich father now gets thirteen times more from the State than the poor father in recognition of the dependent needs of childhood.

Housing is another field of social policy which merits analysis from the point of view of redistribution. Here we have to take account of the complex interlocking effects of local rate payments, public housing subsidies, interest rates, tax deductibles for mortgage interest and other factors. When we have done so we find that the subsidy paid by the State to many middle-class families buying their own homes is greater than that received by poor tenants of public housing (local government) schemes.[26]

These are no more than illustrations of the need to study the redistributive effects of social policy in a wider frame of reference. Hitherto, our techniques of social diagnosis and our conceptual frameworks have been too narrow. We have compartmentalised social welfare as we have compartmentalised the poor. The analytic model of social policy that has been fashioned on only the phenomena that are clearly visible, direct and immediately measurable is an inadequate one. It fails to tell us about the realities of redistribution which are being generated by the processes of technological and social change and by the combined effects of social welfare, fiscal welfare and occupational welfare.

How far and to what extent should redistribution take place through welfare channels on the principle of achieved status, inherited status or need? This is the kind of question which, fundamentally, is being asked in Britain today. And it is being directed, in particular, at two major areas of social policy—social security and housing. Both these instruments of change and redistribution have been neglected for a decade or more. We have gone in search of new gods or no gods at all. It is time we returned to consider their roles afresh and with new vision. Perhaps we might then entitle our journey "Ways of Extending the Welfare State to the Poor."

## NOTES

1. A. Macbeath, *Can Social Policies Be Rationally Tested?* Oxford University Press, London, 1957.

2. For some discussion of the problems of definitions see H. L. Wilensky and C. N. Lebeaux, *Industrial Society and Social Welfare,* Russell Sage Foundation, New York, 1958; *Social Welfare Statistics of the Northern Countries,* Report No. 9, Stockholm, 1964; Gunnar Myrdal, *Beyond the Welfare State,* Yale University Press, 1960; and Richard M. Titmuss, *Essays on the "Welfare State,"* Allen and Unwin, Ltd., 1958.

3. See, for example, A. V. Dicey, *Law and Opinion in England During the Nineteenth Century,* London, 1905.

4. Karl Polanyi, *Origins of Our Time,* Beacon Paperbacks (No. 45), London, 1945, page 63.

5. *Reports of the Royal Commission on the Poor Laws,* His Majesty's Stationery Office, London, 1909.

6. H. H. Gerth and C. W. Mills, *From Max Weber: Essays in Sociology,* Oxford University Press, New York, 1946.

7. See, for example, *Annual Reports of the National Assistance Board, 1950–63,* Her Majesty's Stationery Office, London, and *Seventh and Eighth Reports on the Work of the Children's Department,* Home Office, Her Majesty's Stationery Office, London, 1955 and 1961.

8. Illustrated in the recommendations of the Beveridge Report (*Social Insurance and Allied Services,* Cmd. No. 6404), His Majesty's Stationery Office, London, 1942.

9. M. P. Hall, *The Social Services of Modern England,* Routledge, London, 1952.

10. Richard M. Titmuss, *Income Distribution and Social Change,* chapter 9, Allen and Unwin, Ltd., London, 1962.

11. Richard M. Titmuss, *Essays on the "Welfare State,"* Allen and Unwin, Ltd., London, 2nd ed., 1963.

12. *Reports of the Royal Commission on the Taxation of Profits and Income, 1952–55,* Her Majesty's Stationery Office, London, 1955.

13. *Final Report of the Royal Commission on Taxation,* Cmd. 9474, Her Majesty's Stationery Office, London, 1955, page 68. See also A. Rubner, *Fringe Benefits,* Putnam, London, 1962.

14. See references in Richard M. Titmuss, *Income Distribution and Social Change*, chapter 7, and *British Tax Review*, Jan.–Feb. 1964.

15. Richard M. Titmuss, *The Irresponsible Society*, Fabian Tract No. 323, London, 1959.

16. *Reports of the Royal Commission on the Taxation of Profits and Income, 1952–55*, Her Majesty's Stationery Office, London, 1955.

17. *Ministry of Education, Grants to Students*, Cmd. No. 1051, Her Majesty's Stationery Office, London, 1960.

18. *Report of the Working Party on Educational Maintenance Allowances*, Her Majesty's Stationery Office, London, 1957.

19. National Insurance Act, 1946, section 17 (2) and *Digest of Commissioner's Decisions*, Her Majesty's Stationery Office, London, 1946–64.

20. *See Report of the Public Welfare Crisis Committee*, Metropolitan Washington Chapter of the National Association of Social Workers, Washington, 1963.

21. J. Hudson, *Royal Commission on Marriage and Divorce*, M D P/1952/337, Her Majesty's Stationery Office, London, 1952.

22. A. Lindsey, *Socialized Medicine in England and Wales*, University of North Carolina Press, 1962.

23. Richard M. Titmuss, *Essays on the "Welfare State,"* appendix on the National Health Service, second edition, Allen and Unwin, Ltd., London, 1963.

24. *Robbins Report on Higher Education*, appendix 2, volumes A and B, Her Majesty's Stationery Office, London, 1964.

25. *The Economist*, London, Oct. 26, 1963.

26. D. Nevitt, *Essays on Housing*, Occasional Papers on Social Administration (No. 9), Codicote Press, London, 1964.

# 6   The Role of Government in a Free Society

## MILTON FRIEDMAN

A common objection to totalitarian societies is that they regard the end as justifying the means. Taken literally, this objection is clearly illogical. If the end does not justify the means, what does? But this easy answer does not dispose of the objection; it simply shows that the objection is not well put. To deny that the end justifies the means is indirectly to assert that the end in question is not the ultimate end, that the ultimate end is itself the use of the proper means. Desirable or not, any end that can be attained only by the use of bad means must give way to the more basic end of the use of acceptable means.

From *Capitalism and Freedom* by Milton Friedman, pp. 22–36. Copyright © 1962 by the University of Chicago Press. Reprinted by permission of the publisher and author.

To the Liberal, the appropriate means are free discussion and voluntary co-operation, which implies that any form of coercion is inappropriate. The ideal is unanimity among responsible individuals achieved on the basis of free and full discussion. This is another way of expressing the goal of freedom. . . .

From this standpoint, the role of the market, as already noted, is that it permits unanimity without conformity; that it is a system of effectively proportional representation. On the other hand, the characteristic feature of action through explicitly political channels is that it tends to require or to enforce substantial conformity. The typical issue must be decided "yes" or "no"; at most, provision can be made for a fairly limited number of alternatives. Even the use of proportional representation in its explicitly political form does not alter this conclusion. The number of separate groups that can in fact be represented is narrowly limited, enormously so by comparison with the proportional representation of the market. More important, the fact that the final outcome generally must be a law applicable to all groups, rather than separate legislative enactments for each "party" represented, means that proportional representation in its political version, far from permitting unanimity without conformity, tends toward ineffectiveness and fragmentation. It thereby operates to destroy any consensus on which unanimity with conformity can rest.

There are clearly some matters with respect to which effective proportional representation is impossible. I cannot get the amount of national defense I want and you, a different amount. With respect to such indivisible matters we can discuss, and argue, and vote. But having decided, we must conform. It is precisely the existence of such indivisible matters—protection of the individual and the nation from coercion are clearly the most basic—that prevents exclusive reliance on individual action through the market. If we are to use some of our resources for such indivisible items, we must employ political channels to reconcile differences.

The use of political channels, while inevitable, tends to strain the social cohesion essential for a stable society. The strain is least if agreement for joint action need be reached only on a limited range of issues on which people in any event have common views. Every extension of the range of issues for which explicit agreement is sought strains further the delicate threads that hold society together. If it goes so far as to touch an issue on which men feel deeply yet differently, it may well disrupt the society. Fundamental differences in basic values can seldom if ever be resolved at the ballot box; ultimately they can only be decided, though not resolved, by conflict. The religious and civil wars of history are a bloody testament to this judgment.

The widespread use of the market reduces the strain on the social fabric by rendering conformity unnecessary with respect to any activities it encompasses. The wider the range of activities covered by the market, the fewer are the issues on which explicitly political decisions are required and hence on which it is necessary to achieve agreement. In turn, the fewer the issues on which agreement is necessary, the greater is the likelihood of getting agreement while maintaining a free society.

Unanimity is, of course, an ideal. In practice, we can afford neither the time nor the effort that would be required to achieve complete unanimity on every issue. We must perforce accept something less. We are thus led to accept majority rule in one form or another as an expedient. That majority rule is an expedient rather than itself a basic principle is clearly shown by the fact that our willingness to resort to majority rule, and the size of the majority we require, themselves depend on the seriousness of the issue involved. If the matter is of little moment and the minority has no strong feelings about being overruled, a bare plurality will suffice. On the other hand, if the minority feels strongly about the issue involved, even a bare majority will not do. Few of us would be willing to have issues of free speech, for example, decided by a bare majority. Our legal structure is full of such distinctions among kinds of issues that require different kinds of majorities. At the extreme are those issues embodied in the Constitution. These are the principles that are so important that we are willing to make minimal concessions to expediency. Something like essential consensus was achieved initially in accepting them, and we require something like essential consensus for a change in them.

The self-denying ordinance to refrain from majority rule on certain kinds of issues that is embodied in our Constitution and in similar written or unwritten constitutions elsewhere, and the specific provisions in these constitutions or their equivalents prohibiting coercion of individuals, are themselves to be regarded as reached by free discussion and as reflecting essential unanimity about means.

I turn now to consider more specifically, though still in very broad terms, what the areas are that cannot be handled through the market at all, or can be handled only at so great a cost that the use of political channels may be preferable.

## GOVERNMENT AS RULE-MAKER AND UMPIRE

It is important to distinguish the day-to-day activities of people from the general customary and legal framework within which these take place. The day-to-day activities are like the actions of the participants in a game when they are playing it; the framework, like the rules of the game they play. And just as a good game requires acceptance by the players both of the rules and of the umpire to interpret and enforce them, so a good society requires that its members agree on the general conditions that will govern relations among them, on some means of arbitrating different interpretations of these conditions, and on some device for enforcing compliance with the generally accepted rules. As in games, so also in society, most of the general conditions are the unintended outcome of custom, accepted unthinkingly. At most, we consider explicitly only minor modifications in them, though the cumulative effect of a series of minor modifications may be a drastic alteration in the character of the game or of the society. In both games and society also, no set of rules can prevail unless most participants most of the time conform to them without external sanctions; unless that is, there is a broad underlying social consensus. But we cannot rely on custom or on this consensus alone to interpret and to enforce the rules; we need an umpire. These then are the basic roles of government in a free society: to provide a means whereby we can modify the rules, to mediate differences among us on the meaning of the rules, and to enforce compliance with the rules on the part of those few who would otherwise not play the game.

The need for government in these respects arises because absolute freedom is impossible. However attractive anarchy may be as a philosophy, it is not feasible in a world of imperfect men. Men's freedoms can conflict, and when they do, one man's freedom must be limited to preserve another's—as a Supreme Court Justice once put it, "My freedom to move my fist must be limited by the proximity of your chin."

The major problem in deciding the appropriate activities of government is how to resolve such conflicts among the freedoms of different individuals. In some cases, the answer is easy. There is little difficulty in attaining near unanimity to the proposition that one man's freedom to murder his neighbor must be sacrificed to preserve the freedom of the other man to live. In other cases, the answer is difficult. In the economic area, a major problem arises in respect of the conflict between freedom to combine and freedom to compete. What meaning is to be attributed to "free" as modifying "enterprise"? In the United States, "free" has been understood to mean that anyone is free to set up an enterprise, which means that existing enterprises are not free to keep out competitors except by selling a better product at the same price or the same product at a lower price. In the continental tradition, on the other hand, the meaning has generally been that enterprises are free to do what they want, including the fixing of prices, division of markets, and the adoption of other techniques to keep out potential competitors. Perhaps the most difficult specific problem in this area arises with respect to combinations among laborers, where the problem of freedom to combine and freedom to compete is particularly acute.

A still more basic economic area in which the answer is both difficult and important is the definition of property rights. The notion of property, as it has developed over centuries and as it is embodied in our legal codes, has became so much a part of us that we tend to take it for granted, and fail to recognize the extent to which just what constitutes property and what rights the ownership of property confers are complex social creations rather than self-evident propositions. Does my having title to land, for example, and my freedom to use my property as I wish, permit me to deny to someone else the right to fly over my land in his airplane? Or does his right to use his airplane take precedence? Or does this depend on how high he flies? Or how much noise he makes? Does voluntary exchange require that he pay me for the privilege of flying over my land? Or that I must pay him to refrain from flying over it? The mere mention of royalties, copyrights, patents; shares of stock in corporations; riparian rights, and the like, may perhaps emphasize the role of generally accepted social rules in the very definition of property. It may suggest also that, in many cases, the existence of a well specified and generally accepted definition of property is far more important than just what the definition is.

Another economic area that raises particularly difficult problems is the monetary system. Government responsibility for the monetary system has long been recognized. It is explicitly provided for in the constitutional provision which gives Congress the power "to coin money, regulate the value thereof, and of foreign coin." There is probably no other area of economic activity with respect to which government action has been so uniformly accepted. This habitual and by now almost unthinking acceptance of governmental responsibility makes thorough understanding of the grounds for such responsibility all the more necessary, since it enhances the danger that the scope of government will spread from activities that are, to those that are not, appropriate in a free society, from providing a monetary framework to determining the allocation of resources among individuals.

In summary, the organization of economic activity through voluntary exchange presumes that we have provided, through government, for the maintenance of law and order to prevent coercion of one individual by another, the enforcement of contracts voluntarily entered into, the definition of the meaning of property rights, the interpretation and enforcement of such rights, and the provision of a monetary framework.

## ACTION THROUGH GOVERNMENT ON GROUNDS OF
## TECHNICAL MONOPOLY AND NEIGHBORHOOD EFFECTS

The role of government just considered is to do something that the market cannot do for itself, namely, to determine, arbitrate, and enforce the rules of the game. We may also want to do through government some things that might conceivably be done through the market but that technical or similar conditions render it difficult to do in that way. These all reduce to cases in which strictly voluntary exchange is either exceedingly costly or practically impossible. There are two general classes of such cases: monopoly and similar market imperfections, and neighborhood effects.

Exchange is truly voluntary only when nearly equivalent alternatives exist. Monopoly implies the absence of alternatives and thereby inhibits effective freedom of exchange. In practice, monopoly frequently, if not generally, arises from government support or from collusive agreements among individuals. With respect to these, the problem is either to avoid governmental fostering of monopoly or to stimulate the effective enforcement of rules such as those embodied in our anti-trust laws. However, monopoly may also arise because it is technically efficient to have a single producer or enterprise. I venture to suggest that such cases are more limited than is supposed but they unquestionably do arise. A simple example is perhaps the provision of telephone services within a commmunity. I shall refer to such cases as "technical" monopoly.

When technical conditions make a monopoly the natural outcome of competitive market forces, there are only three alternatives that seem available: private monopoly, public monopoly, or public regulation. All three are bad so we must choose among evils. Henry Simons, observing public regulation of monopoly in the United States, found the results so distasteful that he concluded public monopoly would be a lesser evil. Walter Eucken, a noted German liberal, observing public monopoly in German railroads, found the results so distasteful that he concluded public regulation would be a lesser evil. Having learned from both, I reluctantly conclude that, if tolerable, private monopoly may be the least of the evils.

If society were static so that the conditions which give rise to a technical monopoly were sure to remain, I would have little confidence in this solution. In a rapidly changing society, however, the conditions making for technical monopoly frequently change and I suspect that both public regulation and public monopoly are likely to be less responsive to such changes in conditions, to be less readily capable of elimination, than private monopoly.

Railroads in the United States are an excellent example. A large degree of monopoly in railroads was perhaps inevitable on technical grounds in the nineteenth century. This was the justification for the Interstate Commerce Commission. But conditions have changed. The emergence of road and air transport has reduced the monopoly element in railroads to negligible proportions. Yet we have not eliminated the ICC. On the contrary, the ICC, which started out as an agency to protect the public from exploitation by the railroads, has become an agency to protect railroads from competition by trucks and other means of transport, and more recently even to protect existing truck companies from competition by new entrants. Similarly, in England, when the railroads were nationalized, trucking was at first brought into the state monopoly. If railroads had never been subjected to regulation in the United States, it is nearly certain that by now transportation, including railroads, would be a highly competitive industry with little or no remaining monopoly elements.

The choice between the evils of private monopoly, public monopoly, and public regulation cannot, however, be made once and for all, independently of the factual circumstances. If the technical monopoly is of a service or commodity that is regarded as essential and if its monopoly power is sizable, even the short-run effects of private unregulated monopoly may not be tolerable, and either public regulation or ownership may be a lesser evil.

Technical monopoly may on occasion justify a *de facto* public monopoly. It cannot by itself justify a public monopoly achieved by making it illegal for anyone else to compete. For example, there is no way to justify our present public monopoly of the post office. It may be argued that the carrying of mail is a technical monopoly and that a government monopoly is the least of evils. Along these lines, one could perhaps justify a government post office but not the present law, which makes it illegal for anybody else to carry mail. If the delivery of mail is a technical monopoly, no one will be able to succeed in competition with the government. If it is not, there is no reason why the government should be engaged in it. The only way to find out is to leave other people free to enter.

The historical reason why we have a post office monopoly is because the Pony Express did such a good job of carrying the mail across the continent that, when the government introduced transcontinental service, it couldn't compete effectively and lost money. The result was a law making it illegal for anybody else to carry the mail. That is why the Adams Express Company is an investment trust today instead of an operating company. I conjecture that if entry into the mail-carrying business were open to all, there would be a large number of firms entering it and this archaic industry would become revolutionized in short order.

A second general class of cases in which strictly voluntary exchange is impossible arises when actions of individuals have effects on other individuals for which it is not feasible to charge or recompense them. This is the problem of "neighborhood effects." An obvious example is the pollution of a stream. The man who pollutes a stream is in effect forcing others to exchange good water for bad. These others might be willing to make the exchange at a price. But it is not feasible for them, acting individually, to avoid the exchange or to enforce appropriate compensation.

A less obvious example is the provision of highways. In this case, it is technically possible to identify and hence charge individuals for their use of the roads and so to have private operation. However, for general access roads, involving many points of entry and exit, the costs of collection would be extremely high if a charge were to be made for the specific services received by each individual, because of the necessity of establishing toll booths or the equivalent at all entrances. The gasoline tax is a much cheaper method of charging individuals roughly in proportion to their use of the roads. This method, however, is one in which the particular payment cannot be identified closely with the particular use. Hence, it is hardly feasible to have private enterprise provide the service and collect the charge without establishing extensive private monopoly.

These considerations do not apply to long-distance turnpikes with high density of traffic and limited access. For these, the costs of collection are small and in many cases are now being paid, and there are often numerous alternatives, so that there is no serious monopoly problem. Hence, there is every reason why these should be privately owned and operated. If so owned and operated, the enterprise running the highway should receive the gasoline taxes paid on account of travel on it.

Parks are an interesting example because they illustrate the difference between cases that can and cases that cannot be justified by neighborhood effects, and because almost everyone at first sight regards the conduct of National Parks as obviously a valid function of government. In fact, however, neighborhood effects may justify a city park; they do not justify a national park, like Yellowstone National Park or the Grand Canyon. What is the fundamental difference between the two? For the city park, it is extremely difficult to identify the people who benefit from it and to charge them for the benefits which they receive. If there is a park in the middle of the city, the houses on all sides get the benefit of the open space, and people who walk through it or by it also benefit. To maintain toll collectors at the gates or to impose annual charges per window overlooking the park would be very expensive and difficult. The entrances to a national park like Yellowstone, on the other hand, are few; most of the people who come stay for a considerable period of time and it is perfectly feasible to set up toll gates and collect admission charges. This is indeed now done, though the charges do not cover the whole costs. If the public wants this kind of an activity enough to pay for it, private enterprises will have every incentive to provide such parks. And, of course, there are many private enterprises of this nature now in existence. I cannot myself conjure up any neighborhood effects or important monopoly effects that would justify governmental activity in this area.

Considerations like those I have treated under the heading of neighborhood effects have been used to rationalize almost every conceivable intervention. In many instances, however, this rationalization is special pleading rather than a legitimate application of the concept of neighborhood effects. Neighborhood effects cut both ways. They can be a reason for limiting the activities of government as well as for expanding them. Neighborhood effects impede voluntary exchange because it is difficult to identify the effects on third parties and to measure their magnitude; but this difficulty is present in governmental activity as well. It is hard to know when neighborhood effects are sufficiently large to justify particular costs in overcoming them and even harder to distribute the costs in an appropriate fashion. Consequently, when government engages in activities to overcome neighborhood effects, it will in part introduce an additional set of neighborhood effects by failing to charge or to compensate individuals properly. Whether the original or the new neighborhood effects are the more serious can only be judged by the facts of the individual case, and even then, only very approximately. Furthermore, the use of government to overcome neighborhood effects itself has an extremely important neighborhood effect which is unrelated to the particular occasion for government action. Every act of government intervention limits the area of individual freedom directly and threatens the preservation of freedom indirectly. . . .

Our principles offer no hard and fast line how far it is appropriate to use government to accomplish jointly what it is difficult or impossible for us to accomplish separately through strictly voluntary exchange. In any particular case of proposed intervention, we must make up a balance sheet, listing separately the advantages and disadvantages. Our principles tell us what items to put on the one side and what items on the other and they give us some basis for attaching importance to the different items. In particular, we shall always want to enter on the liability side of any proposed government intervention, its neighborhood effect in threatening freedom, and give this effect considerable weight. Just how much weight to give to it, as to other items, depends upon the circumstances. If, for example, existing government intervention is minor, we shall attach a smaller weight to the negative effects of additional government intervention. This is an important reason why many earlier liberals, like

Henry Simons, writing at a time when government was small by today's standards, were willing to have government undertake activities that today's liberals would not accept now that government has become so overgrown.

## ACTION THROUGH GOVERNMENT ON PATERNALISTIC GROUNDS

Freedom is a tenable objective only for responsible individuals. We do not believe in freedom for madmen or children. The necessity of drawing a line between responsible individuals and others is inescapable, yet it means that there is an essential ambiguity in our ultimate objective of freedom. Paternalism is inescapable for those whom we designate as not responsible.

The clearest case, perhaps, is that of madmen. We are willing neither to permit them freedom nor to shoot them. It would be nice if we could rely on voluntary activities of individuals to house and care for the madmen. But I think we cannot rule out the possibility that such charitable activities will be inadequate, if only because of the neighborhood effect involved in the fact that I benefit if another man contributes to the care of the insane. For this reason, we may be willing to arrange for their care through government.

Children offer a more difficult case. The ultimate operative unit in our society is the family, not the individual. Yet the acceptance of the family as the unit rests in considerable part on expediency rather than principle. We believe that parents are generally best able to protect their children and to provide for their development into responsible individuals for whom freedom is appropriate. But we do not believe in the freedom of parents to do what they will with other people. The children are responsible individuals in embryo, and a believer in freedom believes in protecting their ultimate rights.

To put this in a different and what may seem a more callous way, children are at one and the same time consumer goods and potentially responsible members of society. The freedom of individuals to use their economic resources as they want includes the freedom to use them to have children—to buy, as it were, the services of children as a particular form of consumption. But once this choice is exercised, the children have a value in and of themselves and have a freedom of their own that is not simply an extension of the freedom of the parents.

The paternalistic ground for governmental activity is in many ways the most troublesome to a liberal; for it involves the acceptance of a principle—that some shall decide for others—which he finds objectionable in most applications and which he rightly regards as a hallmark of his chief intellectual opponents, the proponents of collectivism in one or another of its guises, whether it be communism, socialism, or a welfare state. Yet there is no use pretending that problems are simpler than in fact they are. There is no avoiding the need for some measure of paternalism. As Dicey wrote in 1914 about an act for the protection of mental defectives, "The Mental Deficiency Act is the first step along a path on which no sane man can decline to enter, but which, if too far pursued, will bring statesmen across difficulties hard to meet without considerable interference with individual liberty."[1] There is no formula that can tell us where to stop. We must rely on our fallible judgment and, having reached a judgment, on our ability to persuade our fellow men that it is a correct judgment, or their ability to persuade us to modify our views. We must put our faith, here as elsewhere, in a consensus reached by imperfect and biased men through free discussion and trial and error.

## CONCLUSION

A government which maintained law and order, defined property rights, served as a means whereby we could modify property rights and other rules of the economic game, adjudicated disputes about the interpretation of the rules, enforced contracts, promoted competition, provided a monetary framework, engaged in activities to counter technical monopolies and to overcome neighborhood effects widely regarded as sufficiently important to justify government intervention, and which supplemented private charity and the private family in protecting the irresponsible, whether madman or child—such a government would clearly have important functions to perform. The consistent liberal is not an anarchist.

Yet it is also true that such a government would have clearly limited functions and would refrain from a host of activities that are now undertaken by federal and state governments in the United States, and their counterparts in other Western countries. . . . It may help to give a sense of proportion about the role that a liberal would assign government simply to list, in closing this chapter, some activities currently undertaken by government in the U.S., that cannot, so far as I can see, validly be justified in terms of the principles outlined above:

1. Parity price support programs for agriculture.
2. Tariffs on imports or restrictions on exports, such as current oil import quotas, sugar quotas, etc.

3. Governmental control of output, such as through the farm program, or through prorationing of oil as is done by the Texas Railroad Commission.

4. Rent control, such as is still practiced in New York, or more general price and wage controls such as were imposed during and just after World War II.

5. Legal minimum wage rates, or legal maximum prices, such as the legal maximum of zero on the rate of interest that can be paid on demand deposits by commercial banks, or the legally fixed maximum rates that can be paid on savings and time deposits.

6. Detailed regulation of industries, such as the regulation of transportation by the Interstate Commerce Commission. This had some justification on technical monopoly grounds when initially introduced for railroads; it has none now for any means of transport. Another example is detailed regulation of banking.

7. A similar example, but one which deserves special mention because of its implicit censorship and violation of free speech, is the control of radio and television by the Federal Communication Commission.

8. Present social security programs, especially the old-age and retirement programs compelling people in effect (a) to spend a specified fraction of their income on the purchase of retirement annuity, (b) to buy the annuity from a publicly operated enterprise.

9. Licensure provisions in various cities and states which restrict particular enterprises or occupations or professions to people who have a license, where the license is more than a receipt for a tax which anyone who wishes to enter the activity may pay.

10. So-called "public-housing" and the host of other subsidy programs, directed at fostering residential construction such as F.H.A. and V.A. guarantee of mortgage, and the like.

11. Conscription to man the military services in peacetime. The appropriate free market arrangement is volunteer military forces; which is to say, hiring men to serve. There is no justification for not paying whatever price is necessary to attract the required number of men. Present arrangements are inequitable and arbitrary, seriously interfere with the freedom of young men to shape their lives, and probably are even more costly than the market alternative. (Universal military training to provide a reserve for war time is a different problem and may be justified on liberal grounds.)

12. National parks, as noted above.

13. The legal prohibition on the carrying of mail for profit.

14. Publicly owned and operated toll roads, as noted above.

This list is far from comprehensive.

**NOTE**

1. A. V. Dicey, *Lectures on the Relation between Law and Public Opinion in England during the Nineteenth Century* (2d ed.; London: Macmillan & Co., 1914), p. li.

# Chapter Three

# DIRECTIONS OF SOCIAL WELFARE

If social welfare is an emerging institution, it is appropriate to inquire where it is headed. Because institutional developments can be analyzed at many levels, this question does not yield to a singular definitive response. There are many answers, depending on the specific aspects of social welfare under consideration at a given time. We have selected readings for this chapter that discuss some of the trends in social welfare that are taking shape in the 1980s. These developments are concerned with: (1) the size and growth of social welfare programs, (2) the relationship between the public and the voluntary sectors of social welfare, (3) the changing nature of eligibility for social welfare benefits, (4) the planning of social service-delivery systems, (5) the balance between personal services and social reform, (6) the design of income maintenance systems, and (7) the future welfare of female-headed households and the elderly.

Social welfare expenditure data for the United States are readily available in reports of the Department of Health, Education, and Welfare. These reports provide a concise overview of the size and growth of social welfare as indicated by the amounts of money spent according to program categories by various levels of government and the private sector. Several trends may be identified by these data which reveal, for example, that between 1960 and 1974 social welfare expenditures increased from 38 to 55.8 percent of all government expenditures. During this period the federal proportion of these expenditures increased from 47.7 to 57.6 percent. Private expenditures for social welfare also increased slightly more than threefold between 1960 and 1974. However, in 1974 government expenditures accounted for 71 percent of the total spent for social welfare, as compared to 29 percent from the private sector.[1] The most recent estimates indicate that between 1974 and 1977 social welfare expenditures as a percent of all government expenditures continued to increase, going from 56 to 60 percent. During this period the federal proportion of these expenditures also increased from 57 to 60.5 percent.[2]

The relationships between public-government and private-voluntary spending for social welfare are more intricate and of greater significance than might be inferred from the simple proportions noted above. Government spending has not just increased over the years, as Wickenden points out, it has been used increasingly in purchase-of-service arrangements with voluntary agencies.[3] And these arrangements have modified one of the traditional characteristics of the voluntary sector—its financial independence of government. A new "partnership" between government and voluntary agencies has developed along with a series of choices concerning funding arrangements available in this relationship.

Whether under public auspices, private auspices, or some mixture thereof, the tremendous increase in social welfare services has been accompanied by growing demands that those who produce services be held accountable for their performance. But *to whom* should they be accountable? The idea of accountability pertains to various relationships. The federal government provides grants-in-aid to local programs which are then held accountable to the federal bureaucracy. But local taxpayers and consumers believe that social welfare programs should be accountable to them. Alice Rivlin analyzes three service-delivery models that are currently advocated as means to enhance accountability: decentralization, community control, and the voucher system. Rivlin points out that efforts to increase accountability of social services, whether to higher levels of government, taxpayers, consumers, community groups, or whomever, cannot be fully realized by the manipulation of service-delivery arrangements. For social services to be held accountable for their performance, there must be some way to measure and evaluate their accomplishments.[4]

The increasing concern for accountability reflects the fact that social welfare benefits have become available to a wide range of groups in the population over the past 40 years. As claims on welfare benefits are extended, questions of who should be eligible and under what conditions have become fundamental issues in the develop-

ment of modern social welfare systems. These issues often boil down
to the choice of universal versus selective social welfare allocations.
Hoshino traces the movement in Britain toward the allocation of
social services on the basis of universality whereby benefits are made
available to an entire population as a social right, without recourse
to individual tests of need. Similar developments in the United States
are noted. Observing this trend toward universality, Hoshino analyzes the persistence of social services allocated on the basis of selectivity, usually in the form of an individual means test. According to
his analysis selective schemes will continue to be a required feature
of social welfare, but they can and should be administered in a more
dignified manner than is currently the case. There may be a societal
need for means-tested programs, but they need not be mean spir-
ited.[5]

The various trends noted above—increasing scope of social welfare, intermingling of public and private financing, the press for local
accountability, and the drift towards universal eligibility—are drawn
out and examined in the first selection in this chapter, "The Transformation of Social Services" (Reading 7), by Neil Gilbert. This reading
suggests that the collective impact of these changes has brought
social services to the threshold of a new era which opens various
opportunities for the future.

It has been observed by many that during the late 1960s and early
1970s rehabilitation-related activities of traditional individually-ori-
ented social services suffered a considerable decline in public favor
and professional emphasis. And, as these intensive personal helping
services waned, increasing emphasis was placed on reform-related
activities of social action programs. While this shift in the focus and
orientation of social welfare resources has taken place, individual
problems and personal crises have continued to generate great needs
for intensive social services. Alfred Kahn, who has observed this
trend in New York City,[6] has pointed out that while social action and
reform activities are important, they should not submerge the need
for or the contribution of personal social services. He calls for a
revitalization of the personal services and the introduction of greater
balance and coordination in social welfare activities.

We might note that as this book goes to press in 1980, the movement away from personal services and toward social action and reform activities identified by Kahn appears to have run its course. In
the 1960s social welfare and social work were deeply involved in
movements for change, both in professional education and in agency
practice. Gradually, as some new ideas have been implemented,
some have proven to be programmatically and professionally impractical, and others have been found to be politically unfeasible.

The energies of students, teachers, and practitioners appear to be turning toward a renewed interest in refinement of programs and practice.

Social change, of course, is still on the social work agenda. As the turmoil of the late 1960s and early 1970s has abated, the change-oriented approaches have become less rhetorical and more analytical as reflected in Reading 8, "Issues in Welfare Reform," by Martha Ozawa. In this reading Ozawa describes basic approaches to income maintenance and identifies critical policy issues with which any efforts for reform in this area must come to grips. She provides a useful framework for evaluating welfare reform proposals in terms of their immediate impact on specific issues such as equity, efficiency, and stigma, as well as their broader economic and political implications.

In the final selection in this Chapter, "Demographics, Politics, and the Future of the Welfare State" (Reading 9), Mayer Zald addresses the shape of things to come in social welfare. By examining economic, political, and demographic trends Zald constructs a scenario of future demands and resources for social welfare. Among the patterns he discerns are: an increasing demand for services for the elderly and female-headed households; a decrease in new major program initiatives; and a retrenchment of the movement toward universal access to social services (a movement which Gilbert observed, in Reading 7, as gaining momentum between the early 1960s and the late 1970s). Overall, Zald suggests that plans for expansion and further development of the welfare state in the 1980s will not rank high on the list of national priorities. As this book goes to press these sobering predictions look close to the mark for at least the immediate future.

## NOTES

1. Alfred M. Skolnik and Sophie R. Dales, "Social Welfare Expenditures, Fiscal Year 1974," *Social Security Bulletin*, 38 (January 1975): 3–18.

2. Alma McMillan, "Social Welfare Expenditures Under Public Programs, Fiscal Year 1977," *Social Security Bulletin*, 42 (June 1979): 3–13.

3. Elizabeth Wickenden, "Purchase of Care and Services: Effect on Voluntary Agencies," *Issue of the Day: Purchase of Care and Services in the Health and Welfare Field*, ed. Iris Winogrand (University of Wisconsin-Milwaukee, School of Social Welfare, July 1970).

4. Alice Rivlin, *Systematic Thinking for Social Action* (Washington, D.C.: The Brookings Institution, 1971), 120–44.

5. George Hoshino, "Britain's Debate on Universal or Selective Social Services: Lessons for America," *Social Service Review*, 43 (September 1969): 245–58.

6. Alfred J. Kahn, "Do Social Services Have A Future in New York?" *City Almanac*, 5 (February 1971): 1–12.

# 7 The Transformation of Social Services

NEIL GILBERT

From the landmark Public Welfare Amendments of 1962 (P.L. 88-543) to the Social Services Amendments of 1974 (P.L. 93-647), the major programs for social services in the United States have traveled quite a distance. It has been a long and arduous journey, alternating between periods of optimism and of misgiving. That journey is by no means complete; in a sense it never will be, as social services continuously evolve in response to societal needs. During the past fifteen years, however, the social services have experienced a number of significant changes, the results of which are just beginning to coalesce. The emerging shapes are different enough from those of the past to suggest that we are entering a new era in the evolution of social services. The purpose of this paper is to analyze the basic changes that mark this development, to indicate what these changes seem to add up to, and to suggest some of their overall implications for the future of social services and social work.

The focus here is upon social service provisions originally established under Titles I (Old Age Assistance), IV-A (Aid to Families with Dependent Children [AFDC]), X (Aid to the Blind), and XIV (Aid to Permanently and Totally Disabled) of the Social Security Act and recently incorporated into Title XX. There are of course other sources from which social services emanate, including the Economic Opportunity Act of 1964 (P.L. 88-452), the Demonstration Cities and Metropolitan Development Act of 1966 (P.L. 89-754), and Title IV-B of the Social Security Act. The developments of social services in these program areas parallel most of the trends that will be identified in the analysis of Title XX services. The reason that Title XX has been selected as the focal point of analysis is that it provides the largest single source of social service funds. In the most concrete sense it represents the cornerstone of the emerging structure of social services in the United States.[1]

Any discussion of developments in the social services over the last fifteen years must take cognizance of the tremendous increase in federal spending in this area. Between 1963 and 1971 federal grants to states for social services grew more than threefold, from approximately $194 million to $740 million. That was a moderate rate of growth compared with the precipitous rise from $740 million to $1.7 billion that occurred between 1971 and 1972. While $1.7 billion was

Reprinted from the *Social Service Review*, 51 (December 1977): 624–41, by permission of the University of Chicago Press and of the author.

no trifling sum, when state estimates for 1973 indicated a potential increase to $4.7 billion, Congress was prompted to enact a $2.5 billion ceiling on federal expenditures for social services, which is the current limit for federal spending under Title XX.[2]

This unprecedented rise in federal social service grants had less to do with the overall expansion of services offered, though some expansion did take place, than with the transfer of local social service costs from states to the federal government. The elasticity of the 1967 social service legislation, among other reasons, had allowed federal social service funds to be used for the fiscal relief of the states. Martha Derthick's study provides a lucid analysis of how this all came about.[3]

While it is important to appreciate the explosive growth of federal funding as a force in the general development of social services, the main focus of this paper is upon substantive changes in the social services that have accompanied the expanded base of federal support. In this analysis the rise in federal expenditures can be seen perhaps as a quantitative backdrop to the qualitative transformation of social services.

There have been five basic dimensions to changes that signal the transformation in the social services from the time they were first explicitly designated for solid financial support in the 1962 Social Security amendments to the present. These dimensions of change involve social services: (a) clientele, (b) provisions, (c) delivery, (d) finance, and (e) planning.[4] The following discussion will elaborate on the characteristics of change in these service dimensions, as outlined in Table 7–1.

TABLE 7–1
Characteristics of Change in Social Services, 1962–1977

| Dimension of Service | Characteristics of Change |
| --- | --- |
| Clientele | Selective to universal |
| Provisions | Intangible/limited scope to concrete/diversified |
| Delivery | Public to public/private |
| Finance | Grantsmanship to population parity |
| Planning | Centralized to decentralized |

## DRIFT TOWARD UNIVERSALISM

Since 1962 there has been a consistent loosening of social service eligibility standards and a concomitant broadening in the base of social service clientele. Under the 1962 Public Welfare Amendments, eligibility for social services was limited to people receiving public assistance as well as former recipients and others who, in light of their precarious life circumstances, were potential candidates for public assistance. The Bureau of Family Services administratively defined potential recipients as those who might reasonably be expected to need financial aid within one year of their request for services. While these eligibility standards offered the possibility of extending service delivery beyond the immediate public assistance population, in practice this possibility was not realized. At that early stage both program funds and trained social service workers were in relatively short supply. As political support for the 1962 amendments was predicated on the idea that intensive social service could reduce the size of public assistance rolls, the recipient population clearly held first priority on service allocations. Despite those immediate limitations, the possibility of extending service eligibility was established in principle.

The realization of this principle followed shortly, as the 1962 eligibility criteria were extended in two directions by the Social Security Amendments of 1967 (P.L. 90-248). Under these amendments persons become eligible for social services if it had been decided that they might be welfare recipients within the next five years rather than the one year previously stipulated. Even more significant was the introduction of the concept of group eligibility, whereby residents of low-income neighborhoods and other groups such as those in institutional settings became eligible for service.

By 1972 persons not receiving welfare were well represented among the social service clientele and were growing in number. As previously noted, one reason for this development was that the 1967 amendments had provided a loophole through which states began to squeeze many locally funded services into federally funded programs that reimbursed 75 percent of costs to the states. Congressional efforts to stem the tide of universal access to services were reflected in the Revenue Sharing Act of 1972 (P.L. 95-512), which placed the $2.5 billion cap on social service expenditures. The legislation also included a "90/10 restriction," requiring that 90 percent of service expenditures go directly to clients on public assistance, as well as other measures that seemed to reflect growing resistance to the drift toward universalism. While the $2.5 billion ceiling has held, implementation of the 90/10 rule was first postponed and then ignored.[5] Instead, with a suddenness that no one predicted, the drift toward universalism turned into a tide race as the Social Service Amendments of 1974 ushered in a new set of eligibility criteria that extended social service entitlement to the middle class.[6]

Under Title XX there are three basic categories of eligibility for services: *(a)* income maintenance; *(b)* income eligible; and *(c)* universal. People in the income-maintenance category are those currently receiving public assistance, SSI, or medicaid. They are poor according to the means-test standards that income-maintenance applicants must satisfy to receive financial aid. The Title XX regulations require that at least 50 percent of federal funds for service in each state be targeted for people in this category.[7] This allows considerably more latitide for service delivery to the nonpoor than the 90/10 rule endorsed in the 1972 Revenue Sharing Act. Income-eligible recipients include people who earn up to 115 percent of their state's median income, which ranges between $16,000 and $19,000 in most states. The states may offer services free of charge to those whose income does not exceed 80 percent of the state median, which is between $11,000 and $13,000 in most states. For people earning in the range of 80-115 percent of the state's median income, Title XX services may be offered on a subsidized basis for reasonable income-related fees. The universal category refers to services that are available free of charge to all without regard to income.

A catalog of the Title XX Comprehensive Annual Service Plans (which each state is required to submit) indicates that in eight states more than two-thirds of the projected service population would qualify for service outside the income-maintenance category. In eighteen states over 50 percent of the projected service recipients would be eligible, without regard to the income-maintenance means test.[8] We must recognize, however, that these service projections do not represent the actual quantity or quality of services that would be rendered to different groups. For example, the service plan for Arizona indicates that 52 percent of all individuals to be served by the Title XX programs would be eligible under universal standards, but the costs of services to that group would equal only 12 percent of the total for all Title XX programs. This reflects the fact that large numbers of non-poor clients are eligible for inexpensive short-term information and referral services (see Table 7–2).

Data available on the current population actually served by Title XX funds indicate that there were approximately 2.4 million service recipients from October to December 1975.[9] More than 500,000 of these were in the new category of income eligible. (Despite the fact that eligibility criteria for this group often amount to earnings of $16,000–$19,000, they are curiously referred to as the "working poor" in the federal report on Title XX implementation.) More than 250,000 recipients were in the universal category. Thus from the outset more than 30 percent of the Title XX service recipients were not required to qualify for services under the selective means-tested eligibility criteria for SSI, AFDC, or medicaid.

TABLE 7–2

Percentage of Title XX Expenditures and Individuals Served by Categories of Eligibility in Selected States

| | Individuals Service | | | Expenditures | | |
|---|---|---|---|---|---|---|
| | Income Main-tenance* | Income Eligible† | Uni-versal‡ | Income Main-tenance* | Income Eligible† | Uni-versal‡ |
| Arizona | 35.6 | 12.5 | 51.9 | 48.5 | 39.7 | 11.8 |
| California | 32.5 | 10.0 | 57.5 | 78.2 | 17.6 | 4.2 |
| Delaware | 32.7 | 1.9 | 65.4 | 78.5 | 16.8 | 4.7 |
| Illinois | 75.0 | 13.0 | 12.0 | 70.0 | 18.6 | 11.4 |
| Indiana | 42.4 | 18.7 | 38.9 | 48.0 | 33.8 | 18.2 |
| Mississippi | 89.7 | 10.3 | – | 85.2 | 14.8 | – |
| New York | 37.8 | 19.8 | 42.4 | 47.0 | 42.3 | 10.7 |
| Pennsylvania | 30.8 | 23.2 | 46.0 | 50.8 | 39.4 | 9.8 |
| Texas | 25.6 | 41.3 | 33.1 | 43.3 | 22.0 | 34.7 |

Source: Based on data from Candace Mueller and Eileen Wolf, "Title XX–Final CASP Plans, Services Catalogue," mimeographed (Washington, D.C.: Department of Health, Education, and Welfare, January 30, 1976).

*This category includes AFDC, SSI, Essential Persons, and Medicaid recipients.

†This category includes those eligible for service based on varying percentages (usually between 80 and 115) of each state's median income.

‡This category includes those eligible for services without regard to income.

In assessing these eligibility developments, we need to bear in mind that during the first year of Title XX the planning process and public response were rather hurried. Awareness of the new possibilities for middle-class access to social services was faint at best. As public perceptions of these possibilities sharpen, pressure for middle-class access is likely to mount. The initial signs already point in this direction. In Missouri, for example, public response to the Title XX plan included recommendations to expand eligibility for services from those at the 80 percent of the median income level ($10,655), which is the maximum eligibility level set at the state's option, to 115 percent of the median income ($15,317), which is the maximum level permitted under federal guidelines.[10] And in California the planned-parenthood agencies are launching a campaign to have family-planning services for teenagers classified as a universal service under Title XX.

While it would be exaggeration to claim that overnight the Title XX amendments have universalized access to social services, the trend in this direction seems rather pronounced, particularly when we compare the current clientele with the 1962 population of service recipients, almost all of whom qualified for public assistance. This trend toward universal eligibility has been accompanied by changes in the nature of social service provisions.

## DIVERSIFICATION OF SOCIAL PROVISIONS

The nature of social provisions has undergone considerable change in scope and content since the 1962 "service" amendments. At that time social services were aimed primarily at preventing and reducing poverty. This was to be accomplished through intensive social casework services that presumably would rehabilitate the poor, changing their behavior in ways that would help them to become economically independent. Social services also included other basic forms of provision such as homemakers and foster-home care. The essential feature of the 1962 amendments, however, was the provision of social casework services. While this was not specified in the law, Derthick points out that "welfare professionals in the Bureau of Family Services knew more or less what they meant by 'services.' Fundamentally and at a minimum, it meant casework by a trained social worker."[11]

There is an intangible quality about casework service that has made it difficult to specify the exact nature of the provision. This vagueness has led to the cynical observation that such service "is anything done for, with, or about the client by the social worker. If a social worker discusses a child's progress in school with an AFDC mother, a check is made under 'services related to education. . . .' When the discussion turns to the absent father and possible reconciliation a check is made under 'maintaining family and improving family functioning.' "[12] In a similar vein, Handler and Hollingsworth have characterized the service in a public assistance agency as "little more than a relatively infrequent, pleasant chat."[13] At its best, social casework is certainly a more skillful and nurturing enterprise than these comments depict. But large caseloads, demands of eligibility certification (while trying to establish a casework relationship), diversity of clientele (many of whom did not need or want casework services but had to accept them), qualifications of staff (many of whom were not professionally trained), and omnipresent bureaucratic regulations of public assistance administration were hardly conducive to the performance of effective social casework. In any event, whatever its powers and benefits, casework was not a cure for poverty. The addition of almost 1 million recipients to the public assistance rolls between 1962 and 1966 dramatically testified to this point.

Its failure to reduce economic dependency combined with its intangible quality made social casework services a prime target of congressional disillusionment with public assistance. This was reflected in the administration of the 1967 amendments, under which casework services were no longer as prominent as they had been in 1962. The 1967 amendments opened the way for a broader conception of social services that might qualify for federal support than those previously funded. Under the 1962 amendments, federal grants for social service went mainly to pay the salaries of caseworkers.[14] In contrast, the regulations to implement the 1967 amendments contained certain clauses that, as Rein points out, "created such a comprehensive array of specific services that literally almost any service was federally reimbursable."[15] At the same time, greater emphasis came to be placed on the delivery of services that were more tangible than those of social casework. Reporting on this trend, Derthick observes,

> In official language, a distinction soon began to develop between 'soft' and 'hard' services. Advice and counselling from a caseworker were 'soft' in this managerial parlance and presumably less valuable than day-care centers or drug treatment centers, or work training, which were 'hard' and which were much more widely available in 1969 than in 1962 because of the intervening growth of public programs for social purposes. The changed conception and changed social context helped lay the basis for granting funds for a much wider range of activity than the daily routines of caseworkers.[16]

With the passage of the social services amendments, the movement toward diversification of federally financed social services reached new heights. Under Title XX each state is free to support whatever social services are deemed appropriate for its communities. The only requirement is that these services be directed to one of five goals, which are so broadly stated as to encompass almost anything the imagination of social service planners can devise. In the first year of implementation, plans for the fifty states and the District of Columbia specified a total of 1,313 services.[17] Duffy observes the expression of diversity in these services: "There are 51 different sets of services proposed for the developmentally disabled. Even Information and Referral, considered so basic and universal, is not proposed in all State plans. Local needs and local desires have been expressed in a way not possible before. 'I did it my way' is the real theme."[18]

Bringing some order to all this diversity, the Social and Rehabilitation Service of the Department of Health, Education, and Welfare grouped the services with common characteristics into forty-one general categories for purposes of tabulation and analysis.[19] While these categories are not without ambiguity concerning the distinction between most tangible and least tangible services, the data available suggest that the emphasis on delivery of "hard" services which developed in the late 1960s continues to predominate. For example, in the first quarter of Title XX's implementation, among all the services provided to recipients only 9.5 percent fell into the general

category of "counseling" services. At the same time, the clearly more
tangible categories such as day care accounted for 11 percent,
homemaker/chore for 6.5 percent, health-related services for 12
percent, housing improvement for 2 percent, and transportation for
3.5 percent of all services provided to recipients. Care must be taken
in interpreting these figures, because various "hard" categories of
service such as residential care and treatment are the type that often
include a counseling element.

Along with the increasing emphasis on tangible services and the
diversification of service content, a profound reorientation of purpose of the social services is taking place.[20] The services authorized
by the 1962 service amendments that aimed almost exclusively at the
reduction of economic dependency have been replaced by a broad-
scope service network concerned to a large extent with maintenance
and care-oriented services.[21] These services are directed more at
enhancing human development and the general quality of life for
those in need than reducing economic dependency. The first major
step in this direction came in the 1967 reorganization of the Department of Health, Education, and Welfare. With the creation of the
Assistance Payments Administration under the Social and Rehabilitation Services, income-maintenance functions were administratively
divorced from social services in the public assistance program.[22]
Most recently, in 1977, another reorganization of the Department of
Health, Education, and Welfare has refined this administrative separation at the federal level by placing all income-maintenance programs under the Social Security Administration and joining the social
service and human development programs under the Office of Human Development. This trend is reflected in Title XX's emphasis on
services not associated with notions of personal deficiency or lack of
character that in the past marked those dependent on public aid.
Transportation and "meals on wheels" for the elderly, homemaker
services for the disabled, day care for children of all backgrounds,
and many other social services have rapidly gained widespread acceptance.

## INTERMINGLING OF PUBLIC AND PRIVATE AUSPICES

The federal government's promotion of social services through
financial support of private/voluntary agencies can be traced back
well into the nineteenth century. In 1819 the Hartford Asylum for
the Deaf and Dumb, organized by Rev. Thomas Gallaudet, was
awarded a federal land grant which eventually realized $300,000 to
help defray its operating expenses. Gallaudet's institution was among
the first voluntary agencies to receive federal aid for the delivery of

local social series.[23] These early government forays into the private sector of social services did not, however, assume the character of formal ongoing arrangements until recent times. Under the 1962 "service amendments" state public assistance agencies were enjoined from using federal funds to purchase services directly from voluntary agencies. It was possible, however, to purchase these services indirectly, with grants to other public agencies which then might contract for services from the private sector.

Opportunities for purchase of services from private sources were broadened significantly in the 1967 social security amendments and regulations, which authorized purchase arrangements for a wide array of activities. According to Wickenden, this legislative development "represented a major landmark in the evolution of public policy with respect to social services."[24] Nevertheless, one small hitch remained in financing the local matching share for purchase of service arrangements. Although the 1967 amendments allowed state agencies to purchase services directly from private agencies, private-agency donations could not be used as the states' 25 percent matching share of federal social service grants if those contributions reverted to the donor's facility. But there were ways to circumvent this restriction. In practice, for example, it was not uncommon for a donation to be made by a United Fund Organization with the request that their contribution be used to support a particular type of activity in a specified community, one performed only by an agency affiliated with the United Fund Organization.[25] In this fashion private donations could be covertly earmarked as the local share for a designated agency.

Title XX introduced a significant change in policy in regard to financing the states' matching share for social service grants. As with the 1967 amendments, under Title XX private-agency donations that are officially transferred to state agencies may be used as the states' 25 percent matching share of social service grants. The change is that these donations now qualify for the local matching share even when they are used to purchase services for the donating agency; the only restriction on this arrangement for the return of "contributed" funds through purchase of service contracts is that the donor agency must be a nonprofit organization.

Over the last fifteen years, the developments outlined above have produced an enormous expansion in the systematic use of public funds to purchase services delivered by voluntary agencies. The precise magnitude of public purchase of service is difficult to estimate, because the systematic collection of information has not kept pace with the rapid growth of these arrangements. Available data on purchase of services are fragmented. Nevertheless, information from various studies can provide a rough picture of the extent to which public and private auspices have intermingled in the delivery of social services. For example, a study of the trend in government payments to Jewish-sponsored agencies reveals a twentyfold increase in these payments, from $27 million to $561 million, over the period 1962–73. During that time government payments as a proportion of the total income received by Jewish-sponsored agencies rose from 11 to 51 percent.[26] These figures reflect purchase of services by a variety of federal programs. Focusing only on the purchase of services under Title IV-A and the aid-for-adults categories of the Social Security Act, as amended in 1967, a survey indicates that in 1969–70 throughout the State of California approximately $1.7 million was used to purchase services by contracts with private agencies.[27] While comparable statewide data for a later period are not available, the rapid growth in the purchase of services is evident in figures from a recent study limited to 183 private agencies in the vicinity of San Francisco. Data from this study show that by 1974–75 member agencies in the United Way of the Bay Area received more than twice the amount of purchase of service funds through Title IV-A and the categories for adults than had been contracted from these sources to private agencies throughout the entire state in 1969–70.[28]

Much has been written about the potential costs and benefits of this widespread purchase of service.[29] A major concern from the perspective of voluntary agencies is the degree of autonomy they might have to forfeit in gaining access to public funds. The questions they ask are, How much constraint on private-agency activities will accompany the receipt of government funds, and will private-agency activities emerge ultimately as merely the instrument of government policy?[30] The answers are unclear, as few empirical studies of service purchases from voluntary agencies have been concerned with this issue. The limited evidence that is available, however, suggests that private agencies receiving government funds continue to maintain their identity and considerable independence of purpose and style.[31]

## FROM GRANTSMANSHIP TO POPULATION PARITY

The approach to federal financing of social services has undergone a basic reform since 1962. The essence of this reform is that the main factor determining federal social service allocations has changed from state grantsmanship to population parity. Under the 1962 amendments federal financing was open-ended, with the states reimbursed for 75 percent of social service costs. The 1967 amendments expanded the range of services and clientele that might qualify for federal funds. With this expansion the definitions of "social services" and client-eligibility standards were loosely drawn. Whether a particular service for certain clients qualified for federal reimbursement was in large part a matter of local interpretation rather than a clearly defined statutory formula. The most enterprising states made the boldest interpretations and received the largest proportional shares of federal grants for social services. This enterprising quality can be called "grantsmanship." In the states' scuffle for federal funds, grantsmanship was the name of the game, and the biggest winners were New York, Illinois, and California. Together these three states received 58 percent of federal grants for social services in 1972.[32]

The explosive increase in federal social service expenditures engendered by the 1967 amendments came to a halt in 1972, when Congress placed the $2.5 billion ceiling on social service grants. As noted earlier, this sum represents the current limit on federal allocations under Title XX. Together with this limitation on spending has come a change in allocative procedures which ties federal social service allotments to a formula strictly based on state population. This reform means that the size of state grants will no longer be determined by creative interpretation of federal guidelines, enterprising administrative reorganizations, proposal-writing skills, and the general "wheeling-dealing" of the consummate grantsman.

The reform also results in some degree of redistribution of social service grants among the states. Several states that did not excel in grantsmanship are now eligible for substantial increases in federal social service allotments if they supply the 25 percent local matching share. For example, the Title XX allotments for fiscal year 1976 provide Arizona with a ninefold increase and Mississippi with a fifteen-fold increase over the amount of social service funds they received in 1972. The redistributive impact of this reform is illustrated in Table 7–3.

The allocation of Title XX funds on a straight population basis spreads social service grants in a way that should yield a rough form of interstate equalization. However, this mode of finance is not particularly sensitive to the greater needs of poor areas. In this respect the change in the federal approach to financing social services parallels the trend toward universal eligibility standards.

## THE DEVOLUTION OF PLANNING AUTHORITY

It is probably accurate to describe state efforts to develop social service programs prior to Title XX as exercises in "qualifying" rather than in planning. The open-ended matching-grant method of financing was not a device to encourage deliberation in the design and selection of social welfare programs. On the contrary, the incentive

TABLE 7–3

Allocations of Social Service Funds Pre- and Post-Title XX in Selected States

|  | Federal Grants for Services, 1972 (in Millions) | Title XX Allotments, 1976 (in Millions)* | % Change 1972–76 | Difference in Percentage of total 1972–76 |
|---|---|---|---|---|
| Arizona. . . . . . . . | 2.75 | 24.50 | +790 | +.8 |
| California . . . . . . | 198.63 | 245.50 | +23 | −2.0 |
| Delaware. . . . . . . | 12.46 | 6.75 | −85 | −.4 |
| Illinois . . . . . . . . | 188.38 | 133.75 | −41 | −5.9 |
| Indiana . . . . . . . . | 6.53 | 63.25 | +869 | +2.1 |
| Mississippi . . . . . . | 1.83 | 27.25 | +1,389 | +1.0 |
| New York . . . . . . | 588.93 | 217.50 | −171 | −26.5 |
| Pennsylvania . . . . | 51.29 | 141.75 | +176 | +2.6 |
| Texas . . . . . . . . | 53.50 | 140.50 | +163 | +2.4 |

Sources: Martha Derthick, *Uncontrollable Spending for Social Services Grants* (Washington, D.C.: Brookings Institution, 1975), pp. 100–101; and Social and Rehabilitation Service, Department of Health, Education, and Welfare, *A Citizen's Handbook: Social Services 1975* (Washington, D.C.: Department of Health, Education, and Welfare, 1975), pp. 22–23.
*These figures are state entitlements, not actual expenditures.

under this grant arrangement was to qualify for as much as possible. It was unnecessary to gather information and to justify social service decisions on the basis of needs assessments, effectiveness measures, or other information. As Mogulof puts it, "there were no discernible gains for a state in seeking to strengthen its social service intelligence and little to lose if they didn't. The receipt of federal funds did not seem dependent upon this intelligence; the kind of 'planning' enforced by the federal government seemed to require a minimal amount of analysis."[33] The planning that took place typically involved state welfare officials, sometimes aided by outside consultants, interpreting the rather loosely formulated federal social service guidelines to see how various state services might qualify for federal support. There was also discussion and negotiation with federal officials about issues of compliance. On these issues decision-making was centralized at the federal level. The public at large had little input into this process and was generally uninformed about its outcome. As to the quality of planning decisions generated under these arrangements, Mogulof's study of four states in 1973 concludes that "any proposals for change in social service decision making begin with the general acknowledgement that 'there is nowhere to go but up.' "[34] As we shall see, the planning provisions under Title XX offer the potential for movement in a similar direction.

There are several unique features that distinguish social service planning under Title XX from previous efforts. Foremost is the devolution of decision-making authority from the federal to the state level. This decentralization of authority reflects the "New Federalism" philosophy that gained prominence under the Nixon administration. The idea, simply put, is "to set states and localities free—free to set new priorities, free to meet unmet needs, free to make their own mistakes, yes, but also free to score splendid successes which otherwise would never be realized."[35]

Under the New Federalism the states were "set free" from federal guidelines and restrictions through the provision of bloc grants that afford state governments wide discretion in establishing programs tailored to local needs. Strictly speaking, the Title XX funds are not bloc grants (such as states receive under the Comprehensive Employment and Training Act of 1973 and the Housing and Community Development Act of 1974) but, rather, reimbursements to states for money spent for services. Nevertheless, Title XX funds are vested with flexibility similar to that of bloc grants. States are required to develop and submit Comprehensive Annual Service Program (CASP) plans for federal review. This review is mainly to insure that the state planning process has been conducted in accordance with legislative intent rather than to exercise authority over the design of services to be provided and methods of provision. Indeed, the legislation clearly limits federal authority with regard to decisions about program content. The federal agency administering Title XX is not allowed to deny payment "to any state with respect to any expenditure on the ground that it is not an expenditure for the provision of a service or is not an expenditure for the provision of a service directed at [the five Title XX goals]."[36]

Another basic feature of Title XX planning is the provision for public participation, which accompanies the devolution of decision-making authority to the state level. Federal planning regulations include a series of procedures to publicize proposed Title XX CASP plans and to facilitate public review and comment. Final CASP plans for each state must provide a "description of the steps taken to insure that the needs of all residents . . . of the state were taken into account in the development of the plan."[37] Berman depicts the provision for public participation in Title XX planning as "unique in public welfare administration . . . a 'sunshine law,' one which forces government to operate in the open where it can be observed."[38] In the absence of federal oversight, this public observation and involvement at the local level is expected to secure state accountability for social service program content.

It is too early in the history of Title XX to make more than tentative assessments of how public participation will inspire the design of social service delivery systems through planning at the state level. Research on the first year's experience reveals that a variety of public-participation schemes have been employed, including information meetings, public hearings, and questionnnaire and telephone surveys. Service providers participated more frequently than consumers and other members of the public. Overall, involvement during the first planning cycle was characterized by passive forms of participation.[39]

There are indications, however, that the scope and force of public input increased during the second Title XX planning year. A study of planning experiences in eight states cites several developments along these lines: during the second year citizen input was solicited at an earlier phase in the planning process; the role of advisory groups gained importance in the planning process; and efforts were made to tap input from individuals and groups beyond those representing service providers.[40] At this stage perhaps the best that can be said of the Title XX planning process is that it provides a focal point for joining the efforts of local officials, service providers, consumers, and other citizens interested in creating social service systems responsive to local needs. As observed in the conclusion of a recent study, "it is in this sense—as a forum for learning and concern, rather than as a formal strategy for future programs—that the Title XX planning process holds an opportunity for reform."[41]

## A NEW ERA: IMPLICATIONS FOR SOCIAL SERVICES AND SOCIAL WORK

The changes in clientele, provisions, delivery, finance, and planning that have taken place during the last fifteen years signal the beginning of a new era in social services. What these changes have in common is that each in its own way enlarges the strands—of consumers, planners, service providers, and public bodies—that weave social services into the fabric of society. Their collective impact is to strengthen the institutionalization of social service systems nationwide. Under the Title XX framework more types of public and private service agencies, more consumers from all classes, and more state governmental bodies throughout the country have a greater stake than ever before in the establishment of enduring social service networks that form an integral part of modern society.

On the threshold of a new era, the future of social services is uncertain. There are various ways in which current developments can be understood. For example, an emerging middle-class service orientation attends the drift toward universal access to social services. Incorporating a large middle-class clientele may improve the flaccid status of social services, but if the $2.5 billion limit on service allotments remains in force, the supply of services will fall short of the demand generated by these more universal eligibility standards and result in heightened competition for available services. In that competition the poor are unlikely to fare as well as the middle class. On the other hand, a middle-class clientele might create strong pressures to increase the funding level and to elevate the professional standards of social services, both of which might well benefit the poor.

The question of how Title XX will affect professional standards is complicated. Concerns have been voiced about the lack of emphasis of professionalism and the scarcity of federal performance standards in Title XX programs.[42] It is possible that future increases in Title XX funding will be accompanied by stronger federal regulations on program standards. But the recent waiver of the initial Title XX federal staffing standards in day-care programs does not point in this direction.[43]

For the time being at least, the paucity of federal standards presents both a threat and an opportunity to the future of professionalism (especially social work) in social services. The absence of supportive federal guidelines in this regard poses a threat, as without the uniformity imposed by federal strictures each state has considerable latitude to set the level of professional quality in its social services. These service standards are formed through the states' Title XX planning and decision-making processes. With the great variety of service providers eligible for Title XX funding, interest-group politics may come to exert increasing influence on these planning processes. And guardianship of high professional standards has rarely been among the foremost concerns of interest-group politics. Thus, as Title XX unfolds, there are no guarantees that the value of professionalism will receive high priority in locally authorized social services.

The absence of federal standards and guarantees, however, does not preordain the dilution of professional elements in the social services. The other side to this issue is the opportunity it presents. That is, the virtues of federal social service guidelines should not be overrated. Federal regulations, guidelines, and standards have a tendency to assume a life of their own, generating refinements, qualifications, interpretations, revisions, and reporting procedures that grow to cumbersome proportions. Unhampered by these requirements, Title XX funding gives states the chance to initiate flexible and creative responses to the social service needs of their communities. The opportunity exists to institute quality standards and to enhance the value of professionalism in the social services. Whether this opportunity will be realized in the main depends upon who will carry the banner of professional standards. State planners, service providers, and consumers are all potential advocates for professionalism in the social services. The problem is that the agendas of these groups contain other items that may be of more pressing concern; planners must attend to issues of allocation among competing needs, service providers are anxious to obtain their share of program funds, and consumers want their service needs to be reflected in the types of programs funded. For these groups it is likely that involvement in slicing the Title XX service pie will take precedence over concerns about the professional quality of its ingredients.

The list of potential advocates for professionalism in Title XX programs is, however, not limited to planners, service providers, and consumers. The best and most obvious choice for this role is the National Association of Social Workers (NASW), the professional social work organization. The timing could not be better. In 1975 the NASW Delegate Assembly mandated the reorganization of the association's local chapter structure. This reorganization, which merged local chapters into statewide chapters, was completed in 1976. Efforts to staff state NASW chapters have benefited from the consolidation of resources under this new arrangement. It is only coincidental that the recent development of professionally staffed chapters of NASW at the state level dovetails so neatly with the devolution of social service planning from the federal to the state level. But coincidence often travels in tandem with opportunity. While Title XX planning arrangements are still fluid, the state chapters of NASW have a unique chance to carve out a role as gatekeeper of professional standards in Title XX program development. It is an opportunity for NASW to flex its organized energies in an area in which professional expertise is solid and in the process to revitalize social work's commitment to the social services. Such an opportunity may not soon pass this way again.

## NOTES

1. For an outstanding review of the developments leading up to Title XX, see Paul Mott, *Meeting Human Needs: The Social and Political History of Title XX* (Columbus, Ohio: National Conference on Social Welfare, 1976).

2. Martha Derthick, *Uncontrollable Spending for Social Services Grants* (Washington, D.C.: Brookings Institution, 1975), p. 8.

3. Ibid., pp. 7–14. Derthick points out that the states were somewhat encouraged to exploit the 1967 legislation and to seek broad program support from the federal government by HEW officials who expressed a "you hatch it, we match it" attitude toward the social services.

4. This analytic framework is adapted from Neil Gilbert and Harry Specht, *Dimensions of Social Welfare Policy* (Englewood Cliffs, N.J.: Prentice-Hall, Inc., 1974), pp. 28–33.

5. Mott, pp. 24–37.

6. Some of the reasons for this development are analyzed in Neil Gilbert, "The Burgeoning Social Service Payload," *Society* 14 (May–June 1977): 63–65.

7. "Social Services Programs for Individuals and Families: Title XX of the Social Security Act," *Federal Register* 40 (June 27, 1975): 40.

8. Candace Mueller and Eileen Wolff, "Title XX—Final CASP Plans, Services Catalogue," mimeographed (Washington, D.C.: Department of Health, Education, and Welfare, January 30, 1976).

9. These data are taken from the first quarterly report of the statistical series to be published on Title XX in Social Rehabilitation Service, Department of Health, Education, and Welfare, *Social Services U.S.A., Oct.–Dec. 1975*, Publication no. SRS 76–03300 (Washington, D.C.: National Center of Social Statistics, 1975), pp. 2–3.

10. Missouri Department of Social Services, *Final Comprehensive Annual Social Services Program Plan* (Jefferson City: Missouri Department of Social Services, 1975), p. iii.

11. Derthick, p. 9.

12. President's Commission on Income Maintenance, *Background Papers* (Washington, D.C.: Government Printing Office, 1970), p. 307.

13. Joel F. Handler and Jane Hollingsworth, *The Deserving Poor: A Study of Welfare Administration* (Chicago: Markham Publishing, 1971), p. 127.

14. Derthick, p. 19.

15. Mildred Rein, "Social Services as a Work Strategy," *Social Service Review* 49 (December 1975): 519.

16. Derthick, p. 19

17. Social and Rehabilitation Service, p. 7.

18. Thomas Duffy, "Three Axioms for Title XX," *Social and Rehabilitation Record 3* (April 1976): 18.

19. Social and Rehabilitation Service, pp. 5–7.

20. For a cogent analysis of this development, see Rein, pp. 515–38.

21. The evolution of caretaking services is discussed in Robert Morris and Delwin Anderson, "Personal Care Services: An Identity for Social Work," *Social Service Review* 49 (June 1975): 157–74.

22. Gilbert Y. Steiner, *The State of Welfare* (Washington, D.C.: Brookings Institution, 1971), pp. 106–10.

23. Sophonisba P. Breckinridge, ed., *Public Welfare Administration in the United States*, 2d ed. (Chicago: University of Chicago Press, 1938), p. 172.

24. Elizabeth Wickenden, "A Perspective on Social Services: An Essay Review," *Social Service Review* 50 (December 1976): 580.

25. Booz, Allen, and Hamilton, *Purchase of Social Service—Study of the Experience of Three States in Purchase of Service by Contract under the Provisions of the 1967 Amendments to the Social Security Act*, Report Submitted to the Social and Rehabilitation Service, January 29, 1971 (distributed by National Technical Information Service, U.S. Department of Commerce), pp. 40–42.

26. Alvin Chenkin, "Government Support to Jewish Sponsored Agencies in Six Major Fields of Service, 1962–73," mimeographed, background paper prepared for the Sidney Hollander Colloquium, April 24–25, 1967.

27. Booz, Allen, and Hamilton, p. 40.

28. Bay Area Social Planning Council, *Sources of Government Funds Obtained by UWBA Agencies during Fiscal Year 1974–1975* (Oakland, Calif.: Bay Area Social Planning Council, 1975), pp. 1–9.

29. E.g., see Ralph Kramer, "Voluntary Agencies and the Use of Public Funds: Some Policy Issues," *Social Service Review* 40 (November 1966): 15–26; Gordon Manser, "Implications of Purchase of Services for Voluntary Agencies," *Social Casework* 55 (July 1974): 421–27; Eleanor Brilliant, "Private or Public: A Model of Ambiguities," *Social Service Review* 47 (September 1973): 384–96; and Kenneth Wedel, "Government Contracting for Purchase of Service," *Social Work* 21 (March 1976): 101–05.

30. The issue is complicated by the fact that the potential degrees of constraint that might accompany government support of private agencies vary according to the method of financing that is employed. For an analysis of this issue, see Elizabeth Wickenden, "Purchase of Care and Services: Effect on Voluntary Agencies," in *The Emergence of Social Work and Social Welfare*, ed. Neil Gilbert and Harry Specht (Itasca, Ill.: Peacock Publishers, 1976), pp. 149–62.

31. E.g., see Felice Perlmutter, "The Effect of Public Funds on Voluntary Sectarian Services," *Journal of Jewish Communal Services* 45 (Summer 1969): 312–21; and Camille Lambert, Jr., and Leah Lambert, "Impact of Poverty Funds on Voluntary Agencies," *Social Work* 15 (April 1970): 53–61.

32. Derthick, pp. 100–101.

33. Melvin Mogulof, "Making Social Service Choices at the State Level: Practice and Problems in Four States," mimeographed (Washington, D.C.: Urban Institute, August 1973), p. 17.

34. Mogulof, p. 157.

35. Richard Nixon, "Message to Congress on General Revenue Sharing" (February 4, 1971), *Weekly Compilation of Presidential Documents* 7 (February 8, 1971): 170.

36. U.S. Congress, House, *Social Security Amendments of 1974*. Pub L. 93–647, 93d Cong., January 5, 1975, Section 2002(3).

37. *Social Security Amendments of 1974*, Section 2004(2) (G).

38. Jules H. Berman, "Regulations Implementing Title XX of the Social Security Act," *Washington Bulletin* 24 (October 13, 1975): 74.

39. Leilani S. Rose, Frances E. Zorn, and Beryl A. Radin, "Title XX and Public Participation: An Initial Assessment," *Public Welfare* 35 (Winter 1977): 24–31.

40. Gerald Horton and Edmund Armentrout, *State Experiences in Social Services Planning: Eight Case Studies on Social Services Planning in Response to Title XX of the Social Security Act* (Atlanta: Research Group, Inc. 1976), p. 89.

41. Paul Terrell, David S. Franklin, and Stan Weisner, *Planning for Social Services: Title XX in Action in Five Communities* (Los Angeles: Regional Institute in Social Welfare, University of Southern California, 1976), p. 192.

42. Wickenden, "A Perspective on Social Services," pp. 583–84.

43. "Title XX Regulations and Median Income," *Washington Social Legislation Bulletin* 25 (January 10, 1977): 1.

# 8   Issues in Welfare Reform

## MARTHA N. OZAWA

The Nixon administration succeeded partially in welfare reform when Congress enacted legislation for Supplemental Security In-

Reprinted from the *Social Service Review*, 52 (March 1978): 37–55, by permission of the University of Chicago Press and of the author.

come (SSI) in 1972, and now President Carter seems ready to give another try toward achieving reform of the welfare system.

Interest in welfare reform is rising at a time when income-assistance (or income-tested) programs such as AFDC, food stamps, and SSI are perceived as getting out of control in terms of expenditures. Income-assistance programs began to expand faster than social insurance programs in the mid-1960s with the flourishing of the Great Society's War on Poverty. From 1965 to 1976, the annual per capita cost of income-assistance programs, in constant dollars, increased by 313 percent, in comparison with a 177 percent increase for social insurance programs.[1] The estimated total cost of income-assistance programs in 1977, $48.8 billion, is 27 percent of the nation's total outlay for income-maintenance purposes. This contrasts with an estimated cost of $134.2 billion, or 73 percent, for social insurance programs.[2] The increase in income-assistance payments reflects the change in economic conditions as well as policy shifts. In comparison, the increase in social insurance benefit payments, especially social security benefits, reflects demographic shifts, changes in economic conditions, and liberalization of benefits.

The new interest in welfare reform also comes at a time when the nation is finding it necessary to evaluate the basic approach taken during the 1960s in the war on poverty, which shaped the direction of the various cash and in-kind programs that followed. These were developed on the basis of selectivity. The aim was to concentrate the benefits of the programs on a targeted population, with the least amount of waste in expenditures. Housing-assistance programs, Medicaid, SSI, and food stamps all followed this approach. Means tests or income tests were an integral part of the strategy. Combined with the emphasis on economic (or target) efficiency was a concern with the effects of the programs on work incentives. Thus, these programs incorporated work-incentive features by setting the benefit-withdrawal rate at less than 100 percent. However, it was soon recognized that when the same recipient benefited from multiple programs, each having an incentive measure, the cumulative effects of these measures were such that the recipient who increased his work effort often had to give up more in total income than his additional effort brought in. Policymakers and experts in the field faced a conceptual deadlock in the selective approach to income maintenance.[3]

Some, including myself, started worrying about the impact of growing selective programs such as SSI on universal programs such as social security.[4] The more effective SSI becomes in providing a minimum income, the more the role and value of social security are diminished. Furthermore, one of the two principal objectives of social security—social adequacy—begins to be questioned for validity.[5] The other principal objective is earnings replacement.

Welfare reform is becoming an increasingly complex process. Any proposal for initiating a new program or revising an old one needs to be evaluated in the light of multiple and often conflicting policy issues. In addition, any proposal needs to be looked at in broad perspective so that policymakers can assess its effects on the rest of the income-maintenance system.

This article will attempt to identify and discuss pertinent policy issues, show how they are related to each other, and consider their impact within the whole spectrum of income maintenance. Before discussing specific policy issues, it will be useful to categorize and describe briefly the current approaches to income maintenance. It is not the aim of the article to propose or advocate any particular policy or program.[6]

## THREE BASIC APPROACHES

Income-maintenance programs can be broadly classified within three groups: demogrants, social insurance, and income assistance.

*Demogrants.*—A demogrant is a universal provision of a flat payment to the entire population of a country or to all who fall within a certain group, regardless of employment status or income level. Children's allowances, old-age pensions, and maternity benefits are in this category. Benefits of this type are relatively unfamiliar in the United States; however, they are becoming increasingly common in other industrialized societies. For example, sixty-two nations now provide children's allowances of various kinds.[7] During this century, the majority of industrialized nations in the West have also moved toward universal pensions for the aged—some providing a universal flat amount to each individual, others providing a flat amount as the first tier of a social security system plus a second-tier payment based on the individual's earnings.[8] Most of these nations also pay maternity benefits. In the United States, before the enactment of the Social Security Act of 1935, most states had instituted old-age pensions and mothers' pensions, but these were not demogrants, since they provided only for those who proved that they were poor.

*Social insurance.*— Major social insurance programs with the earnings-replacement objective are Old-Age, Survivors, and Disability Insurance (OASDI); unemployment insurance and workmen's compensation; and railroad retirement, unemployment, and disability insurance. Medicare, another major social insurance program, provides for medical care costs. Since medical care costs of the beneficiary population—the aged and the disabled—are a large portion of their living expenses, Medicare has a significant bearing on their income security.

Social insurance programs with the earnings-replacement objective have two basic characteristics: (1) eligibility for benefits depends on previous work in covered employment, and benefit levels are related, although not precisely, to previous earnings; and (2) benefits are granted when a statutorily identified hazard such as unemployment, illness, disability, retirement, or death of an insured worker occurs.

The United States spends a smaller proportion of its GNP for social insurance than do other Western societies. This is mainly because this country lacks a national health insurance program. Even for comparable existing social insurance programs, this country spends less than most other industrialized countries. For example, the United States in 1971 spent 3.42 percent of its GNP for OASDI programs. This compares with 7.59 percent of its GNP spent by West Germany, 6.32 percent by the Netherlands, and 6.03 percent by Sweden. Of nine industrialized nations reporting, only Canada and Japan spent a smaller proportion of their GNP for such programs.[9] To compare the degree of societal commitment to social welfare expenditures in different countries, one needs to include social welfare expenditures made in the private sector. For example, Japanese corporations provide extensive fringe benefits,[10] although the Japanese government does not provide social insurance programs and other social welfare programs as extensively as governments of other countries.

*Income assistance.* — Under this category fall AFDC, SSI, general assistance, veterans' pensions, earned income tax credit, Basic Education Opportunity Grants (BEOGS),[11] Medicaid, food stamps, and housing assistance. The last three are in-kind programs but can be considered as a part of the income-maintenance system because they have a significant bearing on the financial well-being of low-income families. Of the total $48.8 billion estimated to be spent in 1977, expenditures for Medicaid will constitute by far the largest share—$17.2 billion, or 35 percent of the total.[12] All income-assistance programs involve some form of income testing and resource testing.

Since—compared with other industrialized nations—the United States spends a relatively small proportion of its GNP for social insurance programs and has no demogrant programs such as children's allowances and old-age pensions, income-assistance programs must bear a greater burden in meeting the needs of income maintenance than they do in these other countries. (Compared with those in European countries, private sectors in the United States incur a relatively large amount of expenditure for employee-welfare programs. But still, compared with public expenditures, the amount of private expenditures for social welfare purposes is relatively small in this country, except in the field of health care.)[13] And, as already mentioned, the proportion of public expenditures for income assistance versus social insurance has risen sharply in recent years.

## POLICY ISSUES IN PROGRAM PROPOSALS

Policymakers and experts in the field have developed common criteria for evaluating proposals for income-maintenance programs. What are these criteria, and how do they relate to the policy issues of income maintenance?[14]

*Adequacy.* — An income-maintenance program should help a family obtain an adequate minimum income. I define this as the income below which society perceives no family income should fall at a given time in history. Of all the current income-assistance programs in the United States, only SSI explicitly provides a national minimum income. In contrast, on a nationwide basis, AFDC does not pretend to implement the principle of adequacy, and benefits under social insurance programs depend on the level of previous earnings. Thus, the criterion of adequacy cannot be implemented under social insurance unless there are supplemental programs that automatically bridge the gap between the actual benefit levels and the adequacy level.

The concept of adequacy needs to be studied not only in relation to an absolute level of minimum income but also in relation to dynamic changes in living standards. Unless the criterion of adequacy is assessed in the dynamic model, a minimum income adequate for today will become inadequate in the near future. One way to establish the level of adequate minimum income in the dynamic model is to define the minimum income as a percentage of the median family income. Since the poverty-line income defined by the Social Security Administration (SSA) is adjusted every year to account only for the cost-of-living increase and not for the real economic growth, the SSA poverty-line income has become a smaller percentage of the median family income over the years.[15]

*Equity.* —There are two kinds of equity. *Horizontal equity* requires that families of the same size who have the same degree of economic deprivation should receive the same income-assistance payments. *Vertical equity* requires that, even though families are of the same size, those having a greater income need should receive a larger assistance payment. In the case of social insurance, vertical equity requires that those who earned more during their working lives should receive larger benefits when they retire.

At present, the principle of equity is implemented loosely in income-assistance programs. For example, there is wide interstate variation in AFDC payments—with the differential in payments far exceeding the differential in living costs among the various states. Thus, families of the same size with the same degree of income need receive different amounts of assistance payments, depending on where they live. This is a violation of horizontal equity. As of June 1976, basic annual payment levels for a family of four ranged from $720 in Mississippi to $5,196 in Oregon and $6,168 in Hawaii.[16] The preliminary findings of my research show that three independent variables associated with state characteristics mainly account for the difference in state maximum payments. They are, in order of importance in explaining the proportion of variance in maximum payments, (1) the percentage of nonwhite population, (2) per capita personal income, and (3) tax effort. These three variables combined explain 64 percent of the variance in state maximum AFDC payments.[17] Further, assistance payments under different programs vary within states. Families on general assistance generally receive less than those on AFDC, who in turn may receive less than those on SSI, again violating horizontal equity. President Carter's recent welfare-reform proposal attempts to correct the horizontal inequity by consolidating the AFDC, SSI, and food stamp programs into a national program called "A Program for Better Jobs and Income."[18]

The principle of vertical equity dictates that under an income-tested program those who need more should receive more. This principle is often violated in the food stamp program—not in policy but in its implementation. In principle, the net worth of food stamps is inversely related to the level of family income. But many families on AFDC are too poor to buy food stamps. (The program requires that AFDC families spend a certain specified amount of income to buy food stamps; the required amount is often too large for AFDC families to bear.) Thus, many of those who need food stamps most are not taking advantage of the program. President Carter's proposal eliminates the vertical inequity involved in the food stamp program by cashing out food stamps and including their net worth in cash payments.

It is interesting to note that a children's allowance program—which is a type of demogrant—would simultaneously implement both horizontal and vertical equity in a unique way if the allowances were taxable. Children's allowances redistribute income from childless families to families with children, and the latter presumably are in greater financial need than the former. Thus, income redistribution through children's allowances implements horizontal equity. The taxing of these allowances takes away a part of them from financially able families. This implements vertical equity.

*Economic efficiency.*— Economic efficiency requires that assistance payments be concentrated on a targeted population. For example, 100 percent efficiency would be obtained if every $1 of public outlay for an income-assistance program resulted in a $1 gain by the poor.

However, economic efficiency does not operate so neatly and ideally that 100 percent efficiency can be attained in implementing an actual program. In most income-maintenance programs, the criterion of efficiency is entangled with two other criteria, adequacy and work incentives. If work incentives are to be preserved, the benefit-withdrawal rate must be set at less than 100 percent.[19] Thus, a program with a work-incentive feature must compromise either the criterion of adequacy or that of economic efficiency. For example, an income-maintenance program that provides an adequate minimum payment—say, poverty-line income—and incorporates a benefit-withdrawal rate of less than 100 percent must pay benefits to both pretransfer poor and pretransfer nonpoor families up to a break-even point. Thus, it is economically inefficient. On the other hand, if such a program attempts to target benefits solely to the posttransfer poor and incorporates a benefit-withdrawal rate of less than 100 percent, then the basic benefit level has to be less than the poverty-line income, thus undermining the criterion of adequacy.

Children's allowances appear at first glance to be less efficient economically than income-assistance programs such as AFDC and SSI, since these allowances do not involve income testing. However, in general, families with children are presumed to be in greater financial need than childless families because a larger income is required for their support. Therefore, children's allowances are, in effect, targeted to financially needy segments of society. (The concept of presumptive need applies equally to the beneficiary of social insurance programs such as OASDI and unemployment insurance.)[20] If children's allowances are taxable, income testing is in effect incorporated in an indirect way, enhancing the criterion of economic efficiency even further. (The same line of argument applies to taxable old-age pensions.)

It should be noted that economic efficiency does not necessarily bring about the redistribution of a greater amount of income to the poor. Both the rate of economic efficiency and the total expenditures for a program have to be considered in calculating its actual impact. Social security (OASDI), although less economically efficient, in fact redistributes more money to low-income families than does any income-assistance program.[21] This comes about because the expenditures for social security are so much larger.

*Work incentives.* — Most income-assistance programs include work incentives because policymakers and the public in general believe that such programs should not discourage people from working. Whether work incentives are necessary is a debatable point. Empirical findings of an experimental project involving a negative income tax indicate that low-income families generally keep working even when they are provided with income supplements.[22] Programs that in the main are free from the work-incentive question are those that provide income assistance regardless of the employment status of the head of the household or the family's income level. Children's allowances and universal old-age pensions come closest to not involving the incentive question.

Although demogrants such as children's allowances and old-age pensions affect incentives to work of beneficiaries less adversely than an income-assistance program does, they may affect the incentives to work of taxpayers more adversely; as demogrants typically involve a greater magnitude of income redistribution, they require a greater net increase in taxes to finance them.

The work-incentive measure incorporated in SSI is considered an improvement over the one in AFDC. Under SSI, the first $20 of unearned income, the first $65 of earned income, and one-half of the remaining earned income are disregarded in calculating monthly assistance payments. Under AFDC, the first $30 of earned income and one-third of the remaining earned income are disregarded in calculating monthly assistance payments. The program also allows the recipient to deduct work expenses and child-care costs from income when AFDC payments are calculated.

One ought to be aware that the differential in benefit-withdrawal rates of SSI (50 percent) and AFDC (67 percent) is rather misleading. The majority of SSI recipients also benefit from social security programs and other social welfare programs which have their own benefit-withdrawal rates incorporated in them. Furthermore, if the recipient of multiple benefits increases his work effort, he has to pay payroll taxes and often federal and state income taxes. The effect of this is that the composite benefit-withdrawal rate applicable to a person who receives social security benefits and SSI payments while earning $4,820 a year reaches as high as 95 percent.[23] This means, for example, that when a person earns $1 more, he increases his net income by only $0.05. This happens because each income-tested program reduces benefits at a fractional rate as earnings increase; furthermore, the worker has to pay payroll taxes (5.85 percent) and often federal and state income taxes as well. On the other hand, the recipients of AFDC, in calculating assistance payments, are allowed to deduct work and child-care expenses in addition to the earned-income deductions, as mentioned in the previous paragraph. Because of this, the composite benefit-withdrawal rate, even after payroll taxes and federal and state income taxes are taken into account, actually declines to as low as 50 percent for a family of four.[24]

As mentioned earlier, when a family benefits from multiple income-tested programs, the combined incentive features become a composite disincentive. This paradoxical effect is felt, for example, by a family that attempts to earn extra income while simultaneously benefiting from AFDC, veterans' pensions, food stamps, and Medicaid. It is estimated that between 10 and 25 percent of the recipient households benefit from five or more different income-assistance programs.[25]

Medicaid introduces a more serious kind of work disincentive called the "notch problem." This problem is created when a program suddenly cuts off all benefits once family income reaches a certain level. Under Medicaid, a family becomes ineligible for medical care when it leaves AFDC or SSI, if the family is "medically indigent," when its income, after deducting medical expenses, exceeds 133 percent of the state AFDC payment level. Such regulations may encourage families on Medicaid not to increase their income beyond the cutoff level: If they do, they will lose medical care altogether. It is difficult, however, to eliminate the "notch problem" involved in Medicaid, because medical care services cannot be reduced gradually as family income increases.

It is important to note that the advantage of having a low benefit-withdrawal rate in a demogrant program is destroyed in part when multiple income-tested programs supplement it in sequence. The relative differential in benefit-withdrawal rates of a demogrant program and an income-assistance program converges when each of them is supplemented by multiple cash and in-kind transfers in sequence. As a result, the advantage of a demogrant over an income-assistance program, in terms of work incentives, weakens when both are supplemented by other income-tested programs.

*Stigma and self-image of beneficiary.* — Ideally, an income-maintenance program should not impose social stigma or destroy the beneficiary's self-image, and it is generally believed that an income test or a means test tends to do just that. Thus goes the argument that social insurance programs or demogrants, which are not income tested, should be preferred to income-assistance programs. But some argue that income testing per se is not at issue but, rather, how income testing involving the poor is performed.[26] Income testing involving the poor through face-to-face, case-by-case investigation may be stigmatizing, but income testing submerged within income tax returns will not be. Aside from such arguments, one can speculate that the concern about social stigma may be a product of our middle-class value system. Low-income families who daily have to struggle and survive in undesirable and uncertain working conditions may find an income-assistance program an acceptable alternative source of income. All these speculations and questions need to be tested by empirical research.

*Antipoverty effectiveness.* —Two indicators measure the degree of antipoverty effectiveness of a given income-maintenance program: (1) the proportion of pretransfer poor families who are made non-poor by the receipt of program benefits, and (2) the proportion of aggregate income deficit offset for these pretransfer poor families by the program's benefits.[27] A program that is economically efficient in concentrating benefits on pretransfer poor families and does not provide spillover benefits to pretransfer nonpoor families can effi-ciently offset a portion of the aggregate income deficit of poor fami-lies, but it cannot lift a single family above poverty-line income. In contrast, the provision of a basic payment (the level of benefit pro-vided to a family with no income of its own) equivalent to a poverty-line income, with the benefit-withdrawal rate of 50 percent and hence with the break-even point of twice the poverty-line income, will pay spillover benefits to pretransfer nonpoor families, but it will also bring all the pretransfer poor out of poverty. Spillover benefits to the pretransfer nonpoor will be inevitable, though lower, even when the basic payment level is lower than the poverty-line income as long as the break-even point is higher. In the process, some pre-transfer poor families and individuals are pulled out of poverty. Thus, for a program to be effective in bringing poor families out of poverty, it must not only have a high rate of target efficiency but also must be large enough in scope to provide spillover benefits for pretransfer nonpoor families.

These ideas are consistent with research findings. Generally, social insurance programs are more effective in bringing pretransfer poor families out of poverty. More specifically, however, the degree of antipoverty effectiveness in income-maintenance programs varies with the demographic characteristics of beneficiary families. One study shows that social insurance programs have been more effective in bringing out of poverty families headed by the aged than those headed by the nonaged. It indicates, on the other hand, that income-assistance programs have been more effective in bringing out of poverty families headed by the nonaged, especially those with a nonaged female head.[28] Another study shows that social security is a powerful agent for lessening the degree of income inequality among beneficiary families headed by the aged; and public assistance has a similar effect among recipient families headed by a nonaged female.[29] Such differential impacts reflect different demographic groups that a particular social insurance or public assistance program is designed to cover, the scope of expenditures involved in each program, and the degree of selectivity (or concentration on low-income families) involved in each program.

The policy question here is whether it is desirable to continue to depend heavily on income-assistance programs for bringing families headed by the nonaged out of poverty. The selective approach used in income-assistance programs seems to be reaching the limit of tolerance not only in terms of the large government expenditures involved but also in terms of enormous work disincentives created by simultaneous benefits from multiple income-tested programs. Furthermore, the proliferation of income-tested programs is creating horizontal inequity, because not all families with the same level of need benefit from the same set of income-tested programs. President Carter's welfare-reform proposal attempts to improve the situation by cashing out food stamps.

*Effects on the incentive to save.* — It is generally argued that no income-maintenance program should discourage private efforts to save for future rainy days. Thus, policymakers are interested in developing programs that do not discourage these efforts.

Income-assistance programs such as AFDC and SSI provide benefits only when a family has practically exhausted its private resources. Thus, applicants often must "spend down" available resources to be eligible for assistance payments. On the other hand, social insurance provides income to eligible families regardless of the amount of accumulated savings or other types of resources. Thus, social insurance in principle does not discourage saving.

The situation is more complex for families that benefit from both income-assistance and social insurance programs. The case in point is a recipient of both SSI and social security. Social security does not consider the amount of savings in establishing eligibility for benefits or calculating the amount of the benefit. On the other hand, SSI limits the individual's resources to $1,500 and a couple's to $2,250. For a social security beneficiary to supplement a meager benefit with SSI, he has to "spend down" his resources to the stipulated amount.

The founders of social security clearly did not intend that the program should in any way supersede private efforts to save or that it should modify to more than a minor degree the nation's distribution of wealth and income.[30] Nevertheless, recent research shows that social security does decrease private efforts to save and does substantially change the distribution of total wealth—that is, net worth plus social security wealth. The same study finds, however, that when the current value of future social security benefits is included in total wealth the distribution of wealth is less concentrated.[31] These findings imply that social security on one hand "democratizes" wealth but on the other impedes the capital formation necessary for economic growth. Research findings on the effect of social security on private saving, however, are not conclusive. The 1969 Brookings study by Pechman, Aaron, and Taussig shows that private savings expressed as a percentage of disposable income has not declined since the 1950s, even though social security contributions have increased enormously.[32]

*Administrative efficiency.* — On the basis of decades of federal experience in income-maintenance programs since the depression of the 1930s, several generalizations on administrative issues can be made: (1) national administration of a program can be simpler than administration under a state-federal partnership; (2) administration of benefits based on a case-by-case investigation of income and resources—that is, a means test—is more complicated than, for example, a demogrant; and (3) administration of a program is simpler when it has the single objective of providing financial aid than when it has additional objectives such as rehabilitation or social control. Thus, the administration of a social insurance program is simpler and requires a smaller percentage of expenditures than an income-assistance program.

The criterion of administrative efficiency should be evaluated not only in relation to a single program but also with respect to the multiple programs serving the same beneficiaries. An example here is the administration of SSI and social security programs by the Social Security Administration. Unless states choose otherwise, two monthly checks (a yellow check for SSI and a green check for social security benefits) are sent to beneficiaries by the same agency. Better coordination and integration of these programs should be possible.

Since the policy issues involved in specific programs are often interrelated or conflicting, policymakers need to evaluate each program proposal, weighing one criterion against another.

## WELFARE REFORM IN BROADER PERSPECTIVE

The income-maintenance system has become a significant part of the economic life of the nation. Therefore, the broad implications of any welfare proposal should be evaluated as well as its merits in meeting particular needs. Furthermore, the interaction between income-maintenance provisions and the general economy should be examined.

*Singularity versus plurality.* —The interest of the welfare-reform movement in the 1960s and 1970s has revolved around ways to make income-assistance programs such as AFDC more uniform across the nation and ways to consolidate various programs into a single noncategorical one. Enactment of SSI in 1972 partially achieved interstate uniformity by providing national standards for basic benefits. The SSI also consolidated three former state-administered categorical programs: Old-Age Assistance (OAA), Aid to the Blind (AB), and Aid to the Permanently and Totally Disabled (APTD). Politicians and academicians seem to be increasingly interested in nationalizing and decategorizing income-assistance programs even further. The interest of many in a negative income tax (NIT) plan reflects this trend. This approach to welfare reform might be called the "bottom-up singular strategy."

President Carter's welfare-reform proposal follows the bottom-up singular strategy. His proposal involves two separate NIT derivatives but does not use the tax system. One is called "the income support program for the nonworking poor" and the other "the work benefit program for the working poor." Both are further supplemented by earned-income tax credits. His plan attempts to reform the welfare system by providing these national NIT programs, without seriously coordinating with or reforming social insurance programs, introducing a new type of income-maintenance program such as universal old-age pensions and children's allowances, or improving minimum wages.

The bottom-up singular strategy presents at least two problems. First, meeting specific needs and circumstances of various family groups is difficult under a single, gigantic program such as a national NIT plan. To illustrate, if an NIT plan incorporating an incentive measure lumps together the working poor and the nonworking poor, it will be hard to provide an adequate minimum income to the non-working poor without making the break-even point so high that an intolerably large number of families will be eligible for assistance payments. By treating the two categories of poor under two separate programs, the Carter plan escapes this dilemma. His plan succeeds in providing an adequate minimum income to those who are presumed to be unable to work (the aged, the blind, the disabled, and heads of single-parent families with small children) and a high level of work incentives to those presumed to be able to work. Also, by treating the two categories of poor separately, the Carter plan incurs fewer expenditures than a single NIT plan covering all the poor.[33]

Another problem is that this strategy ignores the inherent limits of the role and scope of income-assistance programs in the income-maintenance system. A basically unplanned economy like ours, which can encourage work but cannot enforce it, inevitably has a hierarchical order in its income-maintenance system. This is, for income-assistance programs to be tolerable in scope and nature, social insurance programs which are related to previous wages must be optimally effective in providing income to eligible families. Likewise, for social insurance programs to be a viable vehicle for providing adequate income, wage levels and job security must be adequate.

Policymakers should look at the various components of the income-maintenance system in such a hierarchical order. That is, they might consider the "top-down pluralistic strategy" to welfare reform. If one takes this approach, creating jobs, increasing minimum wages and job security, and improving social insurance programs would become important in welfare reform, as well as streamlining categorical income-assistance programs.

*Economic well-being of children.* — Several income-maintenance programs (e.g., AFDC, SSI, and social security) are concerned with the economic well-being of children. But the government's current ways of providing income support for children create the major stumbling block to systematic welfare reform. An income-maintenance system comprised only of social insurance and income-assistance programs has a built-in constraint against providing adequately for families with children. First, minimum wages cannot be developed that will provide adequate income for families of all sizes. Social insurance programs having benefits related to previous earnings cannot provide for a large number of dependents in addition to the insured worker without jeopardizing two criteria, equity and work incentives. Also, assistance payments under an income-assistance program cannot depart too much from minimum wage levels and social insurance benefit levels without jeopardizing these two criteria.

The inherent constraint results from the fact that the government tries to provide for children through programs directly or indirectly related to the employment status or the wage level of the head of the household. One way to eliminate this constraint is for the government to develop an income-support program for children under which benefits are provided independently of the employment status or the wage level of the head of the household. Some type of demogrant—children's allowances or cashable tax credits for children—might be an option worth considering.

*Balancing various types of income-maintenance programs.* — One source of political discontent with current income-maintenance programs appears to be the growing expenditures for them. When income-assistance programs are overburdened in relation to other types of income-maintenance programs, they tend to provide benefits to too large a number of families whose heads are either working or deemed employable, thus creating a disproportionate amount of political passion. The smaller the scope of income-assistance programs, the less political controversy will be associated with them. That is, income-assistance programs are politically most acceptable when they are truly residual.

Under President Carter's proposal, some of the current welfare mothers and all unemployed fathers covered under AFDC-UP (Unemployed Parents) will be required to work. The plan will also cover a sizable number of working families, some nonpoor, under either the work-benefit program, the earned-income tax credits, or both. Thus the amount of assistance payments to those currently on AFDC may be lower in some cases than at present, but a greater number of families are expected to be included. As a result, the Carter plan, in an effort to streamline the welfare system, will probably enlarge the scope of it, possibly creating political controversy.

If my assessment is accurate, policymakers should develop the income maintenance system so that there will be a healthy balance among various types of programs.[34] They ought to recognize the desirability of strengthening social insurance programs and minimum wages. They might also explore the desirability of introducing another type of income-maintenance program using the demogrant approach. The introduction of universal children's allowances or cashable tax credits for children, which was mentioned briefly above, should assist in attaining at least three objectives: (1) it could help develop healthy hierarchical relationships between minimum wages, social insurance programs, and income-assistance programs; (2) it could lessen the burden placed on income-assistance programs in providing for the poor, thus making these programs truly residual within the system of income maintenance; and (3) together with other types of income-maintenance programs, it could provide adequate income to eligible families of all sizes without creating work disincentives.

*Employment and income maintenance.*—The vitality of an income-maintenance system depends on healthy conditions of employment. For a person to receive an adequate benefit from a social insurance program, he must have been employed for a certain period of time and earned a minimum amount. Similarly, to maintain income-assistance programs at a tolerable residual level, those who are employable must be able to earn adequate income through work.

Government data indicate that in 1971, for example, earnings were the most important source of income even for families with an annual income of $4,000 or less. Earnings constituted 37.1 percent of the total money income of these families.[35] On the other hand, these families, who constituted 13.0 percent of all families, received only 1.2 percent of the total aggregate earnings. In fact, the share of earnings of the bottom fifth of workers seems to have been declining. A study by Henle shows that the share of the bottom fifth of all male workers decreased from 2.75 percent in 1959 to 2.15 percent in 1970. In contrast, the share of the top fifth of all male workers increased from 42.80 percent to 44.95 percent during the same period.[36] That study also shows that the share of the bottom fifth of all year-round, fulltime male workers slightly increased during the same period. These findings seem to indicate that one reason for the declining share of the bottom fifth of male workers is that their rates of unemployment and subemployment had increased over the years.

Policymakers must recognize that there is a relationship between employment and the role of an income-maintenance system. Income-maintenance programs utilizing a politically tolerable magnitude of public expenditures can provide an adequate income for targeted populations of families only when employment provides adequate income for those who are able and willing to work.

*Political considerations.* — So far in this article the framework for understanding and evaluating welfare-reform proposals has been developed with a focus on economic and social policy variables. However, the answer to the question of what kind of welfare/income redistribution system this country eventually will have depends heavily on the political climate of the time.

First of all, the question of what kind of society the public aspires to in the future needs to be addressed. Does it wish to have forever a society in which taxpayers and recipients of income subsidies are clearly exposed and identified? A heavy reliance on the income-assistance approach tends to perpetuate that condition. Or, in contrast, does it wish to have a society in which all contribute in some way and all may benefit from income-redistribution programs at some time in their lives, thus creating the notions of interdependence and mutual help? An increased reliance on social insurance and demogrants would help create such a society. In economic terms, of course, the income-assistance approach is cheaper than the other two, at least in the short run.

Related to the questions above is whether the public is ready to shift from the traditional categorization of deserving and undeserving poor to a new categorization of nonworking and working poor, as the Carter plan proposes. Under the new categorization, all those in need would receive some type of income subsidy, thus enhancing the principle of horizontal equity. Under the Carter plan, which uses the new categorization, nobody will be so undeserving as to be ineligible for any income subsidy. Is the public ready to give up the political scapegoat called "the undeserving poor"?

Another political issue is the extent to which the public wishes to and can provide for those in need from private sources. If the public encourages private approaches, the demand for fringe benefits provided by employers is bound to increase. But even then the government will be called upon to provide a minimum adequate income to those who are not employed by firms able to provide benefits.

A third political issue is whether state legislatures are ready to lose political power by letting the federal government continue its takeover of both financial and administrative responsibilities for income-maintenance and other social welfare programs. According to Handler, states tend to retain their power over income-assistance programs as long as such programs deal not only with the financial need of the recipient but also with the community's need to control the social behavior of the recipient.[37] According to this theory, the public needs to keep a close eye on the recipient when it wishes to impose its values on him. Handing over financial and administrative responsibilities to the federal government would make the political process that imposes the community's values on the recipient more difficult, if not impossible. Recent trends in nationalizing income-assistance programs—SSI in 1972 and the current welfare-reform proposal made by President Carter—would weaken the states' political power to shape and run programs for the poor. State legislatures may resist such a movement, despite the fiscal relief it would provide.

All these political considerations and many more, as well as the economic and social policy aspects discussed earlier, will influence the decision-making process that will shape the future of the income-maintenance system in the United States.

## NOTES

1. Alfred M. Skolnik and Sophie R. Dales, "Social Welfare Expenditures, Fiscal Year 1976," *Social Security Bulletin* 40, no. 1 (January 1977): 9, table 2.

2. U.S. Department of Health, Education, and Welfare, Office of Income Security Policy, Assistant Secretary for Planning and Evaluation, "An Overview of the Income Security System" (Washington, D.C.: Department of Health, Education, and Welfare, n.d.).

3. Robert J. Lampman, "Scaling Welfare Benefits to Income: An Idea That Is Being Overworked," *Policy Analysis* 1, no. 1 (Winter 1975): 1–10; Martha N. Ozawa, "Four More Years of Welfare Nightmare?" *Public Welfare* 31, no. 2 (Spring 1973): 6–7.

4. Martha N. Ozawa, "SSI: Progress or Retreat?" *Public Welfare* 32, no. 2 (Spring 1974): 33–40.

5. For further discussion, see Martha N. Ozawa, "Individual Equity versus Social Adequacy in Federal Old-Age Insurance," *Social Service Review* 48, no. 1 (March 1974): 24–38.

6. I have presented and argued for my own comprehensive proposals elsewhere. See, e.g., the following: Martha N. Ozawa, "Redistribution and Social Insurance," in *Jubilee for Our Times*, ed. Alvin L. Schorr (New York: Columbia University Press, 1977), pp. 162–77; "Welfare and National Economic Policy," in *Social Welfare Forum, 1973* (New York: Columbia University Press, 1974), pp. 91–102; "SSI: Progress or Retreat?"; and "Family Allowances and National Minimum of Economic Security," *Child Welfare* 50, no. 6 (June 1971): 314–16.

7. James C. Vadakin, *Children, Poverty, and Family Allowances* (New York: Basic Books, 1968), pp. 45–55.

8. For further discussion, see Margaret S. Gordon, "The Case for Earnings-related Social Security Benefits Restated," in U.S. Congress, Joint Economic Committee, *Old Age Income Assurance. Part II: The Aged Population and Retirement Income Programs* (Washington, D.C.: Government Printing Office, 1967), pp. 312–19.

9. Max Horlick, *National Expenditures on Social Security in Selected Countries, 1968 and 1971,* Research and Statistics Note no. 29–1974, DHEW

Pub. no. (SSA) 74–11701 (Washington, D.C.: Department of Health, Education, and Welfare, Social Security Administration, Office of Research and Statistics, October 18, 1974).

10. For understanding the interrelation between transfer payments by relatives, private industries, and the government, see Robert J. Lampman, "Transfer and Redistribution as Social Process," in *Social Security in International Perspective*, ed. Shirley Jenkins (New York: Columbia University Press, 1969), pp. 29–54.

11. The BEOGS program was enacted in 1972 to benefit low-income postsecondary students. Students of any age may qualify for a grant if they are enrolled at least half time in an accredited school which requires a high school diploma for admission. An estimated 1.9 million persons will receive an estimated $1.8 million in BEOGS payments in fiscal 1977. See Department of Health, Education, and Welfare (n. 2 above).

12. *Ibid*.

13. Skolnik and Dales (n. 1 above), p. 17, table 10.

14. See U.S. Department of Health, Education, and Welfare, Office of Income Security Policy, Assistant Secretary for Planning and Evaluation, "Income Security System: Purposes, Criteria, and Choices," Welfare Reform Analysis Series, Briefing Paper no. 2 (Washington, D.C.: Department of Health, Education, and Welfare, February 14, 1977); Ozawa, "Family Allowances and a National Minimum of Economic Security"; and Scott Briar, "Why Children's Allowances?" *Social Work* 14, no. 1 (January 1969): 7–9.

15. In 1959, the official poverty-line income represented about one-half of the median income of all Americans. But by 1974, the poverty threshold for an urban family of four persons had dropped to just over one-third of median family income. See Winifred Bell, "Family Structure and Poverty: A Collision Course," in *Welfare Policy*, by Martha N. Ozawa, Alvin L. Schorr, and Winifred Bell (New York: New York University, Graduate School of Social Work, Center for Studies in Income Maintenance Policy, 1975), p. 33.

16. U.S. Department of Health, Education, and Welfare, Social and Rehabilitation Service, Office of Information Systems, National Center for Social Statistics, *Aid to Families with Dependent Children: Standards for Basic Needs, State Maximum and Other Methods of Limiting Money Payments, Federal Matching Provisions under the Social Security Act, July 1976*, DHEW Pub. no. (SRS) 77-03200, NCSS Report D-2(7/76) (Washington, D.C.: Government Printing Office, February 1977).

17. Martha N. Ozawa, "An Exploration into States' Commitment to AFDC" (unpublished manuscript available from the George Warren Brown School of Social Work, Washington University, St. Louis, Missouri 63130). In this study, data for the states of Hawaii and Alaska were excluded.

18. President Carter's welfare message to Congress, August 6, 1977.

19. The benefit-withdrawal rate means the rate of fractional reduction in benefits as earnings increase. E.g., when a program reduces benefits by $1 for $1 of additional earnings, as done in the AFDC programs before 1967, the benefit-withdrawal rate is 100 percent.

20. As social insurance programs provide benefits based on presumptive need, they do not involve income testing. The programs presume the worker to be in financial need once he encounters a risk stipulated under the law such as retirement, unemployment, death, and disability. This does not mean, however, that social insurance programs provide an adequate minimum income for all beneficiary families.

21. Martha N. Ozawa, "Income Redistribution and Social Security," *So-*

*cial Service Review* 50, no. 2 (June 1976): 209–23; Sheldon Danziger, "Income Redistribution and Social Security: Further Evidence," ibid., 51, no. 1 (March 1977): 179–84.

22. David Kershaw and Jerilyn Fair, *The New Jersey Income-Maintenance Experiment,* vol. 1, *Operations, Surveys, and Administration* (New York: Academic Press, 1976), pp. 20–21.

23. Michael K. Taussig, "The Social Security Retirement Program and Welfare Reform," in *Integrating Income Maintenance Programs,* ed. Irene Lurie (New York: Academic Press, 1975), p. 221, table 8.1.

24. Leonard J. Hausman, "Cumulative Tax Rates in Alternative Income Maintenance Systems," in Lurie, p. 44, table 2.1.

25. Department of Health, Education, and Welfare (n. 2 above); and U.S. Congress Joint Economic Committee, Subcommittee on Fiscal Policy, *Public Income Transfer Programs: The Incidence of Multiple Benefits and the Issues Raised by Their Receipt: A Study,* Studies in Public Welfare, Paper no. 1, 92d Cong., 2d sess., April 10, 1972 (Washington, D.C.: Government Printing Office, 1972), pp. 28, table 9; 30, table 10.

26. Lewis Mariam, *Relief and Social Security* (Washington, D.C.: Brookings Institution, 1946), p. 841.

27. The term "poor" means those who fall below the official poverty-line income established yearly for each family size by the Social Security Administration. The poverty-line income is further refined to be applicable to family heads of different sexes and ages. E.g., the poverty-line income for a nonfarm family of four persons was $5,820 in 1976. The poverty-line income is the amount thought necessary for a family in the United States to have a minimum standard of living. In this instance, the concept of poverty is absolute. On the other hand, the concept of poverty can be relative. In comparison with poor people in other countries or in earlier years, poor people in the United States are relatively less poor. Thus, the concept of poverty may be interpreted as absolute or relative, depending on the point of reference for comparison.

28. Michael C. Barth, George J. Carcagno, and John L. Palmer, *Toward an Effective Income Support System: Problems, Prospects, and Choices* (Madison: University of Wisconsin Institute for Research on Poverty, 1974), pp. 26, table 5; 28, table 6.

29. Danziger, p. 179, table 1.

30. Edwin E. Witte, *Social Security Perspectives* (Madison: University of Wisconsin Press, 1962), pp. 11, 111.

31. Martin S. Feldstein, "Social Security, Induced Retirement, and Aggregate Capital Accumulation," *Journal of Political Economy* 82, no. 5 (September/October 1974): 905–26; "Social Security and Private Savings: International Evidence in an Extended Life Cycle Model," in *The Economics of Public Services, Proceeding of a Conference Held by the Economic Association at Turin, Italy,* ed. Martin S. Feldstein and Robert D. Inman (London: Macmillan Press, 1977), pp. 174–205; and "Social Security and the Distribution of Wealth," *Journal of the American Statistical Association,* Applications Section, 71, no. 356 (December 1976): 800–07.

32. Joseph A. Pechman, Henry J. Aaron, and Michael K. Taussig, *Social Security: Perspectives for Reform* (Washington, D.C.: Brookings Institution, 1968), p. 186.

33. Under the Carter plan, the break-even point for a given family size is the same for both the working and nonworking poor, providing, however, a lower basic payment to the working poor. The basic payment continues to

be provided without deduction until the family earnings reach a certain level. E.g., a family of four continues to receive $2,300 a year until its earnings reach $3,800 a year. for further discussion on the Carter plan, see Martha N. Ozawa, "Anatomy of President Carter's Welfare Reform Proposal," *Social Casework*, vol. 58, no. 12 (December 1977).

34. "Healthy" in the sense that other types of income-maintenance programs as well as minimum wages and jobs are maximized in their effects on preventing poverty, redistributing income to the poor, and assuring an adequate minimum income to all.

35. Ozawa, "Income Redistribution and Social Security," p. 214, table 2. In this table, "families" includes both families and persons.

36. Peter Henle, "Exploring the Distribution of Earned Income," *Monthly Labor Review* 95, no. 12 (December 1972): 20, table 4.

37. Joel F. Handler, *Reforming the Poor: Welfare Policy, Federalism, and Morality* (New York: Basic Books, 1972), pp. 58–71.

# 9   Demographics, Politics, and the Future of the Welfare State

## MAYER N. ZALD

Partly reacting to Watergate, Vietnam, the OPEC oil boycott, and the turbulence of the 1960s, all of which seemed to indicate a major shift in America and the world system, a number of eminent social analysts have attempted to read the emerging shape of the future. Starting from different assumptions, distinguished writers such as Heilbroner, Bell, Nisbet, and Huntington have attempted to portray the shape of things to come.[1]

I want to join this group of august writers in thinking about the future, but in more "pedestrian" fashion. Rather than soaring on the clouds of grand concepts, or basing my argument on tendentious assumptions,[2] I wish to explicate some basic social and demographic trends, and draw out their implications for the next several decades.

The topic is the future of the Welfare state in the United States. Some aspects of the economics, demographics, and politics of our society in the years ahead will be brought in, but my primary concern is income distribution and especially, or centrally, income transfer programs. I take the core of the Welfare state to be income support programs—OASDHI Supplemental Security Income, AFDC

Reprinted from the *Social Service Review,* 51 (March 1977): 110–124, by permission of the University of Chicago Press and of the author.

(Aid to Families with Dependent Children), and unemployment compensation. Moreover, for reasons that will become apparent, I take as a major problem of the future Welfare state its support for children in female-headed households and its system for maintaining the elderly.

To project the future we need to have some idea of where we are today and how we have gotten here. But before doing that, I need to state some assumptions of the whole exercise. They are, in a sense, exogenous variables and events to the system to be described. If events falsify these assumptions the story is undone. Over the next twenty-five years I am assuming that there will be no nuclear war that leads to large-scale mobilization, no major or prolonged depression, and that the third world nations will not attempt or be able to strangle the industrial super powers. Finally, I assume that American democracy, even if in a more attenuated form, will prevail.

These are large assumptions, not made lightly. But they permit me to address my problem in the context of incremental change and policy options, rather than in a situation where root and branch analysis would be required.

## THE CONTEMPORARY SCENE

Where are we today and how have we gotten here? First, the relationship of the economy to the welfare state (that state which promotes the welfare of most groups, regardless of income or employment status), and to the Welfare state. It ought to be clear to anyone not obsessed with rhetoric and parochial self-interest that over the long haul of the last half-century there has been a massive transformation of the state of poverty in America (and, for that matter, in all industrialized nations). This decline in poverty is related to technological advances and investment in education, both of which have combined to produce a massive growth in economic productivity. It is related to the growth of governmental activity to manage the economy and to subsidize and provide incentives for individual and corporate benefits—farm product price supports, stabilizing banks, providing interest write-offs for home mortgages, and helping the airline industries to grow. The decline of poverty also has been fueled by the core legislation of the Welfare state aimed at caring for the unemployed, the indigent, the old aged, the bereft, the abandoned, and the incapacitated.

One economist has recently argued that if our present poverty standards had been in effect in 1936, 56 percent of the population in 1936 would have been impoverished, as compared to 12 percent today.[3] Much of this decrease in poverty is related to general affluence, the rise of gross national product per capita. Thus, median family income, in constant dollars, increased from $5,483 per year in 1947 to $10,285 in 1971.[4]

Not only has the growth of the economy raised family income, but government has had a massive role in effecting the creation of social services and in transferring income. Alfred M. Skolnik and Sophia R. Dales have presented data which dramatically illustrate the massive increase in social welfare expenditures, broadly conceived.[5] Between 1950 and 1975 total public welfare expenditures (federal, state, and local), in constant dollars, increased 485 percent, from 49 to 286 billion dollars. Education expenditures increased 299 percent, while the core Welfare areas of social insurance and public aid increased 744 percent and 451 percent respectively. (Per capita social insurance increased from 67 to 567 dollars, public aid from 34 dollars to 187 dollars.)

The figures are also dramatic for the decade 1965–75, which includes the start of new programs, such as Medicare and Medicaid (classified by Skolnik and Dales under social insurance and public aid, respectively), as well as broadened eligibility requirements and increased benefits. In constant dollars social insurance and public aid increased 154 percent and 272 percent in a decade.[6]

Moreover, there has been a clear tendency for the federal government to assume a larger role in the provision of funds. In 1950, 43 percent of social insurance was provided by the federal government; by 1975 the figure was 80 percent; in 1950, 44 percent of public aid was provided by the federal government, in 1975, 66 percent. Except in the case of education, a state and local function in the American system, most other social welfare functions have become dominated by federal funding.

Of course, one could assert that these data are deceptive because all federal expenditures were increasing at the same rate. Whoever so asserted would be wrong. Between 1965 and 1974 defense expenditures fell from 9 percent to 6 percent of GNP, while nondefense expenditures of government (all levels) rose from 20 percent of GNP in 1965 to 27 percent in 1974. Or again 53.7 percent of the federal budget in 1960 went for foreign affairs (state department, foreign aid, defense); that allotment was down to 33 percent in 1974. In 1960 22.3 percent of the federal budget went for cash income maintenance, by 1974, 31 percent.[7]

Some people look at these statistics and argue that they are misleading—"Poverty is worse, just look at our ghettos." Of course ghettos still remain, and in many ways the quality of life in urban ghettos may have worsened. But one should not confuse poverty with cultural and social disorganization as a cause of quality of life. Moreover, even if poverty is a major part of life in the ghetto, visible pockets of poverty should not be confused with the overall case. Consider the statistics on one aspect of the quality of life that many can accept: rooms per person; how many people are there in overcrowded conditions? Of course overcrowding is socially defined. What is considered overcrowding in New York is considered normal in Hong Kong. But most would agree that a decrease in the number of persons per room throughout the American population is a good index of better housing conditions.

Carnahan, Gove, and Galle have examined trends in household densities for the American population since 1940.[8] In 1940, 20 percent of the total population lived in residences with more than one person per room (Carnahan et al.'s definition of overcrowding); by 1970 the figure was down to 8 percent.[9] Even in central cities the percentage of people living in overcrowded conditions declined from 13.3 percent to 8.5 percent between 1950 and 1970. Residential congestion has diminished in the nation *and* in central cities for blacks as well as whites. In 1940, 40 percent of the black population lived in overcrowded conditions; by 1970 the figure was down to 20 percent.

So far, I have argued that there has been an increase in income (consumption standards), an increase in government social welfare expenditures, and a decline in poverty. Not only that, and contrary to the conventional wisdom, it is likely that there has been a decline in income *inequality*. If one uses the traditional measures of income inequality (either gini coefficients, which measure the extent to which, starting from the lowest unit, successive units receive less than an equal proportion of income, *or* the percentage of income or total income going to the lowest quintile), then there has been a slight decline in inequality since 1929, and also in the most recent decade.[10] But if one takes into account in the measurement of inequality the fluctuation of earnings over the life cycle (younger families and older families typically receive less income than families in the middle years), and the changing age composition of the population, the trend of income inequality has been dramatically downward.[11]

Lest you think the argument to be Pollyannaish, let me point out several items. First, important segments of our population still live in desperation, not all of it silent. There is little joy in Detroit when unemployment reaches 25 percent of the labor force and when unemployment benefits are exhausted. The impoverished state and cultural despair of the American Indian is a national disgrace. Many of our mental hospitals and prisons are not only mainly custodial; they are disasters of inhumanity.

Second, our affluence and the decline of poverty have not led to a stable happy society. Trend figures on cirrhosis of the liver (a good indicator of excessive alcoholism), divorce, violence, and mental hospital admissions over the period 1940–70 help make the point. The violent crime rate (murder, forcible rape, robbery, and aggravated assault) increased from 117 per 100,000 population to 361; mental hospital admission rates, from 140 to 330; divorce rates per 1,000 women 15 years or older, 8.8 to 13.4, and cirrhosis of the liver, from 8.6 per 100,000 deaths to 15.8.[12]

Clearly, by these indices of pathology the decline of poverty which has occurred has not turned us into a happy contented people.[13] (If the purpose of the Welfare state is to make us happier, the jury is out on the question.)

There are some lessons to be learned from this brief summary of the evolution of the welfare and Welfare state and some of its programs. First the overriding importance of the growth of economy cannot be stressed enough. The growth of the economy provides higher income; as such it aids the bureaucrat and the worker, as well as the capitalist. Second, deficit spending and inflation and economic growth fuel a large federal budget which translates into welfare spending.[14] Welfare programs tend to be explicit redistribution programs. They take money from one group and give to another. Especially in American society, our individualistic competitive values make this hard to justify. It's easier to justify incentive programs (implicit redistribution programs)—such as home mortgage interest deductions or low-tuition higher education, which in the first instance benefit the middle class and seem to be targeted at shared values—than gifts (explicit redistribution), which are "give-aways." But explicit redistribution programs meet less resistance if they are being funded out of an ever enlarging pie.[15] Third, a point I have only alluded to above but which will be expanded upon below, our provision of human services is ineffective. Fourth, pathology seems to be increasing.

Put another way, if we were to draw up a balance sheet on the human service side of the welfare state, we would find a confusing state of paradoxes: we have a vast array of treatment technologies and programs, an extraordinary range of programs for treating any imaginable social pathology. Some of these are efficient and effective. Yet the level of pathology increases; no one believes we have fully developed the range of necessary services. In other words, although we have provided a vast array of programs, demand for more seems unlimited.

## PROJECTING THE FUTURE

Now that I have touched on how we have gotten to where we are, what can we say about the future? That depends upon your assumptions and projections. First, what assumptions can be made about the growth of the economy? Can we expect renewed growth at a moderate or high level? Or is it the case over the long run, as the ecologically minded tell us, that the scarcity of resources and the negative externalities of economic activity will lead to a decrease in per capita income, or, more important, a decreasing standard of living?

Second, what are the population trends? Are we going to have a young population, an older population, a more dependent population? Or are we going to have a shift in the forms of dependency? These questions affect the shape of the Welfare state. Are we going to have increasing demands for social security pension programs, for health insurance, for child care programs? If so, how are we to finance them? With what consequences for other programs and budgets? Third, what expectations do we have about the different personal maladies and problems that require the human services side of the Welfare state? Can we expect the diminution of, say, mental illness or family problems, or are we likely to be able to solve the problems in a cheaper and more efficient way? Finally, what are the political trends relevant to the Welfare state; do they favor massive expansion, retrenchment, or steady state funding? The answers to these questions go far to predicting the future of the Welfare state.

### Demographic Components

There are three aspects of the shape of our population around the turn of the century that deserve comment: age structure, family formation, and labor force participation. Using the midpoint of current projections, our total population will grow from 209 million in 1972 to 275 million in the year 2,000.[16] At the same time projected population under twenty years old will grow from 77 to 90 million, and population over sixty-five will increase from 21 to 29 million. The population under twenty, as proportion of the total, actually will decrease 4 percent, while the percentage of the population over sixty-five will hold about steady. Stated still another way, child care and educational facilities will have to make way for an 18 percent increase (assuming current proportions of age groups continue to enroll), whereas our social security system and services for the old aged will require an increase of 38 percent. But of course, neither of these increases in sheer population is necessarily that worrisome, for the productive labor force will also have increased.

The best projections of labor force participation take us only to 1990.[17] But the trends are relatively clear. For the rest of the century adult women will increase their labor force participation. They will do this most dramatically before they have children and after children are in school. On the other hand, as early retirement programs take place, and as more people are covered by social security, there will be a decline in the percentage of men over fifty-five in the labor force. Altogether, the projections for 1990 suggest a slight rise (2 percent) in labor force participation.

Thus, by the year 2000 we will not have a very much increased ratio of social security beneficiaries to labor force participants. But, if current low birth rates stay low, whereas we now have thirty beneficiaries to 100 people in the work force, by A.D. 2030 we will have forty-five.[18] Funding social security will become problematic (though funding for education will become much less so).

Now let us turn to relevant trends in family and household formation. The general proposition is that there are increasing populations at risk—divorced and widowed women, mothers with illegitimate children, and the elderly out of the work force, and that they increasingly live in separate households.[19]

Consider female-headed households: Between 1970 and 1975 the number of female-headed households increased from 2,924,000 to 4,402,000, an increase of 50 percent. During this same period the number of husband-wife families decreased 378,000, from 25,547,-000 families to 25,169,000 families, a 1.5 percent decrease.[20] The number of children in husband-wife families declined in this period from 58,399,000 to 52,611,000. The number of children in female-headed households increased from 6,695,000 to 9,221,000. (These rate increases should not be simply projected forward on a linear base. At this rate the number of female-headed households would exceed the number of husband-wife families by the year 2000!)

Increasing separation and divorce may or may not be good for the people involved (after all, at least one party is unhappy with the marriage), but we know that it is disastrous for family income. Female-headed households have incomes roughly one-third of husband-wife families. And even where the female head is employed household income is less than 50 percent of husband-wife families.[21] Thus, in the short run the demand for humane care from the state will increase.[22] However, if birth rates remain low, by the end of the century the proportion of women at risk will be declined.

A parallel development has occurred among the elderly. We all know that three-and four-generation families have declined. For a variety of reasons, including increasing social security benefits, there has been a massive change in where the elderly live. In 1950, 2,-300,000 people over sixty-five lived in separate households. In 1970, 5,444,000 lived in separate households, outstripping the growth of elderly. Similarly, there has been a rapid increase in the number of elderly in homes for aged (from 217,000 to 804,000), and in nursing homes.[23] If these trends continue, there will be increasing demands for services for the elderly.

Divorced, widowed, or single women with or without children do not move into or stay at home with their parents. Elderly parents do not move in with their grown children, if they can help it. The general point is that a desire to live in separate households becomes part of the "taste structure" underpinning demands on the welfare state.

These are some of the sociodemographics of the welfare state. They are important components of the future. However, without knowing something about our changing readiness and ability to fund programs, to define areas of priority and need, we are not yet in a position to predict the future of the welfare state.

## The Recognition of Social Welfare Problems and Solutions

Some societal, medical, and individual problems do disappear. After years of research, infantile paralysis has vanished; the health threat to our cities caused by bad water, horse dung, and inadequate sewage has largely been eradicated. But there are perverse sociological "laws" at work that suggest the inevitability of the *pressure* to expand the Welfare state (not the actual expansion).

First, as the late Richard Titmuss taught us,[24] the increasing division of labor in modern society and the increasing differentiation of roles, status, organizations, and situations lead to new categories for concern and new areas for service.[25] As we make finer and finer distinctions among types of people and their situations, we create demands for new forms of organizations and programs. And as we recognize "pathologies," problems, and their increasing rates we find new service professions and programs contributing to the growth of the service society.[26] Contrast the range of conceivable programs today for prisoners, for example, with the range of discussed programs for prisoners in 1930. This law merges both supply and demand considerations in the growth of the Welfare state. Let us separate them.

Second, on the supply side, as professional cadres grow and differentiate they invent new programs at an exponential rate. A corollary is that professional groups never write themselves out of business. A second corollary: suppliers of social services attempt to create demand by advertising and raising standards and expectations (these corollaries parallel Galbraith's view of the mature corporation's ability to protect itself).

Third, on the demand side, as clientele become more sophisticated, they demand a wider range of services. Although sophistication is correlated with education, the proposition applies to all clientele groups. Prisoners, housing project tenants, college students, and other clients of the welfare state read and hear about what is happening on the next reservation. They then ask for services and programs which, in turn, create greater differentiation, new professions, and the like.

Finally, just as new drugs and surgical procedures and higher rates of treatment increase the number of iatrogenic disorders (disorders induced by treatments themselves), so in modern society is there a sociogenic machine—solutions (planned or unplanned) to one problem create new disorders—for example, the introduction of new technology displaces workers; new fertilizers create pollution of water; better nutrition lowers the age of fecundity and the ability to carry the fetus to birth, leading to higher rates of illegitimacy; introduction of minimum wage laws contributes to teenage unemployment.

Although the above propositions are largely true, they do oversimplify the matter. Some solutions aimed at reforming aspects of society have only marginal negative spillovers. Laws aimed at eliminating child labor have been largely successful, even though their introduction met with great resistance and they are still a source of loose ends of controversy. (Child labor laws, combined with compulsory school attendance, do create higher educational costs.) Disability insurance in relationship to work-incurred injuries has been very successful even though it still has controversial elements (and even though the negative externalities of new technologies may now be outrunning our ability to keep up with them.)

What conclusions can be drawn from these perverse laws? First, there are few "quickie" technological and legal fixes for human problems. Usually the identification of welfare problems requiring state action demands more manpower and more money. Second, although sometimes there are ways of simplifying and eliminating welfare programs the more usual course is for differentiation and expansion. Third, even where there are quickie fixes, as in relaxed abortion laws, ethical and political considerations are often deeply implicated.

Another aspect of the delivery of welfare *services* is that they tend to be labor intensive; they have a high ratio of labor to machines and capital in producing their "product." In labor-intensive industries there are few opportunities to increase productivity by technological innovation. Thus expanded demand is not met or accompanied by lower unit costs. One consequence is that, as compared to capital intensive sectors, it is more difficult for income gains to workers to be accompanied by stable prices. That is, when wages go up in capital-intensive industries increased technological productivity also occurs and wage increases do not lead to price increases. In the human services (where revenues are allocated by central fund raising agencies, public or private), any attempt to increase wages leads agencies to ask for larger budgets without delivering improved or increased services.

There are several solutions offered to the burgeoning organizational component of the welfare state. First, federalization may lead to economies of scale in operation by eliminating duplication, lowering the ratio of supervisors to employees, and so on. But lower administrative costs are not inherent in federalization, since federal wage scales tend to be higher than the states. A second solution to the growth of administrative-labor components is the use of standardized techniques in the delivery of service in the welfare state. One can offer standardized techniques in two different ways. One can deliver them through machines, or one can break out parts of the unstandardized tasks into standardized aspects, using paraprofessionals and technical aides rather than professionals. The use of paraprofessionals has been a vogue of late, and it may, in some cases, lead to cheaper unit costs. But it should be noted that more often than not it just leads to the delivery of more refined services. Does anyone believe, for instance, that the use of casework aides or teacher assistants has actually reduced the cost of service? (Of course, there are social benefits in creating such jobs, even though unit costs are not reduced.) The general point is that in those parts of the welfare state which deliver labor-intensive services, it may very well become more and more difficult to fund them.

### Economics and Politics of the Welfare State

Any projection of the future depends upon your projection of the growth of the economy and governmental revenue. Short of major political upheavals, welfare state programs aimed at providing service and money for those unable to work or pay must compete with a host of other demands for public services, from road building to defense, from fire protection to free colleges. The economic question is, will there be significant growth in the economy so that, short of large changes in taxation rates, new monies will come available for welfare programs. The political question involves changes in taxation rates and changes in willingness to fund social welfare type programs relative to other needs.

What bets are you taking for growth rates from now until the end of the century? For instance, between 1947 and 1971 family income in constant dollars almost doubled. Now that the post-Vietnam recession has ended, will the future of the economy allow for growth, decline, stagnation? Will we double income in the next twenty-five years, or not? Some say we are in for a long-term decline in gross national product as resources become scarcer, energy more expensive, and so on. Others believe that abundant coal, direct solar energy, and solar derivatives will provide us with new sources of cheaper energy, once we have harnessed them. It would appear that at least for the next decade energy costs will be a drag upon economic growth.

Nor can the supporters of an expanded welfare state count on continuing inflation to fuel it. Inflation has a complex set of relations to the welfare state. First, with income tax schedules kept at preinflation rates, inflation leads to a larger share of personal income going for taxes as wages are inflated upward. Second, if benefits are pegged to inflation, inflation leads to higher government outlays for welfare, without any expansion of programs. Third, and most important, if inflation in the United States is now below that of major international competitors and suppliers, the U.S. economy is likely to suffer increased unemployment.

A moderate prediction would be that until the end of the century growth rates will be substantially lower than they have been for the past quarter century, unemployment will be higher than it has been for the last quarter-century (though family participation rates will be higher), and returns on education will be lower. Thus, we are unlikely to see an expanded Welfare state fueled out of a burgeoning economy.

But what about taxation rates? Surely, as Harold Wilensky has recently argued,[27] we can increase the take there. It is true that the United States lags behind many western European countries such as Sweden, France, and Germany in taxation rates, but its taxation rates are ahead of many other industrialized countries such as Canada, Belgium, and Japan.[28] And if private nonvoluntary taxation is included (pension programs and medical insurance),[29] the extent to which we are a laggard in percentage of GNP devoted to social welfare is quite minimal. Moreover, even if taxation rates were increased, there is little reason to believe they would fund new welfare programs. For one thing, experts argue that to keep pace with mandated increases in annuity payments properly funded, our present social security program requires an increase from our present rate of employee and employer taxes of about 11 percent to between 16 and 20 percent.[30] Second, the long-term (1955 onward) increasing deficits of the federal government have fueled growth *and* inflation, but I believe that there will be little taste in the next decade or two for increasing the size of that deficit. Recent changes in congressional budgeting procedures will at least operate as a constraint on the social pork barrel tendencies of Congress. And, indeed, there may be pressures to use increased taxation to reduce deficits.

But let us examine the political question more directly. Is there a possibility of a revived New Deal labor coalition that will make an extension of the welfare state a central task for the next two decades? First, the interests of women, of blacks, and of poorly educated youths often clash with those of organized labor.[31] Issues of seniority and the negative effects of minimum wage laws are going to be with us for some time. Second, labor's interest in redistribution is secondary to its interest in jobs. There is little likelihood they will coalesce with blacks, Chicanos, and left-liberals to push for broad gauge redistribution programs. Third, labor's interest in jobs has recently led it to support nuclear power. So, a consumer-environment-labor coalition is unlikely.

But more profound than all this is the transformation of politics in this postindustrial, postclass, postpolitical machine era. Our political parties are not dead, but they have been weakened. Politicians have more direct relation to voters. There has been a rise in specific issue politics; there has been a professionalization of reform and a professionalization of social movements.[32] There is an enduring split between the executive and Congress, based upon their different constituencies and relations to national and local elites and interest groups. These factors combine to make a coalition across many issues increasingly unlikely.[33] All of this leads me to believe that the class politics which was the political motor of the Welfare state has become secondary. To state it another way, symbolic reform and incrementalism are likely to be the order of the day.

Finally, is there any major group in America which poses a major threat to the upper class and the structure of capitalist-corporatist society? Is there any group which is likely to command the political clout and to be organized enough to threaten systematically the stability of the state? My prediction, and it is purely a guess, is that there is no current group that so threatens the stability of the state that massive changes in the structure of services programs and distribution of income will be required.

## CONCLUSION

Predictions by social scientists are notoriously faulty. The value of this exercise lies less in the accuracy of the predictions for the future than in its aid as analysis of our present and emerging condition. Nevertheless, in way of summary, where is the Welfare state headed?

First, I think it is apparent that there will be no new large-scale redistribution program. Second, the major crisis in our Welfare program is likely to come in the area of female-headed households. If the recent trend does not soon abate we can expect an extraordinarily high level of demand for services in this area. Third, new programs will be so tailored that they minimize their explicit redistribution effect. Fourth, large and costly new programs will be trimmed so that they only affect the most desperately needy parts of the population. Fifth, labor-intensive social welfare services will find it increasingly difficult to be funded, especially since they so rarely show the benefits their initial advocates proclaim. Thus, many labor-intensive programs will be found serving the middle class who can afford them, rather than the very poor who depend upon government funding for them. Finally, in the overall priority of things, the Welfare state in western industrialized countries will be in low gear.

However, this is not a council of doom and despair; it is to say that an era has ended. The Welfare state was a major domestic political response to the emergence and growth of industrial society, and in some ways we have "socialized" the economy, without nationalization. The new political issues in this postindustrial interdependent society lead to a different focus. We enter into an age in which world interdependence and population-resource-environment problems move to center stage. We do not dismantle the Welfare state in the next twenty-five years, but we work around the edges.

## NOTES

This paper was stimulated by reading recent books by two of my teachers: Harold Wilensky, *The Welfare State and Equality: Structural and Ideological Roots of Public Expenditures* (Berkeley: University of California Press, 1975), and Morris Janowitz, *Social Control of the Welfare State* (New York: Elsevier Scientific Publishing Co., 1976). I have received critical help from Ivar Berg, Walter Gove, Jeffrey Hantover, William R. Hodge, Morris Janowitz, Shanti Kinduka, Joachim Singelmann, Gerry Suttles, David Street, and Benjamin Walter. The paper was first presented to the Middle Tennessee Chapter of the Tennessee Conference on Social Welfare in November 1975. The Vanderbilt University Research Council has provided assistance in its preparation.

1. Robert Heilbroner, "The Human Prospect," *New York Review of Books* (January 24, 1974); Daniel Bell, *The Coming of Post-industrial Society* (New York: Basic Books, 1973); Robert A. Nisbet, *Twilight of Authority* (New York: Basic Books, 1975); Samuel P. Huntington, "Post Industrial Politics: How Benign Will It Be?" *Comparative Politics* 6 (1974): 163–91.

2. It is shocking how seasoned thinkers can mistake mood for fact. Heilbroner cogently and, because he hates what he sees coming, convincingly argues for a coming authoritarian state. But his bedrock assumption leading to the logical necessity of that argument is based upon highly debatable assumptions about the tolerance of the ecosphere for heat emission. Heilbroner quotes as fact a trend for the disturbance of the ecosphere by heat emission, ignoring climatological arguments about the cooling of the earth. Others have projected a glorious view of the future based upon the coming green revolution or the use of the mineral *fruites de la mer.*

3. Stanley Lebergott, "How to Increase Poverty," *Commentary* 60 (October 1975): 59–63. The use of 1936 in Lebergott's example was unfortunate, because unemployment in the depression was close to its peak that year.

Nevertheless one could take any year before World War II and come to roughly parallel conclusions. It should be clear that Lebergott was not saying that 56 percent of the population *believed* they were impoverished. Quite the opposite, the raising of standards reflects changes in perceptions and expectations, not absolute poverty–whatever that is.

4. Murray S. Weitzman, *Family (Money) Income: Summarizing Twenty-five Years of a Summary Statistic*, Technical Paper 35 (Washington, D.C.: Social and Economic Statistics Administration, Bureau of the Census, 1974).

5. "Social Welfare Expenditures, 1950–75," *Social Security Bulletin* 39 (January 1976): 3–20.

6. For a treatment of impact of transfer programs on poverty between 1964 and 1974, see Robert D. Plotnick and Felicity Skidmore, *Progress against Poverty: A Review of the 1964–74 Decade* (New York: Academic Press, 1975).

7. These shifts in public expenditures are discussed in Samuel P. Huntington, "The Democratic Distemper," *Public Interest* 41 (Fall 1975): 9–38.

8. Douglas Carnahan, Walter Gove, and Omer R. Galle, "Urbanization, Population Density, and Overcrowding: Trends in the Quality of Life in Urban America," *Social Forces* 53 (1974): 62–72.

9. It is worth noting that the census used to report the percentage of the population living with more than 1.5 persons per room. So few Americans now live in those conditions that the tabulation has been eliminated.

10. Daniel Radner and John C. Hinrichs, "Size Distribution of Income in 1964, 1970, and 1971," *Survey of Current Business* 54(October 1974): 19–31.

11. Morton Paglin, "The Measurement and Trend of Inequality: A Basic Revision," *American Economic Review* 65 (September 1975): 598–609. As an aside let me note that economists and sociologists alike have bought an extremely simplistic view of income inequality, because, I suspect, it fitted their political bias. Think how much sophistication has gone into the measurement of status inconsistency; compare that with our use of simple statistics on income distribution without further thinking about their meaning. If Kolko and others had used simple percentages to prove that we are really getting more equal, would other left-leaning professors accept them? See Gabriel Kolko, *Wealth and Power in America: An Analysis of Social Class and Income Distribution* (New York: Praeger Publishers, 1962).

12. Carnahan et al.

13. There are several components of these changing rates: real changes in the rates, reporting and diagnostic changes leading to more inclusive counts, changes in the population at risk, etc. For instance, since blacks are now treated more equitably, violence in the black community is more fully reported. Moreover, it is not clear whether some of the statistics imply trends or cycles. Phillips Cutright asserts flatly that the increasing divorce rate reflects demographic and economic patterns that have a cyclical base and are not to be taken as long-term trends. Finally, you may not consider some of these rates indicators of pathology: Is divorce pathological? No matter how you evaluate divorce, it *is* important to recognize that female-headed households are more likely to be poor than ones with husbands in them. Walter Gove and I are attempting to isolate the components of these and other indicators of pathology. On cyclical and secular trend factors in divorce and illegitimacy, see Phillips Cutright, "Illegitimacy and Income Supplements," pp. 90–138 in Studies in Public Welfare, paper no. 12, pt. 1, *The Family, Poverty and Welfare Programs: Factors Influencing Family Instability*, prepared for the subcommittee on Fiscal Policy, Joint Economic

Committee (Washington, D.C.: Government Printing Office, November 1973); Phillips Cutright and John Scanzoni, "Income Supplements and the American Family," pp. 54–89, ibid.; and Richard Easterlin, "Relative Economic Status and the American Fertility Swings," *Social Structure, Family Life Styles, and Economic Behavior,* ed. E. Sheldon (Philadelphia: J. B. Lippincott Co., 1972).

14. See Janowitz.

15. Wilensky, pp. 59–61, convincingly argues that the form or type of taxation system has effects upon the willingness of a population to accept welfare programs.

16. *Statistical Abstract of the United States* (Washington, D.C.: Government Printing Office, 1974).

17. Dennis Johnston, "The U.S. Labor Force: Projections to 1990," *Monthly Labor Review* 96 (July 1973):3–13.

18. Quadrennial Advisory Committee Report on Social Security, report to Committee on Ways and Means, House of Representatives, 1975.

19. See Cutright and Scanzoni.

20. "Children of Working Mothers, March 1975," Special Labor Force report, Bureau of Labor Statistics, August 1975.

21. *Ibid.*

22. An important set of issues, beyond the scope of this paper, is the turnover and composition problem. In the past most divorced women remarried. While the number of female-headed households has increased, we do not know much about the length of time that female-headed households remain in that state. Furthermore, since the increase in female-headed households is occurring among more well-educated women, they may fare better in the job market.

23. *American Families: Trends and Pressures, 1973.* Sub Committee on Children and Youth of the Committee on Labor and Public Welfare, United States Senate, 93d Congress (Washington, D.C.: Government Printing Office, 1974).

24. Richard M. Titmuss, "The Social Division of Welfare: Some Reflection on the Search for Equity," in *Essays on the Welfare State* (London: George Allen & Unwin, 1959).

25. See also Mayer N. Zald, "The Structure of Society and Social Service Integration," *Social Science Quarterly* 50, no. 3 (December 1969): 557–67.

26. Mayer N. Zald and John D. McCarthy, "Organizational Intellectuals and the Criticism of Society," *Social Service Review* 49, no. 3 (September 1975): 344–62. On the transformation of the labor force in industrialized societies, see Joachim Singelmann, "The Sectoral Transformation of the Labor Force in Seven Industrialized Countries, 1920–1960" (doctoral diss., University of Texas, 1974).

27. Harold L. Wilensky, "The Welfare Mess," *Society* 13, no. 4 (May/June 1976): 12–16.

28. Richard Musgrave, *Fiscal Systems,* Studies in Comparative Economics, no. 10 (New Haven, Conn.: Yale University Press, 1969).

29. The issue of whether public programs would be better than private ones in these areas is beyond the scope of this paper.

30. Quadrennial Advisory Committee (n. 18 above).

31. One task of the next two decades may be the reformulation of policy for the interrelations of youth, education, and the economy. As returns to education stabilize or decline, as unemployment among youth in the labor

force remains high, a diverse set of policy options will be required. These include new job placement services, a national youth service, an even greater use of short courses, and easy entry training programs.

32. See Kevin P. Phillips, *Mediacracy: American Parties and Politics in the Communication Age* (Garden City, N.J.: Doubleday & Co., 1975), and the review of Phillips by Michael Malbin, *Commentary* 60 (July 1975): 88–90. Also, see Huntington, "Post-industrial Politics" (n. 4 above), and John McCarthy and Mayer N. Zald, *The Trend of Social Movements in America: Resource Mobilization and Professionalization* (Morristown, N.J.: General Learning Press, 1973).

33. See Janowitz.

*Part II*

# SOCIOLOGICAL CRITIQUE

# Chapter Four

# SOCIOLOGICAL CRITIQUE

In the world of practical affairs both the institutional development of social welfare and professional practices in social work are influenced by political and economic forces. The world of ideas as a source of influence is related to but somewhat removed from the practical pressures of daily operations. While developments in social welfare and social work are immediately sensitive to political and economic forces, they are also responsive to the world of ideas—an intellectual force manifest in what we have referred to as sociological critique. As an intellectual force sociological critique provokes thought and stimulates insight into problems of individual and institutional functioning. The concrete impact of sociological critique on a program area will vary, depending upon the merit of the analysis and the characteristics of the political decision-making system. Occasionally, those engaged in sociological critique attempt to connect their ideas to practice and become activists working to implement new arrangements in social welfare and social work. However, as a professional activity, sociological critique is distinct from social work practice and is conducted outside of social welfare institutions, usually in academic settings.

The focus of sociological critique is wider in scope than social planning needs-assessment studies and program evaluations. Sociological critique comments upon broad issues in society that are seen as problematic for institutional functioning and individual well-being. One well-known example of this genre is Michael Harrington's book, *The Other America.* [1] Writing in the early 1960s, Harrington produced a grim report about poverty in America and a vivid analysis of the bitterness of life under these conditions. His work was an indictment of the "affluent society" which sparked the national conscience; it also inspired a proliferation of literature on the characteristics, effects, and conditions of poverty. [2] As for the impact of Harrington's work on program developments in social welfare, Arthur M. Schlesinger, Jr., noted that President John F. Kennedy read *The Other America* and, in Schlesinger's opinion, this "helped crystallize" Kennedy's determination in 1963 to initiate an antipoverty program. [3] Later, when the War on Poverty was implemented under President Lyndon Johnson, Harrington's advice was sought, and he served as a consultant to the federal government during the early stages of the program's development.

In his work Harrington describes the extent of poverty in America and analyzes why the poor have gone relatively unnoticed. His theoretical explanation for the cause of poverty is a popular version of the "culture of poverty," the idea that the poor are trapped in a self-perpetuating cycle of deprivations that is transmitted from one generation to the next.

Harrington's view represents one theme of the culture-of-poverty idea, and this idea represents one among several theoretical perspectives on the causes of poverty. Other explanations of poverty are based upon theories that focus on different major independent variables, such as material, personal, or institutional factors. [4] These theoretical perspectives are utilized in the development of diverse programs to attack the causes and consequences of poverty. Each of these theoretical perspectives has some degree of validity, and each is embedded in one or another action program that seeks and often competes with others for political, economic, and social support.

Another notable example of sociological critique is offered by Richard Cloward in the first selection in this chapter, "Illegitimate Means, Anomie, and Deviant Behavior" (Reading 10). Cloward sets forth the basic framework of the famous opportunity-structure theory of juvenile delinquency, which was fully developed by Cloward and Lloyd Ohlin in *Delinquency and Opportunity.* [5] Cloward's article integrates two major theoretical perspectives on deviant behavior around the idea of differential opportunity structures. According to this thesis the likelihood of deviant behavior increases when an individual's opportunities to achieve culturally prescribed goals through normal, legitimate institutional channels are restricted and he also has ready access to environments that teach the use of illegitimate means.

Opportunity-structure theory had a forceful impact on the development of social reform programs in the 1960s. The theoretical foundations of Mobilization for Youth, one of the first of a wave of federally funded social welfare programs in the 1960s, rested squarely on the propositions of differential opportunity structure. Cloward, who was one of the major architects of Mobilization for Youth, became the director of research when the program was implemented. His theoretical influence is clearly expressed in the program's proposal:

> . . .We believe that delinquency and conformity generally result from the same social conditions. Efforts to conform, to live up to social expectations, often result in profound strain and frustration because the opportunities for conformity are not always available. This frustration may lead in turn to behavior which violates social rules. In this way delinquency and conformity can arise from the same features of social life: unsuccessful attempts to be what one is supposed to be may lead to aberrant behavior, since the very act of reaching out for socially approved goals under conditions that preclude their legitimate achievement engenders strain.
>
> In summary it is our belief that much delinquent behavior is engendered because opportunities for conformity are limited. Delinquency therefore represents not a lack of motivation to conform but quite the opposite: the desire to meet social expectations itself becomes the source of delinquent behavior if the possibility of doing so is limited or nonexistent.
>
> The importance of these assumptions in framing the large scale program which is proposed here cannot be overemphasized.[6]

Satire as a mode of sociological critique which contrasts with the formal theorizing described above is the approach of Reading 11, "How Community Mental Health Stamped Out the Riots (1968–1978)" by Kenneth Keniston. This article deals with a familiar theme in the history of social welfare—the potential for the expression of oppressive social controls in measures ostensibly concerned with social rehabilitation. Examining this repressive potential in the context of the community mental health movement, Keniston warns that "mental illness" is a label that might be used for political purposes in publicly sponsored programs. The danger, as he sees it, is that the label "mental illness," because of its fuzzy nature, can easily be applied to all forms of individual and group behavior that inconveniences established institutions and is socially disapproved.[7]

From one perspective the Keniston article may be viewed as a caution against public efforts that either inadvertently or by design bring pressures on individuals and groups to conform to a single set of normatively prescribed attitudes, beliefs, and behaviors, leading ultimately to the cultural homogenization of American society. Cultural pluralism is a cherished value which is strongly supported by the voluntary sector of social welfare. Yet this value strains against other equally important values pertaining to the achievement of harmonious intergroup relations and the elimination of ethnic and racial prejudice. Social welfare programs are also engaged in furthering these aims.

There is a substantial literature of sociological critique on the tensions between cultural pluralism and social integration and the role of government in their mitigation. Milton Gordon's study of assimilation in American life is among the significant works in this area.[8] In this book Gordon draws a careful distinction between processes of desegregation and integration. In his view the proper role of government is "to effect desegregation—that is, to eliminate racial criteria —in the operation of all its facilities and services at all levels, national, state, and local." Gordon does not believe that government should attempt to impose integration through the "positive" use of racial criteria or the creation of quotas in programs under its jurisdiction. As he observes:

> To bring racial criteria in by the front door, so to speak, even before throwing them out the back, represents, in my opinion, no real gain for the body politic and has potentially dangerous implications for the future. If racial criteria are legitimate criteria (which I firmly argue they are not), then the way is left open for many ominous disputes as to the merits of any particular racial clause in government operations.[9]

We might note that Gordon's insightful analysis on this issue has had little impact on policy developments.[10] Over the past decade, government policies have increasingly emphasized the positive use of racial criteria in public and private programs and, as Gordon anticipates, a rise in racial and ethnic group consciousness, along with heightened intergroup tensions, has followed in the wake of these policies.

In Reading 12, "The Limits of Social Policy," Nathan Glazer develops a classic line of sociological critique. A central theme here involves the "dilemma of the helping hand." That is, while the mutual support functions of social welfare provide immediate compensations for the breakdown of traditional institutions for meeting human needs (as discussed in Chapter 2), in the long run welfare arrangements may operate to further undermine these institutions. As Glazer puts it: "Our efforts to deal with distress themselves increase distress." This, of course, is a disturbing thesis to those engaged in furthering social welfare objectives. It is also a thesis that has been expressed in various forms since the poor laws first went into effect.

The general influence of this idea on program developments is clearly revealed in the comments made by President Richard Nixon concerning his reasons for vetoing the Child Development Act of 1971, which proposed a universal network of child care centers providing infant care, comprehensive preschool programs, evening care, emergency care, and the like. In the veto message Nixon stressed that "Good public policy requires that we enhance rather than diminish both parental authority and parental involvement with children, particularly in those decisive early years when social attitudes and a conscience are formed, and religious and moral principles are first inculcated."[11]

These arguments suggest that social welfare policy should be designed to support traditional values—it should strengthen family life and provide incentives to work and independence. However, these goals are easier to advocate than to accomplish. In the final selection in this Chapter, "Families, Sex and the Liberal Agenda," (Reading 13) Allan Carlson probes some of the basic reasons for the growing instability in family life since the 1960s. He raises challenging questions about the ability to modify this trend through public intervention. As Carlson's lively analysis suggests, the extent to which social welfare programs can improve the human condition will continue to be a major topic of sociological critique as the institution of social welfare becomes more firmly embedded in the structure of modern society.

## NOTES

1. Michael Harrington, *The Other America* (New York: Macmillan Co., 1962).

2. The outpouring of literature on poverty that followed in the wake of *The Other America* is attested to by the fact that within four years of Harrington's work, at least six major anthologies were produced: two under the title of "Poverty in America," two examining "Poverty in (Amid) Affluence," one declaring "Poverty as a Public Issue," and one offering "New Perspectives on Poverty."

3. Arthur M. Schlesinger, Jr., *A Thousand Days* (Boston: Houghton Mifflin Co., 1965), p. 1010.

4. Martin Rein, "Social Science and the Elimination of Poverty," *Journal of the American Institute of Planners,* 33 (May 1967): 417–45.

5. Richard A. Cloward and Lloyd E. Ohlin, *Delinquency and Opportunity* (Glencoe, Ill.: Free Press, 1955).

6. Mobilization for Youth, Inc., *A Proposal for the Prevention and Control of Delinquency by Expanding Opportunities* (New York, 1961), pp. 44–45.

7. Keniston is not alone in criticizing the community mental health movement as a potential design to limit individual freedom in the publicly

sponsored name of "health." For other influential writings on this issue see
Thomas Szasz, *The Myth of Mental Illness* (New York: Hoeber-Harper,
1961) and "The Mental Health Ethic," *National Review*, 57 (June 14, 1966).

8. Milton Gordon, *Assimilation in American Life: The Role of Race,
Religion and National Origins* (New York: Oxford University Press, 1964).

9. *Ibid.*, p. 248.

10. For additional comments on this issue see Macklin Fleming and Pincus Pollack, "The Black Quota at Yale Law School: An Exchange of Letters,"
*Public Interest*, Spring 1970, pp. 44–52; and Neil Gilbert and Joseph Eaton,
"Favoritism as a Strategy in Race Relations," *Social Problems*, Summer
1970, pp. 38–52.

11. *New York Times*, December 12, 1971, p. 4.

# 10   Illegitimate Means, Anomie, and Deviant Behavior

## RICHARD A. CLOWARD

This paper[1] represents an attempt to consolidate two major sociological traditions of thought about the problem of deviant behavior.
The first, exemplified by the work of Émile Durkheim and Robert K.
Merton, may be called the anomie tradition.[2] The second, illustrated
principally by the studies of Clifford R. Shaw, Henry D. McKay, and
Edwin H. Sutherland, may be called the "cultural transmission" and
"differential association" tradition.[3] Despite some reciprocal borrow-
ing of ideas, these intellectual traditions developed more or less
independently. By seeking to consolidate them, a more adequate
theory of deviant behavior may be constructed.

### DIFFERENTIALS IN AVAILABILITY OF LEGITIMATE MEANS:
### THE THEORY OF ANOMIE

The theory of anomie has undergone two major phases of development. Durkheim first used the concept to explain deviant behavior.
He focused on the way in which various social conditions lead to
"overweening ambition," and how, in turn, unlimited aspirations
ultimately produce a breakdown in regulatory norms. Robert K.
Merton has systematized and extended the theory, directing attention to patterns of disjunction between culturally prescribed goals

Reprinted from *American Sociological Review*, 24 (April 1959): 164–76, by permission of the American Sociological Association and the author.

and socially organized access to them by *legitimate* means. In this paper, a third phase is outlined. An additional variable is incorporated in the developing scheme of anomie, namely, the concept of *differentials in access to success-goals by illegitimate means.* [4]

## Phase I: Unlimited Aspirations and the Breakdown of Regulatory Norms

In Durkheim's work, a basic distinction is made between "physical needs" and "moral needs." The importance of this distinction was heightened for Durkheim because he viewed physical needs as being regulated automatically by features of man's organic structure. Nothing in the organic structure, however, is capable of regulating social desires; as Durkheim put it, man's "capacity for feeling is in itself an insatiable and bottomless abyss."[5] If man is to function without "friction," "the passions must first be limited. . . . But since the individual has no way of limiting them, this must be done by some force exterior to him." Durkheim viewed the collective order as the external regulating force which defined and ordered the goals to which men should orient their behavior. If the collective order is disrupted or disturbed, however, men's aspirations may then rise, exceeding all possibilities of fulfillment. Under these conditions, "de-regulation or anomy" ensues: "At the very moment when traditional rules have lost their authority, the richer prize offered these appetites stimulates them and makes them more exigent and impatient of control. The state of de-regulation or anomy is thus further heightened by passions being less disciplined precisely when they need more disciplining." Finally, pressures toward deviant behavior were said to develop when man's aspirations no longer matched the possibilities of fulfillment.

Durkheim therefore turned to the question of *when* the regulatory functions of the collective order break down. Several such states were identified, including sudden depression, sudden prosperity, and rapid technological change. His object was to show how, under these conditions, men are led to aspire to goals extremely difficult if not impossible to attain. As Durkheim saw it, sudden depression results in deviant behavior because "something like a declassification occurs which suddenly casts certain individuals into a lower state than their previous one. Then they must reduce their requirements, restrain their needs, learn greater self-control. . . . But society cannot adjust them instantaneously to this new life and teach them to practice the increased self-repression to which they are unaccustomed. So they are not adjusted to the condition forced on them, and its very prospect is intolerable; hence the suffering which detaches them from a reduced existence even before they have made trial of it."

Prosperity, according to Durkheim, could have much the same effect as depression, particularly if upward changes in economic conditions are abrupt. The very abruptness of these changes presumably heightens aspirations beyond possibility of fulfillment, and this too puts a strain on the regulatory apparatus of the society.

According to Durkheim, "the sphere of trade and industry . . . is actually in a chronic state [of anomie]." Rapid technological developments and the existence of vast, unexploited markets excite the imagination with the seemingly limitless possibilities for the accumulation of wealth. As Durkheim said of the producer of goods, "now that he may assume to have almost the entire world as his customer, how could passions accept their former confinement in the face of such limitless prospects?" Continuing, Durkheim states that "such is the source of excitement predominating in this part of society. . . . Here the state of crisis and anomie [are] constant and, so to speak, normal. From top to bottom of the ladder, greed is aroused without knowing where to find ultimate foothold. Nothing can calm it, since its goal is far beyond all it can attain."

In developing the theory, Durkheim characterized goals in the industrial society, and specified the way in which unlimited aspirations are induced. He spoke of "dispositions . . . so inbred that society has grown to accept them and is accustomed to think them normal," and he portrayed these "inbred dispositions": "It is everlastingly repeated that it is man's nature to be eternally dissatisfied, constantly to advance, without relief or rest, toward an indefinite goal. The longing for infinity is daily represented as a mark of moral distinction. . . ." And it was precisely these pressures to strive for "infinite" or "receding" goals, in Durkheim's view, that generate a breakdown in regulatory norms, for "when there is no other aim but to outstrip constantly the point arrived at, how painful to be thrown back!"

**Phase II: Disjunction Between Cultural Goals and Socially Structured Opportunity**

Durkheim's description of the emergence of "overweening ambition" and the subsequent breakdown of regulatory norms constitutes one of the links between his work and the later development of the theory by Robert K. Merton. In his classic essay, "Social Structure and Anomie," Merton suggests that goals and norms may vary independently of each other, and that this sometimes leads to malintegrated states. In his view, two polar types of disjunction may occur: "There may develop a very heavy, at times a virtually exclusive, stress upon the value of particular goals, involving comparatively little concern with the institutionally prescribed means of striving toward these goals. . . . This constitutes one type of malintegrated culture."[6] On

the other hand, "A second polar type is found where activities originally conceived as instrumental are transmuted into self-contained
practices, lacking further objectives. . . . Sheer conformity becomes
a central value." Merton notes that "between these extreme types
are societies which maintain a rough balance between emphases
upon cultural goals and institutionalized practices, and these constitute the integrated and relatively stable, though changing societies."

Having identified patterns of disjunction between goals and
norms, Merton is enabled to define anomie more precisely: "Anomie
[may be] conceived as a breakdown in the cultural structure, occurring particularly when there is an acute disjunction between cultural
norms and goals and the socially structured capacities of members of
the group to act in accord with them."

Of the two kinds of malintegrated societies, Merton is primarily
interested in the one in which "there is an exceptionally strong
emphasis upon specific goals without a corresponding emphasis upon
institutional procedures." He states that attenuation between goals
and norms, leading to anomie or "normlessness," comes about because men in such societies internalize an emphasis on common
success-goals under conditions of varying access to them. The essence of this hypothesis is captured in the following excerpt: "It is
only when a system of cultural values extols, virtually above all else,
certain *common* success-goals for the population at large while the
social structure rigorously restricts or completely closes access to
approved modes of reaching these goals for a considerable part of
*the same population*, that deviant behavior ensues on a large scale."
The focus, in short, is on the way in which the social structure puts
a strain upon the cultural structure. Here one may point to diverse
structural differentials in access to culturally approved goals by legitimate means, for example, differentials of age, sex, ethnic status, and
social class. Pressures for anomie or normlessness vary from one
social position to another, depending on the nature of these differentials.

In summary, Merton extends the theory of anomie in two principal
ways. He explicitly identifies types of anomic or malintegrated societies by focusing upon the relationship between cultural goals and
norms. And, by directing attention to patterned differentials in the
access to success-goals by legitimate means, he shows how the social
structure exerts a strain upon the cultural structure, leading in turn
to anomie or normlessness.

## Phase III: The Concept of Illegitimate Means

Once processes generating differentials in pressures are identified,
there is then the question of how these pressures are resolved, or how

men respond to them. In this connection, Merton enumerates five basic categories of behavior or role adaptations which are likely to emerge: conformity, innovation, ritualism, retreatism, and rebellion. These adaptations differ depending on the individual's acceptance or rejection of cultural goals, and depending on his adherence to or violation of institutional norms. Furthermore, Merton sees the distribution of these adaptations principally as the consequence of two variables: the relative extent of pressure, and values, particularly "internalized prohibitions," governing the use of various illegitimate means.

It is a familiar sociological idea that values serve to order the choices of deviant (as well as conforming) adaptations which develop under conditions of stress. Comparative studies of ethnic groups, for example, have shown that some tend to engage in distinctive forms of deviance; thus Jews exhibit low rates of alcoholism and alcoholic psychoses.[7] Various investigators have suggested that the emphasis on rationality, fear of expressing aggression, and other alleged components of the "Jewish" value system constrain modes of deviance which involve "loss of control" over behavior.[8] In contrast, the Irish show a much higher rate of alcoholic deviance because, it has been argued, their cultural emphasis on masculinity encourages the excessive use of alcohol under conditions of strain.[9]

Merton suggests that differing rates of ritualistic and innovating behavior in the middle and lower classes result from differential emphases in socialization. The "rule-oriented" accent in middle-class socialization presumably disposes persons to handle stress by engaging in ritualistic rather than innovating behavior. The lower-class person, contrastingly, having internalized less stringent norms, can violate conventions with less guilt and anxiety.[10] Values, in other words, exercise a canalizing influence, limiting the choice of deviant adaptations for persons variously distributed throughout the social system.

Apart from both socially patterned pressures, which give rise to deviance, and from values, which determine choices of adaptations, a further variable should be taken into account: namely, *differentials in availability of illegitimate means.* For example, the notion that innovating behavior may result from unfulfilled aspirations and imperfect socialization with respect to conventional norms implies that illegitimate means are freely available—as if the individual, having decided that "you can't make it legitimately," then simply turns to illegitimate means which are readily at hand whatever his position in the social structure. However, these means may not be available. As noted above, the anomie theory assumes that conventional means are differentially distributed, that some individuals, because of their social position, enjoy certain advantages which are denied to others.

Note, for example, variations in the degree to which members of various classes are fully exposed to and thus acquire the values, education, and skills which facilitate upward mobility. It should not be startling, therefore, to find similar variations in the availability of illegitimate means.

Several sociologists have alluded to such variations without explicitly incorporating this variable in a theory of deviant behavior. Sutherland, for example, writes that "an inclination to steal is not a sufficient explanation of the genesis of the professional thief."[11] Moreover, "the person must be appreciated by the professional thieves. He must be appraised as having an adequate equipment of wits, front, talking-ability, honesty, reliability, nerve and determination." In short, "a person can be a professional thief only if he is recognized and received as such by other professional thieves." But recognition is not freely accorded: "Selection and tutelage are the two necessary elements in the process of acquiring recognition as a professional thief. . . . A person cannot acquire recognition as a professional thief until he has had tutelage in professional theft, *and tutelage is given only to a few persons selected from the total population.*" Furthermore, the aspirant is judged by high standards of performance, for only "a very small percentage of those who start on this process ever reach the stage of professional theft." The burden of these remarks—dealing with the processes of selection, induction, and assumption of full status in the criminal group—is that motivations or pressures toward deviance do not fully account for deviant behavior. The "self-made" thief—lacking knowledge of the ways of securing immunity from prosecution and similar techniques of defense—"would quickly land in prison." Sutherland is in effect pointing to differentials in access to the role of professional thief. Although the criteria of selection are not altogether clear from his analysis, definite evaluative standards do appear to exist; depending on their content, certain categories of individuals would be placed at a disadvantage and others would be favored.

The availability of illegitimate means, then, is controlled by various criteria in the same manner that has long been ascribed to conventional means. Both systems of opportunity are (1) limited, rather than infinitely available, and (2) differentially available depending on the location of persons in the social structure.

When we employ the term "means," whether legitimate or illegitimate, at least two things are implied: first, that there are appropriate learning environments for the acquisition of the values and skills associated with the performance of a particular role; and second, that the individual has opportunities to discharge the role once he has been prepared. The term subsumes, therefore, both *learning structures and opportunity structures.*

A case in point is recruitment and preparation for careers in the rackets. There are fertile criminal learning environments for the young in neighborhoods where the rackets flourish as stable, indigenous institutions. Because these environments afford integration of offenders of different ages, the young are exposed to "differential associations" which facilitate the acquisition of criminal values and skills. Yet preparation for the role may not insure that the individual will ever discharge it. For one thing, more youngsters may be recruited into these patterns of differential association than can possibly be absorbed, following their "training," by the adult criminal structure. There may be a surplus of contenders for these elite positions, leading in turn to the necessity for criteria and mechanisms of selection. Hence a certain proportion of those who aspire may not be permitted to engage in the behavior for which they have been prepared.

This illustration is similar in every respect, save for the route followed, to the case of those who seek careers in the sphere of legitimate business. Here, again, is the initial problem of securing access to appropriate learning environments, such as colleges and postgraduate schools of business. Having acquired the values and skills needed for a business career, graduates then face the problem of whether or not they can successfully discharge the roles for which they have been prepared. Formal training itself is not sufficient for occupational success, for many forces intervene to determine who shall succeed and fail in the competitive world of business and industry—as throughout the entire conventional occupational structure.

This distinction between learning structures and opportunity structures was suggested some years ago by Sutherland. In 1944, he circulated an unpublished paper which briefly discusses the proposition that "criminal behavior is partially a function of opportunities to commit specific classes of crimes, such as embezzlement, bank burglary, or illicit heterosexual intercourse."[12] He did not, however, take up the problem of differentials in opportunity as a concept to be systematically incorporated in a theory of deviant behavior. Instead, he held that "opportunity" is a necessary but not sufficient explanation of the commission of criminal acts, "since some persons who have opportunities to embezzle, become intoxicated, engage in illicit heterosexual intercourse or to commit other crimes do not do so." He also noted that the differential association theory did not constitute a full explanation of criminal activity, for, notwithstanding differential association, "it is axiomatic that persons who commit a specific crime must have the opportunity to commit that crime." He therefore concluded that "while opportunity may be partially a function of association with criminal patterns and of the specialized techniques thus acquired, *it is not determined entirely in that manner,* and consequently differential association is not the sufficient cause of criminal behavior." (emphasis not in original)

In Sutherland's statements, two meanings are attributed to the term "opportunity." As suggested above, it may be useful to separate these for analytical purposes. In the first sense, Sutherland appears to be saying that opportunity consists in part of learning structures. The principal components of his theory of differential association are that "criminal behavior is learned," and, furthermore, that "criminal behavior is learned in interaction with other persons in a process of communication." But he also uses the term to describe situations conducive to carrying out criminal roles. Thus, for Sutherland, the commission of a criminal act would seem to depend upon the existence of two conditions: differential associations favoring the acquisition of criminal values and skills, and conditions encouraging participation in criminal activity.

This distinction heightens the importance of identifying and questioning the common assumption that illegitimate means are freely available. We can now ask (1) whether there are socially structured differentials in access to illegitimate learning environments, and (2) whether there are differentials limiting the fulfillment of illegitimate roles. If differentials exist and can be identified, we may then inquire about their consequences for the behavior of persons in different parts of the social structure. Before pursuing this question, however, we turn to a fuller discussion of the theoretical tradition established by Shaw, McKay, and Sutherland.

## DIFFERENTIALS IN AVAILABILITY OF ILLEGITIMATE MEANS: THE SUBCULTURE TRADITION

The concept of differentials in availability of illegitimate means is implicit in one of the major streams of American criminological theory. In this tradition, attention is focused on the processes by which persons are recruited into criminal learning environments and ultimately inducted into criminal roles. The problems here are to account for the acquisition of criminal roles and to describe the social organization of criminal activities. When the theoretical propositions contained in this tradition are reanalyzed, it becomes clear that one underlying conception is that of variations in access to success-goals by illegitimate means. Furthermore, this implicit concept may be shown to be one of the bases upon which the tradition was constructed.

In their studies of the ecology of deviant behavior in the urban environment, Shaw and McKay found that delinquency and crime tended to be confined to delimited areas and, furthermore, that such behavior persisted despite demographic changes in these areas. Hence they came to speak of "criminal tradition," of the "cultural transmission" of criminal values.[13] As a result of their observations of slum life, they concluded that *particular importance must be assigned to the integration of different age-levels of offenders.* Thus:

> Stealing in the neighborhood was a common practice among the children and approved by the parents. Whenever the boys got together they talked about robbing and made more plans for stealing. I hardly knew any boys who did not go robbing. The little fellows went in for petty stealing, breaking into freight cars, and stealing junk. The older guys did big jobs like stick-up, burglary, and stealing autos. The little fellows admired the "big shots" and longed for the day when they could get into the big racket. Fellows who had "done time" were the big shots and looked up to and gave the little fellows tips on how to get by and pull off big jobs.[14]

In other words, access to criminal roles depends upon stable associations with others from whom the necessary values and skills may be learned. Shaw and McKay were describing deviant learning structures—that is, alternative routes by which people seek access to the goals which society holds to be worthwhile. They might also have pointed out that, in areas where such learning structures are unavailable, it is probably difficult for many individuals to secure access to stable criminal careers, even though motivated to do so.[15]

The concept of illegitimate means and the socially structured conditions of access to them were not explicitly recognized in the work of Shaw and McKay because, probably, they were disposed to view slum areas as "disorganized." Although they consistently referred to illegitimate activities as being organized, they nevertheless often depicted high-rate delinquency areas as disorganized because the values transmitted were criminal rather than conventional. Hence their work includes statements which we now perceive to be internally inconsistent, such as the following:

> This community situation [in which Sidney was reared] was not only disorganized and thus ineffective as a unit of control, but it was characterized by a high rate of juvenile delinquency and adult crime, not to mention the widespread political corruption which had long existed in the area. Various forms of stealing and many organized delinquent and criminal gangs were prevalent in the area. These groups exercised a powerful influence and tended to create a community spirit which not only tolerated but actually fostered delinquent and criminal practices.[16]

Sutherland was among the first to perceive that the concept of social disorganization tended to obscure the stable patterns of interaction among carriers of criminal values. Like Shaw and McKay, he had been influenced by the observation that lower-class areas were organized in terms of both conventional and criminal values, but he was also impressed that these alternative value systems were supported by patterned systems of social relations. He expressly recognized that crime, far from being a random, unorganized activity, was typically an intricate and stable system of human arrangements. He therefore rejected the concept of "social disorganization" and substituted the concept of "differential group organization."

> The third concept, social disorganization, was borrowed from Shaw and McKay. I had used it but had not been satisfied with it because the organization of the delinquent group, which is often very complex, is social disorganization only from an ethical or some other particularistic point of view. At the suggestion of Albert K. Cohen, this concept has been changed to differential group organization, with organization for criminal activities on one side and organization against criminal activities on the other.[17]

Having freed observation of the urban slum from conventional evaluations, Sutherland was able to focus more clearly on the way in which its social structure constitutes a "learning environment" for the acquisition of deviant values and skills. In the development of the theory of "differential association" and "differential group organization," he came close to stating explicitly the concept of differentials in access to illegitimate means. But Sutherland was essentially interested in learning processes, and thus he did not ask how such access varies in different parts of the social structure, nor did he inquire about the consequences for behavior of variations in the accessibility of these means.[18]

William F. Whyte, in his classic study of an urban slum, advanced the empirical description of the structure and organization of illegitimate means a step beyond that of Sutherland. Like Sutherland, Whyte rejected the earlier view of the slum as disorganized:

> It is customary for the sociologist to study the slum district in terms of "social disorganization" and to neglect to see that an area such as Cornerville has a complex and well-established organization of its own. . . . I found that in every group there was a hierarchical structure of social relations binding the individuals to one another and that the groups were also related hierarchically to one another. Where the group was formally organized into a political club, this was immediately apparent, but for informal groups it was no less true.[19]

Whyte's contribution to our understanding of the organization of illegitimate means in the slum consists primarily in showing that

individuals who participate in stable illicit enterprise do not constitute a separate or isolated segment of the community. Rather, these
persons are closely integrated with the occupants of conventional
roles. In describing the relationship between racketeers and politicians, for example, he notes that "the rackets and political organizations extend from the bottom to the top of Cornerville society, mesh
with one another, and integrate a large part of the life of the district.
They provide a general framework for the understanding of the
actions of both 'little guys' and 'big shots.' "[20] Whyte's view of the
slum differs somewhat from that conveyed by the term "differential
group organization." He does not emphasize the idea that the slum
is composed of two different systems, conventional and deviant, but
rather the way in which the occupants of these various roles are
integrated in a single, stable structure which organizes and patterns
the life of the community.

The description of the organization of illegitimate means in slums
is further developed by Solomon Kobrin in his article, "The Conflict
of Values in Delinquency Areas."[21] Kobrin suggests that urban slum
areas vary in the degree to which the carriers of deviant and conventional values are integrated with one another. Hence he points the
way to the development of a "typology of delinquency areas based
on variations in the relationship between these two systems," depict-
ing the "polar types" on such a continuum. The first type resembles
the integrated areas described in preceding paragraphs. Here, claims
Kobrin, there is not merely structural integration between carriers
of the two value systems, but reciprocal participation by each in the
value system of the other. Thus:

> Leaders of [illegal] enterprises frequently maintain membership in such
> conventional institutions of their local communities as churches, fraternal
> and mutual benefit societies and political parties. ... Within this frame-
> work the influence of each of the two value systems is reciprocal, the
> leaders of illegal enterprise participating in the primary orientation of
> the conventional elements in the population, and the latter, through
> their participation in a local power structure sustained in large part
> by illicit activity, participating perforce in the alternate, criminal value
> system.

Kobrin also notes that in some urban slums there is a tendency for
the relationships between carriers of deviant and conventional values to break down. Such areas constitute the second polar type.
Because of disorganizing forces such as "drastic changes in the class,
ethnic, or racial characteristics of its population," Kobrin suggests
that "the bearers of the conventional culture and its value system are
without the customary institutional machinery and therefore in

effect partially demobilized with reference to the diffusion of their value system." At the same time, the criminal "value system remains implicit" since this type of area is "characterized principally by the absence of systematic and organized adult activity in violation of the law, despite the fact that many adults in these areas commit violations." Since both value systems remain implicit, the possibilities for effective integration are precluded.

The importance of these observations may be seen if we ask how accessibility of illegal means varies with the relative integration of conventional and criminal values from one type of area to another. In this connection, Kobrin points out that the "integrated" area apparently constitutes a "training ground" for the acquisition of criminal values and skill.

> The stable position of illicit enterprise in the adult society of the community is reflected in the character of delinquent conduct on the part of children. While delinquency in all high rate areas is intrinsically disorderly in that it is unrelated to official programs for the education of the young, in the [integrated community] boys may more or less realistically recognize the potentialities for personal progress in local society through access to delinquency. In a general way, therefore, delinquent activity in these areas constitutes a training ground for the acquisition of skill in the use of violence, concealment of offense, evasion of detection and arrest, and the purchase of immunity from punishment. Those who come to excel in these respects are frequently noted and valued by adult leaders in the rackets who are confronted, as are the leaders of all income-producing enterprises, with problems of the recruitment of competent personnel.

With respect to the contrasting or "unintegrated area," Kobrin makes no mention of the extent to which learning structures and opportunities for criminal careers are available. Yet his portrayal of such areas as lacking in the articulation of either conventional or criminal values suggests that the appropriate learning structures—principally the integration of offenders of different age levels—are not available. Furthermore, his depiction of adult violative activity as "unorganized" suggests that the illegal opportunity structure is severely limited. Even if youngsters were able to secure adequate preparation for criminal roles, the problem would appear to be that the social structure of such neighborhoods provides few opportunities for stable, criminal careers. For Kobrin's analysis—as well as those of Whyte and others before him—leads to the conclusion that illegal opportunity structures tend to emerge in lower-class areas only when stable patterns of accommodation and integration arise between the carriers of conventional and deviant values. Where these values remain unorganized and implicit, or where their carri-

ers are in open conflict, opportunities for stable criminal role performance are more or less limited.[22]

Other factors may be cited which affect access to criminal roles.
For example, there is a good deal of anecdotal evidence which reveals that access to the upper echelons of organized racketeering is
controlled, at least in part, by ethnicity. Some ethnic groups are
found disproportionately in the upper ranks and others disproportionately in the lower. From an historical perspective, as Bell has
shown, this realm has been successively dominated by Irish, East-
European Jews, and more recently, by Italians.[23] Various other ethnic groups have been virtually excluded or at least relegated to
lower-echelon positions. Despite the fact that many rackets (especially "policy") have flourished in predominantly Negro neighborhoods, there have been but one or two Negroes who have been
known to rise to the top in syndicated crime. As in the conventional
world, Negroes are relegated to the more menial tasks. Moreover,
access to elite positions in the rackets may be governed in part by
kinship criteria, for various accounts of blood relations among top
racketeers indicate that nepotism is the general rule.[24] It has also
been noted that kinship criteria sometimes govern access to stable
criminal roles, as in the case of the pickpocket.[25] And there are, of
course, deep-rooted sex differentials in access to illegal means. Although women are often employed in criminal vocations—for example, thievery, confidence games, and extortion—and must be
employed in others—such as prostitution—nevertheless females are
excluded from many criminal activities.[26]

Of the various criteria governing access to illegitimate means, class
differentials may be among the most important. The differentials
noted in the preceding paragraph—age, sex, ethnicity, kinship, and
the like—all pertain to criminal activity historically associated with
the lower class. Most middle- or upper-class persons—even when
interested in following "lower-class" criminal careers—would no
doubt have difficulty in fulfilling this ambition because of inappropriate preparation. The prerequisite attitudes and skills are more easily
acquired if the individual is a member of the lower class; most mid-
dle- and upper-class persons could not easily unlearn their own class
culture in order to learn a new one. By the same token, access to
many "white collar" criminal roles is closed to lower-class persons.
Some occupations afford abundant opportunities to engage in illegitimate activity; others offer virtually none. The businessman, for example, not only has at his disposal the means to do so, but, as some
studies have shown, he is under persistent pressure to employ illegitimate means, if only to maintain a competitive advantage in the
market place. But for those in many other occupations, white collar
modes of criminal activity are simply not an alternative.[27]

## SOME IMPLICATIONS OF A CONSOLIDATED APPROACH
## TO DEVIANT BEHAVIOR

It is now possible to consolidate the two sociological traditions described above. Our analysis makes it clear that these traditions are oriented to different aspects of the same problem: differentials in access to opportunity. One tradition focuses on legitimate opportunity, the other on illegitimate. By incorporating the concept of differentials in access to *illegitimate* means, the theory of anomie may be extended to include seemingly unrelated studies and theories of deviant behavior which form a part of the literature of American criminology. In this final section, we try to show how a consolidated approach might advance the understanding of both rates and types of deviant conduct. The discussion centers on the conditions of access to both systems of means, legitimate and illegitimate.

### The Distribution of Criminal Behavior

One problem which has plagued the criminologist is the absence of adequate data on social differentials in criminal activity. Many have held that the highest crime rates are to be found in the lower social strata. Others have suggested that rates in the middle and upper classes may be much higher than is ordinarily thought. The question of the social distribution of crime remains problematic.

In the absence of adequate data, the theorist has sometimes attacked this problem by assessing the extent of pressures toward normative departures in various parts of the social structure. For example, Merton remarks that his "primary aim is to discover how some social structures exert a definite pressure upon certain persons in the society to engage in non-conforming rather than conforming conduct."[28] Having identified structural features which might be expected to generate deviance, Merton suggests the presence of a correlation between "pressures toward deviation" and "rate of deviance."

> But whatever the differential rates of behavior in the several social strata, and we know from many sources that the official crime statistics uniformly showing higher rates in the lower strata are far from complete or reliable, it *appears from our analysis that the greater pressures toward deviation are exerted upon the lower strata....* Of those located in the lower reaches of the social structure, the culture makes incompatible demands. On the one hand they are asked to orient their behavior toward the prospect of large wealth ... and on the other, they are largely denied

effective opportunities to do so institutionally. *The consequence of this structural inconsistency is a high rate of deviant behavior.*[29]

Because of the paucity and unreliability of existing criminal statistics, there is as yet no way of knowing whether or not Merton's hypothesis is correct. Until comparative studies of crime rates are available the hypothesized correlation cannot be tested.

From a theoretical perspective, however, questions may be raised about this correlation. Would we expect, to raise the principal query, the correlation to be fixed or to vary depending on the distribution of access to illegitimate means? The three possibilities are (1) that access is distributed uniformly throughout the class structure, (2) that access varies inversely with class position, and (3) that access varies directly with class position. Specification of these possibilities permits a more precise statement of the conditions under which crime rates would be expected to vary.

If access to illegitimate means is *uniformly distributed* throughout the class structure, then the proposed correlation would probably hold—higher rates of innovating behavior would be expected in the lower class than elsewhere. Lower-class persons apparently experience greater pressures toward deviance and are less restrained by internalized prohibitions from employing illegitimate means. Assuming uniform access to such means, it would therefore be reasonable to predict higher rates of innovating behavior in the lower social strata.

If access to illegitimate means varies inversely with class position, then the correlation would not only hold, but might even be strengthened. For pressures toward deviance, including socialization that does not altogether discourage the use of illegitimate means, would coincide with the availability of such means.

Finally, if access varies *directly* with class position, comparative rates of illegitimate activity become difficult to forecast. The higher the class position, the less the pressure to employ illegitimate means; furthermore, internalized prohibitions are apparently more effective in higher positions. If, at the same time, opportunities to use illegitimate methods are more abundant, then these factors would be in opposition. Until the precise effects of these several variables can be more adequately measured, rates cannot be safely forecast.

The concept of differentials in availability of illegitimate means may also help to clarify questions about varying crime rates among ethnic, age, religious, and sex groups, and other social divisions. This concept, then, can be systematically employed in the effort to further our understanding of the distribution of illegitimate behavior in the social structure.

## Modes of Adaptation: The Case of Retreatism

By taking into account the conditions of access to legitimate *and* illegitimate means, we can further specify the circumstances under which various modes of deviant behavior arise. This may be illustrated by the case of retreatism.[30]

As defined by Merton, retreatist adaptations include such categories of behavior as alcoholism, drug addiction, and psychotic withdrawal. These adaptations entail "escape" from the frustrations of unfulfilled aspirations by withdrawal from conventional social relationships. The processes leading to retreatism are described by Merton as follows: "[Retreatism] arises from continued failure to near the goal by legitimate measures and from an inability to use the illegitimate route because of internalized prohibitions, *this process occurring while the supreme value of the success-goal has not yet been renounced.* The conflict is resolved by abandoning both precipitating elements, the goals and means. The escape is complete, the conflict is eliminated and the individual is asocialized."[31]

In this view, a crucial element encouraging retreatism is internalized constraint concerning the use of illegitimate means. But this element need not be present. Merton apparently assumed that such prohibitions are essential because, in their absence, the logic of his scheme would compel him to predict that innovating behavior would result. But the assumption that the individual uninhibited in the use of illegitimate means becomes an innovator presupposes that successful innovation is only a matter of motivation. Once the concept of differentials in access to illegitimate means is introduced, however, it becomes clear that retreatism is possible even in the absence of internalized prohibitions. For we may now ask how individuals respond when they fail in the use of *both* legitimate and illegitimate means. If illegitimate means are unavailable, if efforts at innovation fail, then retreatist adaptations may still be the consequence, and the "escape" mechanisms chosen by the defeated individual may perhaps be all the more deviant because of his "double failure."

This does not mean that retreatist adaptations cannot arise precisely as Merton suggests: namely, that the conversion from conformity to retreatism takes place in one step, without intervening adaptations. But this is only one route to retreatism. The conversion may at times entail intervening stages and intervening adaptations, particularly of an innovating type. This possibility helps to account for the fact that certain categories of individuals cited as retreatists —for example, hobos—often show extensive histories of arrests and convictions for various illegal acts. It also helps to explain retreatist adaptations among individuals who have not necessarily internalized strong restraints on the use of illegitimate means. In short, retreatist adaptations may arise with considerable frequency among those who are failures in both worlds, conventional and illegitimate alike.[32]

Future research on retreatist behavior might well examine the interval between conformity and retreatism. To what extent does the individual entertain the possibility of resorting to illegitimate means, and to what extent does he actually seek to mobilize such means? If the individual turns to innovating devices, the question of whether or not he becomes a retreatist may then depend upon the relative accessibility of illegitimate means. For although the frustrated conformist seeks a solution to status discontent by adopting such methods, there is the further problem of whether or not he possesses appropriate skills and has opportunities for their use. We suggest therefore that data be gathered on preliminary responses to status discontent—and on the individual's perceptions of the efficacy of employing illegitimate means, the content of his skills, and the objective situation of illegitimate opportunity available to him.

Respecification of the processes leading to retreatism may also help to resolve difficulties entailed in ascertaining rates of retreatism in different parts of the social structure. Although Merton does not indicate explicitly where this adaptation might be expected to arise, he specifies some of the social conditions which encourage high rates of retreatism. Thus the latter is apt to mark the behavior of downwardly mobile persons, who experience a sudden breakdown in established social relations, and such individuals as the retired, who have lost major social roles.[33]

The long-standing difficulties in forecasting differential rates of retreatism may perhaps be attributed to the assumption that retreatists have fully internalized values prohibiting the use of illegitimate means. That this prohibition especially characterizes socialization in the middle and upper classes probably calls for the prediction that retreatism occurs primarily in those classes—and that the hobohemias, "drug cultures," and the ranks of the alcoholics are populated primarily by individuals from the upper reaches of society. It would appear from various accounts of hobohemia and skid row, however, that many of these persons are the products of slum life, and, furthermore, that their behavior is not necessarily controlled by values which preclude resort to illegitimate means. But once it is recognized that retreatism may arise in response to limitations on both systems of means, the difficulty of locating this adaptation is lessened, if not resolved. Thus retreatist behavior may vary with the particular process by which it is generated. The process described by Merton may be somewhat more characteristic of higher positions in the social structure where rule-oriented socialization is typical, while

in the lower strata retreatism may tend more often to be the consequence of unsuccessful attempts at innovation.

## SUMMARY

This paper attempts to identify and to define the concept of differential opportunity structures. It has been suggested that this concept
helps to extend the developing theory of social structure and anomie.
Furthermore, by linking propositions regarding the accessibility of
*both* legitimate and illegitimate opportunity structures, a basis is
provided for consolidating various major traditions of sociological
thought on nonconformity. The concept of differential systems of
opportunity and of variations in access to them, it is hoped, will
suggest new possibilities for research on the relationship between
social structure and deviant behavior.

## NOTES

1. This paper is based on research conducted in a penal setting. For a
more detailed statement see Richard A. Cloward, *Social Control and Anomie: A Study of a Prison Community* (to be published by The Free Press).
   2. See especially Émile Durkheim, *Suicide*, translated by J. A. Spaulding
and George Simpson, Glencoe, Ill.: Free Press, 1951; and Robert K. Merton,
*Social Theory and Social Structure*, Glencoe, Ill.: Free Press, 1957, Chapters
4 and 5.
   3. See especially the following: Clifford R. Shaw, *The Jack-Roller,*
Chicago: The University of Chicago Press, 1930; Clifford R. Shaw, *The Natural History of a Delinquent Career*, Chicago: The University of Chicago
Press, 1941; Clifford R. Shaw et al., *Delinquency Areas,* Chicago: The University of Chicago Press, 1940; Clifford R. Shaw and Henry D. McKay, *Juvenile Delinquency and Urban Areas*, Chicago: The University of Chicago
Press, 1942; Edwin H. Sutherland, editor, *The Professional Thief*, Chicago:
The University of Chicago Press, 1937; Edwin H. Sutherland, *Principles of
Criminology*, 4th edition, Philadelphia: Lippincott, 1947; Edwin H. Sutherland, *White Collar Crime,* New York: Dryden, 1949.
   4. "Illegitimate means" are those proscribed by the mores. The concept
therefore includes "illegal means" as a special case but is not coterminous
with illegal behavior, which refers only to the violation of legal norms. In
several parts of this paper, I refer to particular forms of deviant behavior
which entail violation of the law and there use the more restricted term,
"illegal means." But the more general concept of illegitimate means is
needed to cover the wider gamut of deviant behavior and to relate the
theories under review here to the evolving theory of "legitimacy" in sociology.
   5. All of the excerpts in this section are from Durkheim, *op. cit.,* pp.
247–57.
   6. For this excerpt and those which follow immediately, see Merton, *op.
cit.,* pp. 131–94.
   7. See, e.g., Seldon D. Bacon, "Social Settings Conducive to Alcoholism

—A Sociological Approach to a Medical Problem," *Journal of the American Medical Association*, 16 (May, 1957), pp. 177–81; Robert F. Bales, "Cultural Differences in Rates of Alcoholism," *Quarterly Journal of Studies on Alcohol*, 16 (March, 1946), pp. 480–99; Jerome H. Skolnick, "A Study of the Relation of Ethnic Background to Arrests for Inebriety," *Quarterly Journal of Studies on Alcohol*, 15 (December, 1954), pp. 451–74.

8. See Isidor T. Thorner, "Ascetic Protestantism and Alcoholism," *Psychiatry*, 16 (May, 1953), pp. 167–76; and Nathan Glazer, "Why Jews Stay Sober," *Commentary*, 13 (February, 1952), pp. 181–86.

9. See Bales, *op. cit.*

10. Merton, *op. cit.*, p. 151.

11. For this excerpt and those which follow immediately, see Sutherland, *The Professional Thief*, pp. 211–13.

12. For this excerpt and those which follow immediately, see Albert Cohen, Alfred Lindesmith and Karl Schuessler, editors, *The Sutherland Papers*, Bloomington: Indiana University Press, 1956, pp. 31–35.

13. See especially *Delinquency Areas*, Chapter 16.

14. Shaw, *The Jack-Roller*, p. 54.

15. We are referring here, and throughout the paper, to stable criminal roles to which persons may orient themselves on a career basis, as in the case of racketeers, professional thieves, and the like. The point is that access to stable roles depends in the first instance upon the availability of learning structures. As Frank Tannenbaum says, "it must be insisted on that unless there were older criminals in the neighborhood who provided a moral judgment in favor of the delinquent and to whom the delinquents could look for commendation, the careers of the younger ones could not develop at all." *Crime and the Community*, New York: Ginn, 1938, p. 60.

16. Shaw, *The Natural History of a Delinquent Career*, p. 229.

17. Cohen, Lindesmith and Schuessler, *op. cit.*, p. 21.

18. It is interesting to note that the concept of differentials in access to *legitimate* means did not attain explicit recognition in Sutherland's work, nor in the work of many others in the "subculture" tradition. This attests to the independent development of the two traditions being discussed. Thus the ninth proposition in the differential association theory is stated as follows:

(9) *Though criminal behavior is an expression of general needs and values, it is not explained by those general needs and values since noncriminal behavior is an expression of the same needs and values.* Thieves generally steal in order to secure money, but likewise honest laborers work in order to secure money. The attempts by many scholars to explain criminal behavior by general drives and values, such as the happiness principle, striving for social status, the money motive, or frustration, have been and must continue to be futile since they explain lawful behavior as completely as they explain criminal behavior.

Of course, it is perfectly true that "striving for status," the "money motive" and similar modes of socially approved goal-oriented behavior do not as such account for both deviant and conformist behavior. But if goal-oriented behavior occurs under conditions of socially structured obstacles to fulfillment by legitimate means, the resulting pressures might then lead to deviance. In other words, Sutherland appears to assume that the distribution of access to success-goals by legitimate means is uniform rather than variable, irrespective of location in the social structure. See his *Principles of Criminology*, 4th edition, pp. 7–8.

19. William F. Whyte, *Street Corner Society* (original edition, 1943). Chicago: The University of Chicago Press, 1955, p. viii.

20. *Ibid.,* p. xviii.

21. *American Sociological Review,* 16 (October, 1951), pp. 657–58, which includes the excerpts which follow immediately.

22. The excellent work by Albert K. Cohen has been omitted from this discussion because it is dealt with in a second article, "Types of Delinquent Subcultures," prepared jointly with Lloyd E. Ohlin (mimeographed, December, 1958, New York School of Social Work, Columbia University). It may be noted that although Cohen does not explicitly affirm continuity with either the Durkheim-Merton or the Shaw-McKay-Sutherland traditions, we believe that he clearly belongs in the former. He does not deal with what appears to be the essence of the Shaw-McKay-Sutherland tradition, namely, the crucial social functions performed by the integration of offenders of differing age-levels and the integration of adult carriers of criminal and conventional values. Rather, he is concerned primarily with the way in which discrepancies between status aspirations and possibilities for achievement generate pressures for delinquent behavior. The latter notion is a central feature in the anomie tradition.

23. Daniel Bell, "Crime as an American Way of Life," *The Antioch Review* (Summer, 1953), pp. 131–54.

24. For a discussion of kinship relationships among top racketeers, see Stanley Frank, "The Rap Gangsters Fear Most," *The Saturday Evening Post* (August 9, 1958), pp. 26 ff. This article is based on a review of the files of the United States Immigration and Naturalization Service.

25. See David W. Maurer, *Whiz Mob: A Correlation of the Technical Argot of Pickpockets with Their Behavior Pattern,* publication of the American Dialect Society, No. 24, 1955.

26. For a discussion of racial, nationality, and sex differentials governing access to a stable criminal role, see *ibid.,* Chapter 6.

27. Training in conventional, specialized occupational skills is often a prerequisite for the commission of white collar crimes, since the individual must have these skills in hand before he can secure a position entailing "trust." As Cressey says, "it may be observed that persons trained to carry on the routine duties of a position of trust have at the same time been trained in whatever skills are necessary for the violation of that position, and the technical skill necessary to holding the position in the first place." (Donald R. Cressey, *Other People's Money,* Glencoe, Ill.: Free Press, 1953, pp. 81–82.) Thus skills required in certain crimes need not be learned in association with criminals; they can be acquired through conventional learning.

28. Merton, *op. cit.,* p. 132.

29. *Ibid.,* pp. 144–45.

30. Retreatist behavior is but one of many types of deviant adaptations which might be re-analyzed in terms of this consolidated theoretical approach. In subsequent papers, being prepared jointly with Lloyd E. Ohlin, other cases of deviant behavior—e.g., collective disturbances in prisons and subcultural adaptations among juvenile delinquents—will be examined. In this connection, see footnote 22.

31. Merton, *op. cit.,* pp. 153–54.

32. The processes of "double failure" being specified here may be of value in re-analyzing the correlation between alcoholism and petty crime. Investigation of the careers of petty criminals who are alcoholic may reveal that after being actively oriented toward stable criminal careers they then lost out in the competitive struggle. See, e.g., Irwin Deutscher, "The Petty Offender: A Sociological Alien," *The Journal of Criminal Law, Criminology*

*and Police Science,* 44 (January-February, 1954), pp. 592–95; Albert D. Ull-man *et al.,* "Some Social Characteristics of Misdemeanants," *The Journal of Criminal Law, Criminology and Police Science,* 48 (May-June, 1957), pp. 44–53.

33. Merton, *op. cit.,* pp. 188–89.

# 11   How Community Mental Health Stamped Out the Riots (1968–78)

## KENNETH KENISTON

*One day, after I gave a lecture in a course on social and community psychiatry, a student asked me whether I thought community men-tal-health workers would eventually be asked to assume policing functions. I assured him that I thought this very unlikely, and thought no more about it.*

*That night I had the following dream: I was sitting on the plat-form of a large auditorium. In the audience were thousands of men and women, some in business clothes, others in peculiar blue and white uniforms that seemed a cross between medical and military garb. I glanced at the others on the platform: Many wore military uniforms. Especially prominent was a tall, distinguished, lantern-jawed general, whose chest was covered with battle ribbons and on whose arm was a blue and white band.*

*The lights dimmed; I was pushed to my feet and toward the podium. Before me on the lectern was a neatly-typed manuscript. Not knowing what else to do, I found myself beginning to read from it. . . .*

Ladies and Gentlemen: It is a pleasure to open this Eighth Annual Meeting of the Community Mental Health Organization, and to wel-come our distinguished guests: the recently-appointed Secretary for International Mental Health, General Westmoreland [loud ap-plause], and the Secretary for Internal Mental Health, General Walt [applause].

This year marks the tenth anniversary of the report of the First National Advisory Commission on Civil Disorders. And this meeting of representatives of 3483 Community Mental Health Centers, 247

Published by permission of Trans-action, Inc. from Trans-action, Vol. 5, No. 8.

Remote Therapy Centers, and 45 Mobile Treatment Teams may provide a fitting occasion for us to review the strides we have made in the past decade, and to contemplate the greater tasks that lie before us. For it was in the past decade, after all, that the Community Mental Health movement proved its ability to deal with the problem of urban violence, and it is in the next decade that the same approaches must be adapted to the other urgent mental-health problems of our society and the world.

In my remarks here, I will begin with a review of the progress of the past decade. Arbitrarily, I will divide the years since 1968 into three stages: the phase of preparation; the phase of total mobilization; and the mop-up phase that we are now concluding.

In retrospect, the years from 1968 to 1970 can be seen as the time of preparation for the massive interventions that have since been made. On the one hand, the nation was faced with mounting urban unrest, especially among disadvantaged sectors of the inner city, unrest that culminated in the riots of 1969 and 1970, in which property damage of more than 20 billion dollars was wrought, and in which more than 5000 individuals (including 27 policemen, National Guardsmen, and firemen) were killed. Yet in retrospect, the seeds of "Operation Inner City" were being developed even during this period. As early as 1969, the Cannon Report—a joint product of Community Mental Health workers and responsible leaders of the white and black communities—suggested that (1) the propensity to violence was but a symptom of underlying social and psychological pathology; (2) massive federal efforts must be made to identify the individual and societal dysfunctions that produce indiscriminate protest, and (3) more effective methods must be developed for treating the personal and group disorganization that produces unrest.

From 1968 to 1970, a series of research studies and demonstration projects developed the basic concepts that were implemented in later years. Indeed, without this prior theoretical work by interdisciplinary teams of community psychiatrists, sociologists, social workers, and police officials, Operation Inner City would never have been possible. I need recall only a few of the major contributions: the concept of "aggressive alienation," used to characterize the psychosocial disturbance of a large percentage of inner-city dwellers; McFarland's seminal work on urban disorganization, personal pathology, and aggressive demonstrations; the development, on a pilot basis, of new treatment systems like the "total saturation approach," based upon the concept of "antidotal (total) therapy"; and the recognition of the importance of the "reacculturation experience" in treating those whose personal pathology took the form of violence-proneness. Equally basic theoretical contributions were made by those who began to investigate the relationship between aggressiveness, alienation, and anti-societal behavior in other disturbed sections of the population, such as disacculturated intellectuals and students.

After the riots of 1969, rising public indignation over the senseless slaughter of thousands of Americans and the wanton destruction of property led President Humphrey to create the Third Presidential Task Force on Civil Disorders. After six months of almost continuous study, Task Force Chairman Ronald Reagan recommended that massive federal intervention, via the Community Mental Health Centers, be the major instrument in action against violence. Portions of this report still bear quoting: "The experience of the past five years has shown that punitive and repressive intervention aggravates rather than ameliorates the violence of the inner city. It is now amply clear that urban violence is more than sheer criminality. The time has come for America to heed the findings of a generation of research: *inner-city violence is a product of profound personal and social pathology. It requires treatment rather than punishment, rehabilitation rather than imprisonment."*

The report went on: "The Community Mental Health movement provides the best available weapon in the struggle against community sickness in urban America. The existence of 967 Community Mental Health Centers (largely located in communities with high urban density), the concentration of professional and para-professional mental-health workers in these institutions, and their close contact with the mood and hopes of their inner-city catchment areas all indicate that community mental health should be the first line of attack on urban unrest."

In the next months, an incensed Congress, backed by an outraged nation, passed the first of the series of major bills that led to the creation of Operation Inner City, under the joint auspices of the Department of Health, Education, and Welfare and what was then still called the Department of Defense. Despite the heavy drains on the national economy made by American involvement in Ecuador, Eastern Nigeria, and Pakistan, five billion dollars were appropriated the first year, with steadily increasing amounts thereafter.

As the concept of urban pathology gained acceptance, police officials referred those detained during urban riots not to jails but to local Community Mental Health Centers. Viewing urban violence as a psycho-social crisis made possible the application of concepts of "crisis therapy" to the violence-ridden inner-city dweller. As predicted, early researchers found very high levels of psychopathology in those referred for treatment, especially in the form of aggravated aggressive-alienation syndrome.

But it was obviously not enough to treat violence only in its acute phase. Pre-critical intervention and preventive rehabilitation were also necessary. So city law-enforcement officials and mental-health workers began cooperating in efforts to identify those people whose behavior, group-membership patterns, and utterances gave evidence of the prodrome (early symptoms) of aggressive alienation. New statutes passed by Congress in 1971 empowered mental-health teams and local authorities to require therapy of those identified as prodromally violent. In defending this bill in Congress against the congressional group that opposed it on civil-libertarian grounds, Senator Murphy of California noted the widespread acceptance of the principle of compulsory inoculation, mandatory treatment for narcotics addicts, and hospitalization of the psychotic. "Urban violence," he noted, "is no different from any other illness: The welfare of those afflicted requires that the public accept responsibility for their prompt and effective treatment."

Mental-health workers, with legal power to institute therapy, and in collaboration with responsible political and law-enforcement authorities, were finally able to implement the Total Saturation Approach in the years from 1972 to the present. Employing local citizens as "pathology detectors," Community Mental Health teams made massive efforts to detect all groups and individuals with prodromes of violence, or a predisposition to advocate violence. In many communities, the incidence of prepathological conditions was almost perfectly correlated with racial origin; hence, massive resources were funneled into these communities in particular to immediately detect and help those afflicted.

At this point, it became evident that programs attempting to treat inner-city patients still remaining in the same disorganized social environment that had originally contributed to their pathology were not entirely successful. It was only in 1971, with Rutherford, Cohen, and Robinson's now classic study, "Relapse Rates in Seven Saturation Projects: a Multi-Variate Analysis," that it was finally realized that short-term, total-push therapies were not effective in the long run. As the authors pointed out, "The re-entry of the cured patient into the pathogenic disacculturating community clearly reverses *all* the therapeutic gains of the inpatient phase."

Armed with the Rutherford study, Congress in 1972 passed a third legislative landmark, the Remote Therapy Center Act. Congress—recognizing that prolonged reacculturative experience in a psychologically healthy community (antidotal therapy) was often necessary for the permanent recompensation of deep-rooted personality disorders—authorized the construction of 247 centers, largely in the Rocky Mountain Region, each with a capacity of 1000 patients. The old Department of Defense (now the Department of International Mental Health) cooperated by making available the sites used in World War II for the relocation of Japanese-Americans. On these salubrious sites, the network of Remote Treatment Centers has now been constructed. Although the stringent security arrangements necessary in such centers have been criticized, the retreats now constitute one of our most effective attacks upon the problem of urban mental illness.

The gradual reduction in urban violence, starting in 1973, cannot be attributed to any single factor. But perhaps one idea played the decisive role. During this period mental-health workers began to realize that earlier approaches, which attempted to ameliorate the objective, physical, or legal conditions under which inner-city dwellers lived, were not only superficial, but were themselves a reflection of serious psychopathology. Reilly, Bernitsky, and O'Leary's now classic study of ex-patients of the retreats established the correlation between a patient's relapse into violence and his preoccupation with what the investigators termed "objectivist" issues: housing, sanitation, legal rights, jobs, education, medical care, and so on.

Two generations ago Freud taught us that what matters most is not objective reality, but the way it is interpreted by the individual. Freud's insight has finally been perceived in its true light—as an attitude essential for healthy functioning. The fact that previous programs of civil rights, slum clearance, legal reforms, and so on, succeeded only in aggravating violence now became fully understandable. Not only did these programs fail to take account of the importance of basic attitudes and values in determining human behavior—thus treating symptoms rather than underlying psychological problems—but, by encouraging objectivism, they directly *undermined* the mental health of those exposed to these programs. Today's mental-health workers recognize objectivism as a prime symptom of individual and community dysfunction, and move swiftly and effectively to institute therapy.

The final step in the development of a community mental-health approach to violence came with the development of the Mobile Treatment ("Motreat") Team. In 1972 the Community Mental Health authorities set up a series of 45 Motreat Teams, organized on a regional basis and consisting of between 500 and 1000 carefully selected and trained Community Mental Health workers. These heroic groups, wearing their now familiar blue and white garb, were ready on a standby basis to move into areas where violence threatened. Given high mobility by the use of armed helicopters, trained in crisis intervention and emergency treatment, and skilled in the use of modern psychopharmacological sprays and gases, the Motreat Teams have now proved their effectiveness. On numerous occasions during the past years, they have been able to calm an agitated population, to pinpoint the antisocial-violence leaders and refer them for therapy, and thus to lay the basis for society's prompt return to healthy functioning. The architects of the Mobile Treatment Team found that many of their most important insights were obtained from professionals in the field of law enforcement and national defense—more evidence of the importance of interdisciplinary cooperation.

As you all know, the past four years have been years of diminishing urban violence, years when the Community Mental Health movement has received growing acclaim for its success in dealing with social and individual pathology, years when the early criticism of the Community Mental Health movement by the "liberal coalition" in Congress has diminished, largely because of the non-reelection of the members of that coalition. Today the Community Mental Health movement has the virtually undivided support of the nation, regardless of political partisanship. The original federal target of 2800 Community Mental Health Centers has been increased to more than 5000; the principles of Community Mental Health have been extended from the limited "catchment area" concept to the more relevant concept of "target groups" and beyond; and the Community Mental Health movement faces enormous new challenges.

But before considering the challenges that lie ahead, let us review what we have learned theoretically during the past decade.

Doubtless the most important insight was the awareness that *violence and antisocial behavior are deeply rooted in individual and social pathology,* and must be treated as such. We have at last been able to apply the insights of writers, historians, sociologists, and psychologists of the 1950s and 1960s to a new understanding of black character. The black American—blighted by the deep scars and legacies of his history, demoralized by what Stanley Elkins described as the concentration-camp conditions of slavery, devitalized by the primitive, impulse ridden, and fatherless black families so brilliantly described by Daniel Moynihan—is the helpless victim of a series of deep deprivations that almost inevitably lead to intra-psychic and societal pathology. Moreover, we have begun to understand the communicational networks and group-pathological processes that spread alienation and violence from individual to individual, and that make the adolescent especially prone to succumb to the aggressive-alienation syndrome. To be sure, this view was contradicted by the report that many of the advocates of violence—the leaders of the now outlawed blackpower group and its precursors, S.N.C.C. and C.O.R.E. —came from relatively nondeprived backgrounds. But later researchers have shown that the virus of aggressive alienation is communicated even within apparently intact families. As Rosenbaum and Murphy put it in a recent review paper, "We have learned that social pathology is no less infectious than the black plague."

Another major theoretical contribution has come from our *redefinition of the concept of community.* As the first Community Mental

Health Centers were set up, "community" was defined as a geo-graphically limited catchment area often heterogeneous in social class, ethnicity, and race. But the events of the last decade have made it amply clear that we cannot conceive of the community so nar-rowly. The artificial boundaries of the catchment area do not prevent the transmission of social pathology across these boundaries; indeed, efforts to prevent personal mobility and communication between catchment areas proved difficult to implement without an anxiety-provoking degree of coercion. It became clear that cutting across catchment areas were certain pathogenic "target groups" in which the bacillus of social pathology was most infectious. Recognition of the target-group concept of community was the theoretical basis for much recent legislation. Rarely have the findings of the behavioral sciences been translated so promptly into enlightened legislation [applause].

This recognition of the too-narrow definition of "community" led to the creation of the Remote Treatment Centers. True, removing the mentally ill from the violence-prone target groups has not solved the problem completely. But the creation of total therapeutic com-munities in distant parts of the country has had a salubrious and calming effect on the mental health of the groups the patients came from.

It has also become clear that Community Mental Health efforts aimed solely at the disadvantaged are, by their very nature, limited in effectiveness. The suppression of pathology in one group may paradoxically be related to its sudden emergence in others. Stated differently, pathology moves through the entire community, al-though it tends to be concentrated during any given period in cer-tain target groups. The international events of the past decade, the appearance of comparable psychopathology in Ecuador, Eastern Ni-geria, Pakistan, Thailand, and a variety of other countries, raise the question of whether it is possible to have mental health in one coun-try alone.

Another crucial theoretical advance has been the concept of *total therapy*. Patients and groups must be treated *before* symptoms become acute, because the infectiousness of social pathology in-creases during the acute phase. What has been termed the "pathol-ogy multiplier effect" has been widely recognized: This means that it is essential to prevent the formation of pathologically-interacting groups, especially when organized around societally disruptive ob-jectivist issues like black power, civil rights, or improvement in living conditions. Furthermore, crisis intervention must be supplemented by *prolonged aftercare*, particularly for those whose involvement in violence has been most intense. Of the many post-rehabilitation fol-lowup methods attempted, two of the most effective have been the incorporation of rehabilitated patients into mental-health teams working in localities other than their own, and the new programs of aftercare involving the continuing rehabilitation of discharged patients in such challenging areas as Ecuador, Eastern Nigeria, and Pakistan. You are all familiar with the many glowing tributes to this aftercare program recently released by International Mental Health Secretary Westmoreland [applause].

The past decade has also demonstrated beyond doubt the importance of *inter-agency and inter-disciplinary collaboration.* The effectiveness of such collaboration has shown how unfounded were the concerns of the First Joint Commission on Mental Health over inadequate manpower. In large measure because of better and better relationships between mental-health workers, law-enforcement agencies, local civic authorities, the Department of International Mental Health, the National Guard, the Air Force, and other community agencies, radically new patterns of recruitment into the mental-health professions have been established. Indeed, in many communities effective mental-health efforts have permitted a major reduction in the size of law-enforcement authorities, and the training of a whole new group of para-professionals and sub-professionals who, a decade ago, would have entered law-enforcement agencies.

But lest we become complacent about our accomplishments, let me remind you of the many theoretical problems, difficulties, and challenges that lie before us.

Our program has not been without its critics and detractors, and there is much to be learned from them. To be sure, many of the early criticisms of our work can now be understood either as the result of inadequate understanding of the behavioral sciences, or as symptoms of the objectivist social-pathological process itself. In the years before the liberal coalition became moribund, many so-called civil-libertarian critics persisted in ignoring the humanitarian aspects of our program, focusing instead upon the 19th-century concept of civil rights. The political ineffectuality of this group, coupled with the speed with which many of its leaders have recently been reacculturated, suggests the limitations of this viewpoint.

But even within our own midst we have had critics and detractors. We are all familiar with the unhappy story of the American Psychoanalytic Association, which continued its criticisms of our programs until its compulsory incorporation last year into the Community Mental Health Organization. What we must learn from these critics is how easy it is for even the most apparently dedicated mental-health workers to lose sight of broader societal goals, neglecting the population and the societal matrix in a misguided attachment to outmoded concepts of individuality, "reality factors," and "insight therapy."

In my remarks so far, I have emphasized our theoretical and practical progress. But those of us who were involved in the Community Mental Health movement from its beginnings in the early 1960s must remind others that almost all of the major concepts that underlie the progress of the past decade were already in existence in 1968. Even a decade ago, the most advanced workers in the field of community health *knew* that crisis intervention was not enough, and were developing plans for preventive intervention and extensive aftercare. Furthermore, many of the most important concepts in this field derived from researches done by Freud, Anna Freud, Moynihan, Caplan, Gruenberg, Keniston, and others. Even the concept of aggressive alienation itself is based on earlier research on alienation done, not in the inner city, but amongst talented college students. Thus, our enthusiasm for the progress of the past decade must be tempered with humility and a sense of indebtedness to those in the pre-Community Mental Health era.

Furthermore, humility is called for because of the many questions whose answers have evaded our search. I will cite but one of the most important: the problem of therapeutic failure.

We have much to learn from our failures, perhaps more than from our numerous successes. With some patients, even repeated rehabilitation and maintenance on high doses of long-acting tranquilizers have failed to produce a complete return to pro-social functioning. And the uncooperativeness of the government of Canada has made it extremely difficult to reach those unsuccessfully treated patients who have evaded our detection networks and fled north. Since the Canadian government is unwilling to extradite the large numbers of mentally ill who have flocked to Canadian urban centers, we must support the recent proposal of Secretary Westmoreland that we persuade foreign governments to institute their own programs of Community Mental Health, with the close collaboration and support of American advisors. Indeed, the currently strained relations between Canada and the United States raise a series of far more profound questions, to which I will return in a moment.

Rather than list the many other important research issues that confront us, let me turn to our greatest challenge—the definition of new target groups, and the need to broaden still further the concept of community.

In our focus upon the more visible problems of urban violence, we have neglected other target groups of even greater pathological potential. These new target groups are not always easy to define precisely; but there is a clear consensus that high priority on the list of future targets must be given to college students, to intellectuals with no firm ties to the community, and to disacculturated members of certain ethnico-religious groups who retain close ties with non-American communities.

The passage last year of the College Developmental Act enables us at last to apply to the college-age group the techniques so successfully used in the inner city. This act will enable the setting up of college mental-health centers with a strong community approach. One of the particular strengths of this law should be underlined here: It enables us to treat not only the college student himself, but his professors and mentors, from whom—as recent studies have shown —much of his antisocial acculturation springs.

In our continuing work with new target groups, however, we must not lose sight of certain basic principles. For one, the target-group approach is by its very nature limited. Our practical resources are still so small that we must single out only certain target groups for special interventions. But this should not obscure our long-range goal: nothing less than a society in which all men and women are guaranteed mental health by simple virtue of their citizenship. Thus, the entire community must be our target; we must insist upon *total mental health* from the womb to the grave [applause].

Yet our most serious challenge lies not in America, but outside of our national boundaries. For it has become obvious that the concept of "mental health in one nation" is not tenable. We are surrounded by a world in which the concepts of Community Mental Health have had regrettably little impact. Recent studies conducted by the Department of International Mental Health in Ecuador, Eastern Nigeria, and Thailand have shown an incidence of individual and collective psychopathology even higher than that found in American cities ten years ago. The link between objectivism and violence, first established in America, has been repeatedly shown to exist in other cultures as well. Even young Americans serving abroad with the Overseas Mental Health Corps have been exposed to objectivist influences in these countries that have made their renewed rehabilitation necessary, whether on the battlefield or in the special rehabilitation centers back home.

But it should not be thought that the primary argument against mental health in only one country is mere expediency. Our responsibilities as the most powerful and mentally healthy nation in the world are of a therapeutic nature. Were it simply a matter of expediency, the closing of the Canadian and Mexican borders has shown that it is possible to limit the exodus of non-reacculturated Americans to the merest trickle. Nor would sheer expediency alone justify our involvement, at a heavy price in materials and men, in the mental-health struggles of Ecuador, Eastern Nigeria, and Thailand. It is not expediency but our therapeutic commitment to the mental health of our fellow men—regardless of race, color, nationality, and creed—that argues against the concept of mental health in only one nation.

Thus, our greatest challenge is the struggle to create a mentally healthy world. Happy historical accident has given American society a technology and an understanding of human behavior sufficiently advanced to bring about the profound revolution in human behavior that men from Plato's time onward have dreamed of. The lessons of Operation Inner City will continue to be of the utmost importance: the concepts of total saturation, remote therapy, and mandatory treatment; the realization of the close link between objectivism and psychopathology; the need for the closest interdisciplinary cooperation. Already, plans evolved by the Department of International Mental Health and this Community Mental Health Organization call for the international deployment of Mobile Treatment Teams and Overseas Mental Health Corps volunteers, some operating with the assistance of local governments, other courageously risking their lives in communities where pathology has infiltrated even the highest levels of governmental authority. In the years to come, the challenges will be great, the price will be large, and the discouragements will be many. But of one thing there can be no doubt: The Community Mental Health movement will play a leading role in our progress toward a mentally healthy society at the head of a mentally healthy world [applause]. . . .

*I stepped back from the podium and tripped. Many hands reached to pull me to my feet. I cried out and awoke to find my wife shaking me. "You've been dreaming and mumbling in your sleep for hours," she said, "and you're feverish." The thermometer revealed a temperature of 103 degrees. I was in bed for several days with a rather severe virus—which, doubtless, explains my dream.*

# 12  The Limits of Social Policy

## NATHAN GLAZER

There is a general sense that we face a crisis in social policy, and in almost all its branches. Whether this crisis derives from the backwardness of the United States in social policy generally, the revolt of the blacks, the fiscal plight of the cities, the failure of national leadership, the inherent complexity of the problems, or the weakening of the national fiber, and what weight we may ascribe to these and other causes, are no easy questions to settle. I believe there is much

Reprinted from *Commentary*, 52 (September 1971), pp. 51–58, by permission; all rights reserved.

at fault with the way we generally think of these matters, and I wish to suggest another approach.

The term "social policy" is very elastic. I use it to describe all those public policies which have developed in the past hundred years to protect families and individuals from the accidents of industrial and urban life, and which try to maintain a decent minimum of living conditions for all.* The heart of social policy is the relief of the condition of the poor, and it is in that sense I use the term here.

There are, I believe, two prevailing and antagonistic views of social policy.

One—I will call it the "liberal" view—operates with a model of the social world in which that world is seen as having undergone progressive improvement for, roughly, the past hundred years. The unimproved world, in this view, was the world of early and high industrialism. Market forces prevailed unobstructed, or nearly so. The enormous inequalities they created in wealth, power, and status were added to the still largely unreduced inequalities of the pre-industrial world. This situation, which meant that most men lived in squalor while a few, profiting from the labor of the many, lived in great luxury, was seen by a developing social conscience as both evil and dangerous. It was evil because of the huge inequalities that characterized it and because of its failure to insure a decent minimum at the bottom levels; and it was dangerous because it encouraged the destitute to rebellion against industry and the state. Consequently, in Bismarck's Germany, and somewhat later on in England, conservative states grew worried about rebellion and workingmen began to be protected against complete penury in old age or in times of unemployment through industrial accident and illness; small beginnings were also made in helping them cover some of the costs of medical care. Gradually, such measures of protection were extended to cover other areas like housing, and were made available to broader and broader classes of people.

In the liberal view, then, we have a sea of misery, scarcely diminished at all by voluntary charitable efforts. Government then starts moving in, setting up dikes, pushing back the sea and reclaiming the land, so to speak. In this view, while new issues may be presented for public policy, they are never really new—rather, they are only newly

---

*This definition excludes measures aimed at influencing the entire economic or physical environment, even though such measures certainly have some claim to be considered as falling within the realm of social policy and may well be evaluated in terms of their effect on those vulnerable elements of the population who are the special target of social policy. Education, too, falls increasingly into the sphere of social policy, particularly when it is seen as a means of protecting people from poverty and destitution. The same is true of the control of crime, particularly if we see it as a response to poverty and destitution. I shall, however, exclude both these areas from my discussion.

*recognized* as issues demanding public intervention. Thus the liberal point of view is paradoxically calculated to make us feel both guiltier and more arrogant. We feel guilty for not having recognized and acted on injustices and deprivations earlier, but we also feel complacently superior in comparison to our forebears, who did not recognize or act on them at all.

I have given a rather sharp and perhaps caricatured picture of the liberal view. Liberals are of course aware that new needs—and not simply new recognitions of old needs—arise. Nevertheless, the typical stance of the liberal in dealing with issues of social policy is blame —not of the unfortunates, those suffering from the ills that the social policy is meant to remove, but of society, of the political system and its leaders. The liberal stance is: for every problem there is a policy, and even if the problem is relatively new, the social system and the political system must be indicted for failing to tackle it earlier.

There is another element in the liberal view. It sees vested interests as the chief obstacle to the institution of new social policies. One such interest consists simply of those who are better off—those not in need of the social policy in question, who resist it because of the increase in taxes. But other kinds of obstructive interests are also there: real-estate people and landlords in the field of housing, employers subject to payroll taxes in the field of social security, doctors in the field of medical care, and so on.

Despite the assumption here of a conflict pitting liberals against conservatives, I would suggest that the main premises behind this general picture of social policy are today hardly less firmly held by conservatives than they are by liberals. In the American context, conservatives will differ from liberals because they want to move more slowly, give more consideration to established interests, keep taxes from going up too high. They will on occasion express a stronger concern for traditional values—work, the family, sexual restraint. But on the whole the line dividing liberals from conservatives grows steadily fainter. The Family Assistance Program, the major new reform of the welfare system proposed by the Nixon administration, will illustrate my point. Anyone who reads through the Congressional hearings on this proposal will be hard put to distinguish liberals from conservatives in terms of any naive division between those who favor the expansion of social policy and those who oppose it.

It is not only in America that one sees the merging of liberal and conservative views on social policy, and not only today. Bismarck after all stands at the beginning of the history of modern social policy. In the countries of northwest Europe, the differences over social policy between liberals and conservatives are even narrower than they are in this country. In England, very often the issue seems to turn on such questions as what kind of charges should be imposed by the National Health Service for eyeglasses or prescriptions. It was this kind of reduction in the conflicts over basic values in advanced industrial societies that in the 1950s led Raymond Aron and Daniel Bell to formulate their ideas about "the end of ideology." And while in the 1960s all the old ideologies returned to these countries in force, it remains true that ideological battles between major political parties have been startlingly reduced in intensity since World War II.

Having incorporated the conservative point of view on social policy into the liberal, I will go on to the only other major perspective that means much today, the radical. The radical perspective on social policy comes in many variants, but they can all be summed up quite simply: If the liberal, and increasingly the conservative, believes that for every problem there must be a specific solution, the radical believes that there can be no particular solutions to particular problems but only a general solution, which is a transformation in the nature of society itself.

This point of view has consequences, just as the liberal point of view does. If, for example, the conservative proposes a guaranteed annual income of $1,600 for a family of four, and the liberal proposes that the figure be doubled or tripled, the radical will feel quite free to demand an even higher minimum. He knows that his figure is unlikely to be adopted, but he also knows that he can cite this failure as proof of his contention that the system cannot accommodate decent social demands. If, on the other hand, his policy or something like it is taken seriously, he can hope for a greater degree of class conflict as demands that are very difficult to implement are publicized and considered. And even if his policy is implemented, the radical remains firm in his faith that nothing has changed: the new policy is after all only a palliative; it does not get to the heart of the matter; or if it does get to the heart of the matter, it gets there only to prevent the people from getting to the heart of the largest matters of all. Indeed, one of the important tenets of radicalism is that nothing ever changes short of the final apocalyptic revolutionary moment when everything changes.

As against these two perspectives—the one that believes in a solution to every problem, and the other that believes in no solution to any problem save revolutionary change—I want to present a somewhat different view of social policy. This view is based on two propositions:

1) Social policy is an effort to deal with the breakdown of traditional ways of handling distress. These traditional mechanisms are

located primarily in the family, but also in the ethnic group, the neighborhood, and in such organizations as the church and the *landsmanschaft*.

2) In its effort to deal with the breakdown of these traditional structures, however, social policy tends to encourage their further weakening. There is, then, no sea of misery against which we are making steady headway. Our efforts to deal with distress themselves increase distress.

I do not mean to suggest any automatic law. I do suggest processes.

One is the well-known revolution of rising expectations. This revolution is itself fed by social policies. Their promise, inadequately realized, leaves behind a higher level of expectation, which a new round of social policy must attempt to meet, and with the same consequences. In any case, by the nature of democratic (and perhaps not only democratic) politics, again and again more must be promised than can be delivered. These promises are, I believe, the chief mechanisms in educating people to higher expectations. But they are, of course, reinforced by the enormous impact of mass literacy, the mass media, and expanding levels of education. Rising expectations continually enlarge the sea of felt and perceived misery, whatever may happen to it in actuality.

Paralleling the revolution of rising expectations, and adding similarly to the increasing difficulties of social policy, is the revolution of equality. This is the most powerful social force in the modern world. Perhaps only Tocqueville saw its awesome potency. For it not only expresses a demand for equality in political rights and in political power; it also represents a demand for equality in economic power, in social status, in authority in every sphere. And just as there is no point at which the sea of misery is finally drained, so, too, is there no point at which the equality revolution can come to an end, if only because as it proceeds we become ever more sensitive to smaller and smaller degrees of inequality. More important, different types and forms of equality inevitably emerge to contradict each other as we move away from a society of fixed social orders. "From each according to his abilities, to each according to his need"; so goes one of the greatest of the slogans invoked as a test of equality. But the very slogan itself already incorporates two terms—"abilities" and "needs" —that open the way for a justification of inequality. We live daily with the consequences of the fact that equal treatment of individuals does not necessarily lead to "equality" for groups. And we can point to a host of other contradictions as well which virtually guarantee that the slogan of "equality" in any society at all will continue to arouse passions and lead to discontent.

But in addition to the revolution in rising expectations and the revolution of equality, social policy itself, in almost every field, creates new and, I would argue, unmanageable demands. It is illusory to see social policy only as making an *inroad* on a problem; there are dynamic aspects to any policy, such that it also *expands* the problem, *changes* the problem, *generates* further problems. And for a number of reasons, social policy finds it impossible to deal adequately with these new demands that follow the implementation of the original measures.

The first and most obvious of these reasons is the limitation of resources. We in this country suffer from the illusion that there is enough tied up in the arms budget to satisfy all our social needs. Yet if we look at a country like Sweden, which spends relatively little for arms—and which, owing to its small size, its low rate of population growth, and its ethnic homogeneity, presents a much more moderate range of social problems than does the United States—we will see how even the most enlightened, most scientific, least conflict-ridden effort to deal with social problems leads to a tax budget which takes more than 40 percent of the Gross National Product. And new items are already emerging on Sweden's agenda of social demands that should raise that percentage even higher. For example, at present only a small proportion of Swedes go on to higher education. Housing is still in short supply and does not satisfy a good part of the population. And presumably Swedish radicals, growing in number, are capable of formulating additional demands, not so pressing, that would require further increases in taxation—if, that is, any society can go much beyond a taxation rate of 40 percent of its Gross National Product.

In this country, of course, we still have a long way to go. By comparison with Sweden and with other developed nations (France, West Germany, and England) our taxes are still relatively low, and there is that huge 8 percent of the GNP now devoted to arms and war that might be diverted, at least in part, to the claims of social policy. But social demands could easily keep up with the new resources. We now spend between 6 and 7 percent of the GNP on education, and about as much on health. It would be no trick at all to double our expenditures on education, or on health, simply by taking account of proposals already made by leading experts in these fields. We could with no difficulty find enormous expenditures to make in the field of housing. And quite serious proposals (I believe they are serious) are now put forward for a guaranteed minimum income of $6,500 for a family of four, with no restrictions.

My point is not that we either could not or should not raise taxes and use the arms budget for better things. It is that, when we look at projected needs, and at the experience of other countries, we know that even with a much smaller arms budget and much higher taxes, social demands will continue to press on public resources. And we may suspect that needs will be felt then as urgently as they are now.

A second limitation on the effectiveness of social policy is presented by the inevitable professionalization of services. Professionalization means that a certain point of view is developed about the nature of needs and how they are to be met. It tends to handle a problem by increasing the number of people trained to deal with that problem. First, we run out of people who are defined as "qualified" (social workers, counselors, teachers, etc.). Second, this naturally creates dissatisfaction over the fact that many services are being handled by the "unqualified." Third, questions arise from outside the profession about the ability of the "qualified" themselves to perform a particular service properly. We no longer—and often with good reason—trust social workers to handle welfare, teachers and principals to handle education, doctors and hospital administrators to handle health care, managers to handle housing projects, and so on. And yet there is no one else into whose hands we can entrust these services. Experience tells us that if we set up new agencies it will be only a very few years before a new professionalism emerges which will be found limited and untrustworthy in its own turn. So, in the poverty program, we encouraged the rise of community-action agencies as a way of overcoming the bad effects of professionalism, and we already find that the community organizers have become another professional group, another interest group, with claims of their own which have no necessary relation to the needs of the clients they serve.

The third limitation on the effectiveness of social policy is simply lack of knowledge. We are in the surprising position of knowing much more than we did at earlier stages in the development of social policy—more about income distribution, employment patterns, family structure, health and medical care, housing and its impact, etc.— and simultaneously becoming more uncertain about what measures will be most effective, if effective at all, in ameliorating pressing problems in each of these areas. In the past, there was a clear field for action. The situation demanded that something be done; whatever was done was clear gain; little as yet was expected; little was known, and administrators approached their tasks with anticipation and self-confidence. Good administrators could be chosen, because the task was new and exciting. At later stages, however, we began dealing with problems which were in some absolute sense less serious, but which were nevertheless irksome and productive of conflict. We had already become committed to old lines of policy; agencies with their special interests had been created; and new courses of action had to be taken in a situation in which there was already more conflict at the start, less assurance of success, and less attention from the leaders and the best minds of the country.

Thus, if we look at the history of housing policy, for example, we will see that in the earlier stages—the 20s and 30s—there was a good deal of enthusiasm for this subject, with the housing issue attracting some of the best and most vigorous minds in the country. Since little or nothing had been done, there was a wide choice of alternatives and a supply of good men to act as administrators. In time, as housing programs expanded, the issue tended to fade from the agenda of top government. (Indeed, it has been difficult to get much White House attention for housing for two decades.) Earlier programs precluded the possibilities for new departures, and as we learned more about housing and its effects on people, we grew more uncertain as to what policies—even theoretically—would be best. Housing, like so many other areas of social policy, became, after an initial surge of interest, a field for experts, with the incursions of general public opinion becoming less and less informed, and less and less useful. This process is almost inevitable—there is always so much to know.

Perhaps my explanation of the paradox of knowledge leading to less confident action is defective. Perhaps, as the liberal perspective would have it, more knowledge will permit us to take more confident and effective action. Certainly we do need more knowledge about social policy. But it also appears that whatever great actions we undertake today involve such an increase in complexity that we act generally with less knowledge than we would like to have, even if with more than we once had. This is true for example of the great reform in welfare policy—which I shall discuss below—that is now making its way through Congress.

But aside from these problems of cost, of professionalization, and of knowledge, there is the simple reality that every piece of social policy substitutes for some traditional arrangement, whether good or bad, a new arrangement in which public authorities take over, at least in part, the role of the family, of the ethnic and neighborhood group, or of the voluntary association. In doing so, social policy weakens the position of these traditional agents, and further encourages needy people to depend on the government, rather than on the traditional structures, for help. Perhaps this is the basic force behind the ever growing demand for social policy, and its frequent failure to satisfy the demand.

To sum up: Whereas the liberal believes that to every problem there is a solution, and the radical believes that to any problem there is only the general answer of wholesale social transformation, I believe that we can have only partial and less than wholly satisfying answers to the social problems in question. Whereas the liberal be-

lieves that social policies make steady progress in nibbling away at
the agenda of problems set by the forces of industrialization and
urbanization, and whereas the radical believes that social policy has
made only insignificant inroads into these problems, I believe that
social policy has ameliorated the problems we have inherited but
that it has also given rise to other problems no less grave in their
effect on human happiness than those which have been successfully
modified.

The liberal has a solution, and the radical has a solution. Do I have
a solution? I began this discussion by saying that the breakdown of
traditional modes of behavior is the chief cause of our social problems. That, of course, is another way of saying industrialism and
urbanization, but I put it in the terms I did because I am increasingly
convinced that some important part of the solution to our social
problems lies in traditional practices and traditional restraints. Since
the past is not recoverable, what guidance could this possibly give?
It gives two forms of guidance: first, it counsels hesitation in the
development of social policies that sanction the abandonment of
traditional practices, and second, and perhaps more helpful, it suggests that the creation and building of new traditions must be taken
more seriously as a requirement of social policy itself.

A nation's welfare system provides perhaps the clearest and sever-
est test of the adequacy of its system of social policy in general.
Welfare, which exists in all advanced nations, is the attempt to deal
with the distress that is left over after all the more specific forms of
social policy have done their work. After we have instituted what in
America is called social security (and what may generally be called
old-age pensions); after we have expanded it to cover widows, dependent children, and the disabled; after we have instituted a system to
handle the costs of medical care, and to maintain income in times of
illness; after we have set up a system of unemployment insurance;
after we have enabled people to manage the exceptional costs of
housing—after all this there will remain, in any industrial system,
people who still require special supports, either temporarily or for
longer periods of time.

In thus describing the place of welfare, or "public assistance," in
a system of social policy, I am of course describing its place in an *ideal*
system of social policy. I do not suggest for a moment that our programs of social security, health insurance, unemployment insurance,
housing, are as yet fully adequate (though as I understand these
matters, even if they were better, they would still not be seen as fully
adequate). The strange thing, however, is that even if we go to
countries whose systems of social insurance could well serve as models of comprehensiveness and adequacy, we find that the need for
welfare or public assistance still remains, and on a scale roughly

comparable to our own. In Sweden, the number of persons receiving public assistance was 4.4 percent of the population in 1959, and it was in the same year less than 4 percent in America. In England, despite the broad range of social policy there, the number of those on Supplementary Benefits—the English welfare, formerly known as National Assistance—is of the same order of magnitude. In Sweden and England, too, we find concern, though much less than here, over the stigma of welfare, over the effects of a degrading means test, over the problem of second- and third-generation welfare families.

Why, then, do we have, or consider that we have, a greater problem than they do? One reason is that, whereas in Sweden the proportion of those on welfare declines as other forms of social insurance broaden their coverage and become more effective, quite the opposite has happened here. In this country, there has been a rise in the number of people on welfare during the past decade. The rise is not phenomenal—from 4 to 6 percent of the population. Nor, interestingly enough, despite the increased cost of welfare, does it form a really heavy burden on the budget. The cost of welfare, though rising, still accounts for only a bit more than one percent of the Gross National Product, and 6 percent of the federal budget. However, it forms a greater share of state and local revenues, and in some larger cities up to 15 percent of the population is on welfare. That is one reason it has become a serious problem.

But there are more important reasons. In Sweden and England a high proportion of those requesting public assistance are the aged; in America the aged constitute a smaller proportion of the welfare population, and families a much larger share. Indeed, our increase over the past ten years has been almost entirely concentrated in the family population, those assisted under the federal program called Aid to Families with Dependent Children (ADC). Here the situation is quite startling. In 1955, 30 out of every thousand American children received welfare; by 1969 this had doubled to more than 60 out of every thousand. In New York City, where eligibility has always been broad, and where the city and the state provide welfare to families not covered by the federal statute, the increase has been even more dramatic. In 1960, there were 328,000 persons on welfare in New York City, of whom 250,000 were in the family categories (children and their parents). In 1969, there were 1,012,000—about 12 or 13 percent of the population—of whom 792,000, or four-fifths, were in the family categories. Yet during the same period, there seems to have been a drop in the number of families in poverty— from 13 to 10 percent of all families—and the rate of unemployment was halved, from 6 percent to 3 percent.

A second reason why welfare is a more serious matter in America than in Sweden or England is that in those countries it is a problem of the backward areas, whereas here it is a problem of the most advanced. A third and final reason is that welfare has come to be seen in America as a *regular* means of *family* support. In England and Sweden welfare is thought of as emergency aid, provided in response to a special crisis, and meant to put a destitute family back on its feet. In America the situation of the destitute family is increasingly considered a more or less permanent condition for which provision over a very long period of time must be made.

Why should all this be so? One of the most popular explanations to be advanced is that no jobs are available for the men—mainly unskilled—who would ordinarily support these families. In fact, however, unskilled jobs were widely available in the latter part of the 60s, just when the number of families on welfare increased so impressively. It is true that these jobs did not generally pay enough to support a family, but it is also true that large numbers of the urban unemployed were young and unmarried men and women who were not as yet required to support families on their own, though they might well have been capable of contributing to the support of the parental household in which they presumably lived. (The majority of American families, as it happens, are supported by two earners, or more.)

There is a modified form of the argument that no jobs are available, which is that since the actually available jobs do not pay enough to support a family, and since there is no way for working husbands to get supplementary assistance, they are encouraged to defect in order to make their families eligible for help. But let us consider the advanced jurisdictions, like New York State, where complete families *are* eligible for support and have been for a long time, and where a working husband *can* have his income supplemented to bring it up to some necessary minimum for the support of his family. It is just in these jurisdictions that we have had the most remarkable increase in the number of families broken up by abandonment. In 1961 there were about 12,000 deserted families on welfare in New York City. In 1968, there were 80,000, a more than sixfold increase during a period when the population of the city, in overall numbers, remained stable. During the same period, there was a more moderate increase in the number of welfare families that consisted of mothers and illegitimate children, from 20,000 to 46,000. In other words, the family welfare population shifted to one overwhelmingly consisting of abandoned women and their children.

Another effort to account for the situation argues that high welfare payments in New York and other Northern cities encouraged migration from the South and from the rural areas. This probably played some role. But there is no evidence that abandoned families in these areas moved to New York in larger numbers in the 60s than in the

50s. And if the abandonment took place in New York, in a brisk job market, we would want to know why it took place, and migration would not be the explanation.

Then there is the view which holds that in the 1960s—with the spread of concern about poverty, with the development of community organizations, and with the rise of such groups as the National Welfare Rights Organization—more and more of the poor discovered their entitlement to welfare, more and more became willing to apply for it, and higher and higher proportions of those applying were accepted. According to this explanation, then, it was not the poor who increased in numbers, but only the poor on welfare. This is undoubtedly part of the story. But think once again of that huge increase in the number of abandoned families on welfare. If there were just as many, or almost as many, before, what did they do to stay alive?

Still another interpretation emphasizes the fact that the levels of welfare aid in New York became higher during the 60s. This would certainly mean that more and more workers could apply for income supplements. But why would it mean a six-and-a-half times increase in the number of abandoned families?

One must take developments in New York seriously because in many respects they can be considered a test run of the Family Assistance Program, the reform in the welfare system proposed by the Nixon administration and still working its way, after various revisions, through Congress. Without going into detail, and leaving aside the fact that welfare would acquire a national floor and a national administration, there are, I believe, four major features that distinguish the Family Assistance Program from the system we have at present.

The most important is that the working poor would be included in the same system as the non-working poor. The reasoning behind this feature is as follows. Welfare levels cannot be raised if people on welfare get as much as, or more than, people who are working. This would first of all lead to political resistance and resentment on the part of the working poor. Further, they would try to redefine themselves as incapable of work in order to get the higher benefits of the non-working poor. If, however, the working poor are also included, their resistance to higher levels of welfare will decline, and they will have less incentive to become non-working.

A second major difference is that a substantial incentive to work is built into the program. Thus, working leads not to the loss of welfare benefits but to an overall increase in the family income. Family Assistance payments are reduced when there is more earned income, but only as a proportion of the increased earnings.

Third, the grant would in part be divorced from services and from the stigma of investigation. It cannot be fully divorced from investigation—it is after all a grant based on need—but the hope is that in its administration it will become more of an impersonal income-maintenance program and less involved in the provision of help through services rather than through money.

A fourth feature of the new law is that, in addition to building in an incentive to work, it contains a *requirement* that everyone capable of work register for job training or for employment. If there is a father, he must register; if there is no father, the mother must register unless she has children still below school age. (This feature has been the target of much criticism, because of the element of compulsion.)

What are we to conclude about the prospects of the new system? Since all four of its features are in large measure already in existence in New York State, whose condition is not exactly of the happiest, we can be sure that Family Assistance will not succeed in "solving" the problems of welfare. What it will do is redistribute more income, and put more money into the pockets of the poor. It will raise the abysmally low welfare payments in large areas of the South. It may, by moving some part of the way toward national standards, reduce immigration to the big cities of the North. It will provide some relief —but relatively little—to the states and local jurisdictions that now are heavily burdened with welfare costs. All this is to the good. But what the new system will not do, I believe, is strengthen the family or substantially increase the number of those on welfare willing to enter the labor force. If it does, the accomplishment will be a mystery because similar arrangements have not done so in New York, nor in any of the other states in which families with unemployed males are eligible for welfare, or where a work requirement exists. The forces leading to the breakdown of male responsibility for the family among some of the poor seem greater than those the new program calls into play to counteract them.

This brings us back to my original point, and to a possible answer to the question I posed earlier as to how we can account for the dramatic increase in recent years of abandoned families on welfare. The constraints that traditionally kept families together have weakened. In some groups they may not have been strong to begin with. Our efforts to soften the harsh consequences of family breakup speak well of our compassion and concern, but these efforts also make it easier for fathers to abandon their families or mothers to disengage from their husbands. Our welfare legislation has often been harsh, and its administration harsher. But the steps we take in the direction of diminished harshness must also enhance the attractions of either abandonment or disengagement and encourage the recourse to welfare.

And yet, what alternatives do we have? This Family Assistance

Program is after all the most enlightened and thoughtful legislation to have been introduced in the field of welfare in some decades.

My own tendency, following from the basic considerations I have suggested, would be to ask how we might prevent further erosion of the traditional constraints that still play the largest role in maintaining a civil society. What keeps society going, after all, is that most people still feel they should work—however well they might do without working—and most feel that they should take care of their families—however attractive it might on occasion appear to be to desert them. Consequently we might try to strengthen the incentive to work. The work-incentive provision is the best thing about Family Assistance, but we need to make it even stronger. Our dilemma is that we can never make this incentive as strong as it was when the alternative to work was starvation, or the uncertain charity of private organizations. Nor is it politically feasible to increase the incentive by reducing the levels at which we maintain the poor—if anything, the whole tendency of our thinking and feeling is to raise them, as indeed FAP does. The only alternative, then, is to increase the incentive to work by increasing the attractiveness of work. I do not suggest that this is at all simple (we know the ambiguous results, for example, of raising the minimum wage). Could we, however, begin to attach to low-income jobs the same kind of fringe benefits—health insurance, social security, vacations with pay—that now make higher-paying jobs attractive, and that paradoxically in some form are also available to those on welfare?

The dilemma of income maintenance is that, on the one hand, it permits the poor to live better, but on the other, it reduces their incentive to set up and maintain those close units of self-support—family in the first case, but also larger units—that have always, both in the past and still in large measure today, formed the fabric of society. The administration proposal is a heroic effort to improve the condition of the poor without further damage to those social motivations and structures which are the essential basis for individual security everywhere. But does not the history of our efforts to expand policies of income support suggest that inevitably improvement and damage go together?

In other critical areas of social policy, too, the breakdown of traditional measures, traditional restraints, traditional organization, represents, if not the major factor in the crisis, a significant contribution to it. Even in an area apparently so far removed from tradition as health and medical care, the weakening of traditional forms of organization can be found upon examination to be playing a substantial role, as when we discover that drug addiction is now the chief cause of death—and who knows what other frightful consequences—among young men in New York.

Ultimately, we are not kept healthy, I believe, by new scientific knowledge or more effective cures or even better-organized medical-care services. We are kept healthy by certain patterns of life. These, it is true, are modified for the better by increased scientific knowledge, but this knowledge is itself communicated through such functioning traditional organizations as the school, the voluntary organization, the family. We are kept healthy by having access to traditional means of support in distress and illness, through the family, the neighborhood, the informal social organization. We are kept healthy by decent care in institutions where certain traditionally-oriented occupations (like nursing and the maintenance of cleanliness) still manage to perform their functions. I will not argue the case for the significance of traditional patterns in maintaining health at length here; but I believe it is a persuasive one.

One major objection, among many, that can be raised against the emphasis I have placed in tradition has to do with the greater success of social policy in a country like Sweden which shows a greater departure from traditionalism than America does. And it is indeed true that social services in Sweden, and England as well, can be organized without as much interference from tradition-minded interest groups of various kinds (including the churches) as we have to contend with in this country. Certainly this is an important consideration. But I would insist that behind the modern organization of the social services in the advanced European countries are at least two elements that can legitimately and without distortion be called traditional.

One is authority. Authority exists when social workers can direct clients, when doctors can direct nurses, when headmasters can direct teachers, when teachers can discipline students and can expect acquiescence from parents. Admittedly this feature of traditionalism itself serves the movement *away* from tradition in other social respects. The authority will be used, as in Sweden, to institute sex education in the schools, to insure that unmarried girls have access to contraceptives, to secure a position of equality for illegitimate children.

But then another feature that can legitimately be called traditional —ethnic and religious homogeneity—sets limits in these countries on how far the movement away from the traditional—toward indeed a new tradition—may be carried. In America, by contrast, it is the very diversity of traditions—ethnic, religious, and social—that makes it so hard to establish new forms of behavior that are universally accepted and approved, and that also makes it impossible to give the social worker, the teacher, the policeman, the judge, the nurse, even the doctor, the same authority they possess in more homogeneous countries.

But there is a more basic sense in which tradition is stronger in the countries of Western Europe than here. Whatever the situation with sex education and with the laws governing illegitimacy, divorce is less frequent in Sweden and England, responsibility for the rearing of children is still consistently placed within the family, and the acceptance of work as a normal pattern of life is more widespread and less challenged. In England and Sweden it is still taken for granted that the aim of welfare is to restore a man to a position in which he can work, earn his living, support his family. And indeed the psychological damage that renders a man unfit for work, and the ideology arguing against the desirability of work, are so little known in England and Sweden that the restoration of family independence is a fair and reasonable objective of welfare. But this is no longer a reasonable view of welfare for substantial parts of the American population. It is in this core sense that America has gone further in the destruction of tradition than other countries. In doing so, America comes face to face, more sharply than any other country yet has, with the limits of social policy.

# 13   Families, Sex, and the Liberal Agenda

## ALLAN C. CARLSON

The concept of "family policy" has attracted unprecedented attention within liberal political circles over the past four years. This attention, in turn, has generated numerous proposals aimed at strengthening American family life through government action.

The arguments of family-policy advocates follow a fairly standard analytical line. They begin by calling for a new emphasis, which Kenneth Keniston described for the Carnegie Council on Children as "abandoning the tendency to deal with children in isolation from their families or the society they live in. . . . " This change, advocates continue, involves a whole new perspective on public policy. The 1978 report by the National Commission on Families and Public Policies of the National Conference on Social Welfare (NCSW) suggests that the family-policy concept "may well provide fresh insight into social welfare, new perceptions of the individual's relationship to society, [and] a new formulation of the role of government in human affairs. . . . " The analysis then commonly turns to a presenta-

Reprinted with permission of the author from *The Public Interest*, 58 (Winter 1980), pp. 62–79. © 1980 by National Affairs Inc.

tion of statistics reflecting family stress, break-up, or change—such as a rise in the number of single-parent families, the growing percentage of working mothers, the swelling divorce rate, illegitimacy figures, rising welfare dependency, figures on teenage pregnancies, suicides, and runaways, and the number of unmarried, cohabitating couples.

Assessments of cause for this evident stress in American family life usually follow. The Carnegie Council's report faults in part the "American myths" of family independence, personal responsibility, technological advance, economic growth, and *laissez faire.* In addition, the report points to "the broad ecological pressures on children and their parents," chemicals in food, nuclear power, the unplanned nature of broadcasting, and "the economic drain of children" on parents, as forces undermining families' "capability to perform." The NCSW group cites the rigidification of the nineteenth-centrury American family ideal around a work-devoured, paycheck-oriented male tied to an economically and socially dependent woman and a brood of children, who are isolated from traditional sustaining institutions such as the extended family, neighborhood and community. The Advisory Committee on Child Development of the Assembly of Behavioral and Social Sciences of the National Research Council (NCR), in its 1976 report *Toward a National Policy for Children and Families,* sees family difficulties related in significant degree to poverty, racial and sexual inequality, the decline of cities, poor housing, unemployment, inadequate health care, lack of transportation, the deterioration of the environment, and poor education. Every source agrees that existing governmental programs supporting children and families are totally inadequate and often destructive of family life.

In developing their family-policy proposals, advocates posit two principles: comprehensiveness and pluralism. Concerning the first, the Carnegie group argues for a United States family policy "as comprehensive as its defense policy," involving "coherent" social and economic planning, a multitude of services, and a multifaceted approach to the issues. As for "pluralism," advocates all agree that it requires recognition of "the many life-style choices that may produce a wide range of family forms." "Life style" choices with some legitimate claim to family status are said by some to include "child free" couples, unmarried couples, single-parent families, "single persons" families, homosexual pairings, communal arrangements, and—to fill in the gaps—assorted "minority life styles."

While varying in emphasis, specific family-policy proposals tend to include the following:

*Income Security.* All family-policy proponents agree that family income in the United States remains significantly maldistributed. They support establishment of a guaranteed annual family income, or "decency standard," representing half of the U.S.'s median income. Means to that "family stabilizing" goal vary. The NCSW group advocates a taxable federal family allowance of $750 per dependent (to replace the personal income-tax deduction), at a cost of approximately $70 billion. The Carnegie group proposes a comprehensive "credit income tax" scheme, granting households a refundable $1500 tax credit for each family member, tied to an adult work requirement (no work, no credit) and a straight 50-percent tax on all income above the credit line. The NRC report leans toward an unspecified "negative income tax."

*Full Employment.* Joseph Califano stated in his widely praised September 1976 memo to Presidential candidate Jimmy Carter on American families: "[T]he most severe threat to family life stems from unemployment and lack of an adequate income." Most other advocates agree, and call for legally guaranteed jobs to all heads of households, tied to more and better central economic planning.

*Affirmative Action.* Given particular emphasis by the Carnegie report is the belief that current efforts at eliminating racial, sexual, and other forms of discrimination are moving with intolerable slowness. Equality of opportunity, many contend, is not enough to insure a stable basis for family life among minorities, women, and the handicapped. Greater affirmative-action effort is needed.

*Health Care.* Citing the American preoccupation with individuals, the relatively high infant-mortality rate among minorities, and the lack of pre- and post-natal maternity care for the poor, family-policy advocates call for a national health policy emphasizing preventive health care for all children. Their means to better health include "integration" of the health-care-delivery system with other family services, public accountability, more research, and national record keeping and monitoring of children's health.

*Social Services.* Finding the existing 280 federal programs aiding families and children to be "inadequate, uncoordinated and patchwork," the NCSW, and the NRC and Carnegie groups as well, support the creation of integrated family-support services funded at appreciably higher levels.

*Day Care.* All family-policy advocates agree that the government has a responsibility to ensure that families needing child care during working hours have available a wide range of substitute choices.

*Sexual Law.* While avoiding most references to sex, family-policy advocates do tend to cite the need for more sex education and wider availability of contraceptives to reduce teenage pregnancy. Many support widening access to abortion.

*Family Law.* While emphasis varies, family-policy supporters tend to argue for stronger legal supports for families (including guaranteed due process in child-removal situations), greater legal autonomy for children, and reform of such abuse-prone areas of government involvement as foster care.

*Work Law.* All advocates support changes in work laws and new government incentives to accommodate the child-care needs of working parents.

*Government.* All sources agree that the government should be more aware of its impact on families. Most advocates support the idea of requiring that "family impact statements" be attached to proposed legislation and regulations.

In sum, family-policy advocates offer, as the way to reinvigorate American family life, virtually the entire liberal agenda: greater income redistribution, guaranteed minimum incomes, full employment policies, more social and economic planning, more and better integrated social services, reorganization and public funding of health care, more affirmative-action programs, better sex education, increased availability of contraceptives and abortion, government-funded day care, an emphasis on legal rights, work-law reforms, and a more sensitive, activist, and reorganized government.[1] They are focusing their attention on the scheduled 1980 (formerly 1979) White House Conference on Families. A "Coalition for the White House Conference" was organized in 1978 with a membership list "representing dramatically different family life styles and values" and including—together with more traditional family advocates such as the U.S. Catholic Conference and the YWCA—such reform-oriented groups as the American Association of Sex Educators, Counselors, and Therapists, the Child Welfare League of America, the National Council of Churches, the National Gay Task Force, the National Organization of Non-Parents, Women's Action Alliance, and Zero Population Growth.

## WHAT IS A FAMILY?

Family-Policy advocates are certainly correct in their perception of stress and basic change. For though several recent studies—notably Mary Jo Bane's *Here To Stay*—have argued that American families are adjusting well to current social pressures, statistical evidence reflects fundamental alterations in the nation's family life. The divorce rate, for example, rose 150 percent between 1958 and 1974, with the annual number of divorces climbing to nearly 1 million. The number of children affected by divorce each year rose from 379,000 in 1957 to 1.1 million in 1974. The fertility rate (births per 1,000 women aged 15–44) has fallen from 122.7 in 1957 to 66.7 in 1975, reflecting a major retreat from child-bearing. The illegitimacy ratio (illegitimate births per 1,000 live births) has tripled in less than two decades, reaching 142.5 in 1975. The percentage of single-parent families, relative to all families with children under age six, rose from 8 percent in 1960 to 17 percent in 1974. In 1977, nearly 18 million U.S. children lived with only one parent—a 100-percent rise since 1960. Yet despite their appropriate emphasis on such changes, family-policy advocates have stumbled into definitional, attitudinal, and analytical errors that compromise their proposed policy response.

*First, while paying deference to a "pluralism of family forms" may appear to reflect a sound liberal principle, the refusal of most family-policy advocates to set any identifiable norms at all leaves critical policy-related issues begging the question: What exactly is a "family"?* If there can be no definition that excludes any form of human cohabitation, then what is a family policy trying to save, or restore, or strengthen, or help? And if all forms of human cohabitation are essentially equal, why have an expensive policy aimed at no particular goal? Inflation alone will ultimately compel most people to live with others. The "pluralism" school of family sociology, when translated into public policy, founders on the hollowness of its basic concept.

*Second, many family-policy advocates appear to be ambivalent toward birth and children.* All Western European family policies developed in the 1930s and 1940s were predicated on pro-natalist sympathies. The state enthusiastically welcomed babies and encouraged parents to bear larger families. This gave some logical coherence to efforts to socialize child-rearing costs and justified the clearly stated policy preference for traditional nuclear families. However, many American liberals are now committed to a version of neo-Malthusianism that emphasizes over-population as a national threat and a relatively high birthrate as a cause of continuing poverty and ecological distress. Births—especially of third or later children, or among teenagers or the welfare population—are not particularly welcomed. In line with their ideological commitment, family-policy advocates usually buttress support for family allowances and the like with evidence that such measures will have no pro-natalist effect. Rhetorical support for infants and children, it would seem, has a somewhat airy core.

*Third, family-policy activists have built their reform proposals on misinterpreted statistical evidence.* The most significant and startling change—revealed by virtually every measure of family stability (divorce rate, number of children affected by divorce, illegitimacy ratio, fertility rate, juvenile-delinquency rate, or percentage of single-parent families)—is from a remarkable health and vitality for the American "nuclear" family in the 1946–60 period, followed by a striking shift toward marked instability *after* 1960. This historical shift of bewildering proportions has been ignored by most family-policy advocates, because their analysis of the causes behind contemporary family problems cannot explain the extraordinary change from evident family vitality in the late 1940s and 1950s to accelerating instability after 1960.

Examine, for instance, the "poverty argument": that poverty and low incomes create family stress and instability. Personal income, in fact, was everywhere rising and poverty progressively declining throughout the 1960s, and at rates far more rapid than during the 1950s. The percentage of children below the poverty line actually fell from 27 percent in 1959 to 15 percent in 1968. Yet at the same time, families clearly began to fragment.

Or take the "jobs argument": that unemployment is a chief cause of troubled families. During the 1960s unemployment rates for white and black workers progressively declined to levels equal to or below those achieved during the 1950s. Yet family disintegration in the post-1945 era began to accelerate only after 1960.

All other explanations similarly fall short. The 1960s experienced unprecedented advances in incomes, jobs, and status by racial minorities and women. Inflation remained at tolerably low levels from the early 1950s through the late 1960s. The movement of women into the post-World War II labor market began during the late 1940s, not the 1960s. Medicare and Medicaid extended health coverage in the 1960s to many of the aged and poor, part of an extraordinary nationwide expansion of quality health care. Social services grew dramatically during the 1960s under the auspices of hundreds of new federal and state programs. The number of social workers tripled in that decade alone. The presumed pressures of technology—television, nuclear power, processed foods—had their counterparts in the 1950s without appreciable results. The "myths" of technological advance, economic growth, family independence, personal responsibility, and *laissez faire*, all existed with equal or greater virulence in the late 1940s and 1950s without apparent effect on families. In fact, under the causal analysis and policy recommendations advanced by recent family-policy advocates, the 1950s should have been marked by family turmoil and instability, while the 1960s should have evidenced a new blossoming of family life. But exactly the opposite happened. Why?

## THREE DEVELOPMENTS

The instability characterizing American family life since 1960 results from the interplay of three developments: one demographic, one physiological and attitudinal, and one broadly ideological. None is amenable to intervention by a democratic state.

*1. The Demographic Bulge.* The very success of family life in the 1940s and 1950s generated the occasion of subsequent turmoil—a vast age cohort that began reaching adolescence in the early 1960s. The most unstable stage of an individual's life, adolescence is characterized by confused emotions, rebellion against parental and other authority, and the questioning of values and ethical constraints. To deal with adolescents, parents and other responsible adults require confidence in their own values, personal strength, and willingness to administer discipline tempered by understanding and love. Yet, apparently overwhelmed by the surging numbers of youth during the 1960s, American adults and the institutions they controlled collectively showed few such qualities. Only now is the last of the "baby boom" generation passing into the more stable young-adult years. In a complex manner, this demographic bulge certainly conditioned, and to some degree caused, the other two developments.

*2. The "Second" Sex Revolution.* Historian Edward Shorter argues for the existence of two sex revolutions in Western history: The first occurred in Europe between 1750 and 1850 (the United States, he suggests, was "born modern"), and was marked by the initial incursion of premarital sexual intercourse into the lives of the unmarried. The second, says Shorter, began between 1955 and 1965, and saw the generalization of intercourse among the majority of unmarried.

In the United States, the evidence reflecting major discontinuities after 1960 in the erotic life of the average young, white, unmarried woman seems conclusive. Among unmarried white women, ages 15 to 19, the illegitimacy rate was relatively stable through the 1950s—rising from 5.1 per 1,000 in 1950 to only 6.5 in 1962. Thereafter—and despite the spread of "the pill" and the widening availability of abortion—it climbed steadily, and reached 12.1 in 1975. A series of surveys from the 1960s shows as well startling increases in American "nonvirginity rates." Within a typical group of adolescent women questioned in 1971, nearly half had experienced intercourse by age 19, compared to only 17 percent in Alfred Kinsey's study during the 1940s. And the pace of this change is accelerating: A recent study found a 54-percent jump between 1971 and 1976 in the number of 16 year olds having had intercourse at least once. Interestingly, the illegitimacy rate among non-white females rose through the 1950s in conjunction with the surge of marital fertility, but began to *fall* in 1961. In many respects, the "second" sex revolution was a white, middle-class phenomenon.

It soon spread from youth to other parts of the population. In a major 1972 statistical study commissioned by the Playboy Foundation, Morton Hunt discovered that all Americans in the early 1970s

—young and old alike—were having more sex, doing it in different ways, with a greater variety of partners, and feeling less guilty about it afterwards, than did their Kinsey-survey counterparts. Whereas 41 percent of married females ages 35 to 44 had experienced pre-marital sex, 81 percent of married females ages 18 to 24 had. While only 14 percent of Kinsey's "adolescent to age 25" group of white males had used cunnilingus in premarital foreplay, 69 percent of the same age cohort in 1972 said they had. Kinsey reported a median weekly marital coitus figure of 2.45 for persons ages 16 to 25; Hunt found a median of 3.25 for the 18-to-24 age group, with similar increases for all older cohorts.

Even more striking are the shifts in sexual attitudes evident in the period after 1960. Opinion surveys among college students show that virginity was still a mythically prized virtue in the late 1950s; a poll in 1970 found that three out of four students thought it unimportant whether or not they married a virgin. Whereas legal and easy abortion had been unthinkable in the United States in 1963, by 1972 it was legal, subject to certain limitations, in half a dozen states and was to be legally available everywhere only one year later. In the 1973 "Sorenson Report," researchers described the growing predominance of situation ethics in the sexual liaisons of young people. Rejecting laws or religious dogma as irrelevant to the problems of sexual partners, distrusting lifelong monogamy, suspicious of the restraints of fidelity, and believing "family" to interfere with sexual fulfillment, a growing number of youth placed sexual satisfaction at the center of their personal relationships.

What caused this upheaval in American sexual actions and attitudes after 1960? Among background factors were advances by the biological sciences, such as oral contraceptives; physiological changes such as earlier menstruation and later menopause; the dramatic growth in higher education, which drew together large numbers of unmarried youth; and changes in the national mood, including the decline in religious values and a new emphasis on "rights" which led to an obsession with self. Sexual researchers, from Freud through Kinsey to Masters and Johnson, moved emphasis ever further away from the idea of the sex act as an expression of human love toward preoccupation with the nature of the physiological release and "health" of the sex organs.

Perhaps more critical was what Vance Packard calls "the crumbling of traditional controls" over youth sexuality. The decline in parental authority over the awakening process, the decrease in community scrutiny, and the rise of a youth subculture, made it vastly more difficult to assure female virginity until marriage. Surveys from the 1940-to-1960 period show a clear correlation between religious devoutness and abstinence from premarital coitus. Yet with the apparent American retreat from religious belief starting in the late 1950s, church leaders grew pliable and non-judgmental in matters of personal morality. In addition, the spread of "the pill" and waning concern about social stigmatization led to a decline in the fear that sexual activity might lead to premarital pregnancy.

Allan Sherman—in his episodic, rude, but nonetheless insightful *The Rape of the A\*P\*E\** (\**American \*Puritan \*Ethic*)—offers a "conspiracy" theory of the sexual revolution. Sherman traces the sexual revolution's origins to the social upheaval of World War II, follows it through an underground existence in the 1950s, to its full-blown emergence after 1963 and final victory in the 1973 Supreme Court abortion decisions. Led by scattered members of the generation reaching adulthood in the 1940s who were bent on the "obscening of America," the attack centered on the sexual restraints imposed by nineteenth-century bourgeois culture—such as the repression of obscenity, pornography, indecent exposure, nudity, premarital sex, extra-marital sex, abortion, divorce, desertion, perversion—and on the whole "incredibly clean-cut and impossibly wholesome" American world of Disney, church socials, Shirley Temple, the YMCA, Blondie and Dagwood, *The Saturday Evening Post*, Motherhood, miniature golf, Coca-Cola, Apple Pie, and Hot Dogs. By the late 1960s, writes Sherman, "Legions of Lolitas joined the battle with battalions of Babbitts and platoons of Portnoys. Manners and morals and great institutions bit the dust. Waterbeds splashed and vibrators jiggled. And when the air was cleared ... the world was never going to be the same again. No one knew exactly how, but Western Civilization had been caught with its pants down."

And the impact of the sex revolution? Sherman suggests that it "removed America's backbone and revealed our awful secret: Stripped of the Puritan ethic, we have no morals at all." He adds that "nothing was reduced to less recognizable rubble than the revered ... Institution of Marriage." Edward Shorter, a less euphoric coroner, considers the nuclear family of the 1970s wracked by some form of final tubercular spasm.

The institution of monogamous marriage is clearly in trouble, for the sexual revolution has made it vastly more difficult to retain monogamy's monopoly on sex. Marriages predicated mostly on sexual capability and erotic arousal prove fragile. Parents abandon and adolescents reject all sense of lineage, which monogamy alone can provide. The latter turn instead to peer groups and their own subculture in search of values and sexual gratification. As Pitrim Sorokin once observed: "A sex revolution drastically affects the lives of millions, deeply disturbs the community, and decisively influences the future of society." Families, simply put, were major casualties of the Western world's "second" sex revolution.

FROM "FATHER KNOWS BEST" ...

*3. Collapse of the Nuclear Family Norm.* The emergence of industrial capitalism and bourgeois society in the period from 1750 to 1850, according to Shorter, was tied to a dual revolution in "sentiments": heightened sexuality and gushing maternal love. The former change, rising among men and women of the European industrial class who were newly liberated from the sexual restraints of traditional agrarian communities, produced the "first" sex revolution referred to above. The latter change in sentiment welled up among the bourgeoisie, for economic growth had liberated women from other labor and allowed them to devote more time to better mothering and infant care.

Family life took shape about the home. The vital center of this new domesticity was the infant. An emotional web was spun around mother and baby, predicated on a new sense of the preciousness of infant life. Lloyd de Mause has compiled a large body of evidence showing the sweeping improvement in child-care practices that accompanied the rise of the bourgeoisie. Shockingly widespread practices of swaddling, child beating, infanticide, wet nursing (virtually an institutionalized form of infanticide), abandonment, sexual abuse, and even the sale of children, gave way to a surge of parental affection, as demonstrated by the rising popularity of maternal nursing, dramatic drops in infant-mortality rates, a new popular emphasis on the joys of domesticity and family life, and recognition of the priceless importance of infants and children. This valuation spread even to prenatal life. Nineteenth-century campaigns against abortion were largely a bourgeois phenomenon.

Girded by this value structure, the bourgeois nuclear family emerged as the Western family norm. Its characteristics were a stable heterosexual coupling based on love, the exclusiveness of the male-female sexual bond in marriage, the primacy of family attachments, the expectation of children, economic security for women and children, the obligation among family members for mutual support in crises, the acceptance of sex-determined roles within the family, and the prolongation of childhood. There was as well a linkage to bourgeois values of hard work, delayed gratification, and self-imposed restraints on personal behavior. The bourgeois nuclear family certainly never extended to a majority of American households. But like any social or cultural norm, it stood into the twentieth century as the ideal form of American family life, as the measure of normality or deviance, and as the mark of responsibility and respectability. It drew support from most other American social institutions—including law, government, organized religion, neighborhood, the media (such as it was), and the educated elite.

The American nuclear family first ran into trouble during the late nineteenth century, as evidenced in rapidly rising (although still relatively low) divorce figures and falling fertility. A retreat from parenthood grew more evident in the interwar period, primarily in the form of a significant rise in childless marriages. This apparent decline of family life led to the pessimistic sociological formulations of the 1930s which described the family's loss of function and approaching demise.

The post-1945 era, however, witnessed a remarkable and totally unexpected surge of familism and re-emergence of the belief that a family was incomplete without children. Fueled by the flood of GI's returning home to build normal lives, the period was marked by a dramatic rise in the marriage rate, a downward movement in average marriage age, swelling fertility among the married, increasing remarriage, and even higher fertility among the remarried. Sociologists now gave optimistic, supportive assessments of American family life. Capping this genre was William Goode's *World Revolution and Family Patterns,* which argued (with a heady dose of New Frontierism) that the "conjugal family" found in the industrial West—and linked to an ideology first shaped by Protestant asceticism—was the emerging norm among virtually all developing peoples.

## ... TO "THREE'S COMPANY"

In the mid-1960s, however, the nuclear family came under sustained ideological attack. The New Left revived the Marxist critique of the bourgeois family, viewing it as predicated on property relations, male supremacy, and the boredom of domestic bliss. Bourgeois marriage represented the crassest prostitution of both men and women and the domestic slavery of wives. Inspired by Friedrich Engels, the left stressed the relationship between heightened sexuality and the approaching demise of bourgeois family values. Unrestrained sexual intercourse and "true" sexual love demanded the dissolution of the "home," the transformation of housekeeping into a social industry, the collectivization of child care and education, and elimination of the concept of "illegitimacy."

For their part, radical minority spokesmen derided the "racist cultural imperialism" of the white middle class in imposing its family norms and supposedly alien morality on blacks, Hispanics, Native Americans, and other ethnic groups. Feminists drew on the Marxist analysis, arguing that the purpose of the family had been to secure men's ownership of women and children and to sustain male domination over women deprived of any life other than a restraining and debilitating motherhood. "Populationists" resurrected the Malthusian fear of resource shortages and economic decline arising from overpopulation, and opened their assault on the reproductive energies of the nuclear family. Casting parenthood in a negative or, at best, ambivalent role, they argued for "micro" or "childfree" families to save the world from disaster.

In face of this onslaught, institutions once sustaining the nuclear-family norm either proved crippled themselves, or deserted to the other side. Remnant white ethnic groups, which once served a supportive function for families in European immigrant communities came under regular government and media attack during the 1960s as racist and reactionary. Minority groups found their destinies tied to federal power and the schemes of intellectuals. Neighborhood communities were broken apart by federal urban-renewal and housing programs, and by court-ordered busing.

Many churches, once supportive centers of nuclear family life, shifted ground. By the early 1970s, liberal Protestant and Jewish groups had abandoned many traditional moral and social precepts, including normative support for the nuclear family. For instance, a panel representing one large Protestant body affirmed in 1976 that "there is a diversity of types or forms of family existing in modern American society." Defining family as "a relationship community of more than one person," its list of variant forms includes two-parent, one-parent, childless, parentless, and "single persons" families. The traditional family norm found occasional support and sustenance only among culturally-derided Roman Catholic, Mormon, and scattered evangelical Protestant and orthodox Jewish groups.

The media, attracted to protest and evidence of unsettling change, wandered from the nuclear-family norm it had supported in the 1950s. Documentaries probed the failings and pathologies of the American family. Newscasts riveted attention on the New Left, youth culture, minority protests, and the dissolution of old values. *Father Knows Best, Leave It to Beaver,* and *I Love Lucy* gave way to *One Day At a Time, Three's Company,* and *Miss Winslow and Son.*

The corporate world followed the lure of money and struck its Faustian bargain with the anti-nuclear-family cause. Large corporations proceeded to publish books and magazines, press records, produce motion pictures, and sponsor television shows that struck at the heart of middle-class family values.

Legal institutions began to be reshaped. Research showed that most state marriage laws presumed lifelong commitment, a first marriage, procreation as an essential element of marriage, some division of labor in the family, middle-class status, and the Judeo–Christian ideal of a monogamous, heterosexual union. Stripped of their normative character—and portrayed as elements of bourgeois cultural imperialism—these family laws came under challenge; many have already been changed. In its 1973 *Roe* and *Doe* decisions, the U.S. Supreme Court struck down existing state abortion statutes that sustained the bourgeois belief in the sanctity of prenatal infant life. The Court's 1976 *Danforth* decision denied that abortion was in any sense a "family issue" and prohibited interference by a husband, or by a parent of a minor, with the absolute right of a woman to undergo an abortion during the initial three months of pregnancy.

## THE DESERTION BY THE PROFESSIONALS

The abandonment of the nuclear-family norm was most dramatic among family counselors, social workers, and sociologists. Articles appearing in the mid-1960s exposed and critically dissected the nuclear-family mythology encrusting family sociology and family counseling. Authors termed this mythology dangerous, arguing that because it served as the standard used by marriage and family counselors in judging family health it led to culturally biased advice. Starting in the late 1960s, a veritable flood of sociological books and essays attacked all aspects of middle-class family life. One searches in vain during this period for an authoritative voice defending the rapidly collapsing nuclear-family norm.

Revealing evidence of desertion from the old normative family concept comes from a comparison of successive editions of family-sociology textbooks. Those published before 1972 continue to view the middle-class nuclear family as the American norm. Those appearing after 1972 abandon normative concepts altogether.

For instance, Ira Reiss's 1971 text, *The Family System in America*, stresses the continuity and stability of the nuclear-family model, which he terms a system undergoing only "moderate change," not radical transition. The nuclear-family norm forms the book's ordering principle, and is used to identify deviant behavior such as premarital pregnancy and homosexuality. Reiss then saw the rest of the world as moving toward the American model.

In his 1976 edition (revealingly pluralized as *Family Systems in America*), however, Reiss emphasizes that "choices in all stages of the family are now legitimate far beyond what they were just five or ten years ago." The nuclear family no longer serves as the ordering principle of his text. In fact, there are no longer any family norms: "We are now involved in a society with a variety of life styles that necessitates that people be able to feel that their life style is proper to them, even though it may not be a proper life style for other people."

Bert Adams, in his 1971 text, *The American Family: A Sociological Interpretation*, essentially describes an American nuclear-family norm that, "[b]arring a major historical upheaval . . . is likely to persist over the next generation." Such an upheaval apparently occurred, for his 1976 edition, *The Family: A Sociological Interpretation*, stresses alternatives to the old nuclear family and the need for personal choice of an appropriate family life style.

Gerald Leslie, in his 1967 edition of *The Family in Social Context*, clearly states that the "white, Anglo-Saxon, Protestant, middle-class family is a kind of prototype for the larger society. . . . Its patterns are "ideal" patterns for much of the non-white, non-Anglo, non-Protestant, non-middle-class segment of the population . . .In twentieth-century America, however, *an increasing proportion of the population is achieving the ideal"* (emphasis added). Among the values found in this ideal family are: marriage as the dominant life goal for men and women; marriage based on love and free choice; the expectation that marriage should produce happiness for both partners; the belief that life has much to offer the young; the idea that childhood should be protected and prolonged; the confinement of sexual relations to marriage; the belief that husbands and wives have some traditional roles to play; and the idea that individual fulfillment should be sought in family living. This family model is clearly the classic bourgeois family.

Yet Leslie's 1976 edition not only discards the "middle class" family as the cultural norm (he finds it rejected by, among others, blacks, Chicanos, Indians, and Jews who are fighting "forced cultural homogenization"), but even attributes new values to the middle-class family that are radically different from those in his 1967 list. These are: equality of the sexes, including a flexible division of tasks between men and women; democracy in all status and power roles among and between parents and children; permissive, person-centered mate selection, including free sexual experimentation for youth and the right of men and women to enjoy sex, including premarital liaisons; a strong emphasis on sexual and conjugal companionship, tied to continuing functions such as child bearing, socialization, and economic cooperation; the professionalization of marriage and parental roles, including counseling and classes on marriage, childbirth, and parenthood; and a turn to divorce if counseling and classes fail.

Given the startling changes to be found in sociology textbooks, one might assume that the number of nuclear families fell dramatically in this period. But the proportion of nuclear families relative to all households in fact remained relatively steady through 1970. Prevailing family structures were not radically altered; but *the normative concept of the nuclear family*—attacked from many sides in the 1960s and abandoned by most theretofore supporting institutions—effectively collapsed in the early 1970s.

Cultural and social norms provide a civilization with its ordering principles, its measures of morality and deviance, and its legacy to subsequent generations. They define for individuals the nature of responsibility, the ultimate purposes of social life, and the proper basis for human relationships. Nuclear families, now deprived of such a normative nature and the support thereby entailed, have fallen progressively into disarray.

In place of the nuclear family, the dominant voices in sociology and family-counseling professional journals are now describing the emergence of new normative concepts to define acceptable family life in the post-bourgeois era. While varying their emphases, such professionals cite certain values with regularity:

*1. Mutability.* There are no constants in moral questions nor in personal relationships.

*2. Choice.* There should be no bias towards marriage and children. Everything is open. All habitual and cultural attitudes may be questioned. All values are on trial.

*3. Experimentation.* Since there are no family or sexual norms, no traditions worthy of universal emulation, and no restraints, persons must be free to experiment with a variety of sexual partners and practices to find the sexual and family life styles appropriate for themselves.

*4. Self-fulfillment.* Morality demands freedom for people to realize their own potentials—and their own needs, desires, and tastes— with a minimum of social rules and regulations. Relationships should last only so long as they are mutually self-fulfilling.

*5. Uninhibited Sexuality.* Sexual gratification represents one of life's ultimate values. Access to regular sexual satisfaction should be viewed as a basic human right. There is no true humanness devoid of sexuality.

*6. The Problem of Children.* Sexuality must be viewed as totally separated from procreation. Parenthood should be undertaken only after a careful weighing of social, cultural, and economic costs. The burden of social proof is shifted away from the right of persons to remain "childfree" to questioning the right of persons to procreate. Given the problem of overpopulation, reproduction may have to be viewed as a privilege granted by a government working towards the goals of decreasing the quantity while increasing the quality of humankind. Unwanted pregnancies should be aborted.

In sum, any human relationship involving cohabitation that produces self-gratification and sexual fulfillment has some claim to valid family status. "Human actualizing" contracts, progressive monogamy, group marriage, polyandry, polygyny, communal arrangements, homosexual pairings, open marriage (involving group sex, swinging, or revolving mates), heterosexual and nonmonogamous cohabitation, "singlehood," *and* the old nuclear family, are all legitimate family "life styles." "Immorality" in sexual matters or "deviance" in family structure have become empty concepts.

Such new values are supported by and particularly evident among elements of the college-educated upper-middle class. While reassuring voices are correct in arguing that most Americans still live in traditional nuclear families, post-bourgeois family norms are starting to make a statistical dent. In 1970, for instance, there were 1,046,000 unmarried adults sharing living quarters with one person of the opposite sex; by 1977, the figure had swelled to 1.9 million. While such households still form only 2 percent of all "couple households," the 12-percent figure now found in Sweden may suggest the immediate American future.

## THE HELPING HAND THAT HARMS

American family life is being fundamentally altered by two forces: from within, by the impact of the "second" sex revolution on male-female ties and on the linkage of generations; and from without, by the cultural abandonment of the nuclear-family norm and the normative embrace of amoral family and sexual ethics by elements of the educated upper-middle class. Even if a majority of Americans thought it desirable, a democratic government could not check or reverse these trends. On the one hand, the state cannot undo the sex revolution. It might as easily try to reverse the Industrial Revolution or any other nexus of social change that has substantially altered our national evolution. On the other hand, while the government of a free people may reflect a social norm and give it legal recognition and support, it cannot create such a standard, nor long sustain a normative concept devoid of cultural recognition.

Nor will state intervention on behalf of families succeed. Full-employment policies might achieve sound economic goals, and a national health-insurance program could democratize the provision of health care. Day-care subsidies would certainly ease the financial costs of single-parent or two-earner families and free more women for paid labor. Family allowances might help many children, and legal reforms could secure more legally enforceable rights for families and children. *But these measures will not strengthen families.*

The results, in fact, would probably be the opposite. In his review of Soviet attempts to strengthen family life in the Stalinist era, Lewis A. Coser was led to the conclusion that the state, by its very interference in the lives of citizens, must necessarily undermine the parental authority it seeks to restore. Recent research on the effects of Sweden's 1937 marriage-loan act—which was intended to encourage earlier marriage and more children per family—shows that the couples participating had *fewer* children than the unbenefited control population. And while defensive explanations abound, the fact remains that U.S. Department of Health, Education and Welfare experiments with income-maintenance programs have seen divorce, separation, and desertion figures significantly higher among families receiving a guaranteed federal income than among control families receiving no benefits. *The disconcerting reality appears to be that state social intervention on behalf of families actually weakens or destroys families.*

Harvard sociologist Carle Zimmerman concluded his massive 1947 study on the relationship of family and civilization by predicting that the final collapse of the traditional Western family would occur before the end of this century. "The results," he added, "will be much more drastic in the United States because, being the most extreme and inexperienced of the aggregates of Western civilization, it will take its first real 'sickness' most violently."

Can this reckoning be avoided? Viable family life may somehow survive in a normative vacuum. Or, echoing the experience of the 1950s, certain bourgeois family values—now enjoying something of an underground existence in little-noticed movements such as La Leche League International—might re-emerge as normative guides. Or, a new legitimate ordering principle for family life could evolve. The one certainty, though, is that the liberal family-policy agenda cannot overcome—for in some ways it actually reflects—the shallowness and confusion of prevailing cultural norms and the personal hedonism dominating American life.

## NOTES

1. The political strategy being followed by American family-policy advocates has historical precedents. European social democrats have regularly used "family policy" as a potent argument, attracting conservative backing for a variety of welfare-policy proposals designed to save the family from dissolution or sterility. Swayed by the pro-natalist arguments of the 1942 Beveridge report, a number of British Conservatives lent their support to social-welfare policies such as children's allowances and creation of a national health service. They hoped such measures would stabilize family life, raise the United Kingdom's birth rate, and continue to people the Commonwealth with British stock. When Alva and Gunnar Myrdal advanced a sweeping pro-natalist family policy in 1934 that involved the socialist reconstruction of Swedish society, even the veteran conservative economist Gustav Cassel had to acknowledge the strength of their arguments and the need for some state intervention to support families.

*Part III*

# SOCIAL WORK

# Chapter Five

# EMERGENCE OF THE PROFESSION

## BEGINNINGS

The profession of social work has its origins in the late nineteenth century. The functions performed by social workers have, of course, always been carried out in communities, mostly by the family, and during the Middle Ages and the early period of industrialization by the church. As the power of the church declined with the growth of the nation-state, and as social welfare developed as an institution, many of these functions were picked up as voluntary philanthropic efforts. Harry Specht, in the first selection in this chapter, "Origins of the Profession" (Reading 14), describes the early development of these functions in organizations concerned with aiding individuals such as the Charity Organization Society, and organizations concerned with social reform such as the settlements. Specht also describes the development of the organizational structure of the profession itself.

Early social work practice was not theoretically based. It was only in the 1920s and 1930s, with the emergence of Freudian and other psychologically-based theories, that social work began to incorporate a knowledge base that was distinct from the practice method. Social casework, as Howard Goldstein notes, developed without a "commitment to an articulation of the philosophical conception of man" that underlies the practice. Practice of this sort, Goldstein says, "based mainly on a set of pragmatic methods and necessarily incomplete theories, is flimsy and subject to change when new approaches come along."[1]

## THE PROFESSION

In Reading 15, "Attributes of a Profession," Ernest Greenwood describes the major characteristics of professions. A *knowledge base* that draws upon well-developed theory from which the practitioner can formulate testable propositions is one of five major characteristics of a profession. The other major attributes of professions identified by Greenwood are *authority, community sanction*, an *ethical code*, and a *culture. Authority* refers to the client's belief in the superior knowledge of the professional. Unlike marketplace exchanges wherein customers may judge for themselves the quality of merchandise, in the professional relationship it lies with the professional to judge what is in the client's interest. For this reason Everett Hughes has suggested that the appropriate motto for this relationship is *credat emptor*—let the buyer believe—rather than the traditional *caveat emptor* of the marketplace.[2] In order to earn and ensure this belief, and to prevent those who are not properly credentialed from deluding the public, a profession seeks to win the *sanction of the community*, which may take different forms such as registration, certification, and licensing.[3] These different forms of sanction award different degrees of authority and autonomy to the professional, such as privileged communication and the right to set standards for what is considered acceptable professional behavior. Professional *codes of ethics* are created as the means by which the community is reassured that the privileges awarded will be used in the interests of the community. Finally, a *professional culture* representing the values, norms, and symbols of the enterprise, inevitably takes shape to mark the professional identification. This culture operates, for example, in recruitment, screening, and socialization of new entrants to the profession; it also provides the means by which recognition and status are awarded and discipline maintained within the profession.

Greenwood's "Attributes of a Profession" has been the definitive statement on this subject for several decades. Other scholars who write about the profession—whether they agree with Greenwood or not—must invariably address themselves to his formulation. There are many people who believe that the profession itself is an unwholesome influence on the behavior of social workers. Haug and Sussman, for example, describe the reasons why clients are in "revolt" against professional autonomy. The professional, they say "draws upon organizational power as well as the power of his expertise to control the circumstances under which service is given."[4] These circumstances include such items as who is served, at what costs, and when, where, and how. Thus, the question of autonomy is a most important one. Currently, many sociologists and social workers have expressed the belief that professionalism is nothing more than a means by which to protect privilege and self-interest. In this view, the *knowledge* of professions is only self-protective credentialism rather than expertise; *authority* is more a means of controlling clients than a device by which clients can deal with the awesome nature of the professional's superior knowledge and skill; *sanction* is bestowed by, and in the interests of, the established power structure rather than by and for clients; *ethical codes* are developed not to protect the community but, rather, to protect the profession from meddling outsiders; and, finally, the norms, values, and beliefs that constitute the *culture* of a profession are no more altruistic and sacrosanct than any other group that works for wages, fees, and profits; they only represent different paths to success.[5]

Paul Halmos, a British sociologist, has a quite different view of the causes of antiprofessionalism. He points out that, in large part, virulent antiprofessionalism emanates from the United States. "American sociologists of the professions," he says, "are averse to dwelling on the less jaundiced impressions which the personal service professions can and do create." Halmos believes that these ideas are relevant to problems that are uniquely American and not attributable to American professions in particular nor to other countries in general. Moreover, he believes that these views of American sociologists are not well balanced. He says:

> They leave little or no margin of their sociological attention to the fact that facts are not exhausted by the marshalling of all that is tough, combative, competitive, or downright unattractive, reprehensible, and evil in the practising personal service professional. A sociological account of the personal service professions in terms of the basic categories of power, status, prestige, income, and the like, is not in itself mistaken; but when it refuses, almost with a masochistic fervour, to explore what minor and not so minor sociological significance might be found in categories of self-transcendence, such as sympathy, empathy, rapport, affection and the like, it is plainly guilty of a loss of objectivity.[6]

In Reading 16, " 'Attributes of a Profession' Revisited," Ernest Greenwood reviews and analyzes various critiques of professionalism that have been put forth over the last quarter century. He assesses soberly critiques of the profession and professionalism. Greenwood concludes that *specialized knowledge* is the sine qua non of the professional. His carefully reasoned analysis ends with a warning that a profession imperils itself when it fails to recognize the centrality of this attribute.

## SOME SPECIAL CHARACTERISTICS OF SOCIAL WORK

In discussing the other selections it will be useful to bear in mind three characteristics of social work that have made it somewhat different from other professions. *First,* social work began as a private, voluntary enterprise in the philanthropic movements. *Second,* the profession started as a congeries of specializations which were viewed as auxiliary functions to other professions in a variety of organizational contexts. *Third,* in the first half of this century the profession was composed almost exclusively of women. Each of these developmental characteristics has had an important effect on the profession, and each is the source of continuing strain within it.

### Beginnings of a Voluntary Private Enterprise

Because of its origin as a voluntary, private enterprise (which essentially reflected the "residual" view of social welfare), the earlier intervention methods of social work supported individualistic solutions to social problems rather than communalistic ones. By "individualistic solutions" we refer to services performed on behalf of clients that focus on the deficiencies of the clients rather than on institutional deficiencies. The classic individualistic solution, in this sense, is therapeutically-oriented psychiatric casework. Communalistic solutions focus on the reform of institutions and allocative procedures.

Throughout this century social work has grown as a professional enterprise, expanding as social welfare has moved toward fuller institutional status. It has become, like social welfare, a big business in which well over 300,000 employees share responsibility for dispensing benefits valued in billions of dollars.[7] Social work is, clearly, no longer a professional function concerned with meeting residual needs. This continual expansion is responsible, in part, for the great strains social work has experienced throughout its history between its social change and clinical functions that are reflected in the profession's responsibility to provide direct personal services and its responsibility for creating, maintaining, and reforming the institutional context within which it operates.

This strain was articulated by Porter Lee in 1929 in his classic paper "Social Work: Cause and Function."[8] Lee viewed this strain as arising from a "change in the nature of social work from that of cause to that of function." Observing the growth of social work both in numbers of professionals and size of allocations, he warned that the community would demand higher degrees of accountability from social workers and some means for assuring that their conduct is guided by ethical considerations. In effect, Lee was saying that social work would have to acquire the attributes of a profession.

In our view, these dual commitments of social work inhere in the relationship between the profession of social work and the institution of social welfare and will always be present in some degree. In Reading 17, "The Incomplete Profession," Neil Gilbert and Harry Specht argue that social work has not developed sufficiently the techno-methodological capacity to deal with its commitments to development and reform of the institution (or what Lee called "cause").

## Beginnings as Unrelated Specializations

Social work began as a group of unrelated specializations in search of a profession, specializations in the service of other professions (e.g., medicine, education) in specific organizational settings (e.g., hospitals, schools). Many consequences have followed from this. We will discuss the profound impact of these early organizational contexts in the next chapter. But it should be noted that some of the attributes of professions (e.g., professional authority, a code of ethics, a culture) may come into conflict with characteristics of organizations because bureaucratic organizations establish their own hierarchy of authority, rules, and procedures. Therefore, with the growth of professionalism came the increased likelihood of organizational strain for social workers.

Additional consequences follow because social work had been wedded to a variety of other professional disciplines. Often, these affiliations encouraged social workers to use theoretical frameworks (e.g., Freudian theory) that were not well suited to implement Richmond's "person in the situation" conception of social work (a rather simple conception, but one that has endured longer than any other). The mix of Jane Addams, Mary Richmond, and Sigmund Freud, along with sociological theories such as those of Louis Wirth and Robert MacIver, not to mention the theories of progressive education brought in by social group work and the rational businesslike approach contributed by community organization, was sometimes exciting but not easy for the community and for the social workers themselves to comprehend.

## Preponderance of Women

The third characteristic of the profession mentioned above is that in its early development it was composed almost exclusively of women; men began entering the profession in significant numbers only after World War II.[9] The predominance of females supported, in part, the low status and low salaries for what was considered a relatively unimportant, residual function. This composition also both caused and supported the profession's nurturing and humanistic orientation. As the profession and the institution expanded and became more significant financially and politically, many more men were attracted to it. The increased numbers of males in the profession supports, in part, the more technical and rational orientations required by the expanding profession and institution. (Some of our readers may take offense at our attributing the profession's humanistic values to women. We do not mean to suggest that men cannot be nurturing, nor that women cannot be technical and rational; however, in the emergence of social work this seems to have been how things were.)

## A PROFESSION IN PROGRESS

In the last selection of this chapter, Reading 18, "Social Work as a Profession in Process," Thomas Owen Carlton analyzes how some of the major features of social work that we have described and some others have shaped the profession. Carlton's paper integrates the several themes discussed in the preceding papers. He describes how various ideas about mission, specialization, and interest in professionalization have interacted (and continue to interact) to shape the profession. We recommend that after completing all three chapters in this part of the book, the reader review the five articles in this chapter. In rereading this chapter they will see how elements in the organizational context of social work (chapter 6) and current issues in social work (chapter 7) are directly related to the emergence of social work as a profession.

As the profession has expanded, the strain between the nurturing-humanistic and technical-rational orientations to social work practice has been intensified in the field. To some extent this strain underlies the issues discussed in the papers by Gilbert and Specht, and Carlton. These haunting dilemmas occur, as Henry Miller has noted, because the social worker "cannot disengage himself from the moral concerns of his client."[10] While professionalism calls for behavior that is scientific, knowledge-based, objective, and rational, we are constrained by the humanistic, caring, and nurturing values of social work which demand that we be deeply and actively involved in furthering the moral well-being of clients and society. Dilemmas of this sort will, no doubt, continue unabated in the practice of social work for the foreseeable future.

## NOTES

1. Howard Goldstein, *Social Work Practice: A Unitary Approach* (Columbia: University of South Carolina Press, 1973), p. 41.

2. Everett C. Hughes, "Professions," *Journal of the American Academy of Arts and Sciences,* 92 (Fall 1963): 657.

3. Paul E. Weinberger and Dorothy Z. Weinberger, "Legal Regulation in Perspective," *Social Work,* 7 (January 1962): 67–74; also, *See* Reading 26.

4. Marie R. Haug and Marvin B. Sussman, "Professional Autonomy and the Revolt of the Client," *Social Problems,* 17 (Fall 1969), p. 155.

5. Neil Gilbert and Harry Specht, *Dimensions of Social Welfare Policy* (Englewood Cliffs, N.J.: Prentice-Hall, Inc., 1973), pp. 128–29.

6. Paul Halmos, ed., *Professionalization and Social Change* (Sociological Review Monograph, December 1973), p. 9.

7. David Hardcastle, "The Profession, Professional Organizations, Licensing, and Private Practice," *Handbook of Social Services,* eds., Neil Gilbert and Harry Specht (Englewood Cliffs, N.J.: Prentice-Hall, Inc., 1980); and Alma MacMillan, "Social Welfare Expenditures Under Public Programs," *Social Security Bulletin,* 42:6 (June 1979), pp. 3–12.

8. Porter R. Lee, "Social Work: Cause and Function," *Proceedings of the National Conference of Social Work* (Chicago: University of Chicago Press, 1929), pp. 3–20 .

9. Sex ratios in the profession are discussed by Henry J. Meyer and Sheldon Siegel, "Profession of Social Work: Contemporary Characteristics," *Encyclopedia of Social Work,* Vol. II, ed. John B. Turner (New York: National Association of Social Workers, 1977), pp. 1067–1981.

10. Henry Miller, "Value Dilemmas in Social Casework," *Social Work,* 13 (January 1968): 27–33.

# 14   Origins of the Profession

## HARRY SPECHT

The origins of the profession of social work lie in the late nineteenth century, with nurses, settlement workers, and the "friendly visitors" of the Charity Organization Societies—mostly middle- and upper-class young women who engaged in charitable activities to help lower-class people. These activities evolved into what has become known as social work. Because these activities usually were ancillary to the work of other professionals, carried out in well-established institutions such as schools, hospitals, and charitable societies, early social work was actually a collection of subprofessional specializations (Bartlett, 1970, pp. 20–36). These origins laid the basis for the organization of the profession up through the 1940s. During most of that period, social work was organized along functional area lines, which became known as "fields of practice," and most social work training and professional organizations followed suit. Thus, by the 1920s there were five fields of practice: family, child welfare, medical, psychiatric, and school social work. Social group work and leisure-time services, community organization, corrections, and public assistance were added in later years (Bartlett, 1970).

Mary Richmond was the first person to formulate these activities in a systematic fashion. Her books *Social Diagnosis* (1917) and *What Is Social Casework?* (1922) represent landmarks in the literature of "scientific helping." "Social diagnosis," she said, is "the attempt to make as exact a definition as possible of the situation and personality of a human being in some social need—of his situation and personality, that is, in relation to the other human beings upon whom he in any way depends or who depend upon him, and in relation to the social institutions of his community" (Richmond, 1917, p. 357). Richmond's definition of social diagnosis presents a conception of social work practice that is as useful today as it was at the beginning of the century. Interestingly, she preferred the words *social treatment* over *social casework,* and the former was the term of choice of many social workers until the 1920s (Richmond, 1930). *Social treatment* carried with it a much broader conception of the target of social work action than the term *social casework,* because it placed the focus on the person and the situation rather than on the case alone. Her conception of the "situation and personality of a human being in some social need" required an understanding of the client and his family, friends, relatives, work situation, and community social agencies.

Richmond's work is not theoretical in a technical sense; it is more of a how-to-do-it guide. But in those early years of the profession, no one else had put together these thoughts in one volume. Her rationalization of social treatment was part of a general movement in philanthropic work. She lived in the age of developing rationalization in industry; only a few years before she wrote her books, Henry Ford had organized the first industrial assembly line. It was not surprising, then, that the philanthropic organizations (financed largely by the great philanthropists of business and industry) would support the development of systematic and rational methods of handling charitable activities. At the same time as the publication of Richmond's books, the community chest and council-of-social-agencies movements were taking shape, reflecting in the giving of charity the same motive force at work in the rationalization of social casework (Gilbert and Specht, 1977).

The theoretical underpinnings of late nineteenth- and early twentieth-century social work were largely unarticulated. Major ideas came from scientists like Charles Darwin and Herbert Spencer; physicians like Benjamin Rush, Emil Kraepelin, and Henry Meyer; and political scientists like Adam Smith and Robert La Follette. The vision of society that underlay philanthropic activity was one in which the fortunes of humankind were determined largely by physical and biological forces that a benevolent and enlightened upper class could attempt to control by social engineering, using many of the new tools of science that were emerging rapidly in that day. The science of eugenics and the newly developing sciences of society—such as sociology, anthropology, and psychology—were of great interest to social workers of those days. Like the developments taking place in industry, these sciences were preoccupied with mechanics; the social sciences were based essentially on the philosophical assumptions that underlay the more fixed social class structure of the times, a structure in which the responsibility for helping "the poor" —that is, the majority of society—lay with the upper classes.

In the late 1920s, an explicit theory of human behavior, mostly Freudian, was integrated into social work thinking as a means of explaining and directing practice. This was a daring and innovative step, because Freudian theory was neither popular nor widely understood. It gave social casework a basis for understanding and interpreting human responses to social forces that theretofore had been lacking in the profession. Freudian and other psychologically-based theories were the first theoretical systems used by social workers; and, regardless of the limits of these kinds of theories, they provided a powerful knowledge base for the development of professional practice.

Another significant stream of activity in the development of social work and social welfare was the work of the social settlements. Settlement leaders like Jane Addams and Florence Kelley were more interested in social reform and social legislation than in charity and scientific helping. In a sense, their methods of work were *un*scientific because they required immersion in the community rather than objectivity; they lived with and experienced with their clients, and they were somewhat put off by the detachment and cautiousness that professionalism appeared to generate. Not until the 1930s and 1940s, when social group work methods and community organization practice were incorporated into social work, were the settlements absorbed into the community of social work agencies, because these new methods were more compatible with the existential here-and-now orientation of the settlements.

The first formal training for social work began at the end of the nineteenth century as in-service training for groups such as the workers of the Charity Organization Societies. Training programs in colleges and universities were introduced at the beginning of the twentieth century. All this early training was essentially education for social casework (Lubove, 1965).

Although Richmond's work had laid the basis for a generic form of social casework practice, professional education for the fields of practice continued into the 1940s. The notion underlying generic casework is that there are basic concepts that all social work practitioners use.* This idea represented a step forward in social work because it meant that the profession was not merely a series of adjunctive activies carried on in separate institutions such as schools and hospitals. Rather, certain *general* principles and concepts of helping could be applied across institutional areas. Generic practice, therefore, was an increment to the developing body of social work knowledge. This body of knowledge, in the 1920s, consisted largely of the principles and methods described by people like Richmond (1917) and Cannon (1951) and Freudian-type theory as interpreted by people like Marcus (1929), Towle (1931), and Robinson (1930).

Along with development of ideas about generic social casework practice and the introduction of explicit theory, two new specializations developed in social work in the 1930s and 1940s: social group work and community organization. These specializations were based in theoretical and philosophical systems of thought different from those of social casework. Social group work was rooted in the philosophy of John Dewey and associated with schools of progressive education. It was concerned largely with how social groups (that is, family, peer groups, social clubs, and community groups) affect socialization and social development. Social group workers like Coyle (1948) and Wilson and Ryland (1949) brought to the field of social work an interest in the capacity of the social group to support individuals and solve social problems. They were more interested in education for citizenship, and development of social capacities than in treatment of social illness (Papell and Rothman, 1966). Community organization was not concerned with the kinds of therapeutic interventions undertaken by social caseworkers. It came into social work more as a function than a professional practice. That is, the community chests and councils of social agencies (which constituted the major part of the field of community organization up to the 1950s) were the fundraising and fund-distributing subsystem of the field of social welfare, concerned primarily with philanthropic fund raising for voluntary agencies (Gilbert and Specht, 1977). In these early years, social group workers and community organizers tried to make their modes of practice look as much as possible like social casework, the predomi-

---

*The notion of a generic casework was introduced formally to the profession by the report of the Milford Conference in 1929. The Milford Conference was a consortium of social workers who had begun in 1923 to discuss social work practice (American Association of Social Workers, 1929).

nant mode of practice in the field. Thus, social group work gradually became more clinical and less focused on citizenship training and community action; and much of the literature on community organization described it as a social work method concerned predominantly with "intergroup work" processes and development of healthy social relationships (Gilbert and Specht, 1977).

The Depression of the 1930s had a great impact on the institution of social welfare. The Social Security Act of 1935 marked the entry of the federal government into the social welfare field on a large scale. Since that time, government has become the major source of support for social welfare and social service programs of all kinds. The immediate effect of this shift in sources of support for social welfare was to nudge the profession in the direction of more clinical types of work and away from serving poor and disadvantaged populations. As the federal government assumed primary responsibility for income maintenance programs for the poor, the voluntary agencies, which hired most of the professional social workers, shifted their focus to other types of social services, such as family counseling and leisure-time services. This, too, was a period in which social workers were extremely concerned about professionalization; the clinically oriented types of services were particularly attractive because of the more clearly developed and high-status technologies available in the medical and psychiatric fields.

In the 1930s and 1940s, there was no broad public acceptance of the psychotherapeutic arts of social caseworkers or of some of the ideas borrowed from progressive education by social group workers. A beachhead for the ideas of Freud, Horney, and Dewey had been established in the middle-class intellectual and artistic communities; by and large, however, these were not popular treatments. Most people did not seek them out, and there was no basis on which to build support for them in programs serving the masses. Some social workers did work in public assistance programs at that time, but the majority of "professionals" (that is, MSWs) did not. Psychiatric social work was where it was at for most social workers in the 1930s and 1940s. In terms of status and prestige, after psychiatric social work came child welfare and medical social work.

The disengagement of most professional social workers from the poor may be somewhat difficult to understand from the perspective of the late twentieth century. Today it is fairly well established that income support, social services, and psychotherapy are necessary and useful to all social classes in the community. But at the beginning of the century, income support services and social treatment were something that the upper class provided for the "worthy" poor, based on sentiments of *noblesse oblige* and the sanctity of charitable giving. Psychotherapy, for the most part, was for the rich only.

When income support types of philanthropy were taken over by government, and the private agencies moved into psychosocio-therapeutic types of work, questions about social class bias in the social services simply were not raised. The concept of social class in American life was first studied by sociologists in the 1930s. The term *social class* entered professional vocabularies in the 1940s; it was not until the 1950s, with the publication of Hunter's (1953) *Community Power Structure*, that ideas about differential distributions of social resources and power became an issue for professional discussion and action by social workers, city planners, sociologists, political scientists, and other professionals and academics. Alinsky (1946), writing in the 1940s, was an exception, but his ideas did not achieve currency in the professions until the 1960s.

For all these reasons, professional social work in the 1930s and 1940s drifted in the direction of clinical treatment and psychosocio-therapeutic types of work, and most social work professionals were employed in agencies that did not serve the neediest population groups.

By the 1940s social casework, social group work, and community organization had become the three major specializations in social work, with social casework by far the largest. At that time, a person considering a career in social work was confronted with a much simpler set of choices than those existing today. A "professional social worker" was a person with an MSW degree, and the majority of MSWs were social caseworkers who worked in clinically-oriented settings. A smaller number were social group workers, most of whom worked in leisure-time agencies such as settlement houses, community centers, and youth services. A small group was in community organization and was composed predominantly of older, "seasoned," male professionals who usually worked for community chests and health and welfare councils.

These divisions were reflected in the several professional organizations of social workers. The American Association of Social Workers, organized in 1921 and composed principally of caseworkers, was the largest professional organization. The American Association of Group Workers, organized in 1936, was a smaller fledgling organization for social group workers. The Association for the Study of Community Organization, established in 1946, was a comparatively informal group. (Community organization was recognized by the Council on Social Work Education as a legitimate specialization in social work education only in 1962. Until then, students could take courses in community organization, but they would have had to be trained first in social casework or social group work.)

In 1955 the different social work organizations (seven in all) combined to form the National Association of Social Workers (NASW), a clear indication that the social casework-social group work-community organization trinity in social work was not to remain for long the pattern of organization of the profession. Even so, the specialization of social casework appears to be a viable entity today. The *Social Casework* journal still is considered an important one in the field, and, despite the unification of professional social workers in NASW, societies of clinical social work for social workers in private practice are growing in size and influence. There is now a National Federation of Societies of Clinical Social Work, which publishes its own journal and engages in other professional activities to promote private practice (Levin, 1976).

## ELEMENTS OF CHANGE IN SOCIAL WORK PRACTICE

The social upheaval of the 1960s—largely a revolution in human rights—brought about significant changes in American society, which in turn effected some changes in social work practice. The civil rights revolution began in 1954, when the United States Supreme Court declared school segregation unconstitutional. The Warren Court's decision sparked the latent power of the black community and kindled large-scale demonstrations to protest numerous grievances. The movement for blacks' rights to equal access to public facilities and opportunities for jobs and education was supported by many Americans. The sit-ins, marches, civil disobedience, and other forms of nonviolent action in the following years were supported by social workers as professionals and citizens.* The initial successes of the civil rights movement were reflected in the Economic Opportunity Act of 1964, the Civil Rights Act of 1964, and the Elementary and Secondary Education Act of 1965. The legislation enforced constitutional rights to access to public facilities and voting and created programs to increase opportunities for education and jobs for minority groups and other deprived people. However, early results of the civil rights movement left many people frustrated; it was apparent that these programs would not make an immediate impact on the American minorities' source of anger and despair—the ever present existence of *inequality.* By the mid 1960s, public support for nonviolent black protest was submerged by reactions to the violence in communities such as Watts and Detroit and the violent protests on college campuses to the war in Vietnam. After the mid 1960s, the movement for rights extended to other groups in American society

*In the summer of 1964, the profession was especially shaken by the deaths of three young social workers in Philadelphia, Mississippi. James Chaney, Andrew Goodman, and Michael Schwerner, workers in a voter registration project, were brutally murdered. The Michael Schwerner Memorial Fund, Inc., organized by social workers in their memory, continued in this work (Kurzman, 1971).

who felt that they, too, bore the burdens of inequality and oppression: American Indians, Spanish-speaking people, women, homosexuals, the aged, welfare clients, prisoners and released offenders, mental patients, students, and others.

During these years of protest, many people—social workers included—cast a critical eye on the profession's contribution to the perpetuation of inequality and racism. All professions were subject to similar scrutiny, but many believed that social work was an especially glaring example of malfeasance, because it represented the failure of what was supposed to be society's means of preventing poverty and discrimination. The greatest grievance against the profession was its clinical/therapeutic orientation, which was perceived to be society's way of "blaming the victim," of putting the burden for social problems on the people who suffered from inequality, rather than eliminating the causes of inequality. The profession's response to this critique generally was to acknowledge its failures and reaffirm earlier commitments. In particular, attention was given to the social work function of advocacy, which spoke to the profession's responsibility to support clients' rights to dignified and human treatment (Ad Hoc Committee on Advocacy, 1969). Increased social work resources were devoted to social action; and, with support from the economic opportunity programs, many social agencies devoted greater attention to community organization, development of consumer groups, support for increased citizen participation in policymaking, development of community care to replace institutional care, and other social change activities. These efforts expanded the profession's involvement in social welfare programs that were closer to the person-in-the-situation conception of practice described by Richmond than to a classical therapeutic approach.

The renewed interest in the advocacy function was accompanied by a new articulation of professionalism in social work. In this view, adherence to *professional* standards and ethics, as distinct from the concerns of an employing agency, is necessary if services provided are to be in a client's best interests. From the advocacy perspective, the job of the social worker is to help clients utilize the systems around them to their best advantage. Briar (1967, p. 32) expressed this view: "The advocate . . . function requires that caseworkers have much greater *professional* [emphasis added] autonomy and discretion than now prevail in many, if not most, social agencies. Ninety percent or more of all caseworkers practice in bureaucratic organizations, and the demands of such organizations have a tendency to encroach on professional autonomy. Every attempt by the agency to routinize some condition or aspect of professional practice amounts to a restriction of professional discretion, and for that reason probably should be resisted, in most instances, by practitioners." This increased attention to social reform and social change enhanced the profession's concern for the institution of social welfare, which in the view of some, had been neglected too long by social workers (Gilbert and Specht, 1974).

Reform of the profession itself also was needed to counteract what many considered to be the elitism of the MSW as the sine qua non of professionalism. Social work became the spearhead of the "new careers" movement for paraprofessionals (Brager, 1965). The essential thought behind this movement is that the attributes of professionalism are not attained only through formal education. People learn from life experience with such problems as poverty and racism; some poor and disadvantaged people in the populations served have qualities that many professionals, because of their middle-class origins and life-styles, do not have. NASW gave formal recognition to the profession's rejection of elitism in 1971, when requirements for membership in the association were changed to allow full membership to BSWs; in addition, anyone doing social work with any kind of baccalaureate degree qualified for associate membership.

Members of the profession were not of one mind about these changes. Some believed that the elements in the "new" social work represented *deprofessionalization* because they downgraded professional knowledge and skill. The new professionalism, in this view, encouraged professionals to be too political, freeing them to pursue their social and political interests regardless of the particular needs of a specific client (Specht, 1972). The concern expressed here is that the rights of clients are jeopardized when the ethical base of the profession is undermined (Gilbert and Specht, 1976).

Developments in civil rights pressed social work to move in new directions, and the explosion of social science knowledge in mid-century created several directions in which to move. Sociology, psychology, anthropology, political science, and economics are the primary theoretical disciplines useful in social work practice. Many universities began doctoral programs in social work and social welfare, increasing the profession's capacity for synthesizing theory for practice from the disciplines and generating its own theory for practice.

In the 1970s the course chosen in social work education was to allow "a thousand flowers to bloom." Essentially, the field moved in many directions at once (Pins, 1971). At a time of great ferment and strain in society, it was not likely that any single course of action could be approved by all. Schools of social work organized training in many ways. Some maintained the sturdy trinity of the 1940s; some became generalist, training social workers to utilize all methods to solve problems. Other schools organized programs of training to focus on special problems and population groups (aged, community mental health, the black community, poverty). And some developed their programs by dividing the field into what appeared to be two distinctive streams: direct and indirect services, or a clinical track and a social change track.

## REFERENCES

AD HOC COMMITTEE ON ADVOCACY. "The Social Worker as Advocate: Champion of Social Victims." *Social Work,* 1969, 14, 16–22.

ALINSKY, S. *Reveille for Radicals.* Chicago: University of Chicago Press, 1946. (Reprinted by Vintage Books, 1969.)

AMERICAN ASSOCIATION OF SOCIAL WORKERS. *Social Casework—Generic and Specific: An Outline. A Report of the Milford Conference.* Studies in the Practice of Social Work, No. 2. Washington, D.C.: American Association of Social Workers, 1929.

BARTLETT, H. M. *The Common Base of Social Work Practice.* Washington, D.C: National Association of Social Workers, 1970.

BRAGER, G. "The Indigenous Worker: A New Approach to the Social Work Technician." *Social Work,* 1965, 10, 33–40.

BRIAR, S. "The Current Crisis in Social Casework." In S. Briar (Ed.), *Social Work Practice.* New York: Columbia University Press, 1967.

CANNON, I.C. "Medicine as a Social Instrument: Medical Social Service." *New England Journal of Medicine,* 1951, 244, 715–25.

COYLE, G. L. *Group Work with American Youth.* New York: Harper & Row, 1948.

GILBERT, N., and SPECHT, H. "The Incomplete Profession." *Social Work,* 1974, 19, 665–74. (Reading 17)

GILBERT, N., and SPECHT, H. "Advocacy and Professional Ethics." *Social Work,* 1976, 21, 288–93. (Reading 24)

GILBERT, N., and SPECHT, H. "Social Planning and Community Organization: Approaches." In J. Turner (Ed.), *Encyclopedia of Social Work.* Vol. 2. Washington, D.C.: National Association of Social Workers, 1977.

HUNTER, F. *Community Power Structure: A Study of Decision Makers.* Chapel Hill: University of North Carolina Press, 1953.

KURZMAN, P. A. (Ed.). *The Mississippi Experience.* New York: Association Press, 1971.

LEVIN, A. M. "Private Practice Is Alive and Well." *Social Work,* 1976, 21, 356–62. Also, see Reading 25.

LUBOVE, R. *The Professional Altruist.* Cambridge, Mass.: Harvard University Press, 1965.

MARCUS, G. F. *Some Aspects of Relief in Family Casework: An Evaluation of Practice Based on a Study Made for the Charity Organization Society of New York.* New York: Charity Organization Society, 1929.

PAPELL, C. B., and ROTHMAN, B. "Social Group Work Models: Possession and Heritage." *Journal of Education for Social Work,* 1966, 2, 66–68.

PINS, A. M. "Changes in Social Work Education and Their Implications for Practice." *Social Work,* 1971, 16, 5–15.

RICHMOND, M. *Social Diagnosis.* New York: Russell Sage Foundation, 1917. (Rev. ed., 1930.)

RICHMOND, M. *What Is Social Casework? An Introductory Description.* New York: Russell Sage Foundation, 1922.

RICHMOND, M. "Some Next Steps in Social Treatment." In J. C. Colcord and R. S. Z. Mann (Eds.), *The Long View.* New York: Russell Sage Foundation, 1930.

ROBINSON, V. P. *A Changing Psychology in Social Case Work.* Philadelphia: University of Pennsylvania Press, 1930.

SPECHT, H. "The Deprofessionalization of Social Work." *Social Work,* 1972, 17, 3–15.

TOWLE, C. "Review of a Changing Psychology in Social Case Work." *American Journal of Orthopsychiatry,* 1931, 1, 545–53.

WILSON, G., and RYLAND, G. *Social Group Work Practice: The Creative Use of the Social Process.* Boston: Houghton Mifflin, 1949.

# 15   Attributes of a Profession

## ERNEST GREENWOOD

The professions occupy a position of great importance on the American scene.[1] In a society such as ours, characterized by minute division of labor based upon technical specialization, many important features of social organization are dependent upon professional functions. Professional activity is coming to play a predominant role in the life patterns of increasing numbers of individuals of both sexes, occupying much of their waking moments, providing life goals, determining behavior, and shaping personality. It is no wonder, therefore, that the phenomenon of professionalism has become an object of observation by sociologists.[2] The sociological approach to professionalism is one that views a profession as an organized group which is constantly interacting with the society that forms its matrix, which performs its social functions through a network of formal and informal relationships, and which creates its own subculture requiring adjustments to it as a prerequisite for career success.[3]

Within the professional category of its occupational classification the United States Census Bureau includes, among others, the following: accountant, architect, artist, attorney, clergyman, college professor, dentist, engineer, journalist, judge, librarian, natural scientist, optometrist, pharmacist, physician, social scientist, social worker, surgeon, and teacher.[4] What common attributes do these professional occupations possess which distinguish them from the nonprofessional ones? After a careful canvass of the sociological literature on occupations, this writer has been able to distill five

Reprinted with permission of the National Association of Social Workers and the author from *Social Work,* 2: 3 (July 1957): 45–55.

elements, upon which there appears to be consensus among the students of the subject, as constituting the distinguishing attributes of a profession.[5] Succinctly put, all professions seem to possess: (1) systematic theory, (2) authority, (3) community sanction, (4) ethical codes, and (5) a culture. The purpose of this article is to describe fully these attributes.

Before launching into our description, a preliminary word of caution is due. With respect to each of the above attributes, the true difference between a professional and a nonprofessional occupation is not a qualitative but a quantitative one. Strictly speaking, these attributes are not the exclusive monopoly of the professions; nonprofessional occupations also possess them, but to a lesser degree. As is true of most social phenomena, the phenomenon of professionalism cannot be structured in terms of clear-cut classes. Rather, we must think of the occupations in a society as distributing themselves along a continuum.[6] At one end of this continuum are bunched the well-recognized and undisputed professions (e.g., physician, attorney, professor, scientist); at the opposite end are bunched the least skilled and least attractive occupations (e.g., watchman, truckloader, farm laborer, scrubwoman, bus boy). The remaining occupations, less skilled and less prestigeful than the former, but more so than the latter, are distributed between these two poles. The occupations bunched at the professional pole of the continuum possess to a maximum degree the attributes about to be described. As we move away from this pole, the occupations possess these attributes to a decreasing degree. Thus, in the less developed professions, social work among them, these attributes appear in moderate degree. When we reach the midregion of the continuum, among the clerical, sales, and crafts occupations, they occur in still lesser degree; while at the unskilled end of the continuum the occupations possess these attributes so minimally that they are virtually nonexistent. If the reader keeps this concept of the continuum in mind, the presentation will less likely appear as a distortion of reality.

## SYSTEMATIC BODY OF THEORY[7]

It is often contended that the chief difference between a professional and a nonprofessional occupation lies in the element of superior skill. The performance of a professional service presumably involves a series of unusually complicated operations, mastery of which requires lengthy training. The models referred to in this connection are the performances of a surgeon, a concert pianist, or a research physicist. However, some nonprofessional occupations actually involve a higher order of skill than many professional ones. For example, tool-and-die making, diamond-cutting, monument-engraving, or cabinet-making involve more intricate operations than schoolteaching, nursing, or social work. Therefore, to focus on the element of skill per se in describing the professions is to miss the kernel of their uniqueness.

The crucial distinction is this: the skills that characterize a profession flow from and are supported by a fund of knowledge that has been organized into an internally consistent system, called a *body of theory*. A profession's underlying body of theory is a system of abstract propositions that describe in general terms the classes of phenomena comprising the profession's focus of interest. Theory serves as a base in terms of which the professional rationalizes his operations in concrete situations. Acquisition of the professional skill requires a prior or simultaneous mastery of the theory underlying that skill. Preparation for a profession, therefore, involves considerable preoccupation with systematic theory, a feature virtually absent in the training of the nonprofessional. And so treatises are written on legal theory, musical theory, social work theory, the theory of the drama, and so on; but no books appear on the theory of punch-pressing or pipe-fitting or brick-laying.

Because understanding of theory is so important to professional skill, preparation for a profession must be an intellectual as well as a practical experience. On-the-job training through apprenticeship, which suffices for a nonprofessional occupation, becomes inadequate for a profession. Orientation in theory can be achieved best through formal education in an academic setting. Hence the appearance of the professional school, more often than not university affiliated, wherein the milieu is a contrast to that of the trade school. Theoretical knowledge is more difficult to master than operational procedures; it is easier to learn to repair an automobile than to learn the principles of the internal combustion engine. There are, of course, a number of free-lance professional pursuits (e.g., acting, painting, writing, composing, and the like) wherein academic preparation is not mandatory. Nevertheless, even in these fields various "schools" and "institutes" are appearing, although they may not be run along traditional academic lines. We can generalize that as an occupation moves toward professional status, apprenticeship training yields to formalized education, because the function of theory as a groundwork for practice acquires increasing importance.

The importance of theory precipitates a form of activity normally not encountered in a nonprofessional occupation, viz., theory construction via systematic research. To generate valid theory that will provide a solid base for professional techniques requires the application of the scientific method to the service-related problems of the profession. Continued employment of the scientific method is nurtured by and in turn reinforces the element of *rationality*.[8] As an orientation, rationality is the antithesis of traditionalism. The spirit of rationality in a profession encourages a critical, as opposed to a reverential, attitude toward the theoretical system. It implies a perpetual readiness to discard any portion of that system, no matter how time honored it may be, with a formulation demonstrated to be more valid. The spirit of rationality generates group self-criticism and theoretical controversy. Professional members convene regularly in their associations to learn and to evaluate innovations in theory. This produces an intellectually stimulating milieu that is in marked contrast to the milieu of a nonprofessional occupation.

In the evolution of every profession there emerges the researcher-theoretician whose role is that of scientific investigation and theoretical systematization. In technological professions[9] a division of labor thereby evolves, that between the theory-oriented and the practice-oriented person. Witness the physician who prefers to attach himself to a medical research center rather than to enter private practice. This division may also yield to cleavages with repercussions upon intraprofessional relationships. However, if properly integrated, the division of labor produces an accelerated expansion of the body of theory and a sprouting of theoretical branches around which specialties nucleate. The net effect of such developments is to lengthen the preparation deemed desirable for entry into the profession. This accounts for the rise of graduate professional training on top of a basic college education.

## PROFESSIONAL AUTHORITY

Extensive education in the systematic theory of his discipline imparts to the professional a type of knowledge that highlights the layman's comparative ignorance. This fact is the basis for the professional's authority, which has some interesting features.

A nonprofessional occupation has customers; a professional occupation has clients. What is the difference? A customer determines what services and/or commodities he wants, and he shops around until he finds them. His freedom of decision rests upon the premise that he has the capacity to appraise his own needs and to judge the potential of the service or of the commodity to satisfy them. The infallibility of his decisions is epitomized in the slogan: "The customer is always right!" In a professional relationship, however, the professional dictates what is good or evil for the client, who has no choice but to accede to professional judgment. Here the premise is that, because he lacks the requisite theoretical background, the client cannot diagnose his own needs or discriminate among the range of possibilities for meeting them. Nor is the client considered able to evaluate the caliber of the professional service he receives. In a nonprofessional occupation the customer can criticize the quality of the commodity he has purchased, and even demand a refund. The client lacks this same prerogative, having surrendered it to professional authority. This element of authority is one, although not the sole, reason why a profession frowns on advertising. If a profession were to advertise, it would, in effect, impute to the potential client the discriminating capacity to select from competing forms of service. The client's subordination to professional authority invests the professional with a monopoly of judgment. When an occupation strives toward professionalization, one of its aspirations is to acquire this monopoly.

The client derives a sense of security from the professional's assumption of authority. The authoritative air of the professional is a principal source of the client's faith that the relationship he is about to enter contains the potentials for meeting his needs. The professional's authority, however, is not limitless; its function is confined to those specific spheres within which the professional has been educated. This quality in professional authority Parsons calls *functional specificity*. [10] Functional specificity carries the following implications for the client-professional relationship.

The professional cannot prescribe guides for facets of the client's life where his theoretical competence does not apply. To venture such prescriptions is to invade a province wherein he himself is a layman, and, hence, to violate the authority of another professional group. The professional must not use his position of authority to exploit the client for purposes of personal gratification. In any association of superordination-subordination, of which the professional-client relationship is a perfect specimen, the subordinate member— here, the client—can be maneuvered into a dependent role. The psychological advantage which thereby accrues to the professional could constitute a temptation for him. The professional must inhibit his impulses to use the professional relationship for the satisfaction of the sexual need, the need to manipulate others, or the need to live vicariously. In the case of the therapeutic professions it is ideally preferred that client-professional intercourse not overflow the professional setting. Extraprofessional intercourse could be used by both client and professional in a manner such as to impair professional authority, with a consequent diminution of the professional's effectiveness.

Thus far we have discussed that phase of professional authority which expresses itself in the client-professional relationship. Professional authority, however, has professional-community ramifications. To these we now turn.

## SANCTION OF THE COMMUNITY

Every profession strives to persuade the community to sanction its authority within certain spheres by conferring upon the profession a series of powers and privileges. Community approval of these powers and privileges may be either informal or formal; formal approval is that reinforced by the community's police power.

Among its powers is the profession's control over its training centers. This is achieved through an accrediting process exercised by one of the associations within the profession. By granting or withholding accreditation, a profession can, ideally, regulate its schools as to their number, location, curriculum content, and caliber of instruction. Comparable control is not to be found in a nonprofessional occupation.[11] The profession also acquires control over admission into the profession. This is achieved via two routes. First, the profession convinces the community that no one should be allowed to wear a professional title who has not been conferred it by an accredited professional school. Anyone can call himself a carpenter, locksmith, or metal-plater if he feels so qualified. But a person who assumes the title of physician or attorney without having earned it conventionally becomes an impostor. Secondly, the profession persuades the community to institute in its behalf a licensing system for screening those qualified to practice the professional skill. A *sine qua non* for the receipt of the license is, of course, a duly granted professional title. Another prerequisite may be an examination before a board of inquiry whose personnel have been drawn from the ranks of the profession. Police power enforces the licensing system; persons practicing the professional skill without a license are liable to punishment by public authority.[12]

Among the professional privileges, one of the most important is that of confidentiality. To facilitate efficient performance, the professional encourages the client to volunteer information he otherwise would not divulge. The community regards this as privileged communication, shared solely between client and professional, and protects the latter legally from encroachments upon such confidentiality. To be sure, only a select few of the professions, notably medicine and law, enjoy this immunity. Its very rarity makes it the ultimate in professionalization. Another one of the professional privileges is a relative immunity from community judgment on technical matters. Standards for professional performance are reached by consensus within the profession and are based on the existing body of theory. The lay community is presumed incapable of comprehending these standards and, hence, of using them to identify malpractice. It is generally conceded that a professional's performance can be evaluated only by his peers.

The powers and privileges described above constitute a monopoly granted by the community to the professional group. Therefore, when an occupation strives toward professional status, one of its prime objectives is to acquire this monopoly. But this is difficult to achieve, because counter forces within the community resist strongly the profession's claims to authority. Through its associations the profession wages an organized campaign to persuade the community that it will benefit greatly by granting the monopoly. Specifically the professional seeks to prove: that the performance of the occupational skill requires specialized education; that those who possess this education, in contrast to those who do not, deliver a superior service; and that the human need being served is of sufficient social importance to justify the superior performance.

## REGULATIVE CODE OF ETHICS

The monopoly enjoyed by a profession vis-à-vis clients and community is fraught with hazards. A monopoly can be abused; powers and privileges can be used to protect vested interests against the public weal.[13] The professional group could peg the price of its services at an unreasonably high level; it could restrict the numbers entering the occupation to create a scarcity of personnel; it could dilute the caliber of its performance without community awareness; and it could frustrate forces within the occupation pushing for socially beneficial changes in practices.[14] Were such abuses to become conspicuous, widespread, and permanent, the community would, of course, revoke the profession's monopoly. This extreme measure is normally unnecessary, because every profession has a built-in regulative code which compels ethical behavior on the part of its members.

The profession's ethical code is part formal and part informal. The formal is the written code to which the professional usually swears upon being admitted to practice; this is best exemplified by the Hippocratic Oath of the medical profession. The informal is the unwritten code, which nonetheless carries the weight of formal prescriptions. Through its ethical code the profession's commitment to the social welfare becomes a matter of public record, thereby insuring for itself the continued confidence of the community. Without such confidence the profession could not retain its monopoly. To be sure, self-regulative codes are characteristic of all occupations, nonprofessional as well as professional. However, a professional code is perhaps more explicit, systematic, and binding; it certainly possesses more altruistic overtones and is more public service-oriented.[15]

These account for the frequent synonymous use of the terms "professional" and "ethical" when applied to occupational behavior.

While the specifics of their ethical codes vary among the professions, the essentials are uniform. These may be described in terms of client-professional and colleague-colleague relations.

Toward the client the professional must assume an emotional neutrality. He must provide service to whoever requests it, irrespective of the requesting client's age, income, kinship, politics, race, religion, sex, and social status. A nonprofessional may withhold his services on such grounds without, or with minor, censure; a professional cannot. Parsons calls this element in professional conduct *universalism.* In other words, only in his extraoccupational contacts can the professional relate to others on particularistic terms, i.e., as particular individuals with concrete personalities attractive or unattractive to him. In his client contacts particularistic considerations are out of place. Parsons also calls attention to the element of *disinterestedness* in the professional-client relationship.[16] In contrast to the nonprofessional, the professional is motivated less by self-interest and more by the impulse to perform maximally. The behavior corollaries of this service orientation are many. For one, the professional must, under all circumstances, give maximum caliber service. The nonprofessional can dilute the quality of his commodity or service to fit the size of the client's fee; not so the professional. Again, the professional must be prepared to render his services upon request, even at the sacrifice of personal convenience.

The ethics governing colleague relationships demand behavior that is co-operative, equalitarian, and supportive. Members of a profession share technical knowledge with each other. Any advance in theory and practice made by one professional is quickly disseminated to colleagues through the professional associations.[17] The proprietary and quasi-secretive attitudes toward discovery and invention prevalent in the industrial and commercial world are out of place in the professional. Also out of place is the blatant competition for clients which is the norm in so many nonprofessional pursuits. This is not to gainsay the existence of intraprofessional competition; but it is a highly regulated competition, diluted with co-operative ingredients which impart to it its characteristically restrained quality. Colleague relations must be equalitarian; intraprofessional recognition should ideally be based solely upon performance in practice and/or contribution to theory.[18] Here, too, particularistic considerations must not be allowed to operate. Finally, professional colleagues must support each other vis-à-vis clientele and community. The professional must refrain from acts which jeopardize the authority of colleagues, and must sustain those whose authority is threatened.[19]

The ways and means whereby a profession enforces the observance of its ethical code constitute a case study in social control. Self-discipline is achieved informally and formally.

Informal discipline consists of the subtle and the not-so-subtle pressures that colleagues exert upon one another. An example in this connection is the phenomenon of consultation and referral.[20] Consultation is the practice of inviting a colleague to participate in the appraisal of the client's need and/or in the planning of the service to be rendered. Referral is the practice of affording colleagues access to a client or an appointment. Thus, one colleague may refer his client to another, because lack of time or skill prevents his rendering the needed service; or he may recommend another for appointment by a prospective employer. Since professional ethics precludes aggressive competition and advertising, consultation and referral constitute the principal source of work to a professional. The consultation-referral custom involves professional colleagues in a system of reciprocity which fosters mutual interdependence. Interdependence facilitates social control; chronic violation of professional etiquette arouses colleague resentment, resulting in the cessation of consultation requests and referrals.

A more formal discipline is exercised by the professional associations, which possess the power to criticize or to censure, and in extreme cases to bar recalcitrants. Since membership in good standing in the professional associations is a *sine qua non* of professional success, the prospect of formal disciplinary action operates as a potent force toward conformity.

## THE PROFESSIONAL CULTURE

Every profession operates through a network of formal and informal groups. Among the formal groups, first there are the organizations through which the profession performs its services; these provide the institutionalized setting where professional and client meet. Examples of such organizations are hospital, clinic, university, law office, engineering firm, or social agency. Secondly, there are the organizations whose functions are to replenish the profession's supply of talent and to expand its fund of knowledge. These include the educational and the research centers. Third among the formal groups are the organizations which emerge as an expression of the growing consciousness-of-kind on the part of the profession's members, and which promote so-called group interests and aims. These are the professional associations. Within and around these formal organizations extends a filigree of informal groupings: the multitude of small, closely knit clusters of colleagues. Membership in these cliques is based on a variety of affinities: specialties within the profession; affiliations with select professional societies; residental and work propinquity; family, religious, or ethnic background; and personality attractions.

The interactions of social roles required by these formal and informal groups generate a social configuration unique to the profession, *viz.*, a professional culture. All occupations are characterized by formal and informal groupings; in this respect the professions are not unique. What is unique is the culture thus begotten. If one were to single out the attribute that most effectively differentiates the professions from other occupations, this is it. Thus we can talk of a professional culture as distinct from a nonprofessional culture. Within the professions as a logical class each profession develops its own subculture, a variant of the professional culture; the engineering subculture, for example, differs from the subcultures of medicine and social work. In the subsequent discussion, however, we will treat the culture of the professions as a generic phenomenon. The culture of a profession consists of its *values, norms,* and *symbols.*

The social values of a professional group are its basic and fundamental beliefs, the unquestioned premises upon which its very existence rests. Foremost among these values is the essential worth of the service which the professional group extends to the community. The profession considers that the service is a social good and that community welfare would be immeasurably impaired by its absence. The twin concepts of professional authority and monopoly also possess the force of a group value. Thus, the proposition that in all service-related matters the professional group is infinitely wiser than the laity is regarded as beyond argument. Likewise nonarguable is the proposition that acquisition by the professional group of a service monopoly would inevitably produce social progress. And then there is the value of rationality; that is, the commitment to objectivity in the realm of theory and technique. By virtue of this orientation, nothing of a theoretical or technical nature is regarded as sacred and unchallengeable simply because it has a history of acceptance and use.

The norms of a professional group are the guides to behavior in social situations. Every profession develops an elaborate system of these role definitions. There is a range of appropriate behaviors for seeking admittance into the profession, for gaining entry into its formal and informal groups, and for progressing within the occupation's hierarchy. There are appropriate modes of securing appointments, of conducting referrals, and of handling consultation. There are proper ways of acquiring clients, of receiving and dismissing them, of questioning and treating them, of accepting and rejecting them. There are correct ways of grooming a protégé, of recompensing a sponsor, and of relating to peers, superiors or subordinates.

There are even group-approved ways of challenging an outmoded theory, of introducing a new technique, and of conducting an intra-professional controversy. In short, there is a behavior norm covering every standard interpersonal situation likely to recur in professional life.

The symbols of a profession are its meaning-laden items. These may include such things as: its insignias, emblems, and distinctive dress; its history, folklore, and argot; its heroes and its villains; and its stereotypes of the professional, the client, and the layman.

Comparatively clear and controlling group values, behavior norms, and symbols, which characterize the professions, are not to be encountered in nonprofessional occupations.

Our discussion of the professional culture would be incomplete without brief mention of one of its central concepts, the *career* concept. The term career is, as a rule, employed only in reference to a professional occupation. Thus, we do not talk about the career of a bricklayer or of a mechanic; but we do talk about the career of an architect or of a clergyman. At the heart of the career concept is a certain attitude toward work which is peculiarly professional. A career is essentially a *calling*, a life devoted to "good works."[21] Professional work is never viewed solely as a means to an end; it is the end itself. Curing the ill, educating the young, advancing science are values in themselves. The professional performs his services primarily for the psychic satisfactions and secondarily for the monetary compensations.[22] Self-seeking motives feature minimally in the choice of a profession; of maximal importance is affinity for the work. It is this devotion to the work itself which imparts to professional activity the service orientation and the element of disinterestedness. Furthermore, the absorption in the work is not partial, but complete; it results in a total personal involvement. The work life invades the after-work life, and the sharp demarcation between the work hours and the leisure hours disappears. To the professional person his work becomes his life.[23] Hence the act of embarking upon a professional career is similar in some respects to entering a religious order. The same cannot be said of a nonprofessional occupation.

To succeed in his chosen profession, the neophyte must make an effective adjustment to the professional culture.[24] Mastery of the underlying body of theory and acquisition of the technical skills are in themselves insufficient guarantees of professional success. The recruit must also become familiar with and learn to weave his way through the labyrinth of the professional culture. Therefore, the transformation of a neophyte into a professional is essentially an acculturation process wherein he internalizes the social values, the behavior norms, and the symbols of the occupational group.[25] In its frustrations and rewards it is fundamentally no different from the acculturation of an immigrant to a relatively strange culture. Every profession entertains a stereotype of the ideal colleague; and, of course, it is always one who is thoroughly adjusted to the professional culture.[26] The poorly acculturated colleague is a deviant; he is regarded as "peculiar," "unorthodox," "annoying," and in extreme cases a "troublemaker." Whereas the professional group encourages innovation in theory and technique, it tends to discourage deviation from its social values and norms. In this internal contradiction, however, the professional culture is no different from the larger culture of society.

One of the principal functions of the professional schools is to identify and screen individuals who are prospective deviants from the professional culture. That is why the admission of candidates to professional education must be judged on grounds in addition to and other than their academic qualifications.[27] Psychic factors presaging favorable adjustment to the professional culture are granted an importance equivalent to mental abilities. The professional school provides test situations through initial and graduated exposures of the novice to the professional culture. By his behavior in these social situations involving colleagues, clients, and community, the potential deviant soon reveals himself and is immediately weeded out. Comparable preoccupation with the psychic prerequisites of occupational adjustment is not characteristic of nonprofessional occupations.

## IMPLICATIONS FOR SOCIAL WORK

The picture of the professions just unveiled is an ideal type. In the construction of an ideal type some exaggeration of reality is unavoidable, since the intent is to achieve an internally coherent picture. One function of the ideal type is to structure reality in such manner that discrete, disparate, and dissimilar phenomena become organized, thereby bringing order out of apparent disorder. We now possess a model of a profession that is much sharper and clearer than the actuality that confronts us when we observe the occupational scene. What is the utility of this model for social work?

The preoccupation of social workers with professionalization has been a characteristic feature of the social work scene for years. Flexner,[28] Johnson,[29] Hollis and Taylor,[30] and others have written on the subject, proposing criteria which must be met if social work is to acquire professional status. Whenever social workers convene, there is the constant reaffirmation of the urgency to achieve the recognition from the community befitting a profession. The union of the seven separate organizations into the National Association of Social Workers is generally regarded as an important milestone in social work history, precisely because of its potential stimulus toward professionalization.

In view of all this, it is proper for social workers to possess clear conceptions of that which they so fervently seek. The model of the professions portrayed above should contribute to such clarification; it should illuminate the goal for which social workers are striving. It is often contended that social work is still far from having attained professional status.[31] But this is a misconception. When we hold up social work against the model of the professions presented above, it does not take long to decide whether to classify it within the professional or the nonprofessional occupations. Social work is already a profession; it has too many points of congruence with the model to be classifiable otherwise. Social work is, however, seeking to rise within the professional hierarchy so that it, too, might enjoy maximum prestige, authority, and monopoly which presently belong to a few top professions.

The model presented above should also serve to sensitize social workers to anticipate some of the problems that continued professionalization must inevitably precipitate. The model indicates that progressive professionalization will involve social workers in novel relationships with clients, colleagues, agency, community, and other professions. In concluding this paper we refer briefly to one such problem. It is no secret that social workers are not all uniformly enthusiastic about the professionalization of social work. Bisno[32] has given verbalization to a prevailing apprehension that social workers might have to scuttle their social-action heritage as a price of achieving the public acceptance accorded a profession. Extrapolation from the sociologists' model of the professions suggests a reality basis for these fears. It suggests that the attainment of professional prestige, authority, and monopoly by social workers will undoubtedly carry disturbing implications for the social action and social reform components of social work philosophy. The anticipated developments will compel social workers to rethink and redefine the societal role of their profession.

These and other dilemmas flowing from professionalization are bound to tax the best minds among social workers for their resolution. In this connection a proper understanding of the attributes of a profession would seem to be indispensable.

## NOTES

1. Talcott Parsons, "The Professions and Social Structure," *Social Forces*, Vol. 17 (May 1939), pp. 457–67.

2. Theodore Caplow, *The Sociology of Work* (Minneapolis: University of Minnesota Press, 1954).

3. Oswald Hall, "The Stages of a Medical Career," *American Journal of Sociology*, Vol. 53 (March 1948), pp. 327–36; "Types of Medical Careers,"

*American Journal of Sociology*, Vol. 55 (November 1949), pp. 243–53; "Sociological Research in the Field of Medicine: Progress and Prospects," *American Sociological Review*, Vol. 16 (October 1951), pp. 639–44.

4. U.S. Bureau of the Census, *1950 Census of Population: Classified Index of Occupations and Industries* (Washington, D.C.: Government Printing Office, 1950).

5. The writer acknowledges his debt to his former students at the School of Social Welfare, University of California, Berkeley, who, as members of his research seminars, assisted him in identifying and abstracting the sociological literature on occupations. Their conscientious assistance made possible the formulation presented in this paper.

6. The occupational classification employed by the U.S. Census Bureau is precisely such a continuum. The categories of this classification are: (a) professionals and semiprofessional technical workers; (b) proprietors and managers, both farm and nonfarm, and officials; (c) clerical, sales, and kindred workers; (d) craftsmen, skilled workers, and foremen; (e) operatives and semiskilled workers; and (f) laborers, unskilled, service, and domestic workers. (U.S. Bureau of the Census, *op. cit.*)

7. The sequence in which the five attributes are discussed in this paper does not reflect upon their relative importance. The order selected has been dictated by logical considerations.

8. Parsons, *op. cit.*

9. A technology is a profession whose aim is to achieve controlled changes in natural relationships. Convention makes a distinction between technologists who shape nonhuman materials and those who deal with human beings. The former are called engineers; the latter practitioners.

10. Parsons, *op. cit.*

11. To set up and run a school for floral decorating requires no approval from the national florists' association, but no school of social work could operate long without approval of the Council on Social Work Education.

12. Many nonprofessional occupations have also succeeded in obtaining licensing legislation in their behalf. Witness the plumbers, radio operators, and barbers, to mention a few. However, the sanctions applied against a person practicing a nonprofessional occupation are much less severe than is the case when a professional occupation is similarly involved.

13. Abraham Flexner, "Is Social Work a Profession?" in *Proceedings of the National Conference of Charities and Corrections* (Chicago: 1915), pp. 576–90; Robert K. Merton, "Bureaucratic Structure and Personality," in Alvin Gouldner, ed., *Studies in Leadership* (New York: Harper & Brothers, 1950), pp. 67–79.

14. Merton, *op. cit.*

15. Flexner, *op. cit.*; Parsons, *op. cit.*

16. Parsons, *op. cit.*

17. Arlien Johnson, "Professional Standards and How They Are Attained," *Journal of American Dental Association*, Vol. 31 (September 1944), pp. 1181–89.

18. Flexner, *op. cit.*

19. This partly explains why physicians do not testify against each other in malpractice suits.

20. Hall, *op. cit.*

21. The term *calling* literally means a divine summons to undertake a course of action. Originally, it was employed to refer to religious activity. The Protestant Reformation widened its meaning to include economic activ-

ity as well. Henceforth divinely inspired "good works" were to be both secular and sacred in nature. Presumably, then, any occupational choice may be a response to divine summons. In this connection, it is interesting to note that the German word for vocation is *Beruf*, a noun derived from the verb *berufen*, to call.

22. Johnson, *op. cit.*

23. The all-pervading influence of work upon the lives of professionals results in interesting by-products. The members of a profession tend to associate with one another outside the work setting (Oswald Hall, "The Stages of a Medical Career," *op. cit.*). Their families mingle socially; leisure time is spent together; "shop talk" permeates social discourse; and a consensus develops. The profession thus becomes a whole social environment, nurturing characteristic social and political attitudes, patterns of consumption and recreation, and decorum and *Weltanschauung* (Caplow, *op. cit.*, and William H. Form, "Toward an Occupational Social Psychology," *Journal of Social Psychology*, Vol. 24 (February 1946), pp. 85–99).

24. Oswald Hall, "The Stages of a Medical Career" and "Types of Medical Careers," *op. cit.*

25. R. Clyde White, " 'Social Workers in Society': Some Further Evidence," *Social Work Journal*, Vol. 34 (October 1953), pp. 161–64.

26. The laity also entertain a stereotypic image of the professional group. Needless to say, the layman's conception and the professional's self-conception diverge widely, because they are fabricated out of very different experiences. The layman's stereotype is frequently a distortion of reality, being either an idealization or a caricature of the professional type.

27. Oswald Hall, "Sociological Research in the Field of Medicine: Progress and Prospects," *op. cit.*

28. Flexner, *op. cit.*

29. Johnson, *op. cit.*

30. Ernest V. Hollis and Alice L. Taylor, *Social Work Education in the United States* (New York: Columbia University Press, 1951).

31. Flexner considered that the social work of his day was not a profession. Hollis and Taylor regard present-day social work as still in its early adolescence.

32. Herbert Bisno, "How Social Will Social Work Be?" *Social Work*, Vol. 1 (April 1956), pp. 12–18.

# 16  "Attributes of a Profession" Revisited*

## ERNEST GREENWOOD

### INTRODUCTION

The only permanent feature of social phenomena is their impermanence. A tendency to undergo change over time is their prime characteristic. Hence, the population census must be repeated

*© 1980 by E. Greenwood

decennially and the cost-of-living index revised periodically. When I was a graduate student, the then current sociology textbooks taught me that juvenile delinquency was a phenomenon largely confined to the lower socioeconomic stratum; that petty theft, drug traffic, violence, vandalism, and unmarried pregnancies were concentrated predominantly in the slum areas (they were not called "ghettoes" then) of large cities; and that as one traced a line out toward the middle class suburbs, these indicators of social disorganization (sic) decreased markedly in relative frequency. But within a generation juvenile delinquency vaulted over the social factors confining it, landing into the suburbs to become a middle-class phenomenon as well. Therefore, empirical generalizations about any social phenomenon should be regularly tested for current verity by reobserving the latter to determine if the phenomenon has changed in the interim. Such regular reexamination is a "should" for another reason. Not only the object observed but those who observe it can and do change over time. A tendency to spawn ever new concepts is a prime characteristic of every field of study. The novel concepts change the perspective of the investigators therein. This leads them to reobserve the same familiar phenomenon, this time identifying hitherto unsuspected properties, and, hence, deriving new or different generalizations about it. That post-Freudian generalizations about the human psyche differ from pre-Freudian ones, is not because human beings changed in the interim, but because Freud's novel concepts changed our perspective upon the latter. Therefore, the emergence of any new idea(s) regarding a phenomenon should prompt a reexamination of currently held generalizations about it.

It was with the above considerations in mind that I undertook to review an article of mine, now two decades old, which was an attempt to ascertain the defining attributes of the professions (22).* The article set forth five attributes as distinguishing the professions from the nonprofessions, namely, systematic theory, authority, community sanction, ethical codes, and a culture. The perspective reflected in that article Cullen has called the "definitional approach" (6). Recent students of professionalism, viewing the accumulation of researches into the phenomenon, have identified in these efforts two distinct though related guiding perspectives or, as they prefer to call them, theoretical approaches (5, 26, 44). These are: the profession as structure and professionalization as process. What has been called the definitional is actually subsumable under the structural approach.

---

*Numbers in parentheses refer to the numbered references in the Bibliography at the end of the paper.

## Structural Versus Processual

The structural approach focuses upon profession *per se,* as is. It is premised on the assumption that professions comprise a class or type structurally distinct from other occupations which, by implication, are non-professional. Thus, the aim of investigations guided by the structural approach is a quest for the essentials differentiating the type from others. More specifically, it is to identify those occupational characteristics which may be said to constitute the distinguishing attributes of professions. The writings of Goode are prime illustrations of the structural approach (19, 20, 21). My own article is another. The processual approach focuses upon the transformation of a nonprofessional occupation into a profession. It is premised on the assumption that this is an evolving process consisting of sequential stages through which all would-be professions pass and, furthermore, that the stages are ascertainable. Accordingly, the aim of investigations guided by this approach, is to trace this evolution; it is to describe what sociologists would call "the natural history" of professionalization, to formulate a model that typifies this process. In addition, it is to identify those social factors, both internal and external to occupations, which facilitate or impede the professionalization process (3:139–40, 8, 23). Wilensky's oft-quoted article on professionalization is a prime illustration of the processual approach (54).

Investigators employing the processual approach have produced evolutionary models which differ widely regarding the number of stages comprising the professionalization process. On that account the approach has drawn criticism. The critics claim that no two occupations go through the same sequence to become professions, so that it is not possible to construct an evolutionary model which would fit all or even most of the thirty odd existing professions (20). But so has the structural approach, including my own earlier effort, been the target of criticism (6, 7, 44, 50). Since they emanate from diverse sources, these criticisms are not always reenforcing, but at times actually contradictory. Nevertheless, taken singly, each merits consideration. It is this imperative which motivates the present paper. One criticism concerns the validity of the structural approach because of its dubious premise. A second questions the representativeness of the samples studies by structuralists. A third relates to the reliability of the structural approach as a method. A final criticism questions the theoretical adequacy of the structuralist position for its neglect of the attribute of power in professionalism. I will discuss each one of these criticisms in that order, and then conclude with a relevant note regarding the social work profession.

## 1. ON THE MATTER OF VALIDITY

Critics challenge the validity of the structural approach by questioning its underlying premise that there exists a class of occupations with attributes essentially so different as to merit the label "professional" exclusively. They argue that all occupations are essentially similar. Every occupation is a specific socially approved activity which calls for some skill, which is pursued by a group of persons, which results in something that has a market value because it is in demand, and which, therefore, is a legitimate source of steady income. Hence, as one critic puts it, in essentials the so-called professions are indistinguishable from other occupations, so that there is no logical basis for the proposed differentiation. The only possible difference, if any, between what the structuralists call the professions and the nonprofessions, is that the former tend on the whole to exhibit in somewhat greater degree certain characteristics which the latter tend on the whole to exhibit in somewhat lesser degree. In other words, there is an occupational continuum; all occupations are distributed along this very same continuum (45). It is the sociologist who then approaches the latter with his *a priori* structural perspective and proceeds to cut the continuum at some arbitrary point of his own choosing, thereby creating two occupational classes of doubtful validity (6). In summary, the professional versus nonprofessional dichotomy has no counterpart in reality.

### Commentary

But does the above criticism itself possess validity? The class of entities called "the professions" is by no means the creature of the sociological imagination. It is a social reality. After all, why does our language contain the term "profession" if not to stand for a distinct class of referents? Why are there organizations in Western societies termed "professional schools" and "professional associations"? Clearly because there are professions. As the tertiary (i.e., nonagricultural and nonmanufacturing) sector of our economy expands, there is an increase in the white-collar service occupations largely manned by persons with some college education; for example, real estate and stock broker, insurance and travel agent, business manager and interior decorator. Students of the phenomenon have pointed to the uniform aspiration on the part of members of these occupations to acquire the status and trappings of "profession" (27:564, 54). Are the latter aspiring after something that is nonexistent? Hardly so. As occupations, the professions have a history which antedates the appearance of sociologists. The professional versus nonprofessional dichotomy is an objective fact of social life, which is precisely why sociologists are studying the phenomenon.

It is, of course, true that a continuum exists along which the many occupations may be arrayed with respect to any and all attributes, including those we associate with the professions. To a discussion of this very continuum I devoted a lengthy paragraph in my previous article. So, the existence of an occupational continuum is not at issue here. The issue is really a methodological one: is it in accord with scientific method to focus on the occupations at the poles of this continuum and conceptualize them as two contrasting types, viz., professions versus nonprofessions? The answer is that social scientists have been doing just that constantly in describing social regularities. Note such dichotomies as: free-market vs. planned economies, directive vs. nondirective therapies, ascribed vs. achieved statuses, and folk (*gemeinschaft*) vs. mass (*gesellschaft*) societies, to name only a few. The construction of polar types is an accepted procedure premised on the logic that two groups which differ, with regard to a combination of attributes, sufficiently in *degree* are probably different in *kind.* On this issue Freidson, himself a critic of the structural approach, gave the verdict when he wrote that the professions "represent a distinct kind of ocupation" (18).

## 2. ON THE MATTER OF SAMPLE REPRESENTATIVENESS

A second criticism challenges the representativeness of the data from which the structuralists construct their ideal type of profession. The writings of the latter, so the criticism goes, indicate quite clearly that the attributes comprising their model are derived almost entirely from one profession, medicine (26:xi, 44). The earliest effort to define the attributes of a profession is to be found in the classic paper by Flexner, whose occupational identification was with medicine (15). The structuralists, so argue the critics, have reverentially followed in Flexner's footsteps since (50). Preoccupation with medicine has dominated their studies of professionalism and has, therefore, largely determined the composition of the professional model which these studies have produced (47). Medicine, however, is atypical.

Medicine in the U.S. is a free, entrepreneurial profession whose practitioners operate, in the main, individually, exercise considerable control over their practice, and are involved in a fee-for-service relationship with their clients (7). These features of medicine have strongly colored the structuralist's model of the professions as being essentially entrepreneurial and individualistic (10). The preoccupation with medicine is explainable on several grounds: its preeminent position in the occupational hierarchy; its great prestige and privileges in society; and its market monopoly unmatched by any other profession (26:38). But its very singularity renders medicine an unrepresentative choice for a case study intended to yield information about professions in general. Some critics, Ritzer among them, contend that the practice of medicine, as it has evolved in the U.S., is really an aberrant case of professionalism (44). Hence, its repeated use by structuralists as the prototype of the professions yields an erroneous picture of reality.

## Commentary

The criticism that the structuralists, including myself, have constructed a professional model derived entirely from medicine, the entrepreneurial profession *nonpareil*, is not quite true. It is true that Flexner, the first structuralist (if he may be so labeled), was affiliated with the medical profession. It so happened that in the early part of this century medical education in the U.S. was chaotic and retarded compared to that in Western Europe. Cognizant of the need for radical reform, the American Medical Association appealed to the Carnegie Foundation for a critical study of the medical schools. To undertake the study, the Foundation engaged Flexner, who was by background an educator and not a physician. The rest is history. The recommendations of the Flexner Report, when implemented, transformed the medical curriculum in the U.S. (26:37). As a leading architect of professional education in the country, Flexner was subsequently invited to address the then predecessor organization to the National Conference on Social Welfare on the question whether social work was a profession. His classic paper on professional attributes, to which its proponents and opponents repeatedly refer, was delivered on that occasion.

Flexner's approach to his subject was to examine the then generally recognized professions so as to identify their common attributes which might serve him as criteria whereby to gauge social work's claim to professional status. While medicine featured importantly in his analysis, the professions he considered included law, ministry, and engineering as well (15). In formulating the archetypal profession described in my earlier article, I had uppermost in mind those that had been considered by Flexner plus the professions of the university professor and the research scientist. Goode refers to four professions which have been most used by students of professionalism: law, medicine, ministry, and university teaching (21). The truth is that structuralists have employed all of the occupations thus far enumerated plus the officialdom of the military and of the civil services. Furthermore, the professions which have been so utilized are not all of the entrepreneurial, fee-for-service kind. Medicine, law, engineering, yes. But the ministry, university teaching, scientific research are bureaucratic professions. In the latter professionals practice as salaried employees in a large organization which assigns tasks to them and subjects them to its rules. Clearly, the structuralist's typical professional cannot be characterized as drawn solely from the entrepreneurial professions generally and the medical profession specifically.

A review of the array of professions actually employed by the structuralists to derive their model indicates that they share one feature in common. All the professions are relatively old, traditional, with long histories. They originated in the preindustrial era of Western societies; they came to maturity in the industrial era; and in the current postindustrial era they constitute what Carr-Saunders has called the "old established professions" (4, 43). As Larson has observed, it is these well established professions that have furnished the elements from which students of professionalism have constructed their ideal types (26:38). Such exclusive concentration upon the most mature and established professions requires no elaborate explanation. Precisely because they are mature and established, these professions manifest with maximum clarity the distinguishing attributes of their class. They are the ones clustered at the professional pole of the occupational continuum. They, therefore, comprise the cases most appropriate for observations intended to identify the attributes of a profession.

## 3. ON THE MATTER OF RELIABILITY

Thirdly, the critics challenge the reliability of the structural approach by pointing to the confusing variation in the results that its use has yielded. They contend that investigators who employ this approach, although conceptualizing the phenomenon of professionalism similarly, nonetheless come up with lists of attributes which differ from one another. A review of the writings of the latter, so argue the critics, reveals not agreement but disagreement regarding the numbers and kinds of attributes characterizing the professions (28). Which of the several lists available is to be regarded as *the* attributes distinguishing the professions from the nonprofessions? Lortie has criticized sociologists as still not having reached agreement on a single set of criteria for defining a profession (33).

## Commentary

In preparation for this paper I reviewed the writings of two dozen investigators* who have concerned themselves with identifying the distinctive attributes of professions. Of these, eighteen published during the 1960s and 1970s, in other words, since the appearance of my earlier article. Hence, the sample reviewed is, in the main, representative of the more recent crop of students of the subject. The review highlights two points.

All together the authors cited a dozen separate and distinct attributes as setting the professions apart from the nonprofessions. At one extreme an author cited a single attribute as being solely distinctive of a profession, while at the other extreme an author cited nine attributes, with the remaining twenty-two authors distributed in between. The average (median and mode) of the distribution was four attributes cited per author. While many authors cited the identical attribute and while many cited the same number of attributes, no two authors were similar as to both the numbers and the identical attributes cited. Accordingly, the criticism that the structural approach yields a picture of variation among those employing it, contains a truth. However, it does not contain the whole truth, which brings me to the second point highlighted by the review.

Interestingly enough, underneath the variation exists a surprising degree of consensus. Thus, of the dozen attributes cited by our sample, half were cited fewer than six times. Just four attributes alone received well over half of the total citations. Hence, the citations were concentrated around a few attributes. The shape of the distribution here described is comparable to a leptokurtic curve which, while having a large range, actually has a relatively small variance, because of the heavy concentration of frequencies in a few intervals (here discrete categories). Several recent writers have referred to this same anomaly, viz., that although the lists of attributes of the ideal-type profession proffered by students of the phenomenon do vary, nonetheless a certain few attributes keep recurring on every list, thereby indicating an underlying, though obscured, unanimity (18, 26:x). Goode summarized it well when he wrote that the characteristics attributed to the professions, on being tabulated, reveal a "hidden similarity ... suggesting that their foundation is a shared observation of reality" (21).

---

*Those reviewed were: Buckley (2), Carr-Saunders & Wilson (4, 43), Denzin & Mettlin (8), Dyer (9), Epstein (11), Etzioni (13), Feldbaum (14), Flexner (15), Goode (19, 20, 21), Hall (23), Larson (26), Laski (27), Lewis (28), Levy (29), Light (31), Lorber (32), Marshall (35), Moore (36), Nosow & Form (38), Parsons (39), Ritzer (44), Toren (49), Vollmer & Mills (52), and Wilensky (54).

The above described anomaly is explainable. The attributes which we associate with the professions are not all of the same logical order. A number of writers have pointed out that certain of these attributes generate other secondary ones; stated conversely, certain attributes are derived from more basic ones. To illustrate, one-fourth of the authors whom I reviewed cited as a distinguishing attribute that professionals enjoy greater income, prestige and political influence than do nonprofessionals. This attribute is clearly a derived one, a consequent of professionalism. For an occupation is a profession, not because its members enjoy these advantages, but just the reverse; the latter derive these advantages, because they are members of a profession. Conceptual clarity, therefore, calls for a dichotomy of professional attributes: the generating or basic ones versus the consequential or derived ones (5, 2, 21, 31). The basic professional attributes are few and essential, the derived ones are many and varied. Examine the lists of professional attributes proffered by students of the subject and you will find that it is with respect to the derived attributes that they differ so widely. As Goode has suggested, reduce the lists by subtracting from them the derived attributes, and the remaining ones, viz., the basic attributes, will show remarkable and satisfying consistency among them (19).

If my earlier article is to be faulted, it should be for having failed to propound the distinction between basic and derived professional attributes and for having lumped them together indiscriminately. Actually the basic attributes reduce to only three. Significantly they are the same three which were most frequently cited by the two dozen authors who were reviewed. What are these attributes?

## Basic Professional Attributes

To begin with, there is the attribute which has been referred to as the cognitive or intellectual component of professionalism (26:x). Thus, the expertise of the professional is grounded in a body of theory (e.g., physics) or principles (e.g., law) or doctrine (e.g., theology), which is relatively abstract, systematic, and communicable, which is constantly replenished with concepts and data derived from disputation and research, and mastery of which requires higher education that is carefully planned and intellectually demanding. This is what distinguishes a profession from a trade. An apprentice can acquire the skill of his trade by simply watching his master's technique as the latter moves from task to task. A similar didactic approach in the case of a profession would prove entirely inadequate.

A second basic attribute is one which has been varyingly referred to as the collectivity orientation and the normative or service component of professionalism (26:x). Thus, the proper performance of the professional role requires that the practitioner render at all times the highest caliber service of which he is capable, irrespective of the identity and finances of the recipient, and that he invariably subordinate his personal needs and material interests to the latter's welfare should he be confronted with a choice between them. This is what distinguishes professions from commerce. The maximization of profit is a proper motivation for behavior in business; it is inappropriate in a profession.

The third basic attribute is the monopolistic component of professionalism. It is the exclusive privilege of the profession's members, conferred on them by the community and legally sanctioned, to be the sole recognized practitioners of the professional skill. This fact thereby invests them with the control of the following: recruitment and education of neophytes; accreditation of professional schools; definition of licensing requirements; and regulation, evaluation, and when appropriate, censure of the professional behavior of colleagues. In this regard a profession is comparable to a craft guild, and the modern professions are, indeed, descendants of the medieval guilds (38).

In my earlier paper the cognitive, normative and monopolistic attributes were conceptualized and termed systematic theory, ethical codes and community sanction, respectively. The present conceptualization and terminology is much more accurate and clear. And for this I am indebted to others whose writings have been so instructive. These three, then, are the essentials of professions and all the other attributes we associate with the latter are derivatives. That professional education is characteristically prolonged and, in fact, unending, is a derivative of the cognitive or intellectual component of professionalism. Similarly, professional autonomy, viz., the practitioner's right to act on his own judgment in given cases without interference from the laity, is a derivative attribute, a consequent of the monopolistic and the service components combined. And from the combination of all three components derives what I referred to in my earlier article as the professional culture.

Within a given profession the three basic attributes are manifest in varying degrees, with the result that a profession may rank higher on one attribute than on another (42). This phenomenon Cullen has called "status inconsistency" (6). Thus, Toren reminds us, the social work profession has a highly developed service ethic coupled with a considerably less developed fund of scientifically tested knowledge (49:41). This suggests that each of the basic attributes constitutes a continuum. This fact, in turn, calls for a revision of our customary conception of professionalism as a one-dimensional (linear) continuum to be replaced by a three-dimensional one. It is into such a three-dimensional space that we must locate the thirty odd existing professions.

## 4 ON THE MATTER OF THEORETICAL ADEQUACY

A fourth and more fundamental criticism of the structural approach emanates from a new school of investigators who employ a power orientation toward professionalism (1, 7, 18, 45). The power advocates challenge the professional model proffered by the structuralists as exaggerating the harmony between the professions and the community and conveying no hint of the conflict of interest between them. The structural approach, so the criticism goes, is really rooted in functionalist social theory according to which society is a functioning system, self-corrective, and tending toward equilibrium (40). Functionalist theory provides a perspective on society as a stable normative order, integrated around universally held values, and organized around compatible social institutions. Hence, functionalism deemphasizes the existence of intrinsic discord and of necessary conflict in society, and neglects the importance of power as an instrument for redefining social relationships and for rectifying disequilibrium (34). Rooted in functionalist theory, the structuralists have likewise ignored the element of power in both the evolution and the operation of professions. They have failed to see that the distinguishing difference between professions and nonprofessions is to be found in the attribute of organized power (17).

### Power Approach to Professions

Power is the capacity of a group to attain its goals in the face of resistances and, once attained, to retain them. Power is latent; it is manifested as control on the part of the group, both control over its own actions and, correspondingly, control over the actions of others (40:121). As applied to occupations, power is maximum collegial control over the content and conditions of work performed by the occupation's members with minimum interference from the laity (18, 26:xii). Specifically this means control over recruiting, training, accrediting, licensing, regulating, and disciplining members of the profession, and in effect, excluding all nonmembers from professional practice and privileges. Freidson, considered the dean of the power school, has argued that the only important and uniform attribute for distinguishing professions from other occupations is their position of legitimate control over work (45). To be sure, such control over a service market can and does assume varying degrees. Hence, what is customarily referred to as an occupational continuum, is really a power continuum. The professions are the occupations which possess the greatest power to control the conditions of their work, whereas the nonprofessions possess the least (1, 44). Thus, as between two collaborative professions, that one is the more professional which controls the other; good examples are the relationships of physician to nurse and psychiatrist to social worker.

The power approach to professionalism is rooted in social conflict theory according to which society is a collection of rivalrous interest groups, among them occupations, competing for a limited supply of economic goods and prestigious statuses. When a nonprofessional occupation strives to obtain exclusive control over a service market and thereby to achieve professional status, it invariably encounters strong opposition to its aspirations from other interest groups, especially from some competing occupation intent on the same objective (44). The resultant competition between the two occupations is essentially a zero-sum game, for the success of one is at the expense of the other (19). The collective endeavor on the part of the members to elevate their occupation to professional status, Larson has called a "collective [social] mobility project" (26:67). Their indispensable instrument is the professional association, the organization of which creates a power source (53). In behalf of its members the professional association embarks on a prolonged and complex series of transactions with the community so as to establish the boundaries of its service market and to acquire exclusive control over it (21). The professional association operates as a typical pressure group employing a variety of public relations techniques to influence public policy toward directions in its favor. While the association appeals its case to a wide potential client public, special targets for its persuasion are groups which possess the power to influence the state. The aspiring profession forms organic ties with a segment of the power elite which is able to move the state apparatus to legalize the would-be profession's claims. The success of the occupation's drive toward professional status is, thus, largely determined by that group among society's elite which is willing to act as its sponsor (45). Many of the occupations considered nonprofessional are such only because they lack the necessary resources to enlist powerful groups in their behalf (1, 5).

As for the attributes of knowledge and service, do they feature in the power theory at all? Power advocates point to the fact that an invariable element in the professionalization process is the development by the members of the aspiring profession of an elaborate rationale justifying their claim to professional status. Whatever else it may include, this rationale must revolve around the twin concepts of specialized knowledge and commitment to service (7, 45). The segment of the power elite whose sponsorship is sought, must be persuaded that the occupation's members possess superior knowledge which gives them a rare skill (6). But equally important, the sponsor must be persuaded that their commitment to the service ideal is likewise out of the ordinary (55). No emerging profession can afford to admit harboring motives that are parochial and selfish. Only by conveying an image of competence and altruism can it hope to persuade others that granting it a service monopoly is in the public interest (18). While the professional association and the trade union resemble each other in goals, which are basically economic for both, they differ widely in the rhetoric they employ. As Haug and Sussman point out, trade unions stress the concepts of equity, grievances, needs, and rights, whereas professional associations stress the concepts of knowledge, performance, service and skill (25). Actually, it is not demonstrable empirically that the aspiring profession's cognitive and normative attributes are as superior as claimed (17). However, once having gained recognition as a profession, its claims become *ipso facto* unquestioned. Henceforth the profession is by definition all that it presumes to be. To sum up, the cognitive and the normative are not essential attributes of a profession, but form a rationalization which both motivate and facilitate its efforts to attain and to retain professional status (26:xiii). Hence, from the power perspective these two concepts comprise the "ideology" of professionalism (7, 18, 45).

## Commentary

The power advocates offer a unified theory describing both what a profession is (structure) and how it came to be (process). Instead of the structural and processual approaches, they propose a single, and presumably more sophisticated, approach revolving around the concept of power. In that endeavor they impart to the term "power" a dual meaning, which could generate misunderstanding. As Ritzer has observed, there is power as the motor force in the professionalization process and then there is power as a defining attribute of professions (44). Actually, the structural and power approaches do have two points of congruence. For one, both approaches are based on the premise that the professions comprise a structurally distinct class, possessing distinguishable attributes. Secondly, both lead to the conclusion that exclusive control over its work is a prime attribute of a profession. The criticism that the structuralists have ignored the attribute of power in professionalism is not substantial. One of the dual meanings imparted to the term "power" by the power advocates is an occupation's exclusive control over the content and conditions of its work. According to this last definition, the structuralists have indeed integrated the attribute of power into their professional model. Although not labeled as "power," the monopolistic component in the structuralist's model symbolizes the concept of power in the meaning of occupational self-control. In this same sense, my earlier article contained forty-three references to "power" broadly conceived. To be sure, in only eight does the word itself appear; in the remainder synonyms are used (viz., authority, control, dictate, immunity, monopoly and privilege). But none of this is meant to gainsay the sharp antithesis between the structural and power perspectives to professionalism. In the professional model advanced by the power advocates the single and only defining attribute is the monopolistic one. If the structuralists are to be criticized for devaluing "power," then the power advocates are to be criticized for overvaluing it. The power theory of professionalism has the merit and the demerit characteristic of all single-factor explanations of complex phenomena.

The power perspective does have the merit of offering a salutary corrective for the errors to which the structural approach is prone. For one, it compels the structuralists to scrutinize, more than they heretofore have done, the customary sources of their data. These have been by and large the content of publications by and interviews with practitioners of whatever profession is being investigated. But the information thus obtained might well tell us not so much what the profession actually is, but what its members believe it or pretend it or wish it to be. Hence, the face validity of information from such sources requires greater scrutiny than it has perhaps received thus far (1, 26:xv). Secondly, the power perspective compels a reconsideration of the assumption that, because the professions are essential to the functioning of our society, the interests of the two are, therefore, always compatible. Thus, the lengthy socialization process required for entry into a profession plus its guild-like structure generate a collegial solidarity and a concern for occupational goals which could lead to actions by its members that are profession-centered and conflicting with their responsibility to the community (7). Also, the profession's monopoly whereby none but its own members may provide a service, is this not a contradiction of the free market principles that govern the distribution of goods and services in our society (18)? Lastly, the power perspective compels the structuralists to question their assumption that the basic attributes of professions are reenforcing and, accordingly, to prompt them to search for possible antitheses among them. For example, some students of professionalism have suggested that the expansion of theoretical knowledge and technical expertise in a profession is accompanied by an impersonalization of the service; that by fostering an increasing absorption on the part of practitioners in the technical aspects of their practice, it results in a diminished concern for their clients as persons. In other words, it is possible that the intellectual component in a profession grows at the expense of the commitment to the service ideal (10, 14, 49:21). A similar tension between the service and the monopolistic components has likewise been noted (7).

Its admitted merit aside, the serious demerit of the power theory is in its single-factor approach to the professions. In positing power as the sole propelling and sustaining factor in professionalism, the power advocates have in their own way oversimplified a complex phenomenon, the very thing for which they criticize the structuralists (47). Consider briefly what actually is involved in attaining and retaining what Light has aptly characterized as a social contract between the profession and the community (30). As is true of all such contracts, it has the following features.

First, the contract is the product of a very long series of negotiations between the maturing profession and the community. Wilensky obtained for each of thirteen selected professions the dates of certain crucial events marking stages in the professionalization process (54). From his data it is deducible that the average (median) time interval from the establishment of the first training school for a nascent profession to the passage of the first licensing legislation, thereby granting it official recognition, is twenty-eight years; that the average time interval from the organization of its first professional association to the licensing of the profession, is twenty-four years. In other words, the process of professionalization, whereby an aspiring profession achieves its contract with the community, lasts decades. The second feature about the process is that it is completely public. The successes and derelictions of the aspiring profession are topics for review in all media of communication. Its intellectual, ethical and practical claims for a service monopoly are subjects for dissection in legislative hearings and commission reports. It must defend itself against challenges from competing occupations which are threatened by its claims. Goode has amply documented the struggle waged by clinical psychologists during the 1950s and 1960s to gain certification and licensure in the various states against the intense opposition on the part of medically trained psychiatrists (19).

Third, the basis of every social contract is reciprocity. The profession must be able to offer some *quid pro quo* to obtain the privilege of self-control. What the profession has to offer is a matter not of conjecture but of record, the record of many years' performance. Given the long duration and public character of the professionalization process, there is ample opportunity for all agencies to scrutinize whether the profession has established what Larson has called "its social credit" (26:56). The community possesses the mechanisms needed to evaluate whether the profession's record demonstrates its members to be, as Goode puts it, responsible masters of their craft (19). A fourth feature of the social contract between profession and community is that the latter can annul it unilaterally for good cause. If the profession's fund of knowledge is not updated with the times, or if its skills are surpassed by rival occupations, or if its performance comes to have little relation to the needs of society, the service monopoly will be revoked. The very same forces that provided support in the occupation's struggle toward professional status can also withdraw it. From time to time the community subjects given professions to reassessment; the current public debate over the social role of medicine in the U.S. is a good case in point (48). Such a reassessment can lead, if not to the termination of the social contract, to its revision resulting in a drastic reduction of the power of the profession concerned.

It is in the light of the above that the power approach should be viewed. Thus, it is undoubtedly true that a powerful sponsor can facilitate an occupation's difficult ascent to professional status and that this has actually been the case for certain professions. But it is more hypothesis than fact that the cognitive and normative elements are generated by the professionalization process primarily as public relations devices for enlisting influential people in high places in the profession's behalf. Several power advocates have gone so far as to characterize professional ethical codes as self-advertisements and frauds (7, 46). To view the professions through such dark-colored lenses is as simplistic as to view them through rose-tinted ones. Every bit equal to an influential sponsor as a source of power for a profession, is a solid knowledge base combined with a collectivity orientation. Lacking the latter, resort to the cleverest public relations techniques will hardly persuade anyone, including likely sponsors (who are also potential clients), that the profession possesses what in fact it does not. No occupation can attain and retain professional status on the basis of fraudulent claims. Inasmuch as the efficient functioning of the modern economy and polity is dependent upon professional knowledge and skills, it would be dysfunctional for the community to confer a service monopoly upon an occupation which lacks an adequate cognitive base. And for any authority, including professional authority, to become institutionalized and legitimized, it must, by its very nature, be grounded in a collectivity orientation (40:464).

## A NOTE ON THE SOCIAL WORK PROFESSION

The preoccupation of sociologists with the formulation of a generally acceptable model of the professions has perhaps placed them in the position, doubtless unintended, of being arbitrators of what is and is not a profession (1). The result has been that the journals of occupations aspiring to professional status are replete with articles which might more appropriately be entitled, "Model, Model on the Wall, Are We a Profession After All?" A perusal of the social work journals over the years yields ample proof of the frequency with which social workers pose this question to themselves. And when they do not, others pose it for them. The answers forthcoming still fail to reflect consensus. Flexner in his classic paper reached the conclusion that social work, as it was practiced in his time, did not meet the criteria for inclusion in the class of professions (15). In my earlier paper I concluded that social work, while still evolving, nonetheless coincided with my model at sufficient points to warrant its classification among the professions (22). In the four decades separating the appearances of the two papers social work had, in my view, matured. However, Etzioni, who has studied the less established and newer professions, has reached a negative verdict about social work (12). On the other hand, Vigilante insists that the current structural model of the professions is inapplicable to social work (50).

Etzioni and his colleagues have devoted much study to the professions which originated in the late industrial era and are only currently maturing. Included in this group are accounting, administration, counseling, journalism, librarianship, nursing, optometry, pharmacy, social work and teaching. Etzioni points out that these newer professions have understandably been greatly influenced by models which have been derived from studies of the older, well-established professions, and, have, therefore, patterned their own aspirations accordingly. Their collective goal appears to be to achieve a status comparable to that of the established professions (7, 26:38). But, Etzioni contends, this aspiration is unrealistic and the goal is unattainable (13, 20). The reason for this is to be found in what he considers to be the most important component of professionalism, the cognitive. In these newer professions the cognitive infrastructure is relatively weak. The skills employed in their daily work by practitioners in such professions are not grounded in a fully developed theoretical base (49:41). What preparatory knowledge they must acquire to qualify professionally is usually not sufficiently abstract, esoteric, organized nor very original. In the case of librarianship, for example, the knowledge consists of large amounts of concrete details (20). In the case of social work the basic information is a patchwork largely borrowed from the social sciences and allied helping professions. The prognosis that these newer professions will or even can eventually remedy their cognitive deficiencies is not favorable (21, 32). The plain fact is that these professions are more technical than intellectual disciplines. Their members are urged by Etzioni to recognize the intrinsic imperfections of their professions and to accept a middle status along the occupational continuum above the non-professions but below the old established professions. Etzioni has, therefore, labeled these middle range professions the "semi-professions" (12, 13).

To Vigilante the defect lies not in social work but in the structural model to which social work is constantly compared. In our postindustrial society, so goes his reasoning, the professions have grown both in numbers and variety. The most marked expansion has occurred among what Halmos has called the personal service professions, which includes social work (24). The service provided by these professions is a desired change, whether physical, intellectual, psychological or social, in the person of the client/patient. To these newer professions the model of the structuralists is not applicable. The model, having been derived from the old traditional professions, is simply outmoded. To be specific, in the structural model of professionalism there is an exaggerated emphasis on the cognitive, especially the scientific, component. Actually, the presumed superior knowledge of the older professions has become a potent and less than benevolent instrument of social control. By contrast, Vigilante contends, the mark of the true professional is and must be not only nor so much the specialized knowledge that he possesses, but rather what he does with that knowledge, how he uses it (50). In other words, when classifying an occupation as either a profession or a nonprofession, its structural attributes are less important than are the attitudes and behaviors of its members. And the latter, of what do they consist? On this point Vigilante is not specific, but in this connection Lewis has suggested the following list of attributes: a commitment to the task, a sense of responsibility, a striving for excellence, self-discipline, disinterestedness, and rationality (28). To summarize, it is not the structure and the organization of the occupation that marks it as a profession, but it is what Hall has called the attitudinal attributes of its members, as reflected in their behaviors in the work setting (23), that makes the distinguishing difference. Posed in such terms, the question whether social work is a profession answers itself.

Etzioni's classification of professions into the full-fledged and the semi-professions is useful. However, it is not new. Years ago Carr-Saunders offered a five-fold classification, with what he labeled "the semi-professions" as one of its categories. The latter, according to him, emphasize precise technical skills rather than theoretical learning, as exemplified in pharmacy and optometry (4, 43).* Etzioni may well have borrowed the label from Carr-Saunders. It is a fact of

*The Carr-Saunders classification of professions is as follows: old established, new, semi-, would-be-, and marginal (4, 43).

nature that no class is ever completely homogeneous. The units comprising it invariably differ, either in degree or in kind, with respect to the very attribute(s) that unites them into a class. Hence, the genus subdivides into species, the type into subtypes. The professions are no exception and attempts to classify them into subtypes merit consideration. Etzioni's negative prognosis regarding the likelihood of a semi-profession evolving to full-fledged status by perfecting its cognitive base may be unduly pessimistic. Transmutation, whereby one social type evolves into another, does occur. Thus, the accountant evolved from the bookkeeper, the optometrist from the lens grinder, and the social worker from the friendly visitor. Having themselves evolved from nonprofessional occupations, cannot certain ones among the semi-professions continue to evolve to full-fledged professions in time? Goode, accepting Etzioni's classification of social work as a semi-profession, predicts that over the next generation social work will develop a sufficient knowledge base to achieve full professional status (21).

As for Vigilante, I would not dispute his argument that a certain posture or disposition toward one's work, call it "a professional attitude," is an important attribute of professionalism. I would, however, dispute the implication of his argument that this attribute has been ignored by the structuralists. Far from it. What Lewis lists as the indicators of a distinctive professional attitude are subsumable under the cognitive and the normative components, especially the latter, of the structural model. Thus, my earlier article contained thirty-one references to the professional attitude broadly conceived, i.e., the attitude that members of professions are expected to manifest in their behaviors toward clients, colleagues, and community; in seven of them terms identical to those on the Lewis list were used. In that same article I devoted a lengthy paragraph to the concept of "calling" in professionalism as manifested in a commitment to one's chosen work and in the personal satisfaction derived from maximal performance (22). So, the importance of a professional attitude is not in dispute here.

More relevant in this context is Vigilante's perspective upon professionalism as contrasted with Etzioni's and its implications for the social work profession. To Etzioni it is specialized knowledge, the cognitive, which is the principal, the primary component in professionalism; to Vigilante the cognitive is secondary, subordinate to something more important, a special attitude. In this connection I would strongly caution against any deemphasis and downgrading of the knowledge component of professionalism by the leaders of a semi-profession, such as social work, which is already regarded as having a relatively weak cognitive base. To repeat an earlier point, without a solid knowledge base no occupation can lay claim to professional status (47, 54). The professional is unlike a merchant who has a usable commodity for sale; all he has to offer is his knowledge. As Buckley so well phrased it, without its specialized knowledge a profession would be without a saleable product (2). It would, therefore, be a serious error were social workers to reject as outmoded the knowledge component in the structuralist's model on the grounds that the latter was derived from the now old and traditional professions. As so many others before me have asserted, ours is a knowledge society; for its efficient functioning it feeds on knowledge, always more and more of it. Hence, I share Vigilante's concern lest professionals employ their esoteric knowledge as a less than benevolent instrument of social control. The remedy for that, however, is not to deemphasize the cognitive but to reemphasize the normative component in professionalism. The masthead of every professional journal should remind its readers lest they forget that the profession exists by virtue of its social contract with the community. But should the members of any profession begin, from whatever noble motives, to downgrade the importance of knowledge for their craft, they would take the first steps down the road marked "Deprofessionalization."

## BIBLIOGRAPHY

1. Berlant, Jeffrey L., Review of *The Professions and Their Prospects* (by Eliot Freidson, ed.), *Contemporary Sociology*, Vol. 4 (May 1975), pp. 261–63.

2. Buckley, John W., "An Exploration of Professional Identity," in Stephen E. Loeb, ed., *Ethics in the Accounting Profession*, John Wiley, 1978.

3. Caplow, Theodore, *The Sociology of Work*, University of Minnesota, 1954.

4. Carr-Saunders, A.M. and P.A. Wilson, "The Emergence of Professions," in Nosow and Form, eds., *op. cit.*

5. Cullen, John B., "Professionalism, Licensure, and Examinations," unpublished, 1977.

6. ———, "Structural Aspects of the Architectural Profession," *Journal of Architectural Education*, Vol. 31 (Spring 1978), pp. 18–25.

7. Daniels, Arlene Kaplan, "How Free Should Professions Be?" in Freidson, ed., *op. cit.*

8. Denzin, Norman K. and Curtis J. Mettlin, "Incomplete Professionalization. The Case of Pharmacy," in Pavalko, ed., *op. cit.*

9. Dyer, Preston M., "How Professional Is the BSW Worker?" *Social Work*, Vol. 22 (November 1977), pp. 487–92.

10. Engel, Gloria V. and Richard H. Hall, "The Growing Industrialization of the Professions," in Freidson, ed., *op. cit.*

11. Epstein, Cynthia F., "Encountering the Male Establishment. Sex-Status Limits on Women's Careers in the Professions," *American Journal of Sociology*, Vol. 75, (May 1970), pp. 965–82.

12. Etzioni, Amitai, ed., *The Semi-Professions and Their Organization,* Free Press, 1969.

13. ———, "Preface," in Etzioni, ed., *op. cit.*

14. Feldbaum, Eleanor G., "Professionalism and Client Orientation," unpublished, 1977.

15. Flexner, Abraham, "Is Social Work a Profession?" *Proceedings of the National Conference of Charities and Corrections,* 1915, pp. 576–90.

16. Freidson, Eliot, ed., *The Professions and Their Prospects,* Sage Publications, 1973.

17. ———, "Professions and the Occupational Principle," in Freidson, ed., *op. cit.*

18. ———, "The Futures of Professionalization," in M. Stacey, *et al.,* eds., *Health and the Division of Labor,* Croom Helm, 1977.

19. Goode, William J., "Encroachment, Charlatanism, and the Emerging Professions," *American Sociological Review,* Vol. 25 (December 1960), pp. 902–14.

20. ———, "The Librarian. From Occupation to Profession," in Vollmer and Mills, eds., *op. cit.*

21. ———, "The Theoretical Limits of Professionalization," in Etzioni, ed., *op. cit.*

22. Greenwood, Ernest, "Attributes of a Profession," *Social Work,* Vol. 2 (July 1957), pp. 44–45.

23. Hall, Richard H., "Professionalization and Bureaucratization," *American Sociological Review,* Vol. 33 (February 1968), pp. 92–104.

24. Halmos, Paul, "Sociology and the Personal Service Professions," in Freidson, ed., *op. cit.*

25. Haug, Marie R. and Marvin B. Sussman, "Professionalization and Unionism," in Freidson, ed., *op. cit.*

26. Larson, Magali S., *The Rise of Professionalism. A Sociological Analysis,* University of California, 1977.

27. Laski, Harold J., *The American Democracy,* Viking Press, 1948.

28. Lewis, Lionel S., "The University and the Professional Model," in Freidson, ed., *op. cit.*

29. Levy, Charles S., "The Context of Social Work Ethics," *Social Work,* Vol. 17 (March 1972), pp. 95–101.

30. Light, Donald, Jr., "Professional Superiority," unpublished, 1974.

31. ———, "The Structure of the Academic Professions," *Sociology of Education,* Vol. 47 (Winter 1974), pp. 2–28.

32. Lorber, Judith, Review of *Professions and Professionalization* (by J.A. Jackson, ed.), *Contemporary Sociology,* Vol. 1 (November 1972), pp. 533–35.

33. Lortie, Dan C., "The Balance of Control in Elementary School Teaching," in Etzioni, ed., *op. cit.*

34. Mack, Raymond W., "The Components of Social Conflict," in Ralph M. Kramer and Harry Specht, eds., *Readings in Community Organization Practice,* Prentice-Hall, 1969.

35. Marshall, T. H., "The Recent History of Professionalism in Relation to Social Structure and Social Policy," *Canadian Journal of Economics and Political Science,* Vol. 5 (August 1939), pp. 325–40.

36. Moore, Wilbert E., "Economic and Professional Institutions," in Neil J. Smelser, ed., *Sociology: An Introduction,* John Wiley, 1967.

37. Nosow, Sigmund and William H. Form, *Man, Work and Society. A Reader in the Sociology of Occupations,* Basic Books, 1962.

38. ———, "Professions," in Nosow and Form, eds., *op. cit.*

39. Parsons, Talcott, "The Professions and Social Structure," *Social Forces,* Vol. 17 (May 1939), pp. 457–67.

40. ———, *The Social System,* Free Press, 1964.

41. Pavalko, Ronald M., ed., *Sociological Perspectives on Occupations,* Peacock, 1972.

42. ———, "Professional Marginality," in Pavalko, ed., *op. cit.*

43. Reiss, Albert J., Jr., "Occupational Mobility of Professional Workers," *American Sociological Review,* Vol. 20 (December 1955), pp. 693–700.

44. Ritzer, George, "Professionalization, Bureaucratization and Rationalization," *Social Forces,* Vol. 53 (June 1975), pp. 627–34.

45. ———, "Power and the Professions," unpublished, 1975.

46. Roth, Julius, "A Codification of Current Prejudices," letter to the Editor, *The American Sociologist,* Vol. 4 (May 1969), p. 159.

47. Reuschmeyer, Dietrich, "Doctors and Lawyers. A Comment on the Theory of the Professions," in Pavalko, ed., *op. cit.*

48. Starr, Paul, "Medicine and the Waning of Professional Sovereignty," *Daedalus,* Vol. 197 (Winter 1978), pp. 175–92.

49. Toren, Nina, *Social Work. The Case of a Semi-Profession,* Sage Publications, 1972.

50. Vigilante, Joseph L., "The Future. Dour or Rosy?" *Social Work,* Vol. 17 (July 1972), pp. 3–4.

51. Vollmer, Howard M. and Donald L. Mills, eds., *Professionalization,* Prentice-Hall, 1966.

52. ———, "The Concept of Professionalization," in Vollmer and Mills, eds., *op. cit.*

53. ———, "Professional Associations and Colleague Relations," in Vollmer and Mills, eds., *op. cit.*

54. Wilensky, Harold L., "The Professionalization of Everyone?" *American Journal of Sociology,* Vol. 70 (September 1964), pp. 137–58.

55. Zola, Irving Kenneth and Stephen J. Miller, "The Erosion of Medicine from Within," in Freidson, ed., *op. cit.*

# 17   The Incomplete Profession

## NEIL GILBERT AND HARRY SPECHT

The profession of social work is incomplete: it has developed a commitment to services but has failed to develop a commitment to welfare. This incompleteness is one reason for its difficulty in responding effectively to demands placed on it by a society in transition and upheaval.

This diagnosis of the state of the profession is not original. It follows a recurrent theme on the duality of social work practice, played under different titles throughout the profession's history. In 1905 Richmond wrote of the "wholesale" and "retail" methods of social

Reprinted with permission of the National Association of Social Workers, from *Social Work,* 19, 6 (November 1974): 665–74.

reform; in 1929 probably the best known and most enduring variation was composed by Lee under the title of "cause" and "function";
in 1958 Burns spoke of the distinction between "social work" and
"social welfare"; in 1963 Schwartz discussed the "service" and the
"movement"; and in 1972 Richan identified different underlying
language systems in social work.[1] And this is only a partial list.[2]

While duality still exists, in recent years its nature has changed
substantially. The balance has shifted from services to welfare, and
the consequences are now filtering into the field with results disap-
pointing for the profession's commitment to both welfare and services. The purpose of this article is, first, to examine this shift and the
adjustments that have been made and, second, to propose a course
of action designed to fulfill a substantive commitment to welfare
while maintaining the integrity of social work's commitment to services—not to mitigate but to invigorate the duality inherent in social
work practice.

In this discussion the authors refer to *services* as the specific and
concrete activities that professionals engage in to assist those in need.
They include all direct-service activities such as therapy, counseling,
education, advocacy, information gathering, and referral. Such activities are the major concern of casework, group work, and those aspects of community organization in which direct services are
provided to community groups and organizations.[3] These activities
will be discussed collectively as social work services and direct services and the professionals engaged in them will be referred to as
social work specialists and direct-service workers.

*Welfare*, in the framework of this article, deals with the professional activities that focus on both change in and maintenance of the
institution of social welfare. *Institution* in this instance refers to the
system of programs conducted by public and private agencies that
have the express purpose of providing mutual support for individuals, families, and groups.[4] Professional activities involved in social
welfare include indirect services such as planning, policy analysis,
program development, administration, and program evaluation. The
social welfare specialist does not deal directly with those in need, but
rather focuses on the institutional structure through which those in
need are served. These activities will be referred to as indirect services and social welfare, and the professionals engaged in them will
be referred to as indirect service workers and social welfare specialists.

## SERVICES AND WELFARE

In 1958, in a paper entitled "Social Welfare Is Our Commitment,"
the keynote address to the National Conference on Social Welfare,
Burns described the difference between the two commitments and

provided the framework for developing the profession's other side.
Burns indicated that the conference had changed its name from
"social work" to "social welfare" because social work had come to
signify only "certain categories of people who are involved in our
social service," those with "a specific series of skilled services."[5] She
stated that there was nothing undesirable about the professionalization of certain types of social welfare activities, but that the term
"social work" focused too narrowly on professional functions. "Social
welfare," on the other hand "seemed most comprehensively to embrace the entire field of social welfare and the concerns of all those
who were interested in it regardless of their functions, professional
orientation, skills, and affiliations."[6] Ironically, the table of contents
of the conference mistakenly lists Burns's address as "Social Work Is
Our Commitment," and, unfortunately, the profession of social work
appears to have little understood and been little affected by her lucid
and instructive charge.

This result was not entirely unforeseen; Burns identified three
obstacles to the fulfillment of social work's commitment to welfare.
First, the techical skills and knowledge required to affect the structure of welfare services were in short supply in social work. Second,
social workers perceived themselves as lacking the influence and
political power needed to affect public policy decisions. Third, the
profession had no commitment to a cause.[7]

A significant proportion of social workers today have a surfeit of
commitment to causes and no longer suffer from a lack of belief in
their political acumen. However, there has been little development
of the knowledge, skill, and technical expertise that Burns thought
necessary for fulfilling a commitment to welfare. In the current processes of change, the commitment to services has been drastically
diluted, if not completely erased, as resources, practice skills, and
knowledge designed for the service enterprise have been stretched
and twisted in efforts to accommodate new departures. Rein's observation in 1970 is much to the point.

> Individual social workers may, of course, function as reformers in the
> areas of employment, income distribution, and political power—but these
> activities are marginal to their professional tasks. In this sense they are
> professionals who are radical rather than members of a radical profes-
> sion.[8]

How did all this come about?

## IMPULSE FOR CHANGE

Social work's commitment to services was made at the beginning of this century. At that time, as Austin points out, strate-

gies for societal change were rejected in favor of a concentration on services:

> Particularly significant in the conflict between these two approaches was the decision made in 1910 by the board of directors of the New York School of Philanthropy to concentrate on the training of caseworkers for direct service positions in charity agencies. In doing so they explicitly rejected the recommendation ... that social workers should concern themselves with the issues of public policy rather than with the provision of financial assistance on a case-by-case basis ... The practitioner-oriented curriculum which the New York School adopted, built around the personnel needs of locally based individual and neighborhood centered programs, was to become the model for all schools of social work until the 1960s.[9]

In the early 1960s, along with the general national impulse for social justice, social work was gripped by an impulse to make social welfare an instrument to deal with societal inequities. Social workers' belief systems and orientations were profoundly affected by three developments: (1) the civil rights movement, which was part of and probably the cause of a general revolution in human relations; (2) the evolution of national programs such as the War on Poverty and Model Cities, which were directed at producing large-scale social change; and (3) the growing concern at the start of the 1970s with questions of institutional inequality.[10]

The social work profession, as Austin notes, became the whipping boy for the advocates of institutional change because social casework failed to develop effective means for dealing with poverty:

> The high point of the assault was the speech by Sargent Shriver ... in 1964 announcing that there was no place for casework in the war-on-poverty-programs. ... The attack on casework and the organized social work profession continued throughout the [War on Poverty] together with strong support for the principle of using nonprofessionals and generalists rather than social work specialists as staff in community action programs. This attack which was also supported by many professional social workers was so successful that the membership of the professional association voted in 1969 to overturn the principle established ... in the 1920s that social work was a distinctive profession based exclusively on a systematic program of professional education at the graduate level.[11]

With individual services suffering a crisis of confidence, how did the profession express the impulse for social justice? One might say that it attempted to deal rather with injustice, but in poor form. The National Association of Social Workers, the Council on Social Work Education, and schools of social work and social welfare were not prepared with a substantive, distinctive means by which social work could address problems of poverty, discrimination, and inequality. An impulse is not a commitment but only a feeling pushed on by energy without any direction. Demonstration, disruption, confrontation—the tactics of Saul Alinsky based on the idea that "power is all," and the tactics of the civil rights movement—were adopted by many social workers as behaviors of choice for committed professionals.

Caught short, social workers used the only means available to the profession at the time for responding to demands for change—its services.[12] Many concluded that casework was not effective for any purpose, and those who provided services to clients in need began to address themselves politically to social problems. Custodial care, institutionalization, supportive services, and clinical intervention were to become almost anathema in the social services—all seen as variations of "blaming the victim." Attention and resources were devoted to protest activities, street people, social action, and manifestations of social ferment like drug abuse, sexual liberation, and new forms of communication. Many practitioners attached themselves to causes that were written in the day's headlines and that changed almost as frequently.

The authors attended a recent meeting of social workers, called by the school's faculty to discuss what professionals in the field believed the school should teach. As the list of problems having priority grew longer and wider in range, one professional who works with the State Senate inquired, "Is there any problem that you think you cannot deal with?" He then said he finds it difficult to convince the Senate —a legislative body reasonably sensitive to the concerns of social welfare—that social workers can do *anything* well. Apparently this sentiment is not peculiar to the California State legislature. At about this same time the Family Service Association of America issued the following statement:

> It will be impossible for graduates to be prepared for [direct-service-giving] positions if the school has set an educational goal for them that is too general and has encouraged them to place no value on working with the individual predicaments and life problems of people.... Many students do not achieve in graduate schools of social work a fundamental grasp of [the competence needed for casework practice]. They do not develop a commitment to, or even an awareness of, the need for working with and for individuals and families. They do not emerge with an adequate theoretical base for practice in usable form.[13]

The social work profession responded inadequately to the impulse for change because the training, skill, and knowledge required for a sustained and meaningful commitment to welfare were lacking. Social workers enthusiastically rushed to engage themselves in one new programmatic arrangement after another with little to show for the effort either in social change or increased knowledge and competence. All the heat did not forge a commitment to welfare, but rather served to consume the substance on which the commitment to services is based.

## SEARCH FOR UNITY

Many factors internal and external to the profession influenced its response to the social forces at play since the 1960s. One internal factor of central concern to social work educators was that the profession's perennial search for unity hampered change and the development of a commitment to welfare.

Many have long considered that the duality of social work practice is a source of strain within the profession. Proposals for mitigating this strain generally have been couched in terms of unity, which would seem desirable. Indeed, unity is an objective hard to resist in almost any context (man with man, man with nature, nation with nation, husband with wife). The problem is not the objective, but the means proposed to achieve it in social work.

Achieving unity has been equated with mixing the educational elements required to produce the direct-service practitioner and the social welfare specialist. For instance, there are proposals to create the generic social worker by fusing service and welfare commitments into a single function, such as the mediating one described by Schwartz.[14] Levin proposes "a social policy base for unifying the component sequences of the curriculum and for shaping their content."[15] And Richan suggests that the unifying elements may be found in developing a common professional language.[16]

The common thrust of most of these proposals is toward achieving unity by creating a core curriculum in which direct-service practitioners and welfare specialists mingle in the same core courses. The degree to which the identities, skills, knowledge, and practice orientations of the two groups are fused depends on the extent of the core curriculum.

These proposals tend to ignore or at least do not directly address another meaning of unity that has to do with the distinction between mixing and linking. *Mixing* implies creating a new whole by fusing separate identities of constituent elements. *Linking* implies creating a new whole by connecting separate identities of constituent elements.

## A UNIFIED SINGLE FUNCTION

In response to proposals that there should be separate systems of social work education for direct-service practitioners and social welfare specialists, Schwartz states the argument for a unified single function—the unity-through-mixing orientation-as follows:

> To create a "department" for each would in fact *institutionalize* the very evils they mean to solve. The "clinicians" would be shielded from any further pressures to bring weight of the experiences with people in trouble to bear on the formation of public policy; and the "social planners" would be set free from the realities of practice and left alone to fashion their expertise not from the struggles and sufferings of people but from their own clever and speculating minds.... The planner who has not practiced will be as shallow in his policy-making as the practitioner who has not made his impact on policy will be in his work with people.
>
> Thus the question for the profession is whether it now gives itself over to the polarization of the individual and the social, building it into its very structure, or tries to see more deeply into the connections between the two so that it may create a single vision of the professional function. [Italics added.][17]

Schwartz raises an important issue. Is it possible to prepare professionals who can carry a commitment to welfare without first becoming skilled direct-service practitioners? Can they plan for, administer, and evaluate services if they have not been directly engaged in providing them? One way to put this issue to rest is to point out that much significant work on social welfare policy, program, administration, and research and evaluation is by non-social workers or those with little direct-practice experience. Among these, to mention a few, are Eveline Burns, Frances Piven, Nathan Glazer, Daniel Moynihan, Edwin Witte, Arthur Altmeyer, Herman Somers, Mollie Orshansky, Wilbur Cohen, Sar Levitan, Gilbert Steiner and Robert Lampman—all welfare experts known for work they have done skillfully, with compassion and commitment. No one knows or cares whether they have mastered the "conscious use of self" that is legitimately expected of the direct-service worker.

## DUALITY OF THE PROFESSION

Another approach to this issue recognizes that the profession of social work is, in reality, divided into two branches. In actual day-to-day practice, professionals are clearly engaged in either direct or indirect services, carrying out a commitment to services or a commitment to welfare. If social workers ignore this reality, they are merely leaving it to others to fulfill their commitments. As long as the profession does not fulfill its commitment to welfare it will not have a serious handle on its own future. If social workers are to deal with social welfare, then educators and social planners had better begin to build the programs and the professional support system that will encourage them to do so.

The call to arms should not be so thunderous as to drown out the practical wisdom of those who caution against polarization of the profession. When Schwartz stated that "the question for the profession is whether it now gives itself over to the polarization of the individual and the social," this implied division and disaffection between competing elements in the profession. But another outcome might be possible: separate functional identities that are complementary and mutually supporting might be developed. However, the duality in the profession has manifested itself more in division and disaffection than in complementarity and mutual support.

The rejection of Schwartz's proposition that the planner or welfare specialist who has not practiced will be as "shallow in his policy-making as the practitioner who has not made his impact on policy will be in his work with people" does not mean that the authors favor the complete separation of the welfare specialist and the social work practitioner nor that they condone either one's ignorance of the other's line of practice. On the contrary, to the extent that each knows and understands the other's practice, his own grasp of the profession is enhanced and the profession benefits from the support each provides the other. The question is one of substance and degree. The goal is the development of separate functional identities within the framework of a unified profession.

## IMPLICATIONS FOR EDUCATION

The search for unity may be summarized in terms of the following four broad models of social work education: the generic model, integrated core model, linkage model, and independent model. (See Fig. 17–1.)

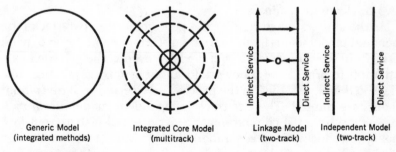

| Generic Model | Integrated Core Model | Linkage Model | Independent Model |
| (integrated methods) | (multitrack) | (two-track) | (two-track) |

FIGURE 17–1
Educational Models for Integrating Social Services and Social Welfare

*Generic model.* Essentially, this model—which represents the extreme of unification through mixing—prepares professionals for direct service to individual clients, families, or groups. In some instances students will have courses in community organization and social planning. This type of program produces professionals whose major commitment is to service and who have a good deal of information about organizations, planning, and welfare systems. Frequently professionals so trained know a little bit about a lot of things but are not well enough versed in the practice requirements of any specific area to offer a substantial contribution to either service or welfare.

Clearly, a commitment to services is important and worthy of professional development. But it is not the same as a commitment to welfare nor should it be. Those who want to provide direct services to people, whether through therapy, counseling, advocacy, or leisure-time activities, are obligated to master relevant knowledge and skill about inter- and intrapersonal interventions, group dynamics, social and individual pathology, and professional behavior in working with clients, agencies, and other professionals. Attempting to expand their functions to include all types of social intervention and social change efforts can only have deleterious results. Their professional equipment is likely to be a thin patchwork quilt. Training for a commitment to services should aim to produce professionals who are as highly skilled as possible at what they do.

*Two-track independent model.* At the other extreme, the two-track independent model calls for a clear separation in developing professional practitioners for welfare and service functions. One track trains for clinical practice (direct services); the other trains for social planning, research, and administration (indirect services).[18] The distinctive feature of this model is that training for one functional track is so independent of training for the other that an entire school of social work may specialize in either area. There is no reason why both tracks must be located in one school and, if they are, there is no curriculum requirement that forces students and faculty of the two tracks to intermingle.

As the authors see it, neither the generic nor the two-track independent model seems likely to train satisfactorily both types of workers within the framework of a unified profession. The generic model attempts to provide a framework for unity by mixing practice functions so thoroughly that, in the process, service and welfare commitments are diluted. The two-track independent model attempts to produce substantial commitments to service and welfare, but in so doing introduces sharp separations and divisions that increase the likelihood of polarization.

*Multitrack integrated core model.* In this model the various tracks may be found under the traditional labels of casework, group work, and community organization; microsystem, mezzosystem, and macrosystem; or direct and indirect services. Or they may focus on problem areas such as community mental health, aging, and child welfare.

The integrated core of these educational programs may vary in size from a few courses to a substantial part of the curriculum (at which point this model takes on aspects of the generic one). Usually the integrated core includes, at a minimum, courses in human growth and development, research, and social policy, in which students from all tracks mix. These core courses are designed, first, to provide students with a body of knowledge relevant to the pursuit of their various lines of practice and, second, to provide the academic binding for unification within the school and profession. Thus they offer a substantive answer to the question: What is it that unites these various specialists in one profession?

Compared to the curriculum for training direct-service practitioners, the programs for indirect services are relatively new to schools of social work and generally not as well formulated. This is not to suggest that all is well with the direct-service training or that the area does not need new curriculum developments, experimentation, and change.[19] However, the focus of this discussion is on curriculum requirements for indirect services. The following four major areas in which the social welfare specialist must have expertise suggest the depth and complexity of the knowledge base for the curriculum of the multitrack model:

1. Problem analysis. This includes skills in research, data collection, and interpretation of findings to reveal linkages between causes and problems; and assessment of needs and resources.

2. Program design. This includes skills in organizational analysis and understanding of alternatives in the construction of service delivery systems; skills in budgeting, cost-benefit analysis, and other forms of systems analysis such as the planning-programming-budgeting system (PPBS); and planning for coordination and resource acquisition.

3. Development of and work with decision-making systems. This includes political organization and processes; uses of priority-setting schemes, organizational operations, and knowledge and skill in the structuring of planning and administrative agencies; and the acquisition and promotion of needed technical support (e.g., for economic development, therapeutic programs, or manpower training).

4. Evaluation. Like the first area, this includes skills in research and data collection but also calls for political and organizational skills. The function of evaluation differs from problem analysis in terms of its objective, which is to enable the community to determine the extent to which social service programs meet their goals.[20]

The authors see a crucial distinction between the essence or core of the welfare specialist's practice orientation and that of the direct-service practitioner. With the understanding that any effort to extract the essence of phenomena as complex as the skill and

knowledge base of social work practice must in some measure sim-
plify reality, the differences may be stated as follows:

■ The core practice orientation of the direct-service worker deals
with individual and group problem-solving methods, drawing upon
social-psychological interpretation and relating mainly to personal
and interactional variables.

■ The core practice orientation of the indirect-service worker deals
with the methods of applied social research, drawing upon empirical
interpretation and relating mainly to structural and organizational
variables.

By requiring students in both the direct- and indirect-service
tracks to take the same set of courses, the integrated core model
tends to emphasize the objective of professional unity at the cost of
functional relevance.

*Two-track linkage model.* What and how much knowledge should
be shared by direct- and indirect-service workers? The main distinction between the integrated core model and the two-track linkage
model is the manner in which this issue is addressed in the curriculum. Both models might include, for example, research, policy
analysis, and human growth and development courses for the direct
and indirect services. In the integrated core model the substance of
these courses would be the same for the direct and indirect services.
These and perhaps other courses are, in effect, what form the integrated core. In the two-track linkage model the substance of these
courses would be different.

Although it is not the authors' intent to design a curriculum, we
will attempt to convey a sense of how this model might be put into
operation. Consider, for instance, the research requirement. In the
indirect-service track, planning and evaluation of social welfare programs are among the skills that must be mastered. Students in this
track would take research courses designed to maximize these objectives; students in the direct services, in which the knowledge of
*applied* research methods is less central to practice, would take a
substantially different type of research course, designed mainly to
produce intelligent consumers or users.

The responsibility for creating the linkage, for teaching direct-
service practitioners something about the practice of the indirect
services and how they might collaborate with social welfare specialists, falls to the indirect-service instructors. Similarly, it would be the
responsibility of instructors in the direct-service track to develop, for
example, special courses designed to give social welfare specialists an
understanding of the nature and requirements of practice in the
direct services. Precisely what courses would fall in each track and
the most appropriate points for creating linkages are matters open
to detailed analysis and experimentation.

There is another type of course in which students from both tracks might intermingle. This would be a course dealing with the history of the profession and its role in developing the institution of social welfare. Such a course would highlight what it is that unites these two types of specialists in one profession—their common interests in the problems, issues, clients, and programs of social welfare and the complementary skills they bring to bear on them.

Finally, there is the question of the kinds and degrees of specialization that an MSW program designed according to the two-track linkage model might have. There can be a wide variety of arrangements for specialization within each of the two major tracks.

## CONCLUSION

Recently, a number of schools of social work have developed programs for training professionals for social welfare, which suggests that the field may be attempting to fulfill its dual commitment.[21] But the appearance of these programs causes a high degree of uneasiness in the profession, and opposition may be expected from a number of sources. What seem to be some of the bases for opposition to a commitment to welfare?

A commitment to welfare entails an abstract, reflective, and long-range outlook. As Burns notes, such a commitment is "a state of mind which conceives of one's own job as part of a wider whole and where attention is focused always on the wider objective."[22] This approach is at variance with that of the political activists, who are more inclined toward immediate action and engagement in the current struggle rather than toward the deliberate study and systematic evaluation that mark a commitment to welfare.

The current ideological demands of minority faculty, students, and practitioners for curriculum emphasis on the Third-World perspective of racial minorities involve a narrower and more particularistic outlook than that required for the training of welfare specialists. This struggle between the universal and the particular is an important one in the profession. It is related to the problem of finding the proper balance between our commitments to services and welfare only because it has emerged out of the same historical currents. However, it is a different and, as Hughes notes, perennial problem:

> This strain . . . is found in some degree in all professions . . . The professional may learn some things that are universal in the physical, biological or social world. But around this core of universal knowledge there is likely to be a large body of practical knowledge which relates only to his own culture. . . . While professions are, in some of their respects, universal, in others they are closely ethnocentric. In fact, inside most professions there

develops a tacit division of labor between the more theoretical and the more practical; once in a while conflict breaks out over issues related to it. The professional schools may be accused of being too "academic"; the academics accuse other practitioners of failure to be sufficiently intellectual.[23]

The debate over the appropriate balance between general knowledge and group-specific knowledge in which the social work profession is now engaged will no doubt continue, along with the search for unity between direct and indirect services. However, the latter search deals with a different dimension of professional development which constitutes a strain in all professions, as Hughes also notes:

> Every profession considers itself the proper body to set the terms in which some aspect of society, life or nature is to be thought of, and to define the general lines, or even the details of public policy concerning it.[24]

That is, every profession must come to grips with the problems created by its duality of commitments.

A third and potentially the strongest source of opposition is from the direct services. Direct-service practitioners have taken quite a battering. Seemingly endless studies demonstrating the ineffectiveness of casework—coupled with a decade-long assault on services by the social action-community organization-social planning-social policy analysis axis—have devastated them.[25] Coming after the collapse of the "grand illusion " of casework's bright future contained in the service amendments to the Social Security Act in the 1960s, it is no wonder that in the 1970s direct-service practitioners are anxious about their place in the field. From their viewpoint, welfare specialists are "the enemy." The notion of complementary and mutually-supporting functions may be unpersuasive in light of these experiences. On the contrary, there is deep-seated concern in the profession that the development of our commitment to welfare will require giving up our commitment to services.

Given these various strains, is it possible for social work to develop the capacity to fulfill a commitment to services and a commitment to welfare to become a complete profession? Perhaps, but such developments await the best efforts that social work professionals have to give. Social workers might begin by ceasing the useless and debilitating attacks on one another, reaffirming the profession's commitment to offering services of high quality, and seeking ways to foster the development of the profession's other side. A reassessment of educational models for the purpose of enhancing the functional integrity of services and welfare within a unified professional framework may be a useful first step in this direction.

## NOTES

1. *See* Mary Richmond, *The Long View* (New York: Russell Sage Foundation, 1930), pp. 214–221; Porter Lee, *Social Work as Cause and Function and Other Papers* (New York: Columbia University Press, 1937), pp. 3–24; Eveline Burns, "Social Work [sic] Is Our Commitment," *The Social Welfare Forum, 1958* (New York: Columbia University Press, 1958); William Schwartz, "Small Group Science and Group Work Practice," *Social Work,* 8 (October 1963), pp. 39–46; and Willard C. Richan, "A Common Language for Social Work," *Social Work,* 17 (November 1972), pp. 14–22.

2. For a concise review of the variations on this theme, *see* William Schwartz, "Private Troubles and Public Issues: One Job or Two?" *The Social Welfare Forum, 1969* (New York: Columbia University Press, 1969), pp. 22–43.

3. Community organization (CO) does not fit neatly into the distinction between service and welfare activities. CO practice, as Rothman points out, may be categorized under locality development, social planning, and social action. Locality development is mainly concerned with service activities, and social planning with welfare activities, but the social action model seems to contain the potential for both types. *See* Jack Rothman, "Three Models for Community Organization Practice," *Social Work Practice, 1968* (New York: Columbia University Press, 1968), pp. 16–47.

4. For a more detailed explanation, *see* Neil Gilbert and Harry Specht, *Dimensions of Social Welfare Policy* (Englewood Cliffs, N.J.: Prentice-Hall, 1974).

5. Burns, op. cit., p. 4.

6. Ibid., p. 3

7. Ibid., pp. 15–19.

8. Martin Rein, *Social Policy* (New York: Random House, 1970), p. 297.

9. David M. Austin, "The Anti-Poverty Wars of the 20th Century," p. 10. Unpublished paper (Waltham, Mass.: Florence Heller School for Advanced Studies in Social Welfare, Brandeis University, 1972).

10. For a thoughtful analysis of the impact of these changes in one city, *see* Alfred Kahn, "Do Social Services Have a Future in New York?" *City Almanac, 5* (February 1971).

11. Austin, op. cit., p. 33.

12. *See* Harry Specht, "The Deprofessionalization of Social Work," *Social Work,* 17 (March 1972); Don C. Marler, "The Nonprofessionalization of the War on Mental Illness," *Mental Hygiene,* 55 (July 1971); and James D. Orten, "Political Action: Ends or Means?" *Social Work,* 17 (November 1972).

13. Family Service Association of America, "Position Statement of Family Service Agencies Regarding Graduate Schools of Social Work" (New York, 1972). (Mimeographed.)

14. Schwartz, "Private Troubles and Public Issues: One Job or Two?" pp. 36–43.

15. Herman Levin, "Social Welfare Policy: Base for the Curriculum," *Social Work Education Reporter, 17* (September 1969), p. 40.

16. Richan, op. cit.

17. Schwartz, "Private Troubles and Public Issues: One Job or Two?" pp. 35–36.

18. For descriptions of this model of practice, *see* Harriett M. Bartlett,

*The Common Base of Social Work Practice* (New York: National Association of Social Workers, 1970); Howard Goldstein, *Social Work Practice: A Unitary Approach* (Columbia: University of South Carolina Press, 1973); and Allen Pincus and Anne Minahan, *Social Work Practice: Model and Method* (Itasca, Ill.: F. E. Peacock Publishers, 1973).

19. For an example of what some of these changes might look like, *see* Rein, op. cit.

20. For additional discussion, *see* Burns, op. cit., pp. 9–12; and Gilbert and Specht, op. cit., pp. 9–12.

21. For example, *see* program statements of School of Social Work, University of Washington; School of Applied Social Sciences, Case Western Reserve University; School of Social Work and Community Planning, University of Maryland; and School of Social Work, University of Minnesota.

22. Burns, op. cit., p. 21.

23. Everett C. Hughes, "Professions," *Journal of the American Academy of Arts and Sciences,* 92 (Fall 1963), pp. 661–668.

24. Ibid., p. 657.

25. For example, *see Social Service Review* (entire issue), 46 (September 1972); *see also* Joel Fischer, "Is Casework Effective? A Review," *Social Work,* 18 (January 1973), pp. 5–20, and Reading 23.

# 18   Social Work as a Profession in Process

## THOMAS OWEN CARLTON

Early in its history, Flexner (1915) assessed social work and concluded that it had not yet achieved professional status. While not all social workers accepted his criteria, a significant number did take his negative assessment seriously. As a result, efforts to integrate existing knowledge, to develop practice methodologies, and to establish professional organizations were accelerated (Pumphrey & Pumphrey, 1961). Despite achievements in these areas since 1915, social work has remained preoccupied with its status as a profession. Recognition by other professionals and the community has been a perennially recurring focus of concern (Brown, 1932; Frankel, 1969; Greenwood, 1957; Johnson, 1944; Tufts, 1923).

The attention given to social work's heritage and past achievements at the 20th Anniversary Professional Symposium of the National Association of Social Workers (Dumpson, Note 1) and the 22nd Annual Program Meeting of the Council on Social Work Education

Reprinted with permission of author and publisher from *Journal of Social Welfare,* 4:1 (Spring 1977), pp. 15–25.

(Wilson, Note 2) suggests that social work is once again in the process of assessing its professional status (Lewis, 1976; Tropp, 1976).

To a large extent, formal assessments of social work's professional status have reflected developments in the sociology of professions that emphasize functional models. Such models view professions as relatively homogeneous communities whose members share common identities, values, role definitions, and interests; they stress norms, codes, cohesiveness, structure and organization, and the induction of recruits into the common ranks (Bucher & Strauss, 1961).

Greenwood's focus on systematic theory, professional authority, community sanction, a regulatory code, and professional culture is perhaps the best known application of a functional model to social work (Greenwood, 1957). Functional models, however, overlook professional differences in interests and values and the implications of these differences for change within a profession (Bucher & Strauss, 1961).

Given the nature of its historical development, it can be argued that social work does not yield easily to the criteria for functional assessment of its professional status. Professions such as medicine and law have tended to emerge with one or two specialties, out of which other segments and specialties have evolved. Unlike other professions, however, social work emerged as the coming together of many segments to form a profession: charity organization, family casework, settlement work, hospital social work, child saving, corrections, for example. These segments tended to emanate from two major social movements: the Charity Organization Movement and the Settlement Movement. An alternative approach might, therefore, yield more productive assessments.

## A PROCESS VIEW OF SOCIAL WORK

Bucher and Strauss (1961) have developed a process model for the study of professions which turns on the concepts of segmentation and specialization and focuses on the variables of: (a) sense of mission, (b) work activity, (c) methodology and technique, (d) clientele, (e) colleagueship, (f) interest and association, and (g) unity and public relations.

Bucher and Strauss assert that segments reflect different values and interests. They may develop coalitions in opposition to other segments. Major segments become specialties within the profession, but even within specialties, segments develop that decrease unity within the specialty.

These segments develop specific identities, a sense of the past, and they posit specific goals and objectives for the future. Their activities are organized to secure an institutional position through which they can implement their distinctive missions. Segments take on the character of social movements, and competition and conflict between them may shift the organization of the profession.

Social work consists of many segments and specialties motivated by distinctive values and objectives that influence the organization of social work activity. These segments and specialties are bound together by the profession's overall purpose and responsibility for affecting "adjustments and changes in the relationship of society and its individual members for the purpose of increasing individual human functioning and well-being" (Gatza, Note 3).

A review of selected social work developments from a process perspective, with an emphasis on social casework and general social work practice, might help social workers to summarize and reconceptualize some commonly held ideas about the profession and redirect their thinking about social work's professional status.

## The Sense of Mission

As a new segment emerges within a profession, unique missions are delineated for which the new segment claims to be uniquely fitted. The Charity Organization Movement, with its mission of eradicating pauperism and saving the industrial city (Lubove, 1965), developed an approach based upon a case-by-case relationship between a friendly visitor and an individual or family. The relationship aimed at individual and family uplift and change through precept and example, rather than the giving of alms. Refinement of this approach expanded its knowledge base and with publication of *Social Diagnosis* (Richmond, 1917), social casework achieved a major conceptual foundation and an extensive explication of techniques. While always a segment of major importance, there could be little doubt after 1917 that social casework was a major social work specialty.

Social caseworkers continued to refine and adapt the basic fundamentals of casework theory to their specific needs within particular settings and areas of function. With the end of World War I and the emergence of psychoanalytic theory in the United States, however, the emphasis on socioeconomic factors that had predominated in the older casework formulations tended to give way to emphasis on the intrapsychic needs of individuals. As a result, psychiatric casework emerged as a major segment and rapidly grew into one of the most influential social work segments.

Nevertheless, segmentation within social casework did not end despite the fact that social casework became rooted in an individual psychology. Further segmentation within the specialty evolved from competition between the followers of Freud, who developed the theoretical basis for diagnostic casework, and those of Rank, who formulated and advocated the functional approach.

In contrast to social casework, other segments with historic roots in the Settlement Movement advocated different approaches and sought to operationalize their mission of improving environmental factors. Emphasis was given to legislative action, social reform, and elicitation of "the collective and corporate initiative of . . . people" (Woods & Kennedy, 1922). From this latter thrust, the social group work approach, stressing democratic processes and procedures, developed as a segment within settlement work. People were helped with developmental tasks, but unlike psychiatric casework, group workers did not view the problems presented as psychopathological or the people served as being in need of a clinical type of help (Falck, Note 4). In time, with its activities focused on the enhancement of social functioning "and commonly perceived behavior, as contrasted with illness-oriented diagnostic categories," or group psychotherapy (Tropp, 1971), social group work grew into a specialty in its own right.

Community organization approaches, dating back to colonial America and asserting the need to organize social systems and people for the benefit of both the individual and society as a whole, continued to develop in the Charity Organization and Settlement Movements. By 1939, community organization achieved recognition as a social work specialty (Lane, 1939; Rice, 1939). But despite refinements in theory and practice, community organization, legislative action, and social reform were scarcely reflected in the overall practice of social work and its professional educational processes from the 1920s through the 1950s (Cohen, 1958; Reynolds, 1963). In fact, during this period social work was generally believed to consist almost totally of ameliorative, individualized, therapeutic approaches (Meyer, 1971).

During the 1950s a group of social work educators began to move toward the conclusion that preparation for professional practice within a specific method or field of practice specialty was insufficient for meeting the accelerating and increasingly complex needs of the consumers of social work services. As this crystallizing belief moved into the 1960s, the assumption that social casework was basic to all social work practice came under serious challenge. Community organization, which had received only token acceptance in schools of social work and in practice, was looked at anew and social group work was increasingly considered in settings that had hitherto relied solely upon casework approaches.

Spurred on by the chaotic social conditions in America during the 1960s these educators became advocates of a new approach to social work practice that stressed a form of specialization based upon a broader foundation than any of the social work segments or specialties previously developed (Selby, Note 5). The mission of this new segment, rooted institutionally in graduate social work education, was to prepare future practitioners for "responsible entry into the profession with skills in work with individuals, families and non-family groups combined with appropriate responsibility to the community and to the profession" (Northen, Note 6). The segment stressed a "common core of knowledge, values, attitudes, philosophy, and concepts," out of which generic educational and practice principles for the general social work practitioner were developed (DiPaola, Note 7).

By 1967, general social work practice had grown into a major segment with a flexible conceptualization of methodological approach and professional identification (Northen, 1968). By 1970, the segment had become a specialty with approximately fifty percent of the accredited graduate schools of social work in the United States offering programs of generic preparation for general social work practice (Lowenberg, 1970).

Bucher and Strauss (1961) point out that "while specialties organize around unique missions, as time goes on segmental missions . . . develop within the fold." As segments had developed earlier within social casework and other specialties, at least three segmental missions have appeared within the specialty of general social work practice: the generic content model, the generic methods model, and the generic processes model (Kolevzon, 1977). Each of the models, to some extent, appears to exacerbate the competition between the advocates of general social work practice and those of the earlier methodological specialties.

### Work Activities

Social work is carried on in varied settings and employs differentiated strategies or methods of professional intervention. Bucher and Strauss note that various segments and specialties within a profession develop different definitions of the kind of work in which the profession should be engaged, and they suggest the major thrusts the profession should undertake.

In defining its conception of the profession, each segment offers its own organizational and structural definitions of the tasks that segment advocates. Within the specialty of social casework, the diagnostic segment conceptually transformed the case-by-case approach into an essentially one-to-one relationship ordered and structured around the concept of individual illness requiring treatment. In contrast, the functional segment employed a psychology of health and growth and organized service around the concepts of process and agency function.

Because of the segmentation within professions, ideal models of professional practitioners are slow to develop. Diagnostic caseworkers see the social worker as a professional psychotherapist involved in the treatment of emotional or mental illness. The functionalist views the professional social worker as one whose role is to help the client make appropriate use of the service offered. The diagnostic caseworker is at the center of the relationship in a treatment approach based closely on the medical model, whereas the functional caseworker and the client engage in a helping process as equals, each having appropriate responsibilities in the giving and taking of service. While both segments place great emphasis on the acquisition of knowledge and the development of practice skill, their differing conceptions of work activity did not facilitate the emergence of an idealized image of a professional practitioner for the specialty as a whole.

Segmentation within general social work practice has made conceptualization of work activities and an ideal practitioner model even more difficult for the generalists than was true for social caseworkers. Consensus does seem to exist among advocates of the generalist specialty, however, that the work activities of the general social work practitioner cut across the boundaries of method and specific social service delivery systems.

While the integration of individual, group, and community modalities has been conceptualized in generic theory and general practice, it has been concepts from administration, policy formulation, social planning, and research that have posed the greatest problems in the development of a theoretical model for the social work generalist.

## Methodology and Technique

As noted, efforts to achieve professional status for social workers centered largely around the development, refinement, and acceptance of the social casework method until the 1960s. A core of knowledge and practice, common to all of the settings in which social casework is practiced, was developed. In 1929, representatives of the various fields of service in which social casework was practiced— charity organization or family social work, children's institutions and placing-out societies, medical and psychiatric institutions, and probation—met at Milford, Pennsylvania, where, after considerable deliberation, they concluded that social casework was a methodology generic to all fields and settings (American Association of Social Workers, 1929). This core of knowledge and practice methodology came to dominate social work to such an extent that for much of its history, social work became synonymous with social casework.

It is in the area of methodology and technique that the practice of the social work generalist differs most markedly from that of other social work segments and specialties. The generalist is not committed to a single method. While the social caseworker deals essentially on a one-to-one basis, the generalist draws on a broad knowledge base and the way in which he engages in professional practice is determined by the nature of the client system with which he interacts and the problems that system presents. Such flexibility in the use of self allows the generalist to intervene and work with individuals, groups, organizations, and communities. As the generalist seeks to facilitate growth and development within an individual client, his service, rooted in the needs of that single individual, might well involve him in interactions with numerous other systems as they relate to the person being served. The reverse may be true when the primary system to which the generalist offers service is a community or a neighborhood or an organization.

Richmond conceived of a more active involvement of the social caseworker in the client's social environment than came to characterize social casework when the social emphasis in Richmond's conceptualization was superseded by that of an individual psychology (Richmond, 1922, 1930; Robinson, 1930). The social work generalist has adapted aspects of this earlier model, but does not see environmental factors as phenomena to be dealt with essentially within a one-to-one relationship or as factors requiring auxiliary services. The generalist views all social systems as potential areas of service in which she might become actively involved.

## Clients

Bucher and Strauss (1961) posit that "specialties, or segments of specialties, develop images of relationships with clients which distinguish them from other . . . groupings." Originally motivated by instincts of personal charity and scientific philanthropy, social work grew out of 19th century efforts to work with the poor and disadvantaged. Social casework developed out of the movement to organize charities that focused on individuals and families. The Settlement Movement, in contrast, sought to improve the conditions under which the poor and disadvantaged lived.

Social casework, however, moved increasingly toward an organization of its services for middle-class clients and took on an increasingly therapeutic role. In contrast, social group work remained focused on the present, even though the Settlement Movement moved away from social reform in favor of socialization and recreational activities. Even community organization achieved its status as a method specialty, not through efforts to bring about social reform, but through efforts to coordinate services to individuals and groups (Gurin, 1971).

"Characteristically, members of professions become involved in sets of relationships that are distinctive in their own segment. Wholly new classes of people may be involved in their work drama whom other segments do not have to take into account" (Bucher & Strauss, 1961).

In theory, social casework views the client as an individual to be helped through a relationship with a caseworker. Social group work focuses on the group as the client system and seeks to help group members to help themselves, particularly in relation to their potential for social functioning and related objectives. Community organization views the neighborhood, society, or the organization as its client system.

In contrast to these conceptions of the clientele served, the generalist views the individual, the family, the small group, the neighborhood, the organization, the community, or a combination of some or all of these systems as potential clients. The general practitioner's strategy of intervention is defined by the client system and its interactions with other systems and by the nature of the problem or problems requiring service, rather than by a specific methodology associated with any of the other social work specialties.

## Colleagueship, Interest, and Association

Colleagiality is a sensitive indicator of segmentation within a profession (Bucher & Strauss, 1961). The association of one member of the profession with another may alienate her from a third member. If the association develops into a grouping with a unique mission, it may result in the first member no longer sharing a mission with others in the same profession.

The differing conceptions of social work to which the various specialties and segments are committed have produced disagreements over the nature of the profession. These differences have led to serious divisions and minimal communication between some social work segments. During the 1960s, for example, as segments advocating institutional change and social reform gained ascendency, clinical social workers came to regard themselves as separate from the rest of social work. Assertions that casework was "irrelevant" and that casework was "ineffective" deepened the division. The formation of the National Federation of Societies for Clinical Social Work in 1971 and the increasing numbers of psychotherapeutically oriented social caseworkers moving from agency settings to private practice are indicators of the sense of separateness that characterizes this segment. Differences between clinical social workers and other social work segments and specialties, in terms of their conceptualizations of professional practice and the tasks to which the profession should address itself, stem, in part, from the recent interest of social workers in social reform, social action, and advocacy and the move of many segments and specialties away from the medical model of practice (Leff, 1975).

According to Bucher and Strauss (1961), identification with a segment directs relationships within the profession and also has a significant impact on relations with allied professions. They suggest the term "alliance" to distinguish this phenomenon from colleagueship within a profession. Social workers interested in policy formulation and social planning, for example, often find a natural affinity with the professions of law and physical planning, whereas social workers in the health field often seek association with physicians, nurses, and allied health professionals. Social caseworkers who view the mission of social work within a psychotherapeutic context look to psychiatry and psychology for cross-professional interaction. As Bucher and Strauss assert, such alliances often "dramatize the fact that one branch of a profession may have more in common with elements of a neighboring occupation than with their own fellow professionals."

Former social caseworkers and social group workers who developed and advocated the generalist approach also conceptualized a mission for social work that differed from that of their former specialty colleagues. But the generalist's cross-method approach has mitigated, to some extent, the potential for conflicts of interest and association within this general practice specialty. A generalist, for example, may find alliances and interests shifting from health professionals to physical planners to legal counselors and so on as the nature of the client system and the problems for which help is sought change.

On the other hand, the recent upswing of interest in specific method skills (Lewis, 1977; Tropp, 1976) and the tensions between the method specialists and the generalists (Clearfield, 1971; Smalley, 1967), together with the current issues relating to the bachelor-master level continuum in social work education (Kolevzon, 1977), have led to shifting interests and changes in colleaguial association in many social work segments and specialties.

## Unity and Public Relations

The Bucher and Strauss model assumes that the seeming unity within a profession suggested to the lay public by such factors as codes of ethics, licensure, and professional association may not necessarily be evidence of homogeneity and consensus. Rather, they may be evidence of the power of a certain segment, or group of segments, to control these factors. Also to be considered is the concept of "those who control the professional associations also control the organs of public relations."

Seven distinct professional social work associations were established between 1918 and 1949, reflecting both method and field-of-practice specialization. In 1950, these seven associations formed an interim association as the result of perceived unity and began to develop plans for a single professional organization, the National Association of Social Workers, which began operation on October 1, 1955. During the same period the Council on Social Work Education was established. Together, these two associations, supported by their publications, created an image of professional unity that suggested that no single specialty or combination of segments dominated social work practice. While it may be argued that method and field-of-practice segments and specialties were rather evenly represented during this period, by the late 1960s the segments advocating institutional change and reform, including efforts to combat institutional racism and poverty, had succeeded in setting these goals as priorities for the profession as a whole.

These developments coincided with the emergence of the generalist segment and its development into specialty status. Both thrusts were sanctioned by a flexible curriculum policy formulated by the Council on Social Work Education, which stressed the development of "loyalty to the social well-being of the persons who are served by the profession, concern for a truly social role ... a sense of self-respect for the social contributions of the profession and an objective attitude toward clients" (Tyler, 1952).

The generalist and institutional change thrusts reached an apex in the early 1970s and were followed by (a) the move of the generalist segment to the undergraduate level when the Council on Social Work Education began to accredit bachelor level professional curricula and (b) the appearance of micro/macro, fields of practice, and other specializations at the graduate level in response to an upswing in concern with the unique missions and practice needs of various social work specialties.

Similarly, the appearance of unity suggested by the National Association and the Council in the middle of the 1970s must be considered in light of this upswing in segmental and specialty interests.

These thrusts, often along the lines of the older associational group-ings, are evidenced in the recent appearance of or soon-to-be-pub-lished, journals responsive to specialty missions, interests, and needs: *Clinical Social Work Journal* (1972); *Health and Social Work* (1975); *Social Work in Health Care* (1975); *Social Work with Groups* (1977); *Journal of Social Service Research* (1977); *Administration in Social Work* (1977); and the transformation of *Abstracts for Social Workers* into a more specialized journal in 1977.

## CONCLUSIONS

From a process perspective, social work can be viewed as a loose amalgamation of "segments pursuing different objectives in different manners and more or less delicately held together at a particular period of history" (Bucher & Strauss, 1961) by its overall purpose and social mandate. Internally, differences exist between social work spe-cialties and segments as each pursues its unique mission within the profession. To expect all of the social work method and field-of-practice segments and specialties to possess the same sense of mis-sion, work activities, methodology, clientele, and so on is no more reasonable than to expect obstetricians and orthopedists, or criminal and corporate lawyers, to do the same.

Social work, like the society in which it exists, is neither fixed nor static, and segments emerge and develop into specialties in response to the changing needs of society and its shifting mandate to the profession, from which services evolve. Viewing social work from a process perspective makes possible, therefore, assessments of its ca-pacity for development, modification, growth, and change. In turn, it is this capacity that makes possible social work's ability to respond differentially to the changing needs of society. The degree to which social work attains and maintains this ability is the pivot upon which its status as a profession turns.

To achieve the purpose of social work and to fulfill its mandate from society, much remains to be done. Social work's "place in soci-ety makes this a difficult but challenging charge" (Towle, 1952).

## NOTES

1. Dumpson, J. *The state of social work skill.* Paper presented at the 20th Anniversary Professional Symposium of the National Association of Social Workers, Hollywood-by-the-Sea, Florida, May 1975.
2. Wilson, G. *A hundred years of social work education.* Paper presented at the 22nd Annual Program Meeting of the Council on Social Work Educa-tion, Philadelphia, Pennsylvania, February 1976.

3. Gatza, M. *The essentiality of certain social worker characteristics for organization change.* Unpublished manuscript, School of Social Work, University of Pennsylvania, 1974.

4. Falck, H. S. *Crisis theory and social group work.* Paper presented at the National Association of Social Workers Mid-Continent Regional Institute, Topeka, Kansas, November 1967.

5. Selby, L. G. *Steps and process toward change in the teaching of methods: One school's experiment.* Paper presented at the 12th Annual Program Meeting of the Council on Social Work Education, Denver, Colorado, January 1965.

6. Northen, H. *The social work practice course at the University of Southern California.* Paper presented at the 12th Annual Program Meeting of the Council on Social Work Education, Denver, Colorado, January 1965.

7. DiPaola, J. *The revised curriculum: Some issues and problems of field work.* Paper presented at the Annual Field Work Institute, School of Social Work, University of Southern California, May 1967.

## REFERENCES

American Association of Social Workers. *Social casework, generic and specific.* New York: Author, 1929.

Brown, E. L. Social work against a background of other professions. In National Conference of Social Work (Ed.), *Proceedings of the National Conference of Social Work.* Chicago: University of Chicago Press, 1932.

Bucher, R., & Strauss, A. Professions in process. *The American Journal of Sociology,* 1961, 66, 325–34.

Clearfield, S. M. Merged method in social work education: A group worker's somewhat jaundiced view. In L. C. Deasy (Ed.), *Doctoral students look at social work education.* New York: Council on Social Work Education, 1971.

Cohen, N. E. *Social work in the American tradition.* New York: Dryden Press, 1958.

Flexner, A. Is social work a profession? In National Conference of Charities and Corrections (Ed.), *Proceedings of the National Conference of Charities and Corrections.* Chicago: The Hildmann Printing Co., 1915.

Frankel, C. Social work values and professional values. *Journal of Education for Social Work,* 1969, 5, 29–35.

Greenwood, E. Attributes of a profession. *Social Work,* 1957, 2, 45–55.

Gurin, A. Social planning and community organization. In National Association of Social Workers (Ed.), *The encyclopedia of social work* (Vol. 2). New York: Author, 1971.

Johnson, A. Professional standards and how they are attained. *Journal of the American Dental Association,* 1944, 31, 1181–89.

Kolevzon, M. S. The continuum in social work education: Destiny not so manifest. *Journal of Education for Social Work,* 1977, 13, 83–89.

Lane, R. P. The field of community organization. In National Conference of Social Work (Ed.), *Proceedings of the National Conference of Social Work.* New York: Columbia University Press, 1939.

Leff, B. A club approach to social work treatment with a home dialysis program. *Social Work in Health Care,* 1975, 1, 33–40.

Lewis, H. The structure of professional skill. In B. Ross & S. K. Khinduka (Eds.), *Social work in practice.* Washington, D.C.: National Association of Social Workers, 1976.

Lewis, H. The cause in function. *Journal of the Otto Rank Association,* 1977, 11, 18–25.

Lowenberg, F. (Ed.). *Statistics on social work education.* New York: Council on Social Work Education, 1970.

Lubove, R. *The professional altruist.* Cambridge: Harvard University Press, 1965.

Meyer, H. J. The profession of social work: Contemporary characteristics. In National Association of Social Workers (Ed.), *The encyclopedia of social work* (Vol. 2). New York: Author, 1971.

Northen, H. An integrated practice sequence in social work education. *The Social Work Education Reporter,* 1968, 16, 29–31, 37–39.

Pumphrey, R. E., & Pumphrey, M. W. (Eds.). *The heritage of American social work.* New York: Columbia University Press, 1961.

Reynolds, B. *An uncharged journey: Fifty years of growth in social work.* New York: The Citadel Press, 1963.

Rice, S. A. The factual basis of community planning. In National Conference of Social Work (Ed.), *Proceedings of the National Conference of Social Work.* New York: Columbia University Press, 1939.

Richmond, M. E. *Social diagnosis,* New York: Russell Sage Foundation, 1917.

Richmond, M. E. *What is social case work?* New York: Russell Sage Foundation, 1922.

Richmond, M. E. *The long view.* New York: Russell Sage Foundation, 1930.

Robinson, V. P. *A changing psychology in social case work.* Chapel Hill: University of North Carolina Press, 1930.

Smalley, R. E. *Theory for social work practice.* New York: Columbia University Press, 1967.

Towle, C. The distinctive attributes of education for social work. *Social Work Journal,* 1952, 33, 62–72.

Tropp, E. Social group work: The developmental approach. In National Association of Social Workers (Ed.), *The encyclopedia of social work* (Vol. 2). New York: Author, 1971.

Tropp, E. The challenge of quality for practice theory. In B. Ross & S. K. Khinduka (Eds.), *Social work in practice.* Washington, D.C.: National Association of Social Workers, 1976.

Tufts, J. H. *Education and training for social work.* New York: Russell Sage Foundation, 1923.

Tyler, R. W. Distinctive attributes of education for the professions. *Social Work Journal,* 1952, 33, 55–62.

Woods, R. A., & Kennedy, A. J. *The settlement horizon.* New York: Russell Sage Foundation. 1922

# Chapter Six

# THE ORGANIZATIONAL CONTEXT OF
# SOCIAL WORK PRACTICE

The ubiquitous role of complex organizations in modern society has been succinctly captured in a statement by Peter Blau and Marshall Meyer:

> A large and increasing proportion of the American people spend their working lives as small cogs in complex organizations. And this is not all, for bureaucracies also affect much of the rest of our lives. The employment agency we approach to get a job, and the union we join to protect it; the supermarket and the chain store where we shop, and the hospitals treating our illnesses, the schools our children attend, and the political parties for whose candidates we vote; the fraternal organization where we play, and the church where we worship—all these more often than not are large organizations of the kind that tends to be bureaucratically organized.[1]

As we noted in our introduction to the preceding chapter, one unique characteristic of social work is that it originated within a variety of organizational contexts, often in settings where social workers served as organizational functionaries, usually of lower status and prestige than other professionals in those settings. Other professions, such as medicine and law, began with practitioners who operated as independent entrepreneurs, and only in comparatively recent times have these professionals begun to ply their trades as staff members of complex organizations. Conversely, the idea of private practice in social work has developed only in the past few years. It is a development that many social workers look upon with disfavor.[2] (See Reading 25, by Paul A. Kurzman.)

The vast bulk of social welfare services is provided through large, complex organizations most commonly known as "bureaucracies." This term, Blau and Meyer remark, is often used invidiously to connote unsympathetic inefficiency. Just as frequently, it is used to describe ruthless control and efficiency.[3] These are descriptions of complex organizations for which many concrete examples can be found in the real world. In whatever institutional sphere they operate, complex organizations are powerful social instruments that can be used to achieve a variety of social purposes, both good and evil.

Practicing social workers may choose to follow careers that keep them outside of complex organizations by working as independent consultants and therapists. Increasing numbers of social workers are doing this. However, the majority of social workers will operate in organizations, and their practice and other aspects of their professional lives will be affected in large part by organizational policies and objectives. Moreover, even if the independent road to a career in social work appears attractive, it should be noted that this path too has many organizational byways and bureaucratic detours. Most private practitioners will be paid their fees *by organizations* (such as private and governmental insurance schemes), for services designated *by organizations*, under conditions set *by organizations*. Therefore, if the profession of social work seeks to develop the professional attributes discussed in the preceding chapter, social workers must understand and be able to exercise some control over the organizational context of social work and social welfare.

Most of the literature tends to envision organizations as either *closed* or *open systems*.[4] With a *closed-system* view they are perceived as rational systems, instruments by which to realize expressly announced group goals. Fundamentally, the *closed-system* conception is based on a mechanical model in which the organization is viewed as a structure having manipulable parts, each of which can be modified to enhance the efficiency of the entire organization.[5] With an *open-system view*, emphasis is given to elements in the organization's environment upon which it depends for survival and goal achievement such as clients, funders, staff, and regulatory agencies.[6] It is difficult to synthesize these two approaches. James Thompson conceives of complex organizations as "open systems, hence indeterminate and faced with uncertainty, but at the same time as subject to criteria of rationality and hence needing determinateness and certainty." That is, organizations may be conceived of as open systems striving to achieve the rationality and certainty of closed systems. This is a particularly useful perspective for social workers because they tend to practice in large bureaucratic agencies that exist in politically troublesome environments.

One kind of knowledge that is required of the social worker from a closed-system perspective is bureaucratic skill. As Robert Pruger has noted, these skills are pertinent to the vast majority of social work professionals.[7] However, Pruger points out, although "achieving one's professional goals through a formal organization requires a competence as complex and demanding as any of the others that professional [social work] helpers consciously seek to master . . . training for the role is almost nonexistent." Here, then, is one bit of the "incompleteness" of the profession.

Another kind of knowledge has to do with relationships among organizations and agencies. Sol Levine, Paul White, and Benjamin Paul have analyzed some of the elements in the open-system perspective. They describe how the goals, needs, and problems of organizations are related to the interorganizational relationships they develop. The concepts of "function," "access," and "domain consensus" are used to draw attention to interorganizational dynamics that are frequently ignored.[8]

Max Weber, the sociologist whose work provided the first theoretical model of bureaucracy, said that it "is a power instrument of the first order—for the one who controls the bureaucratic apparatus."[9] It is a well-established proposition of contemporary organizational theory that bureaucracy has democratizing and leveling effects. (That is, everyone is treated alike.) Street, Martin, and Kramer have suggested that there is a theoretical limit to this process in modern society. Their thesis is that bureaucracy is the means by which modern society manages *in*equality.[10] Many other authors have dealt with the relationship between bureaucracy and the social order. Sjoberg, Brymer, and Farris, for example, have described how the lower classes of society are controlled by the mechanisms of bureaucracy. Staff selection and socialization, client selection and socialization, and bureaucratic procedures and routines are mechanisms that can be utilized to reinforce stratification and cleavage along many lines including class, race, sex, and age.[11]

Another well-established proposition in current organizational theory is that professionalization is an anodyne for the pathologies of bureaucracy: by exercise of discretion based upon the authority of expertise, the professional sustains the particularistic and humane qualities of the organization. Street and his colleagues point out, though, that the "professionalization" of staff functions in many public welfare bureaucracies is largely a fiction. Organizational resources are insufficient to provide professional services, and service-giving functions are so fragmented that the development of a professional relationship between worker and client is impossible. Given these circumstances, the system must resort to industrial processing of clients. Gerald Suttles puts it succinctly:

> Without a sensitivity to the need for interpersonal continuity, the tendency will be toward industrial processing brazenly justified by the formulation that specialization means professionalization.[12]

Currently, antibureaucratic sympathies are common to political groups on both the extreme left and the extreme right. This must surely cause professionals in the human services to approach these questions with a great deal of caution. We wonder about the practical implications of recommendations that frequently follow these kinds of critiques of large organizations. A frequent recommendation is for the purposive duplication of bureaucracies in order to inject a degree of competition into what is otherwise a service monopoly, and/or to create agencies that will represent the disadvantaged.[13] Another frequent recommendation is for the debureaucratization of services by creation of agencies organized along the lines of therapeutic communities and collegial systems. However, these choices are based on the assumption that the problems of delivering services to clients are attributable to bureaucratic organization per se. We believe that this assumption bears close scrutiny. Many of the problems of service delivery occur because of poorly run, rigid, and unresponsive bureaucracies in which administrators operate with excessively high degrees of discretion. These qualities are not intrinsic to bureaucracy, even though they may often appear in bureaucratic settings. The proper objective of professionals, it seems to us, is to create complex organizations that are well run, flexible, and responsive, organizations in which the prerogatives of personnel are kept specific to areas in which their expertise is clearly functional. Organizational solutions that decentralize authority at great financial costs (e.g., purposive duplication), that increase the discretion of personnel (e.g., debureaucratization), that create yet more bureaucracy, and that encourage separatism are not necessarily the answers to the problems identified.

While bureaucratic mechanisms may be used to reinforce an unjust social order, a corollary principle to be borne in mind is that explicit rules, regulations, and procedures can be used to enforce just practices and change unjust ones. Saul Alinsky, one of the great social agitators of our time, had this principle in mind when he instructed organizers to: "Make the enemy live up to their own book of rules. You can kill them with this."[14] Alinsky did not believe that any organization could live up to all of its own principles and rules, which is very likely true. However, in the absence of principles and rules there is little toward which we can hope to have organizations aspire.

In Reading 19, "Social Welfare and Organizational Society," Michael Sosin describes the centrality of large-scale formal organizations in contemporary American society. He analyzes how this important feature of our society shapes the character of the institutions of social welfare and the profession of social work. Sosin does not perceive bureaucracy to be the source of deficiencies in services and practice. Rather, he says, because it is the framework through which conflicts among political, social, and economic values are resolved, an understanding of large-scale organizations may be "a useful starting point for policy discussions."

As Gilbert and Specht note in Reading 17, the theoretical frameworks used to describe and analyze practice in the indirect services differs from those used for the direct services. Political science, organizational theory, and economics are the more useful sources of knowledge for indirect-service practice. In "People Processing Organizations: An Exchange Approach," Reading 20, Yeheskel Hasenfeld uses a combination of sociological and economic theory to analyze the effects of different organizational characteristics. Readers who are more familiar with the interactional language used in the direct services may be somewhat put off or intimidated by this reading. We urge you to stick with it. The ideas are not that difficult to grasp and one can attain an understanding of organizations with these ideas. For example, take the following statement by Hasenfeld:

[O]rganizational intelligence about the environment of potential market units is crucial in determining the range and scope of the exchange relations that people-processing organizations can develop.

This is a useful theoretical statement for professionals who work in agencies that are concerned with determining the eligibility of clients for services offered by other agencies, referring clients to other agencies, and advocating for their clients. Essentially, Hasenfeld's proposition states that it is important for the worker to have a good deal of knowledge about other agencies if they are to carry out these tasks effectively. However, the language of sociology and economics is more crisp and efficient than most other social sciences. It is the language that is most useful for discussing the elements of the organizational context which constitute the environment of social welfare and social work. For that reason, social workers should be conversant in economics and sociology.

In Reading 21, the last one in this chapter, Jerry Turem issues "The Call for a Management Stance." Turem believes that it is essential for the future of both social welfare and social work that professionals acquire the conceptual tools and analytic capabilities to be able to plan and be accountable for social welfare services. This includes such knowledge areas as management information systems, methods of program evaluation, cost-effectiveness analysis, and personnel management. This kind of knowledge must be acquired if professionals are to deal appropriately with social work in its organizational context.

## NOTES

1. Peter M. Blau and Marshall W. Meyer, *Bureaucracy in Modern Society* (New York: Random House, 1971), p. 11.

2. See Irving Piliavin, "Restructuring the Provision of Social Service," *Social Work,* 13 (January 1968): 34–41, for the argument in favor; and Sherman Merle, "Some Arguments against Private Practice," *Social Work,* 7 (January 1962): 12–17, for the opposition.

3. *Op. cit.,* p. 4.

4. James D. Thompson, *Organizations in Action* (New York: McGraw-Hill, Inc., 1967), pp. 3–13.

5. Alvin W. Gouldner, "Organizational Analysis," in *Sociology Today,* ed. Robert K. Merton, Leonard Broom, and Leonard S. Cottrell, Jr. (New York: Harper & Row, 1959), pp. 404–05.

6. Thompson, *op. cit.,* pp. 27–28.

7. Robert Pruger, "The Good Bureaucrat," *Social Work,* 18 (July 1973): 26–32.

8. Sol Levine, Paul E. White, and Benjamin D. Paul, "Community Interorganizational Problems in Providing Medical Care and Social Services," *Journal of Public Health,* 53 (August 1963), pp. 1183–95.

9. Hans H. Gerth and C. Wright Mills (eds.), *From Max Weber: Essays in Sociology* (New York: Oxford University Press, 1946), p. 228.

10. David Street, George T. Martin, Jr., and Laura Kramer, *The Welfare Industry: Functionaries and Recipients in Public Aid* (Beverly Hills: Sage Publications, 1979).

11. Gideon Sjoberg, Richard A. Brymer, and Buford Farris, "Bureaucracy and the Lower Class," *Sociology and Social Research,* 50 (April 1966), pp. 325–27.

12. Gerald Suttles, "Foreword" in Street, Martin, and Kramer, *op. cit.,* pp. 11–12.

13. P. Nelson Reid, "Reforming the Social Services Monopoly," *Social Work,* 17:6 (November 1972), 44–54.

14. Saul Alinsky, *Rules for Radicals* (New York: Random House, 1971), p. 128.

# 19   Social Welfare and Organizational Society

## MICHAEL SOSIN

One important tradition in social welfare scholarship considers the links between the helping professions and the broader structure of society. This is often expressed in the United States by studies of effects of industrial conditions on the welfare effort. For example, Wilensky and Lebeaux point out that industrial conditions influence the social problems, programs, and professional structure involved in the organization of American private and public social services.[1]

Unfortunately, while the American effort to develop these links is important, the existing studies are quickly growing out of date. They are premised on the belief that industrialization is the leading edge of social organization—that is, the factor primarily responsible for defining the general character or at least the direction of change in society and social welfare. However, social scientists are coming to believe that contemporary American society is on the verge of entering what some even call a "postindustrial" society in which the role of industry is greatly reduced.[2] An increased level of welfare expenditures, the changing structure of government and of corporations, and the rising demand for noneconomic human rights characterize this coming social order.

This article argues that these fairly recent trends indicate the importance of analyzing a new leading edge, that of the large-scale, formal organization. This structure, only beginning to demonstrate its effects, has already dramatically altered the nature of society and social welfare, and will continue to influence it in the future. Such effects do not completely negate the importance of industrialization, but they do demand a new, if somewhat speculative, analysis link between the broad social structure and the welfare effort.

## LARGE-SCALE ORGANIZATION

The growth of the large-scale formal enterprise is well documented and beyond dispute. In the private sphere, the last four centuries have witnessed the growth of corporations from simple

Reprinted from the *Social Service Review*, 53:3 (September 1979), pp. 392–405, by permission of the University of Chicago Press and the author.

joint-stock enterprises to large-scale social organizations. The importance of the social organization itself is such that managers are now
being taught skills of human relations and organization, not just skills
of the market or of classical economics.[3] Government organization
has also experienced great expansion and rationalization, and the
governmental sector now accounts for about one-third of the nation's
Gross National Product.[4] A communal, amateurish form of public
administration has been replaced by the professional manager. The
government is so pervasive that direct contacts with government are
common to everyone, and in fact one out of five Americans has had
some special contact pertaining to individual benefits or police actions.[5]

The growth of large-scale organizations can be at least partly attributed to the utility of this social form in meeting demands of other
components of the social system. Weber documents that the traditional bureaucracy, with rigid rules and structure, leads to precise,
calculable, and dependable decisions that are important to the early
stages of industrial growth.[6] It has more recently been noted that
organizations may also develop more flexible forms that allow for the
innovation and complex coordination necessary in an advanced,
complex society.[7] Large-scale formal organizations, while not without many deficiencies, are thus able to meet demands for goods,
services, and flexibility in a modern society to a great enough degree
to dominate smaller or less formally organized collectives; their
growth is bound up with the functioning of society.

The growth and features of large-scale organizations are well
known, but researchers are only recently beginning to document
that these units are far more than extensions of the social forces that
give rise to them. As Selznick and Coleman note, once they are in
operation, organizations develop their own interests.[8] Given the in-
dispensability, resources, and power of formal organizations, often
the surrounding population must adapt to organizational demands;
governmental intervention and private corporate decisions are beginning to have broad ramifications for the entire society.[9]

Large-scale organizations have come to do far more than influence
specific decisions; the organization form also restructures welfare-
related social relations in manners that would not be expected from
an analysis of industrialization. Thus Grønbjerg notes that recent
growth in welfare expenditures in communities is determined more
by the character of the welfare bureaucracy than by characteristics
of the economic situation of the local area.[10] Similarly, Angell, who
in 1940 discovered large correlations between community characteristics associated with industrialization (such as mobility and
heterogeneity) and both private welfare expenditures and crime,
noted smaller correlations and a drop in explained variance by two-

thirds when he tested the same model using 1970 data.[11] Perhaps he could only increase explained variance by studying the character of large organizations, as in modern communities welfare efforts are often carried out by well-publicized campaigns that solicit money directly from where people work, while crime is largely defined and dealt with by a police force. In both analyses the nature of the organizations in a community, not the nature of the community itself, is apparently key to the study of current trends in human welfare.

The trend toward large-scale formal organization is also an important element in a dramatic alteration of the nature of work. Between the 1900 and 1970 censuses the percent of the labor force employed in industry remained relatively constant at about 34 percent, while the service sector, which includes occupations that coordinate and control a complex, large-scale society, swelled from 24 to 61 percent of the labor force.[12] Certainly the majority of occupations appear to manipulate interpersonal relations rather than material.

## ORGANIZATION AND SOCIETY

Given these dramatic alterations in specific social relations, it is not surprising that major institutional forces are also undergoing change. Large-scale organization is merely a form, but it demands special new conduct in all aspects of social life. One can trace changes away from the traditionally described industrial mode of organization toward an organizational mode with respect to the polity, economy, stratification system, and culture.

### The Polity

As has been mentioned, the growth in the functions of the central government is one key component of modern, organizationally defined society. As a result, especially since the war on poverty (a watershed in the growth of the large-scale organization in social welfare which extended and changed the philosophy of New Deal programs), national intervention in local and private affairs has come to be taken for granted. For example, direct monetary involvement of the national government in local public schools may lead to new standards concerning desegregation and discrimination. Corporations, too, now not only must adhere to regulations concerning the quality of their products and the honesty of their advertising (however partial implementation may be), but they are also bound by mandates changing internal structure. Businesses thus must now take the public interest into account.[13]

Because the government is so important to society, the decisions reached in the polity are crucial to the future of both corporations and individuals. Accordingly, the struggle for resources once played out in the market is coming to be a political struggle. The polity is the central institution to the extent to which society is dominated by large-scale organizations.

The American polity has been characterized as having a "marblecake"[14] structure in which influence is shared at many levels and in which numerous interest groups have input at each point. While organizational trends do not alter this general description, they do change the form of government and interest groups. Federal and local governmental agencies are obviously growing in size, and perhaps in order to influence such large units, interest groups are also coming to be represented in large organizations. Thus consumer and citizen protection is now embodied in Common Cause and in Ralph Nader's large organization; civil rights organizations seem most effective when organized to lobby on a national basis; huge labor unions and corporations lobby directly with the nation's leaders. Pluralism has always excluded those who cannot organize, but now organization is increasingly a matter of forming large-scale enterprises.

As Daniel Bell and Morris Janowitz point out, a change in political process and culture mirrors this alteration in political organizations.[15] While the traditional American value system calls for individuality and the free play of the market, large-scale groups seem to demand specific services from the government. In Janowitz's term, the groups believe they have equity claims on the government, and that therefore they should directly receive a share of the nation's resources. The change is from the belief that an ability to compete should be assured to the belief that outcomes should be guaranteed, and this then becomes policy. Farmers demand not a free market, but 100 percent parity; civil rights action has evolved to the use of quotas; and the labor unions demand tariffs on the goods of other countries. The nation is thus beginning to be structured by the interplay of organizational interests at the political level.

## Corporate Capitalism

This change to large government and to a demand for equity has not basically changed the emphasis on capitalism (although the corporations are also large-scale entities), but it has changed and is continuing to alter its expression. When government intervention occurs it often takes the form of incentives for management to act in the appropriate manner, and corporations rarely absorb the cost of change. Thus as Harrington points out, government policy toward oil companies has consistently resisted altering the profit structure of the large firms.[16] Changes in tax rates—and now incentives to look for new oil—take the place of alteration in the means of production.

The consequence of government intervention is a growing interdependence of the public and private sector. Quite complicated arrangements develop, most of which favor bureaucratic interests over those of individuals. For example, recent attempts to fund social security involve an increase in tax for both individuals and corporations. However, while individuals must pay the tax, and may at best attempt to recover some of the cost in later wage negotiations, corporations will immediately pass their share of the increase on in higher prices. Under a capitalist system in which profit levels are not challenged, tax policies and many other regulations affect individuals more than organizations.

The result of the interplay between organizations and capitalism must therefore be detrimental to most individuals. Legislation generally attempts to solve specific problems with minimal alterations in the basic structure of organizations. It therefore inevitably affects those individuals who are dependent on organizations far more than it affects corporate interests. Even "affirmative action" tends to pit groups of individuals against each other and does little to change the organizations that may have discriminated in the first place.

In fact, traditional industrial values such as individualism are still important in dealing with those outside of the centers of power. While corporations and trade unions demand quotas as protection from outside interests, race and sex quotas are often attacked as unfair restrictions of the market;[17] while farmers demand subsidies, individuals receiving public assistance are still told that it is their responsibility to somehow find work. A main change is that these values are now imbedded in decision-making units; rather than letting free market work itself out with respect to the nonelite, government and business directly demand that others follow such roles. The Work Incentive Program is an obvious example of institutionalizing values for the poor that others are not required to follow.

## Stratification

An alteration in the degree of stratification seems to accompany the changes in the polity and economy. While evidence is not yet strong, apparently the stratification system is becoming taller as large-scale organizations increase in influence, with more space between the elite and the most needy.[18] In an organizational society, skills in manipulating technology, communications, or interpersonal relations are key, and those with these skills can demand high salaries and prestigious positions. However, those without these skills have problems, as fewer unskilled occupations exist in a society dominated by organizations than in one dominated by industry. In short, those without the background and educational credentials might become a permanent underclass in society, with little chance for intragenerational mobility.

## Culture

The growing disparities of class seem to be combined with a growing disparity of culture. Those who work in middle-range occupations within organizations are engaged with other people, not with machines. Because the emphasis on interpersonal relations in the economic sector overflows into private life, and because it is also supported by the necessity to deal with large organizations in nonwork contexts, a change in cultural values for the middle class as a whole seems to develop.[19] A higher value is placed on interpersonal communication, understanding other people, and finding one's own social world. Leisure time is often spent pursuing individualized, immediate pleasures.[20]

However, one-third of the population is engaged in direct production of factory work, and this percentage may not alter greatly. Individuals in such occupations will not be able to take part in many of the changes in middle-class culture.[21] For a factory worker the work day is spent in a task that does not allow autonomy, a sense of freedom, or interpersonal relations that would encourage different cultural styles. After being treated as an automaton all day, a worker's desire for quiet and an unwillingness to engage in intense interaction is reasonable. Further, expected leisure-time activities are too expensive for many to afford on a regular basis. Finally, the inevitable layoffs stemming from adjustments in the large-scale economy make life quite precarious. The result of all these factors must be that working-class families will face social isolation, conditioned by the stratification system, which separates classes more than does income alone.

## THE CHARACTER OF SOCIAL SERVICES

It is evident that the direct and indirect effects of large-scale organizations have, and will continue to have, an important effect on the welfare effort. Given the growth in stratification and the dichotomy of culture, one can envision the formation of two distinct social welfare systems. One, already growing in social work, will be private in orientation. This part of the social welfare profession might help provide the means for self-expression and personal satisfaction required by the middle class—the current fad toward interpersonal growth may only be a beginning.[22] More central to this paper, the second part of social welfare will be even more closely tied to the government than in the past. It is probable that given the increases in stratification, the underclass of the society will become more dependent on the government for benefits.

There is evidence that a trend toward centralization is one feature of the public welfare sector. Martha Derthick points out that federal intervention gradually forced a state as locally minded as Massachusetts to change from a volunteer-run system of eligibility determination to a strongly centralized and professionalized apparatus.[23] Whether welfare is reformed or not, a trend toward an increasing concentration of power at the national level is predictable.

Given the centralization of the massive social welfare network, attention must be paid to the very character of the welfare bureaucracy. The way it acts toward clients plays an important role in the quality of life experienced by those tied to the welfare system. One view of government organizations stresses that these large-scale units are inefficient, insensitive to clients, and inherently arbitrary in their propensity to decide to provide services on the basis of class, sex, and race, and this view is shared by large segments of the public. For example, Katz et al. surveyed citizens concerning their beliefs about government services.[24] Sixty-one percent responded that the government was inconsiderate, 70 percent said it was inefficient, 58 percent said it was unfair, and 70 percent said it was unable to take care of problems. Certainly, faith in the public bureaucracies in general and the welfare bureaucracy in particular is quite limited.

However, while there are continuing problems in the interpersonal relations between large-scale organization officials and citizens, it is likely that the extent of these problems decreases, rather than increases, as the formalizations of large-scale organizations develop; many presumed consequences of organization are more common when there is not sufficient structure.[25] Formal rules of large organizations tend to call for impersonal treatment for all clients, and individual arbitrariness occurs more often when such roles are not sufficiently developed to control lower-level participants. Further, with the development of more modern management techniques, the ability of organizations to control individual behavior is likely to increase. Some may argue that while organizations have the potential to limit arbitrariness, they have incentives for allowing it to continue in order to reduce demands on the welfare system. However, I believe that most incentives for leaders promote formal rules and standardized actions toward lower-level participants. It is only through such standardization that control can be maintained, which is necessary to avoid challenges from the expanding legal and political system. In fact, often lower-level participants demand certain rules so that they can be sure of the consequences of their actions.[26]

Current research on organizations' treatment of clients consistently supports this position. The most striking example is found in the study of attitudes toward government mentioned above. It has been noted that many individuals believe that government in general is unfair and inefficient. However, when these very same individuals were asked about personal experiences with bureaucracy, different results arise. Only 23 percent said the government was not considerate in their specific case, 28 percent said service was inefficient, 20 percent said the service was unfair, and 29 percent said that the agency could not take care of their problem.[27] The conclusion is inescapable that most large public organizations are not guilty of many of the vices for which they are accused.

Moreover, even the consequences of individual level racism, classism, and sexism are probably often overestimated. In juvenile justice, for example, numerous studies of judges uncover little such discrimination. Even the police, who do show some signs of arbitrariness, do so only in certain conditions, and only for a small percentage of cases—despite attitudes that clearly would favor racial discrimination.[28]

This seems to present a paradox. The public finds government bureaucracies insensitive, yet they do not find their own experiences unsatisfactory. Individuals in the juvenile justice system act almost without discrimination, yet a larger proportion of minority-group members and lower-class children than would be expected on the basis of offense are committed to institutions.[29] Studies of specific behaviors seem to be missing some very important points.

I believe that the crux of the situation lies in organization policies, not individual decisions. That is, while individuals in formal organizations obey a set of rules, these rules themselves are often unfair. In the general view of government, the individuals in Katz's study are not responding to the way in which rules were administered, but to the rules, which impersonally cause many difficulties.

The classic example of problems with rules involves the notion of institutional racism. Despite changes in laws, firms that have minimal traces of bias seem to have problems finding suitable minority candidates. An obvious reason is that the rules and informal procedures established to define qualified candidates act to the disfavor of minority-group candidates. For example, research on the importance of the primary group in industry[30] implies that many jobs are found through friendships with those already in an occupation, and minority members do not have the friendships necessary; educational qualifications also tend to rule out many blacks. Similarly, the availability of welfare payments is a matter of policy. Administration attempts to limit welfare growth depend not on individual worker discretion but on centrally initiated policies involving determination of need, quality control, and computer technology. These techniques decrease, rather than increase, the importance of arbitrary behavior at an individual level.

This pattern is also evident in juvenile justice. While the difference between black and white juvenile crime rates is small, and while police officers seldom discriminate, many more blacks than expected are found in courts and institutions. This occurs due to many unjust policies or rules. Police officers are more likely to arrest when they receive a complaint, and more citizen complaints are lodged against black people; an official hearing occurs more often if it is demanded by the complainant, and this occurs more often in black neighborhoods; in court, judges seem to commit a given number of juveniles with, at best, a look at past arrests.[31] These policies result in many black arrests. Therefore, if discrimination is to be abolished, policies must change. Police officers must take complaints and pressures in a different light, while juvenile-court judges must cease to use past arrests so directly.

This argument is similar to Mannheim's famous distinction.[32] Bureaucracies are formally rational in that they follow sets of rules well. But they are substantively irrational because these rules often do substantive damage. The problem in modern society is less and less a matter of developing formal fairness, and more a matter of finding rules that are more substantively rational. It thus appears that large-scale organization in public social welfare brings a new set of problems, involving not the fairness with which services are carried out, but the organizational policies that give rise to these services. The content of rules, rather than their form, is key in organizational society.

## SOCIAL WELFARE

Implications of organizational trends are also evident in the level of welfare benefits. According to the standard measure based on the price of food, numbers in poverty since 1962 have gone from 21 percent to 12 percent of the total population as a result of government benefits.[33] But this large step toward reducing absolute poverty must be balanced against the observation that the relative level of inequality has not been reduced despite the influx of funds. Indeed, there are slight differences between the findings of experts when measuring levels of relative poverty. For example, Browning believes that the bottom fifth of the population has improved its position in the least two decades, while Budd believes just the opposite.[34] Whatever the differences in specifics, with few exceptions experts agree that changes in relative poverty are minute.[35]

Given the great increase in cash assistance and in food stamps, this lack of change in relative terms is surprising; one would expect that such a transfer of money would have a greater effect. The lack of change can be explained only in relation to the demands, constraints, and resources of an organizational society. First, apparently the level of absolute stratification in society as allocated by the market is increasing, and governmental support merely offsets these changes. In other words, it is reasonable to assume that the great leveling of stratification Wilensky and Lebeaux applaud in their discussion of industrial society is no longer occurring; further changes toward reducing relative poverty must originate with the government.[36]

Second, the interplay of capitalism and government means that policies will not change the distribution of income and wealth as much as might be desired. While there are programs for the poor, tax breaks for encouraging private enterprise, such as for mortgages or capital gains, largely offset them. Monetary policy is therefore only slightly progressive.[37] Indeed, work programs are generally designed to minimize their impact on the private sector by not competing for business or personnel to any large degree. The result is often poorly planned low-wage programs.

Additionally, the balance of pressures and resource constraints presents a pessimistic picture for any great future reductions in relative inequality. As Janowitz points out, resources are limited because the economic growth of modern society is not keeping pace with changes demanded by powerful elements of the populace.[38] When resources are scarce, power helps determine how they are divided. Given that large organizations are coming to be the main forces demanding resources, and that those receiving public assistance do not belong to such groups, the amount of growth in public assistance cannot be expected to keep up with growth in sectors in which more powerful organizations exist.

It thus seems likely that social welfare efforts may be dealing with a permanent underclass. The increased level of stratification in the economy and society along with limited but stable government expenditures result in a large, undersupported group of people who are isolated from society and whose only source of income is the government. The high unemployment rate of youth in cities may foreshadow a continuing dilemma—one that can lead to disruption of the public order, given the lack of political influence of the lower classes.

## PROFESSIONAL SOCIAL WELFARE

Those trends have profound influence on social welfare practice. The welfare professional, tied closely to federal, state, or local governments, is faced with an underfinanced system that has important responsibilities for a large, dependent underclass. Indeed, given the limits of the political system, it is unlikely that the welfare professional will be able to bring about much change in the absolute level of expenditures. Perhaps the potential for change will only be expressed, as Piven and Cloward insist, in periodic disruptions of the public order by the underclass.[39]

Within the limits placed on social welfare by society, professionals have a measure of influence. They have some say in determining the administrative character of the welfare effort, as well as in suggesting legislative changes if other forces make the need for change apparent. An organizational society tends to rely on the expert opinion of professionals in developing proposals to solve complex societal problems, and welfare professionals appear to have some claim to expertise.[40]

Additionally, there is some room for bringing about change within the welfare bureaucracy in order to create more humane internal policies. The largest organizations, especially, are best characterized as loosely coupled decision-making structures in which internal conflicts and bargains are quite likely.[41] Within bureaucratic areas of policy, welfare officials thus can make a difference.

The application of the influence of the professional welfare official toward more humane legislation and internal policies faces two main barriers, socialization and self-interest. Socialization is a powerful weapon of organizations. Faced with the inevitable uncertainty of a new situation, many social workers come to reflect the values of the unit for which they work.[42] This could tend to lead to social work support of policies favoring the organization and not the client. Self-interest can also result in social work advocacy for reforms that are not in the interest of clients. Social workers in Europe, for example, often lobby for changes in the juvenile justice system that increase the control of juveniles by expanding social services.[43] Further control of clients' lives tends to be in the self-interest of organizational participants.

It is unlikely that the tension between humane professional standards and self-interest and socialization will be resolved in either direction; in fact, on occasion self-interest or socialization might even lead to humane policies. More likely, the social welfare profession will experience sizable internal conflicts between those favoring the organization's maintenance and those sacrificing safety for humane services. One can thus envision a division similar to that between the charity organization societies and the settlement houses of nearly a century ago, but with the emphasis now on activity within public, rather than private, organizations.[44]

## CONCLUSION

The growth of large-scale organizations is only one trend in American society, and it cannot account for all aspects of social change. However, this form clearly has large consequences; it encourages large alterations in the policy, economy, and culture and influences social welfare accordingly. The possible resulting pattern of society and social welfare may not be an entirely optimistic one, but its description may be a useful starting point for policy discussions, as it points out the severe limits and barriers to progress existing in the coming social order.

## NOTES

My thanks to Elizabeth Howe and Mary Wylie for comments on an earlier draft.

1. Harold L. Wilensky and Charles Lebeaux, *Industrial Society and Social Welfare* (New York: Free Press, 1958), pp. 14–15.

2. Daniel Bell, *The Coming of Post-industrial Society: A Venture in Social Forecasting* (New York: Basic Books, 1973), pp. ix–xiii.

3. Henry Jacoby, *The Bureaucratization of the World* (Berkeley: University of California Press, 1973), pp. 71–78.

4. *Economic Report of the President* (Washington, D.C.: Government Printing Office, 1974), p. 249.

5. Daniel Katz, Barbara Gutek, Robert Kahn, and Eugenia Barton, *Bureaucratic Encounters: A Pilot Study in the Evaluation of Government Programs* (Ann Arbor: University of Michigan Press, 1975), p. 20.

6. Max Weber, *The Theory of Social and Economic Organization* (New York: Oxford University Press, 1947), pp. 324–85.

7. Alfred Sloan, *My Years with General Motors* (Garden City, N.Y.: Doubleday & Co., 1964), pp. 42–67.

8. Philip Selznick, "Foundations of the Theory of Organizations," *American Sociological Review* 13, no. 1 (1948): 25–35; James Coleman, *Power and the Structure of Society* (New York: W. W. Norton & Co., 1974).

9. Shirley Terreberry, "The Evaluation of Organizational Environments," *Administrative Science Quarterly* 12, no. 4 (1968): 590–613; John G. Maurer, ed., *Readings in Organization Theory: Open System Approaches* (New York: Random House, 1971).

10. Kirsten A. Grønbjerg, *Mass Society and the Extension of Welfare, 1960–1970* (Chicago: University of Chicago Press, 1977).

11. Robert Angell, "The Moral Integration of American Cities. II," *American Journal of Sociology* 80 (November 1974): 607–29. A

12. Robert Heilbronner, "Economic Problems of Post-industrial Society," *Dissent* (Spring 1973), pp. 163–76.

13. Peter F. Drucker, *The Age of Discontinuity: Guidelines to Our Changing Society* (New York: Harper & Row, 1968), pp. 212–42.

14. Morton Grodzins, *The American System: A View of Government in the American States* (Chicago: Rand McNally & Co., 1966), p. 8.

15. Bell (n. 2 above), pp. 339–68; Morris Janowitz, *Social Control of the Welfare State* (New York: Elsevier, 1976), pp. 76–84.

16. Michael Harrington, *The Twilight of Capitalism* (New York: Simon & Schuster, 1976), pp. 236–64.

17. Nathan Glazer, *Affirmative Discrimination: Ethnic Inequality and Public Policy* (New York: Basic Books, 1975), pp. 33–76.

18. Bell, pp. 165–266; William Julius Wilson, *The Declining Significance of Race* (Chicago: University of Chicago Press, 1978).

19. David Riesman, *The Lonely Crowd* (New Haven, Conn.: Yale University Press, 1960).

20. Janowitz (n. 15 above), pp. 106–10.

21. Lillian Breslow Rubin, *Worlds of Pain: Life in the Working Class Family* (New York: Basic Books, 1976).

22. Edwin Schur, *The Awareness Trap: Self-Absorption Instead of Social Change* (New York: McGraw Hill Book Co., 1976).

23. Martha Derthick, *The Influence of Federal Grants: Public Assistance in Massachusetts* (Cambridge, Mass.: Harvard University Press, 1970).

24. Katz et al. (n. 5 above), pp. 118–19.

25. Charles Perrow, *Complex Organizations: A Critical Essay* (Glenview, Ill.: Scott, Foresman & Co., 1979), p. 6.

26. Michel Crozier, *The Bureaucratic Phenomenon* (Chicago: University of Chicago Press, 1964), pp. 187–94.

27. Katz et al. (n. 5 above), pp. 102–09.

28. Robert M. Terry, "Discrimination in the Handling of Offenders by Social Control Agencies," *Journal of Research in Crime and Delinquency* 4, no. 2 (1967): 218–70; Donald Black and Albert Reiss, "Police Control of Juveniles," *American Sociological Review* 35, no. 1 (1970): 63–77; Frank Scarpitti and Richard Stephenson, "Juvenile Court Dispositions: Factors in the Decision-making Process," *Crime and Delinquency* 17, no. 2 (1971): 143–51.

29. Martin Gold, *Delinquent Behavior in an American City* (Belmont, Calif.: Brooks/Cole Publishing Co., 1970), p. 136; Robert Vinter, ed., *Time Out: A National Study of Juvenile Correctional Programs* (Ann Arbor, Mich.: National Assessment of Juvenile Corrections, 1976), p. 25.

30. See, e.g., Harrison White, *Chains of Opportunity: System Models of Mobility in Organizations* (Cambridge, Mass.: Harvard University Press, 1970).

31. Albert J. Reiss, *The Police and the Public* (New Haven, Conn.: Yale University Press, 1971), pp. 63–121; Scarpitti and Stephenson.

32. Karl Mannheim, *Ideology and Utopia: An Introduction to the Sociology of Knowledge* (New York: Harcourt Brace & Co., 1952).

33. Robert Plotnick and Felicity Skidmore, *Progress against Poverty: A Review of the 1965–1975 Decade* (New York: Academic Press, 1975), p. 82.

34. Edgar Browning, "The Trend toward Equality in the Distribution of Net Incomes," *Southern Economic Journal* 43, no. 1 (1976): 912–23; Edward Budd, "Post-War Changes in the Distribution of Income in the United States," *American Economic Review* 60, no. 2 (1970): 247–60.

35. Michael Taussig, "Trends in Inequality of Well-Offness in the United States since World War II," in *Conference on the Trend in Income Inequality in the U.S.* (Madison, Wis.: Institute for Research on Poverty, 1976).

36. Wilensky and Lebeaux (n. 1 above).

37. Joseph Peckman, *Federal Tax Policy* (Washington, D.C.: Brookings Institution, 1977), p. 54.

38. Janowitz (n. 15 above), pp. 41–71.

39. Frances Fox Piven and Richard A. Cloward, *Poor People's Movements: Why They Succeed, How They Fail* (New York: Pantheon Books, 1977).

40. Bell (n. 2 above), pp. 408–55.

41. Crozier (n. 26 above); Michael Cohen, James March, and John Olson, "A Garbage-Can Model of Organizational Choice," *Administrative Science Quarterly* 17, no. 1 (1972): 1–25.

42. Peter Blau, "Orientation toward Clients in Public Welfare Agencies," in *Social Welfare Institutions: A Sociological Reader,* ed. Mayer Zald (New York: John Wiley & Sons, 1965), pp. 654–70.

43. Roger Hood, *Crime, Criminology and Public Policy* (New York: Free Press, 1974).

44. June Axinn and Hermann Levin, *Social Welfare: A History of the American Response to Need* (New York: Harper & Row, 1975), pp. 89–100.

# 20   People Processing Organizations: An Exchange Approach[1]

YEHESKEL HASENFELD

The study of formal organizations whose function is to change the lives of people occupies a prominent position in organizational literature. At the theoretical level, studies have concentrated on conceptualizing such organizations (Goffman, 1961; Vinter, 1963; Lefton and Rosengren, 1966; Wheeler, 1966). At the empirical level, studies on organizations such as schools (Cicourel and Kitsuse, 1963), hospitals (Roth, 1963; Strauss *et al.,* 1964), and correctional institutions (Street, Vinter and Perrow, 1966) have increasingly focused on the effects of organizational characteristics on the fate of the people they serve.

Scant theoretical attention has been paid, however, to the emerging importance of those organizations whose explicit function is not to change the behavior of people directly but to process them and confer public statuses on them. Examples of such organizations are a diagnostic clinic, a university admissions office, an employment placement office, a credit bureau, or a juvenile court. We shall denote these as "people-processing" in contrast to "people-changing" organizations. These organizations shape a person's life by controlling his

Reprinted with permission of author and publisher from *American Sociological Review,* 37 (June 1972), pp. 256–263.

access to a wide range of social settings through the public status they confer; and they may define and confirm the individual's social position when his current status is questioned.

Moreover, processing functions (i.e., classifying, conferring public statuses, and disposing of clients), are an integral part of the technology of people-changing organizations (e.g., Freidson, 1965; Scheff, 1966: 169–87; Scott, 1969). For example, the rationale for the treatment of the psychiatric or physically disabled patient is based on the "ill" status conferred on him. As people-changing organizations increase in size and complexity these processing functions are likely to be delegated to distinct sub-units or organizations. Yet, the organization's requirements in defining the structure and content of their people-processing functions has not been systematically formulated and explored.

This paper analyzes people-processing organizations by focusing on the exchange relations they develop with their environment, and by tracing the effects of such relations on the structure and content of their people-processing functions. Environment here means the organizational network within which the organization seeks to attain its goals (Dill, 1958; Evan, 1966). These organization-environment relations are emphasized for two reasons. First, the core technology of such organizations consists of a set of boundary roles which define the input of clients to the organization and mediate their placement in various external units. Second, the effects of these relations on the development of the organization's technology and its clients' careers is a relatively neglected area of study.[2]

This study identifies systematically key parameters which influence the exchange relations people-processing organizations develop with their environment. In turn, it derives a series of propositions about the effects of such exchange relations on the processing of clients which it illustrates with findings from studies on such organizations.

## THE CHARACTERISTICS OF PEOPLE-PROCESSING ORGANIZATIONS

People-processing organizations can be defined by the nature of their "product" and of their processing technology. Their major "product" is people with changed statuses and locations in various community systems. Vinter and Sarri (1966) analyze the processing technology into four major tasks:

(1) The client's attributes and situation must be assessed to determine whether he is legitimately subject to official action;

(2) The client's attributes and situation must be explored to determine appropriate action alternatives;
(3) Choices must be made from among these alternatives; and
(4) Once an alternative has been chosen, the person's relocation in a new social set must be managed.

Thus, the core technology of people-processing organizations is the classification and disposition of clients.

Again, this organization does not try directly to alter the behavior of people who enter its jurisdiction, as is the case with people-changing organizations. Rather, it produces changes by identifying and defining the person's attributes, social situation, and public identity, which in turn typically results in both societal and self-reactions. It is through these anticipated reactions of significant others that the organization tries to change its clients' social position and future behavior.

Thus, for example, when a diagnostic center "diagnoses" the client's problems, it is presumed that the therapists who receive the diagnosis will determine the nature of the change efforts to be used. Or when an employment placement agency determines that a client qualifies for a certain job or training program, the client's very definition gains him access to the job or program, and thus alters his situation, prospects, and skills.

Furthermore, unlike people-changing organizations, people-processing organizations are organized so that the anticipated reactions to the statuses they confer occur mainly outside their boundaries. That is, those expected to respond to the classified person by working with him or trying to change him are located in an organization external to the definers'. Similarly, the technological activities of such organizations occur primarily at their boundaries. That is, staff activity consists of transactions with clients and their dossiers at input, negotiations with them on a classification-disposition status at output, and exchanges with potential external recipients of the clients. In contrast, the technology of people-changing organizations is more likely to be insulated from the environment and the organization's boundary transactions, particularly as the intensity of the change efforts increases (Wheeler, 1966: 79–80). Finally, since staff-client encounters in people-processing organizations are not organized to change the client's behavior directly, their relative duration tends to be shorter than in people-changing organizations. Table 20-1 summarizes some distinct differences between people-processing and people-changing organizations.

Given these distinguishing characteristics, people-processing organizations must develop direct and systematic links with external recipient units or markets. We shall denote such formally organized external units "market units." They are thus an integral part of the larger organizational network to which the processing organization is linked. In fact, the network order is based partly on the predictability of the responses of the network's market units to the output of the processing organization.

Furthermore, given the unique product of such organizations, their claims of service effectiveness depend, in part, on the response of the receiving units to the clients' statuses. An employment placement agency's effectiveness is measured largely by its ability to classify and refer applicants to potential employers whose responses will agree with the conferred status (Blau, 1963:37–44). In short, the market's reactions to the products of people-processing organizations are crucial to their survival and effectiveness.

TABLE 20–1
Differences Between People-Processing and People-Changing Organizations

| Variable | People-Processing | People-Changing |
|---|---|---|
| Type of product | Altered status | Behavioral change |
| Technology | Classification-disposition | Socialization-resocialization |
| Locus of technology | Organizational boundary | Intra-organizational |
| Relative duration of staff-client encounter | Short term | Long term |

## EXCHANGE RELATIONS AND CLASSIFICATION-DISPOSITION SYSTEMS

It is proposed that the classification-disposition systems of processing organizations will reflect the constraints of their exchange relations with market units. We assume that under the norms of rationality (Thompson, 1967), such organizations will try to develop systems sensitive to the needs of their market units in order to optimize the units' receptivity to their output.

We can analyze the way processing organizations respond, adapt and manage their relations with market units with a power-dependence paradigm. As Thompson (1967:39) defines it:

An organization is dependent on some element of its task environment (1) in proportion to the organization's need for resources or performance which the element can provide and (2) in inverse proportion to the ability of other elements to provide the same resource or performance.

In general, the more a processing organization depends on a given market unit for accepting its product, the more its classification-disposition system will respond to the constraints and contingencies of that market unit.

Given this paradigm, the analysis of the exchange relations between the processing organization and each of its market units must focus on:

(a) the conditions which lead to dependence on a market unit, and
(b) the countervailing forces the organization can mobilize to enhance its independence.

The following conditions tend to increase a processing organization's dependence on a given market unit.

(a) Enforced dependency on the market unit by externally controlling agents such as legal statutes, parent organization, and other regulatory groups.
(b) High discretion exercised by the market unit over its own intake.
(c) Greater need for the client services provided by the market unit.
(d) Greater prestige of the market unit as a validator of the processing organization's goals and performance.
(e) Scarcity of knowledge about potential and alternative market units.

The following conditions tend to increase a processing organization's independence of a given market unit:

(a) Freedom permitted the organization by its externally controlling agents to develop exchange relations.
(b) Possession of strategic resources needed by potential market units.
(c) Availability of alternative market units offering similar client services.
(d) Development of a self-validating organizational ideology.
(e) An effective intelligence system about alternative market units.

The conditions that increase or decrease the organization's dependency on its market units are summarized in Table 20-2 and will be discussed in some detail below. Clearly, in the organization's exchanges with its market units all the above conditions may operate simultaneously. For discussion and illustration, however, they will be treated separately.

## DEPENDENCY VS. FREEDOM IMPOSED BY EXTERNAL POLICIES

In analyzing processing organizations' market relations, one must fully recognize the constraints, requirements, and privileges of policy-regulating external units. The funding agency, the parent orga-

TABLE 20-2

Conditions Which Increase Dependence v. Countervailing Powers

| Condition of Dependence | Countervailing Power |
|---|---|
| Dependence imposed by external policies | Freedom permitted by external policies |
| Intake discretion of market unit | Possession of strategic resources |
| Need for client services of market unit | Availability of alternative client services |
| Market unit as validator of organizational goals | Development of self-validating organizational ideologies |
| Intelligence deficiencies about alternative market units | Intelligence effectiveness about alternative market units |

nization, the legislative unit and the like, may exert direct and indirect influence on two levels: (a) relations with market units; (b) policies vis-à-vis clients.

Policy regulations may restrict the type or range of market units that the organization can use, and may further stipulate the conditions of such transactions. To comply with these policies the organization will have to incorporate such stipulations in the classification-disposition process. For example, government-sponsored manpower agencies are often restricted in the type of employers or training programs they can use for their clients (Levitan and Mangum, 1969). These constraints, in turn, limit the type and range of occupational categories staff can use to classify and refer their clients.

Moreover, external policies may even specify the attributes that potential clients must have to qualify for certain market units. Such policies curtail a staff's discretion and may rigidly restrict the number of classification-disposition categories they can confer on clients. Such is the case for public welfare departments which are controlled by extensive restrictive policies of this kind (Keith-Lucas, 1957).

External policy units may also require specific information about the clients' attributes and situations, and the need to collect such information thus invariably has consequences for the classification-disposition system. Official classifications, at least, will tend to be constrained to reflect these information requirements.

On the other hand, external policies may give much latitude to the processing organization's relations with external units, enhancing its independence. With such freedom it can select the market units most compatible ideologically and can control the type of clients it serves. Scott (1969) in his study of blindness agencies notes, for example, that the near absence of external policy regulations enabled these agencies to select both programs and clients most compatible with their treatment ideologies.

## INTAKE DISCRETION VS. POSSESSING STRATEGIC RESOURCES

Market units can be distinguished by the amount of intake discretion they use in accepting or refusing a processing organization's products. The greater the discretion the greater the processing organization's dependency on these units, a situation reflected, for example, in the relationship between the employment placement office and potential employers. Consequently, the organization's classification-disposition system is more likely to adhere to these units' intake criteria. Nevertheless, when the organization possesses resources essential to these units, it can potentially offset the effects of such dependency. When it is a major supplier of clients, controls economic resources, or largely validates a market unit's claims for competence, it is in a better bargaining position with them. For example, while the private physician depends on the psychiatric hospital to accept his referred patients, he may also validate the hospital's claim for competence, and thus be only partly constrained by its intake discretion. Mishler and Waxler (1963) found that the psychiatric hospitals they studied were far more likely to accept patients referred by private physicans, though the hospitals added rules to their classification systems on age, previous hospitalization and presence of a relative.

On the other hand, market units having little intake discretion tend to require a minimal set of criteria of their clients for entry (e.g., the public school, the mission shelter, the city's general hospital, etc.). When a significant proportion of the market is composed of units with little intake discretion, one would expect the classification-disposition system used by the processing organization also to have a few relatively global typification rules which are insensitive to the client's attributes and situation. Since the relative lack of intake discretion decreases its dependency on the market unit, the processing organization is less likely to expend resources and energies to develop an elaborate classification system vis-à-vis the unit. In Scheff's (1966:128–55) study of psychiatric screening of patients to a state mental hospital, the screening psychiatrists used very few and gross classification-disposition procedures partly because the hospital used minimal intake discretion. Sudnow (1965) describes a similar pattern in the procedures of the public defender's office.

Under these conditions, however, the market units may try to develop various tacit agreements with the processing organization to control their intake informally. When these occur, the formal classification-disposition system takes on classification criteria which may make it irrelevant in the actual routing of classified persons. Thus, for example, correctional institutions receiving young offenders from a state diagnostic center may tacitly agree with the center to consider additional classification-disposition criteria such as space availability, age, and race, which neutralize such other criteria as offenders' psychological and social adjustment problems (Dickson, 1967).

## NEED FOR MARKET UNIT SERVICES VS. AVAILABLE ALTERNATIVES

The need for a given market unit largely depends on the changes in social position or future behavior the processing organization seeks for its potential clients, and the nature of the demands of potential clients. The more functionally specific its processing tasks the more dependent the organization on other units' specialized services. Yet, the availability of other market units providing comparable services increases a staff's discretion. The organization is in a stronger bargaining position with these units and hence may develop its classification-disposition system somewhat independently of them.

Hence, when the organization needs the services of a given market unit having few counterparts, we would expect its system to correspond to constraints imposed by the market unit. On the other hand, having alternative services available potentially frees the organization from such restrictions.

Lacking such units, the organization is under pressure to control either its intake, or its output of clients, or both. Hence, its system may accept only clients for whom disposition resources are available. Similarly, if the organization cannot control its client intake, it is likely to confer a temporary or "holding" status on clients for whom few alternative market units are available. Such a status links the person to the organization, yet defines him as unready for disposition. A study of employment placement agencies indicated that clients for whom employment opportunities were not available were more likely to be classified as requiring counseling than clients similar to them for whom employment opportunities were available (Hasenfeld, 1970).

As we shall note later, the effectiveness of an organization's intelligence system also crucially influences the effective range of available alternatives.

## MARKET-UNITS AS VALIDATORS OF ORGANIZATIONAL GOALS VS. SELF-VALIDATING ORGANIZATIONAL IDEOLOGIES

Potentially, the organization's products are critical to validating its goals, and organizations go to great lengths to use a variety of product measures as indices of their effectiveness and efficiency. For people-processing organizations, the product is placement of a client in one of several market units. Market units differ in their importance in validating an organization's claims of success. This difference is based on: (a) the type of effectiveness and efficiency measures the organization must use with its regulatory groups, and (b) the prestige, importance and amount of crucial resources the market unit controls in the organizational network.

Hence, the greater the organization's dependence on a market unit for validating its goals, the more will it try to devise a classification-disposition system that will assure placing its clients positively in such a unit. For example, state rehabilitation agencies tend to be evaluated by the number of successful job placements; so they are likely to limit the entry of seriously debilitated clients into their programs (Levine and White, 1961:590–92). Similarly, Reiss and Bordua (1967:32–40) suggest that since police departments depend on prosecutors and courts to validate their claim of competence, the criteria they use for disposition of suspects are partly defined through negotiations with these offices.

The proposition, however, is based on the assumption that an organization's critical product for validating its goals is a "placed" client. An organization's usefulness may rest, however, on other products or side payments (Cyert and March, 1963:29) just as critical to its survival as placing clients, if not more so. It may be a source of employment for members of important political groups, or a training ground for jobs considered important by external validating groups. Ohlin's (1960) analysis of the role of interest groups in influencing correctional objectives points up the importance of side payments. These side payments may neutralize the influence of recipient market units. In fact, they may make the processing organization unconcerned with the market unit's response to its clients. Under these circumstances one may find that its classification-disposition system is insensitive to market conditions and that major disjunctures occur between the two.

Similarly, organizations may develop self-validating ideologies as buffers against negative feedback from their market units. Self-validating ideologies are internally generated belief systems about an organization's effectiveness that negate assessment criteria used by external groups, or those based on evaluation of outcomes. Thus, Eaton (1962) found, for example, that treatment-oriented social work agencies were hostile toward evaluative research and preferred symbolic research based, in part, on staff beliefs about treatment outcomes.

Such ideologies minimize the organization's dependence on its market units to validate its goals. A potentially unanticipated consequence of such ideologies is a staff's biased perception of the type and range of market units that could effectively serve its clients. Such perception, in turn, may foreclose potential transactions with a greater variety of market units. Consequently, its classification-disposition system might respond less to market contingencies than to the self-validating belief system.

## INTELLIGENCE EFFECTIVENESS VS. INTELLIGENCE DEFICIENCY

Finally, we propose that organizational intelligence about the environment of potential market units is crucial in determining the range and scope of the exchange relations that people-processing organizations can develop. Such an intelligence system's importance stems from the fundamental fact that environmental stimuli elicit organizational responses only when transformed into bits of information (Dill, 1958). As Wilensky (1967) suggests, the organization's intelligence system profoundly affects the ways an organization interprets its environment and responds to it.

For people-processing organizations the functions of an effective intelligence system would be to:

(a) determine the various intake criteria used by potential market units;
(b) search and identify new market possibilities;
(c) monitor changes in market conditions regarding intake selection; and
(d) provide feedback to the processing organization about its success or failure in disposing of its clients.

Moreover, an intelligence system's effectiveness will be determined not only by the amount and accuracy of its information but also by the extent it disseminates this information among staff who are processing clients.

The greater the effectiveness of the intelligence system the wider the range of market units likely to be considered and the less the organization will depend on a few market units. Hence, its classification-disposition system will become more elaborate, and have varied and specified typification rules. In contrast, an organization experiencing intelligence deficiencies must rely on the few market units that use only minimal intake discretion, or those whose intake criteria are well known in the community. Hasenfeld (1971) noted that the lack of adequate and valid information about community resources by the staff of community action centers serving the poor led, in part, to using market units already well known to the poor themselves. Under these conditions the classification-disposition system will become simplified, and be characterized by a few global typification rules.

## CONCLUSIONS

We have tried to define and develop a perspective on people-processing organizations that emphasizes the effect of the external environment on the classification and disposition of clients. We have suggested that these core activities occur at such organizations' boundaries and are expressed in the form of continuous transactions with clients and other organizations. We suggest, therefore, that an exchange or transaction view of formal organizations provides a potent model for analyzing such organizations and their core activities, particularly in explaining the various patterns of people-processing such organizations develop. This paper identifies some key inter-organizational features which determine the power-dependence relations between the processing organization and its environment, and traces their significance for such an organization's system for classifying and disposing of clients.

Our study is inevitably limited in its scope, and does not address itself to several key variables that clearly influence clients' careers in processing organizations. Among these are the role of the clients and their resources in negotiating with the organization; the characteristics of the organizational processing technologies; and the social position, training and orientation of personnel in such organizations. Nevertheless, the study systematically derives a series of testable propositions about the effects of the organization's power-dependence relations with its market units on client management patterns in people-processing organizations.

## NOTES

1. I am particularly indebted to A. J. Reiss, Jr., R. C. Sarri and R. D. Vinter for their encouragement and their comments and suggestions on earlier versions of this paper.

2. Some of the studies which address themselves explicitly to this issue are Reiss and Bordua (1967); Ohlin (1960); Carlson (1964); Levine and White (1961).

## REFERENCES

Blau, P. M. 1963. *The Dynamics of Bureaucracy.* Chicago: University of Chicago Press.

Carlson, R. O. 1964. "Environmental Constraints and Organizational Consequences: The Public School and its Clients." Pp. 262–76 in *Behavioral*

*Science and Educational Administration.* Chicago: National Society for the Study of Education.

Cicourel, A. and John Kitsuse. 1963. *The Educational Decision Makers.* Indianapolis: Bobbs-Merrill.

Cyert, Richard M. and James G. March. 1963. *The Behavioral Theory of the Firm.* Englewood Cliffs: Prentice-Hall.

Dickson, D. 1967. "Reception: Organization and Decision Making in a Juvenile Corrections Reception Center." Working paper No. 33. Center for Research on Social Organization, the University of Michigan.

Dill, W. 1958. "Environment as an Influence on Managerial Autonomy." *Administrative Science Quarterly 2* (March):409–43.

Eaton, J. W. 1962. "Symbolic and Substantive Evaluation Research." *Administrative Science Quarterly 6* (March):421–42.

Evan, W. M. 1966. "The Organization-Set: Toward Theory of Interorganizational Relations." Pp. 171–91 in James D. Thompson (ed.), *Approaches to Organizational Design.* Pittsburgh, Pennsylvania: The University of Pittsburgh Press.

Freidson, E. 1965. "Disability as Social Deviance." Pp. 71–79 in Marvin B. Sussman (ed.), *Sociology and Rehabilitation.* Washington, D.C.: American Sociological Association.

Goffman, E. 1961. *Asylum: Essays on the Social Situation of Mental Patients and Other Inmates.* New York: Doubleday.

Hasenfeld, Y. 1970. "People Processing Organizations and Client Careers: A Study of Four Anti-Poverty Organizations." Unpublished Ph.D. dissertation. The University of Michigan.

———— 1971. "Organizational Dilemmas in Innovating Social Services: The Case of the Community Action Centers." *Journal of Health and Social Behavior 12* (September):208–16.

Keith-Lucas, A. 1957. *Decisions About People in Need: A Study of Administrative Responsiveness in Public Assistance.* Chapel-Hill: University of North Carolina Press.

Lefton, Mark and William R. Rosengren. 1966. "Organizations and Clients: Lateral and Longitudinal Dimensions." *American Sociological Review 31* (December):802–10.

Levine, S. and Paul White. 1961. "Exchange as a Conceptual Framework for the Study of Interorganizational Relationships." *Administrative Science Quarterly 5* (March):583–601.

Levitan, S. A. and Garth L. Mangum. 1969. *Federal Training and Work Programs in the Sixties.* Ann Arbor, Michigan: Institute of Labor and Industrial Relations.

Mishler, E. G. and Nancy E. Waxler. 1963. "Decision Process in Psychiatric Hospitalization: Patients Referred, Accepted, and Admitted to a Psychiatric Hospital." *American Sociological Review 28* (August):576–87.

Ohlin, L. 1960. "Conflicting Interests in Correctional Objectives." Pp. 111–29 in Richard A. Cloward et al. (eds.), *Theoretical Studies in the Social Organization of the Prison.* New York: Social Science Research Council.

Reiss, A. J. and David J. Bordua. 1967. "Environment and Organization: A Perspective on the Police." Pp. 25–55 in David J. Bordua (ed.), *The Police: Six Sociological Essays.* New York: Wiley.

Roth, J. 1963. *Timetables.* Indianapolis: Bobbs-Merrill.

Scheff, T. J. 1966. *Being Mentally Ill.* Chicago: Aldine.

Scott, R. A. 1969. *The Making of Blind Men: A Study of Adult Socialization.* New York: Russell Sage Foundation.

Strauss, A., L. Schatzman, R. Bucher, D. Ehrlich and M. Saleshin. 1964. *Psychiatric Ideologies and Institutions.* New York: Free Press.

Street, D., R. D. Vinter and C. Perrow. 1966. *Organization for Treatment.* New York: Free Press

Sudnow, D. 1965. "Normal Crimes: Sociological Features of the Penal Code in a Public Defender's Office." *Social Problems* 12 (Winter):255–76.

Thompson, J. D. 1967. *Organization in Action.* New York: McGraw-Hill.

Vinter, R. D. 1963. "Analysis of Treatment Organization." *Social Work* 8 (July):3–15.

Vinter, R. D. and Rosemary C. Sarri. 1966. "The Juvenile Court: Organization and Decision Making." Pp. 173–320 in *Juvenile Court Hearing Officers Training Manual, Vol. II.* Ann Arbor: The University of Michigan, Institute of Continuing Legal Education.

Wheeler, S. 1966. "The Structure of Formally Organized Socialization Settings." Pp. 51–116 in O. G. Brim and S. Wheeler (eds.), *Socialization After Childhood.* New York: Wiley.

Wilensky, H. 1967. *Organizational Intelligence.* New York: Basic Books.

# 21   The Call For a Management Stance

## JERRY S. TUREM

The startling growth of financing for social welfare programs places these programs under increasing pressure to be accountable for the public funds they receive. The programs must become accountable not only for how the money is spent, but for what is accomplished with it. The pressure for such accountability has brought forth a host of concerns formerly ignored or evaded. These concerns relate to the management of those programs.

In a context of increased accountability, management refers to purposive decision-making to achieve certain objectives. Some objectives have to do with making it more certain that auditors, consumers, legislators, or bureaucrats can determine how funds were spent, who received the benefits of the funds, and whether the funds were administered honestly and efficiently. Other objectives have to do with whether the services or materials purchased for social welfare programs—for example, casework, child care, contraceptive devices—had the desired impact on populations and problems to which they were applied. That is, were the resources allocated in the most effective way?

This article will point out the forces that seem to be pushing for greater accountability in social welfare programs. Some of these

Reprinted with permission of author and NASW from *Social Work,* 19:5 (September 1974), pp. 615–23. Copyright 1974, National Association of Social Workers, Inc.

forces probably developed as a function of the conservative federal administrations. Others seem to relate to the size of social welfare and its success in becoming institutionalized. Some of these forces seem to affect social programs regardless of who is in political office. The notions of management to attain specific objectives and of accountability based on results require evidence that an intellectual underpinning directs action in social programs. Does such evidence exist? In which areas do social welfare programs especially need better management tools?

Key points of the issue of accountability include the following:

1. Since social services generally do not exist in the open market, supply and demand do not force effectiveness and efficiency on those providing them.

2. Social service programs tend to rely on public support whether by charitable donations, tax exemptions, or direct tax subsidies.

3. The only corrective for inefficiency, ineffectiveness, and even dishonesty is a system of accountability for results.

4. The essential elements of a system of accountability are to assure honesty at a minimum and to identify the goals, the problems, the resources needed, and the technology necessary to achieve these goals efficiently and effectively.[1]

## DEFINITIONS

To be accountable, programs must be managed. *Management* may be defined as the purposive control and direction of resources to achieve stated goals. This definition includes goal orientation and decision-making aimed at the goals. To be thus goal oriented suggests using information on efficiency and effectiveness as a guide to allocate resources rather than rationing by intuition or value judgments. Rationing is of course essential because resources—whether money, time or talent—are always limited. From a management perspective, the goals can be taken as set forth by the charter and auspices of the organization.

From a broader perspective on accountability, goals should be defined in terms of measurable results. This permits decisions as to whether a particular technique and process are appropriate to achieve the objectives. The largest single shortcoming of current goals of social programs is their focus on what is put into them, along with faith that a salutary relationship exists between what is put in and what comes out. Specifically, goals are often defined in terms of the number of clients a worker sees, the casework hours, and the like. Program planners seldom describe goals in terms of the reduction in unwanted pregnancies, the improvement in children's living conditions, the lowering of recidivism rates, and so on.

*Administration* is often used synonymously with management, but this article will make a distinction. Administration is defined as the process of management. It provides the tools and techniques for collecting necessary information and for controlling and enforcing decisions about how to allocate resources.

Thus administration covers various activities, many of which can be exercised in a relatively routine manner. Management, on the other hand, requires an underlying knowledge base for determining what does or does not "work," what is or is not "efficient."

*Management*, then, is more than establishing and applying administrative techniques, which every organization does to some degree. Rent and salaries are paid, clients are seen, funds are obtained. Management involves marshalling the resources necessary to attain the results. It has to do with the purposes for keeping books, imposing rules, budgeting and allocating resources, hiring staff and assigning tasks, and raising funds. It has to do with cost accounting and with formulating criteria for the acceptance or rejection of clients. Management, in a sense, takes the overall goals that emerge from the system of accountability and, given certain inputs, tries to get the most outputs.

In the past, when funds were more limited, it might have been difficult to justify a full-blown management system of the type described. With expenditures for social welfare programs now in the multibillions, however, using resources in a socially accountable way is a growing necessity. Since resources are so large, competing providers and alternative uses are becoming visible. If the programs are to sustain their growth and resist decline, social workers must develop the knowledge, information, and techniques to show they can manage programs to accomplish social goals.

## CAUSES OF CONCERN

It is clear that social service programs are being examined closely, in part because of their lack of accountability and their poor management. The following developments offer evidence of this scrutiny:

■ Action from two sides hit the social services authorized under the public assistance titles of the Social Security Act: the federal government issued restrictive regulations, and under Title XX, Congress imposed a ceiling on formerly open-ended expenditures for them.

■ Congress dropped a requirement for social services in nursing homes.

■ Public and private provision of services have become less separate with public purchase of services from private agencies and the donation of nontax funds to match the federal contribution to service programs. Public agencies have imposed more contractual requirements on the private sector, and this elaboration of contractual provisions seems likely to continue over time.

■ Competition for funds has been growing among groups providing services—for example, among agencies dealing with vocational rehabilitation, child welfare, or other social services, who compete within the same area of the federal budget. Such competition is likely to demand stronger demonstrations of effectiveness and efficiency, which call for improved management.

■ Growing politization of social services seems to have occurred, both with respect to consumers and to competitors.

■ Many new comprehensive state agencies are increasingly dominated by non-social workers, and it seems clear that the federal bureaucracies will be also, thus weakening the position of professional social workers.

■ For the first time, serious alternatives, primarily at the federal level, pose a threat to the long-nurtured-and-protected social services. These alternatives are revenue sharing and direct provision of cash to the poor in lieu of services.

Similar concerns for management have arisen in the past. In 1952 Schwartz proposed a research project to measure work so that performance might be the basis of budgeting in a child-placement agency. In 1958 the Children's Bureau published the results of a cost study by Schwartz on adoption and foster care and one by Wolins on institutional child care.[2] Little application of these management tools can be discerned. In 1973, Gruber reported on his rediscovery of the high cost of delivering services.[3]

The isolated events mentioned do not of themselves constitute sufficient evidence that a management stance is inevitably emerging, but they indicate that something may be different from events in the previous few years. For those who believe that programs must be managed if they are not to wither, these developments raise concern for improving accountability and management. It should be borne in mind, however, that there may be other consequences besides slowed growth of funds if programs continue with the rudimentary management tools now in existence.

As social service programs evolve, they seem to be achieving the hopes of early pioneers, but with significant unanticipated effects. The weight of expansion is great and the system is ill prepared to bear it. Profound changes in thinking and behavior result when programs become established as "institutional" rather than "residual." As Wilensky and Lebeaux used these terms, there was a movement from care for the stigmatized hindmost to a normal, accepted pattern of services.[4]

A "big money" social service system requires different justification than the "pitch" of doing good that the traditional social agency used — and far different control too. Social welfare programs are moving from services provided by a few dedicated persons for the "unfortunates" of society toward services provided as a normal aspect of life for many persons. This change means less control by a small group of professionals with shared values and a belief in their own way of work.

When programs become large, both the consumers and those who provide the funds begin to have a larger voice in them. Competitors seek a share of the resources. Social workers tend to become more like cogs in a larger system, where who gets what under which conditions is increasingly out of their hands. The ability to make defensible decisions on who gets what and how is the key to management and to program growth. These decisions, in turn, are based on better information than was hitherto available regarding effects, costs, and productivity. The process is, in a sense, irresistible. Now when physicians and lawyers become public servants, paid by public funds, they too are faced with constraints on what they can and cannot do, the patients they can see, and the services they can provide. Sophisticated, doubting, and perhaps cynical governmental officials, taxpayers, and clients will increasingly question programs in which professionals impose values on behavior or activities—such as programs that social workers think are "good" for those they serve. Thus the successful growth of programs calls for improved management and accountability.

## PURCHASE OF SERVICE

Another reason for improved management arises from the traditional private sector of social services. Private agencies are usually supported by some endowment and nurtured by charitable donations. Therefore, some could be relatively autonomous and continue managing or nonmanaging as in the past. Yet the consolidation of sponsorship, planning, and fund raising is bringing about, in many instances, greater demands for management.

In the private sector of social services, the nonprofit agencies primarily associated with United Way—family service agencies, community centers and Ys, Scouts, foster care and homemaker services and the like—have relatively declining financing. In 1968, United Way contributions were $12.06 per $10,000 of personal income. This figure has decreased every year until by 1971 the figure was $10.05 per $10,000.

The United Way and the American Association of Fund-Raising Councils present the increased total of annual contributions as an indication of continued growth and viability. To some extent, even when price adjusted for inflation, a slight increment continued from 1962 until 1970 when a price-adjusted decline appeared. Adjusted to 1967 prices, contributions were $743.9 million in 1969, the high point, but were down to $713 million in 1971. The private sector still raises close to $1 billion a year, but these figures indicate that its relative income is decreasing, thus imposing greater needs to manage what there is.

An additional reason for more management in the private sector is that it is relying increasingly on public funds. Use of public funds demands at least fiscal accountability and hence a need for better tools for reporting. As Chapman and Cleaveland point out:

> There is ample evidence that the distinctions between private and public sectors are disappearing or becoming blurred. Private corporations, both profit and not-for-profit, are engaged in performing public functions.[5]

The public purchase of service from private agencies and the private donation of state shares of public state and federal grant-in-aid programs were becoming accepted ways of cooperation in 1972, but these activities now seem to have slowed considerably. One set of estimates for the public purchase of private services in fiscal 1972 amounted to nearly $440 million in state and federal funds, an 18 percent increase over 1971.[6] This was almost half the total, $915 million, that the 2,224 United Way campaigns raised across the United States and Canada in 1972.[7]

In the program of Aid to Families with Dependent Children, services purchased from private sources doubled from 1971 to 1972, going from $199 million to $386 million. The bulk of the funds went into child care, foster care, and community adjustment for services related to mental health and mental retardation. Under the provisions for adult welfare services, expenditures for private purchased services rose from 1971 to 1972 from $18 million to $54 million, primarily for homemaker and chore services.

Most purchased services tend to be "hard" and tangible. Little has been spent on services related to general recreation, general casework, community planning, or health. The family and child welfare sector of United Way in 1972 took 28.4 percent of contributions (about $280 million). AFDC purchased services in this private sector for child care alone totaled about $238 million. According to these figures, the family and child welfare sector was almost doubling its own budget through purchased services.

Evidence thus indicates that it is less logical to view private and public social services as separate programs to which separate rules apply. Both are subject to increasing concern about accountability and better management.

## OTHER TRENDS

A formal method called Delphi is used in making projections for the future. Experts respond to certain questions. Then the responses are statistically assessed. Subsequently, questionnaires are circulated to explore given dimensions further. The National Academy of Public Administration (NAPA) sponsored such an exercise on "The Changing Character of the Public Services and the Administrator of the 1980's."[8] This study indicated that the following essential trends were important determinants of public service in the next decade:

■ *Pressures for centralization and decentralization.* Certain problems transcend community, city, county, or even state boundaries. Some may go beyond national boundaries. Increasing recognition of this fact creates pressure for centralized decision-making on such issues as environmental protection and economic well-being. Demands for equity in governmental programs require more standardization and thus also encourage centralization. On the other hand, certain problems, as well as decisions regarding implementation that affect distribution of program benefits, push toward greater decentralization of some sectors, probably accompanied by revenue sharing. Chapman and Cleaveland, in reporting the NAPA study, suggest that higher levels of government should determine broad policy, formulate national standards and guidelines, and evaluate data on program execution and service delivery. Then local governmental agencies would directly manage and deliver the services based on the priorities of the unique local area, but within the boundaries set forth.

This generalized orientation is closely related to conclusions drawn by Mogulof in discussing special revenue sharing.[9] Mogulof points out that the opportunities for local flexibility and the demand for measurement of results are both freeing and constricting, but certainly tend to enhance the social services.

■ *Unionization in the public services.* Unionization, including the development of more militant professional associations, is expected to increase. The new and growing unions will try to minimize the authority of public executives and in many instances they will run against the wishes of consumers. An increasingly professionalized and organized work force that is not loyal to given organizations or given policies is likely to make it difficult for management to be oriented to results and may present barriers to the continuation of many programs.

■ *Increasing citizen involvement.* Unilateral bureaucratic or professional decision-making will become more untenable because suits that challenge decisions on the distribution of benefits, equal opportunities, and equity considerations will increase. As consumer groups grow in size, experience, and power, greater politization may occur in many sectors of public administration that were formerly the province of a few administrators accountable only to a committee chairman and one or two constituent groups.

■ *Impact of technological change.* One can, according to this NAPA study, expect public programs to use computers and systems analysis increasingly. The increasing use of technical and quantitative dimensions of program is expected to create organizations in which ad hoc work groups are formed for specific tasks and dispersed after they accomplish these tasks. Such organizations will clearly require managers who can define and rank tasks, allocate resources, and determine how well tasks are accomplished.

Key factors will be orientation to output, team activity, and open review of results by consumers as well as by the legislative and executive branches of government. Planning is expected to improve technically with better analyses, forecasting methods, and the like.

As Chapman and Cleaveland note:

New standards for effectiveness and for accountability will be developed. "Least Cost" was disposed of some time ago as the most important criterion for measuring program success. Even "most services for the money" is considered less than adequate. There is increasing concern about related or secondary impacts of services delivered and the nature of their delivery as well as the process by which public program decisions are reached.[10]

Wald's Delphi exercise emphasizes the same points:

Future public administration will study value preferences but will eschew value judgments. . . . It will shift away from the category of value supremacy (which implies direct and conscious promotion of values and subjects public administration to the service of those preferred values).

In the future, major tools and methods in academic public administration will be the following: (a) system analysis, (b) economic tools (including cost/benefit analysis, cost/effectiveness, PPBS, expenditures analysis, and to a lesser extent discounted flows), (c) decision making (both normative and statistical), (d) survey research, (e) simulation and gaining (including computer simulation, man-machine simulation, and to a lesser extent human simulation) and (f) case studies.

Public policy and policy analysis will be the main area of future research in public administration. It will be addressed to the questions of "who benefits" (emphasizing clientele values), economy and efficiency.... [11]

## KNOWLEDGE BASE

Managing, not merely administering, is based on knowledge or "intelligence" in the military sense of the term. What intelligence informs the decisions made in state social service programs? Mogulof considered this question in a 1973 study. It was hypothesized that, if these programs are "managed," then their shape develops from relatively reasoned decisions to go toward one goal and not another, from choices of one technique and not another—decisions and choices based on evaluation, analysis, and assessment of what works and what does not. Mogulof wished to test the hypothesis that the shape of social service programs develops from such management, but that decisions made may in turn be affected by federal rules, state political influence, and so on.

Four states were selected on the basis of a wide range of dimensions. Social service directors; personnel of federal, regional, and central offices; budget officers, planners, legislators; local administrators of social services, and others were interviewed at length. Mogulof concluded:

... the knowledge situation on the social services is basically "anarchic," thus supporting a decision situation in which values are most influential in making choices. [12]

It is intuition, feeling, or the force of events that push, tug, and pull social service programs. It is not intelligence and it is not assessment of whether anything "works" and is effective. The present system of social services can be called a system based on value judgments, most of which are vaguely and imprecisely stated. One wonders how long a multibillion dollar system can be expected to continue on such a basis.

Two possible reasons why, in the past, social services have not invested in basic conceptual tools and mechanisms for measuring results are these:

1. Until recently not enough pressure has been applied from high-level political officials to generate the necessary activity. Program administrators have tended to be advocates who believe in the intrinsic worth of their programs. The added efficiency of a strong management system may not have been worth the cost of instituting it when budgets were small and administrators were preoccupied with the survival of fledgling programs. The programs can hardly be called fledgling today.

2. Defining outputs, and hence raising the possibility of measuring success, can show inefficiency and ineptness and make one program look better than another. Programs are now operated by competing agencies within the states, and cross-program measures of output can require cooperation between competing groups. If a merger is proposed for the sake of efficiency, independent agencies will resist being integrated into a larger enterprise, even though they overlap greatly in objectives, technologies, and target populations. Thus stiff opposition is likely to arise from the bureaucratic and political consequences of defining outputs.

## MANAGEMENT LACKS

Social work, like law and medicine, is a profession oriented to the practitioner. But law and medicine, unlike social work, are subject to the supply and demand of the marketplace. As social programs become still more public in their nature and their funding, practitioners will be able to make professional decisions about how to treat their selected clients. Which clients and how many are likely to be public decisions based on information about broad groups with definable social problems for which remedy is possible and measurable.

The profession must recognize that advocacy alone will not be enough but must be accompanied by analysis. Much of what now passes for analysis is little more than a brief for a position arrived at by other means. The pseudoanalysis will become less acceptable, and if social workers continue to use it they will lose credibility and influence with policy-makers.

The most pressing problem is the lack of both conceptual tools and analytic capability. It is important to note that few social work academics and practitioners are oriented to program effectiveness and they do not usually consider quantitative and economic factors relevant to their concerns. In a 1973 article Fischer argued that the output of social workers should be evaluated and measured, and he reviewed several studies indicating a lack of effectiveness.[13] A subsequent letter to the editor protested the conclusions as follows:

What these research projects seemed to prove was that it would have been just as well to have left all the clients alone, just as well not to have offered service and have tried to help. But that's a judgment based on statistics; it's not life! Such research projects cannot report adequately on *the quality of help given to and received by specific clients.* In fact, all our case-record dictation, books, and published papers cannot completely capture the *social worker's skills and creativity,* the intricacies and subtle nuances of the treatment relationship and process. [Italics added.][14]

Being so oriented to inputs—that is, to the nature of the procedures regardless of outcome—may be helpful for a professional, but it offers a poor justification for the spending of public monies. If social work were geared to the marketplace, such statements would cause little concern. Employment of social workers in the public sector offers no mechanism to eliminate those who are ineffective and inefficient. Thus alternative correctives are required. Measuring effectiveness and cost in a comprehensive system of accountability is such a corrective.

Elements of management that are badly developed in social welfare programs include personnel appraisal and evaluation based on productivity and output, not style of work; accounting systems that account; and information systems that inform.

*Personnel.* The basic criteria outlined by the National Association of Social Workers (NASW) in its guidelines for personnel policy essentially involve some sort of certification of the worker.[15] The same is true of personnel policies in many civil service systems. Once on the job, unless by his own choice, an employee is likely to stay if there is no evidence of gross incompetence, dishonesty, or mental illness. Some programs have workload standards that must be maintained—for example, a specific number of visits with clients or investigations of eligibility—but few standards for productivity. Thus input is being measured, not output.

One rarely hears of the dismissal of a relatively nice person with an MSW, who met the usual standards of dress, who was cooperative with colleagues, who was on the job when expected, but whose services did not seem to do anyone any good. As one increasingly finds mixes of skills in service teams that include paraprofessionals and professionals from both social work and allied fields, it is only in terms of productivity that efficient management decisions can be made—that is, decisions based not on how many hours were worked, but on what was accomplished.

*Accounting and budgeting.* Social service administrators often complain about inadequate resources but have seldom made fiscal analyses that would permit more efficient use of funds available. The old pinch-penny rules urged economy in the use of pencils, paper, rubber bands, and the like but cost analysis was seldom done nor cost-effectiveness studies used. Cost-effectiveness studies differ from cost-benefit studies in that they seek only the lowest cost for a given level of output, regardless of how benefits are measured.

In many public programs, and private as well, it is virtually impossible at present to allocate costs to given units of service. It is not possible, for example, to determine rationally which of three clients on a waiting list can be seen when limited time or money makes it possible to see only one. Yet a rational decision is necessary because a wrong or or inefficient choice robs those not chosen. Thinking that first-come-first-served is an efficient or effective way to allocate services is a delusion.

Is good management the answer? A manager should know how his budget is allocated according to types of services purchased, wages paid, capital costs, and direct subsidies to clients. He should know which services absorb which costs, how much, and with what result on which clients. The manager of a program—and the professionals who work with him—should then be able to make a rational decision regarding which of three waiting-list clients should be seen.

*Information.* The endless case records provide little information for management. They tell a bit about the objective traits of most clients—age, sex, race, income, and so on—but little about how the services provided affect clients' lives. Routinely collected information, not special evaluations, must be tied to the cost data so that choices can be made among the competing claims to the agency's resources. Adequate information about programs and clients can tell who is using the service, how various restrictions and incentives are affecting users, and whether decisions are accomplishing the desired ends.

## CONCLUSION

Many forces are pushing social welfare programs toward improved management. Services in some sectors are in relative decline and in others have reached a plateau of growth. Increasingly tough questions will be raised about who gets the program benefits and what difference they make in clients' well-being. Forces are pushing many areas of public service toward programs that can be defended analytically. Demands will be increasing that effectiveness and efficiency be proved. Thus the basic needs that improved management can fulfill will become more evident—assembling hard data, having the means to analyze it, developing the skills to use it in decision-making. Armed with the data, the analyses, and the skills, managers can decide what goals they can reasonably expect to attain and how to allocate resources to attain them efficiently and effectively.

To remain viable, social programs must improve their ability to show they are directed toward defensible and measurable ends, that their resources are purposeful and efficiently allocated, and that they achieve the desired impacts. If better management can be equal to the task and the challenge, then the future of social welfare programs will be that much brighter.

## NOTES

1. Edward Newman and Jerry Turem, "The Crisis of Accountability," *Social Work* (January 1974), pp. 5–16.

2. Edward Schwartz, "Adoption and Foster Home Costs" and Martin Wolins, "Cost of Care in Children's Institutions," *Cost Analysis in Child Welfare Services* (Washington, D.C.: Children's Bureau, U.S. Government Printing Office, 1958).

3. Alan Gruber, "The High Cost of Delivering Services," *Social Work*, 18 (July 1973), pp. 33–40.

4. Harold Wilensky and Charles Lebeaux, *Industrial Society and Social Welfare* (New York: Russell Sage Foundation, 1968).

5. R. Chapman and F. Cleaveland, "The Changing Character of the Public Service and the Administrator of the 1980's," *Public Administration Review* (July/August 1973), p. 371.

6. Touche Ross & Co., "Cost Analysis of Social Services, Fiscal Year 1972." Unpublished report to the Social and Rehabilitation Service, February 1973, mimeographed.

7. *Giving USA, 1973* (New York: American Association of Fund-Raising Counsel, 1974), pp. 41–42.

8. Chapman and Cleaveland, *op. cit.*

9. Melvin V. Mogulof, "Special Revenue Sharing and the Social Services," *Social Work*, 18 (September 1973), pp. 9–15.

10. Chapman and Cleaveland, *op. cit.*

11. *Ibid.*, pp. 366–72.

12. Melvin Mogulof, "Making Social Service Choices at the State Level: Practice and Problems in Four States," Urban Institute Working Paper 963–39 (Washington, D.C.: Urban Institute, October 1973). (Mimeographed.)

13. Joel Fischer, "Is Casework Effective?" *Social Work*, 18 (January 1973), pp. 5–20.

14. David Hallowitz, Letter to the Editor, *Social Work*, 18 (May 1973), p. 106.

15. *NASW Standards for Social Work Personnel Practices* (New York: National Association of Social Workers, 1971).

# Chapter Seven

# DIRECTIONS OF SOCIAL WORK

It would be a remarkable bit of prophecy to set down the direction social work will take in the final decades of the twentieth century. Therefore, in entitling this chapter we have taken care to add an evasive "s" to the word "direction." Like Leacock's irrepressible Gertrude the Governess who always "jumped upon her horse and rode off in all directions," social work seems to be moving in several ways at once, presenting a dizzying array of practices, problems, and programs. Some prognostications are dour: Social work is doomed. Others are ebullient: *Real* social work is just about to begin.

Checking through the issues of the past year's *Journal of the National Association of Social Workers* at the time of writing, we found that the list of topics covers a very wide range. Apart from articles aplenty on professional business such as ethics, accountability, methodology, and supervision, there appeared to be no corner of community life untouched by social work. There were articles about social work in police departments, in industry, and with undocumented aliens. Descriptions of practice included social work with single-parent families, step families, and abusing families. There were articles calling for clearer, more supportive family policies, and articles against family policy. There were discussions of social work in relation to lesbians, learned helplessness, legal services, and legislative action. And that is only a sample.

In recent decades there have been many changes in the composition of the profession. Numbers of social workers have increased markedly, the sex ratio has changed as more men have entered the profession, and the scope and range of professional functions have expanded.[1] There are well over 300,000 social workers in the United States. This figure refers to people who are classified as "social welfare workers" on the basis of their jobs, regardless of their educational attainment.[2] It also includes many people who carry out tasks that do not require high degrees of professional expertise, such as eligibility checking and recreational activities. One of the current concerns of the profession is to define the kinds of knowledge and skill that are required for different levels of professional practice so that classifications based on a continuum of training (such as "aide-technician-BSW-MSW-doctorate") will distinguish the different knowledge and skill levels of social workers in a meaningful way.[3] In addition, the profession is crosscut by other classifications based on specializations such as the traditional casework-group work-community organization trinity (which is going out of style in the United States), the direct and indirect types of services, the clinical and the social-change specializations, and the non-specialist classification of the "generalist." Other specializations are based on functional areas of service such as gerontology, community mental health, and child welfare.

The seven readings in this chapter deal with the directions social work appears to be taking in the 1980s. The authors of the articles agree on one thing: There is great ferment and change in the profession. And there the agreement ends. The different and divergent views, and the varied conclusions and recommendations, are a good sample of current thinking in the profession. The reader who finds much that is contradictory and confusing in these readings will have discovered something about the nature of social work in this decade.

Our intent is to focus on the profession as an entity, and not on professional practice. Our aim is not to describe what social workers *do*, nor *where, how*, and *with whom* they do it. Our intention is to consider how the profession as a community presently conceives of itself and the problems and issues it confronts. For these reasons, there is a great deal about social work practice that we do not present here. Each of the different models of social work practice in current use constitutes an area of study that is substantial by itself.[4] Specific approaches and practice techniques such as behavior modification and sexual counseling have a literature that we could not possibly incorporate in the framework of this volume.[5] There are functionally-specific problem areas such as work with oppressed populations (e.g., women, ethnic groups, homosexuals) and with other population groups (e.g., the aged, the mentally ill) each of which merits intensive study.

In Reading 22, Gilbert and Specht describe "Current Models of Social Work Practice" and some of the ways in which these models direct the behavior of the social worker. This reading concludes with an analysis of the different kinds of knowledge that the professional social worker must master. Gilbert and Specht suggest that there are different kinds of general and specific content at various levels of professional competence. A continuing concern of the profession is to achieve an appropriate theoretical and practical integration of these different kinds of knowledge at different levels of professional development.

The "call for a management stance" in the institution of social welfare that is described by Turem in the last chapter (Reading 21) is echoed in the profession by a call for *effective practice.* Since the mid-1960s there has been continuous questioning both from within the profession and from outside about whether social work practice is effective in solving problems. Briar wrote of "the crisis in social casework" in 1967;[6] in 1973, Joel Fischer asked: "Is casework effective?"[7] and concluded that it is not. Augural titles abounded: "Casework Is Dead"[8]; "The Casework Predicament"[9]; "Has Mighty Casework Struck Out?"[10]. The questions have by no means been answered to anyone's satisfaction.[11]

Although other practice specializations (e.g., social planning, administration, community organization) have not proven themselves to be especially more effective than casework, the malaise about practice has focussed primarily upon direct services. We think this occurs because direct-service practitioners are the people on the line, the ones who actually deal with troubled clients. And caseworkers are more likely than other social workers to deal with involuntary clients, i.e., with people who have not sought treatment of their own choice. Moreover, as Specht points out in Reading 14, during the 1960's revolution in human rights there was much criticism of all professions, social work included. But the harshest criticism of all was leveled at therapeutically-oriented professionals such as social caseworkers because they were perceived to be one of the means by which an oppressive society controlled its victims. Finally, indirect-service kinds of practice specializations such as administration and social planning are even more difficult to evaluate than social casework because their objectives are usually long range; frequently, public interest in programs with long-range objectives has ebbed long before the program is completed and can be evaluated.

The thrust of professional criticism about the effectiveness of social work practice is, in a nutshell, that social casework has made no difference in efforts to relieve social stress. While we cannot here undertake an evaluation of the many evaluations of social casework, some brief comments are in order. Most of the studies cited in the literature of criticism are not well suited to the task of evaluating casework. Many of them (particularly those cited by Joel Fischer)[12] deal with client populations who suffer from problems caused by extreme economic deprivation; moreover, many of these client populations did not request the kind of help proffered by the social caseworkers who served them. (Some studies of outcomes of therapeutic interventions have found that casework does make a difference with client groups who have *voluntarily* sought help.[13]) In many evaluative studies, the nature of the casework intervention is not clear, and in some studies where control groups are used it is not clear as to how the stimulus given to the experimental group (i.e., casework) differed from what was given to a control group.[14] By and large, most of these studies have searched for changes in individual and family functioning brought about as the result of clinically-oriented intervention, a highly unrealistic expectation in light of the evidence that interpersonal and intrapersonal factors are not the cause of many of the problems treated.

Reading 23, by Katherine M. Wood, "Casework Effectiveness: A New Look at the Research Evidence," provides a rigorous examination of twenty-two studies of practice effectiveness. Professor Wood's approach differs from other critiques of this kind in several ways. First, she establishes criteria by which to evaluate the studies. (Thirty-one other studies were discarded because they did not meet her criteria.) Second, she compares studies with one another only if the units under study are sufficiently alike. Third, she maintains careful scrutiny of both the outcomes of the research reports *and* the methodology used in the research projects. Dr. Wood's major conclusion is that no major conclusions can yet be drawn about the effectiveness of social work practice on the basis of research done to date. This is not surprising, given the complexity, variety, and changeability of social work practice today. It is, in our view, much too early in the game to search for an answer to the global question, "Is social work practice effective?"

The issues related to choice of models of practice, and questions about the effectiveness of practice, are somewhat grand. The next four readings deal with more specific professional issues. In Reading 24, "Advocacy and Professional Ethics," Neil Gilbert and Harry Specht discuss some issues related to advocacy, an idea that has been both popular and significant in social work for over fifteen years. The notion of advocacy is significant because it underscores that the professional's responsibility is first and foremost to the client. This idea is significant because, as we have noted, social work emerged as a collection of institutional functions that were auxiliary to other professions such as medicine and teaching. For that reason, until fairly recently, social work practice was more directed by the organizational context within which it was practiced than by professional knowledge, sanctions, ethics, values, and culture. However, the person who said "There's no such thing as a free lunch," was right. Gilbert and Specht argue that the higher degrees of professional autonomy and discretion that are implied by the notion of the social worker as advocate require equivalent higher degrees of professional discipline. If social workers are to be free to exercise judgment and make decisions on behalf of clients, then the public must be assured that the professional's behavior will indeed be directed and bounded by a code of ethics that protects the rights and interests of clients.

The private practice of social work is an issue that inheres in its emergence as a profession. That is, if the attributes of a profession are knowledge, authority, sanction, a code of ethics, and a culture, then those that have them are, presumably, free to offer their services to any client who applies. Over the last twenty years, private practice in social work has been gaining professional acceptance. In 1957, NASW acknowledged private practice to be a legitimate form of social work. Minimum qualifications for such practice were adopted by the NASW Delegate Assembly in 1962. The development of private practice introduces complications for the mission and identity of the profession. There is evidence that MSWs in private practice tend most often to identify themselves as "psychotherapists" rather than social workers. This identification with a treatment modality makes no clear distinction between social workers and the wide range of other mental health professionals who employ psychotherapeutic techniques in their work.[15]

In the view of some people in the profession, private practice falls beyond the boundaries of social welfare, which is a field characterized by socially-sponsored formal organizations that operate outside the market economy as nonprofit agencies.[16] Others, however, believe that the professional practice of social work will be enhanced in status and prestige by the further development of private practice.[7] The thinking here is that the autonomy and independence of private practitioners will enlarge the profession's capacity to use knowledge and skill for *its* objectives rather than the objectives of other professions and institutions.

In his paper, "Private Practice as a Social Work Function," Reading 25, Paul A. Kurzman takes a modified-negative position on the issue of private practice. He grants the significance for the profession of the choice to practice privately, but he asserts that the principal mode for delivery of social services must continue to be community sponsorship.

Professional authority and community sanction are necessary attributes for attainment of professional status. These attributes are manifest in the extent to which the public is willing to recognize that particular tasks may be carried out only by people who can demonstrate mastery of specific kinds of knowledge and skill, and to regulate the conditions under which these functions are performed. This public recognition is given in various forms such as registration, certification, and licensing. David A. Hardcastle provides an assessment of social work's achievement of authority and sanction in Reading 26, "Public Regulation of Social Work." Hardcastle is not entirely sanguine about social work's progress in this regard. Regulation based on bogus claims of knowledge and skill, or on legitimate claims that are not backed up by means to substantiate them is, in Hardcastle's view, without value. In the long run, he thinks, arbitrary and insubstantial regulation may undermine the value and status of the profession.

Paul Adams and Gary Freeman's paper, "On the Political Character of Social Service Work," Reading 27, is an analysis of a recurrent issue in practice that excited especially heated debate in the late 1960s and early 1970s. They examine the proposition that social workers can pursue political objectives in their practice.

We have referred throughout this part of the book to the duality of social work. Adams and Freeman address the dramatic dimension of this duality: Should social workers engage in political action to change the social system? This issue was joined very directly in the last decade. Martin Rein, in 1970, for example, wrote about the features of a kind of social work practice that is responsive to political and social issues and community concerns.[18] Rein's description of types of radical and traditional social work captures the major theoretical perspectives on professions, social problems, and social change as they bear upon social work. The "traditional casework" Rein describes represents elements of the repressive, reactionary, and unattractive features of practice; much of the description is of a kind of casework that hardly exists anymore. The new and more socially-oriented elements in the past twenty-five years of casework practice are viewed by Rein as characteristics of the "radical casework." What Rein designates as "radical social policy" reflects sets of activities related to social action and social reform; these are activities that have been a concern of the profession from days of yore. As Rein indicates, this set of activities is somewhat removed from the kinds of issues to which the majority of social workers providing direct services can pay attention in their jobs as professionals. He says:

> Individual social workers may, of course, function as reformers in the areas of employment, income distribution, and political power, but these activities are marginal to their professional tasks. In this sense, they are professionals who are radical rather than members of a radical profession.[19]

Rein brings us back, full circle, to the problem of duality in the profession, which will always be present because it inheres in the relationship between social welfare and social work.

Others challenged the vision of a radical profession for which so many yearn. Specht, for example, described four ideological currents of the 1960s that, in his view, undermine professionalism in social work: activism, anti-individualism, communalism, and environmentalism.[20] In Specht's view, accommodation to these currents, both in practice and in social work education, erodes what is professional in social work. The resolution of some of the strains that are currently working in the profession, Specht suggests, may lie in social work's becoming less professional, while some of the social welfare and indirect-service functions of the field become more a part of the profession. From a practical viewpoint, it is probably the case that for many years social work has put most of its educational resources at too high a level, thereby overproducing MSWs to carry out a range of tasks, many of which do not require advanced training. This is a somewhat reluctant acknowledgment that Dr. Abraham Flexner was at least half-right. The increasing numbers of BSW programs and the use of subprofessional personnel are salutary in this regard. Ultimately, these developments should force education at the master's degree level to become much more selective in the objectives of training and selection of students and curriculum content.

Essentially, Adams and Freeman perceive all social work practice to be political in a sense. However, they believe that the social services are neither a viable means for political change nor an essential support of the status quo. Their analysis, which employs modern

Marxist theory, provides a realistic perspective on the function of social work in a capitalist society.

Throughout this century there have been a variety of efforts to describe the functions, purposes, mission, and theoretical bases of social work practice.[21] In 1976 and 1979, the National Association of Social Workers made two significant efforts to further define a conceptual framework for social work practice.[22] Two full issues of *Social Work* are devoted to reports on these efforts and, more than anything else, they reflect the remarkable diversity, lack of definition, and variety of perspectives that exist in social work today. We conclude the volume with Reading 28, "The Search for Professional Identity" by Neil Gilbert. In this commentary, Gilbert indicates that the absence of a well-articulated conceptual framework that can encompass the spectrum of activities called social work is the source of a long-standing crisis of professional identity. Gilbert suggests that the starting point for social work's professional identity is in its distinctive relationship to the institution of social welfare. However fluid and diverse it may be, the profession's mission, in Gilbert's view, should be shaped and bounded by the objectives and values that society has vested in the institution of social welfare.

We would have liked to conclude this book with a clear and unequivocal statement about how society's best interests can be served by social work. We do have some preferences which we have presented in the selections we have authored and in introductory statements to the chapters. Nonetheless, we believe that the arguments for radicalization, deprofessionalization, and decentralization are as well presented and persuasive as what can be said for professionalization, unification, and rationalization in social work. The uncertainty that is apparent in regard to every significant aspect of the profession is, we think, indicative of the fragile vitality of social work in this era.

## NOTES

1. Henry J. Meyer and Sheldon Siegel, "Profession of Social Work: Contemporary Characteristics," *Encyclopedia of Social Work*, II, ed. John B. Turner (New York: National Association of Social Workers, 1977), pp. 1067–81.

2. David Hardcastle, "The Profession, Professional Organizations, Licensing, and Private Practice," *Handbook of Social Services*, eds. Neil Gilbert and Harry Specht (Englewood Cliffs, N.J.: Prentice-Hall, Inc., 1980).

3. *Ibid.*

4. For descriptions of the three traditional social work methods, see the following: *Social Casework*—Sister Mary Paul Janchill, R.G.S., "Systems Concepts in Casework Theory and Practice," *Social Casework*, February 1969, pp. 74–82, and Ann Hartman, "But What is Social Casework?" *Social Case-*

*work*, July 1971, pp. 411–19. *Social Group Work*—Catherine P. Papell and Beulah Rothman, "Social Group Work Models: Possession and Heritage," *Journal of Education for Social Work*, Fall 1966, pp. 66–77. *Community Organization*—Jack Rothman, "Three Models of Community Organization Practice," *Social Work Practice*, 1968 (New York: Columbia University Press, 1968), pp. 16–47.

5. For detailed discussion of each of these and the following topics the reader is referred to Gilbert and Specht, *Handbook of Social Services*.

6. Scott Briar, "The Current Crisis in Social Casework," *Social Work Practice*, 1967 (New York: Columbia University Press, 1967), pp. 19–33.

7. Joel Fischer, "Is Casework Effective? A Review," *Social Work*, Vol. 18 (January 1973):5–20.

8. Helen Harris Perlman, "Casework Is Dead," *Social Casework*, 48 (1967), pp. 22–25.

9. Scott Briar, "The Casework Predicament," *Social Work*, 13 (January 1968), pp. 5–11.

10. Joel Fischer, "Has Mighty Casework Struck Out?" *Social Work*, 18 (July 1973), pp. 107–110.

11. Edward J. Mullen et al., *Evaluation of Social Intervention* (San Francisco: Jossey-Bass, Inc., Publishers, 1972).

12. Fischer, "Is Casework Effective?"

13. Steven Paul Segal, "Research on the Outcome of Social Work Therapeutic Intervention: A Review of the Literature," *Journal of Health and Social Behavior*, 13 (March 1972):3–17.

14. For example, see Edwin Powers and Helen Witmer, *An Experiment in the Prevention of Delinquency—The Cambridge-Somerville Youth Study* (New York: Columbia University Press, 1971), and Gordon E. Brown, ed., *The Multi-Problem Dilemma: A Social Research Demonstration with Multi-Problem Families* (Metuchen, N.J.: The Scarecrow Press, Inc., 1968).

15. Neil Gilbert, Henry Miller, Harry Specht, *Introduction to Social Work Practice* (Englewood Cliffs, N.J.: Prentice-Hall, Inc., 1980), pp. 26–27.

16. *Ibid.*

17. Irving Piliavin, "Restructuring the Provision of Social Service," *Social Work*, 13:1 (January 1968).

18. Martin Rein, "Social Work in Search of a Radical Profession," *Social Work*, 15:2 (April 1970), pp. 13–28.

19. *Ibid.*, p. 27.

20. Harry Specht, "The Deprofessionalization of Social Work," *Social Work*, 17:2 (March 1972), pp. 3–15.

21. For example, *Social Case Work: Generic and Specific: A Report on the Milford Conference* (Washington, D.C.: National Association of Social Workers, 1974, reprint of 1929 ed.); Ernest V. Hollis and Alice L. Taylor, *Social Work Education in the United States* (New York: Columbia University Press, 1951); Subcommittee on the Working Definition of Social Work Practice for the Commission on Social Work Practice, National Association of Social Workers, "Working Definition of Social Work Practice," as printed in Harriett M. Bartlett, "Toward Clarification and Improvement of Social Work Practice," *Social Work*, 3 (April 1958), pp. 5–9; Werner W. Boehm, *Objectives of the Social Work Curriculum of the Future* (New York: Council on Social Work Education, 1959).

22. The 1976 effort is reported in *Social Work*, 22:5 (September 1977). The 1979 follow-up will be reported in *Social Work* (forthcoming 1980).

# 22   Current Models of Social Work Practice

NEIL GILBERT and HARRY SPECHT

Do models make a difference? That is, does a particular conception of practice determine how a professional will deal with a problem? This is an important question for students, who invest a great deal in their education and who have every right to wonder whether discussion of models is of practical use or merely an academic exercise. And, if it is of practical use, they will want to know how to choose the best model.

A thoughtful response to the question must be somewhat equivocal: models make *some* difference. Currently, there are several models of social work practice. Each attempts to deal with the duality of social work in a different way. This duality refers to the two components of the profession's concern: providing direct services to people in need, and managing the institution of social welfare. The duality of the profession and how to deal with it has been a recurrent theme in the literature throughout the profession's history. Variations on this theme include the following: In 1905 Richmond (1917) wrote of the "wholesale" and "retail" methods of social reform; probably the best-known and most enduring variation was composed by Lee (1937) under the title of "cause" and "function"; Burns (1958) wrote about the distinction between "social work" and "social welfare"; Schwartz (1963) discussed the "service" and the "movement"; Richan (1972) identified underlying language systems in social work; and Gilbert and Specht (1974), declaring the profession to be "incomplete," called for a more balanced and integrated approach to the profession's two sides, "social work" and "social welfare."

The following paragraph is the introduction to a case reported by a social worker at Mobilization for Youth (MFY), an agency organized to provide comprehensive social services to a community on the Lower East Side of New York City:

Mrs. Smith came to an MFY Neighborhood Service Center to complain that there had been no gas, electricity, heat, or hot water in her apartment house for more than four weeks. She asked the agency for help. Mrs. Smith was twenty-three-years-old and the mother of four children, three of whom had been born out of wedlock. At the time, she was unmarried and receiving Aid to Families with Dependent Children. She came to the center in desperation because she was unable to run her household without utilities. Her financial resources were exhausted [Purcell and Specht, 1965, p. 10].

How would different models of social work practice affect a worker's way of helping Mrs. Smith?

If the traditional model of practice were used, the outcome of Mrs. Smith's request for help would depend on which department she had gone to at MFY. Since she had come into the Neighborhood Service Center, which was staffed by caseworkers, the worker (largely through interaction with Mrs. Smith in a series of interviews) would try to help her use her resources to deal with her situation. An advocacy-oriented social caseworker would help Mrs. Smith deal with the institutions that were affecting her situation. Had Mrs. Smith turned up at one of the many group work agencies in the community, the worker probably would have sought to help her through the relevant social group of which she was a part—the tenants who lived in the same apartment house, all of whom were experiencing some of the same problems. And if Mrs. Smith had gone to one of the several community organization agencies on the Lower East Side, the workers there probably would have focused on the agencies and institutions that were part of this problem: the housing agencies, the health department, the welfare department, and so forth.

Why do social workers in different agencies respond so differently? First of all, the workers are not necessarily perceiving the problem differently; rather, there may be any number of problems operating in this situation. Mrs. Smith does need help. To determine what kind of help she needs will require some exploration. Perhaps this woman is in this situation because she is emotionally overwhelmed with her family responsibilities; therefore, intensive counseling might be indicated. Or interventions that focus on Mrs. Smith as an individual may be inappropriate. Possibly her problem is not unique; rather, she may be one member of a group of people in the same predicament because they share the same social-emotional problems. Perhaps they are vulnerable young women who are exploited by men and might profit from an opportunity to explore their social-emotional experiences and provide strength to one another to change. Or perhaps the economics of housing and the regulations of the housing and welfare agencies may have forced Mrs. Smith into this situation. Perhaps the laws and/or the ways in which social agencies function ought to be changed. If that is so, Mrs. Smith and her fellow tenants ought not to be bothered with counseling, group work, or any other kind of intervention that stops short of institutional change.

Another reason why different social workers might respond differently to Mrs. Smith's problems is much simpler to state. Mrs. Smith may be searching for a particular *kind* of help. *She* may want some sort of therapeutic counseling so that she can change. Or she may want some help that enables her, along with her fellow tenants, to try to change some of the elements external to her situation. Or, she may not be interested in changing herself or in being involved in changing other institutions. Perhaps she is interested only in bringing her *situation* to the attention of the agency, in the hope that some way can be found to make her life more bearable by changing laws and agency regulations. Thus, *what the client wants is variable.* Part of a social worker's job is to understand what the client wants, for we can help people do only what *they* want to do.

Finally, social welfare agencies are organized to offer different kinds of help to people with problems. Whether the agency is public or voluntary, it will have written in law or in the bylaws of the agency a "charge" that will direct and limit the services the professional can offer. Thus, one agency is charged to offer counseling services, another to offer group services, and still another to engage in social planning.

The strongest argument for the traditional approach is that social workers trained in one of these three specializations acquire an in-depth knowledge about one kind of practice that they can deliver with a high degree of skill. The major argument against this approach is that it is too narrow and tends to develop practitioners who are too clinical, in the sense that they are consumed by their interest in searching out knowledge about the refined details of a specialized form of practice and unable to understand the interacting and complex social forces that create social problems for people.

The generalist approach (sometimes called the "unitary" or "integrated" approach) is based on the view that most social problems involve a variety of social systems.* Whether articulated or not, all generalist approaches are based on social systems theory. With social systems theory, all kinds of social units are conceived of as *systems* subject to the *same* rules or behavior. Any system has an internal organization that comprises subsystems and is related to other systems in its environment. For example, an individual may be conceived of as a system made up of various physical and emotional subsystems. The individual is related to other individual systems and is a subsystem of larger systems such as the family, the social group, and the occupational group. A social group can be viewed as a system comprising individuals and subgroups who constitute its subsystems; it is a subsystem of a larger system such as an organization or the community. For example, the group of tenants mentioned above is a subsystem of the housing system in New York City, and the housing

---

*Generic practice had reference only to social casework. It established basic underlying principles for casework practice regardless of the functional area involved. The generalist approach establishes basic underlying principles for practice regardless of the size and composition of the client system; that is, regardless of whether the client is an individual, a family, an organization, or a community.

system is a subsystem of the entire ecopolitical system of New York City. Of course, there is more to systems theory than this brief summary statement suggests. It is á complex theory that developed in the physical sciences and later was applied to the social sciences (Bartlett, 1970; Goldstein, 1973; Pincus and Minahan, 1973). The interested reader may want to consult Churchman's (1968) *The Systems Approach* for a more detailed and nontechnical explanation or Emery's (1969) *Systems Theory Thinking* for some of the technical aspects.

In the case of Mrs. Smith, the MFY workers used the generalist approach to the problem. As they stated it:

> Too often, the client system presenting the problem becomes the major target for intervention, and the intervention method is limited to the one most suitable for that client system. However, Mrs. Smith and the other tenants had a multitude of problems emanating from many sources, any one of which would have warranted the attention of a social agency.... MFY's approach to the problem was to obtain knowledge of the various social systems within which the social problem was located (that is, social systems assessment); knowledge of the various methods (including nonsocial work methods) appropriate for intervention in these different social systems; and knowledge of the resources available to the agency.
>
> The difficulties of the families in the building were intricately connected with other elements of the social system related to the housing problem. For example, seven different public agencies were involved in maintenance of building services. Later, other agencies were involved in relocating the tenants. There is no one agency in New York City that handles all housing problems. Therefore, tenants have little hope for getting help on their own. In order to redress a grievance relating to water supply (which was only one of the building's problems) it is necessary to know precisely which city department to contact. The following is only a partial listing:
>
> No water—Health Department
> Not enough water—Department of Water Supply
> No hot water—Buildings Department
> Water leaks—Buildings Department
> Large water leaks—Department of Water Supply
> Water overflowing from apartment above—Police Department
> Water sewage in the cellar—Sanitation Department
> [Purcell and Specht, 1965, p. 72].

Systems theory provides a good orienting perspective for social workers. However, once this dynamic perspective is adopted, systems theory does not provide specific enough guidelines for professional practice. At a high level of generalization, we can think of all organisms (for example, individuals, groups, organizations) as systems. But in practice, individual systems are considerably different from group systems, and each of these is different from organizational and political systems. More middle-range kinds of theories are necessary for day-to-day practice with each of these systems.

The generalist approach does not provide sufficient instruction about which parts of the person and the environment the worker should attend to first. This is a very important question for social workers, who usually work in agencies in which resources are limited. Also, the generalist approach, in attempting to cull common elements of all practice, ascends to conceptual levels that obscure real and important differences. For example, broadly speaking, it may be correct to say that all social workers require knowledge and skills in data collection and assessment. But the data collection skills of the social worker conducting a community-needs survey bear only faint resemblance to those of the caseworker attempting to assess the personal difficulties of individual clients. And though the MFY approach was generalist, the actual help that was given to Mrs. Smith, the other families, and the community was provided by a number of specialists—caseworkers, group workers, and community organizers (Purcell and Specht, 1965). Thus, the major utility of social systems theory, as stated earlier, is that it provided an orienting perspective for the professionals, leading them to achieve a higher degree of coordination in their efforts than otherwise would have been the case.

The problem and population-group approaches to practice are somewhat like the generalist approach, but they call for specialization along functional area lines. With this kind of approach, the attention of practitioners is focused on a specific problem, such as community mental health, or a specific population group, such as the aged; and practitioners attempt to see the *whole* experience and the *entire* social environment in which these problems and population groups exist. Thus, in work with the aged, the social worker must be able to deal with the developmental problems of aging persons, have skill in utilizing therapeutic modes of working with individuals and groups, and use community organization methods to change institutional practices. This approach presents the segmentation of effort that occurs in methodological specializations; at the same time, it allows for an in-depth development of knowledge and skill in respect to the clients served. If this approach had been used in the case of Mrs. Smith, the "ideal" social work professional would be an expert on problems of housing: housing agencies; the economics of housing; the various groups confronting housing problems; the social-psychological aspects of relocation, redevelopment, and urban renewal; and so forth.

While we should not hold too strong a brief against this kind of specialization, neither is there sufficient basis for seeing it as a major organizing principle by which to educate students for the profession. One reservation is that most concerns of social workers are not bounded clearly by populations or problems. Aged people, minority groups, and children have many similar problems—income maintenance, housing, employment, and so forth; and these problems are not all that different for each group. Furthermore, an individual's social problems—such as housing, employment, and family relations —usually are not discrete. Populations that have any one of these problems frequently suffer from a host of associated problems.

Another shortcoming of this approach is that it locks students into a specialization too early in a professional career. Specializations in practice should be selected only after the student attains a broad understanding of the field of social work and social welfare. In addition, this is a questionable approach to career development even from the long-range view. Social problems and population groups are not static. Over the last twenty years social work and social welfare have changed in response to changes in the larger society. A good professional is one who questions given truths, tests new ideas, and has a demonstrated capacity to change and grow rather than one who has a fixed approach and a static view of society. For these reasons, we tend not to favor specializations that are too narrow.

Another model of social work practice—the model supported in this chapter—divides practice into direct and indirect services. *Direct services* are the specific and concrete activities in which professionals engage to help those who are experiencing social problems. These activities include therapy, counseling, education, advocacy, information gathering, referral, and those aspects of community organization in which direct services are provided to community groups and organizations. *Indirect services* focus on the institution of social welfare. Included here are professional social work activities such as planning, policy analysis, program development, administration, and program evaluation. The social worker engaged in provision of indirect services usually does not deal directly with people in need but, rather, focuses on the institutional structure through which services are provided. If the social workers in the MFY example of Mrs. Smith had utilized the direct- and indirect-services approach, one or more of the workers in the agency probably would have been prepared to provide the services needed to work directly with Mrs. Smith and the other tenants. (These professionals would have a mastery of knowledge and skill dealing with the dynamics of interpersonal relationships.) And one or more of the workers would have had the knowledge and skill for indirect work, such as research on housing, analysis of the organizational and legislative arrangements that caused the problems, and planning policies and programs to prevent similar situations. (These practitioners would have knowledge and skill related to organizational and political systems and technical abilities for managing, manipulating, and analyzing large amounts of information.)

In summary, the traditional casework-group work-community organization approach prematurely splits interactional knowledge into three specializations and does not establish for the student a sufficient basis for development of technical knowledge and skill for planning, administration, and policy analysis. In contrast, the generalist approach and the problem and population-group approaches require that the practitioner be able to deal with direct- and indirect-service tasks equally well—which, in our view, demands too much of the practitioner. Systems theory, we believe, does not provide knowledge that is specific enough to do all these tasks. Moreover, the practitioner is likely to become a jack-of-all-trades and master of none. The direct- and indirect-services approach avoids both of these pitfalls; further, it provides a logical organization of practice knowledge.

## GENERALIST AND SPECIALIST CONTENT
## AT DIFFERENT EDUCATIONAL LEVELS

The various levels of competence in practice and the knowledge elements that should be learned at each of these levels are summarized in Table 22–1. On the vertical axis, three levels of competence are listed: (1) *orientation*—the level at which the student acquires a perspective on the profession of social work and the institution of social welfare; (2) *development of in-depth knowledge and skill*—the level at which one acquires somewhat specialized and focused knowledge for practice; (3) *synthesis*—the level at which one develops and synthesizes new knowledge for practice. (These levels of practice are not clearly associated with specific educational degrees. Schools of social work in the United States vary considerably regarding how much of this content is presented at the undergraduate, graduate, and doctoral levels of education. Most BSW programs would include the teaching of a good deal of material that we have allocated to second-level learning. At most schools, six years are needed to complete the BSW and MSW degrees. A few schools, however, have established five-year programs. It should be remembered, too, that there is no reason to assume that people acquire these different levels of proficiency through formal education only. Some persons work their way to higher levels of professional achievement on the job and through independent study.)

The horizontal axis of Table 22–1 indicates the general content at each level of competence and the content specific to the direct and

TABLE 22–1

Educational Content for Different Levels of Competence
in Social Work Practice

| | Types of Educational Content | | |
|---|---|---|---|
| Competence Level | Specific Content for Direct Services | General Content | Specific Content for Indirect Services |
| 1. Orientation: Perspective on social work and social welfare | | a. practice for direct and indirect services<br>b. social welfare policies and programs | |
| 2. Development of in-depth knowledge and skill | a. human growth and development<br>b. social welfare policy<br>c. direct-service methods (that is, counseling)<br>d. research (application of) | knowledge about problems and population groups | a. human growth and development<br>b. social welfare policy<br>c. indirect-service methods (that is, social planning, administration)<br>d. research (for program evaluation, needs assessment, policy analysis) |
| 3. Synthesis: Development of knowledge for social work and social welfare | | knowledge and skill for research, consultation, teaching and training | |

indirect services at each level. At the first level of competence, two bodies of *general* content should be covered: (a) an introduction to social work practice and (b) an introduction to social welfare policies and programs. (By general content, we mean material that *all* social workers should master at the respective level of competence.) Both of these bodies of content are the congruent elements that link the direct and indirect services of the profession, providing a unified foundation for professional identity. These elements are the institutional context of social welfare, social work's mission within that institution, shared professional values, and a perspective on the broad range of functions carried out by social workers.

At the second level of competence, there are four bodies of *specific* content and one body of *general* content that social workers should master in preparation for work in the direct or indirect services. The *specific* content includes (a) human growth and development, (b) social welfare policy, (c) social work methods, and (d) research methods and techniques. One would expect to see differences in the kinds of knowledge included in each of these areas in education for the direct and indirect services, respectively. For example, knowledge of human growth and development is most useful for direct-service practitioners when it illuminates the dynamics of interpersonal interaction. But for indirect-service workers this knowledge is most useful when the worker can apply it in the design, implementation, and evaluation of programs. The sources of this knowledge for both kinds of workers are the same, but the way in which it is packaged and applied is different for each. The *general* knowledge area for second-level competence is knowledge about problems and population groups (knowledge that *all* professionals who choose to work in these fields should have). These kindred targets of concern at this level of competence afford another congruent element that binds into one profession social workers in the direct and indirect services. (The four specific areas mentioned are required content areas for all MSW programs accredited by the Council on Social Work Education. "Problems and Population Groups" has not been defined as a separate content area in social work education. These kinds of courses are most likely to be given as electives in the social policy or human growth and development content areas.)

At the third level of competence, the knowledge requirements, for the most part, are *general*. Professionals who will be in the business of synthesizing and developing new knowledge require primarily the development of skills for teaching, consulting with other professionals, and doing research on all the bodies of knowledge described for the first and second levels of competence.

In an ideal model of education for social work practice, skills and knowledge would be organized into circumscribed areas that possess internal coherence and maintain a logical relationship to the whole. To a certain degree, the three-level model of competence outlined above captures these qualities. The first-level general orientation to social work practice and social welfare provides an internal coherence for all other training. These congruent elements cement the relationship of direct and indirect services to the whole of social work practice. This relationship is reinforced by the problem and population-group knowledge at the second level. But the model is not ideal. Conceptually, the congruent elements may contain too much water and not enough gravel to cement the model firmly. And, while efforts are under way to define an orienting generic base for the direct and indirect services, the task of developing the elements of these practice specializations in detail is far from complete.

## REFERENCES

Bartlett, H. M. *The Common Base of Social Work Practice.* Washington, D.C.: National Association of Social Workers, 1970.

Burns, E. "Social Work [sic] Is our Commitment." In *The Social Welfare Forum,* 1958. New York: Columbia University Press, 1958.

Churchman, C. W. *The Systems Approach.* New York: Dell, 1968.

Emery, F. E. (Ed.) *Systems Theory Thinking: Selected Readings.* New York: Penguin Books, 1969.

Gilbert, N., and Specht, H. "The Incomplete Profession." *Social Work,* 1974, 19, 665–74.

Goldstein, H. *Social Work Practice: A Unitary Approach.* Columbia: University of South Carolina Press, 1973.

Lee, P. *Social Work as Cause and Function and Other Papers.* New York: Columbia University Press, 1937.

Pincus, A., and Minahan, A. *Social Work Practice: Model and Method.* Itasca, Ill.: Peacock, 1973.

Purcell, F. P., and Specht, H. "The House on Sixth Street." *Social Work,* 1965, 10, 69–76.

Richan, W. C. "A Common Language for Social Work." *Social Work,* 1972, 17, 14–22.

Richmond, M. *Social Diagnosis.* New York: Russell Sage Foundation, 1917. (Rev. ed., 1930.)

Schwartz, W. "Small Group Science and Group Work Practice." *Social Work,* 1963, 8, 39–46.

# 23   Casework Effectiveness: A New Look at the Research Evidence

## KATHERINE M. WOOD

In recent years writers have questioned repeatedly whether casework, the major practice method of the social work profession, is "dead" (Briar, 1967 and 1968; and Fischer, 1973b). In Fischer's two surveys of research studies relating to the effectiveness of casework and group work intervention, he answered his own question, "Is

Reprinted with permission of author and NASW from *Social Work,* 23:6 (November 1978), pp. 437–58. Copyright 1978, National Association of Social Workers, Inc.

casework effective?" with a resounding "No" (1973a and 1976). A number of other analysts, however, have concluded that a sweeping generalization to that effect cannot be inferred from the data of the research studies themselves (Hudson, 1974; Geismar, 1972; Perlman, 1968; Berleman, 1976; Polemis, 1976; Gyarfas and Nee, 1973; and Alexander and Siman, 1973).

The basic assumption of this paper is that, as a number of writers have pointed out, attempting to find global answers to global questions such as whether casework is effective makes little sense as a research endeavor in itself. (Geismar, 1972; Hudson, 1976; and Cohen, 1976). As in any research effort, the question to be studied must be formulated in much sharper and more concrete terms, or the researcher risks going beyond the data and instead basing conclusions on personal opinion and polemics. Furthermore, the profession can do little more than become defensive and confused in reaction to such global charges of ineffectiveness since they offer little contribution to developing and improving practice.

The problem may be more usefully posed by such questions as: What can direct practitioners of social work learn from research evaluating practice outcomes? Why was the intervention successful or unsuccessful? What propositions, prescriptions, and proscriptions of practice theory have been validated, invalidated, or modified? What has been added to the empirical base of practice theory? The "study of studies" to be reported in this article departs from earlier analyses in that it was conducted from the standpoint of social work practice and the practitioner, focusing on questions relevant to practice theory such as these.

## SURVEY OF THE LITERATURE

A survey of the literature from 1956 through 1973 located a total of fifty-three studies of the effectiveness of social work direct practice. As a result of a preliminary analysis, twenty-two research projects met the study's criteria of (1) investigating the outcome of direct-practice intervention, (2) having been done under social work auspices or having social work intervention as a major component, (3) having been conducted in the continental United States, and (4) meeting commonly accepted canons of methodological adequacy for experimental or quasi-experimental research. For the latter criterion, a control, comparison, or contrast group had to be utilized in the research design. Projects that utilized as the intervenors social workers who were not at the master's level were included, since many social work practitioners, particularly in large public agencies, have not had graduate-level social work education. Also, the author was interested in comparing MSW practitioners with non-MSWs as to their effectiveness in practice. The twenty-two studies surveyed, some of which were reported in more than one publication, are listed in Tables 23–1 to 23–5 [the five tables in] this article.

The adequacy of these studies as research efforts was intensely analyzed and evaluated according to an eighteen-page instrument that was developed by the author and extensively pretested by a panel of master's and doctoral social work students. The instrument addressed such questions as how well the research problem was conceptualized; how clearly the independent and dependent variables were identified; the adequacy of the research design in measuring those variables and in controlling the independent and intervening variables; the degree of sophistication concerning the impact of the organizational context in which service took place on both workers and clients; adequacy of methods of data collection and data analysis, including statistical tests; and the degree to which the researchers' conclusions were based on the empirical findings.

Since the study's major interest was in what these research projects had added to (or subtracted from) the theory that informs practice in a variety of problem areas, the studies were grouped according to whether their major focus was on service to a particular group of clients (see Tables 23–1 to 23–4) or on the outcomes of different modes of intervention (see Table 23–5). Some studies fell into more than one category, but each appears in only one table. Please see tables for specific dates of studies discussed, and see Bibliography for full reference information.

## STUDIES OF DELINQUENCY

The evidence of the research projects summarized in Table 23–1 regarding the effectiveness of practice with delinquent clients leads to the same preliminary conclusion as that arrived at by Fischer: the casework and group work practiced in these studies was not very effective. Only one of the six studies reported a positive outcome, that by Webb and Riley, but this was a methodologically weak study. None of these studies defined precisely the interventive variables— "casework," "group work," or "psychotherapy"—a major failing that was also found in most of the other studies to be considered later. The studies are therefore severely limited in their usefulness for practice because the reader has no way of telling specifically what the social worker did. In general, however, the outcomes of these studies indicates that group work or psychotherapeutically oriented casework, used alone or as the major intervention, have not been effective in preventing or ameliorating delinquency.

TABLE 23–1
Summaries of Studies of Delinquency

| Author | Setting | Clients | Number of Subjects | | Sample | Major Intervention | Measures of Dependent Variable | Outcome |
|---|---|---|---|---|---|---|---|---|
| | | | Experimental | Control | | | | |
| Berleman & Steinburn (1967, 1968); Berleman, Seaberg, and Steinburn (1972) | Seattle, Washington: settlement house | Primarily black lower-class delinquent seventh-grade boys | 52 | 50 | Random and matching | Primarily group work by MSWs; some individual casework and work with parents; average of 342 contacts with boy and his family over 1–2 years | Police and school disciplinary records | No significant difference |
| Craig and Furst (1965) | New York City: Board of Education Child Guidance Clinic | First grade boys with risk of delinquency according to Glueck Scale | 29 | 29 | Matching | Casework and psychotherapy with children and mothers by clinic professionals; some home visits and concrete services; median contact 50 months | Annual teachers' judgments and delinquency rates | No significant difference |
| Meyer, Borgatta, and Jones (1965) | New York City: Youth Consultation Service (social agency) | Vocational high school girls identified as predelinquent; mixed ethnicity and economic status | 189 | 192 | Random | Initially individual–casework by MSWs, later emphasis on group work; median 17 contacts, but almost half had less; average intensity less than once a month | Personality and sociometric ratings; school attendance and grades; judgments of teachers, workers, and clients | No significant difference |

| Study | Setting | N (exp.) | N (control) | Assignment | Treatment | Measures | Results |
|---|---|---|---|---|---|---|---|
| Miller (1957, 1959, 1962) | Boston, Massachusetts: streets, homes, school | 205 (7 gangs) | 172 (11 gangs) | Matching | Street corner group work with gangs by MSWs; 3.5 contacts per week over 10 to 34 months | Legal offenses; other disapproved behavior; arrests, court appearances, incarceration | Increase in major offenses by males in experimental group, especially younger boys |
| Tait and Hodges (1962) | Washington, D.C.: Maximum Benefits Program | 108 | 57 | Matching | Casework and psychotherapy with children, some with families, usually mothers, by team of MSWs and graduate students; minimal contact with children (4.5 interviews), moderate contact with mothers (10.9 interviews) over 11 months | Police or court involvement | Experimental group more delinquent than controls |
| Webb and Riley (1970) | Pasadena, California: family service agency | 26 | 32 | Random | Primarily individual casework; some work with husbands; more intensive service than regular agency caseload | MMPI; semantic differential; police involvement; probation officers' judgments | Positive personality change of experimental group; better probation reports |

a For full references, see bibliography at end of article.

## Group Work

Particularly throughout the 1950s and 1960s, group work was considered the interventive method of choice for social work as well as for other disciplines interested in adolescent delinquency. Based on the concept from developmental psychology that adolescence is a life stage oriented to the peer group, it was hypothesized that intervention making use of group processes was the way to reach and change delinquent teenagers. Furthermore, it was assumed that intervention in the natural groups of adolescents, such as street gangs, would be the most effective approach, on the premise that skilled group workers, through their relationships with the gang members, could change the delinquency-oriented culture of the gang to one that was more law-abiding in its values, attitudes, and behavior. However, studies by Miller, by Berleman and his associates, and by Meyer, Borgatta, and Jones found no significant differences in outcome between the youngsters treated by group work techniques and their controls. (The latter study of *The Girls at Vocational High* was widely reported as an example of ineffective casework, although the primary intervention was actually group work.)

Furthermore, there is some evidence that the group approach may have had an iatrogenically deteriorative effect when used with younger boys and work with natural gangs. Miller found in his study that major offenses by younger boys in the experimental program actually increased when compared to offenses by the untreated controls (1962, p. 181). Involvement of younger children in programs to combat delinquency may have had the inadvertent effect of solidifying their own and others' tentative perception of them as delinquents. In addition, the interaction of younger boys with more sophisticated older delinquents in the treatment program may have provided them with role models and an education in delinquency. This is a conclusion reached by researchers on delinquency from other disciplines. For example, Empey and Erickson state that for younger offenders "the less intensive a program is, the more effective it may be" (1972, p. 235). Klein also found that increased cohesion in the natural gangs, stimulated by the presence of the professional, was accompanied by an increase, not a decrease, in delinquent behavior (1971, p. 239). Empey and Erickson concluded that adult sponsorship of adolescent gangs may serve only to reinforce deviant values and behavior and recommended that "nothing should be done, therefore, to make them more cohesive" (1972, p. 74).

## Casework

Casework fared no better in studies of delinquency. The Tait and Hodges project seemed to have defined casework primarily as a form of verbal psychotherapy with children and their mothers, as did the Craig and Furst study. The latter adds a brief note that the workers also "reached out" to the families and engaged in such other activities as brokerage and advocacy, but the quantity and quality of these activities are not detailed. The Webb and Riley study also seems to have relied exclusively on verbal interviews with the delinquent young women and, occasionally, with their husbands. The Tait and Hodges study of the effect of psychotherapeutic casework alone, like some of the group work studies, found the experimental group to be more delinquent than the controls after the treatment period. Craig and Furst report no significant differences between the treated and untreated groups on measures of delinquency. This study was one of the methodologically weaker ones because the control group used was not comparable to the experimental group.

Webb and Riley were the only researchers to report positive changes in the treatment group; however, this study was also, as noted earlier, methodologically weak because of the failure to report any statistical analyses of the behavioral correlates used as an outcome measure and the contaminating knowledge of the probation officers who served as judges of whether the subjects had been in experimental or control groups. Also, this project dealt with a somewhat different client group than the other studies of delinquency since the clients were young adults rather than adolescents.

## What Went Wrong

Perhaps the best conclusion the practitioner-reader can draw from the mixed results of these less-than-rigorous studies is something like this: "No matter what else I do with delinquent adolescents, I probably should not 'do' group work. It is likely to be ineffectual at best and harmful at worst. It has not been demonstrated whether psychotherapeutically oriented casework consisting primarily of talking interviews focused on feelings and the development of insight is effective with delinquent clients, but existing evidence suggests that this is not the best approach either."

These are useful, albeit depressing conclusions, but they are not useful enough; they give the practitioner no guidance concerning what to do differently or better. But closer analysis of the research projects does offer some clues about what went wrong with the interventions in these projects. None of the studies began with the adolescents' own perceptions of what their problems were and what help they needed. Rather, the researchers and practitioners involved in these studies appeared to start with their own theoretical and ideological orientations, which they applied to their clients like a magic formula. They did not explore and assess the problems being experienced by individual clients; instead, the professionals assumed that they knew what ailed their young clients and what was good for them. The intervention did not grow out of a contract between helpers and helped concerning problems and goals that were meaningful to the clients. Thus there could be no investment in or commitment to change on the part of the clients, that is, no "motivation." With no agreed-on problem areas for work and no contracted goals, neither clients nor workers could have been clear about what was the clients' share of the change task and what was the workers' responsibility. The intervention applied bore no clear conceptual or logical connection to the problems in these adolescents' lives. How could a group experience or the provision of "insight" be expected to change the reality problems these disadvantaged young clients were struggling with? In these projects, any intervention directed to the reality needs of the clients was only a sideline to the "real" treatment of group or individual therapy.

Both the Miller and the Berleman et al. projects claimed to be "system-oriented," but an analysis of the intervention offered indicates that they were anything but that. Attention to aspects of the adolescents' lives other than interaction with their peer group was given theoretical lip service, not focused intervention. The Miller study may be more open to criticism on these grounds than the others, since this project made a commitment to interventions "directed at three of the societal units seen to figure importantly in the perpetuation of delinquent behavior—the community, the family, and the gang" (1962, p. 169). However, the actual intervention was focused primarily on group interaction processes. The same criticism of failing to consider all the relevant variables in the problem situation can be directed at the casework interventions described in these studies. The workers who focused casework only on intrapsychic variables generally met with the same poor results as the workers who focused only on group interaction variables.

## STUDIES OF CHILDREN

The four studies located that dealt with interventions in the problems of preadolescent children and met the research criteria are summarized in Table 23–2. Two of those considered in the group of delinquency studies, Tait and Hodges and Craig and Furst, also belong in this category since they focused on preventing later delinquency by intervention with children while they are young.

The McCabe et al. study was not concerned specifically with preventing later delinquency but with improving the "ego capacities"

TABLE 23–2
Summary of Studies of Intervention with Children[a]

| Author[b] | Setting | Clients | Number of Subjects | | Sample | Major Intervention | Measures of Dependent Variable | Outcome |
|---|---|---|---|---|---|---|---|---|
| | | | Experimental | Control | | | | |
| Levitt (1957); Levitt, Beiser, and Robertson (1959) | Chicago: Illinois Institute for Juvenile Research (child guidance clinic) | Follow up study of children and mothers who had received at least 5 treatment interviews from 1944–1954; average age 10½; 69 percent male | 237 | 93 | Random from pool of all such cases and from contact; "defectors", groups later matched on a number of variables | Casework and psychotherapy; 76 percent of individuals seen by MSW staff, rest by other professionals and graduate students; average number of interviews 18; usually mother and child or mother only | Psychological tests; objective indexes such as school completion; evaluations of adjustment by parents, children, and inter viewers | Only significant difference was that treated group liked school more but was more anxious |
| McCabe et al. (1967) | New York City: Community Service Society (large family service agency) | Intellectually gifted but socially deprived children of both sexes, aged 7–11; mixed ethnicity, mostly Black and Puerto Rican | 42 | 25 | Matching and random | Weekly group work over period of 18–24 months with children and bimonthly group work with parents by "trained and experienced" group work staff | 58 indicators including Ego Functioning Scale, academic achievement tests, family functioning | Controls increased more in general functioning; more subjects in experimental group decreased in general functioning; only positive results for treated group were that Black subjects improved significantly in reading and soundness of judgment, and Puerto Rican subjects general improvement was greater than controls |

[a]Two of the studies on delinquency, Tait and Hodges and Craig and Furst, also fall in this category. (See Table 23–1.)
[b]For full references, see bibliography at end of article.

of bright but poor children living in a slum environment. It is difficult to comprehend why the researchers chose a peer group experience to accomplish this rather than interventive efforts directed at softening the impact of an environment identified as "pathogenic" or at providing more intellectually stimulating educational experiences than were available to these children in a ghetto public school.

The most important finding of this study was that the majority of the children were doing quite well, not as a result of the professional intervention, but as a result of the ability of their families to provide for the youngsters' development of "ego capacities" despite their environment. The study might have been more useful if it explored what there was about these families that helped their children succeed when other families were destroyed by the ghetto. For example, why did Puerto Rican children in the experimental group make more gains than the controls, while Black children, by and large, did not? Exploration of such questions might have been more useful in resolving basic practice issues, such as how and when to intervene and with whom, than the by-now familiar finding that there is no magic in the formed-group experience.

Unlike the other studies in this group, which were field research into ongoing treatment, the project of Levitt and his associates was a retrospective study of treatment given over the preceding ten years to preadolescents in a child guidance clinic. The researchers went to great lengths to locate treated and "defector" cases—those clients who decided to withdraw from the clinic before receiving any treatment interviews—and to match the two groups on a number of variables. They found no significant differences between them. Defectors from treatment are, however, inherently different from clients who decide to continue. Were these children healthier, were their presenting problems less severe or their families better able to cope? In light of the children's subsequent fairly good adjustment, perhaps the parents were right and the clinic wrong in their differing perceptions of whether the children needed professional treatment.

If the researchers had done within-group analyses (which few of the studies reviewed did), their findings would be more useful. The two groups were matched on initial diagnoses, but in child guidance parlance this usually refers to an assessment of such characteristics as intrapsychic conflict or development of ego capacities, not to the child's specific problem. Thus, the reader does not know the distribution of presenting problems within the two groups—for example, how many children were enuretics, how many were nonlearners, or how many were aggressive. Did as many of the bed wetters in the untreated group get over this difficulty as the enuretics who received treatment? Did the nonlearners who had no treatment improve their school performance as much as the treated children, or did both groups continue to do poorly in school?

In other words, it would have been more useful for this study to have focused on the different kinds of children, families, problems, professionals, approaches, and techniques involved, and how different combinations of these factors affected whether the children benefited from treatment. A finding that the untreated group of bed wetters did as well as the treated children might contribute information about enuresis in developing children, the necessity of treating this symptom, and the ability of families themselves to help children get over the problem. If, on the other hand, overaggressive children were found to become less aggressive as a result of treatment, this would be valuable knowledge, but even more specific information would be needed. What kinds of aggressive children from what kinds of families in what kinds of social circumstances did better in treatment? If children treated by a particular social worker did better than those treated by a psychiatrist, what did these practitioners do differently, and how did it affect the outcome?

As it stands, the Levitt study as well as the other three studies of intervention into children's problems are of little pragmatic value for the field. Like many of the other studies reviewed, this research leaves practitioners depressed and defensive, feeling nothing they have been doing is useful or effective, but does not tell them anything about how to make their practice more effective. There is no way to put this research to use in practice. The studies present only negative evidence to indicate that neither a formed-group experience nor one-to-one insight-oriented therapy is effective *in itself* in changing the course of children's problems.

The most important questions these studies raise are the ones that the researchers did not address. What kinds of children's problems need direct professional intervention focused specifically on the child and his or her problem? For which problems should the focus, instead, be on teaching the parents specific techniques for dealing with the troublesome behavior? For what kinds of children's problems should the focus be on the functioning of the family as a system rather than on the child alone? Which problems require attempts to change the environment rather than attempts to change the child or the family? It cannot be emphasized too strongly that the basic issue for both practice and research is to determine the approaches and the techniques that, when used by professionals in different settings, produce the best results with different types of clients, depending on the kinds of families, natural groups, and social circumstances the clients come from and the different problems in living they have.

Practitioners worked with parents in all four of these studies, but they were seen separately from their children and as individual clients. However, the problems of one family member, particularly a child, are intimately connected with and may be an expression of problems in the transactions of the family system. Perhaps the children's problems should have been perceived in this way and interventive efforts focused on the family setting in which the problem was occurring. Perhaps the problems should have been defined as the effects of poverty and the interventions directed at ameliorating some of the harsh realities with which the children and parents were struggling rather than at trying to change what went on inside their heads.

As in the delinquency studies, the negative outcomes encountered in the research on intervention with children may be partly related to the narrow manner in which presenting problems were defined. All these projects seem to have started from an assumption that because the child had a problem, the problem was primarily inside the child. There is then a quasi logic to the corollary that intervention should be focused inside the child, rather than on real situations in the child's life that may require the problem behavior. The negative outcomes may also have resulted from setting the intervention in advance, regardless of the kinds of problems to be treated and the kinds of people who had them. McCabe et al. decided in advance that social group work should be the intervention without an adequate rationale for why a group experience would better enable bright children to use their intellectual abilities than intervention focused on improving their educational stimulation. The clinics involved in the other three studies were in the business of dispensing a particular service—insight-oriented psychotherapy—to all clients, regardless of individual differences among them and their problems. In all the projects, the goals of treatment were global and amorphous—for example, "development of ego capacities"—and no clear and logical connection was spelled out between the goals and the problems under consideration. Thus, the findings that the interventions were ineffective are not surprising.

## STUDIES OF THE POOR

Recipients of public welfare and other clientele of programs to aid the poor were studied extensively during the 1960s. Nine studies were identified that dealt with this client group and met the research criteria. (See Table 23–3.)

TABLE 23–3
Summary of Studies of Clients of Poverty Programs

| Author[a] | Setting | Clients | Number of Subjects | | Sample | Major Intervention | Measures of Dependent Variable | Outcome |
|---|---|---|---|---|---|---|---|---|
| | | | Experimental | Control | | | | |
| Behling (1961) | Columbus, Ohio: large public welfare agency | Public welfare recipients, 58 percent white, 42 percent nonwhite | 200 | 200 | Random | Intensive casework with "small" caseloads of 75 (compared to control caseloads of 150–250); workers at BA level | Community Service Society (CSS) Movement Scale; "chronicity score"; open or closed status of case at end of service; financial costs | Experimental group had greater improvement on CSS Movement Scale, but higher costs, higher chronicity scores, and more open cases |
| Brown (1968); Warren and Smith (1963); Wallace (1967) | Chemung County, New York: county welfare agency | Public welfare recipients | 50 | Control: 50; Hidden control: 50 | Random | Intensive casework with small caseloads, average of 25, by MSW workers; median of 2 contacts per month over 31 months | CSS Movement Scale; St. Paul Family Functioning Scale | No significant difference |
| Geismar and Krisberg (1967) | New Haven, Connecticut: Neighborhood Improvement Project (created agency plus consortium of community agencies) | Predominantly white, lower-class, multi-problem families in public housing project | 30 | 51 | Matching | Intensive casework, average 4.4 interviews per month over 18 months; group work, community organization; caseworkers both MSW and BA; group workers untrained but had professional supervision | St. Paul Family Functioning Scale; measures of juvenile and adult delinquency and of economic dependency | Experimental group improved 7 steps on St. Paul Scale, controls less than 1 step; no differences on measures of delinquency and economic dependency |

TABLE 23–3
(Continued)

| Author[a] | Setting | Clients | Number of Subjects — Experimental | Number of Subjects — Control | Sample | Major Intervention | Measures of Dependent Variable | Outcome |
|---|---|---|---|---|---|---|---|---|
| Geismar (1971); Geismar and Krisberg (1966a and b); and Geismar et al. (1972) | Newark, New Jersey: Family Life Improvement Project (experimental agency) | Young, low-income families with first child; 1/3 unmarried mothers, mixed ethnicity | 177 | 175 | Random | Intensive casework including brokerage and advocacy; caseloads from 14–29; BA workers under MSW supervision; 3 years duration; intensity of contact varied, modal frequency 12 contacts | Income; family structure; "legal deviance"; use of community resources; assessment of change in Family Functioning Profile based on St. Paul Scale | Mixed: improvement in childrearing, health, housekeeping; no significant differences in other areas |
| Mullen, Chazin, and Feldstein (1970, 1972) | New York City: collaborative project of Community Service Society (family service agency) and N.Y.C. Department of Social Services | Newly dependent public welfare recipients; 2/3 single mothers; mixed ethnicity | 88 | 68 | Random | Regular service from BA welfare worker plus collaborative counseling from MSW family agency worker; 15 median interviews by latter over 14 months | Interview instrument completed by graduate students of 83 items dealing with family functioning and amount of help received from professionals and organizations | Experimental group received more help with housing conditions, medical services, personal and family problems; no other significant differences |
| Olson (1968, 1970) | Baltimore, Maryland: county welfare department | New AFDC cases; primarily young single mothers; 87 percent white | 66 (in two groups) | 65 (in two groups) | Random | Higher or lower welfare grants and inexperienced or experienced BA workers; average case open 7 months | Individual and family functioning; health, housekeeping, money management, morale, and use of community resources; judged by interview by outside research firm | Higher grant cases better on all criteria than controls; experienced workers enhanced improvement of high-grant cases, but made no difference in low-grant group |

| Study | Location/Agency | Population | | | Assignment | Treatment | Measures | Findings |
|---|---|---|---|---|---|---|---|---|
| Schwartz (1966); Schwartz and Sample (1967, 1972) | Chicago, Illinois: large public welfare agency | Public welfare recipients, families and individuals; 90 percent black | 164 | 150 | Random | Test of team versus conventional service delivery with high and low caseloads; BA workers; experimental supervisors MSWs, control supervisors BA | Personnel morale: questionnaires and absence and turnover rates; client improvement on CSS Movement and St. Paul Family Functioning Scales | Greater client improvement for experimental teams and low caseloads |
| Wilkinson and Ross (1972) | Rural Mississippi: welfare agency | Black AFDC mothers and children | 125 (in three groups) | 56 | Random | *Group A:* Work training and placement; supplemental income; adult basic education; individual counseling from BA worker. *Group B:* Intensive individualized counseling from BA worker; medical and dental services; clothing and educational supplies for children; group sessions on nutrition, banking, and so on; adult basic education; no additional income. *Group C:* Additional income; adult basic education; no special casework service | Before-and-after interviews concerning employment status, nutritional habits, housekeeping standards, use of medical and dental services, participation in community activities, attitudes toward work, and attitudes toward welfare | No significant differences |
| Wilson (1966, 1967) | Delaware: welfare agency | AFDC families | 163 | 151 | Not known | Intensive casework by BA workers with professional supervision | Follow-up interviews and analysis of case records | Experimental group more likely to become independent of welfare help |

a For full references, see bibliography at end of article.

**Intensive Casework with Welfare Recipients**

Seven of these studies dealt with assessing the impact of intensive casework by public agency workers with welfare recipients. In four of them the clients in the experimental conditions improved more than the controls, but in three projects the interventions failed.

Because of this disparity, these studies have limited utility for practice. Practitioners interested in intervening more effectively with clients receiving Aid to Families with Dependent Children (AFDC) cannot derive useful information concerning what is helpful and what is not. The predilection of all twenty-two studies reviewed to report results only in terms of differences between groups and not within groups obscures the most relevant information for practice—differences in outcomes among different clients and among different workers. The failure of most studies to define adequately such variables as the kind of interventions, workers, clients, problems, and circumstances renders the findings of success or lack of it not clearly explainable and therefore not useful.

The studies offer some clues or at least conjectural hypotheses about the reasons for success or failure of the interventions. Although the experimental group in the study by Mullen, Chazin, and Feldstein reported that they had received more help than the controls in improving their housing conditions, in obtaining medical services, and with personal and family problems (although it is not reported whether these problems improved), the researchers found no differences between them on the dimensions of family functioning or decreased dependency on welfare. This should not have been surprising since the female heads of household were the central figure in most of the families, and two-thirds of these women needed welfare because their husbands were gone, one-fourth were in economic need because the wage earner had lost a job, and another one-fourth because the wage earner was ill. Furthermore, in most of the families the female head was unable to work because she was needed at home for child care. The areas in which the MSW-level casework was successful, therefore, were in achieving the only realistic and feasible goals that could have been set for this intervention: connecting people with the resources they needed. Clearly, individual caseworkers could not affect variables such as the lack of day care facilities for mothers who wished to work, a tight job market or lack of marketable skills resulting in the unemployment of the wage earner, illness of the wage earner, or the absence of a husband who had disappeared.

The assumption seems to have been made over and over in these studies with welfare recipients that poverty is necessarily the result of personal and family inadequacy and pathology. Given this assumption, the target and method of intervention made a specious kind of sense: to treat the individuals in the family with intensive casework so they would not be so economically dependent. However, in his analysis of the policy and practice implications of a number of poverty studies, Geismar speculates that projects which focused on poor clients' economic and other instrumental needs, rather than on their expressive needs, were more likely to be successful.

> There is no basis for declaring casework intervention either effective or ineffective without examining the total context within which the service is rendered. The studies, generally speaking, suffer from a failure to define what Helen Harris Perlman calls change targets and rigorously to aim services at these targets. Most of the action-research projects had as their goals helping lower-class families, yet none of the service programs provided adequate economic aid. . . . Marriage counseling, child guidance, or family planning may be an important corollary of—but no substitute for —economic aid. . . . [1971, p. 464].

### Partialization

The moral of these studies of welfare clients for the practitioner and the profession seems to be that the broad range of helping services loosely classified as social casework are effective to the degree that the interventions selected are related to the client's problem. Since many of the human problems with which social work deals are complex Gordian knots, one of the primary skills of the worker must be "partialization"—picking apart that tangled knot, assigning priority status to the pieces of the problem that can be worked with most realistically and feasibly, and then choosing interventions that are sharply focused on these problems. Since the priority problem of poor clients is their poverty, this must be dealt with first.

It may be that the confusing and contradictory results found in these studies is attributable to the greater skill of the workers in the successful projects in analyzing the situations facing them and their clients, partializing the problem and setting priorities, involving the clients in working toward goals that they understood and for which they were "motivated," and choosing interventions that were related to the foregoing. Partialization has long been a basic principle of casework theory. It is perhaps understandable that the researchers did not know this, but it is indefensible that the practitioners seem not to have or that they failed to educate the researchers.

The Olson and the Schwartz and Sample studies seem to bear out this interpretation. The Olson project focused on the effect of giving more money to the welfare families involved as well as on the impact of experienced compared with inexperienced bachelors' level workers. The researcher found that the cases receiving both more money and more experienced casework help made more gains on the outcome measures than the other groups. Cases that received more money but had inexperienced workers made more gains than those receiving smaller grants, but slightly less than those who also had experienced workers. Olson concludes that:

> The worker's experience had little effect on whether AFDC recipients had enough to eat.... This might be assumed as obvious without an experimental study, but in many instances the emphasis upon the AFDC family's need for service has seemed to rule out of consideration the need for adequate food [1970, p. 97].

The Schwartz and Sample project experimented both with the effect of high and low caseloads and with another use of MSWs in a welfare setting. Rather than attempting to use trained direct practitioners to give intensive casework themselves, these researchers set up an administrative arrangement in which MSWs were primarily responsible for diagnostic assessment of the needs of individual cases and for planning a strategy of intervention related to that assessment —the aspect of casework that was left out in several of the other studies. The MSWs utilized the services of bachelor's level workers to carry out partial tasks related to the goals of treatment, but they retained overall responsibility for the intervention strategy. Greater improvement was reported for the experimental teams that used this arrangement and that had the lower caseloads necessary for it to work.

These findings suggest that a basic function of the MSW worker in welfare or in other social agencies is to think. The MSW may also provide some of the particular interventions that are beyond the level of knowledge and skill of the bachelor's level worker, for example, intervention in complex intrapersonal and interpersonal problems or in institutional and other situational problems. The MSW's primary responsibility, however, is to accurately define the problems in the case, what is causing them, and what can realistically be done about them within the limits of available time and service; to see that what can be done is done; and to evaluate the effects of the intervention in terms of the original problem and goals. This is precisely the scientific process—the process of research itself. In the majority of the twenty-two studies under consideration, the first step was ignored. And since the problem was defined inaccurately, the goals were inaccurate, the interventions were off target, and the evaluations told nothing.

## Two Projects

The two projects conducted by Geismar and his associates were somewhat different from the other studies of efforts with poverty clients. The Neighborhood Improvement Project (NIP) in New Haven, Connecticut, reported by Geismar and Krisberg, differed in that it attempted to intervene in the total system affecting the lives of the "multi-problem" families. The project created a range of new community resources such as a nursery school, recreation programs, and services for youth and the aged. Casework focused not only on counseling but also on what the researchers called "energetic intervention" on the families' behalf with social systems such as the medical system, welfare agencies, and so on. There was "greater emphasis on environmental change" than on intrapsychic change (Geismar and Krisberg, 1967, p. 113). The worker's role was conceptualized as that of a "two-way change agent," focusing on changing the way that social systems and their personnel responded to the family and its needs as much as on helping the family itself to change.

The families in the experimental group gained almost seven steps on the St. Paul Scale of Family Functioning—mostly in use of health care, relationship with worker, use of community resources, and family relationships—whereas control families gained less than one step. Comparisons of the experimental and control groups on measures of delinquency and economic dependency were inconclusive. No differences in outcomes were found according to whether the workers were MSWs or BAs, although the authors suggest that because the less-educated but experienced caseworkers were more oriented to concrete problems, they may have been more appropriate and helpful for this group of clients.

The Family Life Improvement Project (FLIP), which Geismar and his associates conducted some years later in Newark, New Jersey, built on the experience of the NIP study and also on that of an earlier study in St. Paul, Minnesota (which is not reported here because its experimental design did not involve a control group [Geismar and Ayres, 1960]). Both of these other projects deal with low-income families defined as multiproblem. FLIP was different from Geismar's earlier studies and from other studies considered here in that it was preventive, addressing itself to young, low-income families, living in one of the worst inner-city environments in the country, before they developed problems. Its basic hypothesis was that social work intervention might make a difference for these families in terms of the development of later individual and family problems as a result of the impact of increased responsibility as children were added to the original family group and the increasing impact of social forces and stresses.

Only mild success was reported. Treated families showed significantly more positive change than controls in only three out of eight areas. As in several studies considered previously, improvement was found in the use of health care resources, but FLIP also demonstrated effectiveness in improving the families' adequacy in dealing with their children and in running the family as an organizational unit. This added success may have resulted because the project started mostly with families that did not yet have major problems. But the FLIP effort was less successful than NIP, which dealt with more difficult, multiproblem families. The researchers account for this difference on the basis of the greater difficulty the FLIP workers encountered with intervening in the clients' social system, particularly in " . . . a service structure that was both less adequate in relation to local need and more impervious to pressure . . . " (Geismar, 1971, p. 461).

Some speculative conclusions may be drawn from the studies of clients in poverty programs. It would seem, as with the other studies considered earlier, that accurate definition and assessment of the client's problem situation must precede the intervention and that dysfunctional social system variables must be highlighted in both assessment and intervention. "Treatment" that focuses on changing the relationship of the social system to the client or family and on connecting people with resources may be the priority intervention for problems associated with poverty, before interventive efforts with other problems can be effective.

## STUDIES OF THE AGED

Table 23-4 summarizes two projects that studied the impact of social work intervention on problems of the aged, both done by Blenkner with others. In a 1964 study in New York City, Blenkner, Jahn, and Wasser found that aged persons in the community who had received service improved more than untreated controls in health care and in social participation. On the nine other criteria used to measure outcome, however, there were no differences between the treated and untreated groups. Improvement of clients' health care was achieved by the two experimental programs, one utilizing a short-term format and intervention by either an MSW or a public health nurse, the other not limited as to time but requiring collaborative teamwork between the social worker and nurse. The contrast program offered only routine unspecialized agency services and did not particularly focus on health problems. The collaborative program was not found to be superior to that in which one worker took

TABLE 23–4
Summary of Studies of the Aged

| Author[a] | Setting | Clients | Number of Subjects Experimental | Control | Sample | Major Intervention | Measures of Dependent Variable | Outcome |
|---|---|---|---|---|---|---|---|---|
| Blenkner, Jahn, and Wasser (1964) | New York City: Community Service Society (family service agency) | Persons over age 60: younger men and all but very old women underrepresented | Short-term: 139; Collaborative Service 133 | Contrast: 142 Control: 133 | Random | *Short-term*: counseling, concrete service; referral by either MSW or public health nurse; time restricted to 2 months and 4 interviews *Collaborative Service*: teamwork of MSW and public health nurse; no time or interview limit *Contrast group*: standard agency service; usually referral by MSW or graduate student to community resources; no time limit *Control group*: no service | Interviews 6 months after termination; assessment of problem status; social adjustment using components of Movement Scale; costs to agency of service | Experimental programs effective on 3 out of 12 criteria concerning health care and social participation; short-term more effective than longer-term services; higher institutionalization and death rate in collaborative service |
| Blenkner, Bloom, and Nielson (1971) | Cleveland, Ohio: Benjamin Rose Institute (agency serving the aged) | Persons over age 60 in need of protective services; sample skewed toward females, whites, native born, not presently married | 76 | 88 | Random | Intensive casework with aged person and collaterals by experienced MSWs; range of concrete services; average of 31.8 interviews with clients over 1-year period | Interviews of client at intake, 3 months, 6 months, after 1 year service period, and throughout 5-year follow-up period; interviews of collaterals; workers' judgments | Experimental group had improved physical environment, received concrete assistance, and had reduced stress on collateral; no difference in physical or mental functioning or contentment; higher death and institutionalization rates |

[a] For full references, see bibliography at end of article.

responsibility, and the long-term design was not more effective than short-term treatment.

The findings of this study, like some of the others previously considered, indicate that social work services individualized to a person or a family can make a particular impact in connecting people with health care. In addition, with this client group at least, short-term intervention that was specifically focused on identified problems appeared to be more effective than more diffuse, longer-term service.

Blenkner, Bloom, and Nielson repeated the experiment in Cleveland several years later. Here the focus was on the older person in need of protective service because of inability to care for him- or herself and the absence of family or other networks of care and protection. The experimental variable was the provision of intensive service by trained and experienced caseworkers, compared with services from a variety of other community agencies and resources that did not specialize in helping the aged. The focus of the program was on "social therapy" rather than psychotherapy—on providing concrete services, enlisting environmental supports for the client, and restructuring the situation to compensate for the older person's deficiencies.

The treated group did not differ significantly from the contrast group on outcome measures of the degree of deterioration they experienced. This raises the question of whether the expectations set and outcome criteria used were realistic goals in view of the definition of the problem. The aged clients had already been identified as being so "deteriorated" in their physical and mental competence that they were in need of protective intervention. Was it reasonable to expect that casework—or any other intervention—could have reversed deterioration attributable to advanced age and previous lack of care?

In both these studies, the experimental group was found to have a higher death rate than the control group. All the reasons for this are not known, but the researchers speculated that it might have been related to the tendency of the workers for the experimental group to arrange for institutional placement of their clients. They conclude that:

> The findings on functional competence together with those on death and institutionalization force consideration of the hypothesis that intensive service with a heavy reliance on institutional care may actually accelerate decline [Blenkner, Bloom, and Nielson, 1971, p. 494].

Again, this finding points to the failure of these studies—and, one must presume, of the social work practitioners involved in them—to consult the clients about their own perceptions of the problem and what they wished to have done about it. Elderly people are characteristically fearful of institutionalization; typically, their goal is to remain in their own homes, often at any cost and even when those homes are severely inadequate. It is not unreasonable to speculate that institutional placement was not something the old people in this project wanted or saw as the solution to their problems; rather, it may be conjectured that this was a solution arranged for them by undoubtedly well-meaning helpers. It must also be remembered that the workers in the Cleveland project had at their disposal additional funds and resources of the agency to provide such services as home health care and homemakers, which are designed to provide alternatives to institutionalization and to make it possible to maintain aged clients in their own homes. In this situation, again, social work treatment was applied to people, without the people themselves being consulted about the problems they were experiencing and on which they were therefore the ultimate experts.

## TYPES OF INTERVENTION

Table 23–5 summarizes the last group of studies considered, those that compared the effects of different forms of intervention. The 1964 study by Blenkner, Jahn, and Wasser also belongs in this category since it examined the comparative effects of short- versus long-term treatment and treatment by one professional versus a social worker-nurse team. Similarly, the Schwartz and Sample study, which examined the effects of an innovative administrative arrangement of service personnel, also falls into this group.

Reid and Shyne conducted one of the best-known studies of the comparative effectiveness of short- and long-term treatment. Their client group consisted of working- and middle-class clients voluntarily applying for help with marital or parent-child problems. They also examined the comparative effects of "modifying" and "supportive" casework treatment according to the Hollis (1972) typology and of individual versus joint interviews. They found Planned Short-Term Service (PSTS) to be superior to the more open-ended and diffuse Continued Service (CS). The same proportion of cases in each group (27 percent) experienced considerable alleviation of their problems, but 57 percent of those in the PSTS group had their problems slightly alleviated as compared to only 37 percent in the CS group. In addition, only 17 percent of the cases served by this mode of treatment experienced no change in or aggravation of the problem situation as compared with 37 percent in the CS group. No differences were found between cases assigned to "modifying" or "supportive" treatment; in fact, the researchers found that workers used a combination of both techniques in all cases and that this was

TABLE 23–5
Summary of Studies of Interventive Modalities[a]

| Author[b] | Setting | Clients | Number of Subjects | | Sample | Major Intervention | Measures of Dependent Variable | Outcome |
|---|---|---|---|---|---|---|---|---|
| | | | Experimental | Control | | | | |
| Cohen and Krause (1971) | Cincinnati, Ohio: family service agency | Wives of alcoholics, sometimes alcoholic husbands; primarily white and lower-middle class | 74 | Two contrast groups: 41 each; Control group: 23 | Random | Casework with wives and, when possible, with alcoholic husbands, by MSW workers specially trained in treating alcoholism; mean of 21.8 interviews over 17 months | Pre- and posttest interviews with marital partners by research interviewers concerning status of husband's drinking problem, partners' attitudes and satisfaction in marriage, and family functioning | Differences not significant at less than .10 level |
| Langsley, Pittman, and Flomenhaft (1968); Langsley et al. (1968); Flomenhaft, Kaplan, and Langsley (1969) | Denver, Colorado: psychiatric hospital | Psychotic and other acutely disturbed persons clinically evaluated as in need of immediate hospitalization; wide range of age, sex, ethnicity, and duration of problem | 150 | 150 | Random | Family crisis intervention by team of psychiatrist, MSW, social worker, and psychiatric nurse; therapy in brief, active format focused on immediate problems; high intensity over brief period (6 contacts over 3 weeks) | Social adjustment inventory, personal functioning scale, rehospitalization rates, measure of days lost from functioning | Experimental group had lower hospitalization rates and only 1/3 the time lost from functioning; no other differences |

| Reid and Shyne (1969) | New York City: Community Service Society (family service agency) | Middle class clients with problems in family relationships | 60 | 60 | Random | Comparison of casework by MSW staff under conditions of Planned Short-Term Service (PSTS) and Continued Service (CS) treatment; also compared effectiveness of "modifying" and "supportive" techniques and comparing individual and joint interviews | Interviews by separate research interviewers at intake, termination, and 6 months after termination, focused on individual and family functioning and status of presenting problem | PSTS group changed more for better, less for worse, than CS group; no difference between "modifying" and "supportive" treatment or between individual and joint interviews |

a The studies by Schwartz and Sample on the poor and by Blenkner, Jahn, and Wasser on the aged also fall in this category. (See Tables 23–3 and 23–4.)
b For full references, see bibliography at end of article.

therefore not a pure or discrete typology. Nor were there any essential differences according to the format of the interview.

Reid and Shyne note that the short-term approach brought about slight alleviation in most of the cases treated this way, but point out that no higher proportion of cases was appreciably helped by the longer and more intensive treatment mode. This was in spite of the fact that the MSW workers had no previous experience with planned short-term treatment and adhered to the notion that personality change must occur through some degree of insight for change in the problem to occur. Reid and Shyne observe that short-term treatment had only to "tie" with the lengthier and more intensive approach, in terms of the number of successful outcomes, to "win" (1969, p. 175).

It may be speculated that the basic reason for the superior performance of the short-term modality was that it forced both clients and workers to arrive rapidly at an accurate, delimited definition of the problem, to set priorities and partialize the problem, to take more responsibility for their own roles and accountability in ameliorating the problem, and to work with and consult each other. The worker could not afford to be only a passive listener but had to assume a more active, risk-taking role. He or she had no time to engage in lengthy academic analyses of the underlying dynamics accounting for the clients' behavior; rather, he or she was forced to concentrate on the here-and-now problem situation. In short, since the clients are assumed to have been comparable because of the randomization procedures used, the difference must have been in the workers' use of themselves.

Reid and Shyne's findings are similar to those in the project directed by Langsley and associates. (Fischer excluded this project from his study on the basis that "caseworkers were only a small minority of the treatment team." However, one of the codirectors of the project is a social worker, and social workers represented one-third of the treatment team, along with a psychiatrist and psychiatric nurse.) Langsley et al. sought to explore if persons suffering from acute psychiatric symptoms could be helped as effectively or better than they would be by hospitalization by a family-system and crisis-therapy approach focused on keeping the individual out of the hospital and returning him or her to previous levels of functioning as soon as possible. The experimental treatment proceeded from the theoretical assumption that although intrapsychic factors are certainly involved in situations of severe psychiatric decompensation, there is also a disturbance or crisis in the family or social system. The experimental group did better than the hospitalized controls on indexes of return to functioning (defined as resumption of responsibilities such as job, housekeeping, or school attendance), continued diminution of psychiatric symptoms, and lower rates of rehospitalization. The researchers did not claim that they had cured mental illness; rather, their focus was on immediate solution of the difficulties being experienced by the individuals and families, return to functioning, and avoidance of the iatrogenic effects of the "sick role" and the label of psychiatric patient.

Again, results of the Reid and Shyne study indicate that an approach focused on the aspects of the immediate problem that are amenable to change, on involvement of the client, and on changing specific behaviors of environmental factors rather than the personalities of the people involved works better than diffuse approaches focused more on the process than on the outcome. This was also the only study of the twenty-two that focused on the family as a system and that utilized it as a problem-solving resource.

The last study to be considered in this group was done by Cohen and Krause with the wives of alcoholics. The report is unclear about the difference between the experimental treatment offered by MSW caseworkers specially trained in working with alcoholism and that by regular MSW workers in the same agency, other than an increased emphasis on education of the alcoholic and his wife to the idea that alcoholism is an illness. Unfortunately, if there was a difference, it did not show up in the outcome—except that there were more marital separations in the families in the experimental group.

The failure of this effort may be seen again as related to the failure of the workers to focus sharply on the specific problems, in concrete and pragmatic terms, that the wives were experiencing as a result of their husbands' drinking behavior. Alcoholism is certainly an individual problem, but by its nature it also becomes a problem in the family system by disrupting its normal roles and rules. A family-oriented approach would therefore seem sensible. Yet treatment in this study was located almost entirely in the worker's office—and the agency was open only one evening per week! Failure to involve the alcoholic husband was by no means, therefore, due only to his "resistance."

## IMPLICATIONS FOR PRACTICE

The question posed at the beginning of this article was, What can be learned from these studies to add to or change social work's theories about direct practice? Unfortunately, the answer seems to be, with a few exceptions, not a great deal. It is difficult to draw prescriptive conclusions from the group of studies as a body for a number of reasons. A lack of standardization among outcome measures makes cumulative evidence difficult to assess. The interventive variable is either different among the studies, inadequately defined, or inadequately controlled. The relationship of the definitions and measures of outcome to the problem being intervened in varies, and the outcome measures also vary in the degree of validity and reliability achieved. A number of studies are characterized by weaknesses in design, or in analysis of the data. Perhaps most important, it is difficult for the reader to determine specifics about clients, conditions, interventions, and changes since the most essential details are lacking. Such research can give little information about whether practice is effective or how to make it more effective.

However, the evidence of the studies does lead to the not-so-startling conclusion that poor practice is indeed ineffective. The interventions of the social work practitioners described in some of the studies that reported negative outcomes are of poor quality; in others, not enough descriptive detail is given to come to a conclusion about the quality of the practice. Studies that reported positive outcomes—that demonstrated effectiveness of the casework or group work interventions applied—appear to have involved a better quality of practice.

Six principles of "quality practice" can be extracted from the foregoing analysis of the twenty-two studies:

■ Accurate definition of the problem
■ Analysis of the problem—factors creating or maintaining it and factors that can help resolve it
■ Assessment of the problem's workability and setting of goals
■ Negotiation of a contract with client
■ Planning a strategy of intervention
■ Evaluation

Not one proposition in this definition of good practice is in any way new; each has long been a part of practice theory.


## DEFINING THE PROBLEM

The problem in living with which the client is struggling must be stated in clear and straightforward terms, preferably in plain English. The statement must refer to the actual problem itself. If this seems obvious, the reader is invited to peruse the case records of many agencies in which clear statements of what workers and clients were working on are largely lacking. Often, the problem will be stated in such terms as "lack of ego capacities" or "difficulty in object relationships." Neither the worker nor, certainly, the client can do anything about a problem defined in this way.

Working with the client toward a simple and clear statement of the problem with which he or she wants help achieves two purposes: it helps the client begin to comprehend what he or she needs and wants to change in his or her life situation and what he or she wants to work toward; and it helps the worker to achieve clarity and focus about the purpose of the interaction with the client or client system. Of course, clearly stating the problem implies that the worker has assumed accountability for working on it and attempting to do something about it. It is thus easier for supervisors or others to measure the effectiveness of the intervention and more difficult for the worker to avoid responsibility.

A clear statement of the problem to be studied is also the first step in the research process. Without this, neither practice nor practice research can answer the question most relevant for both: with what types of problems and circumstances are particular types of interventions and practitioners helpful?

A corollary of this principle is that the definition of the problem must include a dimension of measurability, that is, the problem must be stated in such a way that its incidence and severity can be measured, not only at the beginning of the case, but also when worker and client later evaluate whether the intervention has been successful (Hudson, 1978).

The assumption underlying this first principle is that helping people solve or at least ameliorate their problems in living is what social work direct practitioners should be concerned about. The direct practitioner is responsible for helping people with the problems they are experiencing, not for restructuring their personalities or giving them "growth" experiences. Sometimes these positive results may occur as a result of skillfully helping clients come to grips with their specific problems and achieve some mastery over them. But amorphous goals such as "growth" may not be ethically substituted for focused work on the clients' specific problems.

As noted, this step of defining the problem was ignored in several of the studies which found evidence that the interventions might have had a negative effect. Was the "problem-to-be-worked" in the two studies by Blenkner and her associates the advanced age of the clients? Is that amenable to change? In several of the welfare studies the problem appeared to be the dependency on welfare of women who could not themselves support their families. In this circumstance, is getting such clients off the welfare roles an appropriate problem-to-be-worked?

Reid and Shyne's study, on the other hand, is an illustration of the pragmatic usefulness of this practice principle. Because the workers in that project were bound by a tight time constraint, they were forced (in many instances, according to the researchers, against their grain) to define with the client the problem or problems to be worked on as a crucial first step. Langsley et al. also focused sharply and clearly on the problem for work, defined as that of helping the psychiatrically decompensated clients to stay out of the hospital and return as fully as possible to their former responsibilities—in other words, helping them continue functioning at the best level that could be managed, in spite of their psychiatric illness. These practitioner-researchers did not define the problem as the cure of mental illness or the client's need for a growth experience or other fuzzy and unworkable goals.

A definition of the problem, therefore, must be phrased in terms that make it "workable," that is, amenable to change. However, the next steps of analyzing the problem, setting goals, and contracting increase the workers and client's understanding of the problem, and the worker may need to reformulate the original definition as a result.

## ANALYZING THE PROBLEM

Analysis of the problem means identifying, weighing, and assessing the factors in the client's intrapersonal, interpersonal, and social systems that are contributing to the problem or that might be enlisted in resolving or ameliorating it. All three of these systems must be involved in this analysis. To focus on only one to the exclusion of the others is to deny the influence of the other powerful variables, and therefore to skew the direction of the case. All three sets of system variables are involved in every case to different degrees.

In some of the studies that were examined, the researchers' and practitioners' focus was placed arbitrarily on only one of these sets of factors. With few exceptions, many of the studies began from an implicit assumption that the problem existed only within the personality of the person who had it, confusing the problems with the people who had them. Once this assumption is made, there is a kind of quasi logic in an interventive strategy focused on changing people internally, in spite of the social circumstances that are requiring the adaptive behavior labeled as the problem. If the assumption that everybody needs a formed-group experience is substituted for analysis of the three systems in the client's life as they relate to the problem, then the results of the narrowly focused intervention can be no more effective than the results that were found in the studies by Berleman and associates, McCabe et al., Meyer, Borgatta, and Jones, and Miller.

Of all twenty-two studies that were reviewed, only the project by Langsley and associates made use of the tremendous potential power of the family's natural interpersonal system to help its troubled member. A number of the studies claimed to have a "family focus" or to have used a "family approach," but on close examination, all that was meant was work with one or a few key family members around either their own particular problems or the problems of the identified client. This is totally different from a focus that uses the great power of the natural small-group system to influence and often to direct the behavior, attitudes, and feelings of its members. The most important influence on clients are always the people with whom they share their lives and to whose needs and individual personalities they must adapt. Clients are most responsive to the dynamics of this group system, and no individual worker can ever have this kind of influence in the lives of his or her clients.

Long before the current family therapy movement, social work knew about the powerful forces of the natural-group system from the "practice wisdom" of the profession's own social group work method and from research on small groups from the behavioral and social sciences. These sources confirmed empirically what many group workers had experienced—the potency of the group process to control and influence the behavior, attitudes, and feelings of the group members. But social workers have not put this knowledge to full use in their practice.

However, many of the research studies that did utilize such natural-group processes as that of the adolescent gang also experienced poor results. Perhaps this was because they failed to meet several important criteria for using the natural group as a medium for intervention. First, the natural-group system must be an important variable in the problem of its individual member, and the worker must be able to support and document this diagnosis. The family or other natural-group system does not have a major involvement in every case situation. Second, the worker must be able to show that certain specific changes in the natural-group system will create reverberations that will force the individual member to change also in response. Third, the natural system must be in a state that renders it open to and capable of change. General systems theory, organizational theory, and crisis theory all make clear that for change to occur in any human system, a state of critical imbalance in its normal system processes must exist or be brought about (Buckley, 1967; Etzioni, 1964; Katz and Kahn, 1966; Hall, 1977; and Parad, 1962).

Thus, Miller's project with natural gangs did not take into account that a system must be in an unstable state before change can occur; rather, the group workers in this study sought to make the group more cohesive. Conversely, one reason the Langsley et al. project did work may have been that these researchers were working with a natural system in a state of disequilibrium. Not only were the patients in a state of severe crisis, but, even more important, so were their natural family systems. The intervenor's role may be considered that of an "irritant" in the system, either causing or exacerbating disequilibrium as a first step toward change in individual or small-group natural systems (Wood, 1973).

Given the kinds of people and problems with which social work deals, social system variables are often the most salient of the three dimensions of intrapersonal, interpersonal, and social system factors. Certainly this was true for the AFDC clients involved in the welfare studies, yet the researchers focused on the intrapersonal dimension. Olson's project had positive results because the intervention she designed changed the social system's relationship to the clients by giving them more money. Provision of more experienced casework service also helped, but not for those clients who did not also receive additional funds. Geismar and his associates concluded that one of the reasons they experienced only mild success in their FLIP project of intervention with poor, young families was that both the clients and the workers experienced the social system as immovable.

If the worker's diagnosis is that all three dimensions are involved in the genesis and maintenance of the problem situation, as is often the case, then he or she must plan to target the interventions toward all three, concurrently or sequentially. In general, the old practice wisdom to "start from the outside of the case and work in" makes sense, that is, start with needed and possible environmental change. The worker may not, professionally or ethically, force the data into a preconceived theoretical orientation focused on only one of the three dimensions—as the researchers and practitioners in many of the studies appear to have done.

## WORKABILITY AND GOALS

The worker's next professional task is to assess with the client how amenable to change the problem situation is. He or she must determine what changes in the three sets of variables are needed to resolve or ameliorate the problem and which of these changes are possible to achieve. To "make my husband stop drinking," to "get these clients off the welfare rolls," or to reverse the process of aging are not workable goals.

To set vague goals or to set them unreasonably high is to subject clients to a cruel and destructive experience in disappointment, frustration, and erosion of their confidence in their own capacities. It may also mean that the worker is ignoring other and more immediate goals that might be possible to achieve. This occurred in many of the research projects examined; goals were usually set in advance by researchers, clients were not consulted, and goals were, in some instances, impossible to achieve. In the more successful projects, the researchers and workers appeared to aim for goals that were realistic and feasible.

## NEGOTIATING A CONTRACT

The client must "do" the "casework." The worker's skill is in supporting or challenging the client to do it. With the obvious exception of situations in which the client lacks material resources to which the worker has access, the worker cannot resolve or ameliorate the intrapersonal and interpersonal problems of the client or make them go away. The worker's professional task is to help the client figure out ways to resolve or ameliorate the problem and to support and challenge him or her through the painful process of attempting to bring about change.

For this to happen, the client must be clear about what problem is targeted for change and what kind of efforts the client and the worker will have to make. The client must also be clear about what his or her responsibility is and for what tasks the worker is accountable. This means that a contract must be negotiated between the client and the helping agent. The contract may need to be renegotiated, perhaps several times, as they work together and learn more about the problem, what is causing or maintaining it, what needs to be changed to resolve or ameliorate it, and what is possible to change within the limits of time and resources available to each of them.

The evidence from the studies suggests that some kinds of contract did exist in the studies by Langsley et al., Reid and Shyne, Olson, and in some aspects of the two projects headed by Geismar. Contracts do not appear to have existed in the unsuccessful studies, in which researchers and workers apparently decided what was good for the clients. The clients were not "motivated" toward the goals the workers were seeking to impose on them, and therefore, did not see much point in expending energy on the tasks set for them.

The contract may be seen as the heart of the casework or change effort, which cannot start until some kind of contract is firmly agreed on. The contract may have to be altered if understanding of the situation changes, but some agreement must be arrived at for the work of problem-solving to begin. Contracting may have to be accomplished in stages, perhaps beginning with something as minimal as the client's agreement that he or she will allow the worker to continue talking with him or her about the situation in the hope that ways can be found to improve it.

If the problem involves a natural interpersonal system, the concept of the contract must be extended to agreement among the members of that group on their perception of the problem and the changes they individually and collectively would like to see brought about. The process of change does not begin until the worker has succeeded in helping the members perceive the problem as a family one, rather than the exclusive possession of the identified patient, in terms of each member's investment in changing the way the family operates. Then the worker must get some degree of agreement that all members will share in the responsibility for change.


## PLANNING INTERVENTION

The worker and client must map out together what needs to be done to achieve the goals contracted for. Intervention, treatment, and casework are not esoteric concepts comprehensible only by the professional elite, to be kept as closely guarded secrets from the client. Workers in most of the unsuccessful studies examined seemed to believe that the less the client knew and understood about the intervention being applied, the more powerful that intervention was likely to be. Little provision appears to have been made for the client to give the worker his or her perception of the efficacy of the intervention or its relevance to the problem. To the degree that a client does not understand the intervention or the relationship it bears to the problem and the goals he or she would like to achieve ("How will talking treatment help?") the client will not be invested in the change effort and will resist the worker's interventions.

The strategy of intervention must bear a logical and conceptual relationship in the previous stages of the process; it must flow naturally from them. The worker must be able to present an adequate rationale as to why the particular interventions he or she is planning are reasonable means to achieve the goals posited, rather than any other intervention. The plan of intervention must fit the previously defined problem, the assessment of the three systems of variables involved in that problem, the goals, and the contract. The unsuccessful research studies failed to explain the relationship their interventions bore to these factors. It is not only an invitation to failure, but unethical for the worker to impose on the client some pet intervention of his or her own, whether or not it fits the problem, the assessment, the goals, the contract—or the client.

Although psychoanalytic and ego psychology have probably been more heavily utilized by casework than any other theories, both as descriptive theories of personality and as prescriptive theories of intervention, a major strength of casework is that it has never formally subscribed to any theory in particular (Wood, 1971). Casework practice and theory are sufficiently broad that they can include a wide range of subtheories and intervention techniques. Which one to select depends on the case, not the worker's predilection. The worker, therefore, needs a pluralistic knowledge of descriptive theories about the kinds of problems social work deals with and prescriptive theories of interventive technology. The caseworker should be a craftsman—an expert in helping people to solve problems in living

—not a priest or a guru attempting to impart his or her own theoretical "religion" on unsuspecting clients. It is difficult to understand self-appellations such as "I'm psychoanalytically oriented," or "behaviorally oriented" or "group oriented" or "transactional-analysis oriented," since none of these theories and ideologies are, in themselves, broad enough to suit the variety of human problems with which social workers must deal.

Total pluralistic knowledge and competence—in-depth knowledge of all old and new theories and interventive technology—is clearly impossible for any ordinary social work direct practitioner to ever attain. But it is still a requirement of professional responsibility and scholarship, if only as a life-long goal. "Pluralism," furthermore, is by no means the same thing as "eclecticism" which, as commonly used, seems to mean that the worker does not know a great deal about any theory or intervention, but has stitched together a hodgepodge out of bits and pieces of various theories.

The strategy of intervention must also include an active role for the client. It is not therapeutic for the client to be relegated only to a role of sitting and absorbing the worker's wisdom. The client can best become invested in change by becoming an active participant in change.

## EVALUATION

There are two aspects to the process of evaluation: ongoing evaluation and terminal evaluation. The former is an assessment of the validity, accuracy, and efficacy of each step of the helping process as it occurs, and the latter is an appraisal of the final effects or outcomes of the treatment in terms of the original definition of the problem and the contracted goals.

The nature of evaluative research is inquiry into final outcomes. Each of the studies examined in this article investigated whether a given problem in living had been resolved or ameliorated, according to predetermined criteria for improvement, by means of the interventions utilized. In most of the studies, the findings were rather dismal (although the conclusions can often be challenged on the basis of the poor quality of the research and of the practice).

However, evaluation of the ongoing type also needs to be applied in every case. Each of the stages of the casework process described interlocks with all the others. In practice, the worker is always moving back and forth among the stages, renegotiating the contract or redefining the problem, for example, as the worker and client run into snags. The worker must constantly raise the question, both with him- or herself and with the client, of whether difficulty at a particular interventive stage is a result of defining the problem inaccurately, of misdirected goals, or of a contract that does not provide an agenda that is meaningful to the client.

This appears to be another aspect of casework that was not engaged in by the workers in the unsuccessful studies. There is no description of the workers soliciting their clients' input about the meaningfulness and relevance of their work together or where they were heading. Rather, the studies give the impression that, pushed on by the researchers, the workers in turn pushed the clients in a direction in which they did not wish to go. In such successful outcome studies as those by Langsley et al. and by Reid and Shyne, the researchers reported that workers and clients were required to "check out" with each other as the case progressed.

## RESEARCH IMPLICATIONS

The processes of casework that have been described are exactly the same processes as those of research. These include formulating the problem for study; setting hypotheses; defining the dependent variable; defining the independent variable; applying and monitoring the independent variable; collecting and analyzing data; evaluating the outcome; and drawing inferential conclusions that are supported by the data.

Researchers, particularly in the 1960s, seemed to be single-mindedly focused on only one model of research: the group-comparison experimental model. However, Reid has summarized the implication of the kind of social work studies that have been done to date as follows:

> The proper target for criticism is the research and development strategy as a whole, a product of the joint efforts of researchers and practitioners. . . . In short, the whole treatment-research paradigm has failed to pay off . . . its results have provided little guidance for the improvement of practice [Reid, 1976, pp. 263–64].

For practitioners, one of the results of such research has been learning that interventive techniques they had considered valuable do not, in fact, seem to be particularly useful, at least for the particular problems to which they were applied. Practitioners and theory-builders are then obligated to devise and evaluate other modalities that may work better. The social work researcher has a similar obligation: if the group-comparison experimental model has not proved useful, then other research models must be sought. Research is undoubtedly as subject to cycles and fashions as is practice, and it is as hard for researchers to give up a model in which they have placed their faith as it is for practitioners.

However, a number of social work writers have recently been calling for a "moratorium" on group-comparison evaluative research and for exploration of alternative research paradigms (Fischer, 1976, p. 152; and Hudson, 1976, p. 222). Models are needed that examine both the process and the outcome of treatment. It is possible to build examination of process into the group-comparison experimental design, although admittedly it is difficult and calls for a much more complex design. An alternative model has been proposed using the individual case as its own control, rather than comparing the mean results of groups. This paradigm is sometimes called "$N = 1$" model (Howe, 1974; Dukes, 1965; and Gottman, 1973). Dukes urges the wider use of the single-case study on the basis that

a brief scanning of general and historical accounts of psychology will dispel any doubts about the importance [of this kind of research], revealing, as it does, many instances of pivotal research in which the observations were confined to the behavior of only one person or animal [1965, p. 74].

Single-case studies of process and outcome of behavior modification have accomplished appreciable advances in this area. Gottman points out that "in outcome research, it may be misleading to average data over individuals" and that an "analysis of the effectiveness of psychotherapy could be misleading if only means of grouped change scores were inspected" (1973, p. 93).

The "$N = 1$" model, a quasi-experimental design, uses an interrupted time-series design in which two periods of observation are separated by application of the intervention. The "$N = 2$" paradigm is a time-lag control design in which an intervention is applied to one subject after a base observation period but is withheld temporarily from another subject. After an experimental period, the intervention is applied to the second subject, and both subjects are monitored for a second experimental period. These models present research problems of their own, notably those of statistical inference, representativeness, and generalizability. Some of these can be solved at least in part by replication over many cases.

It may be necessary for research to return at least partially to the case study, the earliest and still major source of knowledge for the profession. The crucial difference between the case-study model as it was applied in the beginnings of social work and the way in which it can be applied now is the availability of greatly improved research methodology. Earlier case studies had to be highly subjective and were impervious to control across different investigators and practitioners. Research methodology now exists that can insure more objectivity, more replicability, and thus more generalizability—although further development and refinement are certainly needed.

The group-sample model is still needed, especially if it can incorporate study of the experimental variable itself (Jayaratne, 1977). One of its disadvantages is that the direct practitioner cannot carry out this type of research alone; it is expensive in terms of both money and personnel—factors that are not under the control of the individual practitioner. An advantage of the single-case models, on the other hand, is that they can be used by practitioners themselves. Every case can and should be a research project for the practitioner.

## IMPLICATIONS FOR EDUCATION

The profession must face the possibility that the reason so many of the research studies reviewed showed negative outcomes is that the practitioners involved in them—MSWs as much as or perhaps more than BAs—were not competent. The research does not present definitive evidence of this, but its possibility or even probability cannot be ignored. Many of the studies give the impression that neither researchers nor practitioners adhered to a logical conceptualization of the process of intervention. They skipped or carried out inadequately one or more of the crucial steps in the practice process and instead imposed on clients their preferred ideology of intervention.

Various types of intervention, such as the formed-group experience, insight-oriented psychotherapy, behavior modification, or social therapy, are each useful for some people with some problems in some circumstances. These techniques are merely tools, good only for the job for which they are fitted. In the course of their graduate study, some MSWs become enamored of ideologies related to one or another interventive theory or technique, but techniques or theories are things, and things are not appropriate objects for dedication and commitment. None of the very wide range of approaches and techniques subsumed under the broad rubric of casework are either bad or good in themselves. They are good when they fit the problem, the client, and the goals, and they are bad, that is, ineffective, when they do not. Thus, it is necessary for the MSW to possess a wide repertoire of interventive theories and skills. The direct practitioner cannot afford to be wedded to one set of techniques or to one ideology of the helping process. Social work is the most difficult of the helping professions because it deals with the widest range of people and problems and the most difficult problems that often are not accessible to the skills of the other helping professions. But social work has the shortest training period of the major helping disciplines, and the current trend seems to be to shorten it even farther.

One conclusion of this study was that the primary role of the MSW, who is more often being used in supervisory and other middle-management roles, is to think—to take responsibility for the processes of analyzing and defining problems, setting goals, devising strategies of intervention, and monitoring and evaluating the effectiveness of the intervention. In view of this conclusion, the growing trend to prepare supervisory personnel for practice agencies through graduate social work programs in administration rather than in practice is disturbing. Such programs may teach knowledge of organizational theory and skills relating to the complex administrative bureaucracies of social agencies better than did the more traditional curricula in casework and group work, but they leave another vacuum that is even more serious. The new MSW supervisors know little about direct practice itself, which is the program of their agencies and the content they must teach to the practitioners under their supervision who are working directly with clients. As a result of the MSWs' inability to teach skills they have not learned themselves, the quality of the practitioners' work with clients and the effectiveness of the agency's program will be poor. Graduate social work education needs collaborative programs that offer the best of both direct-practice and administration curricula.

The interventions studied in this group of research projects were, with some exceptions, skewed toward the individual in the overall configuration of "person-in-situation." A number of studies reported efforts to reach out to and intervene with pathogenic factors in the social system that affected their clients' lives, but this was apparently casework or group work. It is necessary, therefore, for caseworkers and group workers to develop, refine, and teach techniques of intervention in the social system such as brokerage, advocacy, confrontation, manipulation of systems, bargaining, and negotiation. Social work has not given to these approaches anywhere near the amount of work on conceptualizing and abstracting principles of practice that it has given, for example, to conceptualizing the use of relationship in casework or the use of group process in group work. But this dimension of practice may be the basis for knowledge-building in the theory and practice of direct intervention.

A number of studies have found that practitioners are not particularly interested in research (Rosenblatt, 1968; Kirk, Osmalov, and Fischer, 1976; and Wood, 1977). One reason may be that practitioners do not see the similarity of the professional process they engage in to that utilized by researchers. There is still controversy over whether, as Gilbert and Specht believe, "practitioners are primarily responsible for fulfilling the service-giving obligations of the profession" and not for building knowledge (1975, p. 339). As Brown states, this view creates a false and hollow dichotomy; knowledge is available from the field as well as from academia. Social workers in their practice are engaging in research. They may not be aware of it, and it may not be done in a systematic manner.... [1975, p. 501].

Practitioners need to treat every case as an opportunity to experiment with and test their practice theory. However, graduate social work education is not doing very well in educating students to be research-minded. As Hudson states,

we have done a generally feeble job of teaching clinical workers methods that will enable them to monitor their own progress with single clients. Instead, we teach them group research procedures knowing full well that the overwhelming majority of these workers will never utilize such knowledge or skill within the context of their practice and its evaluation. In short, we have not shown our students that research is relevant to practice, and that may be a very large reason for the usually dismal outcomes obtained in typical experiments designed to evaluate casework treatment. That is, the research methodology employed in such studies may simply not be relevant to the problem at hand [1976, p. 211].

Research should be taught to graduate students by practice teachers so that it can be integrated from the beginning with the teacher and learning of practice itself.

## CONCLUSIONS

Has research proved that casework and group work are dead? The empirical evidence from these studies leads to an answer of "no," but also indicates that the direct practice methods of social work may need some vigorous therapy themselves if they are to survive and to demonstrate their usefulness. Recommendations drawn from this "study of studies" are that practitioners must become more aware of the similarity between the practice process and the research process and must apply the thought and methodology of research to practice; that graduate schools of social work must improve their teaching of research and make it more relevant to the needs of students of direct practice; that teachers of direct practice must incorporate teaching of research methodology into their teaching of practice; and that researchers must generate studies that focus on process as well as on outcome and that lead to prescriptions for practice.

## BIBLIOGRAPHY

*Readers will note that bibliographical style has been used for references
in this article. It is used only for reviews of the literature.*

Alexander, Leslie B., and Siman, Alan. "Fischer's Study of Studies," *Social
Work,* 18 (July 1973), pp. 104–106.

Behling, John. *An Experimental Study to Measure the Effectiveness of
Casework Service.* Columbus, Ohio: Franklin County Welfare Department,
1961.

Berleman, William. "A Cautionary Cheer: Some Reservations Regarding
the Interpretation of Findings," in Joel Fischer, ed., *The Effectiveness of
Social Casework,* Springfield, Ill.: Charles C Thomas, 1976, pp. 169–75.

––––––, and Steinburn, Thomas. "The Execution and Evaluation of a Delinquency Prevention Program," *Social Problems,* 14 (Spring 1967), pp. 413–
23.

––––––. *Delinquency Prevention Experiments: A Reappraisal.* Seattle,
Wash.: Seattle Atlantic Street Settlement, 1968.

Berleman, William; Seaberg, James; and Steinburn, Thomas. "The Delinquency Prevention Experiment of the Seattle Atlantic Street Center: A Final
Evaluation," *Social Service Review,* 46 (September 1972), pp. 323–46.

Blenkner, Margaret; Bloom, Martin; and Nielson, Margaret. "A Research
and Demonstration Project of Protective Services," *Social Casework,* 52
(October 1971), pp. 489–506.

Blenkner, Margaret; Jahn, Julius; and Wasser, Edna. *Serving the Aging: An
Experiment in Social Work and Public Health Nursing.* New York: Community Service Society, 1964.

Briar, Scott. "The Current Crisis in Social Casework," in National Conference on Social Welfare, *Social Work Practice, 1967.* New York: Columbia
University Press, 1967, pp. 19–33.

––––––. "The Casework Predicament," *Social Work,* 13 (January 1968),
pp. 5–11.

Brown, Gordon E. (ed.). *The Multi-Problem Dilemma.* Metuchen, N.J.:
Scarecrow Press, 1968.

Brown, John. "Research by Practitioners," letter, *Social Work,* 20 (November 1975), p. 501.

Buckley, Walter. *Sociology and Modern Systems Theory.* Englewood
Cliffs, N.J.: Prentice-Hall, 1967.

Cohen, Jerome. "A Brief Comment: Evaluating the Effectiveness of an
Unspecified 'Casework' Treatment in Producing Change," in Joel Fischer,
ed., *The Effectiveness of Social Casework.* Springfield, Ill.: Charles C
Thomas, 1976, pp. 176–89.

Cohen, Pauline, and Krause, Merton. *Casework with Wives of Alcoholics.*
New York: Family Service Association of America, 1971.

Craig, Maude M., and Furst, Philip W. "What Happens After Treatment?
A Study of Potentially Delinquent Boys," *Social Service Review,* 39 (June
1965), pp. 165–71.

Dukes, William F. "N=1," *Psychological Bulletin,* 64 (July 1965), pp.
74–79.

Empey, LaMar, and Erickson, Maynard. *The Provo Experiment.* Lexington, Mass.: Lexington Books, 1972.

Etzioni, Amitai. *Modern Organizations.* Englewood Cliffs, N.J.: Prentice-
Hall, 1964.

Fischer, Joel. "Is Casework Effective? A Review," *Social Work,* 18 (January 1973a), pp. 5–20.

——. "Has Mighty Casework Struck Out?" *Social Work,* 18 (July 1973b), pp. 107–110.

—— (ed.). *The Effectiveness of Social Casework.* Springfield, Ill.: Charles C Thomas, 1976.

Flomenhaft, Kalman; Kaplan, David; and Langsley, Donald. "Avoiding Psychiatric Hospitalization," *Social Work,* 14 (October 1969), pp. 38–45.

Geismar, Ludwig. "Implications of a Family Life Improvement Project," *Social Casework,* 52 (July 1971), pp. 455–65.

——. "Thirteen Evaluative Studies," in Edward J. Mullen and James R. Dumpson, eds., *Evaluation of Social Intervention.* San Francisco: Jossey-Bass, 1972, pp. 15–38.

——, and Ayres, Beverly. *Patterns of Change in Problem Families: A Study of the Social Functioning and Movement of 150 Families Served by the Family Centered Project.* St. Paul, Minn.: Family Centered Project, Greater St. Paul Community Chest and Council, 1960.

Geismar, Ludwig, and Krisberg, Jane. "The Family Life Improvement Project: An Experiment in Preventive Intervention: Part I," *Social Casework,* 47 (November 1966a), pp. 563–70.

——. "The Family Life Improvement Project: An Experiment in Intervention: Part II," *Social Casework,* 47 (December 1966b), pp. 663–67.

——. *The Forgotten Neighborhood.* Metuchen, N.J.: Scarecrow Press, 1967.

Geismar, Ludwig et al. *Early Supports for Family Life: A Social Work Experiment.* Metuchen, N.J.: Scarecrow Press, 1972.

Gilbert, Neil, and Specht, Harry. "Training for Direct Service," letter, *Social Work,* 20 (July 1975), p. 339.

Gottman, John. "N-of-one and N-of-two Research in Psychotherapy," *Psychological Bulletin,* 80 (August 1973), pp. 93–105.

Gyarfas, Mary, and Nee, Robert. "Was It Really Casework?" *Social Work,* 18 (July 1973), pp. 3–4.

Hall, Richard. *Organizations: Structure and Process.* 2nd ed. Englewood Cliffs, N.J.: Prentice-Hall, 1977.

Hollis, Florence. *Casework: A Psychosocial Therapy.* New York: Random House, 1972.

Howe, Michael. "Casework Self-Evaluation: A Single Subject Approach," *Social Service Review,* 48 (March 1974), pp. 1–23.

Hudson, Walter. "Casework as a Causative Agent in Client Deterioration: A Research Note on the Fischer Assessment," *Social Service Review,* 48 (September 1974), pp. 442–49.

——. "Special Problems in the Assessment of Growth and Deterioration," in Joel Fischer, ed., *The Effectiveness of Social Casework.* Springfield, Ill.: Charles C Thomas, 1976, pp. 197–224.

——. "First Axioms of Treatment," *Social Work,* 23 (January 1978), pp. 65–66.

Jayaratne, Srinika. "Single-Subject and Group Designs in Treatment Evaluation," *Social Work Research and Abstracts,* 13 (Fall 1977), pp. 35–42.

Katz, Daniel, and Kahn, Robert. *The Social Psychology of Organizations.* New York: John Wiley & Sons, 1966.

Kirk, Stuart A.; Osmalov, Michael J.; and Fischer, Joel. "Social Workers' Involvement in Research," *Social Work,* 21 (March 1976), pp. 121–24.

Klein, Malcolm. *Street Gangs and Street Workers.* Englewood Cliffs, N.J.: Prentice-Hall, 1971.

Langsley, Donald G.; Pittman, Frank; and Flomenhaft, Kalman. "Family Crisis Therapy—Results and Implications," *Family Process,* 7 (September 1968), pp. 145–58.

Langsley, Donald G., et al. *The Treatment of Families in Crisis.* New York: Grune & Stratton, 1968.

Levitt, Eugene. "The Results of Psychotherapy with Children: An Evaluation," *Journal of Consulting Psychology,* 21 (June 1957), pp. 189–196.

———; Beiser, Helen; and Robertson, Raymond. "A Follow-up Evaluation of Cases Treated at a Community Child Guidance Clinic," *American Journal of Orthopsychiatry,* 29 (April 1959), pp. 337–347.

McCabe, Alice et al. *The Pursuit of Promise.* New York: Community Service Society, 1967.

Meyer, Henry; Borgatta, Edgar; and Jones, Wyatt. *Girls at Vocational High: An Experiment in Social Work Intervention.* New York: Russell Sage Foundation, 1965.

Miller, Walter B. "The Impact of a Community Group Work Program on Delinquent Corner Groups," *Social Service Review,* 31 (December 1957), pp. 390–406.

———. "Preventive Work with Street-Corner Groups: Boston Delinquency Project," *Annals of the American Academy of Political and Social Sciences,* 322 (March 1959), pp. 97–106.

———. "The Impact of a 'Total Community' Delinquency Control Project," *Social Problems,* 10 (Fall 1962), pp. 168–91.

Mullen, Edward; Chazin, Robert; and Feldstein, David. *Preventing Chronic Dependency.* New York: Community Service Society, 1970.

———. "Services for the Newly Dependent: An Assessment," *Social Service Review,* 46 (September 1972), pp. 309–22.

Olson, Irene. *Some Effects of Increased Financial Assistance and Improved Social Services for Families Receiving Aid to Families with Dependent Children Grants.* Baltimore, Md.: Baltimore County Social Services, 1968.

———. "Some Effects of Increased Aid in Money and Social Services to Families Getting A.F.D.C. Grants," *Child Welfare,* 49 (February 197C), pp. 94–104.

Parad, Howard (ed.). *Crisis Intervention.* New York: Columbia University Press, 1962.

Perlman, Helen Harris. "Casework and the Case of Chemung County," in Gordon Brown, ed., *The Multi-Problem Dilemma.* Metuchen, N.J.: Scarecrow Press, 1968, pp. 47–71.

Polemis, Bernice. "Is the Case Closed?" in Joel Fischer, ed., *The Effectiveness of Social Casework.* Springfield, Ill.: Charles C Thomas, 1976, pp. 232–61.

Reid, William. "Needed: A New Science for Clinical Social Work," in Joel Fischer, ed., *The Effectiveness of Social Casework.* Springfield, Ill.: Charles C Thomas, 1976, pp. 262–72.

———, and Shyne, Ann. *Brief and Extended Casework.* New York: Columbia University Press, 1969.

Rosenblatt, Aaron. "The Practitioner's Use and Evaluation of Research," *Social Work,* 13 (January 1968), pp. 53–59.

Schwartz, Edward E. "Strategies of Research in Public Welfare Administration: The Field Experiment," in *Trends in Social Work Practice and Knowledge: NASW Tenth Anniversary Symposium.* New York: National Association of Social Workers, 1966, pp. 164–78.

————, and Sample, William C. "First Findings from Midway," *Social Service Review,* 41 (June 1967), pp. 113–51.

————. *The Midway Office.* New York: National Association of Social Workers, 1972.

Tait, Columbus, and Hodges, Emory. *Delinquents, Their Families, and The Community.* Springfield, Ill.: Charles C Thomas, 1962.

Wallace, David. "The Chemung County Evaluation of Casework Service to Dependent Multiproblem Families: Another Problem Outcome." *Social Service Review,* 41 (December 1967), pp. 379–89.

Warren, Roland, and Smith, Jesse. "Casework Service to Chronically Dependent Multiproblem Families." *Social Service Review,* 37 (March 1963), pp. 33–40.

Webb, Allen P., and Riley, Patrick. "Effectiveness of Casework with Young Female Probationers," *Social Casework,* 51 (November 1970), pp. 566–72.

Wilkinson, Kenneth, and Ross, Peggy. "Evaluation of the Mississippi A.F.D.C. Experiment," *Social Service Review,* 46 (September 1972), pp. 363–77.

Wilson, Robert. *Evaluation of Pilot Project in the Rehabilitation of Dependent Families.* Wilmington: Community Services Council of Delaware, 1966.

————. "An Evaluation of Intensive Casework Impact," *Public Welfare,* 25 (October 1967), pp. 301–6.

Wood, Katherine. "The Contribution of Psychoanalysis and Ego Psychology to Social Casework," in Herbert Strean, ed., *Social Casework: Theories in Action.* Metuchen, N.J.: Scarecrow Press, 1971, pp. 45–122.

————. "The Therapist as Irritant: Paradigmatic Interventions in the Client's Closed System," *Clinical Social Work Journal,* 1 (Summer 1973), pp. 118–29.

————. "The Impact of Social Work Outcome Research on Social Work Direct Practice." Unpublished doctoral dissertation, Graduate School of Social Work, Rutgers—The State University, 1977.

# 24   Advocacy and Professional Ethics

## NEIL GILBERT AND HARRY SPECHT

Advocacy became prominent among social work practitioners in the 1960s. But prominence should not be mistaken for novelty: advocacy was a part of social work practice long before it was labeled as such in the 1960s. Since the beginning of social work practice, as Levy points out, many social agencies have included advocacy among their functions, and, certainly, many individual social workers

Reprinted with permission of NASW from *Social Work* 21:4 (July 1976), pp. 288–93. Copyright 1976, National Association of Social Workers, Inc.

defended the interests of their clients before advocacy activities were explicitly defined.[1]

Advocacy, then, was not a new concept in the sixties. On the contrary, social workers throughout this century have discussed and tried to resolve the problematic issue of advocacy's place in social work practice. This issue is, according to Schwartz, the "grand-daddy" of social work dilemmas, for it embodies the conflict of the "social" versus the "psychological" and involves "[social work's] responsibility for social reform on the one hand, and individual help to people in trouble on the other."[2] A dilemma for generations of social workers, this problem has been identified anew by each generation in its own terms.[3]

Although practitioners throughout the century have tried to clarify advocacy's role in social work practice, between 1935 and 1960 concern with this issue was often submerged. During these years the profession's attention was focused more on therapeutic and clinical modes of intervention than on social issues such as poverty, discrimination, and client rights. In the 1960s, however, the civil rights movement and other more general societal pressures for social justice led to the reaffirmation of social work's concern with the client's overall treatment by society and the profession's advocacy functions. That reaffirmation was made explicit and a degree of professional legitimacy lent to advocacy by the publication in *Social Work* in 1969 of a statement framed by the Ad Hoc Committee on Advocacy.[4] The committee, which had been established by the National Association of Social Workers' (NASW) Task Force on the Urban Crisis and Public Welfare Problems, issued a statement that was based on four significant papers on advocacy-related topics written by Grosser, Briar, Miller, and Brager, respectively.[5]

Since the late 1960s and the publication of the Ad Hoc Committee's statement, a rash of papers has appeared on the subject of advocacy. By and large, these papers have used as a starting point the statement of the Ad Hoc Committee and the four papers on which it was based. Because the term "advocacy" has various connotations, those who have written about the subject have actually discussed a wide range of behaviors that, although referred to as advocacy, are considerably different. In the literature, for example, one finds the word used to describe consumer education, civil rights and social protest actions, referral and social brokerage activities, and a big brother program for the developmentally disabled.[6] It would seem, therefore, that "advocacy" has come to mean all things to all workers.

Thus, on one hand, applying the abstract notion of advocacy to the practice of social work has some felicitous results: everyone is free to dream their own dreams and hope their own hopes, most of which are not detrimental to practice. Further, as a symbolic response to the demands that social work become more relevant to the quest for social justice, the call for advocacy has been attractive to the profession. Had the call been merely for sound and ethical social work practice, it would have seemed an old and familiar appeal; advocacy seemed to be something new.

However, the theoretical delineation of advocacy functions has had certain disadvantages. As the authors have noted elsewhere, the expediency of abstraction provides advantages to social welfare policies and social work that are often only short-lived.[7] Abstract ideas such as advocacy contain implicit directives for behavior. As an idea increases in popularity, efforts to specify those directives also increase. Certain problems arise here. For among the illustrations and operational definitions of advocacy there is much mischief and some downright harmful notions concerning how social workers should behave in discharging advocacy functions. In this article the authors examine some of the operational directives for advocacy that they consider to be out of keeping with sound professional conduct. Their objective is to demonstrate how the concept of advocacy has been subtly transformed to legitimate a form of social work in which the client is relegated to a position that would be highly problematic for any profession.

## TWO DEFINITIONS

In its statement in *Social Work* in 1969, the Ad Hoc Committee on Advocacy presented two different definitions of advocacy with the observation that they "overlap at many points."[8] The first definition was taken from Briar, who describes the advocate as "... his client's supporter, his adviser, his champion, and, if need be, his representative in his dealings with the court, the police, the social agency, and other organizations that [affect] his well-being."[9] Briar further explicitly notes that the social worker's primary allegiance should be to his client, not to the agency that employs him.[10]

Briar's definition reflects a shift in the relationship between social workers and agencies that took place in the 1960s.[11] Up to that time, the majority of social workers had been taught that, as professionals, they were extensions or representatives of their agencies. Many of them modified this view by the early sixties and began to emphasize that adherence to professional, as distinct from agency, standards and ethics was necessary if services that were in the best interests of the client were to be provided. The employing agency was now seen as part of, or only an agent of, a larger system of government. The professional's job was to help his client better utilize the systems around him, which included the client's family, the workers' employing agency, other social service agencies, and the government.

The Ad Hoc Committee's first definition of the advocate was not accepted without reservation by all members of the profession. Certain aspects of the advocate's defined role seemed to raise troublesome issues. Schwartz, for one, was concerned about the perspective voiced by Briar on the relationship between the employing agency and the social worker as advocate. He argued that the "agency-bad, client-good" distinction was oversimplified and that the polarity created by such a distinction encouraged a shallow analysis of client-agency practice. Schwartz pursued his point this way:

> [The advocates] subvert their own real identification with the poor and the oppressed by their neglect of the dialectics of the client-agency relationship. An agency is not a static organization with no play of internal forces; and those who insist that it is must cut themselves off from the most progressive elements within it, and take their clients with them. . . .
>
> The basic relationship between an institution and its people is symbiotic; each needs the other for his own survival. . . . It is a form of social contract; and when the arrangement goes wrong, as it frequently does, those who claim that the contract is broken do no service to the people or to the agency. The arena of need remains the same, and the symbiosis remains intact—merely obscure to the unpracticed eye.[12]

The Ad Hoc Committee did not delve into the troublesome issues about the worker-agency relationship that were raised for some practitioners by its first definition. The second definition presented by the committee pursued the notion that the interests of the client were the first concern of the advocate. This definition was taken from Brager, who stated that the advocate

> . . . identifies with the plight of the disadvantaged. He sees as his primary responsibility the tough-minded and partisan representation of their interests, and this supersedes his fealty to others. This role inevitably requires that the practitioner function as a political tactician.[13]

## CODE OF ETHICS

Both definitions of advocacy put forward by the Ad Hoc Committee are in substantial harmony with the social worker's Code of Ethics. The code was adopted in 1960, nine years before the Ad Hoc Committee's pronouncements on advocacy.[14] Among the Code's provisions, which are approximately as general as the Ad Hoc Committee's definitions, is the statement that the social worker's primary obligation is to the welfare of his client, whether that client is an individual or a group. Furthermore, the Code indicates the worker's responsibility for modifying agency practices that are unethical or that prevent workers from conducting themselves in keeping with the Code.[15] The Code's description of the social worker's responsibilities, then, is in several important respects actually echoed by the definitions of the Ad Hoc Committee. In fact, the advocate as defined by the committee appears to be nothing more than a social worker who conducts himself in accord with the standards of behavior set forth in the profession's Code of Ethics.*

Beyond symbolically reaffirming ethical practice, what purpose is served, then, by applying the advocacy label to social work functions? Why is the image of the ethical social worker so unappealing that it must be clothed in the guise of advocacy to attract the profession's attention? The latter problem is clearly exemplified in the discussion of the "advocacy challenge" by Wineman and James:

> Imagine the student—caseworker, group worker, or community organization practitioner—who is witness to an act of client dehumanization. *If* [italics added] he wants to enter the lists of advocacy in behalf of a client, only one condition is necessary and sufficient for initiating such action: that his school will regard his action with enthusiasm and support.[16]

Certainly, ethical practice would dictate that no "ifs" be operative regarding instances of client dehumanization. It would also deem a professional to be in violation of the Code of Ethics if he did not support action on behalf of his client in such an instance.[17] Would the advocate social worker and the ethical social worker behave differently in this situation? As described by Wineman and James, there seems to be a choice here between advocacy and some other acceptable form of practice.

The only potentially discordant note between the Code of Ethics and the Ad Hoc Committee's definitions of advocacy involves Brager's reference to the practitioner as "political tactician." This reference is potentially discordant because the phrase "political tactician" has many disturbing connotations. Brager's interpretation of the advocate's role emphasizes "the conscious rearranging of reality to induce a desired attitudinal or behavioral outcome."[18] He claims that the advocate as political tactician is sometimes justified in manipulating others. Schwartz's comments on this aspect of the advocate's role reflect the deeply troublesome issues that such notions present for practitioners. "We find ourselves," he says, "developing a literature of guile, with Machiavelli as the new culture hero."[19] Nevertheless, the Ad Hoc Committee put forward Brager's definition of advocacy

---

*Editors' Note.: In November 1979, NASW adopted a new Code of Ethics, effective July 1, 1980, which differs considerably from the 1960 code.

without explicitly commenting on this issue. In fact, in a specific example of proper conduct that it cited and that will be examined shortly, the committee apparently condoned Brager's interpretation.

## PROFESSIONAL BEHAVIOR

If the levels of discourse on advocacy were all as general as the definitions cited above, this article would not have been written. The authors would have been content to view advocacy as simply another expression of the profession's commitment to the well-being of the people it serves. However, not all efforts to specify advocacy and its behavioral correlates are harmless exercises in drawing superficial distinctions. Indeed, there are a few important exceptions in which attempts to distinguish advocacy behavior are neither superficial nor harmless. These formulations seem to have gained a degree of legitimacy and popular acceptance that far outweighs their merits as guidelines for professional behavior. They are sharply illustrated in the behavioral prescriptions for advocacy put forth by the Ad Hoc Committee.

Recognizing that its general definitions of advocacy raised a number of unresolved issues about specific choices in practice, the Ad Hoc Committee attempted to provide some behavioral guidelines. Two of these guidelines in particular warrant close scrutiny.

First, the committee proposed the following dilemma: What should the advocate do if the promotion of his client's interests in obtaining a scarce resource would deny that resource to someone else? What if this person's need were as great as or greater than the advocate's client? Considering that needy clients and scarce resources are not the exception but the rule in the social services, a dilemma such as the one outlined by the committee would arise, in all likelihood, in the majority of situations with which the advocate social worker deals. And in circumstances involving competing claims on resources between the advocate's client and others in need, the Ad Hoc Committee advised the advocate to weigh the relative urgency of respective claims before deciding to support his client's interest:

> Suppose, for instance, that a child welfare worker has as a client a child who is in need of care that can only be provided by a treatment institution with limited intake. Does he then become a complete partisan in order to gain admission of his client at the expense of other children in need? What of the public assistance worker seeking emergency clothing allowances for his clients when the demand is greater than the supply? Quite

clearly, in either case the worker should be seeking to increase the total availability of the scarce resource. But while working toward this end, he faces the dilemma of competing individual claims. In such a situation, professional norms would appear to dictate that the relative urgency of the respective claims be weighed.[20]

This is an incredible piece of advice which, if taken seriously, would virtually immobilize all advocacy efforts, if not all direct social work practice. Consider the committee's example of a placement in a child welfare institution. Suppose that the institution serves a medium-sized city and has fifty placements and a waiting list of approximately one hundred and fifty applicants at any given time. Its research staff estimates that there are about four hundred additional children in the population who have never been referred but who would potentially qualify to receive the institution's services. These figures are arbitrary, but they are not exceptionally high; there are many social service agencies that are larger, serve broader geographic regions, and have higher numbers on waiting lists and greater estimates of undiscovered need.

In the example of the above institution, how would the advocate follow the behavioral guideline of weighing the relative urgency of respective claims before seeking to gain placement for his client? At the least, he would have to compare his client's need to that of one hundred and fifty other applicants. Moreover, a rigorous application of the Ad Hoc Committee's behavioral prescription would require him to seek out the other estimated four hundred children in potential need and make a relative assessment of their claims.

Aside from the prohibitive time and cost factors that make such behavior impractical, certain questions arise. What criteria are social work advocates going to use in weighing the relative urgency of respective claims? Furthermore, who gives an advocate license to decide whether one client is more deserving of service than another? These questions are not intended to imply that mechanisms for mediating among competing claims for social service resources are. unnecessary. Such mechanisms are needed, and they exist. The examples given by the Ad Hoc Committee of the child welfare agency and the public welfare department imply that organizations of these types have elaborate sets of rules and policies governing client intake and allocation of scarce resources. These mechanisms may be imperfect and in need of change. But superseding them with the individual judgment of the worker and calling this substitution "advocacy" does not represent an improvement. Imagine a physician telling his patient that he needs an operation. Imagine him then saying that before making a referral to the hospital he must assess, *according to his own criteria,* the relative urgency of all other operations pending at the hospital! Such a professional might be called many things, but surely not an advocate.

## SECOND GUIDELINE

The second behavioral prescription offered by the Ad Hoc Committee concerns the situation in which advocacy on behalf of an individual client is incompatible with advocacy on behalf of class interests and institutional change:

> To what extent does one risk injury to his client's interests in the short run on behalf of institutional changes in the long run? It seems clear that there can be no hard-and-fast rules governing such situations. One cannot arbitrarily write off any action that may temporarily cause his clients hardship if he believes the ultimate benefits of his action will outweigh any initial harm.[21]

The community may well be skeptical of a profession's announcement that its members are free to discomfort or disadvantage their clients whenever *they* believe such action will, in the long run, produce beneficial institutional changes. The argument that these changes will ultimately benefit the clients themselves may not mollify the individual client, who may be doubtful about being around "in the long run" to reap the benefits of the hoped-for change.

The issue here is not whether the individual client should or should not suffer temporary hardships for the greater good of institutional change and class interests. An individual's sacrifice for the greater good may be either a noble gesture or enlightened self-interest, depending on whether the greater good redounds to that individual's ultimate benefit. Rather, the issues are these: Who will weigh the potential losses and benefits in a given situation? Who will choose to act out of noble impulse or enlightened self-interest? Who will determine just how long the "long run" will be? And who will decide whether any sacrifice will be made? Contrary to the prescription of the Ad Hoc Committee, the authors believe that a professional understanding, a "hard-and-fast rule," exists that governs situations similar to those the committee described. This rule dictates that the professional *cannot* act on behalf of a client without the client's desire and permission; it is the client, furthermore, not the professional, who decides whether injury to the client's interests in the short run is to be risked to gain institutional changes in the long run.

Generally speaking, the short-term consequences of any given ac-

tion can be predicted more accurately than its long-term consequences. Therefore, in weighing actions that might produce
short-term injury and long-term benefits, the social worker should be
mindful that short-term injury is more likely than benefits to be
reaped in the long run. Under such circumstances, perhaps, another
hard-and-fast rule should be followed: *primum non nocere,* the medical aphorism meaning, "First of all, do no harm." Such a rule would
certainly inspire more client confidence in the social work profession
than the Ad Hoc Committee's license for advocates to risk injuring
their clients' interests on behalf of institutional changes.

Nevertheless, the committee's behavioral prescription seems to
have gained a following in the profession. Panitch, in carrying the
committee's prescription to greater specificity, first presents a case
situation:

> A recent state law eliminated clothing grants. Three children in a family
> receiving public aid were sent home the first day of school because of
> inadequate clothing. The presumption is that there was insufficient fund-
> ing for necessary school clothes. Mismanagement resulted when clothing
> was not bought because other more pressing bills had to be paid.[22]

He then presents the advocate's stance and considerations in such a
situation:

> The social worker could arrange a donation of clothing from a local
> source, help the mother through her presumed depression, and help her
> with budgeting, which probably kept her from managing her funds from
> the outset. These are possible solutions, but they are not positions of
> advocacy. In a position of advocacy, the worker would address questions
> about children being denied their right to education by the new welfare
> law. For instance: Is the mother risking a charge of child neglect because
> of the new state law? The worker might also begin a concerted action to
> lobby for higher income provisions by referring the mother to a constit-
> uent group that deals with welfare rights, while he simultaneously initi-
> ates action in a professional association.[23]

Here is a situation in which a worker could have provided concrete
assistance to a client. Clothing allotments, interpersonal psychological support, and instruction in budgeting skills would have been of
immediate benefit to the client. According to Panitch, however, the
advocate would be more concerned with referring the mother to a
welfare rights group and pressing for institutional change than with
providing her concrete forms of immediate assistance. The short-
term injury that presumably will result from the advocate's choice
of priorities is that the children will continue to go without clothing

and will be unable to attend school, that the mother's state of depression will linger on, and that the financial mismanagement will persist. With advocates like this, who needs adversaries?

## SELF-DETERMINATION

Panitch's example is as instructive for what it omits as for what it contains, for what is omitted is any notion of client self-determination. What if the client simply wants clothing for her children to enable them to go to school? Or would like to receive some psychological support and also learn some budgeting skills? Or does not want to be a test case for the new state welfare law? Or is not interested in joining a welfare rights group? The champions of advocacy often forget that it is the right of the client to make these decisions. Perhaps it is easier to endorse professional arrogance when support is called for in the name of "social victims" and "the disadvantaged." But one of the finer aspects of preadvocacy ideas about professional behavior was that the worker was not taught to regard his client as a passive victim of society on whose behalf he, the professional, would act. Instead, the old-fashioned, ethical social worker perceived that his clients, although perhaps social victims, were nevertheless self-determining people who, given appropriate respect, support, and opportunities, could decide what was in their best short-term and long-run interests.

Recent articles on advocacy proclaim the social worker's obligation to act on his client's behalf as the worker sees it; the use of manipulation in such circumstances is also sanctioned. The idea of client self-determination is not much heralded in social work circles these days. Even in the NASW Code of Ethics, which enjoins workers not to practice discrimination in rendering services and pledges them to respect client privacy, the worker's duty to facilitate opportunities for the exercise of client self-determination is not mentioned.

Self-determination may not be an absolute or supreme value, but neither are privacy and nondiscrimination. To be sure, it is as difficult to define self-determination operationally as it is to define advocacy. Keith-Lucas points out that in one respect client self-determination is simply a fact: certain kinds of decisions, such as the decision to seek help, to change, and to grow can be made only by the client.[24] In another respect, client self-determination is an illusion: certain categories of clients, such as infants and the severely retarded, are incapable of making choices. But between the fact and the illusion there is a broad area of social work practice in which clients are capable of making choices but are not always knowledgeable about opportunities available for exercising a choice. Professionals can facilitate client self-determination by maximizing these opportunities. The difficulties involved in drawing boundaries around the elusive concept of client self-determination should not deter the worker from applying this important concept in professional practice. As Bernstein puts it,

> While self-determination is not supreme, it is supremely important. Only through the rich utilization of this concept can we fully honor the human worth value. This is in line with the best in democratic traditions. As we study and diagnose each situation, our concern should be for maximizing the choices for the people we serve. . . . Even with young children, there are appropriate matters about which they should be helped to make decisions.[25]

The NASW is planning within the not-too-distant future to ask the Delegate Assembly to revise the Code of Ethics.* Among the issues that should be on the agenda for discussion is whether maximizing opportunities for client self-determination merits more specific recognition than it is currently receiving in the code. At the same time, a determination should be made whether the behavioral prescriptions for the social worker as advocate that are found in the literature adequately reflect the ethical strictures of the profession. The implications for professional behavior that stem from social work's commitment to advocacy and to client self-determination must be examined, and appropriate limits for professional behavior in these areas must be defined. Specifying these limits and implications is both an intellectual challenge and a professional responsibility. The forthcoming revision of the Code of Ethics will enable the profession to address this challenge and fulfill its responsibility by clarifying, and possibly reordering, the standards of conduct contained in the code. The first step toward dealing with these issues is to recognize that the fervor and good intentions surrounding recent prescriptions for advocacy must be tempered by equally intense concern for client self-determination.

## NOTES

1. Charles Levy, "Advocacy and the Injustice of Justice," *Social Service Review*, 48 (March 1974), pp. 39–50.
2. William Schwartz, "Private Troubles and Public Issues: One Social Work Job or Two?" *The Social Welfare Forum, 1969*, proceedings of the 96th Annual Forum of the National Conference on Social Welfare (New York: Columbia University Press, 1969), p. 25.

---

*See Editors' Note earlier in this chapter.

3. *Ibid.,* pp. 26–27. *See also* Mary Richmond, "The Retail Method of Reform," in Joanna C. Colcord, ed., *The Long View* (New York: Russell Sage Foundation, 1930), pp. 215–16; Porter R. Lee, *Social Work as Cause and Function and Other Papers* (New York: Columbia University Press, 1937), p. 3; Kenneth L. M. Pray, *Social Work in a Revolutionary Age and Other Papers* (Philadelphia: University of Pennsylvania Press, 1949), p. 231; Clarke A. Chambers, "An Historical Perspective on Political Action *vs.* Individualized Treatment," in *Current Issues in Social Work Seen in Historical Perspective* (New York: Council on Social Work Education, 1962), p. 54; and William Schwartz, "Small Group Science and Group Work Practice," *Social Work,* 8 (October 1963), pp. 40–41.

4. The Ad Hoc Committee on Advocacy, "The Social Worker As Advocate: Champion of Social Victims," *Social Work,* 14 (April 1969), pp. 16–22.

5. Charles F. Grosser, "Community Development Programs Serving the Urban Poor," *Social Work,* 10 (July 1965), pp. 15–21; Scott Briar, "The Current Crisis in Social Casework," *Social Work Practice,* 1967 (New York: Columbia University Press, 1967), pp. 19–33; Henry Miller, "Value Dilemmas in Social Casework," *Social Work,* 13 (January 1968), pp. 27–33; and George A. Brager, "Advocacy and Political Behavior," *Social Work,* 13 (April 1968), pp. 5–15.

6. Malinda Orlin, "A Role for Social Workers in the Consumer Movement," *Social Work,* 18 (January 1973), pp. 60–65; Mildred Pratt, "Partisan of the Disadvantaged," *Social Work,* 17 (July 1972), pp. 66–73; Grosser, *op. cit.;* Briar, *op. cit.;* Brager, *op. cit.;* and Charles W. Smiley, "Citizen Advocates for the Mentally Retarded," *Social Work,* 18 (January 1973), pp. 110–12.

7. Neil Gilbert and Harry Specht, *Dimensions of Social Welfare Policy* (Englewood Cliffs, N.J.: Prentice-Hall, 1974), pp. 91–92.

8. The Ad Hoc Committee on Advocacy, *op. cit.,* p. 17.

9. Briar, *op. cit.,* p. 28.

10. Scott Briar, "The Social Worker's Responsibility for the Civil Rights of Clients," *New Perspectives,* 1 (Spring 1968), p. 90.

11. Briar, "The Current Crisis in Social Casework," p. 32.

12. Schwartz, *op. cit.,* p. 34 and p. 38.

13. Brager, *op. cit.,* p. 6.

14. *Code of Ethics,* NASW Policy Statements, No. 1 (rev. ed.; New York: National Association of Social Workers, 1967).

15. *Ibid.*

16. David Wineman and Adrienne James, "The Advocacy Challenge to Schools of Social Work," *Social Work,* 14 (April 1969), p. 28.

17. *Code of Ethics, op. cit.*

18. Brager, *op. cit.,* p. 8.

19. Schwartz, *op. cit.,* p. 32.

20. The Ad Hoc Committee on Advocacy, *op. cit.,* p. 19.

21. *Ibid.*

22. Arnold Panitch, "Advocacy in Practice," *Social Work,* 19 (May 1974), p. 329.

23. *Ibid.*

24. Alan Keith-Lucas, "A Critique of the Principle of Client Self-determination," *Social Work,* 8 (July 1963), pp. 70–71.

25. Saul Bernstein, "Self-determination: King or Citizen in the Realm of Values?" *Social Work* (January 1960), p. 8.

# 25   Private Practice as a Social Work Function

## PAUL A. KURZMAN

The role of private practice in social work is currently the subject of considerable thought and discussion within the profession. This development is not new, for eight years ago Piliavin recommended that the private entrepreneurial model replace agency-based practice.[1] However, even those who strongly believe that the profession should give more attention to the legitimate needs of colleagues engaged in full-time or part-time private practice are at times troubled by the suggestion that private practice is a "superior service delivery mechanism" and by the implication that social work should reconsider its traditional focus on agency-based service delivery. Without denying the important contribution that private practitioners make to the profession, it is helpful to examine certain limitations of the private practice model before reaching a conclusion about its adoption.

Private practice applies the principles of private enterprise to the proprietary provision of professional services. The fields of medicine and law have largely adopted this model, and because they are old, well-established professions, a consideration of the influence of this model can be instructive. It would seem that the clients who are best served by these professions are those who have the ability to pay for their services. Consequently, the clients who are given the fewest options for service are those whose income or coverage do not allow them to pay on a fee-for-service basis. Therefore, in providing a supplement to agency services, private practice can be helpful to those who have the ability to pay. As the primary or exclusive source of clinical services, however, it would tend to rule out many who are in need. As the *Handbook on the Private Practice of Social Work* clearly states, the private practitioner "is limited to accepting only those clients who can find a way to pay for his services."[2] The serious underservicing of low-income people by the legal and medical professions is well documented, and such clients generally become the responsibility of voluntary or publicly sponsored agencies, such as the Community Action for Legal Services, the Legal Aid Society, public clinics, and municipal hospitals.

Although it is questionable whether Title XIX (Medicaid) legislation has improved the quality of service to patients, more low-

Reprinted with permission of author and NASW from *Social Work* 21:5 (September 1976), pp. 363–68. Copyright 1976, National Association of Social Workers, Inc.

income citizens are now being served, and that is an asset. It is not certain, however, whether the proprietary model, which is heavily underwritten by Medicaid legislation, is the most appropriate model for service delivery. The crucial variable is whether proprietary systems are the best way of directing quality services to a largely underserviced population.

Most professionals in private practice are free to determine which clients they accept. Although the client's ability to pay, even on the basis of a sliding scale, may be one factor in such decisions, other considerations are also important. Clients with severe illnesses accompanied by disruptive acting-out behavior may be considered less desirable than others, both for reasons of setting and because of the relative difficulty in engaging many such clients in the treatment process. Although agencies have their own, sometimes more subtle, justifications for selecting clients, they tend to operate within a community context and do not have the same freedom as private practitioners in choosing or rejecting clients. In making their selections, public and voluntary agencies are influenced by their sources of funding, by oversight of the communities they service, and by the standards of the public or private boards to which they are accountable.

Client service policies are sometimes ineffective because organizations have maintenance needs and thus can be self-serving. Therefore, accountability to the client community can be inadequate in both individual and agency settings. Individuals as well as institutions have survival goals, and a tendency for "goal displacement" can develop when there is an inversion of ends and means.[3] Fortunately, most agencies are subject to self-corrective mechanisms that monitor the selection of clients. Governmental agencies have a public mandate, and voluntary agencies that receive major funding from the public sector must accept the clientele required by their sources of funding. Therefore, intake control is provided by agency sponsors rather than through third-party arrangements or the judgment of an individual practitioner.[4]

Organizations generally have a capacity as well as a mandate to commit resources to outreach arrangements, even when there is no guarantee of immediate return. In attempting to help mental health professionals improve their service to blue-collar families, Glasser and his colleagues found that psychiatrists in private practice would not participate in labor union efforts to orient them about the mental health needs of their members unless they were paid their usual fees.[5] However, Glasser's report continues, "these attitudes were not usually evident among the psychiatrists and other mental health personnel associated with community mental health centers and other organized mental health programs."[6] The distinction would appear not to be between the attitudes of psychiatrists and social workers, but between practitioners in private practice and those in agencies.

The experience of the Arthur Lehman Counseling Service, an organization that was funded principally through client fees, is ably recorded by Fizdale.[7] Reporting on service over a fifteen-year period (1954–69), she indicates that clients were heavily concentrated in "professional and highly technical occupations . . . well-educated . . . [and] economically advantaged."[8] Fees were initially set at an amount less than those generally charged by psychiatrists, but considerably higher than those charged by other voluntary agencies. Furthermore, the fees waived because of clients' inability to pay during the period 1968–69 was less than one-quarter of one percent of the organization's total counseling income. It is difficult to be critical of the remarkable performance that Fizdale and her staff have documented, but it should be noted that the ability to pay is highly correlated with the characteristics of the clients who can be accepted in an essentially fee-for-service arrangement.

Therefore, despite some proprietary advantages, the private enterprise model ultimately raises the question of which clients should be served. The current priorities of the social work profession, as established by the 1975 Delegate Assembly, are the alleviation of poverty and racism. It would be helpful, therefore, to determine whether a change in the social work service delivery system from primary reliance on agency-based services to an essentially entrepreneurial model would help in achieving the priorities of the profession.

## ACCOUNTABILITY AND PEER AID

It is sometimes said that private practice is more accountable to the client than agency service. Financial considerations aside, it is true that a client who is dissatisfied with one private practitioner can seek out another. But in reality, many clients who are involved in a helping relationship are not in a position to make such a change. For example, severely troubled clients with character disorders or psychotic symptomatology are in a poor position to make such assessments. In general, a client involved in a transference relationship may have difficulty in holding the therapist accountable. What alternatives do such clients have, and how are they to exercise and assess them? Such questions are not merely charitable, but are a reality of practice, as anyone knows who has worked clinically with severely troubled clients.

For sophisticated clients whose judgment also is relatively intact, the accountability process may work effectively. However, even in selecting a medical professional, such as a surgeon, many people rely not merely on evidence of a practitioner's medical expertise, but on such matters as hospital affiliation. Therefore, in addition to professional affiliations, a practitioner's organizational affiliations are important because of the tendency to place significance on the organizational context within which treatment is given. For there are situations in which even those who have relatively sophisticated lay judgment do not have the expertise or the emotional distance with which to reach an informed decision. In such situations, it is helpful to know the organizational context within which the professional functions and the institutional supports for his or her practice.

One of the difficulties of private practice in general, and for individual private practitioners in particular, is the "possible crisis of professional isolation."[9] Although it is helpful to keep current with the literature and to attend professional symposia, such activities may not be adequate substitutes for the peer exchange and stimulation that take place in organizational settings. Agencies tend to foster a system of peer learning that is more informal than planned. Discussion over lunch or a cup of coffee can be a source of new information or insight. Agencies also provide peer resources and support, especially concerning new and difficult practice problems related to clinical assessment and intervention. Agency peers can supply information derived from a variety of prior experience and training and concerning a wide range of practice specializations. This knowledge is available to all members, and it forms a system of mutual aid and expertise.

Agencies themselves may develop an organizational wisdom that builds on the experience and collective contributions of their members. Such organizational expertise tends to become greater than the sum of the knowledge of individual members, because it includes the experience of former as well as present workers, and because it draws on formal and informal organizational arrangements within both geographical and functional communities. Such resources, access, expertise, and wisdom are simply beyond what individual and group practitioners generally can provide for themselves or can expect to accumulate as a support for their practice.

## PROBLEMS OF IDENTITY

There is certainly a tendency for social workers, perhaps most often for those in full-time private practice, to think of and call themselves "psychotherapists." This is not a new development, for it was observed by Peek and Plotkin in their pilot study of private practice more than twenty-five years ago.[10] They reported that of the case-workers in private practice they interviewed (all with prior training or experience in agency settings), twenty-seven out of thirty called their clients "patients" and twenty-eight out of thirty called their own activities "psychotherapy" or "psychoanalysis."[11] Moreover, it is clear from experience with the *NASW Register of Clinical Social Workers* that many social work clinicians in private practice prefer not to identify themselves as social workers either to their clients or to the public. Their professional business cards and letterheads often identify them solely as psychotherapists, with no reference to their membership in the social work profession. This is contrary to the recommendations of the National Study Group on Private Practice as defined in the *NASW Handbook on the Private Practice of Social Work,* which explicitly states:

> The private practitioner carefully represents himself as a member of the social work profession. Although he may describe his specific area of practice in terminology that is most meaningful to another profession, it is within the context of his being a social worker.[12]

The question of identification is important. The use of psychotherapy as a treatment modality is qualitatively different from seeing oneself—and asking to be identified by others—as a psychotherapist. Competence in social work is a blend of knowledge, skill, and values derived principally from training in an accredited graduate school of social work and receiving professional sanction through such training rather than through a modality of psychotherapy.

The problem of identification is illustrated by a comment from an experienced caseworker who recently entered private practice:

> When I first started, I noticed that I tended to vacillate in identifying myself sometimes as a psychotherapist, other times as a counselor, and occasionally as a social worker. I usually called the people I saw "patients." Since I have become more secure of my identity in private practice outside an agency, however, I now identify myself consistently as a social worker, and this often provides an early opportunity to structure the treatment process with the client—and he is called a client.[13]

Although the dilemma of this practitioner is understandable, it is perhaps reassuring that she has come to terms with her professional identity. For, once again, the essential basis of competence and the authority for practice derives not merely from a modality of intervention, but from professional preparation and continued identification with an established profession.[14] Indeed, when social workers see themselves as "psychotherapists" they give up much that is uniquely their own.

## FOCUS ON FUNCTION

If practitioners lose their identity as social workers, they also relinquish the concept of professional function. Private practice under any identity tends to focus, and understandably so, on the direct-service role of professional practice. Under such conditions, practitioners tend either to relegate social policy and program development aspects to other colleagues or to see those responsibilities as a separate part of the professional function. However, program development and the formulation of social policy are not simply the domain of the community organizer, administrator, and social planner, but are the province and responsibility of all social workers, including clinicians. Moreover, they are not separate functions, assigned to attention after hours.

In this respect, the *NASW Handbook on the Private Practice of Social Work* states, "In addition to paid work time, most private practitioners allow substantial time for community and professional activities that are part of a professional person's obligations."[15] Such an implied dichotomy, however, is inappropriate, for a professional's attempts to bring about systemic change must derive organically from practice with clients. C. Wright Mills points out the distinction between what he calls the "personal troubles of milieu" and the "public issues of social structure," positing that each must be integrally stated in terms of the other.[16] He also believes there is a continuing institutional responsibility to "translate troubles into issues and issues into the terms of their human meaning for the individual."[17] In this sense, any attempt to separate private troubles from public issues cuts off each from the reinforcing power of the other. As Schwartz states: *"There can be no 'choice'—or even division of labor—between serving individual needs and dealing with social problems."*[18] He emphasizes that the professional's dual responsibility to service "personal troubles of milieu" (private troubles) and "public issues of social structure" (public issues) is an integrated social work function.[19] "Social work and social living," writes Reynolds, "instead of being in contrast, or being artificially brought together, are inextricably mixed, and inseparable."[20]

Social agencies are the arena for the conversion of private troubles into public issues, Schwartz notes, and for the integration of both functions into professional practice. Indeed, as Austin comments, casework is intrinsically bound up with the use of social services and with the development of new programs to meet client needs and strengthen social functioning; "For this reason," she states, "an institutional sponsorship seems mandatory."[21] Through the interaction of their clients and practitioners, social agencies provide the organizational auspices for attacking social problems. Frequently, social agencies can reach these goals more effectively than individual clients or practitioners, because they have the institutional framework, resources, and mandate to accomplish these goals in the larger community. If practitioners do not see themselves as engaging in social work and do not see the necessity for an integrated professional function, they are giving up not only the actual strength inherent in institutional practice, but the very opportunity that in many ways is unique to the profession.

## ACTIVITIES OF NASW AND CSWE

Questions are raised periodically regarding the nature of NASW's support for clinical practice and its recognition of the needs of the private practitioner. In its early years (1955–61), NASW showed little concern for clinical issues or the question of private practice. Levenstein notes that the predecessor organizations of NASW also neglected the issue of private practice, although they had received requests by chapters for such activity beginning in 1926.[22] In 1957, the NASW Commission on Social Work Practice acknowledged that private practice was within the working definition of social work practice and proposed interim minimum standards.[23]

The first significant NASW activity was the adoption by the national board of directors in 1961 of a definition of private practice. This was followed by the establishment of several standards (minimum qualifications) for private practice by the Delegate Assembly in 1962. In December 1964, NASW officially recognized private practice as a legitimate area of social work practice in meeting human needs; at the same time, it affirmed that "practice within socially sponsored organization structures must remain the primary avenue for the implementation of the goals of the profession."[24]

Also in 1964, NASW created the National Study Group on Private Practice, which published the first *Private Practice Handbook* in 1967. Based on the accomplishments of the study group and on a growing recognition of the needs of members in private practice, the board of directors expressed its commitment to private practice when it established a council on private practice. Obviously, the early response of the association was slow and generally inadequate in recognizing the legitimate needs of its members in private practice.

Precise figures on just how many NASW members are currently in fulltime or part-time private practice are difficult to obtain. In 1975, only 2.4 percent of association members responding to a manpower questionnaire designated private practice as their primary setting, but a surprising 22.6 percent of those indicating a method of "second employment" cited "psychotherapy." Of these, 73.6 percent indicated that they spent less than ten hours a week in such practice.[25] The NASW executive director conservatively estimates that between 8,500 and 10,000 social workers are currently in full-time or part-time private practice and that this number is expected to increase.[26]

Recent activity by NASW on behalf of private practitioners in particular and clinical practitioners in general has been substantial. Attempts to achieve recognition of social workers as third-party vendors have been a principal focus for staff and membership activity, and the efforts and achievements in this area are worth noting:

■ Independent vendor status has been achieved for qualified clinical social workers with several major insurance carriers.

■ Active negotiations have been conducted with the Health Insurance Association of America, the central agency of the insurance industry, to provide the acceptance of NASW standards for vendorship coverage by additional member companies.

■ Testimony has been given before the Senate Committee on Labor and Public Welfare, which in effect governs the health benefit coverage for 8.5 million federal employees and their dependents. The purpose of the testimony was to gain professional approval of qualified clinical social workers as individual mental health vendors.

■ Legislation has been drafted and sponsorship has been secured in both branches of Congress to provide direct reimbursement to clinical social workers under both Title XVIII (Medicare) and Title XIX (Medicaid).

■ A written agreement has been reached with the U.S. Internal Revenue Service, specifying that in both agency and private practice settings, clinical social work services are fully tax-deductible as medical services by clients.

■ Legislation has been passed in six states to amend their insurance codes to mandate the direct reimbursement of clinical social workers by insurance carriers essentially on a par with other mental health professionals.

■ Chapter directories of social workers in private practice were published in many states.

■ Local recognition was achieved for the right of clinical social workers to establish a private practice in their homes in areas zoned only to permit practice of traditionally recognized private-practice professions.

■ Provisions were established for a comprehensive yet inexpensive professional malpractice insurance plan for agencies and for individual members in private practice. Currently, over 15,000 members have obtained insurance through NASW arrangements.

■ A *Register of Clinical Social Workers* has been published, providing distinctive recognition of the clinical practitioner to third-party vendors and the public.[27]

NASW has also taken aggressive leadership in promoting the legal regulation of social work practice. It has promulgated a model licensing statute, which has become the basis for successful efforts of its chapters in achieving legal regulation for social work in twenty-two states and Puerto Rico. The association has placed licensing bills before the legislatures of twenty other states that do not have licensing provisions. Furthermore, the NASW Competence Certification Board, which sponsors the ACSW examination, is now developing specialty examinations—starting with clinical social work—that will be used to provide further recognition of practice specializations and to support autonomous clinical practice standards.

Thus, from a modest beginning, the professional association would appear to be taking a strong advocacy position on behalf of the clinical practitioner. Programs designed specifically for clinicians in part-time or full-time private practice are clearly an explicit priority in this effort; and the focus, appropriately, is on full recognition of professional social workers for the receipt of third-party payments.[28]

### Implications for Education

The Council on Social Work Education (CSWE) and graduate schools of social work have been requested by some social work clinicians to reorient their educational focus toward preparing "psychotherapists for private practice." The author would approach this request with concern, however, and suggests that schools of social work should train not psychotherapists or private practitioners, but professional social workers who will be able to make skillful use of several social work methods in a variety of settings and deploy a range of practice modalities.

Schools of social work and the CSWE should be committed to the social work profession, not to psychotherapy. They should foster the serving of a variety of clients in public, private, and voluntary settings on a publicly sponsored, prepaid, or fee-for-service basis, with a clear guarantee to the client that he or she is receiving a professional social work service founded on the collective expertise of the profession. This mandate represents a challenge, but it is more helpful to meet such challenges than to look for or accept simplistic solutions. If this position seems idealistic or philanthropic, it should be remembered that it is the very uniqueness of the social work mandate that has drawn many to the profession. For most students and practitioners the meeting of this challenge is a decision of choice and represents the reason they have chosen social work over other mental health professions.

## TOWLE AND HAMILTON

It has been suggested that private practice represents the values and traditions of Charlotte Towle and Gordon Hamilton. Such a suggestion should be approached with some caution and concern. Virtually all of Towle's career was spent in teaching and in agency-based practice. Historically, her impact was on practice and adminis-tration in the public sector, above all in establishing the concept of public assistance as a "right" and not "charity." As a teacher, she stressed the need for a generic social work curriculum. This was based on her conviction that all caseworkers, not just "psychiatric social workers," needed knowledge about human behavior and should master a broad range of treatment modalities and ap-proaches.[29]

For almost forty years, Gordon Hamilton was one of the most forceful advocates of a close link between social casework, social welfare, and social action. In fact, as interest in the strictly psycholog-ical aspects of casework treatment increased following the publica-tion of Virginia Robinson's *A Changing Psychology in Social Casework* in 1930, Hamilton effectively pointed out that casework-ers must affirm their commitment to working with poor families and to altering the economic and social policy factors that help create family distress and disorganization.[30] She further stated that it might be regressive for social work to abandon its model of agency-based practice in favor of the development of private practice. And there seems to be no evidence that either Hamilton or Towle adopted the model of private practice for their own careers in clinical practice.[31]

## CONCLUSIONS

Some readers might interpret the author's position as a denial of the need for private practice. Nothing, however, could be further from the truth. There is no doubt that private practice supplies a vital service both to clients and to the profession, and that it is a legitimate and respected social work function. All of the recent work of NASW at the local and national level supports this conclusion, and the writer has long had an explicit personal commitment both to third-party payments and to increased professional recognition of clinical practi-tioners. Rather, the question that is raised is whether private practice is a superior service delivery mechanism that should substantially replace the agency-based service tradition of the profession. This is the central issue.

The author believes that NASW should continue to give aggressive leadership to members of the profession who opt for full-time or part-time private practice. At the same time, however, NASW should continue to recognize the strengths inherent in the agency-based model of practice and should reaffirm its appropriateness as the principal social work service delivery system for the future.

This conviction is based on a recognition of the nature of the social work function and its responsibility to deal with both "private troubles" and "public issues." There is also a responsibility to serve not only those who can afford to pay, but those who cannot; to help not only those who seek services, but those who need protective care and are in a relatively poor position either to request or to pay for such services. In every aspect of practice, social workers should manifest their understanding of the dual commitment to social service and social action, which is the hallmark of the social work profession.

## NOTES

1. Irving Piliavin, "Restructuring the Provision of Social Services," *Social Work*, 13 (January 1968).

2. *Handbook on the Private Practice of Social Work* (Washington, D.C.: National Association of Social Workers, 1974), p. 16.

3. *See* Robert K. Merton, *Social Theory and Social Structure* (rev. ed.; New York: Free Press, 1968), pp. 253 ff. For an application of this question in a social work context, *see*, Paul A. Kurzman, "Rules and Regulations in Large Scale Organizations: A Theoretical Approach to the Problem," *Administration in Social Work*, 1 (Winter 1977)

4. For a discussion of the applicability of the private practice model to community organization, *see* Paul A. Kurzman and Jeffrey Solomon, "Beyond Advocacy: A New Model For Community Organization," in *Social Welfare Forum, 1970* (New York: Columbia University Press, 1970), p. 67.

5. *See* Melvin A. Glasser, Thomas J. Duggan, and William S. Hoffman, "Obstacles to Utilization of Prepaid Mental Health Care," *American Journal of Psychiatry*, 132 (July 1975).

6. Ibid., p. 715.

7. *See* Ruth Fizdale, *Social Agency Structure and Accountability* (Fair Lawn, N.J.: R. E. Burdick Publishers, 1974).

8. Ibid., pp. 59; 94–95; 200–1.

9. *Handbook on the Private Practice of Social Work*, op. cit., p. 16.

10. *See* Josephine Peek and Charlotte Plotkin, "Social Caseworkers in Private Practice," *Smith College Studies in Social Work*, 21 (June 1951).

11. Ibid., pp. 165–97.

12. *Handbook on the Private Practice of Social Work*, op. cit., p. 28.

13. Ibid., p. 16.

14. For a discussion of the need for a "profession of psychotherapy," *see* William E. Henry et al., *The Fifth Profession: Becoming a Psychotherapist* (San Francisco: Jossey-Bass, 1971).

15. *Handbook on the Private Practice of Social Work*, op. cit., p. 22.

16. C. Wright Mills, *The Power Elite* (New York: Oxford University Press, 1957), p. 319.

17. C. Wright Mills, *The Sociological Imagination* (New York: Oxford University Press, 1959), p. 8.

18. William Schwartz, "Private Troubles and Public Issues: One Social

Work Job or Two," *Social Welfare Forum, 1969* (New York: Columbia University Press, 1969), p. 38. Emphasis added.

19. Ibid.

20. Bertha C. Reynolds, *Social Work and Social Living,* "NASW Classics Series" (Washington, D.C.: National Association of Social Workers, 1975), p. viii.

21. Lucille Austin, quoted in Sidney Levenstein, *Private Practice in Social Casework* (New York: Columbia University Press, 1964), p. 63.

22. Sidney Levenstein, *Private Practice in Social Casework* (New York: Columbia University Press, 1964), p. 67.

23. Margaret A. Golton, "Private Practice in Social Work," in *Encyclopedia of Social Work* (Washington, D.C.: National Association of Social Workers, 1971), p. 950.

24. Ibid.

25. *See Manpower Data Bank Frequency Distributions* (Washington, D.C.: National Association of Social Workers, 1975). (Mimeographed.)

26. *See* Chauncey Alexander, *Testimony to Subcommittee on Comprehensive Coverage* (New York: Health Insurance Association of America, 1976).

27. *See Professional Social Work Recognition: Vendorship Report* (staff memorandum, Nov. 10, 1977); *The NASW Register of Clinical Social Workers* (Washington, D.C.: National Association of Social Workers, 1976); and recent issues of *NASW News.*

28. *See* Paul A. Kurzman, "Third-Party Reimbursement," *Social Work,* 18 (November 1973).

29. *See* "Charlotte Towle," in *Encyclopedia of Social Work* (Washington, D.C.: National Association of Social Workers, 1977), p. 1556-7.

30. *See* "Gordon Hamilton," in *Encylopedia of Social Work* (Washington, D.C.: National Association of Social Workers, 1977), pp. 517-19.

31. *See* Gordon Hamilton, *The Theory and Practice of Social Casework* (2d ed.; New York: Columbia University Press, 1951, pp. 303-4.

# 26   Public Regulation of Social Work

## DAVID A. HARDCASTLE

A major contemporary movement in social work's efforts to attain recognition as a full profession is the move toward public regulation. The National Association of Social Workers, for example, has taken strong action to further this objective, as illustrated in the following resolution approved by its 1969 Delegate Assembly:

> *Resolved:* That the various combinations of Chapters, working in concert at a state level, be authorized to pursue licensing of Social Work practice within each state. . .[1]

Reprinted with permission of author and NASW from *Social Work,* 22:1 (January 1977), pp. 14-20. Copyright 1977, National Association of Social Workers, Inc.

The public or legal regulation of a profession occurs when the public, through formal legislation and the regulatory or legal powers of the state, defines and regulates professional behavior and conduct. Although the regulated profession may be involved in formulating the definitions and in the processes of regulation, it is the mandate and sanction of the state that ultimately defines the profession. Social work currently has some form of public regulation in Arkansas, California, Colorado, Delaware, Idaho, Illinois, Kansas, Kentucky, Louisiana, Maine, Maryland, Michigan, New York, Oklahoma, Puerto Rico, Rhode Island, South Carolina, South Dakota, Utah, and Virginia.

This article analyzes the conceptual foundation of legal regulation, and develops a classificatory scheme of legal regulation according to its major variables. It also analyzes and classifies existing legal regulations according to the variables.


## PROFESSIONALIZATION

There is general consensus on the attributes of a profession, and they have been well discussed by Greenwood and Feldstein, among others.[2] Basically, these attributes are (1) a systematic and defined theory or a system of abstract propositions, (2) defined and specialized skills, (3) a regulatory code of ethics governing conduct, (4) a supportive professional culture or community with normative standards, values, and symbols, (5) professional authority which holds that professional behavior can only be evaluated by professionals' peers, and (6) the sanction of the community to exercise such authority.

The second point—defined and specialized skills—should be a basic prerequisite for public regulation of an occupational activity. These skills describe the activity to be regulated. However, they are not sufficient alone to transform an occupation into a profession nor do they provide all the prerequisites for public regulation.

According to Wilensky, two additional elements are necessary for each transformation.[3] The first element is technical expertise based on systematic knowledge and doctrine acquired through formal training. The neophyte practitioner must have this training to gain the formal knowledge and skills and the implicit or tacit knowledge, values, and norms of the craft. It is the latter—the tacit knowledge, values, and norms—that provide the basis for what is commonly referred to as the "art" of social work. The second critical element is the acquisition of the regulatory norms by the occupational category, which are needed to limit conduct and behavior. Essential to and inherent in the regulatory norms are the following factors: (1) other professionals, rather than clients or "outsiders," must make judgments of competence and appropriate professional conduct, and

(2) service must be the primary motive for the activity. It is the ideal of service or of a "calling," with the practitioner standing above the sordid considerations of the marketplace, that separates the professions from occupations.[4] Although "service calling" does not exclude other motives, it does place service as the dominant and central motive.

Public or legal regulation of a profession and its activity indicates that the profession has received the sanction and mandate of the public. Wilensky holds that a benchmark of professional development, although not necessarily an integral part of its natural history, is attained when occupations engage in political action to gain the support of public law for the protection of their job territory and their sustaining code of ethics. Legal protection is an expedient of an occupation "on the make." It enhances status, protects jobs, and restricts jobholding to those who meet certain requirements, and protects the public from incompetence—that is, from practice by persons without the requisite technology, tacit knowledge, or normative behavior.[5]

Public regulation, therefore, implicitly recognizes the authority of peer judgments, in that the regulatory board is generally composed of professional peers; it also provides explicit community sanctions for the exercise of professional authority. But public regulation per se does not establish an occupational activity as a profession. In contemporary society most occupational activities are regulated in some manner, and many are directly regulated through formal statute. Wilensky, for example, reports that egg graders are regulated in Indiana, well diggers in Maryland, and horseshoers in Illinois.[6] Friedman reports that, as early as 1938, North Carolina regulated 600 occupational activities ranging from medicine to dealing in scrap tobacco.[7] During its 1974 session, when the Kansas legislature was considering a social work regulation bill, it was also considering a bill to license timber harvesters.

## PURPOSES OF REGULATION

The NASW 1975 policy statement, by action of the Delegate Assembly, sets forth the following four purposes for the public regulation of social work:

1. Establishing a public, legal definition of the profession which recognizes the differential levels of social work practice.
2. Protecting consumer and clientele rights and raising standards of service competence of practitioners in both agency and independent practice.

3. Establishing a public accountability in the delivery of social services based on professional standards rather than inconsistent, private standards of performance, and that protects the practitioner in the performance of social work tasks.
4. Provide a basis for the development and enhancement of the profession within the context of other social institutions and professions.[8]

The public justification for legal regulation is more general and succinct and is made on a twofold basis: the protection of the public and the development and protection of the profession.

It is assumed that the vendor engages in activities so complex that they require knowledge, skill, and technology for judgment beyond that reasonably expected for an independent evaluation by a consumer. The state therefore provides an a priori evaluation for the consumer. It is also assumed that the vendor's behavior has an irreversible impact on the consumer. If the vendor does not have the requisite knowledge, skills, and technology, the consumer may suffer severe and irreversible harm. However, as the Virginia statute states, "the potential for harm is recognizable and not remote or dependent on tenuous arguments."[9] A third assumption is the "neighborhood effect" of the activity, in which the impact of the vendor's behavior clearly extends beyond the vendor and consumer and affects the general public. Examples of neighborhood effect may be found in the area of physical safety, within such fields as architecture, engineering, and public health, and perhaps social planning, community organization, and education.

The development and protection of the profession is inherent in the protection of the public, although distinct from it. Through its regulatory powers, the state can impose entry requirements and standards for maintaining performance. Tests of continued competence and the updating of knowledge and skill can be imposed. Although these standards are designed to protect the public, they also protect the competent professional from the deleterious neighborhood impact of charlatans practicing under the umbrella of the profession.

Less altruistic reasons for an occupational activity to promote legal regulation are imbedded in the potential for protection of the job market that such regulation affords. Depending on the restrictiveness of the entry requirements, it has the potential of limiting the supply of the service in relation to the demand for the service. Although rational justification for restrictions can be made on the grounds of protecting the public, if they limit supply in relation to demand, the tendency will be to drive prices up. The potential of legal regulation to provide market control to the vendors or practitioners is related to the degree to which the vendors control the regulatory boards. Friedman cites a 1956 study indicating that 75 percent of the regulatory boards were controlled by persons who had a direct economic interest in the regulated activity.[10] Indeed, it is generally a hallmark of full professional status when the vendors control the licensing process utilizing the regulatory powers of the state.

The potential of public regulation to provide revenue for states cannot be overlooked. Licensing fees and occupational taxes, like the charges for the sale of liquor licenses in certain states, can be a viable source of revenue. The example of North Carolina with its regulations and fee collections for over 600 occupational and economic activities cannot be ignored. In Kansas, 20 percent of the registration fees of social workers go into the state's general fund while 80 percent are used to defray the cost of regulation.

## CATEGORIES OF REGULATION

Public regulation can be parsimoniously classified into three categories according to the state's use of its regulatory powers to enforce its definitions and regulations to protect the public. These three categories are registration, certification, and licensure.

### Registration

This is the state's listing or registry of persons identifying themselves with the activity. Registration provides a self-identified listing of vendors to potential users. The state's utilization of its regulatory powers is limited. There may be specific requirements for registration, such as the possession of certain educational credentials and the payment of fees, but unregistered vendors do not usually draw punitive measures from the state unless they claim registration. It is up to the market—the client, the agency, the payee—to determine the worth of the registered vendor over the unregistered vendor. This form of public regulation exercises the least degree of regulatory power and the least interference with the activity of the marketplace.

### Certification

This is the warranting by the state that the persons certified have attained a specified level of knowledge and skills. Like registration, certification does not prohibit uncertified persons from engaging in the behavior; it merely prevents their use of "certified" or a similar descriptive term with their title. Registration is a requisite of certification. The latter goes further in that it requires that the state make a judgment as to the competence of the vendor. Certification thus provides the public with an a priori judgment of the competence of those using a term such as "certified" with their title. The state defines competence and may test for it, but does not enforce its definition of competence over the activity, only over the use of the title. Consumers and vendors have the choice as to whether they wish to use—and meet—the state's definition of competence. The unregulated vendor can engage in the activity if consumers can be found who are willing to purchase the service.

## Licensure

This is the third and strongest form of legal regulation. It is a mechanism by which the state decrees that persons may not engage in particular economic activities and behaviors except under specific conditions set forth by the authority of the state and under its regulatory powers. Licensure states explicitly the requirements for knowledge and skills, describes how these are to be obtained and demonstrated, and uses the state's regulatory powers to enforce the definition of standards and behaviors. Licensure protects both the title and job activity. It defines the requirements of those who perform the services and limits the activities to those who meet its definition. For example, individuals may use an accountant who is not certified to monitor and record their fiscal affairs or they may use an unregistered architect to design their homes, but their surgery, whether for a fee or free, must be performed by a state-approved practitioner. Licensure combines registration and certification with control.[11]

## REGULATION OF SOCIAL WORK

As mentioned earlier, nineteen states and Puerto Rico have some form of public regulation of social work. The legislation for public regulation in eighteen of these states and Puerto Rico, as well as the NASW Model Licensing Act, were analyzed and classified according to their potential for the protection of the public and the development of the profession.[12] (Delaware's legislation was passed after the completion of this study and is therefore not included in the analysis. Several other states may also have enacted some legal regulation of social work by the time this article appears.)

## Protection of the Public

Each act of public regulation was analyzed in terms of its potential to protect the public. The stronger the potential for public protection, the more likely is public regulation to approach licensure.

Criteria used to examine the legislation for protection of the public aimed to determine whether the legislative acts contained the following:

1. Definitions and specifications of knowledge, skills, and values required for practice.

2. Entry requirements specified in terms of credentials, experience, and examinations.

3. Standards differentiating the knowledge and skills required for the various levels of practice—when these levels of practice are specified, especially if they are arranged in a hierarchy.

4. Utilization of regulatory powers to protect the public definitions and requirements for social work practice.

5. The functional exclusiveness of the definition.

6. Inclusion of the protection of confidentiality.

7. The degree to which "grandfathering" or the waiving of competence examinations for contemporary practitioners is avoided.

8. Requirements for demonstrations of continuing competence, such as reexaminations for competence and requirements for continuing education.

Two of the criteria may need elaboration. "Utilization of regulatory powers" refers to the degree to which the legislation prohibits unregulated persons from engaging in the activity. In other words, does the statute regulate functions and actions or merely restrict the use of certain titles? True licensure requires functional exclusiveness. "Grandfathering" refers to the practice of automatically granting to the contemporary practitioner the credentials of the public regulations. Under grandfathering the practitioner meets the requirements for regulation upon applying and paying fees. The degree to which existing practitioners are grandfathered is critical for the protection of the public. If it is assumed that regulation is necessary to protect the public, the need for public protection must relate to current practitioners as well as future practitioners. Grandfathering, however, could allow current practitioners to practice for perhaps thirty to forty years, untouched by requirements for updating knowledge or for testing of skills.

Certain issues of recertification are related to grandfathering. Without recertification, two tenuous assumptions must be made before any substantial client protection can be inferred: (1) social work knowledge and skills once acquired are mastered for life and (2) the profession is not generating new knowledge and skills so that social work knowledge and skills are static and will not change over the worker's life.

Regulation with extensive grandfathering and without meaningful recertification offers little protection to the client beyond that available without regulation. The current body of professionals and any future group who pass their entry examinations may have an expectancy of approximately thirty-four to forty years of practice life. If so, regulation with grandfathering will have an approximate twenty-year "half-life"; twenty years will elapse before the profession is half certified if one assumes a constant rate of entry into it and attrition from those leaving it. Under the same assumptions of entry and attrition without meaningful recertification for any future point beyond twenty years, only half the profession will have had a testing of competence within a twenty-year span.

Table 26–1 summarizes the review of the regulations by the foregoing criteria. No state's legal regulations meet the criteria for full

TABLE 26–1

Classification of the Legal Regulations of the Social Work Profession in 18 States and Puerto Rico and in the Model Licensing Act of the National Association of Social Workers (NASW)

| Classification | States, Puerto Rico, and NASW Model |
|---|---|
| *Licensure:* Full use of regulatory powers to enforce functional exclusiveness, credentials requirements for entry. and entry examination of knowledge and skills | None |
| *Strong Certification:* Use of regulatory powers for title protection, credentials requirements for entry, entry examination of knowledge and skills, and at least one other major criterion, such as continuing education, to protect the public | Colorado Idaho Illinois Kansas Kentucky Maryland South Dakota Utah NASW |
| *Weak Certification:* Use of regulatory powers to protect preface to title, credentials requirements for entry, and entry examination, but no other major criteria to protect the public | California Louisiana Maine New York Oklahoma Virginia |
| *Registration:* Use of regulatory powers to protect preface only, credentials for entry examination, but no entry examination on knowledge or skills and no other major criteria to protect the public | Arkansas Michigan Puerto Rico Rhode Island South Carolina |

licensure. No state uses its regulatory powers to enforce its definition of social work practice for persons regulated by the legislation. Persons in all states may engage in the economic activity and behaviors without being regulated as social workers. However, they cannot claim the regulated title in the performance of the activity.

### Development of the Profession

The second area for analysis was the potential for the development of the profession. Although public regulation of a profession means that the state, not the profession, assumes regulatory control, legislation can contain mechanisms to promote the development of the profession and of competent professionals. Criteria for analysis included the following:

1. *Exclusiveness of Claim to Professional Praxis*
Exemptions allowed for other professions
Exemptions allowed for social workers employed under certain auspices
Title protection
Protection of functions
Clear criteria for knowledge, skill, and function for differentiating between levels of social work if levels are used.

2. *Recertification Requirements of Professional Growth*
Periodic examinations of knowledge and skills
Continuing education including definitions of what is required

3. *Professional Authority and Autonomy*
Composition of the regulatory board and proportion of social work professionals
Autonomy of the board
Decision-making power of the board
Autonomy of practice and degree of dependence on controls external to the profession

4. *Reciprocity in Terms of Allowances for Interstate Transfer of Requirements*
The criteria under the third category are critical. They determine whether the regulated professional is an autonomous professional or is limited to carrying out practice activity as a professional under the auspices of an agency.

According to Greenwood, Parsons, and other students of professions, the mark of a profession is strong reliance on peers for professional authority and for judgments of professional competence.[13] The requiring of judgment-making by agency personnel in positions of control within an agency's organizational structure—that is, supervisors—is aprofessional. Essentially it substitutes bureaucratic and administrative judgments for professional ones. It does not further the profession but promotes the agency and discourages professional functioning independent of bureaucratic systems. Meaningful public regulation should curtail the need for bureaucratic regulation, not enlarge it.

Utilizing the major criteria to justify public regulation for the protection of clients and the public and for the development of the profession, it appears that public regulation of social work falls short.

## IMPACT ON PROTECTION

No state uses its regulatory powers to define and regulate functional behaviors for the social work profession. In short, licensure does not exist for social work. Only five states protect the unadorned title of "social worker." The remaining states, following the NASW Model Licensing Act, protect the title of social worker only when prefaced by "registered," "certified," or a similar term. Although 75 percent of the states require entry examinations, all but three have liberal grandfathering exclusions, exclusions for related professions, or exclusions from regulation allowed to some social workers because of the auspices of their employment. Recertification requirements are limited to payment of fees with the exception of continuing education required by four states and the NASW Model Licensing Act. Although certification can be revoked, this is done for negative behavior—"thou shalt nots." Recertification does not depend on positive behavior—"thou shalts."

Eighty percent of the legal regulations and the NASW Model Licensing Act specify more than one practice level. None specify functional or behavioral differences between the levels. The major differences relate to educational preparation and occasionally to differences in experience and auspices. Private practice as a regulated social work activity is permitted only for the upper levels.

In summary, protection of the public or clients is little improved by the current body of legal regulations over what existed without regulation. With the exception of the entry examination, the states, Puerto Rico, and the NASW Model Licensing Act appear to be certifying only that the professional has met baseline educational requirements associated with a specific title.

## IMPACT ON THE PROFESSION

Again, the contemporary body of legal regulations appears to do little to promote the development of the profession. Almost all states,

TABLE 26-2

Potential of Public Regulations to Promote the Development of the Social Work Profession, Classified by States and the Model Licensing Act of the National Association of Social Workers (NASW)

| Criteria | States, Puerto Rico, and NASW Model |
|---|---|
| 1. *Exclusiveness of Claim to Professional Praxis* | |
| Exemption of related professions from regulation | California, Colorado, Kansas, Kentucky, Louisiana, Maryland, New York, South Dakota, Utah, Virginia, and NASW Model (others do not specify) |
| Exemption from regulation of social workers employed under specific auspices | California, Kansas, Kentucky, Louisiana, Maryland, Rhode Island, and Virginia |
| Protection of prefaced title, such as "certified social worker" or "registered social worker" | All |
| Protection of unadorned title of "social worker" | Illinois, Maryland, Maine, South Dakota, and Utah |
| Protection of functions | None |
| Explicit criteria of knowledge and skills | None (not applicable in Louisiana, New York, Rhode Island, and South Carolina—which limit legal regulation to MSW degree) |
| 2. *Recertification Requirements Based on Professional Growth* | |
| Periodic reexamination of knowledge and skills | None |
| Continuing education required | Colorado, Kansas, and South Dakota (and Kentucky at board option) |
| 3. *Professional Authority and Autonomy* | |
| Social workers a majority on regulatory board | All except Arkansas and Colorado |
| Autonomous board | All except Kansas and NASW Model |
| Board with decision-making powers | All except Kansas and NASW Model |
| Practice defined as autonomous and independent of nonprofessional controls | California, Idaho, Illinois, Louisiana, Maine, New York, Oklahoma, Puerto Rico, Rhode Island, South Carolina, South Dakota, and Utah |
| 4. *Reciprocity between States* | Colorado, Idaho, Illinois, Kansas, Kentucky, Maryland, Michigan, New York, South Dakota, Virginia, and NASW Model |

either specifically or by implication, exclude from regulation "other professions performing similar functions," whether or not these professions are regulated by other statutes. Approximately 40 percent exclude social workers who are employed under certain auspices. Only five states protect the unadorned title of social worker. Even NASW's Model Licensing Act does not protect it.

Although 80 percent of the legal regulations specify levels of practice, they do not explicitly mention differentials in knowledge and skills, nor are career ladders present. Movement between levels is generally by meeting the next requirement for academic degrees. Notable exceptions are the requirements of experience for autonomous clinical practice and Michigan's experience continuum.

Registration or certification is generally for life, contingent on the periodic payment of fees. No state monitors the maintenance and upgrading of knowledge and skills, except for the requirement of continuing education in four states. It appears unlikely that legal regulation will provide motivation for professional development beyond that existing without it.

On the criteria related to professional authority and autonomy, the legal regulations grade higher. All but two states have regulatory boards composed primarily of social workers. The boards are autonomous and have decision-making powers, with the odd exceptions of the regulatory board in Kansas, which is advisory to the Secretary of Social and Rehabilitation Services, and the board recommended in the NASW Model Licensing Act, which would be advisory to a regulatory agency.

When the statutes contain levels of practice, the autonomy of the professional and the profession is a critical factor. Autonomous practice in the multilevel statutes is limited to the upper levels of practice. Practitioners at lower levels can engage in the practice activity, but generally only under the auspices and supervision of an agency. The agency supervisor need not be a professional social worker or even a professional. Qualifications required for private practice may include supervision by an appropriately certified social worker. The point is not subtle. The practice of professionals in the field of social work, except for a limited number of elites at the upper level of practice, remains under the control of agencies, that is, under aprofessional or nonprofessional control. If this situation is justified on the basis that the lower levels lack the requisite knowledge and skills for autonomous peer-regulated practice, can their status as professionals be simultaneously advocated? This is not an argument against agencies as delivery systems or against administrative supervision and direction. Nor is it an argument against differentiated practice. It is an argument against the inconsistency of requiring by legal regulation that the majority of the activities of the profession be carried on within the confines of an agency in order to be called professional social work practice.

Slightly over half the states allow for reciprocity with states having similar requirements in their legal regulations. To some degree, the free movement of social workers throughout the country may be inhibited because of the lack of reciprocity between the states. However, this restriction probably has a minimal effect since the legal regulations are relatively flaccid.

## CONCLUSIONS

Overall, the existing legal regulations and the provisions of the NASW Model Licensing Act appear to this author to have little potential for the protection of the public, the development of the profession, and greater impact on the profession than exists without legal regulation. The status quo is not significantly altered. According to Briggs, the basic difficulty seems to lie in the uncertainty and lack of preciseness in the definitions of knowledge and skills and the inability or unwillingness of those formulating the legal regulations to include and develop meaningful standards.[14]

If those associated with social work are unable or unwilling to define more precisely the basic competence, knowledge, and skills of the profession, the assumption that they can test and differentiate these appears dubious. However, if they can define more precisely the requisite knowledge and skills, yet fail to test and monitor them, fail to exclude the incompetents and persons with less than full professional attributes from professional practice, and neglect to require periodic reexamination, then it is an unethical profession.

The profession appears to want the status and protection of public recognition without the costs. The dangers of weak legal regulations are that they may preempt stronger ones in that the weak regulations offer the semblance of public protection and development of the profession without their substance.

Social work, as a liberal profession, has the implicit obligation to resist arbitrary and meaningless public regulation as a bogus status-accruing device. Restrictions, even on a limited basis, are contentious if not offset by the strong and obvious potential for protecting the public and developing the profession.

## NOTES

1. "New Policy Statement on Licensing Issued," *NASW News,* 19 (September 1974), p. 12. *See also* "The 1975 NASW Delegate Assembly Actions: Professional Issues; Legal Regulation of Social Work Practice Policies for a

Continuing Effort" and "NASW Celebrates 20th Anniversary; Assembly Passes Reorganization Plan," *NASW News,* 20 (July 1975), pp. 15–17 and pp. 1, 10, respectively; "Legislative Moves Toward Licensure Continue Unabated," *NASW News,* 20 (September 1975), p. 12; and "Licensing Movement for Social Workers Growing in Both Size and Complexity," *NASW News,* 21 (January 1976) p. 8.

2. Ernest Greenwood, "The Elements of Professionalization," in Howard W. Vollmer and Donald L. Mills, eds., *Professionalization* (Englewood Cliffs, N.J.: Prentice-Hall, 1966), pp. 10–19; and Donald Feldstein, "Do We Need Professionals in our Society? Professionalization Versus Consumerism," *Social Work,* 16 (October 1971), pp. 5–11. For a general review of professionalism and professionalization, *see* Vollmer and Mills, eds., *op. cit.*

3. Harold L. Wilensky, "The Professionalization of Everyone?" in Oscar Grusky and George A. Miller, eds., *The Sociology of Organizations* (New York: Free Press, 1970), p. 484–87.

4. *See* Robert MacIver, "Professional Groups and Cultural Norms," in Vollmer and Mills, eds., *Professionalization, op. cit.,* p. 51; Talcott Parsons, *The Social System* (Glencoe, Ill.: Free Press, 1951), pp. 314–15; and Parsons, *Essays in Sociological Theory* (rev. ed.; Glencoe, Ill.: Free Press, 1954), pp. 38–43.

5. *See* Wilensky, op. cit., pp. 489–90. *See also* Committee on the Study of Competence, *Guidelines for the Assessment of Professional Practice in Social Work* (New York: National Association of Social Workers, 1968), p. iii.

6. Wilensky, *op. cit.,* p. 490.

7. Milton Friedman, *Capitalism and Freedom* (Chicago: University of Chicago Press, 1962), p. 139.

8. *NASW News,* 20 (July 1975), p. 15.

9. Virginia Board for Registration of Social Workers, *Regulations* (Richmond: Department of Professional and Occupational Regulation, Commonwealth of Virginia, September 30, 1975), p. 1.

10. Friedman, *op. cit.,* p. 140.

11. For additional discussions of legal regulation, especially of social work, *see* Anthony J. Agostinelli, "The Legal Regulation of Social Work Practice" (Washington, D.C.: National Association of Social Workers, April 25, 1973) (mimeographed); Friedman, *op. cit.,* pp. 137–161; David A. Hardcastle, "Licensing, Senate Bill No. 6, and Social Work," *The Kansas Conference Key,* 22 (December 1973), pp. 1–4; Charles S. Levy, "The Legal Regulation of Social Work: The Broad View" (Evanston, Ill.: The National Clearinghouse for Legal Services, June 13, 1973) (mimeographed); Bradford W. Sheafor, "Why License Social Workers?" *The Kansas Conference Key,* 22 (November 1973), pp. 5–6; Paul E. and Dorothy Z. Weinberger, "Legal Regulation in Perspective," in Paul E. Weinberger, ed., *Perspectives on Social Welfare: An Introductory Anthology* (New York: Macmillan Co., 1974), pp. 439–53; and Wilensky, *op. cit.,* pp. 483–501.

12. *Legal Regulation of Social Work Practice* (Washington, D.C.: National Association of Social Workers, 1973).

13. *See* Greenwood, *op. cit.;* Talcott Parsons, *The Social System;* and Parsons, *Essays in Sociological Theory.*

14. For an elaboration of this point, *see* Thomas L. Briggs, "A Critique of the NASW Manpower Statement," *Journal of Education for Social Work,* 11 (Winter 1975), p. 15.

# 27　On the Political Character of Social Service Work

## PAUL ADAMS and GARY FREEMAN

The analysis of the political role of the social service sector is essential to an understanding of the limits and possibilities of social work and related professions as vehicles of social change or system maintenance. Social service workers face charges of being wasteful and subversive from some quarters, and of being conservative and repressive from others. In particular, the widespread discussion of the conservative political functions of the social services, especially casework, has led to disillusionment and confusion among social service workers. Responding to this, some individuals have dramatically overstated the potentially revolutionary possibilities of "radical" social work.[1]

The issue of the politics of the social services raises a number of thorny questions having to do with the class position, professional character, and socioeconomic function of social workers. We will not attempt to deal with these here. What we wish to do is examine the proposition that social service workers can pursue political objectives through their social service work practice. Although we accept the argument that all social work is in some sense political, we question whether the social services constitute a viable means of basic political change, or an essential support of the status quo. We begin by making some conceptual distinctions between occupations in which the political attitudes of the worker are relevant to the execution of work tasks, and those in which the work itself contributes significantly to maintaining political and economic power relationships. The extent to which a job is political, in either sense, has no necessary relationship to the political leverage of its occupants. We argue that the political potential of social service workers lies primarily in their relationship to their employers rather than to their clients. This assertion is elaborated through an examination of the centrality of the twin functions of the social services: social control and social wage. We close with some observations about recent state strategies for handling the "dysfunctional" demands emerging from the social service sector, especially the current effort to develop means to carry out these functions without the use of social workers.

Reprinted from the *Social Service Review*, 53:4 (December 1979), pp. 560–72, by permission of the University of Chicago Press and the author.

## OCCUPATION AND POLITICS

In contrast to those who have emphasized the professional and technical aspects of social service work, social critics have sometimes argued that all such activity is inherently political. Normally this has involved an interpretation of the conservative nature of such work. As long ago as 1943, Mills described the "professional ideology of social pathologists" in the following terms: "Their activities and mental outlook are set within the existent norms of society: in their professional work they tend to have an occupationally trained incapacity to rise above series of 'cases.' "[2]

More recently, Edelman has analyzed how a symbolic language of pathology and therapy has grown up within the "helping professions," one function of which is to disguise the coercive, politically repressive character of their activities. He attributes to these professionals a pervasive and important role in preserving the political-economic order: "The helping professions are the most effective contemporary agents of social conformity and isolation. In playing this political role, they undergird the entire political structure, yet are largely spared from self-criticism, from political criticism, and even from political observation through a special language."[3]

Radicals within the social service professions have used similar arguments in response to those who charge them with disregarding professional ethics and human needs by introducing politics into their relations with clients. The question is not whether politics should be introduced, they say, for it is there already; the issue is what kind of politics, and how openly acknowledged. In a recent essay, Gil dismisses objections to mixing politics and social work practice since all practice has political implications, whether they are recognized by the worker or not: "To replace prevailing, unintentional, covert political aspects of practice with conscious, overt ones and to hold practitioners responsible for the political perspective of their practice, would seem a more honest, and hence more appropriate, course in ethical and professional terms."[4] Gil calls on social workers to reject "status-quo-preserving, symptom-ameliorating practice models" in favor of "radical, innovative, system-transforming practice."[5] Unfortunately, he does not say how a clinical social worker should go about developing a practice that would be "system-transforming" or where he or she would find work. He does imply, however, a quite extraordinary potentiality for clinical practice as a motor of social change capable of contributing significantly to human liberation and the removal of capitalism.

In responding to the criticisms of their more conservative or professionally oriented colleagues, radical advocates have overestimated the importance of the political role of the social services. If the social services are necessarily political in some sense, it does not follow that they are an effective way of changing society, or of preserving the status quo, nor that they should be judged as if they were. We believe that the present confusion over this matter arises from a failure to distinguish between whether a job is political and whether its occupants enjoy, individually or collectively, real or potential political power. There are two aspects to the political character of occupations: the extent to which the political attitudes of worker are relevant to the execution of work tasks, and the extent to which the job contributes to maintaining (or subverting) power relationships in the social formation.

For many jobs (e.g., work on an auto assembly line), the political attitudes of the worker are clearly irrelevant to the performance of the task itself. One cannot assemble cars in a radical or conservative fashion.[6] Other occupations (such as those of the professional politician or the political scientist) are such that belief and job performance are nearly inseparable. Social service workers obviously fall near the "political" end of this continuum, and some kinds (e.g., community organization, social planning) are nearer than others (e.g., work with families with autistic children or the terminally ill). If we turn our attention toward the political function of the job rather than the attitudes of the worker, the auto worker would again be at the nonpolitical pole. Even though such work contributes to capitalist profits and helps to recreate and maintain the system of production, it is not part of its policing, social control apparatus. Police and soldiers, of course, would fall at the other end, having a direct role in the maintenance of order through coercion.

Social service workers would be located somewhere near the middle of a continuum along which jobs were arranged according to their contribution to the maintenance and reproduction of the social formation. Social service workers occupy this ambiguous position because they perform both a social control and a social wage function in the welfare state. It is the first that has been the subject of much recent criticism by individuals on the Left. As ideological servants of the state, social service workers both engage in deviancy-controlling activities with individual clients and foster the belief in society that complex problems directly caused by capitalism are amenable to social work solutions. But they also contribute to the social wage of the working class, those forms of benefits and services provided to the worker and his or her family by the state as a means of meeting part of the costs of the reproduction of labor power.[7] The idea of the social services' contribution to the social wage is very important because (1) it provides a basis for social service workers to practice their jobs with a minimum of ambivalence or guilt, and (2) it is central to an understanding of their political leverage.

It is clear from this analysis that social service work is substantially more political than many other occupations. But it is also obvious that the social services are not the most politically central occupations, either in terms of the relevance of workers' political convictions or of the importance of their services to the existing regime. But we are not concerned here with the details of these continua. Our point is that the extent to which a job is "political" has no relationship at all to the political leverage the occupants of those jobs can exercise if they are organized. Coal miners, steelworkers, teamsters, though they may gain some measure of control of their work situation, have no possibility of performing their jobs in a radical way. Yet these and other industrial workers have the potential power to stop production. As such they can pose a threat to the existing system that social service workers cannot.

## THE LIMITS OF RADICAL SOCIAL WORK

Responding to charges that the social services help reinforce the labor market and maintain capitalism by translating the problems of poverty and oppression into terms of individual pathology, some writers have tried to establish a framework for the practice of radical social work. Although we have already conceded that all social work is political (though this can be overstated), and although we do not wish to deny that it is desirable and possible to deliver social services in a less repressive and demeaning manner than is often the case, we believe that the potential of a specifically radical mode of social work is strictly limited. Furthermore, to the extent that such activity promises to be effective, it moves closer and closer to being more like traditional labor-movement activity than social work.

The search for a theory of radical social work has tended to produce models of practice either clearly utopian or developed at such a level of generality that their implications for day-to-day practice remain unclear. One of the most common prescriptions for radicals in the social services involves the reinterpretation of the client's problems within the framework of a radical, usually at least quasi-Marxist, analysis of the socioeconomic system. As Galper expresses it: " ... the root of radical practice must be radical analysis. At the heart of such analysis is the effort to place the life situation and the particular problems of the individual in their broadest social, political, and economic perspective. . . ."[8] This entails both a transformation of the consciousness of the social worker and his or her clients. Corrigan and Leonard, in their recent important contribution to this discussion, offer the following advice to workers dealing with family disputes: "Intervention which is concerned with the family as a whole, places emphasis not only on the material needs of the family members, but attempts to develop with the family, as appropriate, a critical consciousness of its internal and external relationships."[9] They also note that such intervention can help family members to understand "precisely how the imperatives of the economy, and the ideological structures to which it gives rise, determine the kinds of roles that are played in the family."[10] They conclude that the point of radical practice is "to transform our understanding *with* the individual client in a way that enables the relevance of the wider features of the capitalist system to be understood and acted upon."[11]

If the conservative impact of social work derives in part from its tendency to individualize social problems, radical social work must surely attempt, as these authors suggest, to repoliticize these "private troubles."[12] Criticism of such proposals on the grounds that their advocates ignore the "real" problems of their clients in order to indulge themselves in ideological rhetoric does not stand up to careful examination.[13] An argument can be made that social work which involves consciousness raising and improved self-images can have therapeutic effects on individuals. Our point is that it is not likely to be politically effective. In order to appreciate this more fully we have to consider radical proposals for organizing clients.

One of the best illustrations of the promise and limits of the client-organization strategy is the experience of the movement of radical social workers organized around the journal *Case-Con,* which flourished for a while in Great Britain in the early seventies.[14] Shortly after its founding, the belief developed that grass-roots community work might offer more scope for radical practice than the much more numerous kinds of jobs in "statutory" agencies (i.e., public agencies with legal duties to place and supervise children, participate in compulsory admission to mental hospitals, or provide assistance). The belief was short lived partly because the community worker tended to be isolated from fellow workers in the local authority social service departments, partly because when community groups, such as claimants' unions (welfare-rights organizations), organized themselves professional social workers were not welcomed, and also because of the inherent political limitations of this kind of local, consumer activity. Nevertheless, *Case-Con* continued to support militant consumer groups such as welfare recipients (claimants' unions) and tenants' organizations and sought to build links between them and the labor movement. The problem with trying to go further, with seeing the central task of radical social workers in terms of client organizing, is that the clients of social workers tend to be the least well-organized elements of the working class—those who are sick, disabled, unemployed, old, young, isolated, and above all, divorced from the workplace. They are, however radicalized, relatively powerless. In Barratt

Brown's words, "It will not be by the very poor and the drop-outs that the welfare state is dissolved and replaced by socialism, however much these groups may reveal of its true nature."[15]

If social workers are, by virtue of their class position and their location in the state apparatus, marginal to the struggle for socialism, the class position of most of their clients is such as to render them more marginal still. However "political" the relationship between social worker and client, it cannot be central to any serious strategy for changing society.

This does not mean that clients should be written off or that the worker's mode of practice is unimportant. On the contrary, it is only when the hubristic notion of transforming the world through social work, shared by many conservative, liberal, and radical social workers alike, is completely rejected that a humane and realistic approach to the possibilities of social work under capitalism is possible.

This point may be brought out by examining the concept of "client refusal." Taylor argues that social workers should refuse to see those with whom they work as "clients" (i.e., candidates for diagnosis and treatment), but rather as political allies against the system. Workers should use this approach in discriminating within their case loads.[16] Galper, in endorsing this view, suggests giving priority to those who are "active in the movement for social change" or those who demonstrate the potential for a "broader awareness."[17] Such an approach lays itself open to charges of exploitation.[18] As in traditional casework, clients enter a negotiation (if they get that far) in which various kinds of help—patronage, intercession with authorities, material aid, warmth, and sympathy—are offered in exchange for developing "insight" (or "awareness"), that is, for accepting the worker's view of the world.

It is not only the inherent weakness of a strategy of client organizations that vitiates the practice of radical social work. There is serious reason to doubt that in the absence of widespread oppositional movements in the society at large, the social service sector will produce a significant number of radicals. Many conservatives are convinced that the social services are a natural breeding ground for egalitarian, anticapitalist values, and generally reformist or revolutionary sentiment. The increasing size of the social services and the service sector in general in advanced capitalist society is, consequently, a cause of concern for them.[19]

Some radicals accept this thesis. Corrigan and Leonard conclude, for example, that social service workers, both because of their contact with the working class and because of their position in the state bureaucracy, are likely to be exposed to anticapitalist influences. Social service workers operate, they suggest, at the heart of a major contradiction of the welfare state, since they are the agents of a social policy which attempts to perform the impossible task of ameliorating the increasingly severe dislocations of capitalism. Experience in their daily work of the failure of this undertaking may lead them to disenchantment and opposition. Furthermore, social service workers, as part of the ideological apparatus, possess considerably more autonomy than the more traditional and directly coercive arms of the state such as the police and army.[20]

We agree that this possibility exists, but we do not believe that there is any inherent or easy relationship between the experiences of the social worker and the development or expression of oppositional political attitudes. On the contrary, given the marginal class position of social workers and the ambiguous nature of their professional status, it is as likely that social workers will take on the political coloring of whatever coalition of economic and social forces is currently dominant. That is, social work exhibits the characteristics of heteronomy, not autonomy, and is consequently especially susceptible to permeation by externally dominant ideologies.[21] This need not lead us to conclude that social workers cannot be a force for political reform, but it does mean that if this is to come about, they will have to be much more closely tied to the labor movement, which has the social weight and oppositional potential that social service workers lack. The primary locus of effective radical activity is not the client-worker relationship, but that between employer and employee.

## POLITICAL LEVERAGE

To argue that social service workers enjoy their most powerful political position in relation to their employers rather than to their clients is not to say that even in that form they are likely to be especially important. This is a complex question beyond the scope of this article, but we would like to suggest several aspects of what would be a satisfactory answer. The issue which must be dealt with in order to understand the potential role of social service workers as organized labor is the extent to which the twin functions of such workers—social control and social wage—are significant enough that the threat of withdrawal of services would be a credible political weapon. We also need to ask whether other traditional types of trade-union demands likely to be pressed by social workers can be integrated into a broader political strategy.

We have noted that many critics of the social services have charged that they perform a vital social control function for the social system as a whole.[22] In one form this involves defusing potential political conflict and contributing to social harmony and order. It is difficult to demonstrate empirically the significance of social service workers to the reinforcement of social norms and processes, because their role is indirect and at least partially masked. It is clear, however, that in a period of crisis the state can and does rely on the overt forces of order: the police, the courts, and the army.

Such flagrant use of coercion is associated with major political costs, however, and is a strategy of last resort; there are means of social control available to the state short of the police. Institutions such as the schools, the media, and the church reach larger numbers of people than do social workers and have a much more pervasive impact on the society. With regard to the regulation of the labor market, which is probably the most important social control function of welfare programs, it appears that the role of social service workers is marginal. In fact, it is a program such as social security which does not significantly involve caseworkers, and public assistance programs, the structures of which are not actually in the hands of such workers, that actually regulate the labor market.[23]

If we turn to the social wage function, the vulnerability of the social service sector is even more evident. The development of the social wage is in part a necessary outcome of capitalist evolution, but it is also the result of working-class political agitation.[24] Consequently, the size of the social wage is not a given—the minimum necessary social wage (or the "social democratic minimum," as Katznelson has recently dubbed it)[25] may be taken as a requirement of a capitalist economy, but anything above that threshold is determined by the balance of class forces at any particular time. Furthermore, the form which the social wage will assume is matter left for the most part to political negotiation. We see no reason why the social wage must involve the kinds of services performed by social workers, at least at the levels at which they now exist. Indeed, there is evidence on a number of fronts of attempts to circumvent the use of social service workers in the provision of the social wage, either through the substitution of an "incomes" for a "services" strategy or through the use of traditional institutions rather than state employees for the delivery of services. These efforts are only partially designed to head off the politicization of the social services. Their more immediate goal is to reduce the cost and increase the efficiency and effectiveness of social welfare programs. As such they are a primary response to the deepening fiscal crisis of advanced capitalist states. Their success will, in any case, mean a greatly reduced role for those social service workers dealing with individual clients.

In both Britain and the United States there has been a clear movement away from a services strategy with respect to the poor and the unemployed toward an incomes strategy.[26] Such an approach seeks to ameliorate the social problems of poverty, delinquency, disease, and joblessness through the relatively direct and antiseptic devices of income transfers (e.g., supplemental security income, negative income tax, vouchers) rather than through the provision of services (counseling, training, therapy). In many ways these innovations are welcome. They grow out of an appreciation of the tenuous empirical base for many of the claims of service strategies. Furthermore, they grant to recipients a greater measure of autonomy and dignity than do some service-oriented approaches. But it is probably only a mild exaggeration to suggest that social service workers who have traditionally pursued an individualized, client-oriented strategy are being displaced by the new policy analysts who use the tools of economic analysis to manage society in the interest of efficiency and rationality. This represents an advancing rationality in social policy to only a limited extent. The policy analyst/economist is much more likely to exhibit political attitudes compatible with dominant interests than are social service workers who, at the least, tend to adhere to a humanistic, charitable tradition. Social service workers may have relatively little autonomy, but they are much more likely to dissent from repressive and ungenerous social programs than are individuals whose professional training exalts least-cost solutions to problems viewed from the perspective of the capitalist economy.[27]

A second dimension of the attack on the social services is the current wave of interest in social policies which work through and reinforce rather than supplant traditional or "mediating" structures.[28] Glazer was one of the first critics systematically to raise the possibility that welfare programs were as much a cause of as a response to the erosion of the family, the community, the church, and other traditional social structures.[29] More recently, Lasch has launched a vehement attack on the invasion of the family by a host of professionals, both private and governmental.[30] Again, some aspects of this critique are sound and are fully consistent with radical analyses from within the social work profession. It is the likely effect of programs designed to avoid such deleterious impacts on traditional structures that is troublesome. One implication is simply the use of income-oriented programs such as we have already discussed. Another, however, is to build welfare programs around the use of nonprofessional community, church, and family groups. Whatever the potential benefit of such programs, they will likely result in a reduction of the social wage and certainly will result in a reduction of the size or rate of growth of the social services sector.

The substitution of an emphasis on self-help, voluntarism, and local initiative for uniform national programs will encourage (indeed, is meant to encourage) a wide variety in the content and level of services in various communities. This is likely to reduce aggregate ser-

vice levels because the most powerful and advantaged groups, able
to satisfy their needs privately or to take advantage of government
money to finance group-specific services, will have little incentive to
press for general welfare benefits. The least advantaged, unable to
handle their needs on their own, and deprived of their more powerful allies, will be relatively worse off. Furthermore, efforts to limit
welfare-state bureaucracies, though often motivated by the desire to
improve the quality of services and to enhance the control exercised
by social service clients, normally find favor with government officials because they promise to reduce costs. The drive to achieve
major cutbacks in spending is well advanced in the context of the
present fiscal crisis and is aimed at reducing the tax burden of the
middle classes, increasing the availability of investment capital, and
removing governmentally created impediments to the incentive to
work.[31]

These developments, taken together, both point out the vulnerability of the social services sector and identify a political agenda for
it. Social service workers, if they were organized and linked to the
labor movement, could help lead the fight against cuts in social
spending. To be successful they must develop allies among the more
traditional working-class unions, in particular among their rank-and-
file opposition where those unions are bureaucratic, corrupt, and
conservative. Through their own organization, and their links to
organized workers, they can also be most effective in resisting the
repressive and authoritarian aspects of their jobs and of social programs in general.

One approach would be to develop and foster formal links between national leaders of such organizations as the National Association of Social Workers and the top officials of the AFL-CIO,
cooperating in the furthering of common goals, such as national
health insurance. Communication at this level, between leaders who
cannot deliver the votes, much less organize concerted political action, will amount to little unless it represents, and is controlled by,
a genuine movement from below. Of much greater significance are
actions at the grass-roots level. Social service workers need to play an
active role in the rank and file of their own unions, not only working
for democratic control of the union by members, for militancy on
issues of pay and working conditions, but also raising broader political questions involved in opposition to racism and sexism, and in
defense of the social wage. They need to support and build links with
rank-and-file caucuses in other unions which work for similar ends,
such as the Teamsters for a Democratic Union, the auto workers'
United National Caucus, or the various dissident groups within the
Communications Workers of America. Defending the social wage

and opposing repressive social policies depend on mobilization of working-class power, but that in turn requires that workers gain control of their own organizations and transform them into bodies that are at once democratic, militant, and politically progressive.

Many obstacles stand in the way of successfully implementing such a strategy, not least the professional illusions and aspirations of many social service workers and the undifferentiated suspicion and hostility which many, even those who see themselves as radicals, feel for organized labor in general. Much depends on developments beyond the control of social service workers, such as the relative success of the rank-and-file movements in the major industrial unions. In any case, whatever potential for political effectiveness social service workers may possess does not lie in their professional practice. It depends on their organizing themselves, rather than their clients, and raising their own political and trade-union consciousness.

## NOTES

1. There has been more interest in this question in Britain than in the United States. See Roy Bailey and Mike Brake, eds., *Radical Social Work* (New York: Pantheon Books, 1976); Paul Corrigan and Peter Leonard, *Social Work Practice under Capitalism: A Marxist Approach* (London: Macmillan Publishing Co., 1978); Geoffrey Pearson, *Ideological Crisis in Social Work* (London: Macmillan Publishing Co., in press); Colin Pritchard and Richard Taylor, *Social Work: Reform or Revolution?* (London: Routledge & Kegan Paul, 1978). For the United States, see Jeffry H. Galper, *The Politics of Social Services* (Englewood Cliffs, N.J.: Prentice-Hall, Inc., 1975), and the journals *Catalyst* and *Social Development Issues*.

2. C. Wright Mills, "The Professional Ideology of Social Pathologists," *American Journal of Sociology* 49, no. 2 (1943–44): 165–80, quote on p. 171.

3. Murray Edelman, "The Political Language of the Helping Professions," *Politics and Society* 4, no. 3 (1974): 295–310, quote on p. 310.

4. David G. Gil, "Clinical Practice and the Politics of Human Liberation," *Catalyst* 1, no. 2 (1978): 61–69, quote on p. 62.

5. *Ibid.*, p. 68.

6. It is true that industrial workers may exercise more or less control, formally or informally, over the conditions of their work, but they cannot make the task itself—mining coal or pressing steel—either radical or conservative.

7. Paul Adams, "Social Control or Social Wage: On the Political Economy of the 'Welfare State,'" *Journal of Sociology and Social Welfare* 5, no. 1 (1978): 46–54.

8. Galper, p. 209.

9. Corrigan and Leonard, p. 137.

10. *Ibid.*, p. 136.

11. *Ibid.*, p. 123.

12. C. Wright Mills, *The Sociological Imagination* (New York: Oxford University Press, 1959), pp. 8–13.

13. Galper, p. 209.

14. The best source of information of the *Case-Con* group is the journal itself. We draw on it and on the experience of one of the present authors, who was for a time the assistant editor of *Case-Con*.

15. Michael Barratt Brown, "The Welfare State in Britain," in *The Socialist Register 1971*, ed. Ralph Miliband and John Saville (London: Merlin Press, 1971), p. 205.

16. Ian Taylor, "Client Refusal: A Political Strategy for Radical Social Work," *Case-Con* 7 (April 1972): 5–10.

17. Galper, p. 214.

18. Stanley Cohen, "It's All Right for You to Talk: Political and Sociological Manifestos for Social Work Action," in Bailey and Brake, pp. 76–95.

19. See Daniel Patrick Moynihan, "The Professionalization of Reform," *Public Interest* 1 (Fall 1965): 6–16; Irving Kristol, "About Equality," *Commentary* 54, no. 5 (1972): 41–47. For a similar argument from a different political perspective, see Claus Mueller, *The Politics of Communication* (New York: Oxford University Press, 1973), pp. 170–78.

20. Corrigan and Leonard, p. 106.

21. See Reuben Bitensky, "The Influence of Political Power in Determining the Theoretical Development of Social Work," *Journal of Social Policy* 2, no. 2 (1973): 119–30; Terence Johnson, *Professions and Power* (London: Macmillan Publishing Co., 1972), and "What Is to Be Known? The Structural Determination of Social Class," *Economy and Society* 6, no. 2 (1977): 194–233.

22. For example, Frances Fox Piven and Richard Cloward, *Regulating the Poor: The Functions of Public Welfare* (New York: Vintage Books, 1971).

23. For a discussion of the manner in which old age pension systems may be designed to manipulate labor markets, see Gaston V. Rimlinger, *Industrialization and Welfare Policy in Europe, America, and Russia* (New York: John Wiley & Sons, 1971), chap. 8. For a detailed examination of the impact of the U.S. retirement system on the labor market and the economy in general, see Alicia H. Munnell, *The Future of Social Security* (Washington, D.C.: Brookings Institution, 1977). On the public assistance program, see Piven and Cloward.

24. Corrigan and Leonard, p. 97.

25. Ira Katznelson, "Considerations on Social Democracy in the United States," *Comparative Politics* 11, no. 1 (1978): 77–99.

26. For evidence on the United States, see Daniel Patrick Moynihan, *The Politics of a Guaranteed Income* (New York: Vintage Books, 1973). British developments are described in J. C. Kincaid, *Poverty and Equality in Britain*, rev. ed. (Harmondsworth, Middlesex: Penguin Books, 1975), chaps. 4 and 6.

27. Katznelson, pp. 90–93.

28. The most direct statement of this view is Peter L. Berger and Richard John Neuhaus, *To Empower People: The Role of Mediating Structures in Public Policy* (Washington, D.C.: American Enterprise Institute, 1977).

29. Nathan Glazer, "The Limits of Social Policy," *Commentary* 52, no. 3 (1971): 51–58.

30. Christopher Lasch, *Haven in a Heartless World: The Family Besieged* (New York: Basic Books, 1978).

31. On Britain, see Kevin McDonnell, "Ideology, Crisis and the Cuts," *Capital and Class* 4 (Spring 1978): 34–69. On the United States, the most general treatment is James O'Connor, *The Fiscal Crisis of the State* (New York: St. Martin's Press, 1973).

# 28 The Search for Professional Identity

## NEIL GILBERT

Regardless of the point at which the search for social work's distinctive identity begins, its pathways often lead back to the central question of purpose. What is social work about (that other professions are not)? What does it seek to achieve (that other professions do not)? Purpose is the nucleus around which the varied activities constituting social work practice coalesce. It would seem that without a sense of common purpose to bond and guide professional activities, meaningful discourse on professional methods and knowledge is difficult to sustain.

The question that remains to be answered is the following: To what extent is there conceptual clarity about a distinct identity for social work practice to which the profession as a whole can subscribe? Two criteria should be considered in this regard: (1) the degree to which statements regarding mission, objectives, and relevant knowledge set social work practice apart from various activities that might otherwise appear similar; and (2) the degree of professional consensus that is elicited by these statements.

Statements about the purposes of social work practice that are vague and abstract may satisfy the second criterion, for everyone may read into them what they please. But statements of this sort create unity through fuzziness, strengthening the practitioner's sense of moral rectitude yet doing little to guide sound practice. Similarly, the first criterion can easily be satisfied by a unique and vivid statement of purpose that is relevant to some circumscribed facet of practice and to which only a small segment of the profession would subscribe. However, such statements frequently elevate fads and fashions to the level of ultimate truths, the result being that practice is guided into narrow paths. The problem, then, is to delineate social work's purpose at a level of conceptualization that achieves the delicate balance required to serve both criteria simultaneously. In this way, a definition of purpose that has both scope and pertinence should be achieved.

### SOCIAL WORK'S MISSION

The mission of social work may be described in a number of ways. At the conceptual frameworks meeting,[1] the following descriptions

Reprinted with permission of NASW from *Social Work* 22:5 (September 1977), pp. 401–6. Copyright 1977, National Association of Social Workers, Inc.

were among those offered: promoting values to be adopted throughout society concerning human dignity, self-determination, and the
right of people to resources enabling them to lead "the good life";
improving the quality of life experienced by individuals; enhancing
and restoring the social functioning of individuals; and promoting
the self-realization of individuals. These descriptions overlap and are
mutually reinforcing. Widespread agreement might be achieved
within the profession that the sum of these statements captures a
large part of social work's broader purpose. At the same time, all sorts
of individuals, groups, and professions can legitimately claim that
they also promote values concerning human dignity and the right of
individuals to resources. For example, in addition to other helping
professions such as public health, education, and psychology, business organizations like General Motors can describe their mission as
"improving the quality of life," and the promise of self-realization is
intimately associated with sources other than social work, such as
religious movements, est, and the writings of Norman Vincent Peale.

However, because others may claim to do some good in this world
is no reason for social work to deny its heritage of helping people.
The difficulty in this regard is that, as they stand, definitions of social
work's so-called helping mission, such as improving the quality of life,
promoting societal values, and encouraging self-realization, do not
provide a distinctive unifying conception of the profession's purpose.
There are simply too many others in this world who call themselves
helpers and resource providers and who undertake these types of
functions. The professional identity of social workers would be better
served if the *differentia specifica* of the profession's mission were
delineated as well as those facets of it that resemble what other
people do in society.

There is a unique aspect of social work's mission that may constitute the basis of a distinctive professional identity. This aspect involves social work's connection to the institution of social welfare and
the functions this institution performs in society. Although the provision of social welfare includes programmatic arrangements that require the services of people from many related professions, social
work is clearly the major source of personnel in this area and is
involved with the broadest range of social welfare programs. One
need look no further than the pages of this journal to discover the
comprehensiveness of social work's role vis-à-vis social welfare. By
virtue of its past history and present representation, social work's
proprietary interests in this area are well established.[2]

The institution of social welfare represents a special helping mechanism devised to aid those who suffer from the variety of ills found
in modern industrial society. Whether the cause be personal failing
on the part of the individual, malfunction on the part of society's

institutions, or plain bad luck, the people most vulnerable to these ills are generally either poor or on the brink of poverty. These groups constitute the majority of those served by social welfare, the remainder of those served coming from the more prosperous segments of society. Whenever other major institutions—be they familial, religious, economic, or educational in nature—fall short in their helping and resource-providing functions, social welfare spans the gap. In the sense that it is like a safety net, expanding and contracting in response to the needs and failures of other institutions, social welfare has sometimes been characterized as serving a residual function.[3] Yet because it is suspended as the final network of protection over the void of utter ruin for individuals without resources, social welfare commands a unique and important position as an institution in society.

Social welfare's position in society and the special protective functions it performs as an institution are related to the distinctive features of social work's helping mission. Perceived from this institutional perspective, the diversity and ferment that characterize professional practice no longer represent the makings of social work's so-called identity crisis, but rather the makings of its identity. Social work has suffered too long from what might almost be called the "Flexner syndrome," or professional insecurity based on an idea advanced by Flexner in 1915 when he argued that because social workers play so many roles in so many settings, social work is "not so much a separate profession as an endeavor to supplement certain existing professions ... "[4] According to this view, the diversity of social work's various activities reflects its lack of a distinct mission or identity. In contrast, this author would agree with Reid's suggestion that social work's uniqueness seems to lie in its diversity.[5] This diversity is not without structure or purpose; rather, it corresponds to the manifold nature of social welfare's protective and helping functions which are designed to compensate whenever the diverse needs of individuals go unmet by other institutions.

The current ferment in social work practice reflects, in part, the dramatic expansion that social welfare services have undergone in recent times. Between 1955 and 1965 the proportion of the gross national product represented by social welfare expenditures in the United States increased at an average rate of approximately one-half of one percent a year; from 1965 on, that increase averaged one percent a year through 1975, at which time social welfare expenditures in this country totaled approximately $388.7 billion, or 27.3 percent of the gross national product. Although most of these increases can be attributed to income maintenance and health services spending, expenditures in the social services category, which includes services in such areas as rehabilitation, child welfare, institutional care, and economic opportunity, increased almost 2½ times between 1970 and 1975. This constitutes the largest proportional increase among social welfare expenditure categories.[6]

The provision of social welfare is a diverse and fluid enterprise that expresses the community's recognition of its collective responsibility for helping its members. Diversity and fluidity are not the stuff out of which hard and clear boundaries emerge. But to the extent that the boundaries of social welfare are even vaguely discernible, they allow social workers to distinguish the common ground that forms the basis of the profession's mission in society.

## OBJECTIVES

As social work's mission informs the broad sense of professional purpose, its objectives represent the operational goals for implementing that purpose. Most of the objectives identified at the meeting on conceptual frameworks relate to problem-solving and social change. That is, in terms of these objectives, social work's mission is manifest through problem-solving aimed at changing people and the circumstances of their environments. Cooper illustrates this general viewpoint in her discussion of the dissenting role of social work. She argues that society needs a mechanism that will continually press for change and that the profession of social work constitutes this mechanism and is the "conscience of the community."[7]

Elaborating on the theme of social work's problem-solving and social change objectives, Reid analyzes four focal points of change efforts.[8] When they are compared, a clear parallel emerges between Reid's system of classification and the objectives of social work practice identified by Minahan and Pincus.[9] What Reid has termed an "environmental" focus corresponds to the objectives outlined by Minahan and Pincus as developing new resource systems and facilitating interactions among resource systems. What Reid has termed a "personal-environmental" focus corresponds to the objective described by Minahan and Pincus as establishing linkages between people and resource systems. What Reid has referred to as an "interpersonal" focus corresponds to the objective described by Minahan and Pincus as facilitating interaction between people within resource systems. Finally, what Reid has called an "intrapersonal" focus corresponds to the objective delineated by Minahan and Pincus as helping people to develop internal resources.

Although Reid agrees with Minahan and Pincus on the broad agenda of problem-solving objectives, their views diverge regarding the best ways to approach these objectives. Reid's approach puts the emphasis on substantive problems and uses specific social problems as points of departure against which a variety of theories and methods are tested. The method that proves most effective in resolving a given problem becomes part of the practice repertoire for dealing with it. By comparison, Minahan and Pincus emphasize the use of a general theoretical perspective on problem-solving that applies to all problem situations. The differences between their approach and that of Reid sharply illustrate the kind of countervailing forces that emerge in all professions as they attempt to balance the universal and the particular aspects of their practice.[10] Each of these approaches possesses certain appealing features. Reid's hard-nosed empiricism demands a degree of rigor that is often lacking in the development and application of social work methods. The broad framework outlined by Minahan and Pincus attempts to create a unified model for practice that promises to provide a basis for a distinctive professional identity.

However, the profession's close adherence to either of these paths might not be without cost. Diversity may be one of social work's strengths, but diversity in professional practice must be informed by a unifying or organizing element. Reid's model of practice is organized around an untold number of problem-specific methods, and one is left searching this model for practice elements that unite these many professional specializations. At the other extreme, Minahan and Pincus buy unity at the price of excessive abstraction. In attempting to cull the common elements of social work activities, their definition of practice ascends to conceptual levels that obscure real and important differences, and this is particularly the case with regard to the distinctions between direct and indirect services. For example, it may be correct to say that all social workers require knowledge and skills in the collection of data and the assessment of problems. But the data collection and assessment skills needed by the social welfare planner conducting a survey of community needs bear only a faint resemblance to those needed by the psychiatric social worker, family counselor, or child welfare worker who must assess the personal difficulties of individual clients.

An alternative vision of social work's objectives that is in lively contrast to an emphasis on problem-solving and social change is offered by Morris, who argues that social work's main objective should be to care for society's casualties.[11] These include neglected and abused children, the mentally ill and addicted, the physically disabled, the delinquent, and the poor. Morris observes that these individuals experience problems that yield slowly, if at all, to efforts toward change and solution. In his view, social workers can more immediately and effectively help many of those afflicted with such problems by providing them with long-term care and supportive services rather than by undertaking curative and preventive measures.

Morris's definition of social work's objectives is marked by an appealing clarity of purpose. However, the widespread adoption of such a viewpoint would in all likelihood serve mainly as a corrective rather than as a guide for the profession. The objective of caring for people through long-term maintenance services is too restrictive as a guide, for it directs social work toward a canyon that is uncomfortably narrow for professional practice. As a proposed corrective, however, it emphasizes a significant area within the institution of social welfare that merits more professional attention and involvement than social work has heretofore devoted to it.

Most of the discussion of social work objectives that took place at the conceptual frameworks meeting revolved around the themes of care and change. However, little discussion was devoted to clarifying the differences between the direct-service and the indirect-service applications of these objectives, a point that warrants some attention. Direct services express social work's helping mission by implementing objectives that relate to the provision of care and the accomplishment of change and that focus mainly on individuals. The aim here is to help people by providing them with the types of maintenance services described by Morris when they need them and, wherever possible, with supports and resources to effect social rehabilitation and psychological change that strengthen human capacities for self-determination. (There are, to be sure, disagreements regarding the point at which the possibility of change ends and the necessity for maintenance services begins.) Although the direct services cannot seek to eliminate all the personal risks of life in modern society, they strive to mitigate the consequences of societal and personal failures.

The provision of care and accomplishment of change are also the basic objectives of indirect services. These services focus on the institutional framework within which direct services are performed and through which those in need are served, and they carry major responsibilities with regard to changing and caring for this framework. These responsibilities are exercised through organizational maintenance and program planning and through activities relating to implementation, evaluation, and efforts at reform.

## SOCIAL CONTROL

In addition to the provision of care and the implementation of change, the enforcement of social control has been identified as a major social work objective. Although Reid was not alone in recognizing social control as a legitimate social work objective, other thoughts on this matter were also voiced at the conceptual frameworks meeting. This is not surprising, for whether social control should be a legitimate objective of social work has been a long-standing issue of debate in the profession.

The very phrase "social control" elicits visions of social work as an oppressive tool of society. Some of the profession's critics have been quick to play on such visions, equating elements of social control that are apparent in social work activities with the heights of professional malefaction.[12] And just enough examples of social work's involvement in oppressive controls can be found to lend these charges some degree of credence.[13] For this reason, social workers often regard social control as a reprehensible objective that should be purged from the profession's repertoire. However, separating activities related to caring and change objectives from activities marked by elements of social control is often impossible. It is difficult to deny that many professional efforts involved in the provision of care and the implementation of change are aimed at getting people to behave in socially acceptable and productive ways. Objectives of social control, therefore, cannot be written off without rejecting a substantial portion of professional activities conducted in the areas of child welfare, probation, mental health, and public assistance.

Social work practitioners must, then, distinguish between oppression and social control. This distinction is often obscured by the rhetoric employed by some members of the profession. But social work can implement social control objectives, as, for instance, in cases of child abuse, without necessarily serving as an instrument of oppression. Indeed, social control functions are necessary for regulating legal, political, and social relationships in a complex society whose members are interdependent. From this viewpoint, social controls are not inherently wicked but can be designed to support ideals of justice and human dignity as easily as they can be designed to undermine them. Whether social workers will become involved with forms of social control that are humiliating or humane depends in large measure on the profession's capacity to see beyond the emotionally charged rhetoric obscuring this topic and to address social control objectives with clarity, intelligence, and compassion.

## BASES OF SPECIALIZATION

The one point of almost universal agreement at the conceptual frameworks meeting was that what social workers know and do to achieve their objectives can be divided into areas of specialization. (Even Minahan and Pincus note that their social work generalist can become a specialist in aging, administration, behavior modification, and the like. And Reid suggests that in certain cases even the practitioner who is a generalist might be considered a kind of specialist.) However, much disagreement arose concerning the central conceptual framework around which these areas of specialization should be developed.

Absent among the principles stressed for organizing practice specializations was attention to the traditional triad of casework, group work, and community organization methods. In place of this configuration, three basic approaches to specialization were represented in papers for the meeting: Reid advocated specializations organized principally around specific social problems; Minahan and Pincus, although primarily concerned with establishing a generic practice base, envisioned a variety of specializations built on that generic base and organized around problems, populations, and ethnic and cultural groups; and Morris emphasized the direct- and indirect-service methods approach with specializations in administration and counseling. Each of these approaches has some validity. The issue, therefore, should not be a choice of the either-or variety but should be a question of synthesis. How can the fecund elements of these approaches be combined to form a coherent model of specialization?

## IMPLICATIONS

As theoreticians muse over social work's mission, objectives, and specializations, in the daily practice of social work the profession continues to respond to the aspirations of its members and society. The internal and external pressures generated by these aspirations lead the profession in directions that are not always in keeping with its conceptual frameworks.

Among the various trends in social work practice discussed at the meeting on conceptual frameworks, none has more salient implications for social work's future than the increasing orientation of social services toward the middle class. As Cooper notes, the realization is growing within society that no group or class of individuals enjoys special immunity from the contingencies of life.[14] Recently enacted social welfare legislation has begun to open the door of universal access to social services. In 1975, Title XX amendments to the Social Security Act extended potential eligibility for certain services to those of middle-class income levels. One analysis of the effects of this legislation suggests that the working class and near poor may be squeezed out of the picture.[15]

In addition to forces operating outside the social work profession, certain forces within the profession are attempting to direct its energies toward the middle class. This trend is exemplified by the increasing numbers of social workers who are engaged in private practice. Indeed, Dean has identified the expansion of private practice as a direct challenge to social work's heritage of concern for the disadvantaged.[16]

The issue raised here is not new. Social workers have long experienced a strain between the ideal of rendering service to those most in need (usually the poor) and the attraction of serving a middle-class clientele, work with whom would probably increase professional status and wealth. In the past, the social work ideal has generally prevailed over this attraction, in part because opportunities for social workers to serve the middle class were rather limited. Recently, however, opportunities in this area have changed. Apparently client demand of a magnitude to support a growing branch of private practice within the social work profession now exists. And with the implementation of Title XX, universal access to social services may soon be a reality.[17] How will social workers respond to these opportunities?

Although it has served some middle-class clients, social work has traditionally been a profession basically oriented toward the poor. A reversal in this status quo may, however, take place. It is possible that in the future social work will become basically oriented toward the middle class while serving some individuals who are poor. It is also possible that social work will develop a more general and expansive service orientation in which the poor and nonpoor are included on an equal footing.[18] In any case, a service orientation toward a middle-class clientele seems to be a latent facet of the profession that will demand increasing recognition.

Social work's emerging middle-class orientation may have many effects. For example, serving large numbers of middle-class clients might enhance the status and respectability of social work, which could use some enhancement after the battering taken by the profession in the 1960s. At the same time, a middle-class clientele might demand more from the profession than is being asked of it at present in the way of systematic knowledge, proven techniques, and concrete benefits of services. If they are not abandoned as clients by the profession, the poor might well benefit from some of the effects of a service orientation expanded to include the middle class. All this remains to be seen. As for the future, it is only safe to say that issues concerning professional identity will continue to mold the agenda of many social work conferences to come.

## NOTES

1. Madison, Wisconsin, May 6–7, 1976; reported in *Social Work*, 22:5 (September 1977).

2. Neil Gilbert and Harry Specht, "The Incomplete Profession," *Social Work,* 19:6 (November 1974), pp. 665–74.

3. Harold L. Wilensky and Charles Lebeaux, *Industrial Society and Social Welfare* (New York: Russell Sage Foundation, 1958), pp. 138–47.

4. Abraham Flexner, "Is Social Work a Profession?" in *Proceedings of the National Conference of Charities and Corrections* (Chicago, Ill.: Hildman Printing Co., 1915), pp. 576–90.

5. William J. Reid, "Social Work for Social Problems," *Social Work,* 22:5 (September 1977), pp. 374–81.

6. Alfred Skolnik and Sophie Dales, "Social Welfare Expenditures, 1950–75," *Social Security Bulletin,* 39 (January 1976), pp. 3–20.

7. Shirley Cooper, "Social Work: A Dissenting Profession," *Social Work,* 22:5 (September 1977), pp. 360–68.

8. Reid, *op. cit.*

9. Anne Minahan and Allen Pincus, "Conceptual Framework for Social Work Practice," *Social Work,* 22:5 (September 1977), pp. 347–52.

10. For a discussion of the balance between the universal and the particular in professional life, see Everett C. Hughes, "Professions," *Daedalus,* 92 (Fall 1963), pp. 655–66.

11. Robert Morris, "Caring for vs. Caring about People," *Social Work,* 22:5 (September 1977), pp. 353–59.

12. For a recent and not very persuasive expression of this view, see Jeffry Galper, *The Politics of Social Services* (Englewood Cliffs, N.J.: Prentice-Hall, 1975).

13. See, for example, Samuel Mencher, "Newburgh: The Recurrent Crisis of Public Assistance," *Social Work,* 7 (January 1962), pp. 3–11.

14. Cooper, *op. cit.*

15. Mildred Rein, "Social Services as a Work Strategy," *Social Service Review,* 49 (December 1975), pp. 515–38.

16. Walter R. Dean, Jr., "Back to Activism," *Social Work,* 22:5 (September 1977), pp. 369–73.

17. For an analysis of this development, see Neil Gilbert, "The Burgeoning Social Service Payload," *Society (Transaction),* 14 (May–June 1977), pp. 63–65.

18. Neil Gilbert, "The Transformation of Social Services," *Social Service Review,* 51:4 (December 1977), pp. 624–41.

# NAME INDEX

# SUBJECT INDEX

# CONTRIBUTORS

*Paul Adams.* Assistant Professor, School of Social Work, University of Iowa, Iowa City.

*Allan C. Carlson.* His article was written while a National Endowment for the Humanities Fellow at the American Enterprise Institute for Public Policy. He is currently Assistant to the President at Gettysburg College, Gettysburg, Pennsylvania.

*Thomas Owen Carlton.* Associate Professor, Health Services Concentration, School of Social Work, Virginia Commonwealth University, Richmond, Virginia.

*Richard A. Cloward.* Professor, Columbia University School of Social Work, New York.

*Gary Freeman.* Associate Professor, School of Social Work, University of Pennsylvania, Philadelphia.

*Milton Friedman.* Professor, University of Chicago.

*Neil Gilbert.* Professor, School of Social Welfare, University of California, Berkeley.

*Nathan Glazer.* Professor of Education and Sociology, Harvard University, Cambridge.

*Ernest Greenwood.* Professor Emeritus, School of Social Welfare, University of California, Berkeley.

*David Hardcastle.* Dean and Professor, School of Social Welfare, University of Kansas, Lawrence.

*Yeheskel Hasenfeld.* Professor, School of Social Work, University of Michigan, Ann Arbor.

*Kenneth Keniston.* Professor, Massachusetts Institute of Technology, Cambridge.

*Paul Kurzman.* Professor, Hunter College School of Social Work, City University of New York.

*James Leiby.* Professor, School of Social Welfare, University of California, Berkeley.

*Samuel Mencher* (1918–1967). Professor, School of Social Work, University of Pittsburgh.

*Martha Ozawa.* Professor, George Warren Brown School of Social Work, Washington University, St. Louis.

*Michael Sosin.* Assistant Professor, School of Social Work, University of Madison, Wisconsin.

*Harry Specht.* Dean and Professor, School of Social Welfare, University of California, Berkeley.

*Richard Titmuss* (1907–1973). Professor, Social Administration, London School of Economics.

*Walter Trattner.* Professor of History, University of Wisconsin, Milwaukee.

*Jerry Turem.* Director, Office of Planning, Research, and Evaluation, Human Development Services, U.S. Department of Health, Education, and Welfare, Washington, D.C.

*Katherine Wood.* Associate Professor, Graduate School of Social Work, Rutgers - The State University, New Brunswick, New Jersey.

*Mayer Zald.* Professor of Sociology and Social Work, University of Michigan, Ann Arbor.

**THE BOOK MANUFACTURE**

*Emergence of Social Welfare and Social Work, Second Edition* was typeset at Datagraphics, Phoenix, Arizona. Printing and binding was at George Banta Company, Menasha, Wisconsin. Cover design was by Jane Rae Brown. Internal design was by F. E. Peacock Publishers art department. The typeface is Caledonia.